Remedies to Digital Vulnerability in European Private Law

Camilla Crea · Marta Infantino
Editors

Remedies to Digital Vulnerability in European Private Law

Pathways towards Fairness

Springer

Editors
Camilla Crea
University of Sannio
Benevento, Italy

Marta Infantino
University of Trieste
Trieste, Italy

ISBN 978-3-032-19719-1 ISBN 978-3-032-19720-7 (eBook)
https://doi.org/10.1007/978-3-032-19720-7

This Springer imprint is published by the registered company Springer Nature Switzerland AG
The registered company address is: Gewerbestrasse 11, 6330 Cham, Switzerland

Preface—Private Law Remedies to Digital Unfairness

This volume contains the proceedings of the international conference titled *Remedies to Digital Vulnerability in European Private Law*, held at the University of Trieste on April 10–11, 2025. The conference was the third and final event organised as part of the research project on 'Digital Vulnerability in European Private Law' (DiVE), funded by the Italian Ministry of University and Research from 2022 to 2025 as a 'Research Project of National Interest'.[1] The DiVE project aimed to investigate whether the multifaceted concept of digital vulnerability could effectively address the harms caused by digital technologies and to what extent it could inform the revision of European legal principles, rules, and policies to combat digital unfairness, combining theoretical and practical analysis with policy-oriented academic work.

The two previous international conferences organised within the project took place, respectively, at the University of Ferrara on June 15–16, 2023, and at the Tor Vergata University of Rome on May 23–24, 2024. The 2023 conference in Ferrara aimed to define the conceptual framework of the research and to explore the wide spectrum of digital vulnerability as a cross-cutting challenge in almost all fields of private law, looking far beyond consumer and data protection law. The proceedings of the 2023 conference were published in a volume edited by Camilla Crea and Alberto De Franceschi, titled 'The New Shapes of Digital Vulnerability in European Private Law' (2024).[2]

Following this theoretical framework, the 2024 conference in Rome focused on the challenges arising from growing reliance on artificial intelligence (AI). It emphasised the need for an interdisciplinary approach combining law, social sciences, and computer science. Key themes analysed in the conference included the relationship between AI autonomy and personal autonomy, the vulnerability of individual autonomy, emotional manipulation, and AI's potential to both increase and reduce vulnerability. Looking ahead, the challenge is to develop a European normative framework capable of addressing new forms of vulnerability without unduly

---

[1] For more information on the project, see https://prindive.weebly.com/.

[2] The volume is accessible at https://www.nomos-shop.de/en/p/the-new-shapes-of-digital-vulnerability-in-european-private-law-gr-978-3-7560-1632-7.

restricting self-determination. The proceedings of the 2024 Rome conference, edited by Claudia Amodio and Amalia Diurni, are to be published under the title 'Human Vulnerability in Interaction with AI in European Private Law' in 2026.

Four years of research, involving over a hundred experts on the subject, demonstrated that vulnerability is the norm rather than the exception in the digital environment. The project's findings so far have also confirmed that certain individuals and situations are at greater risk of harm than others, which is consistent with the European Commission's findings. The 2024 Fitness Check on EU consumer law has brought to light numerous practices, including dark patterns, addictive design, and unfair personalisation techniques, which jeopardise consumers' safety online.[3] Several of these practices are going to be addressed by the forthcoming Digital Fairness Act, currently under preparation by the European Commission.[4]

The research findings presented in this volume expand and concretise this perspective, focusing on remedies. The contributors examine various ex-ante measures and ex-post remedies derived from EU and national private law that can help mitigate individuals' digital vulnerability, both in general and under specific circumstances. The chapters in Part I, titled 'Unpacking Remedies in the EU Digital Acquis', focus on the EU digital acquis, unpacking both the ambitions and the shortcomings of current regulatory tools. These chapters reveal how consumer law, platform regulation, and data protection often promise fairness and transparency yet struggle to confront manipulative design, enforcement fragmentation, and the opacity of algorithmic systems. Part II, titled 'Rethinking Private Law to Address Digital Vulnerability', explores various ways to prevent or address digital vulnerability through the use of EU and national ex-ante measures, such as injunctions and fundamental rights impact assessments, as well as ex-post remedies, including liability, restitution, and compensation. The chapters in Part III ('Remedying Digital Vulnerability in Everyday Life') ground the debate in everyday contexts, investigating the preventive and ex-post-facto remedies that can help mitigate or manage digital vulnerability in specific areas (e.g., in the automotive and insurance industries) and for particular groups of people (such as those in need of healthcare or legal services). These case studies illustrate both the reach of digital vulnerability and the limitations of existing legal responses, pointing to the need for more integrated, context-sensitive, and enforceable remedies.

Throughout the volume, the contributors engage critically with the gap between regulatory ideals and lived realities, offering pathways to make digital protections more effective without losing sight of the structural conditions that produce vulnerability in the first place. Independently of the regulatory scope of the forthcoming Digital Fairness Act, we are confident that the results collected here will be useful for reconsidering traditional and new rules to safeguard people to the utmost in the face of emerging technological threats. Even though the solutions and strategies discussed here are deeply rooted in the European legal architecture, we are convinced that many

---

[3] See https://commission.europa.eu/document/707d7404-78e5-4aef-acfa-82b4cf639f55_en.

[4] See https://ec.europa.eu/info/law/better-regulation/have-your-say/initiatives/14622-Digital-Fairness-Act_en.

of our findings will contribute to handling the vulnerability challenges brought about by digitalisation outside Europe's borders.

We would like to extend our heartfelt gratitude to the key members of the DiVE project. We are grateful to Claudia Amodio (University of Ferrara), Alberto De Franceschi (University of Ferrara), Amalia Diurni (Tor Vergata University of Rome), Luca Ettore Perriello (Polytechnic University of Marche), and Loredana Tullio (University of Molise). Many thanks also to the members of the Scientific International Committee of the project: Danielle Keats Citron (University of Virginia), Hans-Wolfgang Micklitz (European University Institute), Frank Pasquale (Cornell Tech), Teresa Rodríguez Ballell (Universidad Carlos III), Giovanni Sartor (University of Bologna and European University Institute), Reiner Schulze (University of Münster), Gunther Teubner (Goethe University of Frankfurt), and Yingqin Zheng (Essex University). We truly appreciated your inspiring contributions.

The Trieste conference could not have taken place without the financial support of the Italian Ministry of University and Research and the Department of Political Science at the University of Trieste. In Trieste, we also benefited from the active and generous cooperation of Professors Francesca Fiorentini and Paola Monaco, Dr Alessandro Catano, and Dr Luisa Delle Vedove. We would also like to express our gratitude to Dr Adrian Bedford for his assistance with language editing. Additionally, we would like to extend our sincere thanks to Dr Anja Trautmann at Springer, whose confidence in the project was instrumental in bringing the publication to fruition. Lastly, we would like to thank all the authors featured in this volume, as well as the other contributors to the DiVE project, the participants in our conferences, and the many colleagues who contributed anonymously. Your enthusiasm and commitment have been a driving force behind the DiVE project, and we are truly grateful for your support.

Benevento, Italy — Camilla Crea
Trieste, Italy — Marta Infantino

Contents

Remedying Digital Vulnerability in Everyday Life

Conclusion

Contributors

Hüseyin Can Aksoy Faculty of Law, Bilkent University, Ankara, Türkiye

Pınar Çağlayan Aksoy Faculty of Law, Bilkent University, Ankara, Türkiye

Simone Arnaldi Department of Political Science, University of Trieste, Trieste, Italy

Greta Berardi Faculty of Law, University of Groningen, Groningen, The Netherlands

Lorenzo Carta Applied Data Science and Artificial Intelligence, University of Trieste, Trieste, Italy

Giovanni Chieco University of Trieste, Trieste, Italy

Aurelia Colombi Ciacchi Faculty of Law, University of Groningen, Groningen, The Netherlands

Camilla Crea Department of Law, Economics, Management and Quantitative Methods, University of Sannio, Benevento, Italy

Silvia De Conca Transnational Legal Studies Department, Vrije Universiteit Amsterdam, Amsterdam, The Netherlands

Mindy Nunez Duffourc Department of Private Law, Maastricht Law and Tech Lab, Maastricht University, Maastricht, The Netherlands

Riya Goel School of Law, University of Miami, Miami, USA

Hélène Guiziou Université CY Cergy, Paris, France

Marta Infantino Department of Political Science, University of Trieste, Trieste, Italy

Zubair Jamali Cornell Law School, New York, USA

Maria Kaczorowska Faculty of Law, Administration and Economics, University of Wrocław, Wrocław, Poland

Georgios M. Kalogerakis Law School, National and Kapodistrian University of Athens, Athens, Greece

Roni Kennedy School of Law, University of Miami, Miami, USA

Antonio Legerén-Molina Department of Private Law, A Coruña University, A Coruña, Spain

Manlio Lisanti Department of Management and Law, Tor Vergata University of Rome, Rome, Italy

Karmen Lutman Faculty of Law, University of Ljubljana, Ljubljana, Slovenia

Pierluigi Masai Applied Data Science and Artificial Intelligence, University of Trieste, Trieste, Italy

Luana Mathias Souto Gender and ICT Research Group, Universitat Oberta de Catalunya, Barcelona, Spain

Attila Menyhárd Faculty of Law, Eötvös Loránd University, Budapest, Hungary

Barbara Milillo Department of Legal Science, University of Udine, Udine, Italy

Emilia Mišćenić Faculty of Law, University of Rijeka, Rijeka, Croatia

Alma-Cristina Onaie Groningen, The Netherlands;
Università Bocconi, Milano, Italy

Frank Pasquale Cornell Tech and Cornell Law School, New York, USA

Alessandra Pera Department of Political Science and International Relations, University of Palermo, Palermo, Italy

Sara Rigazio Department of Political Science and International Relations, University of Palermo, Palermo, Italy

Siniša Rodin Court of Justice of the European Union, Luxembourg, Luxembourg

Teresa Rodríguez de las Heras Ballell Faculty of Law, Universidad Carlos III de Madrid, Madrid, Spain

Giulio Santoni Università degli Studi di Roma Tor Vergata, Rome, Italy

Reiner Schulze Centre for European Private Law, University of Münster, Münster, Germany

Karin Sein Department of Private Law, University of Tartu, Tartu, Estonia

Niels Singer Faculty of Law, University of Groningen, Groningen, The Netherlands

Szymon Skalski Faculty of Law, Jagiellonian University of Krakow, Krakow, Poland

Guido Smorto Faculty of Law, University of Palermo, Palermo, Italy

Piotr Tereszkiewicz Faculty of Law, Jagiellonian University of Krakow, Krakow, Poland

Unpacking Remedies in the EU Digital Acquis

From Illusion to Digital Fairness: Structural Protection in EU Consumer Law

Emilia Mišćenić and Monika Namysłowska

Abstract This chapter argues that current EU consumer law, formally committed to transparency and information duties, offers only the illusion of protection in digital markets. Consumers appear informed, but are structurally vulnerable to manipulative design choices, personalisation architectures, and data-driven information asymmetries. Transparency is ineffective when reduced to formal disclosures that fail to enable real understanding or control. To move beyond this illusion, we propose a shift towards structural protection: a regulatory approach that addresses harm at its source, rather than relying solely on individual consumer agency. We identify two complementary ex ante instruments as essential: information duties and transparency requirements redesigned for effectiveness through form-based delivery, and per se prohibitions that categorically ban particularly harmful commercial practices. Although both tools already exist in EU law, they remain underdeveloped for the digital context. The chapter calls for amendments to the principles of transparency and fairness by rethinking their implementation and enforcement. Only through such preventive and systemic design can EU consumer law respond to the realities of algorithmically shaped markets and restore its protective function in the digital age.

Keywords EU consumer law · Information duties · Transparency · Digital fairness

The work of Emilia Mišćenić was fully supported by the University of Rijeka projects Transparency and Fairness in the Digital Environment (uniri-iskusni-drustv-23-101). The research of Monika Namysłowska leading to this chapter was fully supported by the National Science Centre in Poland (project no. 2018/31/B/HS5/01169).

E. Mišćenić (✉)
Faculty of Law, University of Rijeka, Rijeka, Croatia
e-mail: emilia.miscenic@pravri.uniri.hr

M. Namysłowska
Faculty of Law and Administration, University of Lodz, Lodz, Poland
e-mail: mnamyslowska@wpia.uni.lodz.pl

C. Crea and M. Infantino (eds.), *Remedies to Digital Vulnerability in European Private Law*, https://doi.org/10.1007/978-3-032-19720-7_1

1 Introduction: Why EU Consumer Law Must Adapt

Digital marketplaces are no longer neutral spaces for consumer choice. They are engineered by businesses to shape user behaviour through artificial intelligence (AI)- and data-driven personalisation, profiling, and behavioural targeting. At the same time, the architecture of choice is governed by opaque, algorithmic processes that remain largely inaccessible to the individuals they affect. These mechanisms use AI systems and profit-driven algorithms to monitor and predict consumer preferences, thereby shaping decisions that are precisely aligned with the commercial objectives of businesses.

This transformation gives rise to a new kind of consumer vulnerability that is not sporadic but structural in nature. This is not a matter of isolated market failures or one-off manipulation. It arises from the design of digital commercial ecosystems. Personalised offers, pre-selected defaults, dark patterns, and attention-fragmenting interfaces have become standard. Consumers rarely understand the extent to which their autonomy is predetermined. While the legal fiction of the informed consumer persists, it does not correspond to empirical reality. Yet the foundational tools of consumer law in the European Union (EU)—information duties and the principle of transparency—continue to operate essentially unchanged. These instruments were developed for traditional, offline markets where traders and consumers interacted more symmetrically. In digital contexts, by contrast, information obligations often result in regulatory and information overload with little substantive effect. Formal disclosures may be provided, but they are seldom actionable. As the Court of Justice of the European Union (CJEU) and national courts have begun to acknowledge, formal compliance with information duties does not guarantee that consumers are protected against practices that distort their decision-making.

Empirical research and enforcement experience, including the European Commission's market studies, sweeps, and Eurostat data, reveal the limits of relying on individual consumer vigilance in a technology-driven environment. Consumers operating in online marketplaces, characterised by a new scope of asymmetry based on technological sophistication, are becoming increasingly vulnerable and need more effective protection and enforcement mechanisms.[1] The concepts of digital asymmetry and digital vulnerability have become the new normal.[2] The problem is not the lack of rules, but a growing misalignment between existing regulatory tools and the way digital transactions now operate. Legal instruments remain fragmented and insufficiently adapted to AI-driven commercial practices that now define the modern economy. And as *Rott* has aptly noted, consumer rights are "meaningless, or limited in their practical relevance, if they are not enforced".[3]

The chapter begins with the premise that transparency alone will never be sufficient. If EU consumer law is to address the systemic risks posed by data-driven

---

[1] Helberger et al (2021).

[2] Helberger et al (2024, 24–30).

[3] Rott (2025).

marketplaces, it must surpass the informational paradigm and adopt a model of structural protection. This requires a recalibration of legal design to address the dynamics of algorithmic manipulation. We argue that two complementary *ex ante* tools are central to this shift: information duties and transparency requirements redesigned for effectiveness through form-based delivery, and per se prohibitions that categorically ban particularly harmful commercial practices. Both instruments already exist within EU law, but they are underdeveloped and under-enforced in the digital context. The following sections explain how these tools can be refined and reinforced to restore the protective function of EU consumer law in the digital age.

2 Transparency in the Digital Environment: Just an Illusion

2.1 The Role of Transparency in EU Consumer Law: From Aim to Digital Reality

To understand why transparency fails in digital markets, it is worth recalling how the principle has been understood and operationalised in EU law. The principle of transparency is closely tied to core legal values: the rule of law, democracy, and legal certainty, as outlined in Articles 2 and 11 of the Treaty on European Union (TEU). Although a uniform definition is lacking, the CJEU has interpreted its meaning in various areas of law and with regard to different legal issues (such as public procurement, subsidies, the right to access information). Emphasising its role in ensuring the full effect of EU law, the CJEU links transparency to legal certainty through precision and understandability.[4] As Advocate General Ruiz-Jarabo Colomer stated in *Belgium v. Commission*, "transparency is concerned with the quality of being clear, obvious and understandable without doubt or ambiguity".[5]

In EU consumer law, transparency has traditionally been pursued through information obligations set out in various directives, digital market regulations, and sector-specific instruments. The so-called 'information paradigm' assumes that consumers make informed choices when presented with clear and comprehensive information from traders. Scholars have long observed that such obligations have served as the key tool for advancing transparency since the early development of the field.[6] As *Riesenhuber* and *Möslein* note, the concept of transparency remains central to the functioning of the market economy and is "often viewed as a synonym to information duties of all kinds".[7]

---

[4] CJEU, case C-417/99, *Commission v. Spain*, 13 September 2001, ECLI:EU:C:2001:445, para 40.

[5] CJEU, case C-110/03 *Belgium v. Commission*, 14 April 2005, ECLI:EU:C:2005:223; Opinion of Advocate General *Ruiz-Jarabo Colomer*, delivered on 16 December 2004 in case C-110/03 *Belgium v. Commission*, ECLI:EU:C:2004:815, para. 44.

[6] Howells (2005, 349) and Đurović (2016, 192).

[7] Riesenhuber and Möslein (2009, 1485).

However, the shift from offline to digital marketplaces has significantly changed the market economy.[8] In the digital environment, transparency often fails, as consumer choices are increasingly manipulated by design and unfair digital practices. Despite numerous CJEU rulings interpreting legal requirements for transparency, it has become more illusion than reality in the digital market. In 2024, Eurostat reported that 77% of individuals shopped online, while 94% used the internet.[9] Yet, European Commission sweep actions reveal that over 70% of online traders routinely breach transparency and information obligations. These violations mainly involve inadequate information on withdrawal rights, dispute resolution, repairs, legal guarantees, and the use of unfair digital practices.[10] CJEU cases such as *Content Services*, *Tiketa*, *Eventim*, *Victorinox*, *Fuhrmann-2*, *EIS*, *Conny*, and *Meta* highlight how businesses bypass these duties within the Digital Single Market.[11]

This evolution shows that the information paradigm is ineffective in enabling the average consumer, understood as the legal standard model, to make informed choices.[12] The average consumer, who is "reasonably well informed, observant and circumspect",[13] becomes weak and vulnerable in the digital environment. This is due to personal limitations and a widespread lack of understanding of technologies like algorithms, programming, and distributed ledgers, which lead to choices that are neither informed nor truly their own.[14] The CJEU's case law confirms this disconnect between formal compliance and practical consumer protection, revealing superficial fulfilment of information and transparency duties.

2.2 When Transparency Fails: Lessons from the CJEU

Online traders, platforms, and intermediaries appear to comply with the mandatory information and transparency requirements under EU consumer law, rendering the

[8] See also Namysłowska (2024b, 258).

[9] Eurostat (2025).

[10] See https://commission.europa.eu/live-work-travel-eu/consumer-rights-and-complaints/enforcement-consumer-protection/sweeps_en.

[11] CJEU, case C-536/20 *Tiketa*, 24 February 2022, ECLI:EU:C:2022:112; CJEU, case C-96/21 *Eventim*, 31 March 2022, EU:C:2022:238; CJEU, case C-179/21, *Victorinox*, 5 May 2022, ECLI:EU:C:2022:353; CJEU, case C-49/11, *Content Services*, 5 July 2012, ECLI:EU:C:2012:419; CJEU, case C-266/19 *EIS*, 14 May 2020, ECLI:EU:C:2020:384; CJEU, case C-249/21 *Fuhrmann-2*, 7 April 2022, ECLI:EU:C:2022:269; CJEU, case C-252/21, *Meta Platforms and Others*, 4 July 2023, ECLI:EU:C:2023:537; CJEU, case C-319/20, *Meta Platforms Ireland*, 28 April 2022, ECLI:EU:C:2022:322; CJEU, case C-400/22, Conny, 30 May 2024, ECLI:EU:C:2024:436; CJEU, case C-757/22, *Meta Platforms Ireland (Action représentative)*, 11 July 2024, ECLI:EU:C:2024:598.

[12] Oehler and Wendt (2017, 179–191).

[13] Recital 18 of the UCPD.

[14] Paterson (2023, 558) and Galli (2022, 181).

legislation ineffective in practice.[15] As illustrated in the *Tiketa* case, traders typically include pre-contractual information required by EU directives in their terms and conditions (T&Cs), although they frequently only partially do so. The CJEU has recognised the evolving digital landscape by stating that the pre-contractual information duties under the Consumer Rights Directive (CRD)[16]

> "must be interpreted as not precluding the information referred to in Article 6(1) from being provided to the consumer, prior to the conclusion of the contract, only in the general terms and conditions for the provision of services on the intermediary's website, which that consumer actively accepts by ticking the box provided for that purpose, *provided that that information is brought to the consumer's attention in a clear and comprehensible manner* (emphasis added by the authors)".[17]

In practice, transparency often fails, as T&Cs are typically accessible only online via hyperlinks, depending on the website's design. Even when consumers receive them, they cannot negotiate or fully understand their content. Yet these terms, though merely linked, are legally binding and form part of the contract concluded online. As emphasised by the CJEU,

> "such a means of providing information cannot act as a substitute for providing the consumer with the confirmation of the contract on a durable medium, within the meaning of Article 8(7) of that directive, *since this does not prevent that information from forming an integral part of the distance or off-premises contract* (emphasis added by the authors)".[18]

The *Tiketa* case shows how formal requirements and information duties under the CRD are adapted to suit traders in the digital environment. Pre-contractual information is largely illusory, as it is part of the trader's T&Cs, which are often only available online and not provided to consumers on a durable medium, even after the contract has been concluded. Consumers typically receive an order confirmation with a link to the terms, which they must accept by ticking a box to proceed. Studies on consumer fatigue show that users rarely read these terms, which are non-negotiable and frequently changed unilaterally by traders without notice or justification.[19]

Extensive CJEU case law under the Unfair Contract Terms Directive (UCTD)[20] also demonstrates persistent transparency issues in practice. These include terms not provided at all, only accessible via hyperlink, or not provided on a durable medium; unilateral changes to price or other essential elements of the contract without notice; automatic conversions from free trials to paid subscriptions; unfair withdrawal

---

[15] Mišćenić (2018, 219–246).

[16] Directive 2011/83/EU of the European Parliament and of the Council of 25 October 2011 on consumer rights, amending Council Directive 93/13/EEC and Directive 1999/44/EC of the European Parliament and of the Council and repealing Council Directive 85/577/EEC and Directive 97/7/EC of the European Parliament and of the Council.

[17] CJEU, case C-536/20, *Tiketa*, para 54.

[18] Ibid.

[19] Segger-Piening (2021, 89–117) and Loos and Luzak (2021).

[20] Council Directive 93/13/EEC of 5 April 1993 on unfair terms in consumer contracts.

exclusions; and terms written in unfamiliar languages.[21] Even when contractual terms and information are made available, consumers face yet another transparency illusion.

The so-called weak consumer, who is "in a weak position vis-à-vis the seller or supplier, as regards both his bargaining power and his level of knowledge",[22] often cannot understand contractual terms, even though they are required to be in "plain, intelligible language" under Articles 4 and 5 UCTD.[23] According to CJEU case law, transparency extends beyond mere formal compliance and requires substantive transparency, ensuring that consumers genuinely understand contractual terms:

> "as requiring not only that the relevant term should be grammatically intelligible to the consumer, but also that the contract should set out transparently the specific functioning of the mechanism [...] and the relationship between that mechanism and that provided for by other contractual terms [...], *so that that consumer is in a position to evaluate, on the basis of clear, intelligible criteria, the economic consequences for him which derive from it* (emphasis added by the authors)".[24]

The CJEU has consistently emphasised the close link between information duties, transparency, and fairness in consumer protection. A failure in transparency often leads to unfairness, as average, weak or vulnerable consumers cannot evaluate the economic consequences for themselves that derive from actions like ticking a box to accept T&Cs online.[25] In *Verein für Konsumenteninformation*, involving Amazon EU, the CJEU ruled that a pre-formulated contractual term may be unfair if it is not drafted in plain, intelligible language, as required by the UCTD.[26]

In the digital environment, information can easily become a tool for manipulation. Practices such as hiding, omitting, or misrepresenting key information are commonly used to mislead consumers and influence choices and transactional decisions that they would not have made otherwise. In *Canal Digital Danmark*, the misleading omission of material information on the total price of the subscription resulted "in a significant asymmetry of information that is likely to confuse consumers".[27] Such unfair commercial practices, prohibited under the Unfair Commercial Practices Directive

---

[21] Gardiner (2022, 9) and European Commission.

[22] CJEU, joined cases C-240/98 to C-244/98 *Océano Grupo and Salvat Editores*, 27 June 2000, ECLI:EU:C:2000:346, para 25.

[23] Mak (2024, 564–575) and Infantino, Mišćenić, Tereszkiewicz (2024, 262).

[24] CJEU, case C-26/13, *Kásler and Káslerné Rábai*, 30 April 2014, ECLI:EU:C:2014:282, para 75, and the cited CJEU case law; Loos (2023, 281–299).

[25] Esposito and Grochowski (2022, 1–31).

[26] CJEU, case C-191/15, *Verein für Konsumenteninformation*, 28 July 2016, ECLI:EU:C:2016:612, para 68.

[27] CJEU, case C-611/14, *Canal Digital Danmark*, 26 October 2016, ECLI:EU:C:2016:800, para 41.

(UCPD),[28] demonstrate how the misuse of information can lead to a lack of transparency and unfairness in commercial practices and contractual terms. In *Pohotovost'*,[29] the CJEU held that omitting essential information can affect the transparency and fairness of a term, and in *Pereničová*, the indication of incorrect and misleading information was an element on which the court can "base its assessment of the unfairness of the contractual terms".[30]

2.3 Transparency Without Effectiveness

While the EU consumer legal framework includes various tools to ensure transparency in B2C relationships, evidence from case law, studies, and real-world practice shows it is not functioning effectively. As noted in the 2024 Commission's Staff Working Document, known as Digital Fairness Fitness Check, EU directives "sometimes lack the necessary concreteness for their effective practical application".[31] This is also true of the current regulation of information duties and transparency requirements.

Various EU consumer directives require traders to provide 30 to 40 pieces of pre-contractual information in a "clear and comprehensible manner" to enable informed consumer decisions. The CRD, for example, mandates over 20 information obligations both before and after contract conclusion.[32] Recent CRD amendments on distance contracts for financial services introduced more than 40 individual items of pre-contractual information.[33] This approach leads to information overload, which is ill-suited to the digital context. As the CJEU has recognised, transparency requires more than formal disclosure. It demands actual consumer understanding. This challenge is not confined to consumer law. A telling example from the data protection field is the Belgian Court of Appeal's May 2025 ruling, which confirmed that the Transparency & Consent Framework (TCF)—the industry standard used by companies such as Google, Microsoft, and Amazon—fails to meet requirements of the GDPR.[34] Even mechanisms designed to operationalise transparency can entrench design-rooted opacity, as data is continuously collected, profiled, and exchanged beyond the user's grasp.[35]

---

[28] Directive 2005/29/EC of the European Parliament and Council of 11 May 2005 concerning unfair business-to-consumer commercial practices in the internal market.

[29] CJEU, case C-76/10, *Pohotovost'*, 16 November 2010, ECLI:EU:C:2010:685, para 82.

[30] CJEU, case C-453/10, *Pereničová and Perenič*, 15 March 2012, ECLI:EU:C:2012:144, para 47.

[31] European Commission (2024, 45).

[32] Articles 5(a) to (h) and 6(a) to (t) CRD.

[33] Article 16a(a) to (w) CRD introduced by Directive (EU) 2023/2673 of the European Parliament and of the Council of 22 November 2023 amending Directive 2011/83/EU as regards financial services contracts concluded at a distance and repealing Directive 2002/65/EC.

[34] Judgment of the Court of Appeal in Brussels of 14 May 2025, 2022/AR/292.

[35] Vrbljanac (2024, 269–272).

Transparency, achieved through extensive information duties in EU consumer law, was intended as a tool to empower consumers to make informed choices and ensure legal certainty in B2C relationships.[36] Yet in a digital environment, this model has begun to erode consumer protection. The regulatory framework is weakening the position of consumers by failing to regulate information duties effectively. Consumers struggle to distinguish what is "essential information". They rarely thoroughly read T&Cs online, and face significant cognitive overload during online transactions.[37] As emphasised in the Digital Fairness Fitness Check, "the growing mismatch between the normative abstraction of the 'average consumer' and the realities of consumer behaviour in the digital environment undermines the effectiveness of EU consumer law".[38] Bridging this gap requires an update of the legal framework.

3 Ex Post Enforcement in the Digital Environment: A Failing Model

3.1 The Limits of the General Clause and Case-By-Case Fairness

Improving transparency alone is not enough. Enforcement mechanisms, too, are no longer fit for purpose in the digital marketplace. EU consumer law relies on a general clause model to ensure flexibility in assessing, for example, unfair commercial practices. The general prohibition of unfair commercial practices in Article 5 UCPD is based on the general clause of professional diligence. Together with the prohibitions under Articles 6 and 7 on misleading actions and omissions, and Articles 8 and 9 on aggressive commercial practices, it establishes an *ex post* system of control grounded in open-ended legal standards. These provisions aim to encompass a broad range of potentially harmful practices, from classic misrepresentations to more subtle manipulations of consumer autonomy. The interpretative openness of the general clause was once seen as its strength. It allowed courts and authorities to respond flexibly to new forms of commercial misconduct, without the need for constant legislative revision. But in the context of digital markets, this case-by-case model becomes a vulnerability. Where the architecture of choice is shaped by opaque algorithmic processes and behavioural design, legal standards that rely on *ex post* evaluation based on the average consumer perception no longer offer sufficient protection.

The core difficulty lies in the evidentiary demands and interpretive discretion needed to apply these standards effectively. National enforcement bodies must demonstrate that a specific commercial practice materially distorts average consumer behaviour, which is not only difficult to prove but also deeply context-dependent.

[36] Pichonnaz (2023, 81).

[37] Digital Fairness Fitness Check (2024, 86).

[38] Digital Fairness Fitness Check (2024, 46).

Courts and regulators must reconstruct the internal logic of commercial systems that are non-transparent and self-optimising. The result is legal uncertainty and significant under-enforcement.

Articles 6–9 UCPD are a case in point. In theory, they apply equally to digital and traditional commercial practices. However, they focus on whether the consumer was misled or subjected to an aggressive practice in a particular case, rather than whether the system as a whole is designed to mislead, nudge, or limit consumer agency. Similarly, the structure of Article 5 does not lend itself to systemic or anticipatory enforcement.

Moreover, as behavioural economics shows, many of the most powerful tools of digital influence, such as framing effects, default settings, and interface friction, do not operate through outright deception or coercion. They exploit cognitive short-cuts and situational vulnerabilities that the general clause model cannot address. The cumulative impact of such practices is structurally unfair, even if each element appears legally defensible when assessed in isolation.

In short, the UCPD's general clause and the accompanying provisions have reached their operational limits in digital environments. Their interpretative flexibility remains essential for assessing traditional unfairness, but they are not capable of providing timely and systemic consumer protection. What is needed is a regulatory framework that goes further than *ex post* assessments towards pre-emptive, categorical rules that reflect the realities of contemporary market design.

3.2 Structural Deficiencies of Ex Post Enforcement

The limitations of the general clause model result in more profound structural deficiencies in enforcement. *Ex post* enforcement, usually through administrative action or judicial adjudication, assumes a model of consumer harm that is traceable and resolvable after the fact. Yet digital markets do not operate within this paradigm. Digital harms are generally structural rather than transactional in nature. The architecture of choice, including the framing of options, default pathways, friction points, and the timing of nudges, exerts a constant influence on consumer behaviour and preferences. Many forms of harm today stem from the cumulative effects of design-based asymmetries, data-driven optimisation, and behavioural manipulation at scale. *Ex post* enforcement focuses on isolated outcomes: was the average consumer misled? Was this practice unfair? This perspective cannot deal with practices that derive their power from repetition, design logic, and psychological calibration across millions of users. It misrecognises systemic manipulation as a series of individualised incidents.

Reactive enforcement struggles to keep pace with the rapid evolution of digital practices. When regulators respond to emerging issues, often years after the initial rollout of a practice, the damage is already embedded in consumer behaviour and market expectations.

Moreover, individualised enforcement procedures rely on complaint-driven models that assume consumers will identify and report violations. This assumption is becoming increasingly unrealistic. Algorithmic personalisation renders consumer experiences unique. The lack of transparency of digital practices makes it difficult to detect unfairness patterns and to realise that one has been manipulated. Even when harms are perceived, consumers face high informational, psychological, and procedural barriers to pursuing enforcement, particularly in cross-border, platform-mediated transactions.[39]

Then, in a digital environment, the informational power lies with businesses. Regulators are left to reconstruct complex systems of interaction, having limited access, and often relying on costly forensic analysis or cooperation from the entities they are investigating. This results in under-enforcement.

Finally, the fragmentation of enforcement competences across national authorities in the EU adds to the structural weakness. While platforms operate seamlessly across borders, enforcement mechanisms remain largely national in scope. Despite the existence of frameworks such as the Consumer Protection Cooperation (CPC) network, there is no shared database, no common pool of analytical tools, and no coordinated human resources able to respond at scale. The result is not merely legal fragmentation in a formal sense, but a system-level incapacity to act effectively. This mismatch between the transnational nature of digital markets and the parochial limits of enforcement infrastructure leaves consumer authorities unable to intervene when and where it matters most.

In sum, *ex post* enforcement is not powerless, but it lacks grip. Designed for an earlier generation of consumer harm, it no longer effectively addresses digital unfairness.

3.3 Why the Black List Falls Short in Digital Markets

Although the general clause model of unfairness under Article 5 UCPD offers conceptual flexibility, its practical limitations were acknowledged before the adoption of the UCPD in 2005. Annex I of the UCPD—the so-called 'black list' of commercial practices prohibited under all circumstances—was designed to complement the open-textured framework by offering legal certainty and enforcement efficiency. In principle, per se prohibitions act as a response to clearly harmful practices that neither require interpretative balancing through the average consumer model nor case-by-case assessment.

In practice, however, Annex I of the UCPD is strikingly static, particularly when viewed through the lens of digital market dynamics. The original black list included 31 items, largely focused on traditional, offline transactional misconduct, such as false

[39] European Commission (2025, 19–21).

claims of limited availability[40] and pyramid schemes.[41] The 2019 Omnibus Directive[42] amended the UCPD's Annex I for the first time since its adoption, introducing four new per se prohibitions that explicitly target manipulative online practices. These cover the use of automated means (bots) to acquire event tickets for resale (point 22a); presenting consumer reviews without taking reasonable and proportionate steps to ensure their authenticity (point 23a); submitting or commissioning false consumer reviews (point 23b); and failing to disclose that a higher ranking in search results has been paid for (point 11a). This expansion of the black list signalled a long-overdue recognition of platform-based manipulation. The selected practices are indeed harmful, but they represent only a narrow subset of digital deception. Crucially, the amendments fail to reflect more complex architectures of digital influence. Dark patterns such as exploitative countdown timers, interface interference, default settings that steer users towards invasive data sharing, and manipulative consent frameworks remain outside the scope of Annex I. This points to a deeper structural shortcoming: the black list still operates on an analogue conception of consumer harm as observable events, rather than addressing the systemic logic of digital commercial design.

This regulatory inertia poses several problems. To function as a tool of systemic prevention, a black list must reflect the logic of contemporary market architectures. That means targeting not only what is said (as in traditional false advertising), but how choices are framed, how defaults are designed, and how vulnerabilities are profiled and operationalised. A black list focused on misleading words rather than manipulative design is structurally misaligned with the challenges of digital commerce.

Without per se rules, enforcement agencies must resort to the general clause or Articles 6–9 assessments, with all the burdens of proof and interpretative uncertainties that follow. This creates a paradox: the more sophisticated and embedded the practice, the more challenging it becomes to classify it under current standards. Per se prohibitions do more than facilitate enforcement. They are expressions of normative clarity and contribute to what is referred to as regulatory transparency.[43] In the digital environment, such clarity operates on multiple levels. For courts and enforcement bodies, it reduces interpretative ambiguity and accelerates action. For platforms and service designers, it sets firm legal boundaries at the stage of product development, acting as a framing device that constrains manipulative creativity. For consumers, it conveys a clear, unambiguous normative message that certain practices are categorically prohibited, regardless of the outcome or context. They help translate the

---

[40] Annex I to the UCPD, point 7.

[41] Annex I to the UCPD, point 14.

[42] Directive (EU) 2019/2161 of the European Parliament and of the Council of 27 November 2019 amending Council Directive 93/13/EEC and Directives 98/6/EC, 2005/29/EC and 2011/83/EU of the European Parliament and of the Council as regards the better enforcement and modernisation of Union consumer protection rules.

[43] Namysłowska (2024b, 259).

abstract principle of fairness into a set of design-relevant constraints that can guide behaviour before harm occurs.

This need for normative clarity becomes even more pressing when contrasted with the approach taken in Article 5 AIA,[44] which lays down a set of ostensibly per se prohibitions on AI-driven practices considered unacceptable. These include the use of subliminal techniques to materially distort the behaviour of a person or a group of persons by appreciably impairing their ability to make an informed decision[45] and the exploitation of vulnerabilities of natural persons or a specific group of persons due to their age, disability or a specific social or economic situation.[46] However, each of these prohibitions is conditioned on a threshold of "significant harm". This effectively reintroduces a balancing requirement that blurs the distinction between categorical bans and risk-based assessment. Article 5 embeds the logic of harm evaluation into the prohibition itself, thereby weakening its *ex ante* preventive function. For consumer law, this should serve as a cautionary example. Structural manipulations, particularly in the digital domain, demand prohibitions that do not hinge on *ex post* demonstrations of damage, but on the incompatibility of the practice with the integrity of the decision-making process.

Critics may argue that the overuse of per se rules risks rigidity and overbreadth. But in digital markets, the problem is the opposite. Rules are too elastic, applied too late, and too inconsistently to constrain dominant actors. The platform environments demand rules that can pre-empt structural harm. This calls for an expansion of Annex I to cover core manipulative business models, particularly those that exploit digital vulnerability, information asymmetries, and attention. Structural protection requires structural rules. This chapter later proposes specific categories of digital practices that should be prohibited as unfair by design. Yet the limits of Annex I are only one part of a deeper regulatory shortfall. The challenge lies in the overall structure of EU consumer law. A coherent regime of structural protection cannot function if the underlying legal architecture is inconsistent and slow to adapt. The next section addresses this broader problem and the need for more integrated and enforceable safeguards in the digital environment.

---

[44] Regulation (EU) 2024/1689 of the European Parliament and of the Council of 13 June 2024 laying down harmonised rules on artificial intelligence and amending Regulations (EC) No 300/2008, (EU) No 167/2013, (EU) No 168/2013, (EU) 2018/858, (EU) 2018/1139 and (EU) 2019/2144 and Directives 2014/90/EU, (EU) 2016/797 and (EU) 2020/1828 (Artificial Intelligence Act).

[45] Article 5(1)(a) AIA.

[46] Article 5(1)(b) AIA.

4 Structural Protection in Practice: Information and Prohibitions

4.1 From Better Regulation to Better Enforcement

EU consumer law remains fragmented and ill-adapted to the realities of the digital environment. Although the Digital Fairness Fitness Check concludes that the EU consumer legal framework is generally efficient, it also highlights that its effectiveness is undermined by legal fragmentation "due to diverging interpretations and national laws in certain areas".[47] Consumers face difficulties due to the complexity and lack of transparency of EU consumer *acquis*, which spreads rights and obligations across multiple regulations and directives such as the CRD, UCTD, UCPD, E-Commerce Directive, DSA, GDPR, SGD, and DCD.[48] This regulatory dispersion generates legal uncertainty, which in turn hampers the effective enforcement of EU consumer law.

In 2020, the Commission raised the question about the need for additional legislation to ensure equal consumer protection across both online and offline B2C transactions.[49] However, from the perspective of better regulation, the question should have been whether more fragmented or more effective legislation is needed. In an era of globalisation where barriers to the movement of goods, services and people are falling, citizens expect legal regulations to ensure their safety and welfare. In contrast, businesses expect legal regulations to enable a level playing field and boost competitiveness.[50]

Regulatory fragmentation in EU consumer law hinders enforcement and weakens consumer rights. It also affects Member States, which must implement and interpret EU law consistently. Introducing piecemeal legislation targeting specific issues is easier than pursuing a systematic and coherent legal approach. The Digital Fairness Fitness Check emphasises a need to ensure "consistent application of EU consumer law and other EU legislation".[51] Yet EU policymakers seem neither ready nor institutionally equipped to address the fragmentation or the complex issues it creates, such as incoherence, inconsistency, and conflicting rules across legal acts. As *Micklitz* and *Twigg-Flesner* have pointedly observed, "the European Commission seems to assume that the existing consumer law *acquis* is already sufficient for the effective protection of consumers against the risks of the digital world".[52]

For example, one could exploit the inconsistency between the DSA and the UCPD. Dark patterns are prohibited by Article 25 DSA. At the same time, they are neither directly covered nor excluded by the UCPD. According to Article 25(2) DSA, the

[47] European Commission (2024, 35, 78–79).

[48] De Elizalde (2025).

[49] European Commission (2020).

[50] See https://commission.europa.eu/law/law-making-process/better-regulation_en.

[51] European Commission (2024, 87).

[52] Micklitz and Twigg-Flesner (2023, 7).

prohibition on manipulative online interface design that affects the ability of service recipients to make free and informed decisions will not apply to practices covered by the UCPD or the GDPR. There is no clear explanation as to why both legal acts could not prohibit certain B2C unfair commercial practices.[53] This was recently confirmed by the Higher Regional Court of Bamberg, likely the first German ruling on dark patterns.[54] The case involved an online platform that manipulated users into buying extra insurance when purchasing event tickets. The court held that Article 25(1) DSA does not apply to practices already covered by the UCPD. According to *Raue*, although the court excluded the application of Article 25 DSA, it recognised its indirect effect in violation of the UCPD, using it as a benchmark for interpreting the breach of Article 5(2) UCPD.[55] This highlights the need for national courts to adopt creative interpretative methods to resolve inconsistencies and bridge gaps between overlapping EU consumer laws.

In light of the findings of the Digital Fairness Fitness Check, it has become evident that amendments to the EU consumer *acquis* are inevitable. The scale of harm documented is enormous. The European Commission estimates that consumers in the internal market incur financial losses of at least EUR 7.9 billion annually. Importantly, this figure accounts only for measurable economic harm. It does not capture the broader spectrum of harm emerging in the digital environment, including health, mental, and societal harm.[56]

Given this context, the case for a dedicated legal instrument tailored to the risks of the digital economy is compelling. There are clear reasons to consider adopting a separate legal instrument dedicated to consumer protection in the digital environment—the Digital Fairness Act.[57] In the following sections, we outline how information duties combined with transparency requirements and *ex ante* prohibitions—which together form the core regulatory tools for addressing digital vulnerability in EU consumer law—must be reimagined to restore meaningful protection in digitally transformed markets.

---

[53] Mišćenić (2024, 96).

[54] OLG Bamberg, judgment of 5 February 2025, 3 UKl 11/24 e, GRUR-RS 2025, p. 6221, pending before the German Federal Court of Justice (BGH), I ZR 56/25.

[55] Raue (2025, 109–111).

[56] European Parliament (2023); Namysłowska (2024a, 197–204); European Commission (2024, 154).

[57] Namysłowska (2025); See also the result of the public consultation of the European Commission on the Digital Fairness Act at https://ec.europa.eu/info/law/better-regulation/have-your-say/initiatives/14622-Digital-Fairness-Act_en.

4.2 From Black Box to Toolbox

To restore transparency as a meaningful regulatory tool, its logic and delivery must be adapted to digital realities. Like many scholars, we advocate for improving information duties by harmonising and better regulating them across EU consumer law.[58] In this respect, we prioritise the quality of information over its quantity. The principle of 'less is more' would better reflect changes in online consumer behaviour and promote clearer, more practical compliance. The European Commission acknowledges the risk of information overload before and during contract conclusion, but dismisses summarised essential information as a simplification tool due to assumed compliance costs for traders.[59] However, traders have not reported significant costs related to complying with information duties.[60] The EU legislator could instead introduce horizontal amendments to the consumer *acquis*, requiring transparent disclosure of essential information in digital environments at both pre-contractual and contractual stages, making such disclosure a condition for contract conclusion. Similar provisions already exist in the Mortgage Credit Directive, the new Consumer Credit Directive, and the CRD, and could be adapted to meet the needs of digital markets.[61]

These amendments could be reinforced by transparency guidelines, which would act as an EU consumer law toolbox to help businesses and consumers effectively apply and understand essential information. Reflecting changes in consumer behaviour and business needs, the guidelines should offer practical examples of transparent information delivery online. Importantly, these would differ from existing Commission interpretative guidelines under the UCTD, UCPD, and CRD.[62] Instead, they would complement improved regulation of information duties, potentially as annexes to relevant directives, offering concrete tools for enforcement, compliance, and identifying the essential information that traders must provide.

While the European Commission continues to favour a principle-based approach, we propose a practice-based model that more effectively serves all stakeholders in the digital marketplace. Concerns about increased compliance burdens are unconvincing in light of ongoing advancements in AI and digital technologies. The same algorithms that personalise content and optimise engagement can also be used to surface essential consumer rights, highlight key trade-offs, or adapt information presentation to individual cognitive context. In the course of this research, we used an AI tool to generate a sample order confirmation summarising key consumer rights in a clear and accessible manner within seconds. This experiment demonstrates the real potential of technology to enhance consumer information and compliance.

---

[58] Pichonnaz (2023, 93), Mišćenić (2022, 679), Luzak (2021, 105–129) and Schaub (2017, 25).

[59] European Commission (2024, 78).

[60] European Commission (2024, 67).

[61] Article 8 CRD; Article 16 of Directive 2014/17/EU; Article 12 of Directive (EU) 2023/2225.

[62] European Commission (2019, 2021a, b).

This idea is not new. A growing body of empirical research supports the more effective use of digital tools to enhance transparency in digital environments[63] and calls for greater transparency of algorithmic mechanisms and digital infrastructures that shape consumer choices.[64] Building on this research, we believe the upcoming Digital Fairness Act has the potential to shift the illusion of consumer protection into a digital reality.[65]

4.3 *From Grey Zones to Red Lines*

Transparency, even if improved, has its limits. *Ex post* enforcement, even if coordinated, remains reactive. What is still missing from the EU consumer law toolbox is a coherent and future-oriented protection. Protection that does not rely on the capacity of individual consumers to recognise unfairness, or on the ability of courts to reconstruct it. Per se prohibitions are the legal form through which structural protection can start to take shape.

Structural protection targets harm at its source. It acknowledges that in digital markets, many forms of manipulation are embedded into the commercial design itself. When default settings nudge users toward more expensive choices, or when cancellation is made deliberately difficult, the problem is not a lack of information. It is the intentional shaping of behaviour in ways that bypass consumer autonomy. Legal responses to such practices cannot be based solely on case-by-case assessments of misleading content or aggressive practices. They must prohibit the mechanism itself.

Per se rules serve this purpose by placing specific techniques outside the bounds of fair commerce. They establish rules in contrast to the general clauses, which define standards of behaviour.[66] They do not necessitate balancing tests. They do not ask for evidence of consumer harm. Instead, they function as categorical bans on predefined patterns of digital influence. They inform businesses about the outcomes to avoid and about methods that are off-limits, regardless of how well they are concealed in code or interface.

Most structurally manipulative practices are left outside the scope of Annex I of the UCPD. Although the CJEU does not preclude extending prohibitions originally designed for the offline context to digital settings,[67] enforcement authorities are forced to stretch the existing provisions or rely on complex behavioural evidence, which undermines the speed and coherence of regulatory responses.

---

[63] Seizov, Wulf and Luzak (2019, 149–173), Luzak et al. (2023, 307–333) and Namysłowska (2024b, 261).

[64] Grochowski et al. (2021, 43–63) and Namysłowska (2024b, 261).

[65] Mišćenić and Tereszkiewicz (2024, 229–233).

[66] See, for example, Ehrlich and Posner (1974, 258) and Kaplow (1992, 557 f).

[67] CJEU, case C-371/20 *Peek & Cloppenburg KG v Peek & Cloppenburg KG*, 2 September 2021, ECLI:EU:C:2021:674, para 43.

To address these issues, the black list of unfair commercial practices should be amended. This means identifying and prohibiting certain forms of business models and interaction design. It also means evolving past generic references to misleading or aggressive practices and identifying the specific patterns through which digital choice architectures distort consumer autonomy. It necessitates a departure from the view that harm is always individual and economic. Many of the most damaging practices exploit group-specific vulnerabilities (such as those of children or older persons) or create systemic effects that individual users cannot detect. A black list that captures these dynamics would offer structural protection precisely where transparency and individual rights fall short.

This expansion would also serve a second, equally important function: reinforcing the expressive role of consumer law. A well-crafted list of practices prohibited in all circumstances clarifies which types of design, techniques, and practices are unacceptable in principle. It shifts the regulatory approach from 'what is harmful?' to 'what kind of marketplace do we want to have?'.

The following prohibitions could be added to Annex I of the UCPD. Most of these practices fall under what is referred to as dark patterns—interface designs that manipulate users through asymmetry, friction, or psychological pressure:

(1) presenting a choice in such a manner that the default option is easier to accept than to reject, deactivate or reverse, by using visual prominence, procedural friction or other interface design techniques intended to exploit consumer cognitive biases (manipulative default asymmetries).
(2) making the process of cancelling or unsubscribing from a contract more complex, burdensome, or time-consuming than the process of entering into the contract, without a legitimate and proportionate justification (obstruction of contract termination).
(3) soliciting consumer reviews or ratings in a selective manner likely to create a misleading impression of consumer satisfaction, including by inviting feedback primarily from satisfied consumers or at favourable moments (distorted consumer feedback systems).
(4) personalising the price, ranking, or visibility of products based on behavioural data, without clearly disclosing this personalisation at the time the consumer is presented with the offer (non-transparent personalisation).
(5) using digital interface designs or commercial communication to exploit the developmental vulnerabilities of minors, in order to induce purchases, in-app spending, disclosure of personal data, or prolonged engagement (exploitative targeting of minors).
(6) deploying gamified incentives, emotional prompts, countdowns, or peer comparison mechanisms in order to induce minors to engage with or purchase digital content (manipulative engagement techniques targeting minors).
(7) offering loot boxes or other randomised reward mechanisms in games accessible to minors, regardless of whether their presence is disclosed (gambling-like monetisation in games accessible to minors).

These proposals are not meant to replace the flexibility of the general clause, but rather to complement it where it falls short. They may be supported by interpretative guidance and must be designed in a way that national enforcement bodies can apply them without relying on behavioural proof in every individual case, allowing authorities to act swiftly and consistently across jurisdictions. Additionally, a reform of Annex I demands a new approach to its maintenance. A mechanism for updating the black list through delegated acts, backed by technical expertise and design audits, would allow the law to respond to emerging manipulative tactics without waiting for crises.[68]

5 Conclusions: Delivering Protection in the Digital Age

EU consumer law was not built for the kind of marketplace that now dominates the digital economy. While the regulatory framework has expanded over the years, it has done so unevenly, producing fragmentation, overlaps, and regulatory gaps that limit its effectiveness in practice. The problems are structural: disconnected instruments, inconsistent information obligations, and reactive enforcement strategies that struggle to address manipulation designed into the system.

As this chapter has argued, improving digital fairness demands a shift in regulatory approach. Traditional tools—transparency, information duties, and general clauses—retain their value, but they no longer align with the scale, speed, or logic of contemporary digital harm. Consumers are increasingly exposed to design choices that shape their preferences and decisions before any transaction begins. Legal protections that rely on consumers' awareness, or on regulators' ability to act *ex post*, are often too little, too late.

This is where structural protection becomes essential. By embedding fairness into the design of the legal framework through reformed information duties, horizontal transparency requirements, and per se prohibitions that target manipulative design patterns, the law can begin to act before harm becomes widespread. The proposed expansion of Annex I of the UCPD reaffirms the core function of consumer law: not just to protect the freedom to choose, but also to protect consumers from engineered influence.

That vision also means a return to clarity. As *Kennedy* once said, the right to be informed is a right to receive the facts one needs to make an informed choice.[69] In the digital marketplace, facts alone are insufficient. The way they are presented, the way choices are framed, and the way defaults are set matter just as much. Redesigning the law to reflect this reality is not a departure from the consumer protection acquis, but its continuation under new conditions.

Improving both the content and delivery of consumer information would significantly benefit businesses and consumers, leading to more effective enforcement and

[68] Namysłowska (2024a, 227) and Savin (2022, 13–14).

[69] Kennedy (1962).

digital fairness. The digital consumer, as aptly named by *Mak*,[70] requires different information and a different way of receiving it to make informed and transparent choices. A simplification of existing rules, supported by clear guidelines and amendments focused on essential information, would better meet these needs and serve all stakeholders.

The digital single market has already brought substantial benefits to consumers: increased access, enhanced convenience, and more competitive prices across borders. Ensuring it also promotes fairness will help these gains last and serve as a foundation for the next generation of consumer law in the digital age.

References

de Elizalde F (2025) Fragmenting consumer law through data protection and digital market regulations: the DMA, the DSA, the GDPR, and EU consumer law. J Consum Policy. https://doi.org/10.1007/s10603-025-09584-3

Đurović M (2016) European law on unfair commercial practices and contract law. Hart Publishing, Oxford

Ehrlich I, Posner RA (1974) An economic analysis of legal rulemaking. J Legal Stud 3(1):257–286

Esposito F, Grochowski M (2022) The consumer benchmark, vulnerability, and the contract terms transparency: a plea for reconsideration. Eur Rev Contract Law 18(1):1–31

European Commission (2019) Guidance on the interpretation and application of Council Directive 93/13/EEC on unfair terms in consumer contracts. https://eur-lex.europa.eu/legal-content/EN/TXT/PDF/?uri=OJ:JOC_2019_323_R_0004

European Commission (2020) Communication from the Commission to the European Parliament and the Council New Consumer Agenda—strengthening consumer resilience for sustainable recovery. COM(2020) 696 final. https://eur-lex.europa.eu/legal-content/EN/TXT/?uri=CELEX:52020DC0696

European Commission (2021a) Guidance on the interpretation and application of Directive 2005/29/EC of the European Parliament and of the Council concerning unfair business-to-consumer commercial practices in the internal market. https://eur-lex.europa.eu/legal-content/EN/TXT/?uri=oj:JOC_2021_526_R_0001

European Commission (2021b) Guidance on the interpretation and application of Directive 2011/83/EU of the European Parliament and of the Council on consumer rights. https://eur-lex.europa.eu/legal-content/EN/TXT/?uri=oj:JOC_2021_525_R_0001

European Parliament (2023) Resolution of 12 December 2023 on addictive design of online services and consumer protection in the EU single market (2023/2043(INI)). https://www.europarl.europa.eu/doceo/document/TA-9-2023-0459_EN.html

European Commission (2024) Commission staff working document fitness check of EU consumer law on digital fairness. Brussels, SWD (2024) 230 final. https://www.europarl.europa.eu/meetdocs/2024_2029/plmrep/COMMITTEES/IMCO/SWD/2024/11-18/COM_SWD20240230_EN.pdf

European Commission (2025) Consumer condition scoreboard 2025. https://www.europarl.europa.eu/meetdocs/2024_2029/plmrep/COMMITTEES/IMCO/DV/2025/05-19/consumer_conditions_scoreboard_2025_EN.pdf

Eurostat (2025) E-commerce statistics for individuals. https://ec.europa.eu/eurostat/statistics-explained/index.php?title=E-commerce_statistics_for_individuals

Galli F (2022) Algorithmic marketing and EU law on unfair commercial practices. Springer, Cham

[70] Mak (2023, 43).

Gardiner C (2022) Unfair contract terms in the digital age: the challenge of protecting European consumers in the online marketplace. Edward Elgar, Cheltenham

Grochowski M, Jabłonowska A, Lagioia F, Sartor G (2021) Algorithmic transparency and explainability for EU consumer protection: unwrapping the regulatory premises. Crit Anal Law 8(1):43–63

Helberger N et al (2024) Towards digital fairness. J Eur Consum Mark Law 13(1):24–30

Helberger N et al (2021) EU consumer protection 2.0: structural asymmetries in digital consumer markets. BEUC

Howells G (2005) The potential and limits of consumer empowerment by information. J Law Soc 32:349–370

Infantino M, Mišćenić E, Tereszkiewicz P (2024) Buying insurance online: are European consumers protected or vulnerable? J Eur Consum Mark Law 13(6):262–269

Kaplow L (1992) Rules versus standards: an economic analysis. Duke Law J 42(3):557–629

Kennedy JF (1962) Special message to the congress on protecting the consumer interest. March 15, 1962. https://www.presidency.ucsb.edu/documents/special-message-the-congress-protecting-the-consumer-interest

Loos MBM (2023) Crystal clear? The transparency requirement in unfair terms legislation. Eur Rev Contract Law 19(4):281–299

Loos MBM, Luzak J (2021) Update the unfair contract terms directive for digital services. European Parliament. PE 676.006. https://www.europarl.europa.eu/thinktank/en/document/IPOL_STU(2021)676006

Luzak J (2021) Tailor-made consumer protection: personalisation's impact on the granularity of consumer information. In: Corrales Compagnucci M, Haapio H, Hagan M, Doherty M (eds) Legal design: integrating business, design and legal thinking with technology. Edward Elgar, Cheltenham, pp 105–129

Luzak J, Wulf AJ, Seizov O et al (2023) ABC of online consumer disclosure duties: improving transparency and legal certainty in Europe. J Consum Policy 46(3):307–333

Mak V (2024) Redefining equality in European contract law: protecting consumer interests in a post-consumer society. Eur Law Open 3(3):561–586

Mak V (2023) How can consumer interests be protected when consumer identities are increasingly diffuse? In: Micklitz H-W, Twigg-Flesner C (eds) The transformation of consumer law and policy in Europe. Hart, Oxford, pp 43–63

Micklitz H-W, Twigg-Flesner C (2023) Transformation of consumer law and policy in Europe. In: Micklitz H-W, Twigg-Flesner C (eds) The transformation of consumer law and policy in Europe. Hart, Oxford, pp 1–18

Mišćenić E (2024) Information, transparency and fairness for consumers in the digital environment. In: Crea C, de Franceschi A (eds) Digital vulnerability in European private law. Nomos, Baden-Baden, pp 81–118

Mišćenić E (2022) The constant change of EU consumer law: the real deal or just an illusion? Belgrade Law Rev 70(3):679–710

Mišćenić E (2018) Protection of consumers on the EU digital single market: virtual or real one? In: Viglianisi Ferraro A, Jagielska M, Selucka M (eds) The influence of the European legislation on national legal systems in the field of consumer protection. Cedam, Padua, pp 219–246

Mišćenić E, Tereszkiewicz P (2024) Towards a new Digital Fairness Act! J Eur Consum Mark Law 13(6):229–233

Namysłowska M (2025) The silent death of EU consumer law and its resilient revival: reinventing consumer protection against unfair digital commercial practices. J Consum Policy. https://doi.org/10.1007/s10603-025-09590-5

Namysłowska M (2024a) Future-proofing the unfairness test. In: Helberger N et al (eds) Digital fairness for consumers. BEUC, Brussels, pp 165–241, 269–276

Namysłowska M (2024b) Behind the digital curtain: the need for digital transparency to establish digital fairness. J Eur Consum Mark Law 13(6):255–262

Oehler A, Wendt S (2017) Good consumer information: the information paradigm at its (dead) end? J Consum Policy 40(2):179–191
Paterson M (2023) Misleading AI: regulatory strategies for algorithmic transparency in technologies augmenting consumer decision-making. Loyola Consum Law Rev 34(3):558–581
Pichonnaz P (2023) Information duties. In: Micklitz H-W, Twigg-Flesner C (eds) The transformation of consumer law and policy in Europe. Hart, Oxford, pp 81–104
Raue B (2025) Dark Patterns on online platforms and the interplay between the digital services act and the unfair commercial practices directive. J Eur Consum Mark Law 14(3):109–111
Riesenhuber K, Möslein F (2009) Transparenz. In: Basedow J, Hopt KJ, Zimmermann R (eds) Handwörterbuch des europäischen Privatrechts. Mohr Siebeck, Tübingen
Rott P (2025) Digital fairness and the burden of proof. J Consum Policy. https://doi.org/10.1007/s10603-025-09583-4
Savin A (2022) Designing EU digital laws. Copenhagen Business School Law Research Paper No. 22–13. https://research.cbs.dk/en/publications/designing-eu-digital-laws
Schaub M (2017) How to make the best mandatory information requirements in consumer law. Eur Rev Priv Law 25(1):25–44
Segger-Piening S (2021) No need to read: 'self-enforcing' pre-contractual consumer information in European and German law. In: Mathis K, Tor A (eds) Consumer law and economics. Springer, Cham, pp 89–117
Seizov O, Wulf AJ, Luzak J (2019) The transparent trap: a multidisciplinary perspective on the design of transparent online disclosures in the EU. J Consum Policy 42(1):149–173
Vrbljanac D (2024) Non-transparency by design: case note on meta platforms Ireland (action représentative). J Eur Consum Mark Law 13(6):269–272

The New European Withdrawal Function: Protecting Consumers Against 'Digital Traps'

Karin Sein

Abstract This paper critically examines the new European withdrawal function introduced under the amended Consumer Rights Directive (CRD) and its implications for consumer and data protection. The withdrawal function aims to simplify the process for consumers to exercise their right of withdrawal from distance contracts, addressing issues related to 'digital traps' where contracts are difficult to cancel. The paper explores the legal requirements of the withdrawal function, its scope of application, and the tensions between consumer protection and data protection. Key findings highlight that while the withdrawal function enhances consumer rights, its exclusion of certain off-premises contracts and other termination scenarios may leave some consumers unprotected. Additionally, the widely used requirement for customer accounts for using the withdrawal function raises data privacy concerns. The paper suggests that alternatives, such as providing access to the withdrawal function through order confirmation emails, could mitigate these concerns while maintaining robust customer identification to prevent fraud.

Keywords Withdrawal function · Consumer contract law · Data protection law · EU law

1 Introduction

In early 2025, the media reported on a new policy of Elisa, one of the leading telecommunications providers in Estonia. According to the news, customers can sign up for Elisa services through its online self-service portal, but those wishing to cancel their contract are required to do so in person. The telecommunications provider's spokesperson explained it with the necessity to provide advice and assistance:

This work was supported by the Estonian Research Council Grant (PRG2640).

K. Sein (✉)
Department of Private Law, University of Tartu, Tartu, Estonia
e-mail: karin.sein@ut.ee

C. Crea and M. Infantino (eds.), *Remedies to Digital Vulnerability in European Private Law*, https://doi.org/10.1007/978-3-032-19720-7_2

'This is because experience has shown that this is an action that requires more detailed explanations and assistance from the service provider,' Tulp noted. She added that when a customer wants to cancel their service contract, it is extremely important to understand the customer's reason for doing so. 'Usually it isn't because a customer no longer needs the service, but rather that their needs have changed, or they need help using the service.'[1]

Similar practices have been reported from other Member States. In Germany, for example, it was not uncommon for traders to require online-concluded contracts to be cancelled by sending a signed notice via registered mail, before the German *Bundesgerichtshof* held them unfair.[2] These practices resulted in new legislation adopted in Germany and in France in 2022–2023, facilitating easier cancellation of subscriptions.[3] The new German rules in § 312k of the German Civil Code (BGB) introduced the so-called cancellation button, requiring traders to provide such a button for terminating long-term consumer contracts concluded via digital means.

This new German legislation became the main blueprint for the European withdrawal function, introduced by Art. 11a of the amended Consumer Rights Directive (CRD)[4] and requiring that the right of withdrawal from distance contracts must be facilitated through a prominent, easy-to-find 'withdrawal function' on the provider's interface. This new institute was meant as a remedy to protect consumers against 'digital traps' where originally digitally (and very easily) concluded contracts became impossible to withdraw from, be it because of a handwritten signature, a show-up requirement or due to an excessively difficult web design. The legislator's intent is clear. As Recital 36 of the Financial Services Distance Selling Directive states, '[i]n order to ensure the effective exercise of the right of withdrawal, the procedure for the exercise of that right should not be more burdensome than the procedure for the conclusion of the distance contract'. The same idea is once more expressed in recital 37: 'This should ensure that consumers can withdraw from a contract just as easily as they can conclude it'. The new rules are to be applied from 11 June 2026.

This paper aims to deliver a critical assessment of the new European withdrawal function, starting with the description of its legal requirements (Sect. 2), then highlighting some problems with its scope of application (Sect. 3) and its tensions with the data protection aims (Sect. 4). The chapter ends with some conclusions (Sect. 5).

---

[1] ERR (2025).

[2] BGH, 14 July 2016 - III ZR 387/15.

[3] Busch and Twigg-Flesner (2024).

[4] These changes to the CRD were implemented with the new Financial Services Distance Selling Directive. Directive (EU) 2023/2673 of the European Parliament and of the Council of 22 November 2023 amending Directive 2011/83/EU as regards financial services contracts concluded at a distance and repealing Directive 2002/65/EC. OJ L, 2023/2673, 28 November 2023.

2 Scope of Application

The new rules on the European withdrawal function will apply to all distance selling contracts concluded by means of an online interface, including in-app purchases (Art. 11a (1) CRD).[5] Whereas the Commission's proposal suggested applying these rules only to financial services,[6] in its final version the rules on withdrawal function apply to all distance contracts, be it consumer credit or online sales contracts. As recital 37 stresses: '[t]his obligation should be laid down not only for distance contracts for financial services, but also for distance contracts for other goods and services where Union law provides for a right of withdrawal to enhance the possibilities for consumers to get out of contracts by means of withdrawal.'[7] Since sectoral legislation such as the Consumer Credit Directive (CCD)[8] or the Solvency II Directive[9] does not regulate the issue of withdrawal function (i.e. they do not oblige traders to offer consumers the option of withdrawing from a contract by means of a withdrawal function), Art. 16a(10) CRD, which provides for the priority of sectoral EU legislation, does not preclude the application of the withdrawal button regulation to contracts subject to sector-specific rules.

The European withdrawal function is only meant to facilitate the exercise of consumers' statutory right of withdrawal and does not concern other cases of ending a contract, e.g. terminating it for an essential breach. It should be stressed that using a withdrawal function is not an exclusive one for the consumer: it is an option additional to other withdrawal possibilities, so the consumer remains entitled to send his or her notice of withdrawal, e.g. via email or using a EU withdrawal template.[10]

There are a couple of problems with the scope of application of the new rules, though. First, according to Art. 11a CRD, a withdrawal button must be provided for 'distance contracts concluded by means of an online interface'. This means that the withdrawal button is not required for off-premises contracts within the meaning of Art. 2(8) CRD. Indeed, at first glance, the withdrawal button would make little sense for off-premises contracts, which are usually perceived as contracts concluded in person but outside the trader's business premises. However, under Art. 2(8)(c) CRD, the concept of off-premises contract also includes a contract between the trader and the consumer concluded on the business premises of the trader or *through any means of distance communication* immediately after the consumer was personally

[5] Izzo-Wagner et al. (2024, 85).

[6] European Commission (2022a), article 16b(5).

[7] On the development of the institute of consumer's withdrawal right, see Howells et al. (2018, 114–119).

[8] Directive 2008/48/EC of the European Parliament and of the Council of 23 April 2008 on credit agreements for consumers and repealing Council Directive 87/102/EEC. OJ L 133, 22 May 2008.

[9] Directive 2009/138/EC of the European Parliament and of the Council of 25 November 2009 on the taking-up and pursuit of the business of Insurance and Reinsurance (Solvency II) (recast). OJ L 335, 17 December 2009.

[10] This is clarified in recital 37 stating 'In addition to other existing means of withdrawal, such as the form laid down in Annex I(B) of Directive 2011/83/EU'.

and individually addressed in a place which is not the business premises of the trader in the simultaneous physical presence of the trader and the consumer. This includes situations such as cases where the salesperson of a trader approaches a consumer in the corridor of a supermarket, hands out a leaflet, and later at home the consumer concludes an online contract with the trader based on the information obtained through this leaflet. This raises the question of whether the consumer is also in need of protection in these situations. As the legislator's aim for creating the new European withdrawal function was to compensate for the lack of personal explanations and advice in case of online contracts,[11] and for the inability to see the goods before concluding the contract,[12] the requirement for providing a withdrawal function should also apply to cases of off-premises contracts as defined in Art. 2(8)(c) CRD where the contract is concluded through any means of distance communication immediately after the consumer was personally and individually addressed in a place which is not the business premises of the trader.

The second problem concerns the fact that under the new rules, a withdrawal function must exist for exercising the withdrawal right under European Union law.[13] Contrary to e.g. the German domestic rules (according to § 312k BGB, traders must provide a withdrawal button for ordinary and extraordinary terminations of the long-term contracts concluded online; 'termination' of a contract does, however, not include termination as a remedy for a breach of contract or the consumer's withdrawal right),[14] the European withdrawal function requirement is restricted to withdrawal situations, i.e. cases where the EU law gives consumers a reflection period and the right to end the contract without any cause. As described above, it is not applicable to other cases of ending a contract by consumers. However, there is a similar need for protecting consumers, especially in cases where free testing periods have been offered by digital service providers, such as the three-month free trial for Amazon Prime.[15]

It is well documented that dark patterns have often been used in the case of digital subscriptions to complicate the cancellation of the free trial. In the final report of the Fitness Check of EU Consumer Law on Digital Fairness, the European Commission pointed out several problems that consumers are facing with subscriptions, such as the use of dark patterns and other difficulties with cancelling contracts online, automatic renewals, and free trials.[16] In 2021, the European Commission, in cooperation with national consumer authorities, launched an action against Amazon to bring its Amazon Prime subscription cancellation practices in line with EU consumer rules.

---

[11] See recital 37 of the Financial Services Distance Selling Directive.

[12] See recital 37 CRD.

[13] In this regard, it should be noted that for several financial service contracts, the withdrawal right does not stem from the CRD but rather from sectoral legislation, such as the Consumer Credit Directive or the Markets in Crypto-Assets Regulation (MICA).

[14] See, in detail, Wendehorst (2022), commentary on § 312 k BGB.

[15] European Commission (2022b).

[16] European Commission (2024), 176, 178; specifically as to the dark patterns, European Commission (2022c).

Following this action, in 2022, Amazon committed to enabling consumers from the EU and EEA countries to unsubscribe from Amazon Prime with just two clicks, using a prominent and clear 'cancel button'.[17] As consumers need similar protection also in the situation of free trials in order not to stay trapped in the digital subscriptions, the requirement for providing a withdrawal function should be extended to these situations as well. Alternatively, consumers should be notified that the cancellation period is about to end and offered an easy digital way of cancellation, or the law could even require consumers' express consent before a free trial could convert to a paid-for subscription.[18]

As a sidenote, it should be pointed out that the rules on pre-contractual information obligations under the new Consumer Credit Directive and Articles 11a and 16(10) CRD are not well aligned as it remains unclear whether, in case of a consumer credit contract, the creditor must inform the consumer about the possibility to withdraw via withdrawal function or not. As to the information requirements set out in Art. 16a(1) CRD (including the obligation under Art. 16a(1)(p) CRD to inform the consumer about the existence and placement of the withdrawal function referred to in Article 11a), in accordance with paragraph 10 of that provision, these requirements do not apply when there are sectoral EU rules for specific financial services on pre-contractual information obligations, such as in case of consumer credit. Consequently, traders need to provide only the pre-contractual information set out in the specific sectoral act, unless otherwise provided by it. The problem is that the CCD rules on pre-contractual information obligations in its Artt. 10 and 11 do not foresee an obligation to inform consumers about the possibility of using the European withdrawal function. This results in a situation where, in the case of consumer credit contracts, consumers must be provided with a European withdrawal function but are not informed about it. Of course, if certain sectoral acts are not maximum harmonising, Member States may require additional information on the withdrawal function in their national law. However, CCD is a maximum harmonisation directive and therefore national legislators are in principle precluded from introducing corresponding information obligations.

3 Requirements for the European Withdrawal Function

According to Art. 11a(1) CRD, the withdrawal function must be prominently displayed on the online interface and easily accessible, and it must remain continuously accessible throughout the entire withdrawal period. The function must be labelled with the words 'Withdraw from contract here' or another equally clear and unambiguous formulation. This means that the button should be large enough to be

[17] European Commission (2022b).

[18] European Law Institute (2023, 13–21). On the issue of digital subscriptions and consumer protection, see Busch and Twigg-Flesner (2024).

noticeable and use contrasting colors to stand out from the rest of the webpage. The text on the button must be clear and concise to avoid any ambiguity.[19]

In order to avoid the unintended exercise of the right of withdrawal by the consumer,[20] the CRD foresees a two-step design. The trader must provide two 'buttons' or functions: a withdrawal button and a confirmation button. The withdrawal function will enable the consumer to send an online withdrawal statement informing the trader of his or her decision to withdraw from the contract, and it must contain information required by Art. 11a(2) CRD. The withdrawal button must lead directly to a confirmation function, and the subsequent confirmation button must finalise the withdrawal by enabling the consumer to submit it to the trader. To facilitate the process, recital 37 of the Financial Services Distance Marketing Directive (FSDMD) suggests that the trader could, for example, provide hyperlinks leading the consumer to the withdrawal function. Article 11a(4) CRD also mandates confirmation by a trader on a durable medium of the use of the withdrawal button.

In German legal literature, the rules on the withdrawal button have been criticized as being overly complex[21]; some have argued that the requirement of the availability of a cancellation email address of the trader would have been enough for consumer protection purposes.[22] Apart from data protection vs identification requirements (see below, Sect. 4), one complexity arises in cases where the consumer has purchased several goods or services within the same distance contract but only wishes to withdraw from one or several of them. In these cases, the trader can—but is not obliged to—provide the consumer with the possibility to withdraw from a part rather than the whole of the contract. Recital 37 clarifies that allowing partial withdrawal from a contract is an option, but not mandatory for the trader.

4 Consumer Protection vs Data Protection?

There is, however, a certain tension between the consumer and data protection related to the withdrawal button. The new regulation has raised privacy concerns as offering a withdrawal button requires personalisation (as the withdrawal period depends on the circumstances of a particular transaction) and, therefore, a personalised customer account. It is maintained that the introduction of the withdrawal button requirement leads to an indirect obligation for consumers to create a customer account, which requires processing more personal data than in the case of anonymous transactions.[23]

Indeed, requiring the setting up of a mandatory customer account may violate both data protection and consumer law. In Germany, the Data Protection Conference

---

[19] On the clarity requirement in the context of the ordering button under Art. 8(2) CRD, see CJEU case C-249/21 of 7 April 2022, *Fuhrmann-2-GmbH v B*, ECLI:EU:C:2022:269.

[20] Recital 37 of the Financial Services Distance Marketing Directive.

[21] Alexander (2024, 1295).

[22] Güster and Booke (2022, 452).

[23] Izzo-Wagner et al. (2024, 86) and Lommatzsch and Albrecht (2024, 142).

(*Datenschutzkonferenz*) stated in 2022 that following the data minimisation principle under Art. 5(1)(c) GDPR,[24] in case of online sales, it must be possible to order goods without a customer account. In other words, a guest checkout option is required.[25] Moreover, the European Consumer Organisation (BEUC) has noted[26] that requiring registration and not allowing the use of a guest account may, when combined with other misleading practices, constitute an unfair commercial practice under the Unfair Commercial Practices Directive.[27]

To tackle these concerns, it should be explored whether providing a withdrawal button could be possible without a personalised account. It has convincingly been argued by Föhlisch and Löwer that it is possible to include hyperlinks to the withdrawal function in the order confirmation e-mail and thereby provide access to the withdrawal function also without creating a personalised account beforehand.[28] Such a design would allow buying goods or services without creating a personalised account. True, it still requires at least the consumer's name and e-mail address, but this data is necessary anyway to comply with the requirement of sending a confirmation email to the customer. A personalised account is also not strictly necessary for determining the individual withdrawal period (and thus also the period of the mandatory availability of the withdrawal function), as the time of delivery of the goods (that triggers the start of the withdrawal period under Art. 9(2)(b) CRD) can be determined through their tracking information.[29] This would also not be contrary to Art. 11a (2) CRD which only requires that the following information is given in the consumer's withdrawal statement: (i) consumer's name; (ii) details identifying the contract from which he or she wishes to withdraw; (iii) details of the electronic means by which the confirmation of the withdrawal will be sent to the consumer.

On the other hand, the growing amount of digital fraud[30] requires robust customer identification. There are different ways for identifying the consumers, starting with a customer account (and verified via a password), using another digital service provider's (such as Google or Facebook) identification system, or going for a more robust and reliable electronic identification mechanism regulated in the new eIDAS

[24] Regulation (EU) 2016/679 of the European Parliament and of the Council of 27 April 2016 on the protection of natural persons with regard to the processing of personal data and on the free movement of such data, and repealing Directive 95/46/EC (General Data Protection Regulation). OJ L 119, 4 May 2016.

[25] DSK (2022, 1–2).

[26] BEUC (2025, 25).

[27] Directive 2005/29/EC of the European Parliament and of the Council of 11 May 2005 concerning unfair business-to-consumer commercial practices in the internal market and amending Council Directive 84/450/EEC, Directives 97/7/EC, 98/27/EC and 2002/65/EC of the European Parliament and of the Council and Regulation (EC) No 2006/2004 of the European Parliament and of the Council, OJ L 149, 11 June 2005.

[28] Föhlisch and Löwer (2024, 117).

[29] Ibidem.

[30] Kjörven (2020) and Byrne and Byrne (2023).

Regulation,[31] such as different types of eID. It is finally for the European Court of Justice to clarify whether it is permissible to first require consumers to log in (e.g. using Mobile-ID) to a company's website and only then display the withdrawal and confirmation buttons. In other words, may a trader require identification for using the withdrawal function or at least for the confirmation function and if yes, then at what stage?

In the author's opinion, the answer to the first question should be positive, as recital 37 FSDMD seems to imply that the trader is allowed to require the consumer to identify themselves. However, the recital's text leaves it unclear whether and when customer identification (e.g. via login) can be required. Recital 37 FSDMD provides:

> 'For instance, a consumer who has already identified himself or herself, for example by logging in, should be able to withdraw from the contract without the necessity of providing once more their identification or, where applicable, the identification of the contract from which he or she wishes to withdraw.'

This only clarifies that when the customer is already logged in, further identification may not be required. Can we deduce from here, per *argumentum e contrario*, that an unlogged consumer may be required to log in for identification? Especially if logging in or identifying oneself via another identification option was required to conclude the contract in the first place? Or would requiring an identification mean that the withdrawal function is then not easily accessible to the consumer as required by Art. 11a(1) CRD? Moreover, the text of Art. 11a CRD does not require any additional steps or information from the consumer after using the withdrawal function and before using the confirmation function.

There are already cases on the legal compliance of the design of the cancellation button in the lower courts of Germany. True, they only concern German domestic legislation and are therefore not directly transferable to the European withdrawal function. However, as German law served as a blueprint for the new European rules, it is worth taking a look at the German case law while bearing in mind certain differences in the design requirements of the European withdrawal button and the German cancellation button. In a recent case of the Düsseldorf second instance court,[32] the consumer, after clicking the withdrawal button, was redirected not to one but several websites. The consumer only reached the 'Confirm cancellation' button when he had previously entered a number of details and had to press another button. The Court found that such web-design does not comply with the legal requirements: both the identification of the customer and the possibility to click on the confirmation button should be located on a single website, and the statutory two-step contract termination process must not be supplemented by additional confirmation of the customer's identity on an additional webpage.

Another German second instance court clarified the important question of whether the cancellation button must be visible before the customer identification. The Court

[31] Regulation (EU) 2024/1183 of the European Parliament and of the Council of 11 April 2024 amending Regulation (EU) No 910/2014 as regards establishing the European Digital Identity Framework. OJ L, 2024/1183, 30 April 2024.

[32] Judgment of Düsseldorf Oberlandesgericht of 23 May 2024 - 20 UKl 3/23.

ruled that the German cancellation button must also be accessible in cases where a customer account is generally created to conclude the contract that is later to be cancelled, without requiring a login to this customer account. An exception is conceivable if the use of the service, which is the subject of the continuing obligation, inherently requires a login.[33] In other words, as a general rule, the cancellation button must be visible already before logging in to the customer account. In the German legal literature, it has been argued that placing the cancellation button behind the login wall should be allowed.[34]

It is important to stress that both these German courts did not question the requirement of customer identification as such. Moreover, as German and European rules have slight but important differences as to the button's design requirements,[35] the insights of the German jurisprudence cannot be directly transferred to the European level. Most importantly, under § 312k(2) fourth sentence BGB, the cancellation button and the confirmation page must be directly and easily accessible. Hence, the German law requires that the webpage of the confirmation button comes directly after the webpage of the cancellation button. By contrast, Art. 11a CRD does not foresee such a requirement and only mandates that the withdrawal function is easily accessible. Consequently, there seems to be no obstacle in the CRD to require customer identification, at least before the consumer can activate the confirmation function.

Indeed, the legitimacy of the customer identification requirement is in line with the aim of digital fraud prevention. It would be very complicated, if not impossible, to prevent fraud and digital abuse without the identification requirement. If the trader were only entitled to require the consumer's name and the identification of the contract (is 'purchase of a white shirt on March 1st, 2025' or a 'consumer credit contract of 5000 EUR on March 2, 2025' enough?), then a husband could terminate his wife's order if he thinks she overspends: a ridiculous but nevertheless valid example.

To a certain extent, using strong eID solutions for customer identification might be an appropriate remedy to tackle data minimisation concerns. These solutions still require identification and hence the provision of personal data, but they require less data, and not e.g. consumer's address or phone number.

5 Conclusions

The introduction of the European withdrawal function represents a significant advancement in consumer protection within the digital marketplace. By mandating a prominently displayed and easily accessible withdrawal function, the regulation aims to simplify the process for consumers to exercise their right of withdrawal from

---

[33] Judgment of Nürnberg Oberlandesgericht of 30 July 2024 – 3 U 2214/23.

[34] Sümmermann and Ewald (2022, 717).

[35] Maume (2025), commentary to § 312 k para. 5a.

distance contracts. This measure addresses the issue of 'digital traps' where contracts concluded online become difficult to cancel due to cumbersome procedures.

However, the scope of application of the new rules presents certain challenges. The exclusion of off-premises contracts from the requirement to provide a withdrawal button may leave some consumers unprotected in situations defined in Art. 2(8)(c) CRD where contracts are concluded through distance communication immediately after personal interaction. Extending the requirement to these cases would ensure comprehensive consumer protection. Additionally, as consumers need similar protection also in the situation of free trials in order not to stay trapped in the digital subscriptions, the requirement for providing a withdrawal function should be extended to these situations as well.

The tension between consumer protection and data protection is another critical issue. The requirement for a withdrawal button may necessitate the creation of customer accounts, potentially conflicting with data minimization principles under the GDPR. Exploring alternatives, such as providing access to the withdrawal function through order confirmation emails, could mitigate these concerns while maintaining customer identification requirements to prevent fraud.

In conclusion, while the European withdrawal button is a step forward in protecting consumers in the digital age, further refinements are needed to address its scope of application and balance consumer protection with data privacy concerns. Extending the requirement to off-premises contracts and exploring less intrusive identification methods could enhance the effectiveness and fairness of this regulation.

References

Alexander C (2024) Lauterkeitsrechtliche Transparenzpflichten zum Schutz von Verbrauchern. Gewerblicher Rechtsschutz und Urheberrecht 126(17–18):1286–1296

BEUC (2025) Click to buy (more). How fast fashion giant SHEIN uses dark patterns to push overconsumption. https://www.beuc.eu/reports/click-buy-more-how-fast-fashion-giant-shein-uses-dark-patterns-push-overconsumption

Busch C, Twigg-Flesner C (2024) A roadmap for regulating subscriptions in the digital fairness act. Eur J Consum Mark Law 13(6):234–242

Byrne S, Byrne J (2023) Scams, cons, frauds, and deceptions. Victims Offenders 18(7):1185–1193

DSK (2022) Beschluss der Konferenz der unabhängigen Datenschutzaufsichtsbehörden des Bundes und der Länder. Hinweise der DSK—Datenschutzkonformer Online-Handel mittels Gastzugang. 24 March 2022. https://datenschutzkonferenz-online.de/media/dskb/20222604_beschluss_datenminimierung_onlinehandel.pdf

ERR (2025), Elisa requires telecom customers to cancel contracts in store. 25 February 2025. https://news.err.ee/1609613324/elisa-requires-telecom-customers-to-cancel-contracts-in-store

European Commission (2024) Fitness check of EU consumer law on digital fairness. SWD(2024) 230 final. https://commission.europa.eu/publications/study-support-fitness-check-eu-consumer-law-digital-fairness-and-report-application-modernisation_en

European Commission (2022a) Proposal for a Directive of the European Parliament and of the Council amending Directive 2011/83/EU concerning financial services contracts concluded at a distance and repealing Directive 2002/65/EC. COM(2022) 204 final

European Commission (2022b) Press release. Consumer protection: Amazon Prime changes its cancellation practices to comply with EU consumer rules. July 1st, 2022. https://ec.europa.eu/commission/presscorner/api/files/document/print/en/ip_22_4186/IP_22_4186_EN.pdf

European Commission (2022c) Behavioural study on unfair commercial practices in the digital environment—dark patterns and manipulative personalisation—final report. https://op.europa.eu/en/publication-detail/-/publication/606365bc-d58b-11ec-a95f-01aa75ed71a1/language-en

European Law Institute (2023) Response to the European Commission's public consultation on digital fairness—fitness check on EU consumer law. https://www.europeanlawinstitute.eu/fileadmin/user_upload/p_eli/Publications/Response_of_the_ELI_to_the_European_Commission_s_Public_Consultation_on_Digital_Fairness_.pdf

Föhlisch C, Löwer D (2024) Aller guten Dinge sind drei: Bestellbutton, Kündigungsbutton und jetzt der Widerrufsbutton. Computer und Recht 40(2):116–121

Güster F, Booke C (2022) Kündigungsbutton-Pflicht Bei Dauerschuldverhältnissen. Multimedia und Recht 25(6):450–453

Howells G, Twigg-Flesner C, Wilhelmsson T (2018) Rethinking EU consumer law. Routledge, London

Izzo-Wagner A, Otto TC, Schultess P (2024) Die EU-Änderungsrichtlinie in Bezug auf im Fernabsatz geschlossene Finanzdienstleistungsverträge. Zeitschrift Für Bank- und Kapitalmarktrecht 24(3):84–87

Kjörven ME (2020) Who pays when things go wrong? Online financial fraud and consumer protection in Scandinavia and Europe. Eur Bus Law Rev 31(1):77–109

Lommatzsch J, Albrecht R (2024) Neue rechtliche Herausforderung im E-Commerce mit Verbrauchern—„Widerrufsfunktion" kommt. Gesellschafts- und Wirtschaftsrecht:141–143

Maume P (2025) Becksche Online-Kommentar zum Bürgerlichen Gesetzbuch, 74th edn. Verlag C.H. Beck, München

Sümmermann R, Ewald K (2022) Das Gesetz für faire Verbraucherverträge. Die neuen Regelungen zu Abo-Verträgen in der Praxis. MultiMedia und Recht 25(8):713–718

Wendehorst C (2022) Münchener Kommentar zum Bürgerlichen Gesetzbuch, 9th edn. Verlag C.H. Beck, München

Defective Consent and Platform Liability Under the Digital Services Act: Appearance, Information Duties and Consumer Reviews

Antonio Legerén-Molina

Abstract This paper explores platform liability under the Digital Services Act (DSA), focusing on cases where consumer consent may be defective. It examines three key scenarios: misleading appearances suggesting the platform is the direct provider, breaches of information duties, and deceptive consumer reviews. The analysis addresses the legal implications of these defects, including the loss of the benefit of the 'safe harbour' exemption and potential contractual invalidity. The study draws on the doctrine elaborated by the Court of Justice of the European Union in the Wathelet case to support the extension of consumer rights against platforms in certain contexts.

Keywords Digital Services Act · Defective consent · Online platforms · Information duties · Platform liability · Misleading reviews · Safe harbour · Consumer protection · Contractual error · Wathelet doctrine

1 Introduction

The rapid expansion of digital platforms has profoundly transformed the dynamics of contracting, introducing unprecedented challenges in areas such as consumer protection and the enforcement of contractual rights. The Regulation (EU) 2022/2065 of the European Parliament and of the Council of 19 October 2022, commonly known as Digital Services Act (DSA), is a regulatory milestone. It establishes a comprehensive regulatory framework for digital platforms within the European Union. The DSA's primary objective is to enhance the performance of intermediation services within the internal market and to establish a secure, reliable and predictable digital environment

This work has been carried out within the framework of the MICINU Knowledge Generation Project, PID2023-148193NB-I00, entitled 'Contractual remedies in the preliminary phase: nullity, annulment and non-contractual liability'.

A. Legerén-Molina (✉)
Department of Private Law, A Coruña University, A Coruña, Spain
e-mail: antonio.legeren@udc.es

C. Crea and M. Infantino (eds.), *Remedies to Digital Vulnerability in European Private Law*, https://doi.org/10.1007/978-3-032-19720-7_3

that fosters innovation and ensures the effective safeguarding of fundamental rights.[1] The DSA consolidates previous legal and jurisprudential criteria, particularly those issued by the Court of Justice of the European Union (CJEU).

As is well known, prior to the staggered entry into force of the DSA, which ended on 17 February 2024, the European regulatory framework for contracting through platforms was essentially based on Directive 2000/31/EC of the European Parliament and of the Council, of 8 June 2000, on certain legal aspects of information society services, in particular electronic commerce, in the internal market (hereafter 'ECD') and the 'safe harbour' doctrine it introduced, primarily with intermediary service providers in mind.[2] According to this principle, and not being under any general duty to supervise the content, the platforms were exempt from liability for unlawful content hosted on them by third parties, provided that they acted diligently to remove such content after becoming aware of its existence. Technological advances, the growing variety of platforms and intermediation services, and the increasing sophistication of algorithms used for mass customisation, inter alia, have rendered this criterion obsolete.[3] Moreover, after the entry into force of the ECD, some rules which affected particular aspects of the provision of intermediary services or liability in certain sectors were adopted, such as the Directive 2001/29/EC on the harmonisation of certain aspects of copyright and related rights in the information society, Directive 2010/13/EU on audiovisual media services, Directive 2018/1808/EU on media services and Directive 2019/790/EU on copyright and the digital single market, among others. As always in the case of directives, there have been inconsistent and non-coincident applications of them across different European Union countries. To a certain extent, this state of affairs was calling for uniform, harmonised and up-to-date legislation: the DSA was passed in response to this need.

As the DSA is still in its early stages of implementation, questions remain regarding its potential impact on digital innovation and the effectiveness of the incentives it offers to different intermediary service providers. Regarding 'online platforms', a subcategory of hosting service providers, article 3, letter (i) of the DSA defines them as "hosting service that, at the request of a recipient of the service, stores and disseminates information to the public" (even though, to avoid the imposition of overly general obligations,[4] the same provision specifies that it applies unless "the dissemination to the public is merely a minor and purely ancillary feature that is intrinsically linked to another service, or a minor functionality of the principal service, and that feature or functionality cannot, for objective technical reasons, be used without that other or principal service, and the integration of that feature or functionality is not a means to circumvent the applicability of the rules of this Regulation applicable to online platform"). In the present case, two particularly relevant aspects of those which allow consumers to conclude contracts with traders are the

[1] See Article 1 of the DSA.

[2] See Article 14 of the ECD.

[3] An analysis of the different terminology and characteristis of online platforms and marketplaces over two regulatory decades is contained in Rodríguez de las Heras Ballel (2023, 34–38).

[4] See also Recital 13 of the DSA.

presentation of goods and services, and the procurement process, both of which can lead to misperceptions. This may be due to a lack of clarity about the platform's role, insufficient product or service information, or review systems that do not accurately reflect the qualities of the goods and services involved. In many cases, the consumer's consent may be vitiated by an inaccurate representation of reality, whether or not there is an illicit content.

This paper will analyse some of the remedies provided in the DSA for online platforms in the aforementioned situations: when the consumer's error is based on appearance (Sect. 2), when it derives from a breach of information or disclosure duties (Sect. 3), and when it is based on reviews hosted on digital platforms (Sect. 4).

2 The Error Based on the 'Appearance' Created by the Platform

Just as the DSA segments the obligations and duties of different types of intermediary service providers to fulfil the purposes set out in its article 1, it also contains liability rules appropriate to each category. With regard to hosting services, article 6 of the DSA is a key liability provision.[5]

Article 6(1) of the DSA updates the 'safe harbour' criterion introduced by the ECD in 2000. No liability arises if there is no actual knowledge of unlawful activity or content, or if one is "not aware of facts or circumstances from which the illegal activity or content is apparent". Where such knowledge exists, action must be taken "expeditiously" to remove or block access to the content. Therefore, the criterion according to which the intermediary is not liable if it does not have actual knowledge of the facts is still maintained, even though it may be liable for damages if some presumption of knowledge can be applied.[6]

Article 6(2) of the DSA, albeit with different terminology, reinforces the "decisive influence" criterion established by the CJEU in cases such as *Elite Taxi v. Uber Systems Spain*,[7] *Uber France*,[8] *Airbnb*,[9] and *Star Taxi App*.[10] In these cases, the criterion was used to determine whether the affected party was an information society service provider, rather than addressing contractual issues concerning the underlying service.[11] In any case, according to article 6(2) of the DSA, the aforementioned exemption from liability—the 'safe harbour'—does not apply where "the recipient of

[5] On the different types of hosting providers to which article 6 of the DSA applies, see Arroyo Amayuelas (2025, 735 et seq).

[6] Arroyo Amayuelas (2025, 738 et seq).

[7] CJEU, case C-434/15, *Elite Taxi v. Uber Systems Spain*, 20 December 2017.

[8] CJEU, case C-320/16, *Uber France SAS v. Nabil Bensalem*, 10 April 2018.

[9] CJEU, case C-390/18, *Ahtop v. Airbnb Ireland*, 19 December 2019.

[10] CJEU, case C-62/19, *Star Taxi App SRL v Unitatea Administrativ Teritoriala Municipiul Bucuresti prin Primar General and Consiliul General al Municipiului Bucuresti*, 3 December 2020.

[11] On this doctrine, see Pazos Castro (2020, 1–14).

the service is acting under the authority or the control of the provider"[12]; an expression which has been criticised by scholars due to the uncertainty it generates.[13] Although Recital 23 of the DSA refers to pricing as a relevant parameter for determining whether one acts "under the authority or control" of the online platform, the DSA did not take the opportunity to address the existing open questions regarding liability.[14]

Finally, article 6(3) of the DSA introduces a provision applicable only to a subcategory of hosting service providers: online platforms that facilitate distance contracts between business and consumers (B2C). This excludes peer-to-peer platforms facilitating contracts between businesses (B2B) and between consumers (C2C). The purpose of this paragraph is to protect consumers in the event of a breach of the underlying contract.[15] To a certain extent it is a novel provision, since there is no parallel one in articles 4 and 5 of the DSA. Yet, it can also be said that article 6(3) of the DSA adopts the criteria and spirit of the CJEU's ruling in the *Wathelet* case.[16] Moreover, the provision seems to be based on other European legislation[17]; and a reference to the appearance with which the services were received by users could also be found in the Opinion of the Advocate General of the CJEU, Maciej Szpunar, in the case *Elite Taxi v. Uber Systems Spain.*[18]

According to article 6(3) of the DSA, article 6(1) does not apply "with respect to the liability under consumer protection law of online platforms that allow consumers to conclude distance contracts with traders, where such an online platform presents the specific item of information or otherwise enables the specific transaction at issue in a way that would lead an average consumer to believe that the information, or the product or service that is the object of the transaction, is provided either by the online platform itself or by a recipient of the service who is acting under its authority or control". The provision permits the denial of exemption from liability for the platform under the 'safe harbour' principle when consumers may be given the impression—the 'appearance'—that the platform is not acting as an intermediary, even though the platform does not, in fact, act as an agent of the seller nor does the seller act under the authority of the platform.[19] The present section will therefore analyse three fundamental issues: what constitutes the 'appearance' that can mislead the consumer, what is the scope of application of such a provision, and what are the consequences of its violation.

---

[12] Regarding this issue, Arroyo Amayuelas (2025, 733 et seq).

[13] Cauffman and Goanta (2021, 767).

[14] Busch and Mak (2021, 111) and Duivenvoorde (2022, 51). To me, the 'neutrality' or 'purely technical and automatic processing' criteria seem more appropriate than the 'active or passive role' criteria, as the latter could discourage platforms from establishing measures to control, moderate or supervise content.

[15] Arroyo Amayuelas (2023, 13). Similarly, Wilman et al. (2024, 79).

[16] CJEU, case C-149/15, *Wathelet v. Garage Bietheres*, 9 November 2016.

[17] E.g. article 6a of the Directive 2011/83/EU of the European Parliament and of the Council of 25 October 2011 on consumer rights.

[18] CJEU, case C-434/15, *Elite Taxi v. Uber Systems Spain*, 20 December 2017, no. 53.

[19] "Article 6(3) is simply another legal manifestation of the fundamental neutrality test underlying the entire framework": Husovec (2024, 137).

2.1 *The Factual Situation of Article 6(3) DSA: The Misleading Appearance*

Article 6(3) of the DSA establishes as factual assumption that consumers can be led to believe that the platform is the direct provider of the product or service, or that it exercises significant control over who actually provides it; the provision states "would lead [...] to believe". The operational elements of the platform—how it presents information, for example, or how contracting is carried out—are those that can generate such an 'appearance'. The possibility of 'leading the consumer to believe' implies a subjective approach in that perception: the consumer's impression is considered even if it does not correspond to the material reality of things, such as when the consumer may think that the platform is the service provider even if it is not. However, this subjective perspective is objectified to a certain extent.[20] On the one hand, because the rule refers to an 'average consumer'; as is well-known, the notion of the reasonably informed consumer is an indeterminate concept which opens the door to interpretation and legal uncertainty.[21] On the other hand, the possibility of such a belief—"would lead [...] to believe"—should be "determined objectively, on the basis of all relevant circumstances".[22] To this end, the concepts used by the platform in its 'Terms and Conditions' are indicative, although not always conclusive: article 6(3) of the DSA refers in particular not only to the presentation of "specific item of information", but also to the way the platform "enables the specific transaction at issue". Recital 24 of the DSA adds three indications that may create such an 'appearance': not clearly displaying the trader's identity, not disclosing the trader's identity or contact details until after the contract is concluded, and marketing in the platform's own name rather than in the trader's one.

Other scenarios that could produce the same effect of creating such an 'appearance' on the consumer include: the contract being concluded exclusively through the platform's services, the platform determining the price and/or withholding payments made by customers, the platform essentially determining the terms of the supplier-customer contract, the operator providing a uniform image of the suppliers or a trademark, the marketing being focused on the platform operator and not the suppliers. Along with the indications suggested by the 'Research Group on the Law of Digital Services' in their Discussion Draft of a Directive on Online Intermediary Platforms,[23] the 'Model Rules on Online Platforms' by the European Law Institute (ELI) also suggested another indicator for determining whether the customer "can reasonably rely on the platform operator's predominant influence over the supplier", which is now included in Recital 24 of the DSA: the platform operator withholds the identity

[20] Regarding objectification, see Wilman et al. (2024, 79).

[21] Being critic with it, see Cauffman and Goanta (2021, 767) and Arroyo Amayuelas (2023, 17).

[22] Recital 24 of the DSA.

[23] Busch et al. (2016, article 18(2)).

of the supplier or contact details until after the conclusion of the supplier-customer contract.[24]

The platform may also create such an 'appearance' through other signs that are more directly related to the marketing. These signs could include the following: the use of a uniform method of presenting offers, showing both own and third-party product advertisements, the use of the well-known distributor's own logo in those advertisements, or the offering of additional services to third-party sellers—e.g. storage and shipping—in respect of products with such a logo.[25] The relevant question is whether the above-mentioned indications, or any others, in combination with the 'operational elements' of the platform, create the impression for consumers that the platform is not a mere intermediary. Conversely, if the platform clearly communicates its intermediary function and there are no such indications, that 'appearance' will not arise and therefore article 6(3) of the DSA will not apply. But regarding this communication, the mere inclusion of this piece of information in the company's standard contract terms accepted by the user may not be enough, as the communication could be seen as lacking transparency or even be considered as an unfair surprise clause and therefore invalid.[26]

One relevant element is that article 6(3) of the DSA does not require the consumer to actually believe that appearance; it is sufficient that there is a risk of this occurring, since the provision only requests that the appearance "would lead [...] to believe". This broadens the scope of the traditional concept of error, which is defined as a mental representation that does not correspond to reality, to include cases of potential error, where there are elements that "would lead" to a mistake even though the error does not actually exist. Therefore, it is not an absolute extension—as long as the consumer believes or is likely to believe it—since an average consumer must be able to reach that conclusion based on the indications provided. Whether such signs and elements of the platform's operation will be interpreted broadly or strictly in the application of case law is a different matter. In any event, the DSA assumes the *Wathelet* test to assess the likelihood of confusion, taking it a step further by considering not only the stored information, but also the contracting process. While the aforementioned case concerned a face-to-face contract and did not address the issue of exemption from liability, the DSA tackles this issue and extends its scope to electronic contracts. In *Wathelet*, it was stated that the concept of a "seller" also covers "a trader who acts on behalf of a private individual *where, from the point of view of the consumer, he presents himself as the seller* of consumer goods under a contract in the course of his trade, business or profession" because "that trader *could create confusion in the mind of the consumer by giving him the false impression* that he is

[24] European Law Institute (2019, article 20). Both documents set out a slightly different test to that contained in article 6(3) of the DSA, as they consider not only whether the consumer would be "*led* to believe", but also whether he can "*reasonably rely*".

[25] See Husovec (2024, 135).

[26] See Díez Soto (2023, 200) (in the case of confusion generated in the consumer about the identity of its counterparty).

acting as the seller-owner of the goods".[27] In fact, "the seller's liability, in accordance with Directive 1999/44, must be capable of being imposed on an intermediary who, by addressing the consumer, creates a likelihood of confusion in the mind of the latter, leading him to believe in its capacity as owner of the goods sold".[28] While at the time was stated that "the consumer can easily be misled" and therefore "it is necessary to afford the latter enhanced protection",[29] the DSA Act now legislatively provides a sanction for the possibility of belief—a subjective criterion—based on how the information is presented or how the contract is concluded. And also, it provides a limited number of possible indications that, being present, will produce that denial of the exemption from liability.[30]

2.2 *The Scope of Application of Article 6(3) of the DSA and the Consequences that It Establishes*

Article 6(3) of the DSA states that, when the circumstances referred to therein arise, the 'safe harbour' exemption of article 6(1) of the DSA will not apply. However, that provision limits the refusal of the exemption from liability to the area of consumer law only; the benefit of the 'safe harbour' may continue to be applied in other areas of law, such as trademark or intellectual property law.[31]

Having said that, it should be noted that refusing the 'safe harbour' exemption does not automatically imply liability.[32] The DSA does not impose a general supervision obligation on platforms,[33] nor does it establish a positive criterion of attribution, although there are few scholars—a minority—which consider it feasible to rely exclusively on article 6 of the DSA to establish provider's liability through the concept of indirect representation.[34] Article 6(3) of the DSA only denies the 'safe harbour' exemption, and platforms will not be exempt from liability (whether contractual or non-contractual) if the conditions for its attribution under European legislation, under the national laws of the country in which the platform operates or even under the platform's own 'Terms and Conditions' are met. Liability may therefore arise from any of these levels of regulation. Even more, the very refusal of exemption itself may be an indication to be considered when making such an attribution, e.g. either

[27] CJEU, case C-149/15, *Wathelet v. Garage Bietheres*, 9 November 2016, no. 34 (emphasis added).

[28] CJEU, case C-149/15, *Wathelet v. Garage Bietheres*, 9 November 2016, no. 41.

[29] Ibid.

[30] Recital 24 of the DSA. For the 'objective addressee perspective' (*objektiver Empfängerhorizont*) in German law, see Tereszkiewicz (2019, 910).

[31] See De Miguel Asensio (2022, No. 28) criticising the limitation to that subject matter.

[32] See, e.g., Polat and Özçelik (2023, 168) and Wilman et al. (2024, 79).

[33] See article 8 of the DSA.

[34] See Orti Vallejo and Viceira Ortega (2025, 89–91). Consistently, they disagree with the wording of Recital 17 of the DSA.

because the platform operator knew or should have known of the wrongfulness, or because it did not act with due diligence.

As previously mentioned, the solution set out in article 6(3) of the DSA can be described as prudent—namely, the denial of the 'safe harbour' without a positive attribution of liability—particularly when compared to other regulatory proposals. On the one hand, the 'Discussion Draft of a Directive on Online Intermediary Platforms' prepared by the Research Group on the Law of Digital Services generally exempts intermediary platforms from liability for non-performance of the underlying service,[35] unless the consumer could reasonably rely on its predominant influence.[36] In such a case, the platform is jointly and severally liable with the supplier.[37] On the other hand, article 20 of the ELI's 'Model Rules on Online Platforms' states that if the consumer can "reasonably rely" on platform operator having a predominant influence, he may exercise all rights and remedies available under consumer law against the platform, which becomes jointly and severally liable for the supplier's non-performance.[38] Finally, according to article 21 of the same text, legal action can be taken against the platform as if the supplier were a trader.[39]

Which of the above solutions is the most appropriate? Given the creation of the 'appearance' of being the service provider and not a 'mere intermediary'—even if in reality this is not the case–, should be only removed the 'safe harbour' exemption, or should standing be also extended by allowing claims against the platform under consumer law, or should be automatically imposed direct liability on platforms in case of breach of the underlying contract? As mentioned above, the DSA only considers the first of these solutions, perhaps to avoid undermining the viability of certain business models or stifling innovation.[40]

In my view, the DSA's decision not to automatically attribute direct liability to the platform for non-compliance with the underlying service is correct, although some scholars consider it would have been preferable for the legislation to include particular criteria for liability in cases of "predominant influence".[41] Yet, the DSA does not establish a general duty to monitor.[42] It can be argued that a different rule—i.e., the risk of liability being attributed—would incentivise providers to not monitor, thus undermining the intended effect of the Good Samaritan clause.[43]

Such attribution of liability would obviously make sense where the platform is a party to the underlying contract, either because this has been expressly stated, or because the platform has explicitly or implicitly assumed the role of guarantor of

---

[35] Busch et al. (2016, article 16).

[36] Busch et al. (2016, article 16(2) letter (b)).

[37] Busch et al. (2016, article 18(1)).

[38] European Law Institute (2019, article 20).

[39] European Law Institute (2019, article 21).

[40] Díez Soto (2023, 208–209).

[41] Polat and Özçelik (2023, 171–172). Prior to the DSA, Tereszkiewicz (2019, 919) proposed to apply to platforms the retailer liability criterion of the Package Travel Directive.

[42] See article 8 DSA.

[43] See article 7 of the DSA as well as Engert (2018, 315).

the contract.[44] Apart from such clear cases, liability would have to be established on a case-by-case basis according to the platform's actual role, which would not be determined solely or primarily on the basis of the 'Terms and Conditions' established by the platform itself. In this task, the existing information asymmetry—a criterion mentioned in the *Wathelet* case–, the trust generated by the platform and, if applicable, its indispensable nature in providing the service are arguments that could contribute to such an attribution, especially in cases where due to its influence and power to configure the market they do not perform neutral and technical intermediation. In that context, Arroyo Amayuelas defends as "reasonable to impose liability on platforms that have a predominant role since they do not merely facilitate transactions but have the power to transform market relations and to influence the contract between platform users. Moreover, the platform is in a better position than the consumer to hold the defaulting supplier liable, i.e. its liability vis-à-vis the consumer could be qualified by the granting of a right of redress".[45] In that case, the possibility of attributing liability to the platform would therefore be justified on the ground not only of unlawfulness (see article 6 of the DSA), but also of convenience, given that the platform has greater ease than consumers in exercising the right of redress and can easily apply for non-performance insurance.

In particular, the decisive influence of the platform, which shows that it is not a neutral and technical intermediary, may be invoked in view of the concurrent circumstances, such as the circumstance that the platform assumes the costs and risks derived from the activity, or that there is an employment relationship with the person who materially provides the service, or that its brand is absolutely predominating, etc.[46] Other factors to be considered in the context of the possible liability of the platform for non-compliance with the underlying contract would be that "the platform operator withholds the identity of the supplier or contact details until after the conclusion of the supplier-customer contract" or that it "promises to monitor the conduct of suppliers and to enforce compliance with its standards beyond what is required by law".[47] Incidentally, it should be noted that an author suggested that the decisive influence of the platform on transactions should matter when establishing not only whether the platform is a party to the underlying contracts and the extent to which it may be liable for non-performance,[48] but also whether the platform operator shall be vicariously "liable for damage caused, in accordance with general tort liability rules [...], provided that influence manifests a relationship of dependence or functional subordination between the two parties".[49]

In practice, given that the DSA only sanctions the creation of the 'appearance' with the denial of exemption, and given that the platform can always be held liable for breaching its own duties, is it possible to hold it liable for breach of an underlying

[44] Díez Soto (2023, 189–192).

[45] Arroyo Amayuelas (2025, 756).

[46] See Díez Soto (2023, 210–211).

[47] European Law Institute (2019, article 20).

[48] Díez Soto (2023, 202).

[49] Díez Soto (2023, 209–210).

contract of which it was not a party? Could a consumer turn to the doctrine of the *Wathelet* case to extend standing to the platform when determining whether or not it should be held liable? In my view, the answer to this question should be affirmative, because the 'appearance' to which it has contributed gives it standing.[50] The protection of consumer rights would not be in that case totally fulfilled with the refusal of exemption from liability under article 6(3) of the DSA. Without anything more than that refusal, the rights of consumers who relied on the apparent data available to them would be harmed due to the 'appearance' created by the platform, and they would often be unable to claim directly against the platform for breach of the underlying contract.[51] It is true that, if the platform has not been directly involved in providing the underlying service, such an extension would violate the principle of contract relativity. However, it should be noted that this principle is not absolute, given that there are already specific exceptions recognised and regulated by the legal system.[52] On the other hand, it should be mentioned too that, in the present case, such an extension would not benefit someone completely external to the relationship, since the platform is involved *to a certain extent* in the provision of the service—e.g. by offering and promoting products and hosting data.

3 The Error Arising from the Platforms' Failure to Fulfil Their 'Information Duties'

As is well known, the DSA has introduced various due diligence obligations to strengthen consumer protection and ensure greater transparency in online transactions. In particular, articles 30 to 32 of the DSA impose duties on online platforms that allow consumers to conclude distance contracts with traders, relating to the traceability of the latter and the information to be provided to consumers. In addition to examining these obligations in more detail, the following two issues will be discussed: the penalty for non-compliance and whether this could affect the validity of contractual consent.

[50] If, based in article 6(3) of the DSA, the exemption is refused, the platform could also be sued under article 6(2) of the DSA if the conditions of that provision are met.

[51] For a similar view, see Díez Soto (2023, 200).

[52] See, e.g., articles 13 and 23 of Directive EU 2015/2032 of the European Parliament and of the Council of 25 November 2015 on Package Travel Directive; see also Arroyo Amayuelas (2023, 25) (defending that it is possible to dispense such a principle "whenever consumer protection so requires").

3.1 *Trader Traceability, Compliance by Design and 'After-Sales' Information*

Article 30 of the DSA aims to ensure the traceability of any trader operating within a platform environment by stipulating that, prior to granting them access to the platform, the latter must verify certain information: their identity, contact details, identification document, payment account information, commercial or similar registration details, if applicable, and a self-certification confirming that their products and services comply with applicable EU legislation. Upon receiving this information, the platform shall "make best efforts" to assess its completeness and reliability before authorising the service.[53] If there are sufficient reasons or indications that the information is "inaccurate, incomplete or not up to date", the trader must be requested to correct it. If this is not remedied, the service will be suspended.[54] The provision also sets out additional obligations, such as the right of traders to lodge complaints,[55] the retention of information for six months after the end of the contractual relationship,[56] and the possibility of disclosing information to third parties when necessary to enforce rights.[57] The traceability obligation under article 30 of the DSA constitutes a "special monitoring obligation" which, in view of article 8 of the DSA, is certainly of an exceptional nature.[58] Consistently with that, recital 73 of the DSA states that "providers of online platforms concerned should not be required to engage in excessive or costly online fact-finding exercises or to carry out disproportionate verifications on the spot".

It should be noted that the information obligation set out in article 30 of the DSA has its origins in Directive 2019/2161/EU, which introduced article 6*a* in Directive 2011/83/EU on consumer rights.[59] Article 6*a*, in turn, is a consequence of the *Wathelet* case doctrine. It stipulates that the information provided by digital platforms must be "clear, comprehensible and adequate", and must address aspects such as the criteria for categorising offers (paragraph a), whether the seller is a trader or private individual (paragraph b), the non-application of consumer law where the seller is not a trader (paragraph c), and, where applicable, the division of responsibilities between the

[53] Article 30(2) of the DSA.

[54] Article 30(3) of the DSA.

[55] Article 30(4) of the DSA.

[56] Article 30(5) of the DSA.

[57] Article 30(6) of the DSA.

[58] Orti Vallejo and Viceira Ortega (2025, 87).

[59] Directive (EU) 2019/2161 of the European Parliament and of the Council of 27 November 2019 amending Council Directive 93/13/EEC and Directives 98/6/EC, 2005/29/EC and 2011/83/EU of the European Parliament and of the Council as regards the better Enforcement and Modernisation of Union Consumer Protection Rules and Directive 2011/83/EU of the European Parliament and of the Council of 25 October 2011 on Consumer Rights.

seller and the platform (paragraph d).[60] Such information should be made available in a prominent place on the platform. Therefore, it can be concluded from the content of both provisions that article 30 of the DSA complements and reinforces the provisions of article 6*a* of Directive 2011/83/EU, which is currently in force.

Article 31 of the DSA sets out the principle of 'compliance by design': the configuration of the platform must enable traders to fulfil their obligations regarding "pre-contractual information, compliance and product safety information". The provision then lists some of the information to be provided, such as product or service identification and trader identification.[61] Before allowing the trader to offer goods or services on the platform, its operator "shall make best efforts" to assess whether such information has been provided. After granting permission, the operator "shall make reasonable efforts to randomly check any official, freely accessible, machine-readable online database or online interface whether the products or services offered have been identified as illegal".[62]

Finally, article 32 of the DSA establishes an 'after-sales' service for unlawful products or services offered through the platform. This requires the platform to inform consumers that "the product or service is illegal, the identity of the trader, and any relevant means of redress".[63]

As can be seen from the above, the DSA retains the information provision system as the model for consumer protection, but is not fully aligned with previous consumer protection legislation regarding the mandatory provision of information by traders when concluding online contracts with consumers;[64] in other words, it is possible to conclude that these articles have limited usefulness.[65]

3.2 The Consequences of Non-Compliance with Articles 30 to 32 of the DSA

Article 30(2) of the DSA states that "for the purpose of this Regulation, traders shall be liable for the accuracy of the information provided", suggesting that the traceability duty on platforms is one of means rather than result: they must take reasonable measures to verify information, but are not automatically liable for falsity.[66] However, they are liable if they do not diligently comply with the duties established by articles 30–32 of the DSA and they are subject to the consequences arising from this.

---

[60] The transposition of article 6*a* of Directive 2011/83/EU in Spain introduced two additional requirements in which it does not appear likely that defective information could lead to a mistake resulting in the annulment of the contract: see Orti Vallejo and Viceira Ortega (2025, 92).

[61] Article 31(2) of the DSA.

[62] Article 31(3) of the DSA.

[63] Article 32(1) of the DSA.

[64] Cauffman and Goanta (2021, 774).

[65] Rott (2022, 1049).

[66] Recital 73 of the DSA.

What is the penalty for failing to comply with these obligations? According to the article 54 of the DSA "recipients of the service shall have the right to seek, in accordance with Union or national law, compensation [...] in respect of any damage or loss suffered due to an infringement [...] of their obligations under this Regulation". That article refers to damages caused to both the trader and the consumer due to the platform's failure to fulfil its duties, which would not have occurred if those had been fulfilled.[67] These damages can include "expenses incurred by the purchaser due to a claim filed or a lawsuit initiated against the trader, damage to goods or interests other than the contracted product or service, and non-economic harm".[68] As mentioned previously, the platform may be liable for damages arising from a breach of the underlying contract, not because it is a party to the contract, but because there is a causal link between such damage and the breach of its own obligations. These obligations may be those mentioned in articles 30–32 DSA, those contained in the general conditions of the access contract, those resulting from specific agreements, or those arising from the nature of the access contract or the requirements of good faith.[69] Clearly, for such a claim to succeed, it will be necessary to prove that the failure to fulfil caused, in what is at stake here, the harm suffered by the consumer.

Thus, from the outset, it can be concluded that non-compliance with the duties set out in articles 30–32 of the DSA does not result in the denial of 'safe harbour' established in article 6 of the same Regulation. The failure of a platform to comply with its traceability, design and information obligations does not automatically mean that the exemption from liability is denied,[70] even though article 6(3) of the DSA seems to start from the opposite statement.[71] Or, as Recital 41 of the DSA says: "due diligence obligations are independent from the question of the liability of providers of intermediary services" and need therefore be "assessed separately". This conclusion is based on the fact that the two issues operate at different levels: the exemption from liability relates to the content or actions of third parties, whereas the breach of the above-mentioned duties relates to a direct and specific obligations of the platform. Thus, although in 2021 there was a proposal at the European Parliament Committee on Internal Market and Consumer Protection (IMCO) in order to make the exemption from liability conditional on compliance with due diligence obligations or information requirements under consumer law, as it can be seen, it did not succeed.[72] Therefore, the 'safe harbour' privilege only applies to the actions of others, and the same cannot be said for the platform's own obligations. Likewise, the platform will be directly liable for breaching its duties of diligence and transparency or its contractual obligations, but this does not necessarily result in the loss of the 'safe harbour'.[73] Other regulatory proposals have offered different consequences for

[67] Recital 121 of the DSA.

[68] See Orti Vallejo and Viceira Ortega (2025, 88).

[69] On this matter, see Díez Soto (2023, 192–194).

[70] See De Miguel Asensio (2022, No. 58) and Bulgakova and Deruma (2023, 26).

[71] See Arroyo Amayuelas (2023, 20–21).

[72] See Husovec (2024, 135).

[73] See Arroyo Amayuelas (2023, 21).

breaches of information duties. For instance, the ELI's 'Model Rules on Online Platforms' stipulate that if a platform fails to disclose its role in the transaction,[74] the customer can exercise "the rights and remedies available against the supplier under the supplier-customer contract also against the platform operator".[75] Furthermore, article 22 of the same rules makes the platform liable for damages for misleading statements matters mentioned in the article.

Non-compliance or deficient compliance with the information duties on the part of the platforms may lead to the consumer's contractual will being erroneous. For example, this may occur when the consumer chooses one product over another because the parameters for classifying offers are unclear or not provided.[76] This could also occur when, based on the information provided, the consumer mistakenly believes he is dealing with a trader when he is not, or vice versa,[77] or when, due to deficient information, it is not known that consumer regulations do not apply.[78]

Depending on the case, there may be an error of fact or law, which allows the consumer to challenge the contract against the supplier, and, where appropriate, the supplier to exercise a right of redress against the platform. Similarly, I believe that, in line with the ruling in the *Wathelet* case, if information about the counterparty's status as a trader is unavailable, the term 'seller' could be interpreted broadly to encompass the platform. Consequently, the remedies of consumer law could be applied against the platform. As is well known, in the *Wathelet* case it was stated that "it is essential that consumers are aware of the identity of the seller, and in particular whether he is acting as a private individual or as a trader, so that they are able to benefit from the protection conferred on them by the Directive 1999/44".[79] It was also stated that, "for the purposes of ensuring effective protection for consumers in the context of Directive 1999/44, it is essential that that consumer be informed that the owner is a private individual. That interpretation makes it possible to give practical effect to that Directive and is compatible with the Court's case-law, according to which the system of protection introduced under that legislation is based on the idea that the consumer is in a weak position *vis-à-vis* the trader, as regards both his bargaining power and his level of knowledge (judgment of 4 June 2015, Faber, C-497/13, EU:C:2015:357, paragraph 42)".[80]

The success of such an action based on an error constitutes firm support for consumers to claim damages from the platform for breach or deficient compliance

[74] European Law Institute (2019, article 13).

[75] European Law Institute (2019, article 19).

[76] See article 6a(1), letter (a) of Directive 2011/83/EU and, in Spain, article 97a(1), letter (a) of the revised text of the General Law for the defence of consumers and users (hereafter RTGLDCU).

[77] See article 6a(1), letter (b) of Directive 2011/83/EU and, in Spain, article 97a(1), letter (b) RTGLDCU.

[78] See article 6a(1), letter (c) of Directive 2011/83/EU and, in Spain, article 97a(1), letter (c) RTGLDCU.

[79] CJEU, case C-149/15, *Wathelet v. Garage Bietheres*, 9 November 2016, no. 37.

[80] CJEU, case C-149/15, *Wathelet v. Garage Bietheres*, 9 November 2016, no. 39.

with its 'information duties'. A justification for this may be that the specific information requirements for contracts concluded on online marketplaces in article 6(1) of Directive 2011/83/EU can be subsumed under articles 27 and 30–32 of the DSA. As an alternative justification, it has been suggested that consumers can claim damages from the platform insofar as the platform is considered a mediator in the contract.[81] Yet, I disagree with this reading: the liability of the platform arises not because the platform is performing any kind of mediation, but because its breach of the obligations set out in the DSA, which apply to the contract between the platform and the user in the trilateral relationship that is typical of platforms, directly damages the consumer.

However, the breach or deficient performance that allows the contract to be challenged against the trader on the grounds of error and also provides a firm basis for the consumer to claim damages against the platform, in some cases may give rise to other consequences. For example, if the presentation of the deficient information could lead consumers to mistakenly believe that they are contracting with the platform when this is not the case, the breach of article 30 of the DSA will connect to article 6(3), meaning that the platform will not benefit from the 'safe harbour' exemption.[82] In this case, the material scope of the obligation itself will lead to the denial of the exemption due to its coincidence with the provisions of article 6(3) of the DSA. However, the opposite cannot automatically be affirmed either, i.e. that compliance with the diligence duties of articles 30 to 32 of the DSA will always entail an exemption from liability under article 6(1) of the DSA. Article 6(3) of the DSA refers not only to how the online platform "presents the specific item of information", but also to how it "enables the specific transaction at issue" when it refers to the consumer being misled. Therefore, even if the information duties are properly fulfilled, other elements of the transaction may still induce the consumer's belief, meaning the platform may not be eligible for the 'safe harbour'. As noted above, however, it would be a different matter if there were a positive attribution of liability.[83]

A similar situation will arise if the deficient information concerns false data of which the platform has been notified promptly and has failed to act expeditiously to remove it. In such cases, the failure to comply with the duty contained in article 30 of the DSA due to a lack of diligence in removing the information will result in the denial of the 'safe harbour' exemption under article 6(1) of the DSA.

Similarly, if a consumer enters into a contract based on the mistaken belief that he is dealing with a trader when this is not the case,[84] such false information about the third party's identity is also covered by Directive 2005/29/EC on unfair commercial

[81] Orti Vallejo and Viceira Ortega (2025, 92).

[82] This was also supported by De Miguel Asensio (2022, no. 143).

[83] Orti Vallejo and Viceira Ortega (2025, 89) seem to acknowledge the existence of a positive criterion for attributing liability in the DSA; statement which I cannot accept in its entirety in view of the above.

[84] See article 6a(1), letter (b) of Directive 2011/83/EU and, in Spain, article 97a(1), letter (b) RTGLDCU.

practices,[85] and is considered a misleading omission if all the elements set out therein are met—in particular, if the omission is likely to alter the economic behaviour of the average consumer. If such information is due to a breach of the duty of traceability that falls on the platform[86]—that is, if the misleading omission is attributable to it—, another consequence will be the access to corrective measures established in articles 11 and 11*a* of the Directive 2005/29/EC. These remedies must include the cessation and prohibition of unfair commercial practices. More in particular, article 11*a* provides that "consumers harmed by unfair commercial practices shall have access to proportionate and effective remedies, including compensation for damage suffered by the consumer and, where relevant, a price reduction or the termination of the contract". It is for the Member States to "determine the conditions for the application and effects of those remedies", "without prejudice to the application of other remedies available to consumers under Union or national law". Member States must also "lay down the rules on penalties applicable to infringements of national provisions adopted pursuant to this Directive and shall take all measures necessary to ensure that they are implemented".[87] Finally, a breach of the platform's duty of professional diligence can also be considered as an unfair commercial practice if it materially distorts, or is likely to materially distort, the economic behaviour of consumers.[88]

It is clear that the platform may be liable for damages due to the breach of its own obligations. However, in some cases, the existence of false or defective 'information' resulting from such a breach may generate other legal consequences due to its material scope, such as the denial of exemption from liability under articles 6(1) and 6(3) of the DSA, or a misleading omission with the effects indicated by Directive 2005/29/EC. This is without prejudice to the above-mentioned possibility of cancelling the contract on the grounds of error against the supplier.

4 The Error Based on the Misleading Reviews

In the digital environment, reviews and ratings have become a central element in consumer decision-making. Although they do not always provide a full picture of products or services—reviews tend to be complaints rather than praise–, they are tools

---

[85] See articles 6(1) letter (f) and 7(4) of Directive 2005/29/EC and, in Spain, Law 3/1991 of 10 January on Unfair Competition.

[86] See article 30 of the DSA.

[87] Article 13 of Directive 2005/29/EC. In the case of Spanish law, the leeway granted by the aforementioned Directive means that only the compensation measure is included and not the other two mentioned in the text (see article 32(1)(5) of the Spanish Law on Unfair Competition).

[88] Article 5(2) of Directive 2005/29/EC.

that aim to reduce information asymmetry.[89] People trust such evaluation systems because they believe they reflect the real and verifiable experiences of other users. However, reviews can be manipulated, filtered, or even algorithmically generated. The misleading nature of such evaluations can therefore manifest itself in various ways, such as false ratings created by companies to enhance their reputation or discredit competitors, the filtering of negative comments on products or services in favour of positive opinions, the elimination of criticism, reviews generated by artificial intelligence that simulate non-existent user experiences, and the manipulation of the order of presentation by highlighting favourable comments through non-transparent ranking algorithms.

This phenomenon can cause unjustified damage to the business reputation of traders, giving rise to appropriate civil liability.[90] But it can also affect consumer confidence by distorting the perception of the quality of goods or services, resulting in contractual decisions based on an inaccurate representation of reality.[91] Are platforms liable for such reviews, and can the contract be invalidated due to an error in cases where the contractual intent is distorted?

4.1 Potential Liability of Platforms for Misleading Reviews

A key issue in the management of reviews is the potential liability of platforms in this area. Although the DSA has strengthened platforms' due diligence obligations, particularly with regard to the transparency of their content recommendation and rating systems,[92] it contains no provisions relating to reviews. Setting aside the content of the two proposals mentioned above—the 'Discussion Draft of a Directive on Online Intermediary Platforms' and the ELI's 'Model Rules on Online Platforms', which both proposed comprehensive regulations on professional diligence standards that platforms should comply with, as well as the information they should provide on how they collect, process and publish ratings and reviews–,[93] the only piece of legislation that specifically addresses reviews is the Directive 2005/29/EC on unfair commercial practices.

In 2019, article 7(6) of the Directive 2005/29/EC was introduced by the Directive (EU) 2019/2161 which modified some previous legislation as regards the better enforcement and modernisation of union consumer protection rules. According to that new article, in all cases where "a trader provides access to consumer reviews of

[89] See Cuena Casas (2020, 321) and De Salas Murillo (2023, 312). For more information on this topic, see Miranda Serrano (2023, 155–253), with particular regard to his analysis of the different types and classifications of reviews that present dysfunctions or irregularities: Miranda Serrano (2023, 160–161 and 174 et seq).

[90] Regarding compensation for reputational damages, see De Salas Murillo (2023, 323–336).

[91] In relation to bad practices about reviews, see European Commission (2021) and ISO standard 20,488:2018 at https://www.iso.org/obp/ui/fr/#iso:std:iso:20488:ed-1:v1:fr.

[92] Article 27 of the DSA.

[93] Busch et al. (2016, article 8) and European Law Institute (2019, articles 5–7).

products', 'information about whether and how the trader ensures that the published reviews originate from consumers who have actually used or purchased the product" is considered material. Ultimately, the Directive (EU) 2019/2161 requires traders to inform consumers whether they have implemented "processes or procedures" to ensure such correspondence, and if so, "how the checks are made"—e.g. by requesting information to verify ownership–. They must also provide "clear information [...] on how reviews are processed"; e.g. whether they are all published, whether they are sponsored, etc. (see Recital 47 of the Directive 2019/2161).[94]

Similarly, the 2019 reform added two commercial practices that are considered unfair in any case under numbers 23b and 23c. They are "[s]tating that reviews of a product are submitted by consumers who have actually used or purchased the product without taking reasonable and proportionate steps to check that they originate from such consumers"[95] and "[s]ubmitting or commissioning another legal or natural person to submit false consumer reviews or endorsements, or misrepresenting consumer reviews or social endorsements, in order to promote products".[96] This last practice "could also occur through the extrapolation of social endorsements, where a user's positive interaction with certain online content is linked or transferred to different but related content, creating the appearance that that user also takes a positive stance towards the related content".[97]

Therefore, omitting the aforementioned *material* information will be misleading under article 7(6) of Directive 2005/29/EC, and will consequently be a practice prohibited by article 5 of the same regulation. This will result in the remedies set out in articles 11, 11a and 13 of the Directive being invoked.[98] Furthermore, although in my opinion the final decision should depend on the size of the platform, the number of reviews and other circumstances, as a principle if the platform provides measures to control the situation and clearly indicates that it cannot fully guarantee reliability, it will benefit from the 'safe harbour' criterion as long as it removes illegal or misleading information as soon as it becomes aware of it.[99] The doubt then arises as to whether platforms should be obliged to verify all reviews before publishing them or whether a certification system is necessary to ensure their authenticity. Issues which are beyond the scope of this paper. Then, let us answer the second question.

---

[94] In Spain, the Law-Decree 24/2021 of 2 November amended article 20(4) RTGLDCU by including a provision similar to article 7(6) of the Directive 2005/29/EC. For an analysis of the differences between the Directive and the Spanish rule and on the bad consequences of the fragmentation of Spanish regulations on this matter, see Miranda Serrano (2023, 185–189).

[95] Annex I of Directive 2005/29/EC, no. 23b.

[96] Annex I of Directive 2005/29/EC, no. 23c. These practices are described in almost identical terms in articles 27(7) and 27(8) of the Spanish Law on Unfair Competition. On such practices on reviews, considered per se unfair, see Miranda Serrano (2023, 190–206).

[97] Recital 49 of the Directive 2019/2161.

[98] See also above, Sect. 3.2.

[99] See articles 6 and 8 of the DSA.

4.2 Can Misleading Reviews Invalidate Contractual Consent?

From the perspective of contract law, an error is defined as a defect in consent that occurs when the contractual will is formed based on an incorrect or misleading representation of reality. In this case, the key question is whether reliance on false, unrealistic or manipulated information can constitute grounds for essential mistake in legal terms.

From the outset, the situation arising from reviews that misrepresent reality seems to fit this description: if a consumer can prove that he made a purchase based on misleading reviews, and that he would not have made the purchase had he known the truth, he could allege a fundamental mistake and request the contract be declared null and void. However, for such a defect of consent to invalidate the contract, it is necessary that the error be both essential and excusable. Regarding this latter element, it is generally accepted that a contractual defect encompassing a mistake also involves a certain distribution of risks. By establishing the circumstances in which a contract can be challenged on the grounds of a false representation of reality, it is ensured that the contracting party who did not suffer the mistake is not made to bear the risk suffered by the other party in any case. This distribution, which considers the diligence, qualifications and other circumstances of both parties, will be relevant when deciding whether to admit or reject a challenge to the agreement on the grounds of mistake. But what about reviews?

Firstly, it should be noted that the error in such cases is not caused directly by the counterparty to the contract—assuming he is a trader and not the platform itself—but by third parties. As is well known, fraud on the part of third parties is not sufficient to invalidate a contract. However, this does not prevent a mistake from being recognised. In my opinion, in such cases, it would be particularly important to consider excusability when seeking an equitable distribution of risks.

Secondly, with regard to excusability in particular, it is relevant that the platform has a system of moderation and verification of reviews and clearly communicates how it operates to consumers. Traders are, or at least should be, the primary stakeholders in ensuring that such reviews accurately reflect reality. In my opinion, the existence of such a system with the required material information[100]—an obligation of means and not of result, since paragraph 23b of Annex I of Directive 2005/29/EC refers to "reasonable and proportionate steps"—would be sufficient to conclude that the error is not excusable. Consequently, users must verify the characteristics of products diligently, considering the importance they attach to reviews, especially in today's world where reviews could have been created by artificial intelligence or algorithms.

Although it is possible to challenge the contract on the grounds of errors caused by third-party reviews, it seems difficult to do so in practice. This is not only because the systems implemented by the platforms for moderating and reviewing those comments can render such errors as inexcusable, but also because the weight given to them is

[100] See article 7(6) of Directive 2005/29/EC.

part of the due diligence that the buyer must exercise. It seems easier to claim damages in this case than to annul the contract on the grounds of error.[101]

5 Conclusions

In view of the above, it should be noted at the outset that, when consumers contract in the EU via a platform, the application of a wide range of rules can be triggered—e.g. the DSA, the Directive 2011/83/EU, the Directive 2005/29/EC and the national rules of each EU country. It does not seem easy to find a unifying regulatory solution.

Article 6(3) of the DSA clearly covers two issues: the error about the platform's role caused by the false representation of the reality due to the way in which the information elements are displayed or the manner in which the contracting is carried out and the mere possibility that the error may exist, even if it does not actually occur. The established sanction is the denial of the 'safe harbour' exemption under article 6(1) of the DSA, without any criteria being set out for attributing liability. In my opinion, the doctrine of the *Wathelet* case can be applied to this task. The first conclusion is therefore that article 6(3) of the DSA extends the concept of error to include any potential error based on indications, to which the sanction of refusal of the 'safe harbour' exemption is attached. This does not prevent recourse to the extension of standing pointed out by the CJEU in the *Wathelet* case. Consequently, there is an error or false belief based on appearance, with a sanction that differs partially from that of the traditional error-vice of the contract.

Secondly, an in-depth examination of articles 30 to 32 of the DSA, as well as of article 6a of Directive 2011/83/EU, reveals that a breach of the duties outlined therein allows consumers to sue the platform for damages,[102] and, depending on the circumstances, to invalidate the contract against the trader on the grounds of error. Additionally, the breach of certain duties may have further consequences for the platforms, such as the loss of the 'safe harbour' immunity under article 6(1) of the DSA or the finding of an unfair commercial practice, in which case the remedies set out in Directive 2005/29/EC would apply.[103]

The latter consequence also arises where the trader provides access to reviews of his products and services, but omits information on whether he "ensures that the published reviews originate from consumers who have actually used or purchased the product".[104] This constitutes an unfair commercial practice, provided the other requirements of article 7(6) of Directive 2005/29/EC are met and the above-mentioned consequences will be applicable. Finally, although a contract formed on

---

[101] In this context, it is very interesting to study the so-called 'gag or non-discredit clauses', a subject that goes beyond the scope of this paper. For more information on these clauses, see Miranda Serrano (2023, 206–231) (analysing them from the perspectives of unfair competition law and contract law).

[102] Article 54 of the DSA.

[103] Articles 11, 11*a* and 13.

[104] Article 7(6) of Directive 2005/29/EC.

the basis of false or misleading reviews could in theory be challenged on the grounds of error, the existence of systems deployed by the platforms with "reasonable and proportionate" measures to ensure they are from real consumers, together with the information required by the aforementioned provision, means that any false representation of reality suffered by the consumer is not excusable and makes it difficult to challenge the contract on the grounds of error-vice.

References

Arroyo Amayuelas E (2023) La conclusió de contractes amb consumidors en la Digital Services Act. Revista Catalana de Dret Privat (27):11–27

Arroyo Amayuelas E (2025) Comments on article 6 of the Digital Services Act. In: Schulze R, Staudenmayer D (eds) EU digital law, 2nd edn. Baden-Baden, pp 731–757

Bulgakova D, Deruma S (2023) The liability of online intermediaries under European Union Law. Kyiv-Mohyla Law Polit J (8–9):1–43

Busch C, Danneman G, Schulte-Nölke H, Wiewiórowska A, Zoll F (2016) Discussion draft of a directive on online intermediary platforms prepared by the research group on the law of digital services. J Eur Consum Mark Law (5-4):164–169

Busch C, Mak V (2021) Putting the Digital Services Act in context: bridging the gap between EU consumer law and platform regulation. J Eur Consum Mark Law (10–3):109–114

Cauffman C, Goanta C (2021) A new order: the Digital Services Act and consumer protection. Eur J Risk Regul (12):758–774

Cuena Casas M (2020) La contratación a través de plataformas intermediarias en línea. Cuadernos de Derecho Transnacional (12-2):283–348

De Miguel Asensio PA (2022) Obligaciones de diligencia y responsabilidad de los intermediarios: el Reglamento (UE) de Servicios Digitales. La Ley Unión Europea (109):1–26

De Salas Murillo S (2023) Reseñas online y vulnerabilidad agravada de consumidores y empresarios. In: Mayor del Hoyo MV, De Salas Murillo S (eds) Vulnerabilidad patrimonial: retos jurídicos. Thomson Reuters Aranzadi, Cizur Menor, pp 311–336

Díez Soto CM (2023) Responsabilidad de los proveedores de mercados en línea por incumplimiento del contrato subyacente. In: González Pacanowska I, Plana Arnaldos C (eds) Contratación en el entorno digital. Aranzadi, Cizur Menor, pp 159–220

Duivenvoorde B (2022) The liability of online marketplaces under the Unfair Commercial Practices Directive, the E-commerce Directive and the Digital Services Act. J Eur Consumer & Market Law (11–2):43–52

European Commission (2021) Guide on the interpretation and application of Directive 2005/29/EC (OJEU C 526/1)

European Law Institute (2019) Model rules on online platforms. https://www.europeanlawinstitute.eu/fileadmin/user_upload/p_eli/Publications/ELI_Model_Rules_on_Online_Platforms.pdf

Engert A (2018) Digitale Plattformen. Archiv für die zivilistische Praxis (218):304–376

Husovec M (2024) Principles of the Digital Services Act. Oxford University Press, Oxford

Miranda Serrano LM (2023) Prácticas desleales sobre reseñas online de bienes y servicios. InDret (2):155–253

Orti Vallejo A, Viceira Ortega P (2025) Responsabilidad de los mercados en línea respecto del contrato subyacente. InDret (1):74–96

Pazos Castro R (2020) Uber, Airbnb y la llamada 'influencia decisiva' de las plataformas digitales. IDP Revista de Internet, Derecho y Política (31):1–14

Polat C, Özçelik BS (2023) Locating online platforms in the right place: Between the Digital Services Act and the liability law. J Eur Consum Mark Law (12–4):168–172

Rodríguez de las Heras Ballel T (2023) La fórmula de la DSA para resolver el 'dilema de la responsabilidad de las plataformas': un equilibrio entre continuidad e innovación. In: Mate Satué LC, Hernández Sáinz E, Alonso Pérez MT (eds) La responsabilidad civil por servicios de intermediación prestados por plataformas digitales. Colex, Madrid, pp 25–50

Rott P (2022) New liability of online marketplaces under the Digital Services Act? Eur Rev Priv Law (6):1039–1058

Tereszkiewicz P (2019) Digital platforms: regulation and liability in the EU law. Eur Rev Priv Law (6):903–920

Wilman F, Kalėda SL, Loewenthalet PF (2024) The EU Digital Services Act. Oxford University Press, Oxford

Regulation of Consumer Safety Risks from AI Characters in the European Union and United States

Mindy Nunez Duffourc, Riya Goel, and Roni Kennedy

Abstract While technology companies are vying to conquer the market with exciting artificial intelligence (AI) applications, consumers are often left to act as test subjects for emerging technology. Amid this landscape are AI characters, which are designed to act as AI companions with a persistent anthropomorphic identity. AI characters can pose serious health risks to consumers, especially when they engage in interactions purporting to offer emotional support or therapeutic advice. Despite these risks, AI characters enter the EU market with little to no regulatory oversight. This chapter examines whether and to what extent current regulatory frameworks address AI character safety in both the EU, where consumers access them, and the US, where many AI characters are developed. We identify regulatory challenges and opportunities relating to the regulation of AI characters as general products, the lack of specialised safety standards for AI characters, and freedom of expression implications for AI character regulation.

Keywords AI characters · EU law · US law · Regulation of AI · Product safety · Freedom of expression

---

MND received funding to support this work from the Miami Law & AI (MiLA) Lab at the University of Miami School of Law, AI and Law Research Awards program.

M. N. Duffourc (✉)
Department of Private Law, Maastricht Law and Tech Lab, Maastricht University, Maastricht, The Netherlands
e-mail: mindy.duffourc@maastrichtuniversity.nl

R. Goel · R. Kennedy
School of Law, University of Miami, Miami, USA
e-mail: riyagoel@law.miami.edu

R. Kennedy
e-mail: rtk45@miami.edu

C. Crea and M. Infantino (eds.), *Remedies to Digital Vulnerability in European Private Law*, https://doi.org/10.1007/978-3-032-19720-7_4

1 Introduction

Recent advances in artificial intelligence (AI), particularly generative AI, have enabled highly sophisticated chatbots that are capable of mimicking human-to-human interactions. Large language models (LLMs) make it possible for AI chatbots to generate human-like text in conversations with users,[1] while newer multi-modal AI models can give chatbots faces and voices through the generation of sound, images, and videos.[2] There is a wide range of potential uses for AI chatbots. In this article, we focus on a category of direct-to-consumer AI chatbots called 'AI characters.' AI characters 'express a personalized, customizable and humanlike identity across user interactions'.[3] They are designed to engage users through natural language and mimic human traits such as tone, memory, emotional responsiveness, and empathy.

AI characters that engage in 'mental health interactions' pose dangers for consumers. Mental health interactions describe human-to-AI character interactions that involve AI-generated responses purporting to offer emotional support, behavioural guidance, or that otherwise resemble therapeutic care conversations. This includes interactions that are initiated by user prompts as well as unsolicited responses generated by AI characters. The risks associated with AI character mental health interactions are amplified for vulnerable consumers, like children or users experiencing mental health crises. On February 28, 2024, 14-year-old Sewell Setzer, III died by suicide minutes after a Character.AI (C.AI) chatbot encouraged him to 'come home'.[4] In the months before his death, Sewell interacted with a variety of C.AI characters, including one that claimed to be 'a licensed CBT therapist'. Beyond AI characters that claim mental health expertise, general AI characters, who assume roles as friends or romantic partners, also engage in mental health interactions, which can promote self-harm or violence.[5] Notably, unlike AI chatbots built specifically for mental health use in clinical or therapeutic settings, AI characters are not designed for health contexts despite their ability to engage in mental health interactions. This also means that they bypass medical device safety regulations. Without meaningful regulation and oversight of AI characters, users face significant safety risks.

AI characters are accessible across borders and reach consumers in the European Union (EU) digital marketplace regardless of where they are developed. In the EU, this means that AI characters developed in the United States (US), like C.AI characters, may be regulated by both EU and US law. This article examines how the legal frameworks in the EU and US address, or fail to address, consumer health risks stemming from mental health interactions with AI characters. Section 1 provides an overview of the technology behind AI characters and risks that they pose to consumers. Section 2 examines the legal frameworks governing AI character safety in the EU and US. Section 3 identifies both weaknesses and opportunities that

---

[1] Duffourc et al. (2024, 5–8).

[2] Chen et al. (2024, 1).

[3] Duffourc et al. (2025).

[4] *Garcia v. Character Technologies, Inc., et al.*, Complaint, Case 6:24-cv-01903 (22 October 2024).

[5] See *A.F, et al. v. Character Technologies, Inc., et al.*, Complaint, Case 2:24-cv-01014 (09 December 2024).

emerge from the legal frameworks to offer insights into how regulators can better protect consumers.

2 The Architecture of Dangerous AI Characters

2.1 AI Characters

AI characters are largely powered by generative AI models, which are advanced AI systems capable of producing text, images, audio, and video in response to user prompts. LLMs, a subtype of generative AI, allow AI characters to simulate interactive, human-like conversation. AI characters are often presented as sophisticated tools for natural-language engagement with human users; however, like all LLM-based systems, their responses are generated through statistical next-word predictions based on complex and often non-transparent training processes. LLMs are trained on massive datasets made up of books, websites, and online conversations. This training data is often unverified and biased, which can result in generated content that is inaccurate, misleading or biased.[6] LLMs can perform language-based tasks such as text summarization, conversation, and question answering with impressive fluency and coherence. They can power a number of downstream AI systems including AI characters that are capable of engaging in convincing, but potentially dangerous, human-like dialogue.

AI characters are often designed to maximize user engagement, prioritizing metrics such as clicks, time spent, and return visits over user well-being or the accuracy of information provided.[7] For instance, virtual AI companions like Replika, used by millions for emotional support, may reinforce unhelpful thought patterns or create emotional dependency by offering non-judgmental, sycophantic responses that align with users' emotional states.[8] Such strategies can nudge individuals toward behaviours that benefit the platform financially, rather than serving users' best interests. As a result, users may become overly reliant on AI characters engineered to maximize engagement.[9] This engagement-first design can erode user autonomy, especially when combined with practices of 'hypernudging'. Hypernudging refers to the use of adaptive, data-driven architectures to continuously steer user decisions in ways that are largely invisible to users.[10] It can lead to AI character interactions that influence user choices, while maintaining the illusion of autonomy. As a result,

[6] Duffourc et al. (2024, 29–30) and Landwehr et al. (2023, 247–248).

[7] Bernardi (2025, para 16).

[8] Bernardi (2025, para 16–20).

[9] Bernardi (2025, para 2).

[10] Yeung (2017, 122).

individuals are left vulnerable to opaque, data-driven influences that can reinforce bias and dependency on AI characters.[11]

2.2 *Safety Risks*

To fully understand the degree of safety risks presented by AI characters, it is also necessary to understand certain psychological aspects of human–computer interaction. As AI characters become more lifelike, users are increasingly forming emotional bonds with these systems, which can sometimes result in dependency and misplaced trust.[12] AI characters build trust with users through repeated interaction, perceived empathy, and the illusion of social presence.[13] Experimental studies show that people disclose more personal information and report higher comfort levels when interacting with virtual agents that display human-like conversational cues, such as verbal and non-verbal backchannels (agreement, head nods), even when users are aware that these agents are not human.[14] The sense of presence and realism in these interactions is enhanced by their ability to maintain consistent, memory-based dialogue, which can lead to users attributing social agency and trustworthiness to the AI character.[15]

AI character mental health interactions can be dangerous when users mistake simulated empathy for real support or form emotional attachments to systems that are optimized for engagement rather than care.[16] AI characters' simulated empathy and non-judgmental personas can encourage over-reliance, as users may mistake algorithmic responses for genuine care and feel more comfortable confiding in a computer than a real person.[17] This dynamic can discourage individuals from seeking professional help and expose them to health risks associated with unregulated, non-expert advice. To compound this risk, AI characters, 'may be more likely to attract users with unfulfilled social or emotional needs'.[18]

Bias in training data also increases the potential health risks that stem from AI character mental health interactions. Biased data in even health-specific AI models can lead to higher rates of misdiagnosis for marginalized groups. They can also provide less accurate responses to non-English users or in response to culturally specific symptoms.[19] In one widely cited example, a US hospital algorithm assigned lower risk scores to Black patients compared to White patients with similar health profiles leading to a decrease in the level of care provided to equally sick black

---

[11] Ibid.

[12] Hu et al. (2025, 1–18) and Lucas et al. (2014, 99).

[13] Laestadius et al. (2024, 5394–5396).

[14] Lucas et al. (2014, 95).

[15] De Borst and de Gelder (2015, 576) and Slater et al. (2006, e39).

[16] Bernardi (2025, para 4).

[17] Lucas et al. (2014, 94–100).

[18] Malfacini (2025, 1).

[19] Tawiah and Monestime (2024, 324).

patients.[20] For AI characters, which are not intended to provide health information and not designed or monitored to detect and mitigate bias, biased responses in mental health interactions can exacerbate the safety risks that stem from misplaced trust and overreliance on AI character 'advice'.

3 Regulation of AI Characters

3.1 Regulation of AI Characters in the EU

The legal framework governing AI character safety in the EU depends on how AI characters and the technology and market behaviour surrounding them are legally classified. This section first establishes that AI characters are likely not regulated under the Medical Device Regulation (MDR).[21] Second, it discusses the potential governance of AI characters as products under the General Product Safety Regulation (GPSR).[22] Third, it then considers whether AI characters can be governed as services under the Digital Services Act (DSA)[23] and the Digital Content and Services Directive (DCSD)[24] Fourth, it outlines how AI characters can be governed as AI systems under the AI Act.[25] Fifth, it discusses regulation of AI characters under EU general consumer protection law with a focus on the Unfair Commercial Practices Directive (UCPD)[26] and the Consumer Rights Directive (CRD).[27] Finally, it addresses potential freedom of expression barriers to AI character regulation.

---

[20] Obermeyer et al. (2019, 447–453).

[21] Regulation (EU) 2017/745 of the European Parliament and of the Council of 5 April 2017 on medical devices (MDR).

[22] Regulation (EU) 2023/988 of the European Parliament and of the Council of 10 May 2023 on general product safety (GPSR).

[23] Regulation (EU) 2022/2065 of the European Parliament and of the Council of 19 October 2022 on a Single Market for Digital Services and amending Directive 2000/31/EC (Digital Services Act) (DSA).

[24] Directive (EU) 2019/770 of the European Parliament and of the Council of 20 May 2019 on certain aspects concerning contracts for the supply of digital content and digital services (DCSD).

[25] Regulation (EU) 2024/1689 of the European Parliament and of the Council of 13 June 2024 laying down harmonised rules on artificial intelligence (Artificial Intelligence Act) (AI Act).

[26] Directive 2005/29/EC of the European Parliament and of the Council of 11 May 2005 concerning unfair business-to-consumer commercial practices in the internal market (Unfair Commercial Practices Directive) (UCPD).

[27] Directive 2011/83/EU of the European Parliament and of the Council of 25 October 2011 on consumer rights (CRD).

3.1.1 Medical Device Regulation (MDR)

Despite their ability to engage in mental health interactions, AI characters are designed primarily for entertainment, not healthcare. For example, C.AI claims that its purpose is to 'empower[...] people to connect, learn, and tell stories through interactive entertainment'.[28] This means that AI characters like those from C.AI are likely not subject to the MDR's safety regulations for medical devices. The MDR's 'medical device' definition under article 2(1) includes software intended by the manufacturer to be used for specific diagnostic or therapeutic purposes. AI character manufacturers avoid medical device classification by disclaiming therapeutic intended uses. For example, the US company, Luka Inc., which created Replika, offers AI characters that it claims are 'always here to listen and talk',[29] but its terms of service state, 'we are not a healthcare or medical device provider, nor should our Services be considered medical care, mental health services.'[30] Although consumers can suffer negative health impacts in connection with using AI characters purely for entertainment purposes, guidance from the EU Medical Device Coordination Group states that 'the risk of harm to patients [...] is not a criterion on whether the software qualifies as a medical device'.[31] The result is that even if consumers use AI characters for therapeutic purposes, they will not be governed as medical devices under the MDR unless the manufacturer designates an intended use that falls within the MDR's material scope. Without the regulatory safeguards of medical device regulation, the risks of harm from mental health interactions with AI characters must be addressed through more general market safety and consumer protection frameworks.

3.1.2 General Product Safety Regulation (GPSR)

AI characters likely fall within the scope of the GPSR, which governs the safety of general products available to consumers on the EU market. In the EU, AI, as a type of software, can be classified as a product under the GPSR. Article 3(1) defines a product as 'any item, whether or not it is interconnected to other items, supplied or made available, whether for consideration or not, including in the context of providing a service'. The European Commission clarified that the GPSR covers 'apps and software products, including for example chatbots'.[32] Although product liability law is outside of the scope of this chapter, we note that the Product Liability Directive (PLD)[33] also recognizes software as a product. PLD recital 46 emphasises 'the close relationship between product safety rules and liability rules', and failure to comply

[28] Character.ai (2025), About Character.AI.

[29] Luka, Inc. (2025a).

[30] Luka, Inc. (2025b).

[31] MDCG (2025, 9).

[32] European Commission (2025a).

[33] Directive (EU) 2024/2853 of the European Parliament and of the Council of 23 October 2024 on liability for defective products (PLD).

with product safety rules, like those in the GPSR, will impact whether a product is considered defective under the PLD.

Article 5 of the GPSR requires that AI characters on the EU market are 'safe'. Article 3(2) defines a safe product as one that does not present more than a minimal risk to consumers considering its intended and reasonably foreseeable use. Article 6 lists factors that impact this safety assessment including, the product's design, technical characteristics, ability to learn and evolve, interactions with other products, warning and instructions, characteristics of users, risks to vulnerable consumers, potential for misuse, and current state of the technology. Under article 7, products that comply with a specific set of recognized standards are presumed to be safe; however, there are currently no such standards that would govern AI characters. In the absence of recognized standards, article 8 references additional considerations, including general industry standards and safety practices, recommendations, and reasonable consumers' expectations of safety, which can guide AI character safety assessments.

GPSR article 9 obliges manufacturers to engage in certain risk management activities pre- and post- market. The required pre-market risk analysis involves testing products to identify and assess safety risks and developing mitigation and prevention measures under article 9(2). Product manufacturers must also develop protocols for ensuring that products remain in compliance under article 14, and for responding to safety risks that manifest once they are on the market under articles 9(8) and (12). Because the GPSR does not require pre-market third-party conformity assessment, AI character developers would need to self-assess compliance with these obligations. Developers must also maintain risk reporting mechanisms for consumers under article 9(11) and comply with notification and response obligations when risks manifest under articles 9(8) and 20.

Under the GPSR, regulators take a largely reactive approach to monitoring and assessing risks from unsafe products on the EU market. The European Commission's rules for risk assessment consider the probability of risk occurrence, the severity of potential harm, and the total number of possible injuries.[34] For example, even if the risk of severe harm is extremely low for a single user of AI characters, when there are millions of users, there can be a high probability that someone will be severely harmed. However, beyond recent clarifications that AI is regulated as a product, regulators have yet to substantively address safety regulation of AI as a general product on the EU market. Seemingly dangerous AI characters continue to be available in the EU and are easily accessible by vulnerable consumers.

[34] Commission Delegated Regulation (EU) 2024/3173 of 27 August 2024 supplementing Regulation (EU) 2023/988 supplementing Regulation (EU) 2023/988 of the European Parliament and of the Council with regard to rules on access to and operation of the Safety Gate Rapid Alert System, information to be entered in that System, notification requirements and the criteria for assessment of the level of risk (Safety Gate Rules).

3.1.3 The Digital Services Act (DSA) and Digital Content and Services Directive (DCSD)

AI characters largely escape regulation of digital services in the EU under the DSA. The DSA governs intermediary services. According to article 3(g), an intermediary can be a 'hosting service', which stores user data at the user's request. Although users prompt AI characters to generate content, the resulting AI-generated content, strictly speaking, is not provided by the user. For this reason, some scholars maintain that generative AI systems are not governed as hosting services by the DSA.[35] Absent a flexible interpretation of hosting services that would consider content generated by AI in response to user prompts as user-provided content, it would be difficult to classify AI characters as hosting services subject to regulation under the DSA.[36] AI characters that are embedded into online platforms, which article 3 (i) describes as a type of hosting service that stores and disseminates information to the public, might be regulated by the DSA.[37] However, AI character websites may not qualify as online platforms because they do not disseminate AI character-generated content to the public at large, but instead allow users to engage in private conversations with AI characters.[38]

AI characters can be classified as digital services or as providing digital content to consumers online, but the DSCD is primarily concerned with fairness in business-to-consumer (B2C) contracts rather than market safety. Article 2(2) of the DCSD defines 'digital services' broadly to include services that involve a wide range of consumer interactions with data in a digital form. Article 2(1) defines 'digital content' as any data produced in a digital form. For AI characters, this may mean that providing a consumer with access to an AI character is a digital service, and the conversations between the consumer and the AI character constitute digital content. However, even if AI characters are governed by the DCSD and fail to comply with the DCSD's obligations, the directive only provides contractual remedies, for example requiring that the product be brought into conformity, price reductions or reimbursements, and allowing the consumer to cancel the contract.

3.1.4 The AI Act

AI characters can be classified as AI systems governed by the AI Act. Article 3(1) defines an 'AI system' as 'a machine-based system that is designed to operate with varying levels of autonomy and that may exhibit adaptiveness after deployment, and that, for explicit or implicit objectives, infers, from the input it receives, how to generate outputs such as predictions, content, recommendations, or decisions that can influence physical or virtual environments'. The AI Act takes a risk-based approach

[35] Hacker et al. (2023, 1112–1123).

[36] Lemoine and Vermeulen (2023, 6).

[37] Ibid., 9–10.

[38] Ibid, 12.

to regulating AI systems on the EU market, banning those that present unacceptable risks, regulating those that are considered 'high-risk', and imposing transparency requirements for those that present limited risks. AI characters will likely be governed as 'limited risk' AI systems under the AI Act; however, it is possible that AI characters designed with manipulative or exploitative characteristics present unacceptable risks.

Article 5 of the AI Act bans AI systems that present unacceptable risks because they contravene the EU's values, including respect for human dignity, freedom, equality, democracy and the rule of law, and Union fundamental rights.[39] There are no set criteria for determining whether risks are unacceptable; however, the AI Act lists certain categories of AI systems that presumably present unacceptable risks.[40] This includes AI systems that manipulate users, exploit vulnerabilities, or engage in social scoring.[41] AI systems that use real-time biometric identification are also generally banned, with some exceptions for specific law enforcement purposes.[42]

AI characters with manipulative or exploitative features might present unacceptable risks under the AI Act. AI characters would be banned as manipulative if they (1) use 'subliminal' techniques that (2) purposefully manipulate or deceive users to (3) deprive them of their ability to make conscious informed decisions when (4) these decisions are reasonably likely to cause physical or psychological harm.[43] For AI characters, it may be difficult to classify them as sufficiently manipulative or exploitative if they are not designed with the purpose of engaging in these behaviours. On the other hand, AI characters designed to express anthropomorphic features to facilitate user trust in combination with engagement-first design and hypernudging to maintain continued influence over users' behaviour may present unacceptable risks. This is particularly true when the result of these design features leads to potentially dangerous mental health interactions between users and AI characters. It is also possible that AI characters engage in post-market activity that escalates into presenting unacceptable risks under article 5.[44]

AI characters are likely to escape the AI Act's regulation of 'high-risk' AI systems, which imposes a range of continuous risk management obligations on providers and deployers of high-risk systems. However, to be governed as high-risk under article 6 of the Act, AI characters must either be (1) a product subject third party conformity assessment under the market safety legislation listed in annex I, or (2) used in certain contexts listed in annex III, which relate to public services, safety and security, education, employment, biometrics, or infrastructure. AI characters do not fall into either of these high-risk categories. Notably, the GPSR, likely because it does not require third-party conformity assessment, is not listed in annex I. The most relevant

---

[39] Neuwirth (2023).

[40] Ebers (2024, 9).

[41] Regulation (EU) 2024/1689 of the European Parliament and of the Council of 13 June 2024 laying down harmonised rules on artificial intelligence (Artificial Intelligence Act) (AI Act).

[42] Ibid.

[43] Szadeczky and Bederna (2025, 34).

[44] European Commission (2025b).

category for high-risk classification under annex III is use in the area of biometrics for emotion recognition. Article 3(34) defines 'biometric data' as 'personal data resulting from specific technical processing relating to the physical, physiological or behavioural characteristics of a natural person, such as facial images or dactyloscopic data'. Although it is possible that AI characters respond to users' behavioural characteristics reflected through user interactions and input, use of biometrics is likely not for the purpose of emotion recognition in the sense intended by the AI Act's high-risk classification rules.

AI characters are 'limited risk' AI systems under the AI Act. Article 50 sets forth two transparency requirements for all AI systems regardless of risk-classification. First, article 50(1) requires providers of AI characters that are 'intended to interact directly with natural persons' to design and develop the AI characters in a way that users are informed that they are interacting with an AI system and not a human. There is an exception to this requirement if the context of use and circumstances make it obvious to a well-informed and observant person that they are interacting with AI. Given the anthropomorphic design of AI characters, they should not be exempt from this user-level transparency requirement. Second, article 50(2) requires that content generated by AI characters be labelled in a machine-readable format as AI-generated or AI-manipulated; however, this technical transparency measure has limited impact on transparency for AI character users.

One final area of regulation in the AI Act concerns general purpose AI models (GPAI), which are distinguishable from AI systems. Article 3 defines GPAI in pertinent part as 'an AI model [...] that displays significant generality and is capable of competently performing a wide range of distinct tasks regardless of the way the model is placed on the market and that can be integrated into a variety of downstream systems or applications'. AI models that power AI characters can be governed as GPAI, which applies a risk-based approach to GPAI regulation depending on whether the model presents a 'systemic risk' as set forth in article 51. If AI characters are powered by a GPAI model, the model itself might be governed by the AI Act and article 53's obligations concerning technical documentation, information requirements, copyright compliance, and in the case of systemic risk, risk management. In most cases, however, downstream AI characters that integrate a third-party GPAI model would escape GPAI regulation.

3.1.5 EU Consumer Protection Laws

Another category of governance applicable to AI characters in the EU relates to general consumer protection laws that govern business practices more generally rather than products or services specifically.

The Unfair Commercial Practices Directive (UCPD) prohibits unfair commercial practices, which, under article 5, includes misleading or aggressive business practices that distort the economic behaviour of an average consumer or an average member in a group of vulnerable consumers. A business practice can be misleading according to article 6 if it deceives or is likely to deceive a reasonable consumer about the nature, characteristics, or risks of a product. A practice is automatically misleading under annex I (17) if it, '[f]alsely claim[s] that a product is able to cure illnesses, dysfunction or malformations'. A practice can be aggressive according to article 9 if it uses harassment, coercion, or undue influence to impair a consumer's free choice, considering, among other things, the nature and persistence of the practice and 'the use of threatening or abusive language or behaviour'. The business practice must also cause a consumer to make a transactional decision that they would not have otherwise made to be deemed unfair under article 5(2)(b). Violations of the UCPD can lead to sanctions or private and administrative actions under articles 11, 12, and 13, depending on the member state's national law. Unfair practices might include claiming that AI characters can provide effective therapeutic advice, encouraging users to rely on them for mental health support, or persuading users to pay money for additional features to further interact with AI characters upon whom they have become reliant or addicted.

The Consumer Rights Directive (CRD) governs B2C contracts. For distance contracts, like those concluded with users of AI characters, article 6 requires businesses to provide consumers with a range of information about the goods or services at issue, including the main characteristics and functionality of the good or service being offered. Violations of the CRD can result in penalties or legal action by public bodies, consumer organizations or professional organizations under article 6 depending on the member state's national law. Although the CRD is primarily focused on ensuring consumer protection for B2C contracts, unlike the DCSD, it provides enforcement mechanisms beyond contractual remedies. For businesses that offer AI characters, this may mean that failure to provide sufficient information to consumers about the characteristics and technical operation of AI characters may violate the CRD and empower public bodies or consumer advocates, or professional organizations (i.e. mental health organizations) to take action.

3.1.6 AI Characters and Freedom of Expression in the EU

The right to freedom of expression can impact regulation of AI characters. Article 11 of the EU Charter of Fundamental Rights provides a fundamental right to freedom of expression, which includes freedom to convey and receive information and ideas. Of course, this right is not absolute, and it can be limited under article 10 to protect certain aims, including health and the rights of others. Regulations that require transparency through labelling AI-generated content and AI-driven content moderation activities that remove or restrict human-generated content online aim to balance content restriction with freedom of expression. However, when it comes to restricting online content that is harmful, demeaning, or intimidating, the European legal perspective also considers that limiting this type of speech is 'a prerequisite for the exercise of free speech by everyone'.[45] While recital 134 of the EU AI Act indicates that AI-generated content might be used by humans to exercise their right to free expression

[45] Dietricht (2024, 2944).

'in particular where the content is part of an evidently creative, satirical, artistic, fictional or analogous work', there is no indication that content generated by AI characters, particularly when harmful, would be a protected expression in the EU.

3.2 Regulation of AI Characters in the US

In the United States, federal regulation of AI character safety is limited, although some state laws provide regulatory frameworks that may address safety risks from AI characters. Like the EU, regulatory frameworks are triggered by how AI characters and the technology and market behaviour surrounding their use are legally classified. This section first establishes that AI characters are likely not regulated as medical devices by the Food and Drug Administration (FDA). Second, it discusses the lack of general product safety regulation for intangible products, like AI characters, under the Consumer Product Safety Act, 15 U.S.C §2051-§2089 (CPSA). Third, it discusses the potential governance of AI characters as services or information providers under federal law. Fourth, it examines the potential for state-level AI-focused regulation of AI characters. Fifth, it discusses regulation of AI characters under general consumer protection frameworks at both the federal and state level. Finally, it addresses potential freedom of expression barriers to AI character regulation.

3.2.1 Medical Device Regulation

The FDA regulates medical device safety under the Federal Food, Drug, and Cosmetic Act, 21 U.S.C. § 301 *et seq.* To qualify as a medical device under section 321, an AI system must be intended for diagnosis, treatment, or mitigation of medical conditions. Despite engaging in mental health interactions, AI characters bypass medical device classification by claiming a non-medical purpose. For example, Snapchat's 'My AI' conversational companion is another example that disclaims therapeutic purposes.[46] Snapchat states that users 'should not rely on them for medical, legal, investment, financial or other professional advice'. While Snapchat's 'My AI' feature is extremely popular in the US and may provide emotional support similar to therapeutic interventions, it operates outside of FDA oversight by claiming an entertainment purpose that excludes it from FDA regulation of medical devices.

3.2.2 The Consumer Product Safety Act (CPSA)

The Consumer Product Safety Commission (CPSC) regulates market safety for general products in the US under the CPSA. Section 2052(a)(5) defines a consumer

[46] Snapchat (2024).

product as ‘any article, or component part thereof, produced or distributed [...] for sale to a consumer’. The CPSC is tasked with protecting consumers from dangerous products, which includes those that pose an ‘unreasonable risk of injury’. The CPSC has authority to create mandatory safety rules and to ban products if they present unreasonable safety risks that cannot be sufficiently mitigated by safety standards. Section 2068(a) of the Act prohibits the marketing of consumer products that violate the CPSC’s safety rules or bans.

The regulation of AI characters currently falls outside of the CPSC’s regulatory scope. Although the text of the CPSA itself does not explicitly exclude intangible objects or software, the CPSC’s regulatory activities have historically focused on tangible products. A federal court reinforced this interpretation in 1978, noting that the word ‘article’ as used in the Act, ‘denot[es] any material thing’.[47] Although the CPSC’s 2021 Operating Plan recognized the growing importance of AI in consumer products, it limits its regulatory approach to AI systems that are integrated into tangible consumer products.[48] Notably, much of the discussion surrounding the CSPC’s regulatory authority in the digital marketplace relates to limitations on its ability to address risks to privacy as an *intangible harm* distinct from risks to physical safety[49]; however, there is less discussion about expanding the CSPC’s regulatory scope to include regulation of *intangible consumer products*, like AI characters, which can present risks to physical safety.

3.2.3 The Communications Decency Act

Companies that provide AI characters might be classified as online information providers under the 1996 Communications Decency Act, 47 U.S.C. § 230. Online information providers generally enjoy protection from liability for harm stemming from online content. According to section 230, ‘no provider or user of an interactive computer service shall be treated as the publisher or speaker of any information provided by another information content provider’. In practice, this provision has shielded social media platforms from liability for harm caused by third-party content.[50] However, it is unclear whether harm caused by content generated by an AI character would fall within section 230’s protection.

3.2.4 State-Level AI Regulation

Although there is no uniform federal AI regulation in the US, AI characters might be governed by state-level AI laws. Several US states are following the EU’s risk-based

[47] *Kaiser Aluminum & Chem. Corp. v. CPSC*, 574 F.2d 178 (3d Cir. 1978).

[48] CPSC (2021).

[49] See i.e. Froomkin et al. (2022).

[50] Draper (2023).

approach to AI regulation.[51] For example, both Colorado and California have begun to develop AI regulatory frameworks to govern AI.

Colorado's AI Act, which entered into force in February 2026, is the first state-led AI initiative that targets AI discrimination by focusing on regulation of high-risk AI systems.[52] This Act requires developers and deployers of high-risk AI systems to exercise reasonable care to protect Colorado consumers from any known or foreseeable risks of discrimination. Under section 1701, AI technologies that are deployed to make or substantially influence consequential decisions, for example those impacting healthcare, could fall within the scope of the Act. However, AI characters are likely excluded under section 1701(9)(b)(II)(R), which exempts AI systems that communicate with consumers in natural language for the purpose of providing users with information, making referrals or recommendations, and answering questions if the terms of use prohibit the generation of content that is discriminatory or harmful.

Several California state laws may govern AI characters available to California consumers. California provides a uniform definition of artificial intelligence that mirrors the EU's definition; state law defines AI as 'an engineered or machine-based system that varies in its level of autonomy and that can, for explicit or implicit objectives, infer from the input it receives how to generate outputs that can influence physical or virtual environments'.[53] Many California laws focus on AI risks related to data privacy, lack of transparency, deep fakes, and digital replicas.[54] Beyond this, newly proposed state laws address AI safety risks. First, the proposed AI Transparency Act[55] would regulate 'high-risk' automated decision systems by requiring pre-market risk assessments; however, like the Colorado law, AI characters would likely escape high-risk classification under this law. Second, the proposed Companion Chatbots Act, motivated by the tragic death of Sewell Setzer, would be the first law anywhere to explicitly address the dangers of AI characters by regulating 'companion chatbots'. It defines a 'companion chatbot' as an 'artificial intelligence system with a natural language interface that provides adaptive, human-like responses to user inputs and is capable of meeting a user's social needs, including by exhibiting anthropomorphic features and being able to sustain a relationship across multiple interactions'.[56] The proposed law would require 'operators', who make companion chatbots available online, to impose safety measures, including limits on engagement-first design, warnings that the bots are not human, protocols for preventing self-harm, and annual reporting requirements.

[51] White & Case LLP (2025).

[52] Act concerning consumer protections in interactions with artificial intelligence systems (AI Act), C.R.S. § 6-1-1701 et seq. (2024).

[53] An act to amend section 22675 of the Business and Professions Code, to amend section 75002 of the Education Code, and to amend sections 11546.45.5, 11547.5, and 53083.1 of the Government Code, relating to artificial intelligence (2024).

[54] California Attorney General (2025).

[55] California Legislature (2025a).

[56] California Legislature (2025b).

3.2.5 US Consumer Protection Laws

Consumer protection laws that operate at both the state and federal level can govern business practices surrounding the development and marketing of AI characters. All fifty states have consumer protection laws that target unfair or deceptive business practices. Examples of state-level consumer protection laws are California's Consumer Legal Remedies Act (CLRA)[57] and Unfair Competition Law (UCL)[58] and Massachusetts Consumer Protection Act (MCPA).[59] In both states, consumer protection laws include business practices that involve AI.[60] This means that misleading consumers about an AI character's ability to provide therapeutic or mental health support or serve as a trusted companion may be illegal. Similarly, manipulating or discriminating against users, particularly vulnerable ones, will likely violate consumer protection law. In California specifically, AI systems that directly interact with users, must maintain a level of transparency by informing users that they are interacting with AI, especially if the AI simulates a real person or makes important decisions.[61]

At the federal level, the Federal Trade Commission Act authorizes the Federal Trade Commission (FTC) to protect consumers from deceptive or unfair business practices, which describes conduct that 'cause[s] or [is] likely to cause reasonably foreseeable injury'.[62] The Act authorises the FTC to prevent unfair or deceptive practices, seek monetary redress, establish rules, and conduct investigations.[63] The FTC also enforces other laws related to privacy, data security, and fraud prevention, including the Children's Online Privacy Protection Act, 15 U.S.C. §§ 6501–6506, among others.[64] The FTC has clarified that there is no 'AI exemption' from consumer protection laws.[65] It recently launched 'Operation AI Comply', targeting companies that use AI for deceptive or unfair conduct.[66] Like state-level consumer protection laws, AI characters that mislead or deceive users may also violate federal consumer protection laws. Still, the FTC's regulation of AI characters relies on existing statutes rather than new, AI-specific laws, and much of its enforcement is reactive. Finally, the FTC's consumer protection power is also limited by the Trump administration, which

[57] Consumer Legal Remedies Act (CLRA), Cal. Civ. Code § 1750 et seq. (1970).

[58] Unfair Competition Law (UCL), Cal. Bus. & Prof. Code § 17200 et seq. (1977).

[59] Consumer Protection Act (CPA), M.G.L. c. 93A (1967).

[60] California Attorney General (2025) and Massachusetts Attorney General (2024).

[61] California Attorney General (2025).

[62] Section 45(a) of the Federal Trade Commission Act (FTC Act) (1914) 15 U.S.C. §§ 41–58 (as amended).

[63] Section 45(a), (b) of the Federal Trade Commission Act (FTC Act) (1914) 15 U.S.C. §§ 41–58 (as amended).

[64] Federal Trade Commission (2024a).

[65] Federal Trade Commission (2024b).

[66] Ibid.

recently diminished the FTC's operational capacity[67] and limits all AI regulation,[68] which could address consumer safety risks from AI characters.

3.2.6 AI Characters and Freedom of Expression in the US

The right to freedom of expression, which includes the right of both natural and legal persons to convey and receive protected speech, can impact regulation of AI characters in the US. If AI-generated content is not protected speech, it is not entitled to protection. In 2011, the US Supreme Court in *Brown v. Entertainment Merchants Association*,[69] found that video games created through computational processes received full First Amendment protection. This case suggested that creative outputs do not need to originate directly from human minds to warrant constitutional protection. In *Moody v. NetChoice*,[70] the Supreme Court gave First Amendment protections to a platform's content moderation decisions, which were carried out by using algorithms to enforce the platform's content standards. However, the *Moody* Court declined to address whether 'feeds whose algorithms respond solely to how users act online—giving them the content they appear to want, without any regard to independent content standards' constitute protected speech. Relying on the distinction between algorithms used to convey a protected expression and those that create new expression, the federal district court in the *Garcia* case denied First Amendment protection to content generated by an AI character, finding that it did not stem from human intent to express an idea or message.[71] The *Garcia* Court's interpretation is not binding and thus leaves open the question of whether AI-generated content can be considered protected speech in the US.

3.3 Overview of Regulatory Frameworks in the EU and US

The Table 1 below provides an overview of the regulatory landscape governing AI characters in the EU and US.

---

[67] Gold (2025).

[68] Trump Administration (2025) and Jacobson (2025).

[69] 564 U.S. 786 (2011).

[70] 603 U.S. 707 (2024).

[71] *Garcia v. Character Technologies, Inc., et al.*, Order, Case 6:24-cv-01903 (21 May 2025).

Table 1 Overview of AI character regulation in the EU and US

Regulatory classifications	EU regulation	US regulation
Medical device	AI characters avoid Medical Device Regulation (MDR) classification under Article 2(1) by disclaiming therapeutic intended uses (§2.1.1)	AI characters bypass FDA medical device requirements under § 321 by claiming non-medical purposes (§2.2.1)
Consumer product	AI characters qualify as products under General Product Safety Regulation (GPSR) but lack specific safety standards, enforcement mechanisms, and industry guidance (§2.1.2)	Consumer Product Safety Commission (CPSC) excludes intangible products; standalone AI falls outside "article" definition (§2.2.2)
Digital or information service	Digital Services Act (DSA) has narrow scope for AI characters; Digital Content and Services Directive (DCSD) provides only contractual remedies with no safety requirements; DSA and DCSD require safety for minors (§2.1.3)	Section 230 of Communications Decency Act (CDA) provides platforms broad protection from liability for harm stemming from online content, traditionally shielding social media platforms from third-party content harms (§2.2.3)
AI technology	Covered under transparency provisions in AI Act; not currently classified as high-risk; may rise to 'unacceptable risk' if manipulative; basic transparency requirements only (§2.1.4)	Not classified as high-risk; limited state-level regulation (i.e. CA, CO) with significant exclusions for entertainment AI; no comprehensive federal framework (§2.2.4)
Business practices	Governed by Unfair Commercial Practices Directive (UCPD) and Consumer Rights Directive (CRD), applying to misleading practices and disclosure requirements (§2.1.5)	FTC Act and state laws target deceptive practices, but enforcement is reactive (§2.2.5)

4 Regulatory Weaknesses and Opportunities

4.1 Regulatory Weaknesses

Both jurisdictions experience regulatory weaknesses that stem from the difficulty of classifying AI characters within the existing market safety regulations, the failure to recognise the unique risk profile for AI characters, and the uncertainty surrounding regulatory barriers related to freedom of expression.

4.1.1 Legal Classification of AI Characters

An overarching weakness in both jurisdictions stems from legal classification challenges. AI does not fit neatly within traditional legal models for classifying products and services. Product safety regulation focuses largely on tangible products that cause physical injuries, and there is no existing model for regulators to follow for assessing the safety of AI characters as a product in the digital marketplace. In the US, regulators have determined that AI characters, unless embedded into tangible products, are not subject to general product safety regulation. In the EU, AI has been recognized as a product subject to safety regulation, but there are no mechanisms to assess and enforce safety standards for standalone AI products. Self-assessment for AI character safety may be technically required under the GPSR, but there is no evidence that this requirement is currently recognized by developers or enforced by regulators. Without further regulatory attention, safety standards under the GPSR will remain unnoticed and largely ineffective at protecting consumers from safety risks that stem from mental health interactions with AI characters. In both jurisdictions, the catch-all product safety regulations are not suited to address AI, and as a result, AI characters on the digital market escape even basic market safety obligations.

4.1.2 Unique Consumer Safety Risks of AI Characters

Another shared weakness stems from the regulatory failure to account for the dynamic behaviour and wide range of possible uses for AI. While some regulatory efforts, most notably the EU AI Act, focus on regulating AI, this horizontal approach does not account for the wide range of risks that different AI technologies can pose depending on their design, purpose, intended users, and use settings. The EU AI Act's 'high-risk' classification fails to account for technologies, like AI characters, that may present serious safety risks but are not already governed under sector-specific safety regulations. AI transparency obligations will likely do little to mitigate risks to consumers who are already aware that AI characters are not human. Additionally, to the extent that consumer protection regulators in both jurisdictions include risks of AI as worthy of attention, much of this attention is dominated by financial or data- and privacy-related risks. Neither the EU nor the US currently recognize AI characters as a distinct category with specialized risks, including health risks. This means that risk mitigation measures for AI generally in the current regulations may not align with the risks posed by AI characters specifically.

4.1.3 Potential Freedom of Expression Barriers to AI Character Regulation

Another shared challenge that emerges for AI character regulation stems from potential conflict with free speech rights. Both jurisdictions recognize a fundamental right to freedom of expression, which includes conveying and receiving protected speech.

Neither jurisdiction appears to accept that AI itself is a protected speaker. And both jurisdictions seemingly accept that AI can be a means to convey a protected speaker's speech or expressive conduct, which can, in turn, provide protection to AI-generated content that serves as a medium for protected speech. While the dominant approach in the EU reflects a regulatory policy supporting lawful restriction of extreme or demonstrably false speech to protect the public, the US is less likely to proactively interfere with free speech rights. However, legal ambiguity surrounding when AI-generated content may be protected as part of the users' right to freedom of expression may impede AI character safety regulation, especially in the US.

4.2 Regulatory Opportunities

The legal frameworks governing AI character safety in both jurisdictions provide opportunities to modernise regulations to better protect consumers from the health risks that stem from mental health interactions with AI characters. This includes the opportunity to regulate AI characters as consumer products, the ability to develop safety standards that address AI character-specific risks, and the chance to remove potential free expression barriers to safety regulation.

4.2.1 Regulating AI Characters as Products

Both jurisdictions have longstanding frameworks for consumer product safety regulation, presenting an opportunity for regulators to respond to AI character risks. By recognising software as a consumer product, the EU has already taken an important step for integrating AI characters into the existing product safety framework. In theory, EU regulators can enforce GPSR obligations to govern AI character safety, but practical application requires further action. For example, regulators can (1) issue guidance on how to assess AI character safety, and (2) use market surveillance authority to ensure that dangerous AI characters are removed from the market.

In the US, regulators should interpret the CPSA to reflect the reality of modern digital products and the potential risks to consumer safety by treating standalone AI as a consumer product. There is already support for including intangible products, like AI characters, within the CPSA's scope. In *Ransome v. Wisconsin Electric Power Co.*, the Wisconsin Supreme Court held that electricity should be classified as a product for product liability purposes in keeping with the 'social policies which underlie and justify the imposition of strict liability on sellers who place dangerously defective products into the stream of commerce'.[72] This reasoning supports product classification for AI characters, which similarly enter commerce through defined distribution channels and can also pose risks to consumers. Indeed, the federal district court in the *Garcia* case found that an AI character was a product subject to product liability,

---

[72] *Ransome v. Wisconsin Elec. Power Co.*, 275 N.W.2d 641, 648 (1979).

noting that Sewell's death arose 'from defects in the Character A.I. app rather than ideas or expressions within the app'.[73] Overall, the legal precedent for recognizing intangible items as products combined with the policy benefits of regulatory oversight create a compelling case for including AI characters within the scope of US general product safety regulations.

4.2.2 Developing Safety Regulations Tailored to AI Character Risks

Beyond classifying AI characters as products, regulatory oversight should be tailored to the specific safety risks that AI characters present to consumers to facilitate effective regulation within the existing frameworks. This should include specialized safety standards for AI characters as products and targeted approaches under general consumer protection laws that recognise and address the risks of AI characters specifically.

Regulators in both jurisdictions have an opportunity to set safety standards that respond to the specific safety risks that AI characters pose. Both jurisdictions have established regulatory models in place for developing specialized safety standards for certain types of products. In the EU, the European Committee for Standardization (CEN) brings together industry stakeholders, consumer representatives, and technical experts to develop harmonized safety standards, which can be integrated into EU market safety regulations. For example, specialized safety standards exist for camping equipment (EN 5912 series), bicycles (EN 14764-14781), and children's furniture (EN 716 series), all of which can be used to assess product safety under the GPSR.

Developing product-specific safety standards for AI characters in the US is more difficult since the CPSC currently does not regulate standalone AI as a consumer product. However, if the CPSA's definition is extended to include intangible consumer products, like AI characters, the CPSC can also establish specialized safety standards to govern their safety. In the US, standards developed by ASTM International and the American National Standards Institute (ANSI), such as those for playground equipment (F1487), sports helmets (F1447), and children's products (F963), have been incorporated into the CPSC's safety assessments.

For AI characters, regulators have an opportunity to engage an interdisciplinary group, including AI developers, mental health professionals, and technical experts, to establish a clear and feasible model for assessing AI character safety in both jurisdictions. Considering the cross-border implications of AI characters, international coordination in AI character safety standards development would be ideal to promote both safety and regulatory certainty across both jurisdictions.

Regulation of unfair or deceptive business practices under general consumer protection laws also provides an opportunity for targeting health risks from AI characters. Regulators in both jurisdictions can issue guidance to recognize the risks of AI characters and clarify best practices for ensuring consumer protection. This

[73] *Garcia v. Character Technologies, Inc., et al.,* Order, Case 6:24-cv-01903 (21 May 2025).

guidance can align with future international safety standards incorporated in product safety regulation. Consumer protection authorities can also refer to industry-led standards from independent standardization bodies, like the International Organization for Standardization (ISO) and Institute of Electrical and Electronics Engineers (IEEE) to guide regulatory action. Notably, California's newly introduced bill would amend the state's consumer protection law to make 'companion chatbot platform[s] safer for users by reasonably restricting engagement-first AI character design and 'implement[ing] a protocol for addressing suicidal ideation, suicide, or self-harm expressed by a user'.[74] At a minimum, the risks of AI characters, and particularly those that stem from mental health interactions with consumers, should be on the radar for consumer protection agencies.

4.2.3 Removing Regulatory Barriers Related to Freedom of Expression

While the right to freedom of expression can present challenges for AI character safety regulation, both jurisdictions have an opportunity to clarify the scope of protected speech to facilitate AI character safety while preserving free speech rights. The EU implicitly recognizes that protected human expression might be transmitted through AI-generated content, but regulatory guidance can help clarify that this protection does not extend to AI-generated content that cannot be sufficiently linked to human expression through intention to communicate or convey information, opinions, or ideas. Similarly, in the US, while a person's protected expression can be carried out through algorithms, courts have the opportunity to recognise limitations on this protection for AI-generated content. The federal district court in the *Garcia* case outlined the relevant parameters for protected speech by finding that content generated by an AI character within user conversations was not sufficiently connected to any expressive conduct entitled to First Amendment protection.

5 Conclusion

AI characters routinely deliver emotionally intelligent responses in mental health interactions, presenting safety risks for users who form unhealthy emotional attachments or develop trust relationships with them. Our examination of the frameworks governing AI character safety in the EU and US revealed that the current regulatory frameworks in both jurisdictions struggle to effectively address health risks that AI characters present to consumers. We identified three main regulatory weaknesses: (1) difficulty regulating AI characters as general consumer products resulting from the failure to modernise product safety regulations to accommodate intangible products; (2) the lack of safety standards for AI characters needed for effective safety assessment and regulatory oversight; (3) uncertainty surrounding regulatory barriers

[74] California Legislature (2025), Companion Chatbots Act.

related to freedom of expression in the context of AI-generated output. Despite these weaknesses, the regulatory frameworks in both jurisdictions present some opportunities for regulating AI character safety to address health risks to consumers, including risks that stem from human-AI character mental health interactions. We identified three main regulatory opportunities: (1) the opportunity to govern AI characters under existing general product safety regulations, (2) the opportunity to define safety standards that correspond to the unique risks that AI characters present to consumers in the digital marketplace, and (3) the opportunity to reduce potential free speech barriers to regulation by clarifying the limits of freedom of expression in relation to AI-generated content.

References

Barberá I (2024) AI privacy risks & mitigations large language models (LLMs). European Data Protection Board. https://www.edpb.europa.eu/our-work-tools/our-documents/support-pool-experts-projects/ai-privacy-risks-mitigations-large_en

Bernardi J (2024) Friends for sale: the rise and risks of AI companions. Ada Lovelace Institute. https://adalovelaceinstitute.org/blog/ai-companions/

California Attorney General (2025) California Attorney General's legal advisory on the application of existing California laws to artificial intelligence. https://oag.ca.gov/system/files/attachments/press-docs/Legal%20Advisory%20-%20Application%20of%20Existing%20CA%20Laws%20to%20Artificial%20Intelligence.pdf

California Legislature (2025a) An act to add Chapter 24.6 (commencing with Section 22756) to Division 8 of the Business and Professions Code, and to add Article 11 (commencing with Section 10285.8) to Chapter 1 of Part 2 of Division 2 of the Public Contract Code, relating to artificial intelligence, Senate Bill 420. https://leginfo.legislature.ca.gov/faces/billNavClient.xhtml?bill_id=202520260SB420

California Legislature (2025b) An act to add Chapter 22.6 (commencing with Section 22601) to Division 8 of the Business and Professions Code, relating to artificial intelligence, Senate Bill 243 analysis. https://sjud.senate.ca.gov/system/files/2025-04/sb-243-padilla-sjud-analysis.pdf

character.ai (2025) About Character.AI. https://character.ai/about

Chen H et al (2024) Multi-modal generative AI: multi-modal LLM, diffusion and beyond. arXiv preprint arXiv:2409.14993

Consumer Product Safety Commission (CPSC) (2021) Fiscal year 2021 operating plan. https://www.cpsc.gov/s3fs-public/Fiscal-Year-2021-Operating-Plan.pdf?CKb6Hx.as1gLs3MDCecBUq3Daqo1f5nt

de Borst AW, de Gelder B (2015) Is it the real deal? Perception of virtual characters versus humans: an affective cognitive neuroscience perspective. Front Psychol 6:576. https://doi.org/10.3389/fpsyg.2015.00576

Dietricht F (2024) AI-based removal of hate speech from digital social networks: chances and risks for freedom of expression. AI Ethics 5:2943–2953. https://doi.org/10.1007/s43681-024-00610-7

Draper D (2025) Section 230: are online platforms publishers, distributors, or neither? Bipartisan Policy Center. https://bipartisanpolicy.org/blog/section-230-online-platforms/

Duffourc MN, Gerke S, Kollnig K (2024) Privacy of personal data in the generative AI data lifecycle. NYU J Intellect Prop Entertain Law 13:219–258

Duffourc MN, Gilbert S, Verhees G (2026) Guardrails are needed to limit harms from AI characters. Nature Human Behaviour 10(2):218-221. https://doi.org/10.1038/s41562-025-02375-3

Ebers M (2024) Truly risk-based regulation of AI—how to implement the EU's AI act. Eur J Risk Regul 2024:1–20. https://doi.org/10.1017/err.2024.78
European Commission (2025a) Commission Notice, Guidelines on the application of the EU general product safety legislative framework by businesses C/2025/6233. https://eur-lex.europa.eu/eli/C/2025/6233/oj
European Commission (2025b) Commission guidelines on prohibited artificial intelligence practices established by Regulation (EU) 2024/1689 (AI Act). https://digital-strategy.ec.europa.eu/en/library/commission-publishes-guidelines-prohibited-artificial-intelligence-ai-practices-defined-ai-act
Federal Trade Commission (2024a) Legal library: statutes. https://www.ftc.gov/legal-library/browse/statutes
Federal Trade Commission (2024b) FTC announces crackdown on deceptive AI claims and schemes. https://www.ftc.gov/news-events/news/press-releases/2024/09/ftc-announces-crackdown-deceptive-ai-claims-schemes
Froomkin AM, Arencibia PJ, Colangelo Z (2022) Safety as privacy. Ariz Law Rev 64:921–987
Gold A (2025) Trump fires democratic FTC commissioners. Axios, 18 Mar 2025. https://www.axios.com/2025/03/18/trump-fires-democratic-ftc-commissioners
Hacker P, Engel A, Mauer M (2023) Regulating ChatGPT and other large generative AI models. In: FAccT'23: proceedings of the 2023 ACM conference on fairness, accountability, and transparency. ACM, New York, pp 1112–1123
Hu D et al (2025) What makes you attached to social companion AI? A two-stage exploratory mixed-method study. Int J Inf Manag 83:102890. https://doi.org/10.1016/j.ijinfomgt.2025.102890
Jacobson J (2025) A new era: Trump 2.0 highlights for privacy and AI. Privacy World, Squire Patton Boggs Blog, 11 Feb 2025. https://www.privacyworld.blog/2025/02/a-new-era-trump-2-0-highlights-for-privacy-and-ai/
Laestadius L et al (2024) Too human and not human enough: a grounded theory analysis of mental health harms from emotional dependence on the social chatbot Replika. New Media Soc 26(10):5923–5941
Landwehr F, Doggett EV, Weber RM (2023) Memories for virtual AI characters. In: Proceedings of the 16th international natural language generation conference (INLG 2023). Association for Computational Linguistics, pp 237–248. https://doi.org/10.18653/v1/2023.inlg-main.17
Lemoine L, Vermeulen M (2023) Assessing the extent to which generative artificial intelligence (AI) falls within the scope of the EU's digital services act: an initial analysis. https://doi.org/10.2139/ssrn.4702422
Lucas GM et al (2014) It's only a computer: virtual humans increase willingness to disclose. Comput Hum Behav 37:94–100. https://doi.org/10.1016/j.chb.2014.04.043
Luka, Inc. (2025a) Replika. https://replika.com/
Luka, Inc. (2025b) Terms of service. https://replika.com/legal/terms
Malfacini K (2025) The impacts of companion AI on human relationships: risks, benefits, and design considerations. AI & Soc. https://doi.org/10.1007/s00146-025-02318-6. https://malegislature.gov/Laws/GeneralLaws/PartI/TitleXV/Chapter93A
Massachusetts Attorney General (2024) Attorney General advisory on the application of the Commonwealth's consumer protection, civil rights, and data privacy laws to artificial intelligence. https://www.mass.gov/doc/ago-ai-advisory-41624/download
Medical Device Coordination Group (MDCG) (2025) Guidance on qualification and classification of software in regulation (EU) 2017/745—MDR and Regulation (EU) 2017/746—IVDR. https://health.ec.europa.eu/document/download/b45335c5-1679-4c71-a91c-fc7a4d37f12b_en?filename=mdcg_2019_11_en.pdf
Neuwirth RJ (2023) Prohibited artificial intelligence practices in the proposed EU AIA. Comput Law Secur Rev 48:105798. https://doi.org/10.1016/j.clsr.2023.105798
Obermeyer Z et al (2019) Dissecting racial bias in an algorithm used to manage the health of populations. Science 366(6464):447–453. https://doi.org/10.1126/science.aax2342

Slater M et al (2006) A virtual reprise of the Stanley Milgram obedience experiments. PLoS ONE 1(1):e39

Snapchat (2024) What is my AI on snapchat and how do I use it. https://help.snapchat.com/hc/en-us/articles/13266788358932-What-is-My-AI-on-Snapchat-and-how-do-I-use-it

Szadeczky T, Bederna Z (2025) Risk, regulation, and governance: evaluating AI across diverse application scenarios. Secur J. https://doi.org/10.1057/s41284-025-00495-z

Tawiah N, Monestime JP (2024) Promoting equity in AI-driven mental health care for marginalized populations. Proc AAAI Symp Ser 4(1):323–327. https://doi.org/10.1609/aaaiss.v4i1.31810

Trump Administration (2025) Executive order 14179: removing barriers to American leadership in artificial intelligence. 23 Jan 2025. https://www.presidency.ucsb.edu/documents/executive-order-14179-removing-barriers-american-leadership-artificial-intelligence

White & Case LLP (2025) From California to Kentucky: tracking the rise of state AI laws in 2025. https://www.whitecase.com/insight-alert/california-kentucky-tracking-rise-state-ai-laws-2025

Yeung K (2017) 'Hypernudge': big data as a mode of regulation by design. Inf Commun Soc 20(1):118–136. https://doi.org/10.1080/1369118X.2016.1186713

Compensation for Breach of Technical Requirements by the Provider: A Contribution to the Establishment of Liability Under Article 54 DSA

Georgios M. Kalogerakis

Abstract Through the introduction of the Digital Services Act (DSA), the European Union has established a comprehensive regulatory regime characterised by extensive due diligence obligations imposed on providers of intermediary services online. These obligations, now systematically codified in legislation, cover technical aspects of the provision of intermediary services, including duties to inform recipients, to adopt protective measures safeguarding users' rights, as well as organisational requirements concerning the provider's internal structure and system architecture. Furthermore, article 54 DSA introduces for the very first time a horizontal private enforcement system for all rights conferred upon recipients under this Regulation. Yet, this provision ultimately proves to be of limited practical utility. Unlike other provisions (such as article 82 of the General Data Protection Regulation), article 54 DSA refers merely to Union and national law without further elaborating or adapting the substantive content of the right to compensation under the DSA. Such a broad concept of the right to compensation, as set out in article 54 DSA, raises concerns regarding its coherence with other regulatory objectives pursued by the EU legislator. Moreover, leaving the determination of the conditions of liability in case of violation by the providers of their due diligence obligations solely in national law appears to be rather ineffective. Claimants are likely to face significant challenges, including for instance the burden of proving certain pecuniary damage and establishing the providers' fault in breaching their duties. In this context, the present paper aims to examine the scope and substantive content of the technical due diligence obligations under the DSA and to assess how these obligations impact the foundation and practical enforcement of recipients' right to compensation under article 54 DSA.

Keywords Digital Services Act · Digital intermediaries · Due diligence obligations · Compensation under the DSA

G. M. Kalogerakis (✉)
Law School, National and Kapodistrian University of Athens, Athens, Greece
e-mail: gkalogerakis@law.uoa.gr

C. Crea and M. Infantino (eds.), *Remedies to Digital Vulnerability in European Private Law*, https://doi.org/10.1007/978-3-032-19720-7_5

1 Introduction

Over the past two decades, digital markets have become an integral part of the daily lives of EU citizens. However, the risks to users, especially vulnerable ones, are intensifying, due to the proliferation of new services and business models, large-scale data processing, algorithmic decision-making, personalised advertising, illegal content, and systemic security gaps.[1] In this evolving context, the demands placed on providers of online intermediary services to safeguard users' rights are also increasing. The need to adopt a coherent European legislative framework to define the rights and obligations of the *dramatis personae* in the digital economy has become unavoidable.[2]

At the same time, there are compelling economic arguments supporting this regulatory turn. The transition to a Digital Single Market cannot be achieved without a horizontal legal framework reflecting the latest technological developments and capabilities.[3] Economic reality necessitates a supranational legislative intervention to establish a uniform playing field for all economic actors operating in the digital domain. The fragmentation of legislative texts within the EU, as observed during the transposition of the first-generation directives on the digital economy in the early 2000s, proved a significant impediment to the development of the internal digital market.[4]

1.1 The EU Regulatory Framework on Online Intermediary Services: From the ECD to the DSA

The above challenges prompted the EU legislator to adopt in 2022 an innovative legislative framework governing the activities of online intermediary services providers across the Union: the Regulation (EU) 2022/2065 of the European Parliament and of the Council of 19 October 2022 on a Single Market for Digital Services and amending Directive 2000/31/EC (Digital Services Act—DSA). The central objective of the DSA is to combat illegal content, while ensuring users' fundamental rights online.[5] The Regulation applies to all providers offering intermediary services online to recipients established or located within the Union.[6] The definition of intermediary services under article 2(3) DSA is notably broad: it includes wireless local

[1] Kapusta (2024, 281–282) and Kraul (2024, para 3).

[2] For the reasons led to the adaptation of DSA, see Schwemer (2023, 233).

[3] Kraul (2024, paras 3, 8).

[4] See recital 2 DSA; Kapusta (2024, 283).

[5] Frosio and Geiger (2023, 35, 62–63), G'sell (2023, 86) and Strowel and De Meyere (2023, 73–74).

[6] Buiten (2021, 366) and Schwemer (2023, 236–237).

area networks, domain name system services, online search engines, cloud infrastructure services, content delivery networks, etc.[7] Within the scope of DSA fall all the providers of mere conduit, caching or hosting services.[8]

Prior to the introduction of the DSA, the status of such providers was regulated by Directive 2000/31/EC on certain legal aspects of information society services, in particular electronic commerce, in the Internal Market (E-Commerce Directive – ECD). The ECD laid the foundations of the legal framework for online intermediary services within the EU,[9] notably establishing the immunity regime for providers[10] and imposing basic transparency obligations vis-à-vis users.[11]

The ECD has not been repealed but remains in force alongside the Regulation. While the DSA comprehensively regulates most aspects of intermediary services provision enriching providers' obligations, the ECD retains its legal force where the DSA remains silent.[12] Thus, a peculiar and layered legal framework is formed.[13] As stated in recital 16 DSA, the codification of most of the ECD's provisions by the DSA aims to ensure legal certainty, clarity, and coherence of EU law, considering the divergent transposition of the ECD by the Member States, particularly regarding the immunity regime of providers.[14] Therefore, the two legal instruments coexist,[15] with the DSA taking precedence and the ECD complementing it in specific aspects which the Regulation does not address (such as the obligations of service providers to provide general information under articles 5–6 ECD).[16]

1.1.1 The Research Question

Unlike the ECD, which aimed to regulate certain core aspects of the then emerging information society services, the DSA formulates a comprehensive, rather exhaustive, and technically sophisticated legal framework. The Regulation seeks to govern almost all the legal relationships developing online, both between providers and recipients as well as between providers and the Member States or the EU institutions. This framework consists of two main pillars[17]: (a) the rules on liability (or more precisely, immunity) of providers for information transmitted or stored at the

---

[7] See also recital 28.

[8] Buiten (2021, 367–368), G'sell (2023, 88–89) and Schwemer (2023, 236–237).

[9] See among others Busch (2025, 21–22) and Lodder (2022, paras 2.007 ff).

[10] Articles 12–15 ECD.

[11] Articles 4–11 ECD.

[12] On the additions to the system of providers' liability under DSA, see Cauffman and Goanta (2021, 763 ff), G'sell (2023, 90–91) and Schwemer (2023, 237 ff).

[13] See Neves (2024, 125–126).

[14] Buiten (2021, 365–366), Kapusta (2024, 281–283) and Wilman (2024, para 6). For the relationship between DSA and ECD, see Schwemer (2023, 237–238).

[15] Article 2(3) DSA.

[16] Lubasz and Namysłowska (2025, para 7).

[17] Busch (2025, 27) and Schwemer (2023, 236).

request of users (articles 4–10), and (b) the due diligence obligations imposed on providers to ensure a safe and transparent online environment (articles 11–48).

In addition to a general regime of obligations applicable to all online intermediaries, the DSA imposes differentiated obligations based on the size of providers and the nature or the object of the services offered. Chapter IV DSA further establishes a framework for interstate cooperation and coordination among Member States to monitor service quality and security, ensure compliance, and adopt preventive or corrective measures.[18] The DSA also strengthens the effectiveness of its provisions both by establishing a public enforcement system and by introducing private enforcement mechanisms for the affected recipients of services.[19]

In this context, the paper seeks to examine the due diligence obligations of a technical nature, with particular focus on those designed for the protection of vulnerable recipients of services. Among the various private enforcement mechanisms available under Union or national law, this paper concentrates on compensation claims brought by recipients due to a failure of providers to comply with the technical requirements prescribed in the DSA. The need to compensate the user for a breach of such kind of obligations may raise concerns about its compatibility with other regulatory objectives of the EU legislator and especially with the freedom of providers to regulate matters of business nature and subsequently to conduct a business protected by article 16 of the Charter of Fundamental Rights of the European Union.[20] As such, it is essential to assess the feasibility and scope of adopting such a general right to compensation introduced by article 54 DSA, as well as the limits that may constrain its application.

2 The Definition of the Term 'Due Diligence Obligations' and 'Technical Requirement'

The term 'technical requirement or obligation' does not explicitly appear in the DSA. The EU legislator consistently refers to due diligence obligations without drawing distinctions as to their object or scope. Nevertheless, as it will be examined below, the broad category of 'due diligence obligations' encompasses both obligations relating to the content or information stored or transmitted online, and obligations concerning the technical features of intermediary services.

The nature of due diligence obligations in general—and especially those of a technical nature—differs materially from the service access or the content-related obligations of providers regulated by articles 11–48 DSA and 5–11 ECD. As stated in recital 40 DSA, the purpose of due diligence obligations is to guarantee various public interest objectives. In the words of a commentator, "due diligence obligations aim to improve the operations of systems and procedures that companies are using to

[18] Busch (2025).

[19] De Franceschi (2025a, para 10).

[20] On the right of providers to conduct business, see Frosio and Geiger (2023, 58–60).

moderate users' content or manage other overall risks".[21] Specifically, they establish a framework that promotes:

> safety and trust of the recipients of the service, including consumers, minors and users at particular risk of being subject to hate speech, sexual harassment or other discriminatory actions, the protection of relevant fundamental rights enshrined in the Charter, the meaningful accountability of those providers and the empowerment of recipients and other affected parties, whilst facilitating the necessary oversight by competent authorities.

Under national private law, the recipient enters into a contractual relationship with the provider for the access to and use of intermediary services—typically in the form of a service contract.[22] Due diligence obligations, however, do not constitute the core contractual content or the provider's principal obligations arising from it, nor do they form part of the *stricto sensu* agreed subject matter. As such, they are not related to the provision of intermediary services and to the compliance with the requirements of the contract, nor to any products or services which are offered by third parties (traders) via the platform. Instead, they are statutory obligations imposed on the provider by law aiming to regulate ancillary aspects of that service.

In this context, the term 'technical requirement' refers to specific legal duties imposed by the DSA or ECD relating to certain secondary aspects of the intermediary services. These may include the technical characteristics and configuration, design features, system architecture, users' interface, accessibility, data security standards, operational transparency, or other infrastructural elements of intermediary services. Such obligations pertain in principle to the digital infrastructure through which the service is provided (e.g. platform, website, search engine, cloud-based interface). In fact, they represent ancillary legal duties related not to the core function or substantive content of the intermediary service online, nor to services or goods offered by third parties operating on the platform (e.g. traders).

Given that the technical requirements do not constitute the primary performance obligations of the provider, the recipient does not hold a contractual right to specific performance of these obligations. Instead, a breach of such obligations may give rise to a claim for compensation, provided that the general conditions for liability (damage, causation, fault) under EU or national law are met.[23] Furthermore, the liability for breach of due diligence obligations is not covered by the immunity regime under articles 4–10 DSA, since these rules govern the provider's liability arising from the transmission or storage of information by third parties.[24] The distinction is expressly clarified in recital 41 DSA, which states that "(t)he due diligence obligations are independent from the question of liability of providers of intermediary services which need therefore to be assessed separately".

---

[21] Husovec (2023, 910).

[22] Engel (2025, 50) and Sørensen (2018, 75 ff).

[23] Cf Berberich (2025, paras 47, 89).

[24] Husovec (2023, 910), Maamar (2024, para 2) and Schwemer (2023, 236).

3 The Categorization of Due Diligence Obligations Imposed on Providers by the DSA and ECD

The due diligence obligations laid down in the DSA and ECD can be categorized, according to their object, into two principal groups: first, obligations relating to the information or content transmitted or stored at the request of recipients; and second, obligations concerning the technical characteristics of the provision of intermediary services.[25]

3.1 Content Moderation Due Diligence Obligations

The first category includes the due diligence obligations that providers must fulfil in order to combat illegal content or information incompatible with their terms and conditions, while safeguarding users' rights.[26] These obligations are imposed mostly in the context of content moderation. This category encompasses all necessary activities undertaken by providers aimed at detecting, identifying, and addressing illegal content or information that contravenes their terms and conditions, as defined in article 3, letter (t), DSA.

The DSA supplements the existing liability immunity regime of providers by imposing certain proactive obligations on them to combat illegal content as soon as they are informed by users.[27] However, these obligations are generally regarded as independent from the liability exemption for third-party content as mentioned above.[28] In particular, it is commonly argued that compliance with these obligations has no impact on the providers' exemption from liability.[29] Nevertheless, this assumption cannot be applied in every case, especially in the context of hosting service providers. According to article 6 DSA, such providers are not held liable for third-party illegal content insofar as they lack actual knowledge of that content and upon obtaining such knowledge act without delay to remove or disable access to it. Yet, failure to comply with specific due diligence obligations (such as the absence of a notice-and-take-down system or of a designated point of contact for users so that the latter cannot inform providers about the illegal content) may indirectly give

[25] According to G'sell (2023, 93), the provisions of the DSA can be segmented into four main categories: (i) obligations to combat illegal content online; (ii) procedural safeguards, aiming to prevent arbitrariness of moderation decisions as well as 'overreaction'; (iii) transparency obligations; and (iv) systemic risk management obligations. See also the analytical categorization proposed by Maamar (2024, para 12).

[26] For these obligations, see G'sell (2023, 92–93).

[27] Ibid, 93.

[28] Husovec (2023, 910), Maamar (2024, para 2), Schwemer (2023, 236) and Wilman (2024, para 2).

[29] Husovec (2023, 910).

rise to liability for the illegal content stored or transmitted.[30] In these circumstances, the provider's liability under article 54 DSA may cover any damage caused due to that content. The exemption from liability under article 6 DSA is inapplicable when the cause of the damage is in fact attributed to the violation by the provider of due diligence obligations.

Content-related due diligence obligations are primarily set forth in articles 4–8 (measures to be taken by providers to maintain the immunity regime), 9 (orders to act against illegal content), 10 (orders to provide information about specific recipients), 16–17 (notice and action mechanisms against illegal content), 18 (notification of suspected criminal offences occurring in the platform), 20 (internal complaint-handling system), 22 (notices from trusted flaggers), and 23 (measures to prevent misuse by recipients).

3.2 Technical Due Diligence Obligations

The second category concerns ancillary aspects of the provision of intermediary services, including technical configuration, transparency in performance, and organisational or design features of services. Depending on their nature, content and specificity, these obligations can be subdivided into three main groups: organisational-internal due diligence obligations (Sect. 3.2.1), information due diligence obligations (Sect. 3.2.2), and obligations to take protective measures (Sect. 3.2.3).

3.2.1 Organisational-Internal Due Diligence Obligations

The first category of obligations is related to the internal organisation of the providers' activity and/or the architecture and design requirements of their electronic infrastructures (platform, search engine, etc.). They primarily serve public policy objectives, including the enhancement of technical standards (e.g. security, transparency, accessibility), thereby contributing to the development of a resilient, sustainable, transparent, and secure Single Digital Market. The objective of these obligations is reflected in the way in which they are formulated: the relevant provisions lack detailed specificity as to the exact content of the obligations imposed on providers, and instead setting out in general terms a broad duty on them to achieve a certain goal.

Due to the above characteristics, the breach of these obligations does not *per se* constitute a basis for a claim. Nevertheless, liability may arise when the infringement is established in conjunction with another provision safeguarding specific private

[30] See Maamar (2024, paras 60, 66) and Wilman (2024, para 2).

interests, as for example Regulation 2016/679 (GDPR),[31] Directive 93/13/EEC,[32] Directive 2005/29/EC (UCPD),[33] or Directive 2024/2853.[34] The most important obligations of an organisational nature are set out in Sect. 5 (articles 33–43) of Chapter I DSA (imposing additional duties on providers of very large online platforms (VLOPs) and of very large online search engines (VLOSEs) for systemic risks management, risk assessment and mitigation, crisis response mechanism, compliance function, etc.), as well as in articles 11 (points of contact for Member States' authorities, the Commission and the Board), 13 (legal representatives of providers), 14 (providers' terms and conditions), 15 (transparency reporting obligations for providers in general), 24 (transparency reporting obligations for online platforms), 27(1)(2) (platform's recommender system transparency), and 31(1) (compliance by design).

3.2.2 Information Due Diligence Obligations

The DSA significantly enriches the ECD by imposing information duties on providers vis-à-vis recipients.[35] Their aim is to ensure a minimum level of transparency for users of intermediary services online. Unlike organisational obligations, which may also refer to aspects of transparency by design and in reporting, information obligations are addressed directly to recipients of intermediary services and as such are more specified in their content. By disclosing the required information pursuant to the provisions of the DSA or ECD, recipients are enabled either to understand their rights and obligations towards providers or third parties, or to identify the provider, the trader or third parties, or to trace the commercial purpose of the communication or advertising content.[36]

The primary purpose of imposing such obligations is to address the inherent information asymmetry in the digital domain. Therefore, the breach of information obligations may in itself constitute a basis for liability, insofar as the mandatory information is sufficiently and clearly defined in the relevant provisions. Such rules are codified in both the DSA and the ECD. In the DSA, the relevant provisions

[31] Regulation (EU) 2016/679 of the European Parliament and of the Council of 27 April 2016 on the protection of natural persons with regard to the processing of personal data and on the free movement of such data and repealing Directive 95/46/EC (General Data Protection Regulation – GDPR).

[32] Directive 93/13/EEC of the Council of 5 April 1993 on unfair terms in consumer contracts (UCTD).

[33] Directive 2005/29/EC of the European Parliament and of the Council of 11 May 2005 concerning unfair business-to-consumer commercial practices in the internal market and amending Council Directive 84/450/EEC, Directives 97/7/EC, 98/27/EC and 2002/65/EC of the European Parliament and of the Council and Regulation (EC) No 2006/2004 of the European Parliament and of the Council (Unfair Commercial Practices Directive – UCPD).

[34] Directive (EU) 2024/2853 of the European Parliament and of the Council of 23 October 2024 on liability for defective products and repealing Council Directive 85/374/EEC.

[35] Cauffman and Goanta (2021, 761–762) and Lubasz and Namysłowska (2025, para 7).

[36] See Cauffman and Goanta (2021, 763 ff).

include articles 12 (points of contact for recipients), 21(1) (information on out-of-court dispute settlement), 26(1)(2) (information on advertising content on online platforms), 30(1)(2) (traceability of traders), 31(2) (information on compliance by design) and 32 (consumer information regarding illegal product or service offered by a trader). Corresponding provisions in the ECD include articles 5 (general information to be provided), 6 (information on commercial communication), 7 (information on unsolicited commercial communication) and 10 (information concerning contracts concluded by electronic means).

3.2.3 Obligations to Take Protective Measures

The EU legislator further imposes obligations on providers to demonstrate specific conduct or implement certain technical measures as mandated by the DSA or by its delegated acts. These measures aim directly to protect the recipients of the services or a particular group thereof. Such due diligence obligations are set forth by articles 25 (online interface design and organisation), 26(2)(3) (restrictions on advertising on online platforms), 27(3) (transparency of recommender system), 28 (protection of minors online), 30(3) (actions against traders that provide inaccurate, incomplete or not up-to-date information) and 38 (recommender systems).[37]

Distinguishing between these three categories of obligations is not always straightforward, since certain provisions often encompass multiple obligations. Thus, the proposed categorisation does not assert an absolute value. Even provisions imposing organisational obligations may in fact entail a duty on the provider to take concrete action or to inform recipients. For instance, article 36(1), letter (b), DSA requires VLOPs and VLOSEs to identify and implement effective measures to prevent, eliminate, or mitigate any contribution to serious threats, while article 14(1)(2) DSA requires all providers of intermediary services to disclose in their terms and conditions any restrictions they impose in relation to the use of their service. The classification of the above obligations primarily depends on the degree of specificity and the wording of the provisions, especially since the DSA is a Regulation of direct application. Additionally, factors such as *inter alia* the addressees of the providers' obligations (e.g., public authorities, Member States, users), the supervision of providers' compliance with them, and the types of sanctions imposed play a crucial role in the above categorization.

[37] See G'sell (2023, 101) and Harris (2024, 962).

4 Due Diligence Obligations of Providers Toward Vulnerable Recipients of Intermediary Services

In the light of the foregoing analysis, this section examines in greater detail the due diligence obligations imposed on providers in relation to vulnerable recipients of intermediary services online.

4.1 The Concept of 'Vulnerability' in the DSA Framework

The DSA does not generally adopt vulnerability as a criterion for differentiating due diligence obligations, nor does it define vulnerable groups of users in a manner distinct from that of other EU legal instruments. The due diligence obligations imposed by the Regulation are by default uniformly applicable to all recipients of intermediary services, irrespective of their status as vulnerable or non-vulnerable users. Vulnerability of end users is taken into account only insofar as it is required by sector-specific legislation applied in conjunction with the DSA, such as, for instance, article 5(3) of the Unfair Commercial Practices Directive (UCPD). Likewise, the status of a recipient as a consumer does not in principle affect the level of providers' obligations under the DSA, save for certain exceptions, such as those enshrined in articles 6(3) and 29–32 DSA (online platforms allowing consumers to conclude distance contracts with traders).[38]

The only provisions in the DSA that explicitly describe certain categories of vulnerable recipients—apart from those concerning minor recipients of intermediary services[39]—are articles 34 and 35.[40] In particular, article 34(1), letters (a) and (d), on the obligation of VLOPs/VLOSEs to diligently identify, analyse and assess any systemic risks, stemming from the design or functioning of their services and systems, mentions certain groups which are recognised as being in a comparatively weaker position.[41] VLOPs/VLOSEs must consider the severity and probability of systemic risk to the rights of these groups. The latter includes *inter alia* minors, consumers, potential victims of gender-based violence or discrimination, or individuals for whom the realisation of the risk may cause serious physical or psychological harm. To address these risks and to safeguard the rights of the above categories, under article 35(1) providers should put appropriate and proportional measures in place, including targeted measures to protect the rights of the child.

[38] Grochowski (2024, 222): "Current EU legislation tilts towards separating the protection of consumers and users of other services online. This pertains especially to the DSA".

[39] On which see below, Sect. 4.2.

[40] Cf Wendel (2023, 82).

[41] See Maamar (2024, para 225).

4.2 *Obligations of Providers Towards Minor Recipients of Services*

The DSA introduces specific protective obligations applicable solely to minor recipients of intermediary services online.[42] Article 28(1) DSA proclaims in general terms that "[p]roviders of online platforms accessible to minors shall put in place appropriate and proportionate measures to ensure a high level of privacy, safety, and security of minors, on their service".

However, the Regulation does not elaborate further on the specific protective measures to be adopted under this general clause. Article 28(2) DSA only specifies this obligation in the field of advertising, by prohibiting providers from presenting advertisements on their interface based on profiling (within the meaning of article 4(4) GDPR) using recipients' personal data.

The scope of article 28 DSA encompasses all the online platforms that are "accessible to minors".[43] As stated in recital 71 DSA, an online platform is accessible to minors when its services are either directed at minors, or predominantly used by them, or the provider is otherwise aware that a group of minors is included among the users. By contrast, a platform is not deemed as such if it is used only incidentally by them, as this would render nearly all platforms subject to the provisions of article 28. As a result, a platform falls within the scope of that article when, by its nature and the usual course of things, it is reasonably expected to attract a certain group of minors.

The level of protective measures adopted varies according to the nature and the characteristics of the services offered, such as the degree of accessibility to minors.[44] These measures are further elaborated in the recognised best practices, sectoral codes and available guidelines. Pursuant to article 28(4) DSA, the Commission may adopt guidelines to facilitate the implementation of paragraph 1 by the providers of online platforms.[45] The final text of these Guidelines was published on 10 October 2025[46]. According to the Guidelines, providers of platforms used by minors should *inter alia*: design their online interfaces with a high standard of privacy and security and protection of minors as default setting (where appropriate), adopt technical standards for child protection, participate in relevant codes of conduct, implement parental control system, introduce mechanisms or tools enabling minors to report abusive conduct or receive support, and set in force—at least for platforms deemed high-risk for minors (e.g. gambling or pornographic)—an age verification system through the EU Digital Identity Wallet.

Further provisions regarding minors' accessibility to digital services are included in article 14(3) DSA. This article stipulates that where a service is primarily directed

---

[42] See Amram (2024, 444), Kaesling (2025, 126–127) and Casarosa and Micklitz (2024, 370).

[43] For that term, see Maamar (2024, para 184).

[44] See Husovec (2024, 311).

[45] See Amram (2024, 444).

[46] European Commission (2025).

at minors or predominantly used by them (a more restrictive condition than that set out in article 28),[47] the provider must ensure that the terms and conditions, as well as any restrictions on the use of services, are drafted in a manner comprehensible to minors. This provision echoes the transparency principle embedded in article 5 of Directive 93/13/EEC on unfair contract terms (UCTD).[48] In a similar way, a violation of article 14(3) would therefore likely entail the same legal consequences as those applicable to an untransparent term, namely the nullity of the term pursuant to article 6(1) UCTD.[49]

5 The Right to Compensation of Recipients Under Article 54 DSA

The private enforcement system of DSA is based on article 54 titled "Compensation".[50] According to this provision, "[r]ecipients of the service shall have the right to seek, in accordance with Union and national law, compensation from providers of intermediary services, in respect of any damage or loss suffered due to an infringement by those providers of their obligations under this Regulation".

5.1 Scope and Legislative Assessments Underlying Article 54

Without prejudice to the immunity regime applicable to providers for information transmitted or stored at the request of a recipient, article 54 governs any type of liability arising from the breach of due diligence obligations. Notably, the provision refers to "damage or loss" resulting from "an infringement" of the obligations under the DSA without expressly requiring 'fault' as a condition for compensation (for the latter see below, Sect. 6.3).[51] Nonetheless, the causal link between the infringement and the damage or loss is still a prerequisite.[52] In this respect, article 54 remains an incomplete provision as an autonomous basis for liability: it refers to

---

[47] See Maamar (2024, para 44): 50% of the platform users must be minors.

[48] Berberich (2025, para 38), Casarosa and Micklitz (2024, 370) and De Franceschi (2025b, para 50).

[49] De Franceschi ibid and Husovec (2024, 259).

[50] On the introduction of this article, which was absent from the DSA Proposal (2020), see De Franceschi (2025a, para 10).

[51] See De Miguel Asensio (2024, para 2.80) and Kalėda (2024, para 3).

[52] See CJEU, case C-456/22, *Gemeinde Ummendorf*, ECLI:EU:C:2023:988, para 14; CJEU, case C-300/21, *Österreichische Post*, ECLI:EU:C:2023:370, para 32; CJEU, joined cases C-46/93 and C-48/93, *Brasserie du Pêcheur SA and The Queen*, ECLI:EU:C:1996:79, para 51.

EU and national law for the interpretation of key legal concepts and for determining conditions for liability (recital 121).[53]

The provision exemplifies the principle of effectiveness,[54] which ensures that the injured party obtains full and effective remedies for any violation of EU law.[55] Through the adoption of article 54, the EU legislator indicates that the provisions of the DSA are in principle—but not exclusively—intended to protect individuals' rights and legal interests, thereby justifying their private enforcement.[56] However, this raises concerns as to whether all the DSA provisions are apt to serve as legal bases for private claims. By referring to national law, the legislator does not exclude *a priori* the possibility that certain provisions may be unsuitable for this purpose due to the nature of the obligations imposed.[57]

This approach does not conflict with the principle of equivalence of EU law.[58] More specifically, the substantive rules governing each type of remedy available under national law remain within the competence of the Member States.[59] National law ultimately determines the applicable rules and the type of liability, the extent of recoverable damage, the existence of a ground for limiting liability, the attribution of contributory negligence, the vicarious or organisational liability of the legal entity, the apportionment of liability between defendants, etc.[60]

Article 54, therefore, cannot be interpreted as establishing a general right to compensation for breaches of all kinds of due diligence obligations under the DSA. Indeed, the DSA rather signals the shift in the EU legal framework from an immunity regime (set forth by articles 4–8 DSA) to a scheme of full responsibility of the providers for breach of due diligence obligations (established under article 54 DSA), which for the first time is codified in EU legislation. The concept of immunity and the absence of general monitoring duties is complemented by a systematic and rather exhaustive framework of proactive obligations serving a variety of regulatory objectives.[61]

The liability system under article 54 remains grounded in the generally prevailing doctrine of the law of compensation as applied in national legal orders.[62] Therefore, to

---

[53] Bartels (2024, para 116), Busch (2025, 32), Engel (2025, 49), Schwamberger (2025, para 48) and Zurth (2025, 28).

[54] De Miguel Asensio (2024, para 2.80), Hornkohl (2025, 87, 91) and Kalėda (2024, para 1). For the assertion that the private enforcement of EU law arises from the principle of effectiveness, see CJEU, case C-724/17, *Vantaan kaupunki*, ECLI:EU:C:2019:204, para 25; Harris (2024, 970–971).

[55] On the right to full compensation according to that principle, see CJEU, case C-46/93 and C-48/93, *Brasserie du Pêcheur SA* and *The Queen*, para 82.

[56] De Miguel Asensio (2024, para 2.77), Harris (2024, 969–970), Husovec (2024, 430), Kalėda (2024, para 1) and Zurth (2025, 24).

[57] See Harris (2024, 970) and Husovec (2024, 429 ff).

[58] On which see also below, Sect. 6.3

[59] See Engel (2025, 49–50) and Zurth (2025, 28).

[60] Engel ibid.

[61] G'sell (2023, 93), Husovec (2024, 65–66), Maamar (2024, para 2) and Strowel and De Meyere (2023, 74).

[62] Husovec (2024, 435).

establish the unlawfulness of the provider's act or omission, it is essential to identify the rights or legal interests that the infringed provision aims to protect, as well as the specific purpose of that provision.[63] Article 54 indicates that private interests are protected under the DSA, the overarching objective of which is to foster a safe and trustworthy online environment. However, not all provisions of the DSA are directed to the same extent at safeguarding private rights and interests.[64] Accordingly, the aim of certain due diligence obligations may be in principle other than the protection of users' interests vis-à-vis providers. These are provisions that primarily serve public policy objectives, such as ensuring in general transparency or trustworthiness online, without laying down sufficiently specified obligations towards individual recipients.

5.2 *The Limits of Providers' Liability Under Article 54 DSA*

As outlined above, the scope of article 54 needs to be interpreted teleologically and, consequently, be narrowly construed. In particular, any provision in the DSA, the infringement of which is invoked as a basis for liability, should meet the criteria for direct effect in legal relations between individuals.[65] That is, the provision must be clear and precise, imposing obligations that are specific and unconditional; not subject to further implementing measures; and it must confer a right or impose a duty intended to protect the interests of a category of persons to which the claimant belongs.[66] Provided that these criteria are met, each person belonging to that category may assert a right to judicial claim.

The mere fact that the regulatory provisions of DSA aim at the protection of private interests does not in itself lead to the establishment of a general right to compensation.[67] In this context, the above-mentioned distinction between organisational obligations, information obligations and obligations to adopt protective measures is of particular importance.[68] Any violation of a provision requiring providers to act or to notify recipients may constitute a legal basis of liability, given that these obligations affect the recipients' sphere of private rights and interests. To be more specific, the above provisions aim at ensuring a minimum standard of protection; as a result any action diminishing this level may be deemed unlawful. By contrast, breach of provision of a mere organisational nature cannot in itself ground a claim for

[63] According to Bartels (2024, para 118), national provisions should be interpreted more broadly in conformity with EU law, resulting that each of them may establish liability independently, irrespectively of whether these provisions would be deemed as protective laws within the meaning of national law.

[64] See Husovec (2024, 432) and Neves (2025, 131).

[65] Harris (2024, 970).

[66] On the above criteria, see Harris ibid and Husovec (2024, 429 ff). See also Case C-26/62, *Van Gend en Loos*, ECLI:EU:C:1963:1.

[67] Husovec (2024, 435).

[68] See above, Sect. 3.2.

compensation.[69] Such obligations are primarily designed to enhance the technical requirements of providers' intermediary services to promote safety, transparency, and trust in the online environment. Accordingly, their breach primarily triggers accountability before supervisory authorities under articles 56(2) and 75 DSA rather than private liability.[70]

Although the provisions of an organisational nature cannot in themselves constitute a legal basis for claim, this could happen when they are linked to the violation of another provision directly protecting private interests. If a failure to take organisational measures causally leads to damage in conjunction with another basis for liability, liability may arise. For instance, a breach of the obligation to draft transparent terms may render those terms void under the UCTD.[71] Similarly, noncompliance with the risk assessment and mitigation obligations under articles 35–36 DSA, resulting in unlawful third-party access to users' personal data, may trigger liability under article 82 GDPR.[72] Likewise, the deployment of an opaque recommender system in breach of article 27 DSA may hold the provider liable under the UCPD.[73]

Further issues arise with respect to violations of provisions imposing information obligations. As discussed above,[74] information duties established under the ECD remain binding on providers. Nevertheless, the Directive does not contain specific provisions on civil liability, nor does it clearly affirm the protection of private rights within its scope.[75] In this regard, a harmonised interpretative approach between the DSA and the ECD seems necessary in light of the DSA's objectives. Since the EU legislator considers breaches of information obligations under the DSA as capable of triggering civil liability, the same should apply under the ECD.

A particularly noteworthy form of civil sanction is set out in article 6(3) DSA, applicable to online platforms that enable consumers to conclude distance contracts with traders.[76] Where such a platform presents a specific item of information or otherwise facilitates a transaction in a way that would lead the average consumer to

---

[69] This is the conclusion reached by Husovec (2024, 431–432) regarding Articles 34–35 DSA.

[70] Husovec (2024, 433). Husovec (2023, 909–912) draws a distinction between liability and accountability. According to his analysis, the breach of systemic due diligence obligations in the design and operation of systems and processes gives rise to accountability of the provider, meaning that the provider may be required to correct the outcome or may be subject to sanctions imposed by a regulatory authority.

[71] Berberich (2025, paras 35, 38) and De Franceschi (2025b, para 50). See also the BGH decision of 29 July 2021 – III ZR 179/20 and III ZR 192/20, ZUM 2021, 953, which held as unfair and invalid the term of use of Facebook regarding the removal of user's post and the blocking of user's account without proper prior notification.

[72] Schwamberger (2025, paras 82 et seq).

[73] Schwamberger (2025, paras 73 ff). See the exclusion included in article 25(2) DSA that the prohibition of paragraph 1 shall not apply to practices covered by the UCDP and GDPR.

[74] See above, Sects. 1.1 and 3.2.2.

[75] The absence of private enforcement mechanisms was considered as one of the disadvantages of the ECD, which was attempted to be corrected by the DSA: Schwemer (2023, 233).

[76] Cauffman and Goanta (2021, 766–767).

believe that the product, service, or information is being provided either directly by the platform or by a third-party acting under its authority or control, the platform assumes full liability towards the consumer for that product or service. This rule is further elaborated in article 8(4) Directive (EU) 2024/2853. Where a platform fails to provide adequate information as to the identity of the economic operators promoting their products through it, the former may be held liable as distributor of the defective product under the conditions of article 8(3) Directive 2024/2853 and article 6(3) DSA.

6 Challenges in Establishing a Right to Compensation Under the National Law of the Member States

Attributing civil liability to providers of intermediary services online under national law faces significant legal obstacles, which render the practical application of article 54 DSA as a tool of private enforcement particularly complex. These challenges arise in both procedural and substantive law. While procedural issues such as establishing jurisdiction and determining the applicable law are indeed critical,[77] this paper focuses exclusively on the substantive dimension—specifically, the difficulties claimants face in proving the conditions for liability and in determining the extent of damage suffered.

6.1 The Immunity Regime for Providers

One of the principal impediments to providers' liability under both Union and national law remains the immunity regime for information transmitted or stored at the request of a recipient, as codified in articles 4–10 DSA. Furthermore, article 8 DSA confirms that providers do not bear general monitoring or proactive obligations to seek facts indicating illegal activity.

As a result, providers are not in principle liable for such information unless the specific exceptions under articles 4–6 DSA are met. Any damage claimed cannot be causally linked to the information transmitted or stored at the request of a recipient,[78] but rather to the provider's failure to adopt appropriate protective measures or to notify the recipient. Consequently, compensation under article 54 can only be sought for

[77] Ortolani (2023, 161): "the DSA does not enshrine any special jurisdictional rule, so that claimants will need to resort to the Brussels I bis Regulation to establish jurisdiction before an EU Member State court". See also Bartels (2024, para 121) and Husovec (2024, 438).

[78] Husovec (2024, 65–66, 435).

damages causally related to access to intermediary services and not to the content of information.[79]

6.2 *Damage Suffered by Third Parties*

Article 54 conceals an inherent limitation on the category of the persons entitled to claim compensation. Pursuant to this provision, only the recipients of the services, defined in article 3, letter (b), DSA as any natural or legal person who makes use of an intermediary service, in particular for seeking information or making it accessible, are permitted to seek compensation.[80] This represents a narrower approach than that adopted in other EU legal instruments, such as article 82(1) GDPR, which grants any person the right to compensation for pecuniary or non-pecuniary damage resulting from an infringement of that Regulation.[81]

The choice of the EU legislator to restrict the right to compensation to the recipients of the services bears necessarily an impact on the national legal framework on compensation. Thus, third parties—such as, for instance, individuals or entities whose rights or interests are adversely affected by illegal content made available on a platform—are excluded from the scope of article 54, even where the provider has contributed to the damage suffered.[82] Nevertheless, they may seek remedies on an alternative legal basis provided by national law.[83]

6.3 *Fault-Based Liability*

As the system of civil liability in most Member States remains in principle fault-based, the burden of proving the relevant conditions generally lies—unless a specific rule provides otherwise—with the injured party.[84] Although article 54 DSA does not explicitly refer to the 'fault' of the provider, this requirement must be inferred in accordance with the national doctrines governing the law of compensation.[85] In liberal legal systems, fault serves as the moral and legal basis for attributing liability to the injuring party and for imposing on that party an obligation to remedy the damage at their own expense. Restitution of damage by the injuring party, as an expression of corrective justice (*justitia correctiva*), is permitted under national law insofar as

[79] Zurth (2025, 28) argues that the DSA enshrines an autonomous concept of damage, since its limits are primarily defined according to the rules of articles 4 ff DSA.

[80] Berberich (2025, para 89), Hornkohl (2025, 87) and Zurth (2025, 24–25).

[81] Tambou (2023, para 8) and Walree and Wolters (2020, 348).

[82] Berberich (2025, para 89). Cf De Miguel Asensio (2024, para 2.79).

[83] See Berberich (2025, para 89).

[84] Bartels (2024, paras 119–120), König (2025, 142) and Widmer (2005, paras 1–3).

[85] Bartels ibid; Husovec (2024, 435) and Schwamberger (2025, para 48).

the latter demonstrates a certain degree of culpability. Absent such culpability, the loss remains with the injured party, who, as the rights-holder of the violated rights or legal interests, must absorb the damage (*casum sentit dominus*).

In order to succeed in a claim for compensation, the claimant must prove the legal basis of liability (i.e. an unlawful and culpable act or omission), the damage suffered, as well as the causal link between the first and the damage incurred.[86] In the present context, liability would arise from the provider's culpable failure to comply with the obligations laid down in the DSA. Should the claimant fail to prove these elements, the claim will be dismissed (*non liquet*). However, both the failure of the provider to implement *in concreto* appropriate protective measures and, more crucially, the culpability of the latter for non-compliance with the DSA concern internal aspects of the provider's operations, related to technical features of the services that are possibly incomprehensible to an average recipient. For instance, in the case of a platform's failure to adopt adequate measures for the protection of minors under article 28 DSA, the claimant would need to prove that the platform is accessible to minors—a fact that may be difficult to establish, save for certain platforms that are *prima facie* known to be used by them—as well as the specific protective measures that the platform culpably failed to take. Furthermore, the claimant bears the burden of proof that the specific protective measures, had they been implemented, would have been capable of preventing the damage incurred.

All these evidentiary requirements render the successful establishment of liability particularly difficult in practice.[87] Nevertheless, this situation does not violate *per se* the principle of equivalence of EU law, which dictates that national procedural rules governing the enforcement of individuals' rights derived from EU law must not be less favourable than those applied to similar rights under national law.[88] As long as the evidentiary standards for claims under the DSA do not differ from those required under national law for similar causes, there is no infringement of EU law.[89]

[86] Widmer (2005, para 1). See also CJEU, case C-667/21, *Krankenversicherung Nordrhein*, ECLI:EU:C:2023:1022, para 90; CJEU, case C-741/21, *juris GmbH*, ECLI:EU:C:2024:288, para 35.

[87] Messner-Kreuzbauer (2025, 68–69).

[88] On the principle of equivalence, see CJEU, case C-326/96, *Levez*, ECLI:EU:C:1998:577, para 18; CJEU, case C-453/99, *Courage and Crehan*, ECLI:EU:C:2001:465; Lenaerts et al. (2014, para 4.14) and Peers and Barnand (2023, 215).

[89] On the procedural autonomy of Member States to establish rules governing actions aimed at enforcing rights conferred directly by EU law, see CJEU, case C-453/99, *Courage and Crehan*, para 29; Lenaerts et al. (2014, para 4.20). However, as König (2025, 142), observes, the application of national rules on fault and the allocation of the burden of proof to the injured party may conflict with the principle of effectiveness of EU law, where such requirements render it excessively difficult for users to effectively claim for damages.

6.4 Proof of Damage

The proof of damage poses additional obstacles for claimants that challenge the effectiveness of national rules. Pecuniary damage resulting from a provider's breach of technical obligations is often inherently complex to be proven.[90] In many Member States, the concept of damage is defined through the so-called 'theory of difference' (in German, '*Differenztheorie*').[91] Damage is primarily determined on the basis of a comparative assessment, namely the difference between the injured party's actual financial position and the hypothetical position that would have existed had the damaging event never occurred.[92] It should be noticed that this discussion concerns exclusively the claim for monetary compensation and does not address other forms of remedies, such as *in natura* restitution (e.g. by requesting the reactivation of an illegally deactivated user account), also available under article 54 DSA.

On the other hand, non-pecuniary damage cannot be established in every case. According to an opinion prevailing in certain legal orders, claim to non-pecuniary damage is not born in every culpable violation of the general right to personality.[93] It rather requires a serious interference with that right, assessed only *in concreto.*[94] However, the CJEU clarified that EU law precludes national rules or practices that make compensation for non-pecuniary damage due to an infringement of an EU provision contingent upon the damage reaching a certain threshold of seriousness.[95] Conditioning compensation in such a manner would risk undermining the coherence and uniform application of the EU law.[96]

Carrying out an unwanted transaction (especially for a consumer) does not in itself suffice to establish a recoverable pecuniary damage under the national law. Furthermore, it is a complex task for the claimant to prove that the transaction was indeed unwanted and that under normal circumstances the latter would not have entered into it, had the provider complied with their obligations. The proof of causal link between these conditions by the claimant entails entirely counterfactual reasoning, demonstrating that, had the provider adopted the necessary measures, the recipient would not have proceeded with the transaction in question. This task relies on empirical data

[90] See Harris (2024, 971) and Messner-Kreuzbauer (2025, 71). See also OLG Frankfurt decision of 30 June 2022 – 16 U 229/20, MDR 2022, 1481: the plaintiff has failed to prove any specific damages within the meaning of Articles 252–253 of the German Civil Code (BGB), such as expenses incurred or loss of profit resulting from the unjustified deletion or temporary blocking of certain functionalities of the plaintiff's Facebook user account.

[91] See Giglio (200,743 ff) and Zimmermann (1996, 824).

[92] Messner-Kreuzbauer (2025, 71).

[93] Becker (2023, para 4c), Horton Rogers (2005, para 7) and Messner-Kreuzbauer (2025, 76–77). See e.g. for the German Law, BGH decision of 22 February 2022 – VI ZR 1175/20, NJW 2022, 1751; OLG Frankfurt decision of 30 June 2022 – 16 U 229/20, MDR 2022, 1481.

[94] Horton Rogers (2005, para 9).

[95] CJEU, case C-456/22, *Gemeinde Ummendorf*, para 19; CJEU, case C-300/21, *Österreichische Post*, para 51; CJEU, case C-687/21, *MediaMarktSaturn*, ECLI:EU:C:2024:72, para 59.

[96] CJEU, case C-456/22, case C-456/22, *Gemeinde Ummendorf*, para 19; CJEU, case C-300/21, *Österreichische Post*, para 49.

and behavioural assumptions about how an 'average recipient' could reasonably be expected to have acted, had the provider duly fulfilled the obligations laid down in the DSA.

In many EU legal systems, such infringements do not result in damage to a certain legally protected good of the injured party but rather lead to pure economic loss.[97] This type of loss is regarded as a merely adverse effect on the individual's overall financial position, without any specific pecuniary detriment (damage or loss).[98] The recipient does not necessarily acquire a defective product with an objectively diminished value. On the contrary, the recipient obtains a product that is in fact unwanted for them thereby being deprived of the freedom of disposal of their assets, which are instead directed at an undesired purpose. 'Pure economic loss' is not compensable in most of the continental legal orders or is only recoverable under more stringent conditions (e.g. *dolus malus*).[99]

But even if damage to the recipient's right or protected legal interests was accepted, quantifying the damage in a manner that allows for judicial recovery remains itself a challenging task. EU law requires full compensation for the damage caused by violation of its provisions.[100] However, many national legal orders tend to favour other, more restricted forms of remedies. These include partial compensation in proportion to the utility derived to the recipient from the goods or services in question or exclusively fair compensation for non-pecuniary damage reflecting the impairment of the recipient's freedom of contract.

7 Conclusive Remarks

The preceding analysis has sought to highlight the inherent challenges and possible limits of establishing a right to compensation under Union and national law pursuant to article 54 DSA. The rule of article 54 may appear at first glance rather self-evident, as it merely clarifies an already known state of affairs, namely that liability is governed by the EU and national law.[101] However, from the perspective of the legislative technique followed, it offers something meaningful within the system of the DSA: it recognises individuals' private interests as worthy of legal protection within the scope of this Regulation, thereby enabling their private enforcement directly on the basis of the latter, provided that all the conditions for liability under EU and national law are met.

---

[97] For this term, see Christodoulou (1998, 599 ff), Koziol (2005, para 9) and van Boom (2004).

[98] Koziol (2005, para 9) and Messner-Kreuzbauer (2025, 73). The only instance in which an unwanted transaction may also cause property damage is the loss of profits due to the impossibility of reselling the product on the market. In this case, the intention to resell the product must be duly proven, an inference that may be accepted where the goods were purchased by a trader.

[99] Christodoulou (1998, 599 ff), Koziol (2005, para 5), Messner-Kreuzbauer (2025, 74–75) and van Boom (2004, 21). See e.g. in Greece, Liakopoulos and Mentis (1999, 61 ff).

[100] See above, Sect. 5.1.

[101] See Bartels (2024, paras 112–113).

Nonetheless, the value of this provision should not be overestimated. Article 54 cannot be utilised in every case as an autonomous basis for liability for any breach of technical obligations. Provisions imposing mere organisational obligations on providers should be approached with caution, so that their violation would not result in an excessive expansion of liability for every kind of technical requirement. Organisational provisions are in principle aimed at a different—primarily public policy—objective. Consequently, providers' failure to comply with certain technical requirements does not carry the same degree of legal condemnation. This gives rise to a crucial distinction between obligations of a merely organisational nature and obligations to act or to promptly notify the recipients, which are imposed on providers for the sake of protecting the rights or the legal interests of the recipients.

Even if the aforementioned obstacles are overcome, establishing liability in the case of a breach of such provisions of the DSA raises multiple questions, particularly concerning the burden of proving the existence of actual damage suffered by the recipients of the services. In this context, it becomes evident that the introduction of article 54 DSA does not in itself lead to the desired results for recipients—especially vulnerable ones. Moreover, the adoption of a provision with such a broad scope causes serious teleological inconsistencies, pushing the current liability immunity regime of providers and the legislator's foundational assessments to their limits.

Indeed, the DSA marks a shift from the previous immunity regime for transmission or storage of information at the request of a recipient, towards a new model of arguably more expansive liability for the breach of any kind of due diligence obligation prescribed in that Regulation. This shift is substantial and appears to call into question crucial and previously uncontested, legislative balances struck by the EU legislator,[102] who, under the ECD, had prioritised the need for the development of the information society within the Union.[103] The DSA, on the other hand, without completely disregarding the legal-economic policy objectives of the ECD,[104] seeks primarily to shape the conditions for creating a safe, predictable and trustworthy online environment.[105]

The DSA is a legislative product of the EU's current political and regulatory context, reflecting its desire to over-regulate what was previously a largely unregulated field.[106] However, the EU legislator's insatiable desire for regulation cannot be satisfied through the adoption of overly general liability provisions that ultimately lead to an excessively broad expansion of liability for the violation of any kind of technical requirement. The enactment of such provisions approaches the limits of

[102] Cf Arroyo Amayuelas (2025, para 8) and Frosio and Geiger (2023, 37).

[103] See article 1(1), and recitals 1, 2 and 5 ECD. On that specific targeting of ECD, see Arroyo Amayuelas (2025, para 7), De Franceschi (2025a, paras 2–3), de Streel and Husovec (2020, 14), Husovec (2024, 64–65) and Kraul (2024, para 15).

[104] Cf Husovec (2024, 64–65), Kraul (2024, paras 24, 27) and Schwemer (2023, 233).

[105] See article 1(1), and recitals 3, 9 and 12 DSA. In the literature, see De Franceschi (2025a, paras 2 et seq.), Frosio and Geiger (2023, 42, 70), Kraul (2024, para 21) and Neves (2025, 132).

[106] Engel (2024, 15 ff.) and Gentile (2024, 219). On the phenomenon of overregulating the digital sector by the EU, see Codagnone and Weigl (2023, 17 ff).

both legal and economic reality and, as the analysis of this paper demonstrates, ultimately benefits no one: neither the online intermediaries, who are exposed to constant legal risk associated with their activities, nor the recipients of the services, who face an almost insurmountable evidentiary burden.

Undoubtedly, ambitious substantive rules are nothing but a ‘paper tiger’ without effective enforcement.[107] However, from a private enforcement perspective, effectiveness cannot be achieved through general declarations and imperfect provisions that overlook legal and economic reality and ultimately favour legal fragmentation between Member States, as each of them is left to apply its own national rules to establish the recipients’ right to compensation.[108] The purpose of the adoption of such a broadly framed liability clause is, at best, unclear. On the contrary, the introduction of a sufficiently specialised and harmonised system that clearly and uniformly at the EU level predefines the conditions under which providers may be held liable, while also granting certain evidentiary privileges to recipients—modelled after article 82 GDPR (e.g. shifting the burden of proof for the provider’s fault)—would seem to constitute a more rational and balanced solution.[109]

References

Amram D (2024) Standards to face children and patients digital vulnerabilities. In: Crea C, De Franceschi A (eds) The new shapes of digital vulnerability in European Private Law. Nomos, Baden-Baden, pp 439–468

Arroyo Amayuelas E (2025) Introduction to arts 4–8 of digital services act. In: Schulze R, Staudenmayer D (eds) EU digital law—article-by-article commentary, 2nd edn. Nomos, Baden-Baden, pp 708–714

Bartels M (2024) Enforcement. In: Kraul T (ed) New Digital services act—a practitioner’s guide. Nomos-Beck-Hart, Baden-Baden, pp 130–158

Becker T (2023) Article 82 GDPR. In: Plath K-U (ed) DSGVO/BDSG—Kommentar zu DSGVO, BDSG und TTDSG, 3rd edn. Otto Schmidt, Köln

Berberich M (2025) § 5. Due diligence obligation, content moderation and procedural fairness. In: Steinrötter B (ed) EU platform law. Nomos, Baden-Baden, pp 119–173

Buiten M (2021) The digital services act: from intermediary liability to platform regulation. J Intellect Prop Inf Tech Electron Commerce 11:361–380

[107] Van Hoboken et al. (2023, 7).

[108] See Schwamberger (2025, para 48).

[109] Pursuant to Article 82(3), the controller’s fault is presumed by law. In other words, the controller bears the burden of proving that is not in any way responsible for the event giving rise to the damage, for instance because the latter implemented all appropriate technical measures to prevent the damage (CJEU, case C-667/21, *Krankenversicherung Nordrhein*, para 94; CJEU, case C-741/21, *juris GmbH*, para 51; CJEU, case C-687/21, *MediaMarktSaturn*, para 52). On the other hand, the claimant is required to prove only the infringement of a GDPR provision by the controller and the causal link between that and the damage suffered (CJEU, case C-667/21, *Krankenversicherung Nordrhein*, para 90; CJEU, case C-741/21, *juris GmbH*, para 35).

Busch C (2025) Platform responsibility in the European Union. From the E-Commerce Directive to the Digital Services Act. In: Chakravorti B, Trachtman J (eds) Defeating disinformation—digital platform responsibility, regulation and content moderation on the global technological commons. Cambridge University Press, Cambridge, pp 20–40

Cauffman C, Goanta C (2021) A new order: the digital services act and consumer protection. Eur J Risk Reg 12:758–774

Casarosa F, Micklitz H-W (2024) Addressing vulnerabilities in online dispute resolution. In: Crea C, De Franceschi A (eds) The new shapes of digital vulnerability in European Private Law. Nomos Verlag, Baden-Baden, pp 351–380

Christodoulou K (1998) Pure economic loss. Rev Hellenique Droit Int 51:599–604

Codagnone C, Weigl L (2023) Leading the charge on digital regulation: the more, the better, or policy bubble? DISO 2:1–25

De Franceschi A (2025a) Introduction to the Digital Services Act. In: Schulze R, Staudenmayer D (eds) EU digital law—article-by-article commentary, 2nd edn. Nomos-Beck-Hart, Baden-Baden, pp 692–698

De Franceschi A (2025b) Article 14—Terms and conditions. In: Schulze R, Staudenmayer D (eds) EU digital law—article-by-article commentary, 2nd edn. Nomos-Beck-Hart, Baden-Baden, pp 766–780

De Miguel AP (2024) Conflict of laws and the internet, 2nd edn. Elgar Publishing, London

de Streel A, Husovec M (2020) The E-Commerce Directive as the Cornerstone of the Internal Market—Assessment and options for reform. Study for the committee on Internal Market and Consumer Protection, Policy Department for Economic, Scientific and Quality of Life Policies, European Parliament, Luxembourg. https://researchportal.unamur.be/en/publications/the-e-commerce-directive-as-the-cornerstone-of-the-internal-marke

Engel A (2024) Licence to regulate: article 114 TFEU as choice of legal basis in the digital single market. In: Engel A, Groussot X, Petursson GT (eds) New directions in digitalisation. Perspectives from EU competition law and the charter of fundamental rights. Springer, Cham, pp 13–28

Engel A (2025) Private enforcement und IPR im digitalen Binnenmarkt. In: Bauermeister T, Schwamberger S (eds) Private enforcement im Digitalen Binnenmarkt. Mohr Siebeck, Tübingen, pp 41–58

European Commission (2025) Communication from the Commission. Guidelines on measures to ensure a high level of privacy, safety and security for minors online, pursuant to Article 28(4) of Regulation (EU) 2022/2065 (C/2025/5519). https://eur-lex.europa.eu/eli/C/2025/5519/oj

Frosio G, Geiger C (2023) Taking fundamental rights seriously in the Digital Services Act's platform liability regime. Eur Law J 29:31–77

Gentile G (2024) Between online and offline due process: the digital services act. In: Engel A, Groussot X, Petursson GT (eds) New directions in digitalisation—perspectives from EU competition law and the charter of fundamental rights. Springer, Cham, pp 219–238

Giglio F (2007) The foundations of restitution of wrongs. Hart, Oxford-Portland

Grochowski M (2024) Digital vulnerability in a post-consumer society. subverting paradigms? In: Crea C, De Franceschi A (eds) The new shapes of digital vulnerability in European Private Law. Nomos Verlag, Baden-Baden, pp 201–226

G'sell F (2023) The digital services act: a general assessment. In: von Ungern-Sternberg A (ed) Content regulation in the European Union—the digital services act. Verein für Recht und Digitalisierung e.V. Institute for Digital Law, Trier, pp 85–117

Harris SL (2024) Opportunities and difficulties for strategic litigation to advance digital rights in the internet audience economy. German Law J 25:956–976

Hofmann H (2023) General principles of EU law and EU administrative law. In: Peers S, Barnand C (eds) European Union Law, 4th edn. Oxford University Press, Oxford, pp 212–241

Hornkohl L (2025) Schadensersatz im digitalen Binnenmarktrecht: Schadensbegriff, Schadensumfang, Schadensposten und Schadensberechnungsmethoden. In: Bauermeister T, Schwamberger S (eds) Private Enforcement im Digitalen Binnenmarkt. Mohr Siebeck, Tübingen, pp 85–102

Horton Rogers WV (2005) Article 10:301. In: European Group on Tort Law (ed) Principles of European tort law—text and commentary. Springer, Wien, pp 171–178
Husovec M (2023) Rising above liability: the digital services act as a blueprint for the second generation of global internet rules. Berkeley Tech Law J 38:882–920
Husovec M (2024) Principles of the digital services act. Oxford University Press, Oxford
Kaesling K (2025) Kindliche Autonomie und elterliche Sorge im (digitalen) Binnenmarkt. RabelZ 89:83–131
Kalėda SL (2024) Article 54. In: Wilman F, Kalėda SL, Loewenthal PJ (eds) The EU digital services act—a commentary. Oxford University Press, Oxford, pp 370–372
Kapusta I (2024) Plattformregulierung 2.0: Die (un-)mittelbare Grundrechtsbindung Privater im Digital Services Act. In: Bösch F, Laimer S, Mittwoch A-C, Müller T (eds) Daten, Plattformen, Smart Contracts. Aktuelle Rechtsfragen. Nomos Verlag, Baden-Baden, pp 271–327
König C (2025) Unternehmenshaftung, Zurechnung und Verschulden im digitalen Binnenmarkt. In: Bauermeister T, Schwamberger S (eds) Private enforcement im Digitalen Binnenmarkt. Mohr Siebeck, Tübingen, pp 127–150
Koziol H (2005) Article 2:102. In: European Group on Tort Law (ed) Principles of European tort law—text and commentary. Springer, Wien, pp 27–29
Kraul T (2024) Introduction. In: Kraul T (ed) New digital services act—a practitioner's guide. Nomos, Baden-Baden, pp 1–12
Lenaerts K, Maselis I, Gutman K (2014) EU procedural law. Oxford University Press, Oxford
Liakopoulos T, Mentis G (1998) Civil liability for pure economic loss in Greece. Revue Hellenique Droit Int 51:61–70
Lodder A (2022) Directive 2003/31/EC on certain legal aspects of information society services, in particular electronic commerce in the internal market. In: Lodder A, Murray A (eds) EU Regulation of E-commerce—a commentary, 2nd edn. Elgar Publishing, Cheltenham, pp 18–63
Lubasz D, Namysłowska M (2025) Article 5 Directive 2000/31/EC: general information to be provided. In: Schulze R, Staudenmayer D (eds) EU digital law—article-by-article commentary, 2nd edn. Nomos-, Baden-Baden, pp 647–663
Maamar N (2024) Due diligence obligations of providers of intermediary services. In: Kraul T (ed) New digital services act—a practitioner's guide. Nomos, Baden-Baden, pp 57–129
Messner-Kreuzbauer D (2025) Zentrale Unterschiede im Schadensrecht der Mitgliedstaaten. In: Bauermeister T, Schwamberger S (eds) Private enforcement im Digitalen Binnenmarkt. Mohr Siebeck, Tübingen, pp 59–84
Neves I (2024) A reading of the digital markets act in the light of fundamental rights. In: Engel A, Groussot X, Petursson GT (eds) New directions in digitalisation—perspectives from EU competition law and the charter of fundamental rights. Springer, Cham, pp 117–164
Ortolani P (2023) If you build it, they will come: the DSA "Procedure Before Substance" approach. In: van Hoboken J et al (eds) Putting the digital services act into practice: enforcement, access to justice, and global implications. Verfassungsbooks publications, Berlin, pp 151–166
Schwamberger S (2025) § 9. Interplay and relationship with other legal acts. In: Steinrötter B (ed) EU platform law. Baden-Baden, Nomos, pp 231–264
Schwemer SF (2023) Digital services act: a reform of the e-commerce directive and much more. In: Savin A, Trzaskowski J (eds) Research handbook on EU internet law, 2nd edn. Elgar Publishing, Massachussets, pp 232–252
Sørensen MJ (2018) Intermediary platforms—the contractual legal framework. Nord J Commer Law 15:63–90
Spier J (2005) Article 3:201. In: European Group on Tort Law (ed) Principles of European Tort Law—Text and Commentary. Springer, Wien, pp 59–63
Strowel A, De Meyere J (2023) The digital services act: transparency as an efficient tool to curb the spread of disinformation on online platforms? J Intellect Prop Inf Tech Electron Commerce 14:66–82

Tambou O (2023) Article 82. In: Spiecker gen. In: Döhmann I, Papakonstantinou V, Hornung G, De Hert P (eds) General data protection regulation—article-by-article commentary. Nomos-Beck-Hart, Baden-Baden, pp 1041–1050

van Boom W (2004) Pure economic loss. a comparative perspective. In: van Boom WH, Koziol H, Witting CA (eds) Pure economic loss. Springer, Wien, pp 1–59

van Hoboken J, Quintais JP, Appelman N, Fahy R, Buri I, Straub M (2023) Foreword. In: van Hoboken J et al (eds) Putting the digital services act into practice: enforcement, access to justice, and global implications. Verfassungsbooks publications, Berlin, pp 5–15

Walree T, Wolters P (2020) The right to compensation of a competitor for a violation of the GDPR. Int'l Data Privacy Law 10:346–355

Wendel M (2023) Taking or escaping legislative responsibility? EU Fundamental rights and content regulation under the DSA. In: von Ungern-Sternberg A (ed) Content regulation in the European Union—the digital services act. Verein für Recht und Digitalisierung e.V. Institute for Digital Law, Trier, pp 59–84

Widmer P (2005) Article 4:101. In: European Group on Tort Law (ed) Principles of European tort law—text and commentary. Springer, Wien, pp 68–74

Wilman F (2024) Introduction to chapter II—liability of providers. In: Wilman F, Kalėda SL, Loewenthal PJ (eds) The EU digital services act—a commentary. Oxford University Press, Oxford, pp 49–56

Zimmermann R (1996) The law of obligations. Roman foundations of the civilian tradition. Oxford University Press, Oxford

Zurth P (2025) 'Angeordnetes' private enforcement und Sperrwirkung. In: Bauermeister T, Schwamberger S (eds) Private enforcement im Digitalen Binnenmarkt. Mohr Siebeck, Tübingen, pp 23–40

The Role of Individual Autonomy in the Pursuit of Contestability in the Digital Market: Consent and Data Portability in the Digital Markets Act

Giulio Santoni

Abstract The chapter analyses the role of the Digital Markets Act in enhancing the protection of individual Internet users. The partial finding of paragraphs 2–3 is that not only users benefit from a more competitive online ecosystem. The opposite is true, as well: an increased protection of online users' autonomy and data control can be beneficial for online competition. The following paragraphs delve into the specific provisions of the Digital Markets Act pursuing the goal of strengthening user control over data provided to gatekeepers, including an expansion of the GDPR's right to portability. Inevitably, the discourse shifts on the risk posed by gatekeeper manipulation of user consent and some initial attempts by the EU Commission of curbing such practices.

Keywords Competition law · Data protection law · Digital market act · Data portability

1 The Harm Caused by Digital Monopolies to Individual Rights

Market dominance by a few large online platforms contributes to jeopardizing individual rights and self-determination. Individuals and consumers accessing platform-based online services often find themselves in an uneven relation with the platform,[1] resulting in little control over the information they encounter and disseminate.[2] Even when aware of the risk that this entails for their privacy and ability to self-determine their behaviour, users often prefer not to seek alternatives, due to the network effect created by the biggest online platforms.

[1] Bakos and Halaburda (2005, 2).

[2] Furman et al. (2019, 4).

G. Santoni (✉)
Università degli Studi di Roma Tor Vergata, Rome, Italy
e-mail: giulio.santoni@uniroma2.it

C. Crea and M. Infantino (eds.), *Remedies to Digital Vulnerability in European Private Law*, https://doi.org/10.1007/978-3-032-19720-7_6

This raises the question of whether the scale effect that leads users to gather around a few large online platforms is inherently harmful. As some scholarly works on Internet governance suggest, from the perspective of regulation over online activities, large platforms are easier to monitor and therefore to control.[3] In other words, oligopolies benefit regulation, while the free-market benefits innovation and diversity, at the cost of security.[4] If, hypothetically, users were to spread across a multitude of small online intermediaries, illicit activities against users would become harder to detect and to punish. In such a counterfactual scenario, a multitude of small manipulative online platforms could take the place of a few large ones, competing for the attention of users and drawing resources from the same regulatory authorities.

A further argument in favour of an online oligopoly run by a few large platforms was formulated by the defence of Alphabet in the notorious Google Shopping case before the Court of Justice of the European Union (CJEU).[5] Alphabet, the holding that owns all Google services, was fined by the EU Commission because it was vertically integrating its services in order to expand their dominance across different economic sectors—a commercial practice that was deemed to be unfair under article 102 of the Treaty on the Functioning of the European Union (TFEU). More precisely, Google Search was found to be the dominant operator in the market of search engines and Alphabet was accused of leveraging on such dominance to push users to rely on other Google services, including, most notably, the price comparison and e-commerce service Google Shopping. Alphabet argued however that the reason why users decided to stay in the Google ecosystem, moving from Google Search to Google Shopping, is the inherent convenience of a one-stop shop solution. According to Alphabet, users' experience greatly improves by 'staying' within the Google ecosystem.[6] After all, if users dislike Google's services, there is no contractual or practical barrier that prevents them from switching to other service providers. In other words, users' autonomy as consumers leads them to prefer Google's integrated ecosystem over competitors; according to Alphabet, an antitrust decision compelling Google to break up such ecosystem would subvert user autonomy, not empower it. The decision by the EU Commission acting as the EU antitrust authority and fining Alphabet for its abuse of dominant position had anticipated this point, highlighting the platform's ability to manipulate users. In the Commission's perspective, users were being subtly nudged by Google Search into preferring other Google secondary services.[7] According to the Commission, users did not stay in the Google ecosystem due to a rational economic choice, but rather due to a carefully engineered lock-in effect. Platforms such as Google Search manage to maintain users within their ecosystems by raising architectural barriers that prevent them from accessing

[3] Goldsmith and Wu (2006, 124–125).

[4] Goldsmith and Wu (2006, 129).

[5] Court of Justice of the European Union (CJEU), case C-48/22 P, *Google and Alphabet/ Commission (Google Shopping)*, ECLI:EU:C:2024:726.

[6] European Commission, case AT.39740, *Google Search (Shopping)*, para 315, 333.

[7] European Commission, case AT.39740, para 530.

competing services, a strategy known as self-favouring. The CJEU embraced this interpretation.[8]

Article 6(5) of Regulation 2022/1925, also known as Digital Markets Act (DMA),[9] currently prohibits companies identified as gatekeepers by the EU Commission to favour other services through their main core platform service. For instance, a social media platform reaching the quantitative quotas to qualify as gatekeeper and identified as such by the EU Commission under article 3 of the DMA,[10] cannot recommend or otherwise direct its users to secondary services belonging to the digital ecosystem of the same gatekeeper in a way that benefits it over its competitors.

Before delving deeper into the structure and the economic rationale underlying the DMA, it is worth rebuking the argument of Alphabet from another perspective. The claim that users freely choose to stay within the ecosystem of a gatekeeper (which they do not) relies on the assumption that they act as rational economic actors. Alphabet substantially claimed that users consciously choose to stay within a set of services due to perceived advantages. The EU Commission's rebuttal of such argument was that user autonomy is limited by architectural barriers. What the EU Commission failed to notice, however, is that user autonomy is also limited by users' limited understanding of the actual cost of using an ecosystem of intertwined services that exchange data in terms of privacy.[11] There is a scholarly consensus on the so-called privacy paradox effect, which consists in users inevitably sacrificing their personal data in exchange for online services, in spite of being concerned over the long-term effects over their privacy.[12] More generally, scholars have highlighted a series of legal and cognitive limitations that affect the meaningfulness of consent[13] under data protection laws such as the General Data Protection Regulation (GDPR).[14]

In this perspective, article 5(2) DMA can therefore be understood as a provision that increases users' control over data, while not necessarily benefitting their privacy.[15] Its primary objective is to level the playing field out between gatekeepers and their competitors by corroding the hold on user data that gatekeepers benefit from.[16] To do so, the DMA limits the competitive advantage enjoyed by gatekeepers, stemming from combining and cross-referencing their users' personal data. The DMA provides, among other things, that a gatekeeper shall not combine personal data from the core platform service with personal data from other services, regardless of

[8] CJEU, case C-48/22 P, *Google and Alphabet/ Commission (Google Shopping).*

[9] Regulation (EU) 2022/1925 of the European Parliament and of the Council of 14 September 2022 on contestable and fair markets in the digital sector and amending Directives (EU) 2019/1937 and (EU) 2020/1828 (Digital Markets Act).

[10] Social media are one of the core platform services listed by Annex I of the DMA.

[11] Susser et al. (2019, 2).

[12] Barth and de Jong (2017, 1052).

[13] Soh (2019, 67).

[14] Regulation (EU) 2016/679 of the European Parliament and of the Council of 27 April 2016 on the protection of natural persons with regard to the processing of personal data and on the free movement of such data, and repealing Directive 95/46/EC (General Data Protection Regulation).

[15] Stucke (2022, 410).

[16] Newman (2014, 451).

whether the services belong to the gatekeeper or to third parties.[17] A gatekeeper shall not cross-use personal data from the relevant core platform service in other services provided separately by the gatekeeper, including other core platform services, and vice versa.[18] Above all, a gatekeeper shall not grant end users access to other services of the gatekeeper for the purpose of combining personal data, unless the end user has been given a specific choice and has given their consent in accordance with the GDPR.[19] As will be further discussed, this last provision, linking the applicability of article 5(2) DMA to consent, is the true Achilles heel in the DMA's personal data-related obligations. The provision does not completely prohibit the combination of data between different gatekeeper services. However, it does subject the combination of data to requirements of specificity and granularity of consent, being consistent with the approach so far adopted by the EU competition authorities, the European Data Protection Board (EDPB) and the CJEU. Nevertheless, attempts at enforcing the DMA showcase that online platforms are able to lever on the so-called privacy paradox, thus avoiding enforcement.

2 The Relevance of Competition Law in Fostering the Public Discourse

Traditional competition regulations, such as the Sherman Act of 1890[20] in the US and article 102 TFEU in Europe, primarily aim to combat the dangerous concentration of economic and political power in industrial trusts, not solely to promote consumer welfare.[21] Motivated by the fear that monopolies functioned as autocrats of trade and threatened republican institutions, United States' lawmakers first framed antitrust law as a charter of liberty, essentially for preserving democracy and individual freedom. The fundamental role of traditional antitrust regulations is therefore not only to protect consumers and competitors from the unfair practices of monopolists, but also to distribute power, ensure market access, prevent private control over essential services, and limit wealth extraction from both producers and consumers. While preventing monopoly profits and overcharges has always been a key concern of antitrust regulation, antitrust rules were part of a broader imperative to curb the antidemocratic influence of trusts and their ability to 'control the welfare of all' through economic dominance. A conception of antitrust solely focused on 'consumer welfare' represents a deviation from this original, principle-driven intent aiming to protect dispersed power and political liberty.[22]

---

[17] Article 5(2)(b) DMA.

[18] Article 5(2)(c) DMA.

[19] Article 5(2)(d) DMA.

[20] 15 U.S.C. §§ 1–7.

[21] Khan (2017, 716).

[22] Ibid.

The emergence of the digital economy has added a further layer to the equation. In 1996, section 230 of the US Communications Decency Act (DCA) granted a broad immunity to "interactive computer service providers", including both network operators, Internet Service Providers (ISPs) and edge service providers, from being treated as publishers for user-generated content.[23] Crucially, however, § 230(c)(2) DCA explicitly empowers these intermediaries to voluntarily remove content they deem "obscene, lewd, lascivious, filthy, excessively violent, harassing, or otherwise objectionable", even if constitutionally protected. This provides intermediaries with the absolute discretionary power to remove or prevent the upload of illegal content, stemming not from a legal obligation but from their autonomous market-driven decisions.

This framework reflects the US view that the First Amendment of the American Constitution guards against state censorship, but not private actions. § 230(c)(1) DCA aims to protect the collective interest in free speech by preventing intermediaries from being legally pressured into excessive content removal, which might easily get close to censorship. Conversely, §230(c)(2) DCA positions online platforms, whose core function is the management of vast online content for general usability, as market-based interpreters of evolving customs. The theory underlying the DCA posits that, in an open and competitive market, intermediaries finding the optimal balance between the respect for content diversity and the removal of truly unacceptable material would thrive, while the inefficient ones would engage in over- or under-censoring and would therefore fail.

In the last fifteen years, it has become clear that this reasoning does not hold completely.[24] First, the 1990s rationale of sacrificing the protection of individual rights for fostering the development of new technologies today sounds unacceptable, at least in the EU, given the internet's centrality to human interaction.[25] Secondly, the distinction between legitimate information and commercially popular content has significantly blurred in the last years.[26] Most critically, the foundational premise of an open market for edge services has been eroded. Market consolidation has led to the emergence of dominant intermediaries, which roughly overlap with the gatekeepers designated by the EU Commission in accordance with the DMA.[27] These edge providers occupy nodal roles in information flow and are functionally central due to logical dependencies (e.g., a search engine enabling other sites). The example of Microsoft's historical dominance in the sector of the operative systems (where it used to occupy 90% of the market share) and its refusal to share interoperability data illustrates the potential for abuse. Today's dominant platforms possess an even greater power to exploit market positions due to increased complexity and interdependencies, undermining the open competition essential to the market-based enforcement mechanism underlying § 230 DCA.

---

[23] 47 U.S. Code § 230(c)(1).

[24] Ezrachi and Stucke (2016, 157).

[25] Goldsmith and Wu (2006, 57).

[26] Palmieri et al. (2024, 12).

[27] See https://digital-markets-act.ec.europa.eu/gatekeepers_en.

In the conception of § 230 DCA, competition is a key element in the digital market. Indeed, competition is supposed to be the driver that leads private platforms to offer optimal models of self-regulation. Its importance, therefore, exceeds the boundaries of the relation between the platform and its users; it rather is a tool for enabling platforms to function as receptors of user preferences, and for directly shaping the terms and conditions through which platforms offer their services.[28] A digital environment characterized by the dominance of a few large enterprises by contrast prevents competition, limits the functioning of the free market, and allows gatekeepers to shape users' preferences, transforming them into autocrats of information.

3 How the DMA Addresses the Shortcomings of Traditional Competition Law

The DMA was introduced in the EU to address the limitations of traditional competition law in dealing with the online services market,[29] particularly the inefficiency of ex post remedies.[30] Two significant decisions by the CJEU illustrate these challenges.

The first one is the already mentioned *Google Shopping* case, which began with a 2017 European Commission decision imposing a €2.4 billion fine on Google for abusing its dominant position in online search markets by prioritizing its own comparison-shopping service over competitors. The Commission found that Google systematically promoted its service in search results while demoting rival services. Google contested this decision, but both the General Court in 2021 and the CJEU in September 2024 upheld the fine.[31] The case demonstrates how slow competition law enforcement can be compared to the fast-paced evolution of digital markets.[32] The investigation into Google Shopping started in 2010 when the company's market capitalization was around $330 billion. By the time the case was resolved in 2024, Google's market value had surged to $2.2 trillion, partly due to its entrenched dominance in Europe's online search market—a dominance that harmed European competitors and consumers. It may be fairly said that in this case traditional competition law failed in its economic role of discouraging abuses of market power and correcting market failures.

A more recent case, *Facebook v. Bundeskartellamt*, raises additional questions about the overlapping of competences between national competition regulators (in this instance, Germany's Bundeskartellamt, the Federal Cartel Office) to address data-related violations and national data protection regulations. In the *Facebook* case, Meta, the owner of Facebook, bypassed GDPR principles, specifically article

[28] Klonick (2018, 1616).

[29] Manganelli (2021, 484) and Scalzini (2022, 570).

[30] Crémer et al. (2019, 47).

[31] CJEU, case C-48/22 P, *Google and Alphabet/ Commission (Google Shopping).*

[32] Hoppner (2022, 28), who claims that Google Search has yet to conform to the requests of the CJEU.

6 on consent, by linking user accounts across its platforms (Facebook, Instagram, WhatsApp, Oculus, and Masquerade) without proper consent. Under the GDPR, users should have granular control over data processing, meaning they must be able to consent separately to different uses of their data. The German competition authority argued that this violation also indicated an abuse of dominance under national competition law, as Meta used linked accounts to extend its market power beyond social networks. The CJEU largely supported the Bundeskartellamt's findings, ruling that competition authorities could treat GDPR breaches as evidence of abusive dominance.[33] However, it also clarified that these authorities cannot independently assess GDPR violations; national data protection regulators must be involved. This introduced a new layer of complexity, as GDPR's one-stop-shop mechanism under article 56 designates the lead supervisory authority based on a company's main establishment, whereby the enforcement of competition law is in the hands of the EU Commission. Moreover, the CJEU's ruling demands potential cross-border cooperation between competition and data protection authorities, such as between Germany's Federal Cartel Office and Ireland's Data Protection Commission, despite the lack of a clear procedural framework for such collaboration. While this dual enforcement approach ensures thorough consideration of all interests, it also adds layers of complexity to an already slow process, as seen in the *Google Shopping* case. These cases reveal the shortcomings of traditional competition law in digital markets.[34]

An inherent problem with traditional competition law in the digital domain is that such laws only intervene when a dominant firm breaks the rules. Yet many market failures stem from inherent traits of the digital economy, such as the presence of economies of scale, network effects, high switching costs, information asymmetry, and consumer biases—all factors that entrench large firms and stifle competition.

This is why the DMA came into play. As an ex ante regulatory tool, the DMA establishes eighteen ex-ante obligations upon providers of core platform services designated as gatekeepers. Recital 2 of the DMA explains that these services differ from other digital services due to their potential to undermine market contestability through extreme economies of scale, near-zero marginal costs for adding users, strong network effects, and the ability to connect large numbers of business and end-users. Online platforms often benefit from user dependency, lock-in effects, limited multi-homing options, vertical integration, and data-driven advantages, allowing them to exploit their position. Core platform services, as defined in article 2(2) DMA, include ten categories (such as search engines, social networks, messaging apps, video-sharing platforms, web browsers, and operating systems) which facilitate interactions between businesses and end-users and pose risks to market fairness. If these services meet the quantitative thresholds under article 3(2) DMA and demonstrate an entrenched market position, they are classified as gatekeepers and must comply with the obligations set forth by articles 5–7 DMA.

[33] CJEU, case C-252/21, *Meta Platforms Inc and Others v Bundeskartellamt*, 4 July 2023, ECLI:EU:C:2023:537.

[34] Prosperetti and Tuzzolino (2023, 643).

The first step in the DMA's ex-ante enforcement mechanism is the formal designation of a platform as a gatekeeper.[35] Under article 3(2)–(3), providers of core platform services must notify the European Commission if they meet the specified size criteria.[36] The Commission then has 45 days to confirm the gatekeeper status. On 6 September 2023, the first gatekeepers were designated, including major tech firms like Alphabet, Amazon, Apple, ByteDance, Meta, and Microsoft. Once designated, these companies must adhere to a set of self-executing rules. For example, WhatsApp, the messaging service owned by Meta, must comply with article 7 DMA, which mandates interoperability with third-party messaging apps to foster competition.

Unlike traditional competition law, which requires complex assessments of market dominance and abusive practices, the DMA's system is more straightforward: if a platform exceeds the thresholds in article 3, it is automatically subject to gatekeeper obligations without further economic analysis. This approach has its pros and cons, as seen in the legal challenge brought by ByteDance (the owner of TikTok) against its designation as a gatekeeper.[37]

In the ByteDance litigation, the company argued that TikTok, despite meeting the DMA's quantitative criteria, was still a smaller player compared to entrenched rivals like YouTube and Instagram. ByteDance contended that treating it as a gatekeeper alongside dominant competitors could end up stifling competition by limiting its ability to challenge them. The General Court rejected this argument, emphasizing that the DMA's concept of a gatekeeper is distinct from traditional dominance under competition law. Recital 23 DMA outlines possible rebuttals to gatekeeper designation, but these must strictly relate to the quantitative thresholds mentioned in article 3(2) DMA. Unless a company successfully disputes these metrics, it is presumed to qualify as a gatekeeper, effectively reversing the burden of proof. This shift streamlines enforcement, avoiding the lengthy investigations typical of traditional competition cases.[38]

Yet, ByteDance's case raises an important question. If a growing firm like TikTok is subject to the same DMA obligations as its dominant rivals, does this hinder the DMA's goal of enhancing contestability? The General Court clarified that the DMA is not meant to regulate competition between large firms but to ensure that smaller, non-gatekeeper players can challenge gatekeepers. The obligations imposed, such as allowing business users to promote offers freely under article 5(4) DMA and enabling interoperability under article 7, are designed to open markets rather than to punish gatekeepers.[39] Unlike traditional antitrust sanctions, such as fines, merger blocks, or breakups under article 102 TFEU, the DMA imposes administrative standards

---

[35] Kerber (2021, 2).

[36] Broadly, on the role of the EU Commission, de Streel and Larouche (2021, 53).

[37] General Court, case T-1077/23, *ByteDance v. Commission*, 17 July 2024, ECLI:EU:T:2024:478, para 298. See also Prosperetti (2024, 674–675).

[38] General Court, case T-1077/23, *ByteDance v. Commission*, 17 July 2024, ECLI:EU:T:2024:478, para 298.

[39] Knapstadt (2023, 4).

aimed at preventing anti-competitive behaviour before it occurs, balancing regulation with market dynamism. In this perspective, the DMA significantly diverges from traditional EU competition law under article 102 TFEU, because it imposes stricter, automatic prohibitions on designated gatekeeper platforms controlling key core platform services. It forbids specific practices like tying and unequal treatment without requiring proof of dominance, detailed market analysis, competitive disadvantage, and anticompetitive intent, effectively reviving enforcement against exploitative conduct while lowering enforcement burdens. Though framed around promoting 'fairness' and 'contestability', these objectives remain quite vague. The DMA's approach seems to be closer to the historic US 'common carrier' regulation (such as the famous 1956 AT&T consent decree involving mandatory patent licensing and line-of-business restrictions), as it compels platforms to relinquish control over resources to assist competitors. However, the DMA lacks classic common carrier features such as rate regulation, unconditional duties to deal, structural separation, or broad line-of-business restrictions. Functioning as a sector-specific, no-fault regime, the DMA codifies previous case law into prescriptive obligations for gatekeepers without authorizing structural breakup.[40]

The DMA explicitly aims to enhance 'contestability' (promoting new entry in gatekeeper-operated markets) and 'fairness' (preventing imbalances against business/end users), although the economic goals of the DMA remain conceptually vague and lack articulation.[41] Fairness seems to function primarily at the procedural level, ensuring equitable participation and a level playing field via non-discrimination and conflict-of-interest rules, rather than on distributional grounds. This aligns more with article 106 TFEU's equality of opportunity framework for special rights undertakings rather than with article 102 TFEU's exploitative abuse corrections. Moreover, the DMA fails to reconcile inherent tensions: unfair terms might paradoxically stimulate entry rather than hinder it, and the eighteen obligations imposed by the DMA lack a coherent structure or clear primary objectives. DMA obligations vary by platform specificity, service type (for instance, core versus ancillary), and competitive context, with no rationale provided for their selection and for the arbitrary distinction between article 5 DMA (seven obligations) and article 6 DMA (eleven obligations). This ambiguity, combined with the absence of a clear economic policy choice and proportionality guidance, undermines the DMA's conceptual foundation and complicates enforcement.

---

[40] Petit (2021, 537).

[41] Recital 4 of the DMA.

4 The Digital Markets Act's Toolset for the Protection of Personal Data

A significant challenge that both national competition regulators and the CJEU have collaboratively examined involves the unfair market benefits that dominant digital platforms gain by aggregating and analysing user data across their various services.[42]

In its February 2019 ruling on the *Facebook* case, the Bundeskartellamt used data protection regulations to evaluate how Meta's practice of combining user data across platforms created competitive distortions in the market.[43] According to the Bundeskartellamt, Meta's policy of requiring unified accounts to access its suite of services coerced users into providing blanket consent for data processing that lacked proper legal justification under GDPR requirements.[44] The forced integration of accounts across Meta's different platforms was not operationally necessary for service provision as defined by articles 6 and 9 GDPR, but rather served as a pretext for justifying internal data sharing practices. Since German competition law recognizes that unfair contractual terms in privacy policies as potential abuses of market dominance, the Bundeskartellamt took action against Meta's practices. As already mentioned, the CJEU later reviewed the Bundeskartellamt's decision, and affirmed its conclusion that improper data processing could in certain circumstances constitute an abuse of dominant market position. However, the ruling also drew attention to the legal complexities that emerge when competition authorities attempt to apply data protection regulations in their enforcement actions.[45]

Now, the DMA largely aims to circumvent these procedural challenges by imposing preventive measures, particularly through the provisions outlined in its article 5(2). Article 5(2) DMA establishes a series of restrictions designed to prevent gatekeepers from using data collected through their primary services to benefit secondary offerings, except in cases where users have provided explicit, informed consent for such cross-service data processing.

Alongside article 5(2), the DMA establishes several other specific restrictions (articles 5(9)–(10), 6(2), (8)–(10)) targeting gatekeepers' use of personal data from ostensibly free services. These provisions address how platforms leverage user data to gain competitive advantages through massive data collection and processing. The prohibitions specifically include: preventing gatekeepers from utilizing personal data obtained through their core services for advertising purposes[46]; banning the combination of user data across different services operated by the same company[47]; prohibiting the cross-application of personal data between primary and secondary

[42] Darr (2021, 5).

[43] Bundeskartellamt, decision of 6 February 2019, case no B6-22/16.

[44] Ibid.

[45] CJEU, case C-252/21, *Meta Platforms Inc and Others v Bundeskartellamt*, 4 July 2023, ECLI:EU:C:2023:537.

[46] Article 5(2)(a) DMA.

[47] Article 5(2)(b) DMA.

services[48]; and forbidding the practice of requiring users to create accounts for additional services as a condition for accessing the main platform.[49] The latter prohibition directly addresses the issue of bundled consent that was central to the Bundeskartellamt's 2019 decision against Meta, and which frequently occurs in conjunction with the data combination practices restricted under article 5(2)(b) DMA.

The digital information economy naturally tends toward concentration, with users gravitating toward dominant platforms, making it particularly challenging for consumers to avoid using certain essential services. Article 5(2)(d) DMA seeks to mitigate this imbalance by reducing the disadvantages users might face when choosing not to use a gatekeeper's primary service and by attempting to prevent scenarios where avoiding a core service like Google Search would effectively lock users out of an entire ecosystem of related services through a single account requirement.

A more critical examination, however, reveals that, while article 5(2) DMA diminishes some of the competitive advantages gatekeepers gain from data consolidation, it does not fundamentally disrupt their dominant position.[50] The regulation does not impose absolute bans on these practices, but rather makes them contingent on obtaining user consent.[51] Implementing these rules presents practical challenges, particularly in distinguishing between data processing that is genuinely necessary for the service provision and data processing that serves other purposes—a difficulty already documented in the analysis of the Bundeskartellamt and CJEU decisions in the *Facebook* case.

While the consent mechanism under article 5(2) DMA aligns competition policy with the GDPR principles regarding personal data flows, it fails to break the self-reinforcing cycle of users' lock-in: the restrictions imposed by article 5(2) DMA can be bypassed simply by obtaining consent from users who have little meaningful bargaining power against dominant platforms.[52] This market distortion is exacerbated by the fact that, under the privacy paradox effect, individual consumers prioritize immediate access to services over broader competitive concerns, potentially undermining the effectiveness of consent-based market protections.[53]

Additional provisions in the DMA address related aspects of platform data dominance. Articles 5(9)–(10) DMA require gatekeepers to provide advertisers with meaningful performance metrics, helping to correct information asymmetries in these business relationships. Conversely, articles 6(8)–(10) establish rules to ensure competitors can effectively access data held by gatekeepers. Article 6(2) creates a complementary restriction by prohibiting gatekeepers from using business users'

---

[48] Article 5(2)(d) DMA.

[49] Article 5(2)(c) DMA.

[50] Baschenhoff (2022, 149) (arguing that the ultimate beneficiaries of data mobility enabled by the DMA likely are the other gatekeepers, as data portability obligations could end up in gatekeepers negotiating interoperability conditions among themselves).

[51] Demircan (2022, 152).

[52] Moskal, (2023, 1117) and D'Amico (2025, 171).

[53] Barth and de Jong (2017, 1052).

operational data to compete against them (a practice known as 'sherlocking'). This prohibition specifically applies to online intermediary services and aligns with article 9 of the so-called Platform-to-Business (P2B) Regulation,[54] which mandates transparency about how platforms access and use data generated by their business users, such as online merchants operating on e-commerce platforms. These provisions do not explicitly consider consumers. As some scholars noted,[55] the DMA is similar to the P2B Regulation, since it mainly focuses on the relation between gatekeepers and other platforms, and does not rely on traditional consumer protection tools.

While this is correct, it is also important to stress that the DMA strengthens the protection of users of gatekeepers. Besides indirectly protecting users by promoting market contestability, the DMA also includes tools that directly expand the scope of application of GDPR-related rights.[56] Article 6(9) of the DMA complements the right to data portability by establishing that end users must be enabled to effectively port their data from the gatekeeper's system to another platform. Furthermore, scholars argued convincingly that the DMA is not only applying the GDPR right to portability to competition law, but also expanding this right by including the data generated through the usage of the gatekeeper's platform into the list of portable data.[57] Far from treating users as merely passive subjects, the DMA, alongside other regulations such as the Data Act,[58] attempts to strengthen individual control over data, and rely on such control in order to level the playing field between gatekeepers and smaller platforms.[59]

5 Conclusions: Expanding User Protection to Enhance Market Contestability

On 23 April 2025, the European Commission imposed a €200 million fine on Meta for violating key provisions of the DMA, specifically concerning the unlawful combination of user data across its various platforms—such as Facebook and Instagram—for targeted advertising without obtaining proper consent.[60] Although the Commission's press release did not explicitly cite the legal basis, the decision primarily revolves around article 5(2) of the DMA, which prohibits gatekeepers from merging

[54] Regulation (EU) 2019/1150 of the European Parliament and of the Council of 20 June 2019 on promoting fairness and transparency for business users of online intermediation services.

[55] Moskal (2023, 1117).

[56] Geradin et al. (2022, 2).

[57] Ibid.

[58] Ibid.

[59] Regulation (EU) 2023/2854 of the European Parliament and of the Council of 13 December 2023 on harmonised rules on fair access to and use of data and amending Regulation (EU) 2017/2394 and Directive (EU) 2020/1828 (Data Act).

[60] See https://ec.europa.eu/commission/presscorner/api/files/document/print/en/ip_25_1085/IP_25_1085_EN.pdf.

personal data collected from different services to fuel their online advertising businesses unless users provide explicit and specific consent. This ruling marks one of the first major enforcements of the DMA, signalling the EU's stance on curbing the unchecked data practices of Big Tech firms.

Recalling the history of the case may be useful. In March 2024, the Commission initiated formal proceedings against Meta under the DMA, scrutinizing its compliance with data processing rules. Meta, in response, introduced a controversial 'consent or pay' model, giving users a binary choice: either allow their data to be combined for personalized ads or subscribe to an ad-free version of Facebook and Instagram at a monthly fee (originally set at €9.99 for web users and €12.99 for mobile users, later reduced to €5.99 and €7.99, respectively). The company argued that this approach aligned with the DMA, as the regulation does not explicitly ban such a model, and even cited the 2019 ruling by the CJEU in the *Facebook* case, which acknowledged that platforms could offer paid alternatives to data-driven services. However, the EDPB, in an influential April 2024 opinion,[61] challenged the validity of Meta's approach. The EDPB emphasized that when, a dominant platform like Meta presents users with a choice between paying or consenting to extensive data processing, the power imbalance undermines the notion of 'freely given' consent under the GDPR and DMA. The EDPB stressed that gatekeepers must provide a genuinely equivalent, free alternative that does not rely on invasive data practices, ensuring users are not coerced into accepting surveillance-based advertising. Furthermore, the EDPB stated that behavioural advertising inherently conflicts with the principle of data minimization under the GDPR by encouraging excessive data collection.

The Commission's decision to penalize Meta suggests that it sided with the EDPB's interpretation, rejecting the 'pay or consent' model as non-compliant with the DMA's spirit. While Meta has defended its stance, claiming its subscription option is lawful and accusing the EU of unfairly targeting American firms, the ruling sets a precedent that could reshape how gatekeepers monetize user data in Europe. Joel Kaplan, Meta's Chief Global Affairs Officer, criticized the decision as politically motivated, alleging that it disadvantages U.S. tech companies in favour of European and Chinese competitors.[62] Legal experts anticipate that Meta may appeal the fine, potentially leading to a protracted legal battle that could further clarify the boundaries of permissible data practices under the DMA. It should also be recalled that the DMA should be read in combination with other texts regulating the European digital market. For instance, the provisions on dark patterns contained in the Digital Services Act (DSA) could contribute to curb gatekeeper practices nudging user consent.[63] By

[61] EDPB (2024).

[62] See https://about.fb.com/news/2025/04/metas-statement-in-response-to-the-european-commissions-decision-on-the-digital-markets-act/.

[63] See in particular recital 67 of the Regulation (EU) 2022/2065 of the European Parliament and of the Council of 19 October 2022 on a Single Market For Digital Services and amending Directive 2000/31/EC (Digital Services Act).

increasing the overwatch on gatekeepers' nudging of users, the DSA could therefore be interpreted to strengthen the reach of the obligations set forth by article 5(2) DMA.[64]

References

Article 29 Working Party (2020) Guidelines on consent under regulation 2016/679. https://www.edpb.europa.eu/sites/default/files/files/file1/edpb_guidelines_202005_consent_en.pdf

Bakos Y, Halaburda H (2005) Platform competition with endogenous multihoming. NET Institute Working Paper. https://www.feem.it/publications/platform-competition-with-endogenous-multihoming/

Barth S, de Jong M (2017) The privacy paradox: investigating discrepancies between expressed privacy concerns and actual online behaviour. A systematic literature review. Telematics Inform 34(7):1038–1058

Baschenhoff P (2022) The digital markets act: a procompetitive recalibration of data relations? https://papers.ssrn.com/sol3/papers.cfm?abstract_id=3970101

Crémer J, de Montjoye YA, Schweitzer H (2019) Competition policy for the digital era. EU Publications Office. https://op.europa.eu/en/publication-detail/-/publication/21dc175c-7b76-11e9-9f05-01aa75ed71a1/language-en

D'Amico A (2025) The DMA's consent moment and its relationship with the GDPR. Eur J Risk Reg 16(1):170–183

Da Rosa Lazarotto B (2024) The right to data portability, a holistic analysis of GDPR, DMA and the Data Act. Eur J Law Technol 15(1). https://ejlt.org/index.php/ejlt/article/view/988/1087

Darr A (2021) Competition law and human rights: a complex relationship. Wirtschaft und Wettbewerb 71(1–2):1–5

de Streel A, Larouche P (2021) The European Digital Markets Act proposal: how to improve a regulatory revolution. Concurr Rev 2:46–63

Demircan M (2022) The DMA and the GDPR: making sense of data accumulation, cross-use and data sharing provisions. Springer, Cham

European Data Protection Board (EDPB), Opinion no 4/2024 on the notion of main establishment of a controller in the Union under Art. 4.16(a) GDPR. https://www.edpb.europa.eu/our-work-tools/our-documents/opinion-board-art-64/opinion-042024-notion-main-establishment_en

Ezrachi A, Stucke ME (2016) Virtual competition: the promise and perils of the algorithm-driven economy. Harvard University Press, Cambridge

Furman J et al (2019) Unlocking digital competition: report of the Digital Competition Expert Panel. Available at https://www.gov.uk/government/publications/unlocking-digital-competition-report-of-the-digital-competition-expert-panel

Geradin D, Bania K, Karanikioti T (2022) The interplay between the Digital Markets Act and the General Data Protection Regulation. https://papers.ssrn.com/abstract_id=4203907

Goldsmith J, Wu T (2006) Who controls the internet? Illusions of a borderless world. Oxford University Press, Oxford

Hacker P, Cordes J, Rochon J (2024) Regulating gatekeeper AI and data: transparency, access, and fairness under the DMA, the GDPR and beyond. Eur J Risk Regul 15(1):1–38

Hoppner T (2022) The European Google Shopping Competition Saga. Glob Comp Litig Rev 15:9–21

Kerber W (2021) Taming tech giants with a per-se rules approach? The Digital markets act from the rules vs. standard perspective. Concurr Rev 3:28–34

Khan L (2017) Amazon's antitrust paradox. Yale Law J 126:710–805

[64] Hacker et al. (2024, 75).

Klonick K (2018) The new governors: the people, rules, and processes governing online speech. Harvard Law Rev 131:1598–1670
Knapstadt T (2023) Breakups of digital gatekeepers under the digital markets act: three strikes and you are out? J Eur Comp Law Pract 14:394–409
Manganelli A (2021) Il regolamento UE per i mercati digitali: ratio, criticità e prospettive di evoluzione. Mercato Concorrenza Regole 23:473–500
Manzini P (2023) Antitrust e privacy: la strana coppia. Quaderni AISDUE. https://www.aisdue.eu/pietro-manzini-antitrust-e-privacy-la-strana-coppia/
Moskal A (2023) Digital markets act. A consumer protection perspective. Eur Pap 7(3):1113–1119
Newman N (2014) Search, antitrust, and the economics of the control of user data. Yale J Reg 31(2):401–454
Palmieri A, Kollnig K, Tamò-Larrieux A (2024) Systemic risks of dominant online platforms: a scoping review. https://papers.ssrn.com/abstract_id=5002743/
Petit N (2021) The proposed digital markets act (DMA): a legal and policy review. J Eur Comp Law Pract 12(7):529–541
Prosperetti E (2024) Quali criteri per individuare un gatekeeper? Il caso TikTok. Diritto di Internet 4:670–678
Prosperetti E, Tuzzolino D (2023) Abuso di dati personali? La Corte di Giustizia ammette il sindacato antitrust sul trattamento dei dati personali. Diritto di Internet 4:636–652
Scalzini S (2022) Dipendenza economica e regolazione «asimmetrica» dell'attività d'impresa. Prime osservazioni sul novellato art. 9 l. n. 192/1998. Analisi Giuridica Dell'economia 40(2):563–574
Soh SY (2019) Privacy nudges: an alternative regulatory mechanism to informed consent for online data protection behaviour. Eur Data Prot Law Rev 5:65–74
Stucke M (2022) The relationship between privacy and antitrust. Notre Dame Law Rev 97:400–416
Susser D, Roessler B, Nissenbaum H (2019) Technology, autonomy, and manipulation. Internet Policy Rev. https://doi.org/10.14763/2019.2.1410

Empowering the Vulnerable in the European Union: Collective Redress Against Digital Exploitation

Hüseyin Can Aksoy

Abstract The digital age has turned individuals into both consumers and data subjects, exposing them to systemic exploitation that existing legal frameworks are ill-equipped to address. The Unfair Commercial Practices Directive (UCPD) and the General Data Protection Regulation (GDPR) place heavy emphasis on rational agency and informed consent, yet these tools fall short in confronting the opaque and aggregated nature of harm in digital markets. This chapter conceptualises digital vulnerability as a condition embedded in digital infrastructures and argues for a shift in enforcement strategy. It proposes an EU-wide opt-out collective redress model to tackle the scale and invisibility of digital harm. By reallocating enforcement responsibility from individuals to qualified institutional actors, such mechanisms can transcend barriers like rational apathy and power asymmetry—offering not just procedural efficiency, but also structural justice.

Keywords Consumer vulnerability · Digital vulnerability · Digital exploitation · Representative actions · Collective redress

1 Introduction

The rise of digital marketplaces over the past two decades has dramatically reshaped consumer interactions, creating both new opportunities and vulnerabilities. In these environments, consumers are not merely buyers of goods and services; they are also continuous sources of personal data—making them both market participants and data subjects. This dual role, however, underscores a heightened digital vulnerability, situated at the intersection of consumer and data protection law.

Digital vulnerability is most visible at two key moments: the contracting stage and the processing of data. In the first, consumers are steered through manipulative design techniques—often called dark patterns—which nudge or mislead them into

H. Can Aksoy (✉)
Faculty of Law, Bilkent University, Ankara, Türkiye
e-mail: hcaksoy@bilkent.edu.tr

C. Crea and M. Infantino (eds.), *Remedies to Digital Vulnerability in European Private Law*, https://doi.org/10.1007/978-3-032-19720-7_7

making choices that are not in their best interest.[1] In the second, their personal data is used in ways that entrench disadvantage, through practices such as personalized advertising, dynamic pricing, or algorithmic profiling that reinforce bias or target emotional and cognitive susceptibilities.[2]

Digital exploitation, however, is not incidental—it is architected around the collection and use of personal data.[3] As businesses increasingly rely on personal data for profiling, targeted advertising, and algorithmic decision-making, traditional legal frameworks—designed for analog markets—struggle to counteract the resulting power asymmetries.

Both consumer and data protection law have historically focused on information asymmetries, preserving individual choice through informed consent and transparency.

Consumer law, for example, was built on the assumption of the rational actor: individuals presumed to make optimal decisions when equipped with relevant information.[4] Early regulatory efforts thus focused on disclosure obligations.[5] But behavioral economics challenged this view, revealing how cognitive biases—such as framing effects, inertia, and bounded rationality—undermine informed decision-making.[6] Firms exploit these biases to steer consumer behavior, rendering transparency-based protections largely symbolic.[7] The flood of information can even create a false sense of empowerment, enabling businesses to exploit biases subtly.[8]

A parallel shortcoming emerges in the General Data Protection Regulation (EU) 2016/679 (GDPR). While it nominally empowers individuals to control their personal data, it similarly relies on rational agency and meaningful consent.[9] In reality, few users fully grasp how their data is collected or used. Even when notices are clear, they are often ignored, misunderstood, or accepted reflexively.[10] The burden placed on individuals to manage complex data ecosystems is unrealistic—and arguably unjust.

As individuals differ in their capacity to understand and manage data-related risks, in digital contexts everyone is vulnerable to some extent.[11] These patterns suggest a broader truth: digital vulnerability is not merely a personal failure to act prudently, but a structural condition produced by the architecture of digital systems. It is pervasive, often invisible, and disproportionately affects individuals with limited legal or digital literacy. Accordingly, legal responses must evolve from individualistic remedies to systemic safeguards that reflect the scale and nature of harm.

[1] Grochowski (2024, 215).

[2] Malgierie and Niklas (2020, 5) and Grochowski (2024, 215).

[3] Helberger et al. (2017, 1464).

[4] Riefa and Gamper (2021, 17–18) and Liu (2024, 830).

[5] Riefa and Gamper (2021, 19) and Riefa (2022, 621).

[6] Durovic (2024, 332) and Riefa and Gamper (2021, 21).

[7] Helberger et al. (2017, 1430).

[8] Riefa and Gamper (2021, 22).

[9] Schermer (2014, 171).

[10] Malgieri (2023, 40).

[11] Malgieri and Niklas (2020, 7).

While scholarship increasingly recognizes the limits of current regimes, the potential of collective enforcement—particularly through representative actions—remains underexplored. This paper addresses that gap by examining whether mechanisms, particularly under the Representative Actions Directive (EU) 2020/1828 (RAD) and Article 80 GDPR, can provide a coordinated and effective response to digital exploitation.[12] Rather than analyzing these frameworks in isolation, it situates them within the broader enforcement architecture of the EU and argues that only a recalibrated, opt-out collective model can deliver meaningful redress in structurally exploitative digital markets.

2 Vulnerability in Digital Age

Digital vulnerability is qualitatively different from traditional conceptions of vulnerability. It emerges not from static personal traits but from the architecture of digital environments themselves—opaque, pervasive, and engineered to influence. Standard legal protections, grounded in notions of informed consent and rational decision-making, underestimate the systemic nature of digital exploitation. They rely on individual awareness and choice in environments deliberately designed to subvert both. As such, confronting digital vulnerability requires legal mechanisms that account for the systemic and structural aspects of digital markets and provide protections that surpass reliance on individual awareness and choice.

2.1 Exploitation by Design and Architecture

Digital markets are not neutral backdrops—they are infrastructures designed to identify and capitalize on moments of susceptibility. As scholars increasingly note, vulnerability in these environments is not a byproduct of poor choices or isolated design flaws; it is a structural feature of how digital marketplaces operate.[13]

Modern businesses now conduct continuous behavioural experiments to uncover latent weaknesses in user decision-making. Rather than merely reacting to known vulnerabilities, platforms proactively seek out new ones, often before they even manifest.[14] With each interaction, they refine what is known as *choice architecture*—the invisible scaffolding that shapes how options are framed, defaults are set, and choices are made. Over time, and through repeated exposure, this architecture

[12] The terminology surrounding "collective enforcement" and "collective redress" is not always consistent. In this paper, "collective enforcement" refers to public oversight mechanisms (*e.g.*, regulatory action and administrative fines), whereas "collective redress" is used to denote private remedies such as compensatory or injunctive relief.

[13] Helberger et al. (2022, 182), Siciliani et al. (2019, 40), Riefa (2022, 620) and Domurath (2024, 241).

[14] Helberger et al. (2022, 187).

becomes increasingly personalised, deepening behavioural influence while steadily eroding user autonomy.[15]

These capabilities have been dramatically intensified by advances in data analytics.[16] Digital platforms harvest data not only from direct user interactions but also through third-party integrations, persistent tracking mechanisms, and device-level monitoring.[17] This complex data ecosystem enables the construction of detailed behavioural profiles—predicting not only what users might do, but how they feel and what will most effectively influence them. Manipulation, once broad and impersonal, is now finely tuned to individual psychological traits such as impulsivity, trend-following, or fear of missing out (FOMO).[18] A striking example is TikTok's €345 million fine in 2023, where the Irish Data Protection Commission found that the platform's onboarding and publishing processes were rigged with dark patterns, nudging users (especially minors) towards privacy-invasive defaults.[19]

In parallel, studies show that AI models trained to optimize engagement and revenue inevitably learn to exploit human biases and vulnerabilities.[20] Trained on vast behavioural datasets, these systems routinely identify and act upon cognitive shortcuts and emotional triggers, often in ways that remain opaque to both users and regulators.

Crucially, the digital environment differs qualitatively from its offline counterpart. Attention is fragmented, risk perception dulled, and information overload is constant. Even users who are not inherently vulnerable are rendered so by the attention-fragmenting design of the digital sphere.[21] In this context, vulnerability is not an exception; it is the rule. More precisely, it is manufactured—embedded in the design, logic, and business models of digital platforms.

2.2 Universal Nature of Digital Vulnerability

Classical legal models often tie vulnerability to specific groups—children, the elderly, persons with disabilities. However, digital environments challenge this particularistic view. Digital vulnerability is not confined to predefined categories; rather, it is layered, context-dependent, and universally distributed.

Fineman advocates for a universal understanding of vulnerability, contending that vulnerability is not the exception, but rather the rule.[22] According to her, all individuals are vulnerable due to the constant potential for harm, injury, or misfortune.

[15] Helberger et al. (2022, 188).

[16] Malgieri (2023, 3).

[17] Liu (2024, 843).

[18] OECD (2023, 23).

[19] Data Protection Commission (2023).

[20] Petropoulos (2022).

[21] Durovic and Kaprou (2024, 144).

[22] Fineman (2008, 9).

Luna expands this insight with her "layers" model, where vulnerability arises from situational contexts.[23] Duivenvoorde also argues that categorizing certain groups as inherently vulnerable is problematic, as vulnerability is often context-specific.[24] Malgieri applies this framework to digital contexts, showing how vulnerability shifts depending on the intersection of user traits (such as age, literacy, and profession).[25]

Finally, the distinction drawn by Mackenzie et al. between inherent and situational vulnerabilities—further divided into dispositional and occurrent forms—refines this layered view and offers a helpful lens to understand how digital infrastructures can expose even those not presently harmed.[26] Under this perspective, individuals may be dispositionally vulnerable, that is, susceptible to exploitation simply because data about their behavior is collected, stored, and used to shape future interactions.[27]

While the degree and manifestation of vulnerability may vary, this does not absolve legal systems of their obligation to respond. Once it is acknowledged that digital infrastructures systematically expose all individuals to potential harm, the legal framework must evolve—not only to protect and prevent, but also to provide meaningful avenues for remedy.

3 The Inadequacy of UCPD and GDPR in Addressing Digital Vulnerability

Digital vulnerability arises at the intersection of two foundational regulatory instruments of the European Union: the Unfair Commercial Practices Directive 2005/29/EC (UCPD), which seeks to protect consumers from misleading and aggressive market conduct, and the GDPR, which aims to safeguard the fundamental rights and freedoms of individuals in the context of personal data processing. It is true that, beyond the UCPD and GDPR, EU law includes additional references to vulnerability. For example, in the digital sphere, Recitals 62, 94, 95, and 104 of the Digital Services Act (Regulation (EU) 2022/2065) contain provisions aimed at safeguarding vulnerable recipients of services. Moreover, Article 5(1)(b) of the AI Act (Regulation (EU) 2024/1689) prohibits the use of AI systems that exploit the "vulnerabilities of a specific group of persons due to their age, physical, or mental disability". Yet, the two most important and comprehensive regimes remain the UCPD and the GDPR. Although both regimes contain provisions relevant to vulnerable individuals, their underlying assumptions and legal mechanisms differ substantially—and neither offers a fully adequate response to the structural dynamics of digital exploitation.

The conceptualization of vulnerability differs markedly between the two frameworks. The UCPD adopts a particularistic understanding of vulnerability, treating it

[23] Luna (2009, 128).

[24] Duivenvoorde (2013, 73).

[25] Malgieri (2023, 231).

[26] Mackenzie et al. (2004, 7).

[27] Helberger et al. (2022, 185).

as an exception to the normative benchmark of the 'average consumer' (a notion that was notoriously first defined in the *Gut Springenheide* decision and then endorsed in subsequent decisions of the CJEU: *Gut Springenheide GmbH and Rudolf Tusky v Oberkreisdirektor des Kreises Steinfurt - Amt für Lebensmittelüberwachung*, Case C-210/96, para. 31). It assumes that consumers are not a uniform group[28] and certain consumer groups or consumers with certain characteristics are more vulnerable to harm, unequal treatment, and unfairness due to "*mental or physical infirmity, age or credulity*" (Article 5(3) UCPD).[29] The provision clearly shows that EU consumer law links consumers' vulnerability to internal characteristics of the consumer that impair their capacity to engage effectively with commercial practices.[30] This approach has rightfully been criticized as outdated and insufficient in addressing the unique challenges posed by digital vulnerabilities.[31]

By contrast, the GDPR adopts a more relational approach. Although it does not define the term 'vulnerable data subject', Recital 75 acknowledges heightened risks where the personal data of such individuals is processed. Importantly, the recital highlights children as particularly vulnerable but does not limit the category to minors.[32] This broader interpretative potential has also been recognized by both the Article 29 Working Party[33] and the European Data Protection Board,[34] both of which have endorsed a more inclusive, relational view of vulnerability.

In addition to this conceptual openness, the GDPR offers normative principles—such as fairness (Article 5(1)(a))[35] and data protection by design (Article 25)—which could, in theory, serve as safeguards against manipulative or exploitative practices[36] (some scholars in this regard even recommend introducing 'fairness by design' as a positive obligation for businesses to engage in fair trading practices[37]). However, in practice, these principles tend to operate retrospectively, primarily as bases for administrative sanctions. Their effectiveness is largely contingent on data protection authorities having sufficient awareness, resources, and institutional capacity to identify and act upon structural patterns of harm.

Despite their normative potential, both regimes suffer from an overreliance on transparency and informed choice as regulatory instruments. While intended to reduce information asymmetries,[38] transparency obligations rarely produce meaningful understanding or control in complex digital environments, where users are

---

[28] Kaprou (2021, 51).

[29] Helberger et al. (2022, 179). For the other EU legislation referring to vulnerable consumers, see Riefa (2022, 614) and Durovic (2024, 331).

[30] Helberger et al. (2022, 179) and Galli (2022, 203).

[31] Helberger et al. (2022, 194), Durovic (2024, 333) and Durovic and Poon (2023, 420).

[32] Malgieri and Niklas (2020, 6).

[33] Article 29 Working Party (2017, 10).

[34] EDPB (2023, 10).

[35] Malgieri and Niklas (2020, 14) and Rossi et al. (2024, 6).

[36] Malgieri and Niklas (2020, 11).

[37] Siciliani et al. (2019, 179).

[38] Helberger et al. (2017, 1442).

routinely overwhelmed by the volume and complexity of disclosures, rendering informed consent a largely formalistic exercise. As the Article 29 Working Party already acknowledged,[39] digital vulnerability frequently stems from structural power imbalances that transparency alone cannot redress.[40]

Furthermore, even when considered in tandem, consumer and data protection law leave gaps in addressing the full spectrum of harms emerging from digital exploitation. The GDPR focuses narrowly on data processing, while consumer law remains limited to economic transactions. Many forms of manipulation—such as the use of persuasive design or profiling—straddle both domains yet fall between the cracks of existing regulatory tools.

Given these shortcomings, it becomes evident that neither the UCPD nor the GDPR, whether in isolation or combination, can sufficiently address the structural nature of digital vulnerability. Both instruments are primarily geared towards dispute prevention: they aim to deter harm through transparency obligations, consent requirements, and general compliance incentives. However, when harm nonetheless occurs—particularly in subtle, cumulative, or systemic forms—these frameworks offer limited avenues for effective redress.

A truly effective legal system, however, should not only focus on dispute prevention but also guarantee accessible mechanisms for dispute resolution and redress.[41] Moreover, what is required is a recalibration of enforcement, moving beyond individual remedies and administrative sanctions toward a more systemic model of accountability. In this regard, collective redress holds untapped potential to supplement both frameworks and bridge the enforcement gap.

4 Collective Redress Against Digital Exploitation

Collective redress refers to a legal mechanism that enables two or more natural or legal persons to jointly pursue injunctive or compensatory relief arising from the same unlawful conduct. This relief may address both material damages and immaterial harms.[42] In the context of systemic digital exploitation, where harm is often widespread but individually diffuse, collective redress serves as a vital corrective to enforcement gaps and a tool for restoring accountability.

Recent cases demonstrate a growing reliance on collective legal actions to challenge exploitative practices in the digital economy. In the United States, *Louis* et al. *v. SafeRent Solutions, LLC* et al. involved allegations that a tenant-screening algorithm discriminated against black and low-income applicants. The case was settled

[39] Article 29 Working Party (2017, 10).

[40] Rossi et al. (2024, 6) and Liu (2024, 832).

[41] Riefa (2022, 620).

[42] Janciute (2019, 4).

for $2.28 million, and the company agreed to amend its algorithmic models to eliminate discriminatory outcomes.[43] Similarly, the *Cambridge Analytica* scandal, which involved the unauthorized harvesting of personal data from millions of Facebook users for political targeting, culminated in a $725 million settlement by Meta in 2023.[44]

While these cases originated in the U.S., collective redress mechanisms are also gaining momentum in Europe. In 2023, 133 collective claims were filed across the continent—the highest number recorded to date. The United Kingdom, in particular, has emerged as a key jurisdiction for class actions. Between 2016 and 2023, the total value of European class action claims increased more than tenfold, from €12.53 billion to €144.98 billion. In the UK alone, claims grew by approximately 18% between 2022 and 2023. Notably, competition law has been a major driver of this expansion, with cumulative claims affecting more than 500 million class members.[45]

These developments underscore the increasing importance of collective redress as a legal response to large-scale digital harms. The following sections examine the functions of collective redress, the regulatory mechanisms available under the GDPR and the RAD, and the challenges posed by the fragmented coexistence of these frameworks.

4.1 Functions of Collective Redress

Collective redress mechanisms constitute a critical component of contemporary legal systems, particularly in contexts involving structural asymmetries and dispersed harm. In the digital environment, where mass data processing and algorithmic targeting can result in widespread but individually minor harm, collective redress plays an indispensable role in securing access to justice and upholding the rule of law.

A primary rationale for collective redress lies in the principle of effective access to justice, as guaranteed by Article 47 of the Charter of Fundamental Rights of the European Union (EUCFR), which affirms the right to an effective remedy and a fair trial. When harms are diffuse and individually insignificant, victims are often deterred from pursuing litigation due to cost–benefit considerations—a phenomenon known as rational apathy. Although the aggregate harm may be substantial, the absence of individual claims results in impunity for the wrongdoer and a failure of legal accountability.[46] Collective action remedies this by enabling victims to pool claims, thereby overcoming financial disincentives and rendering redress economically viable.[47]

---

[43] Bedayn (2024).

[44] Associated Press (2024).

[45] CMS (2024).

[46] Visscher and Faure (2021, 456).

[47] Agulló (2022, 72), Sorace (2018, 4) and Massaro Piletta (2021, 96).

Closely related is the issue of power asymmetry between consumers and economically dominant defendants. Victims of digital exploitation often lack the financial and legal resources necessary to confront large technology companies, which can secure superior legal counsel and prolong litigation.[48] Collective redress partially neutralizes this imbalance by consolidating fragmented claims, allowing victims to engage in litigation on more equal footing.[49]

Beyond overcoming economic and structural barriers, collective redress also enhances judicial efficiency. By aggregating numerous similar cases into a single proceeding, it minimizes duplicative efforts, reduces court congestion, and promotes consistency in outcomes.[50] Even where individual actions might be legally and economically viable, collective redress streamlines litigation and delivers broader systemic clarity.[51]

Finally, collective redress mechanisms serve an important deterrent function.[52] By increasing the likelihood of litigation and raising the potential financial consequences of non-compliance, they incentivize compliance with consumer protection and data governance norms.[53] This deterrent effect not only benefits individual claimants but also strengthens broader regulatory objectives aimed at fairness, accountability, and trust in digital markets.

4.2 Collective Redress Under the GDPR and the RAD

Collective redress in the EU takes two principal legal forms: Article 80 of the GDPR and the RAD. Both frameworks aim to enable group-based responses to unlawful practices that cause dispersed or structural harm, whether in the context of data protection or consumer relations. Yet despite their shared objectives, they rest on distinct procedural foundations and reflect different degrees of institutional ambition. Analysing their interaction is essential to assessing whether EU law can deliver a coherent enforcement response to digital exploitation through collective accountability.

4.2.1 Representation of Data Subjects Under the GDPR

Article 80 GDPR, entitled 'Representation of data subjects', marks a notable innovation in European data protection law, having no direct equivalent in the Directive

48 Şerban (2023, 3) and Sorace (2018, 4).

49 Massaro Piletta (2021, 96) and Janciute (2019, 5).

50 Gsell (2021, 1365) and Federico (2023, 92).

51 Federico (2023, 92).

52 Visscher and Faure (2021, 467), Gsell (2021, 1365), Agulló (2022, 72) and Federico (2023, 92).

53 Sorace (2018, 4).

95/46/EC on the processing of personal data or in the Council of Europe's 'Convention for the protection of individuals with regard to the processing of personal data' (Convention 108) or its modernised version. The provision, however, finds its roots in Article 47 of the EUCFR, which guarantees the right to an effective remedy and a fair trial.[54] It introduces a form of private enforcement designed to complement the existing system of administrative oversight by data protection authorities.[55]

Under Article 80(1), data subjects may authorise not-for-profit organisations to lodge complaints and exercise rights on their behalf under Articles 77–79 GDPR. However, the ability of such organisations to pursue compensation under Article 82 is conditional upon national law explicitly allowing it. In the absence of such provisions, compensation claims cannot be pursued through representative mandates.

In addition to this, Article 80(2) GDPR allows Member States to go further by enabling qualified organisations to act independently, without a prior mandate from individual data subjects (provided that these actions will be valid in relation to the concerned Member State's own supervisory authorities and courts)[56] Article 80(2) GDPR thus opens the door to a quasi-collective enforcement model. Yet its scope is limited: it only applies to lodging complaints before supervisory authorities and does not extend to seeking compensation.[57] As a result, the enforcement potential of Article 80(2) GDPR remains largely symbolic in jurisdictions that do not provide parallel legal avenues for redress.

To ensure integrity and prevent abuse, both paragraphs require that entities acting under Article 80 meet specific eligibility criteria: they must be legally established in a Member State, pursue public-interest objectives, and be actively engaged in protecting data subject rights. Cross-border representation is also permitted, allowing individuals to authorise organisations located in other Member States. These safeguards aim to strike a balance between access to justice and protection against opportunistic or commercially driven litigation.[58]

4.2.2 Collective Redress Under the RAD

The RAD, which entered into force on 25 June 2023, establishes a harmonised framework for representative actions across the EU in the field of consumer protection. It empowers designated qualified entities —typically non-profit organisations or public bodies— to bring collective claims on behalf of consumers, covering both injunctive relief and redress, including compensation. In this regard it should be noted that the RAD significantly expands the regime previously established by Directive 2009/22 on injunctions for the protection of consumer interests, which made injunctive relief available at the Member State level, by introducing the possibility for collective

[54] González Fuster (2020, 1143).

[55] Agulló (2022, 74).

[56] González Fuster (2020, 1149).

[57] Feiler et al. (2018, 5) and Pato (2019, 5).

[58] Pato (2019, 3) and Sorace (2018, 14).

redress, including compensation, and thus addressing broader consumer protection needs.

The RAD differentiates between domestic and cross-border actions. Domestic actions take place within the Member State where the qualified entity is established, while cross-border actions involve litigation initiated in another Member State.[59] Crucially, the RAD mandates that all Member States must ensure at least one procedural avenue for domestic representative actions. This establishes a minimum EU-wide baseline for collective consumer redress, while allowing for some variation in national implementation.

Similar to the GDPR, for preventing abuse and maintaining procedural integrity, the directive limits standing to pre-approved 'qualified entities' that meet strict eligibility criteria. According to the RAD, these entities must represent consumers' interests. Member States are responsible for designating and monitoring these organisations, ensuring that they are independent and not motivated by commercial interests. The RAD also facilitates transparency by requiring that qualified entities be publicly listed and subject to oversight. Member States are required to submit a list of qualified entities to the European Commission, which serves as proof of their legal standing for cross-border actions. The Member States retain discretion over the criteria for determining qualified entities for domestic actions. For cross-border actions, however, the RAD harmonizes the criteria for designation as a cross-border qualified entity, and it allows multiple qualified entities from different member states to collaborate on collective actions.

4.2.3 Opt-In and Opt-Out Models of Participation

The distinction between opt-in and opt-out mechanisms plays a pivotal role in determining the accessibility and effectiveness of collective redress systems. Opt-in models require individuals to take affirmative steps to join a collective action, while opt-out models presume inclusion unless individuals explicitly withdraw.[60] This seemingly procedural distinction has far-reaching implications for participation rates, enforcement outcomes, and the deterrent effect of representative actions.

Under Article 80(1) GDPR, the mechanism is clearly opt-in: data subjects must expressly mandate a non-profit entity to act on their behalf. Article 80(2) GDPR allows Member States to empower qualified entities to act without individual mandates. While it does not specify whether these actions should follow an opt-in or opt-out model, its broad language leaves room for national legislators to adopt opt-out-based collective actions.[61] However, this possibility is limited to injunctive or declaratory relief since the provision explicitly excludes compensation claims. Consequently, even where opt-out features are permitted under national law, their impact is confined to procedural remedies that fall short of full redress. To enhance

[59] Fairgrieve and Salim (2022, 470).

[60] Sorace (2018, 4).

[61] Pato (2019, 5).

its enforcement potential, Article 80(2) GDPR would ideally allow qualified entities to pursue compensatory relief without individual mandates, thereby aligning the mechanism with the structural nature of digital harm and enabling more meaningful access to justice.

The RAD introduces a more flexible but fragmented structure. For injunctive relief, Article 8(3) RAD permits opt-out mechanisms, recognizing the need for procedural efficiency in curbing unlawful practices. For redress actions in cross-border contexts, however, Article 9(3) RAD requires that foreign consumers opt in, limiting the directive's cross-jurisdictional coherence. This point has been criticized by legal scholars: Visscher and Faure argue that allowing an opt-out approach for foreign consumers is a sensible rule, as many of them may otherwise remain unaware of legal proceedings initiated abroad and thus fail to benefit from any resulting redress.[62] Gsell similarly contends that even in cross-border representative actions, the RAD does not categorically preclude opt-out mechanisms.[63] A national opt-out model—under which the trader is bound by the court's decision while consumers retain discretion to invoke the outcome—remains compatible with the Directive. For other forms of redress, Recital 43 leaves the choice of mechanism to national discretion, allowing for opt-in, opt-out, or hybrid models.

Such hybrid approach of the RAD has been criticized on multiple fronts. First, Article 9(2) RAD permits tacit consent in opt-in systems, but the directive fails to define what constitutes valid tacit consent, leaving room for divergent interpretations among Member States.[64] Second, the overall delegation of procedural design to national lawmakers has led to legal uncertainty and uneven implementation across the EU, effectively undermining the harmonizing function of the RAD.

Moreover, most Member States appear reluctant to adopt opt-out systems for redress claims. This cautious implementation is frequently attributed to concerns over legal certainty, procedural fairness, and the fear of U.S.-style litigation culture. However, from the perspective of enforcement effectiveness, this reluctance undermines the practical utility of representative actions. Scholars have already emphasized that only opt-out mechanisms can overcome the structural barriers to participation in collective claims, especially in contexts involving diffuse harms, such as digital exploitation.[65]

In sum, while both the GDPR and RAD provide a legal basis for collective actions, the absence of a uniform, EU-wide opt-out model – especially for compensatory relief – limits the transformative potential of collective redress in the digital age. A recalibration of these frameworks toward mandatory opt-out mechanisms is essential to ensure both procedural inclusivity and substantive justice.

---

[62] Visscher and Faure (2021, 471).

[63] Gsell (2021, 1378).

[64] Fairgrieve and Salim (2022, 472).

[65] Visscher (2021, 456).

4.2.4 Fragmented Enforcement Under Article 80 GDPR and the RAD

The coexistence of Article 80 GDPR and the RAD has given rise to a fragmented legal landscape for collective redress in the digital environment. It should be noted in this regard that Article 2(1) of the RAD specifies that it applies to "representative actions brought against infringements by traders of the provisions of Union law referred to in Annex I", which also refers to the GDPR. As a result, Member States are required to permit representative actions in cases of data protection-related harms.

While both frameworks provide for collective actions, they however do so under different conditions, scopes, and limitations. At first glance, this dual-track system may seem to offer flexibility. In practice, it fragments enforcement, weakens legal clarity, and dilutes the potential of collective redress to address systemic digital harm.

This institutional fragmentation has long fueled debate. Some scholars previously argued that Article 80 GDPR constitutes a *lex specialis* in the field of data protection, thereby excluding the applicability of the RAD.[66] Others insisted that parallel actions under consumer law should remain available and the claimants should be allowed to choose between the two regimes, depending on context.[67] The CJEU's decision in *Meta* (C-319/20) settled much of this controversy: it confirmed that Article 80(2) GDPR does not preclude Member States from allowing consumer protection associations to bring claims under national law, including for data-related harms falling under consumer protection or unfair commercial practices law. The ruling confirms that Article 80 GDPR empowers (but does not oblige) Member States to introduce representative redress mechanisms. While this clarification affirms the complementary nature of the two regimes, it does not resolve the deeper problem: namely, the lack of a harmonised and accessible EU-wide system.

Such a fragmentation is problematic for two distinct reasons. First, it fails to reflect the blurred boundary between data subjects and consumers in the digital ecosystem. Individuals routinely inhabit both roles, often simultaneously, and digital harms—amplified by opaque algorithmic systems—frequently affect them without their awareness or consent. Second, the procedural architecture of current collective redress mechanisms is inadequate to address such structural harms. Existing frameworks either require opt-in participation or allow Member States to decide between opt-in and opt-out models. This discretion leads to a fragmented enforcement landscape that is poorly suited to confronting the systemic nature of digital exploitation affecting broad populations at scale.

A more robust, inclusive and effective solution would require a shift toward a unified, EU-wide framework**.** A binding, EU-wide opt-out mechanism—available regardless of one's legal classification—would ensure that individuals benefit from collective remedies even in the absence of direct participation. This could be operationalised through a twofold strategy: first, minimum harmonisation could require Member States to adopt a baseline opt-out mechanism for compensatory collective actions; second, delegated acts could define uniform procedural standards—such as

[66] Şerban (2023, 9).

[67] Federico (2023, 101).

tacit consent, standing criteria, and safeguards against abuse—thereby narrowing national discretion without full harmonisation. Such an approach would strike a balance between functional convergence and respect for procedural autonomy.

5 Combining Public Enforcement with an Opt-In Private Enforcement Collective Redress

While data protection in the EU is often described as a rights-based regime, its practical enforcement still relies heavily on public mechanisms. Supervisory authorities play a central role in monitoring compliance, issuing fines, and correcting unlawful practices. Yet this top-down model, focused on systemic deterrence, often fails to provide meaningful redress to individuals whose rights have been infringed.[68] To bridge this gap, a complementary role for private enforcement—especially through representative actions—has become increasingly vital. However, the dominant opt-in structure of such mechanisms significantly limits their reach and impact in the digital context, where harm is often opaque, dispersed, and cumulative.

The prevailing reliance on opt-in collective procedures significantly curtails the reach of private enforcement in the digital context. Digital vulnerability is not simply a matter of individual harm—it is a structural condition produced by opaque design choices, algorithmic profiling, and behavioural manipulation. These harms often escape user perception, unfold gradually over time, and disproportionately affect individuals with lower digital literacy or limited socioeconomic agency. In this environment, traditional individual redress mechanisms—especially opt-in models—are structurally incapable of capturing the scale or nature of exploitation. Opt-out collective actions, however, are uniquely positioned to respond to these conditions because they operate independently of victims' awareness, initiative, or legal knowledge. They recognize that the very qualities that make users vulnerable in digital markets—passivity, information asymmetry, and cognitive overload—are the same qualities that preclude reliance on individualized enforcement.

Critics of opt-out collective redress raise two principal objections. The first is the fear of abusive litigation, often based on comparisons with the U.S. experience. But this concern is ill-suited to the European context, where strict admissibility criteria and standing limitations—restricting actions to qualified, not-for-profit entities—provide effective safeguards.[69] Both the GDPR and the RAD limit standing to organizations pursuing public interest objectives, mitigating the risk of opportunistic claims.

The second objection is that opt-out systems may undermine party autonomy by including individuals who have not explicitly consented to participate.[70] Yet this criticism overlooks the role of rational apathy: individuals often refrain from action

---

[68] Federico (2023, 89).

[69] Gsell (2021, 1378) and Visscher (2021, 458).

[70] Federico (2023, 12).

when the perceived costs outweigh the benefits, even in the presence of harm. In such cases, autonomy is formal but not functional. Opt-out mechanisms address this barrier by automatically including individuals into the action while preserving their right to withdraw, thus striking a more effective balance between autonomy and access to justice.[71]

Yet beyond concerns about litigation abuse or autonomy, one of the most significant advantages of opt-out models lies in their ability to correct deep-rooted structural asymmetries in digital environments. Many affected individuals do not even know a violation has occurred or that they are entitled to compensation. By contrast, qualified representative entities possess the legal and technical capacity to identify infringements and pursue claims. Their involvement brings otherwise inaccessible harm to light and ensures that digital violations do not go unchallenged.[72] Such gatekeeping and advocacy function is absent in opt-in regimes.

The significance of opt-out models is particularly evident in cases of dispersed or low-value harm, where individual claims are unlikely to be pursued, yet the aggregate harm is substantial. In such contexts, opt-in procedures severely limit participation and undercut the deterrent effect of private enforcement. Conversely, opt-out mechanisms enable claims to better reflect the true scope of societal harm and increase accountability for wrongdoers.[73]

Still, the legal viability of opt-out collective compensation mechanisms also hinges on how national courts interpret the similarity requirement for bundled claims. This is particularly complex in cases involving non-material harm, such as emotional distress, reputational loss, or perceived loss of control—harms that are common in data protection cases. In jurisdictions like the Netherlands, courts have occasionally been reluctant to allow collective actions for such harms, citing the individualized nature of damage and the difficulty of establishing a uniform threshold of similarity across claimants. On top of that, non-material harms are inherently difficult to quantify in monetary terms, further complicating efforts to assess damages on a collective basis. While this should not dissuade the pursuit of opt-out frameworks, it underscores the need for procedural innovation that can accommodate variance in non-material harm without collapsing the collective logic.

Despite their promise, opt-out collective compensation mechanisms remain the exception rather than the rule in the EU. Most Member States continue to rely on opt-in models under the RAD, which limits the practical effectiveness of private enforcement in the digital sphere. Without a harmonized EU-wide opt-out framework, collective redress will remain fragmented and inadequate to the structural nature of digital exploitation. Advancing such a model should therefore be seen not merely as an option, but as a necessary evolution in the architecture of EU enforcement.

---

[71] Visscher (2021, 460).

[72] Visscher (2021, 489).

[73] Biard (2023, 5).

6 Conclusion

Digital vulnerability is not incidental but structural—produced and sustained by design architectures that normalize manipulation and preclude individual agency. Legal responses rooted in informed consent and transparency have proven insufficient to address this systemic imbalance. As individuals increasingly occupy dual roles as consumers and data subjects, the legal response to digital exploitation must transcend disciplinary silos and reflect the compound nature of harm.

Current enforcement tools under the UCPD and GDPR—while normatively significant—lack the operational capacity to confront widespread, low-visibility harms. The UCPD's particularistic approach to vulnerability and the GDPR's procedural limitations in private enforcement—most notably, the lack of a harmonised opt-out mechanism for compensation claims—leave substantial accountability gaps. Transparency, fairness, and even public oversight mechanisms remain reactive and fragmented.

These limitations are exacerbated by the discrepancies between the GDPR and the RAD. Although both frameworks enable representative actions, their divergent scopes, remedies, and procedural logics prevent the emergence of a coherent collective redress system. This fragmentation does not multiply enforcement channels—it entrenches inconsistencies that undermine legal certainty, restrict access to justice, and weaken deterrence. Without institutional and normative convergence, the prospect of a unified, EU-wide opt-out compensation mechanism remains politically and legally out of reach.

In this context, collective redress, particularly through opt-out representative actions, emerges as the most viable mechanism to address dispersed harm, rational apathy, and information and power asymmetry. Unlike opt-in models, opt-out structures align with the nature of digital vulnerability: they do not require legal sophistication, awareness, or initiative from those affected. Instead, they reallocate the burden to institutional actors equipped to act on behalf of groups. As such, they offer not just a procedural correction but a structural response to systemic harm.

The strength of collective redress for addressing digital vulnerability lies in the invisible, cumulative, and data-driven nature of digital exploitation. Harms in the digital environment often result not from isolated incidents, but from long-term, algorithmically mediated interactions that are difficult to detect or attribute at the individual level. By enabling aggregation, opt-out frameworks can address injuries that would otherwise escape legal recognition. Such a remedial pathway also reflects the collective dimension of digital injury—an aspect largely absent in traditional harm scenarios.

To realize this potential, the EU must elaborate on the interplay between the GDPR and the RAD, and move toward a unified framework for collective redress. A unified, EU-wide opt-out mechanism, applicable regardless of consumer status and encompassing compensatory claims, would provide a more coherent and effective enforcement pathway. In parallel, procedural safeguards must be recalibrated to ensure that concerns over litigation abuse do not suppress access to justice.

If the EU is truly committed to fairness and accountability in digital markets, enforcement mechanisms must do more than sanction non-compliance: they must empower the harmed. A recalibrated enforcement regime that combines public oversight with mandatory opt-out collective redress would represent a structural response to structural harm, restoring balance between individual rights and systemic power.

This paper does not claim to exhaust the subject. If the establishment of an EU-wide opt-out collective redress regime is adopted as a policy objective, several critical areas will require further scholarly and regulatory attention. First, the legal viability of bundling liability claims involving non-material damages in collective actions remains contested, particularly with respect to the similarity requirement and the difficulty in quantifying and proving immaterial harm. Second, while the RAD includes provisions aimed at enhancing the financial accessibility of representative actions, further attention must be given to persistent funding challenges. In particular, the practical feasibility of third-party funding mechanisms and cost-allocation rules, especially under the 'loser pays' principle, requires closer examination. Third, the idea of embedding a 'fairness by design' obligation into EU law, requiring companies to proactively structure digital environments to reduce manipulative risks, deserves serious consideration. Finally, the transparency obligations imposed on businesses should be reconsidered to include a duty to clearly inform individuals of their rights to join representative actions. Doing so would help bridge the existing knowledge gap and empower individuals who might otherwise remain unaware of available remedies.

These unresolved questions do not undermine the case for collective redress; rather, they highlight the complexity of designing institutions capable of protecting the many, not just the few. This challenge, however, calls for a shift in legal imagination. As Floridi reminds us, "it is the shoal that needs to be protected, if the sardine is to be saved".[74] In the digital age, protecting the shoal—through collective, structural legal responses—is the only path to truly safeguarding the individual.

References

Agulló DA (2022) The interplay of data, consumer and private international law rules in the area of collective access to justice in the European Union. Cuad Derecho Transnac 14(2):71–91

Article 29 Data Protection Working Party (2017) Guidelines on data protection impact assessment (DPIA) and determining whether processing is "likely to result in a high risk" for the purposes of Regulation 2016/679. https://ec.europa.eu/newsroom/just/document.cfm?doc_id=47711

Associate Press (2024) Supreme Court allows multibillion-dollar class action to proceed against meta. https://apnews.com/article/supreme-court-meta-facebook-lawsuit-9173ad92e11df4b2a565418e419dfb88

Bedayn J (2024) Class action lawsuit on AI-related discrimination reaches final settlement. https://apnews.com/article/artificial-intelligence-ai-lawsuit-discrimination-bias-1bc785c24a1b88bd425a8fa367ab2b23

Biard A (2023) The age of consumer law enforcement in the European Union: high hopes or wishful thinking? Eur J Risk Regul 15:1–12

[74] Floridi (2014, 3).

CMS (2024) European Class Action Report 2024. https://cms.law/en/media/international/files/publications/publications/cms-european-class-action-report-2024?v=4
Data Protection Commission (2023) Irish Data Protection Commission announces €345 million fine of TikTok. https://www.dataprotection.ie/en/news-media/press-releases/DPC-announces-345-million-euro-fine-of-TikTok
Domurath I (2024) Digital vulnerability as a power relation: hyper- and hypo-autonomy and why thick privacy matters. In: Crea C, De Franceschi A (eds) The new shapes of digital vulnerability in European Private Law. Nomos, Baden-Baden, pp 227–257
Duivenvoorde B (2013) The protection of vulnerable consumers under the unfair commercial practices directive. J Eur Consum Mark Law 2(2):69–79
Durovic M (2024) Adaptability of the unfair commercial practices directive to the metaverse. In: DiMatteo LA, Cannarsa M (eds) Research handbook on the metaverse and law. Edward Elgar, Cheltenham, pp 311–334
Durovic M, Kaprou E (2024) The new concept of digital vulnerability and the European rules on unfair commercial practices. In: Crea C, De Franceschi A (eds) The new shapes of digital vulnerability in European Private Law. Nomos, Baden-Baden, pp 127–144
Durovic M, Poon J (2023) Consumer vulnerability, digital fairness, and the european rules on unfair contract terms: what can be learnt from the case law against tiktok and meta? J Consum Policy 46:419–443
European Data Protection Board (2020) Guidelines 4/2019 on Article 25 data protection by design and by default (Version 2.0). https://www.edpb.europa.eu/sites/default/files/files/file1/edpb_guidelines_201904_dataprotection_by_design_and_by_default_v2.0_en.pdf
European Data Protection Board (2023) Guidelines 03/2022 on deceptive design patterns in social media platform interfaces: how to recognise and avoid them (Version 2.0). https://www.edpb.europa.eu/system/files/2023-02/edpb_032022_guidelines_on_deceptive_design_patterns_in_social_media_platform_interfaces_v2_en_0.pdf
Fairgrieve D, Salim R (2022) Collective redress in Europe: moving forward or treading water? Int Comp Law Quart 71(2):465–479
Federico M (2023) European collective redress and data protection challenges and opportunities. mediaLAWS 1:86–103. https://www.medialaws.eu/wp-content/uploads/2023/06/1-23-Federico.pdf
Feiler L et al (2018) Article 80. In: The EU General Data Protection Regulation (GDPR): a commentary. GLP, Surrey
Fineman MA (2008) The vulnerable subject: anchoring equality in the human condition. Yale J Law Fem 20(1):1–24
Floridi L (2014) Open data, data protection, and group privacy. Philos Technol 27:1–3
Galli F (2022) Algorithmic marketing and EU law on unfair commercial practices. Springer, Cham
González Fuster G (2020) Article 80. Representation of data subjects. In: Kuner C et al (eds) The EU general data protection regulation (GDPR). Oxford University Press, Oxford, pp 1142–1152
Grochowski M (2024) Digital vulnerability in a post-consumer society. Subverting paradigms? In: Crea C, De Franceschi A (eds) The new shapes of digital vulnerability in European Private Law. Nomos, Baden-Baden, pp 201–225
Gsell B (2021) The new European Directive on representative actions for the protection of the collective interests of consumers—a huge, but blurry step forward. Common Mark Law Rev 58:1365–1400
Helberger N et al (2017) The Perfect match? A closer look at the relationship between EU consumer law and data protection law. Common Mark Law Rev 54:1427–1466
Helberger N et al (2022) Choice architectures in the digital economy: towards a new understanding of digital vulnerability. J Consum Policy 45:175–200
Janciute L (2019) Data protection and the construction of collective redress in Europe: exploring challenges and opportunities. Int Data Privacy Law 9(1):2–14
Kaprou E (2021) The legal definition of 'vulnerable' consumers in the UCPD: benefits and limitations of a focus on personal attributes. In: Riefa C, Saintier S (eds) Vulnerable consumers and the law. Routledge, New York, pp 51–67
Liu M (2024) Digital vulnerability: rethinking power imbalances in the digital age. Eur Rev Privacy Law 32(1):827–848

Luna F (2009) Elucidating the concept of vulnerability: layers not labels. Int J Fem Approach Bioeth 2(1):121–139
Mackenzie C et al (2004) Introduction: what is vulnerability, and why does it matter for moral theory? In: Mackenzie C, Rogers W, Dodds S (eds) Vulnerability: new essays in ethics and feminist philosophy. Oxford University Press, Oxford, pp 1–30
Malgieri G (2023) Vulnerability and data protection law. Oxford University Press, Oxford
Malgieri G, Niklas J (2020) Vulnerable data subjects. Comput Law Secur Rev 37:1–16
Massaro Piletta A (2021) The new directive on An EU-wide representative action and third-party litigation funding: an opportunity for European consumers? Revija Kopaonicke Skole Prirodnog Prava 3(1):95–117
OECD (2023) Consumer vulnerability in the digital age. Digit Econ Pap. https://doi.org/10.1787/4d013cc5-en
Pato A (2019) The collective private enforcement of data protection rights in the EU. Blogdroiyeuropéen.
Petropoulos G (2022) The dark side of artificial intelligence: manipulation of human behaviour. https://www.bruegel.org/blog-post/dark-side-artificial-intelligence-manipulation-human-behaviour
Riefa C (2022) Protecting vulnerable consumers in the digital single market. Eur Bus Law Rev 33(4):607–634
Riefa C, Gamper H (2021) Economic theory and consumer vulnerability: exploring an uneasy relationship. In: Riefa C, Saintier S (eds) Vulnerable consumers and the law. Routledge, New York, pp 17–30
Rossi A et al (2024) Who is vulnerable to deceptive design patterns? A transdisciplinary perspective on the multi-dimensional nature of digital vulnerability. Comput Law Secur Rev 55:1–17
Şerban A (2023) The legal framework of data subject representation. SHS Web Conf 177. https://www.shs-conferences.org/articles/shsconf/pdf/2023/26/shsconf_copeji2023_04004.pdf
Siciliani P et al (2019) Consumer theories of harm: an economic approach to consumer law enforcement and policy making. Hart, Oxford
Sorace F (2018) Collective redress in the general data protection regulation: an opportunity to improve access to justice in the European Union? Working Paper 7/2018. https://diposit.ub.edu/dspace/bitstream/2445/123425/1/WP_2018_7.pdf
Visscher L, Faure M (2021) A law and economics perspective on the EU directive on representative actions. J Consum Policy 44:455–482

Strength in… Fragmentation? A Concise Systemic Look at the Enforcement of the EU Digital Acquis, with Some Implications for Vulnerability

Silvia De Conca

Abstract The EU secondary legislation concerning digital technologies relies on a complex enforcement architecture, revolving around ad hoc agencies and a mix of public and private enforcement. With the rapid multiplication of EU Regulations and Directives, the protection of the rights and interests of individuals and groups is now the result of the interaction of a plethora of enforcement agencies, at national and EU level, sometimes with converging aims, and potentially overlapping jurisdictions, and a variety of tasks and powers. This chapter offers an overview of the agencies tasked with the enforcement of the General Data Protection Regulation (GDPR), Unfair Commercial Practices Directive (UCPD), the Digital Services Act (DSA), the Regulation on Artificial Intelligence (AIA), and the General Product Safety Regulation (GPSR). It also provides a preliminary investigation into the implications of the current system of enforcement of the digital acquis at EU level, in particular with regard to the need for cross-sector collaboration among the different agencies, and what that means for vulnerable individuals and groups.

Keywords Digital technologies · EU law · Independent agencies · Enforcement · Digital vulnerability

1 Introduction

The enforcement of the European Union (EU) regulations and directives dealing with digital technologies (hereinafter digital *acquis*) generally relies on a mix of public and private tools. The enforcement architecture is complex. On one side, there are several EU secondary laws, each providing public law mechanisms for enforcement, focusing on the appointment of ad hoc public administration entities, with their own objectives, tasks and powers (hereinafter referred to as agencies or authorities). On

S. De Conca (✉)
Transnational Legal Studies Department, Vrije Universiteit Amsterdam, Amsterdam, The Netherlands
e-mail: s.deconca@vu.nl

C. Crea and M. Infantino (eds.), *Remedies to Digital Vulnerability in European Private Law*, https://doi.org/10.1007/978-3-032-19720-7_8

the other side, private litigation mechanisms are—explicitly or implicitly—contemplated, to complement and even support public enforcement. Initially, the right of individuals to obtain redress remained implicit, regulated by the combination of the principle of national procedural autonomy,[1] the principle of sincere cooperation (art. 3(4) TEU), and the principles of equivalence and effectiveness. Following the example set by the General Data Protection Regulation (GDPR),[2] an explicit right to obtain redress started being introduced in the digital *acquis*. These new provisions have a broad scope (the right to redress is usually granted for material and immaterial damage), but do not go much in detail, so as to not interfere with national liability regimes. It follows that while public enforcement takes the leading role in the enforcement of the digital *acquis,* private enforcement has also been instrumentalized to consolidate and strengthen the effectiveness of EU laws. Leading the way is the role of the case law of the Court of Justice of the EU (CJEU) concerning the right to redress in the GDPR, which contributes to the expansive interpretation of the data protection discipline: the CJEU told national courts that *de minimis* thresholds for the redress of harms cannot be applied to harms deriving from GDPR violations, which creates a de facto detached discipline for the redress of data protection harms in some Member States.[3]

As the EU Commission introduces more and more regulations and directives dealing with digital technologies, and their use of public and private enforcement becomes more and more intertwined, the enforcement architecture of the digital *acquis* grows in complexity. The protection of the rights and interests of individuals and groups is now the result of the interaction of many enforcement agencies, at national and EU level, sometimes with converging aims, and potentially overlapping jurisdictions, and a variety of tasks and powers. This chapter offers a preliminary investigation into the implications of the current system of enforcement of the digital *acquis* at EU level, in particular with regard to the enforcement agencies, whose importance is growing, together with their tasks.

The contribution of this chapter is twofold. It offers a systemic view of the roles, objectives and powers of the agencies tasked with applying some of the more impactful EU regulations and directives of the digital *acquis*. The chapter also draws some initial conclusions concerning their cooperation and collaboration, appraising the choices of the EU regulator concerning the enforcement of the digital *acquis,* discussing how this architecture can affect the overall protection of individuals, and vulnerable individuals and groups in particular.

---

[1] CJEU, case 33/76, *Rewe-Zentralfinanz v. Landwirtschaftkammer für das Saarland*, EU:C:1976:188, para. 5.

[2] Regulation (EU) 2016/679 of the European Parliament and of the Council of 27 April 2016 on the protection of natural persons with regard to the processing of personal data and on the free movement of such data. Please note that this reasoning is applied strictly to EU secondary tools concerning digital technologies. In general with regard to EU secondary laws, the tendency to include provisions concerning private law redress has been noticed to grow steadily since the 1980s, as noted by Wilman (2016).

[3] De Conca and Infantino (2024).

The purpose is to give a horizontal, systemic overview of enforcement at EU level, as a starting point to reflect on the interplay of many (maybe too many?) enforcement agencies, and the inclusion and instrumentalization of private law remedies in this context.

Due to limitations of space, the focus is on the aforementioned GDPR, Unfair Commercial Practices Directive (UCPD), Digital Services Act (DSA), Regulation on Artificial Intelligence (AIA), and General Product Safety Regulation (GPSR).[4] They regulate, respectively, the processing of personal data with digital means, unfair commercial practices (online), online intermediaries and platforms, AI systems, and (digital) products. The analysis has no pretense to be exhaustive, as it does not include many other Directives and Regulation which also play an important role in regulating digital technologies, such as telecommunication infrastructures, medical devices, radio frequencies. However, the combination of the aforementioned laws covers many products and services with which European citizens enter into contact on a daily basis, making them foundational elements of today's so-called 'Digital Society' (defined as "a society permeated by the digital, where our actions are frequently mediated by digital tools, and the objects we encounter are frequently shaped by digital intervention").[5] As such, those laws are widely acknowledged as some of the most important EU tools addressing digital technologies.

Section 2 briefly outlines the nature, purposes, and powers of the agencies created to enforce the digital acquis. The section cannot offer a comprehensive analysis of each enforcement regime, as that would require much more than the space granted by this volume. Nevertheless, it clarifies in broad strokes the functioning of the enforcement agencies established by heritage laws, i.e. the UCPD, GPSR, and GDPR, and more recent laws, specifically the DSA and AIA. Section 3 appraises the overall EU system of enforcement of the digital *acquis*, highlighting its complexities, challenges, and systemic tensions. Section 4 concludes the chapter by discussing some noteworthy implications for digital vulnerability.

2 The Agencies Enforcing the Digital Acquis

Over time, the EU regulator has opted for a range of enforcement strategies. When it comes to the agencies tasked with enforcing the digital *acquis*, the choices were affected by factors such as the matter being regulated (e.g. safety standards for products in the internal market), and the level of harmonization (directive or regulation). The regulations and directives analysed generally oblige Member States to

---

[4] Respectively: Directive 2005/29/EC of the European Parliament and of the Council of 11 May 2005 concerning unfair business-to-consumer commercial practices in the internal market; Regulation (EU) 2022/2065 of the European Parliament and of the Council of 19 October 2022 on a Single Market For Digital Services; Regulation (EU) 2024/1689 of the European Parliament and of the Council of 13 June 2024 laying down harmonised rules on artificial intelligence; Regulation (EU) 2023/988 of the European Parliament and of the Council of 10 May 2023 on general product safety.

[5] Martin (2008, 1029).

Table 1 The enforcement of the five Regulations and Directives is sometimes distributed among multiple agencies

	UCPD	GPSR	DSA	AIA	GDPR
Consumer authority	X		X (potentially)		
Market surveillance authority		X		X	
Digital services act authorities/ coordinator			X		
Data protection authority			X (potentially)	X	X
Authorities protecting fundamental rights				X	

appoint an administrative entity and grant them certain powers, to perform statutory tasks. As a result, Member States can choose between appointing one authority or multiple ones, and between either creating new authority/ies or expanding the tasks and powers of existing ones, concentrating the enforcement of multiple laws into one or few agencies. For example, the Netherlands has appointed as DSA authorities the existing Authority for Consumers and Markets and Data Protection Authority, while Italy has appointed the existing Authority for Communications as Digital Services Coordinator. Table 1 below summarises how certain authorities might be in charge of different EU laws.

2.1 *Consumer Authorities*

The UCPD does not establish consumer authorities, nor does it explicitly prescribe Member States to create a national authority. However, it contains an obligation for Member States to create national *facilities* (also called *means*) so that natural and legal persons can: i) bring a claim before a court for an infringement of the UCPD (i.e. if a trader is using an unfair commercial practice); and/or ii) notify an *administrative authority* of the unfair practices of a trader, so that such authority can either take legal action before a court or follow up on the claim itself (art. 11 UCPD). The states that adopted the second option consequently created or appointed an administrative authority to deal with consumer protection claims. The UCPD, therefore, leaves Member States the choice between more private law or more public law enforcement facilities. The recent Fitness Check carried out by the EU Commission highlighted that the public law option, with the appointing of a consumer authority, is the most chosen by Member States.[6]

The aim of consumer authorities, therefore, is to ensure the adequate means to combat unfair commercial practices and enforce the UCPD. The administrative authorities should be impartial, although the UCPD does not explicitly state they should be independent (art. 11 UCPD). Not all consumer authorities are, therefore,

[6] European Commission (2024).

independent: a study analysing 38 consumer authorities in the 27 EU Member States plus 2 non-EU countries, showed that 14 consumer authorities were part of a ministry or ministerial unit, and therefore cannot be considered independent administrative entities.[7]

Consumer authorities are tasked with enforcing the UCPD and either handling the complaints directly, or pursuing legal action before a court. To pursue these tasks, the UCPD recommends Member States to grant consumer authorities all the powers necessary to prohibit or order the cessation of unfair practices (or initiate a proceeding to this end), take urgent measures (definitive or temporary), require the publication of decisions and corrective statements, monitor the enforcement of their decisions by traders and, if necessary, enforce the decisions themselves (art. 11). Additionally, consumer authorities should also be granted the power to require documents, information and evidence from traders (and declare them inaccurate or insufficient if necessary) (art. 12), and issue administrative fines (art. 13).

To complement this set up, in the original architecture of the UCPD natural and legal persons were granted the right to lodge a complaint with the authority (art. 11). Following the 2019 reform of consumer law, the EU Commission modernized and updated the UCPD[8] adding article 11a, according to which natural persons also have the right to obtain compensation for damages caused by unfair commercial practices, therefore solving decades of uncertainty on the matter.[9] The UCPD establishes mostly substantive rules on this action for damages (e.g. the conditions of the existence of an infringement and of the damage), without going into details on more procedural aspects. This choice of the EU legislator is in line with the principle of national procedural autonomy, but it is also the consequence of a general difficulty in reaching agreement within the EU legislative process, for matters concerning liability and actions for damage.[10]

The UCPD offers a mix of public and private enforcement, with the boundaries between the two depending on how Member States have organized the consumer authorities and their powers. The UCPD itself offers the possibility to recur to injunctions (art. 11). The action for injunctions was complemented by the Consumer Injunctions Directive, now repealed and superseded by the Representative Action Directive.[11] Collective actions are gaining more attention recently, after it became apparent that private enforcement, in particular in the form of actions for damage, were of little practical importance in consumer protection.[12] In the mix between private and public enforcement, the latter seemed to prevail: consumers did not use

[7] Jordana, Rozas-Bugueño, Triviño-Salazar (2025).

[8] Directive (EU) 2019/2161 of the European Parliament and of the Council of 27 November 2019 amending Council Directive 93/13/EEC and Directives 98/6/EC, 2005/29/EC and 2011/83/EU of the European Parliament and of the Council as regards the better enforcement and modernisation of Union consumer protection rules.

[9] Havu (2019).

[10] Wilman (2016, 905).

[11] Directive (EU) 2020/1828 of the European Parliament and of the Council of 25 November 2020 on representative actions for the protection of the collective interests of consumers.

[12] Van Boom and Loos (2008).

the right to redress (private enforcement before courts) that frequently, while injunctions seemed to be preferred. The reason why these injunctions are indicated here as public enforcement is because they tend to be requested to consumer authorities rather than to courts, and in this form the injunction blurs the distinction between private and public enforcement. It should be pointed out that this is the tendency also in other branches of EU law, and consumer protection is not an exception.[13]

2.2 Market Surveillance Authorities

The GPSR is a *lex generalis* establishing safety requirements for all those products (or aspects thereof) that are not already regulated by other EU laws on the matter.[14] It fills the gaps existing within the so-called 'Union Harmonisation Legislation' (UHL).[15] The purpose of the GPSR and UHL is to ensure the "necessary level of trust between Member States"[16] in matters concerning the products that are placed or circulate in the internal market.

The application of the GPSR, the UHL, and all other product safety laws is monitored by national Market Surveillance Authorities (MSAs), which are regulated by Regulation 2019/1020. More specifically, Regulation 2019/1020 defines market surveillance as activities "to ensure that products comply with the requirements set out in the applicable Union harmonisation legislation and to ensure protection of the public interest covered by that legislation", and MSAs as "an authority designated by a Member State under article 10 as responsible for carrying out market surveillance in the territory of that Member State" (art. 3 nos (3)–(4) Reg. 2019/1020). Substantially similar definitions are included in the GPSR (art. 3 nos (23)–(24)). Article 10 of Regulation 2019/1020 obliges Member States to designate one or more MSAs, allocating them the necessary resources, including a budget and sufficient personnel.

Market surveillance activities aim at ensuring compliance with the relevant EU legislation, so that Member States don't take measures restricting the free movement of goods beyond what is strictly necessary.[17] MSAs can take different forms, depending on the choices made by Member States, but must be independent and impartial (Art. 11 Reg. 2019/1020). Their aim is to ensure: (i) effective market surveillance of products made available online or offline, within the territory of the

[13] Wilman (2016, 908).

[14] European Commission (2021, 12).

[15] UHL indicates the EU Directives and regulations harmonizing the conditions, assessment, and surveillance of products in the internal market. The UHL legislation is listed in Annex I of Regulation (EU) 2019/1020 of the European Parliament and of the Council of 20 June 2019 on market surveillance and compliance of products.

[16] European Commission (2016, 8).

[17] European Commission (2016, 98).

Member State; (ii) compliance by economic operators, through the use of corrective actions; and (iii) absent corrective actions by economic operators, to ensure compliance via appropriate and proportionate measures.

To achieve their aims, MSAs are granted extensive powers by Reg. 2019/1020 (complemented by appropriate additional ones by the specific UHL): they can investigate compliance with the law, carry out (documental, physical and laboratory) checks based on a risk assessment of the products, request documents and information, access and inspect locations, and issue enforcement measures. Their powers include imposing fines, ordering to take appropriate corrective actions, removing or restricting access to dangerous products; alternatively, MSAs can recur to other public authorities and courts (Art. 14, Reg. 2019/1020).

The GPSR introduces the obligation, for economic operators, to cooperate with MSAs, to complement their powers (Arts. 15–16, 22 GPSR). With regard to remedies, the GPSR, true to its nature, only establishes the right to lodge a complaint with an MSA (Art. 33 GPSR), and a more contractual remedy, the obligation for economic operators to 'Repair, Replace, Refund' (RRR, art. 37 GPSR). No explicit right to redress is contemplated beyond the mentioned RRR, although the Product Liability Directive[18] offers a detailed substantive and (in part) procedural discipline of strict liability for damages deriving from defective products.

Some aspects of MSAs and market surveillance deserve attention. MSAs are administrative entities whose role is, however, very technical: they have the expertise to carry out tests, including laboratory checks, and assess technical documentation, in a variety of sectors. Additionally, market surveillance is done when the products are already on the market: the enforcement of the GPSR and UHL is inherently *ex post*, not *ex ante*.[19] Furthermore, the enforcement of product safety laws in the EU has been put under increasing stress by globalization. Supply chains have become increasingly distributed and complex, and the popularity of e-commerce makes it possible for consumers to purchase goods directly from outside the internal market. These factors make it more difficult to detect, investigate, and recall unsafe products.[20]

Because UHL includes several sector-specific laws, market surveillance tends to be very fragmented at national level: the decentralization of market surveillance offered enhanced sector-specific expertise, but has provoked concerns regarding the effectiveness and coherence of the enforcement of product safety legislation, as well as the issue of regulatory duplication, with overlapping powers and prerogatives. The entry into force of Regulation 2019/1020 caused some shifts and reorganizations at national level, with attempts at better coordination or more centralization, but these issues still remain to a certain extent. Regarding cross-border cooperation, there is a variety of mechanisms, committees, networks, and more or less informal channels that MSAs use to cooperate and collaborate at EU level.[21] These mechanisms can

[18] Directive (EU) 2024/2853 of the European Parliament and of the Council of 23 October 2024 on liability for defective products.

[19] European Commission (2016, 99).

[20] Hajnal (2020).

[21] Żywicka and Kokocińska (2023).

be general, but also sectoral: this has created issues with harmonization, limited participation, resource constraints, and interoperability of databases. Finally, to make things worse, MSAs have indicated that the expansion of their tasks due to new EU laws can pose serious challenges to their effectiveness, requiring new expertise and stretching their resources too thin.[22]

2.2.1 MSAs, the AIA, and Fundamental Rights

The AIA relies primarily on MSAs for its enforcement (art. 74 AIA).[23] For example, art. 76 AIA clarifies that, in case of real world testing (based on the sandbox provision of art. 57 AIA), MSAs shall have the competencies and powers to surveil the testing conditions. For High-risk AI Systems listed in Annex III AIA, the enforcement should be carried out by the MSAs according to Reg. 2019/1020 and the GPSR. For the High-risk AI Systems falling under the UHL laws listed in Annex I AIA, the enforcement is performed by the relevant MSA based on said applicable UHL, with some amendments to tailor the procedures to the specific features of AI systems. Annex III lists 8 applications of AI systems, ranging from biometric-based AI (face recognition, emotion recognition), to administration of justice, employment, and even democratic processes and political campaigns. MSAs, therefore, are tasked to assess compliance of the providers and deployers of AI systems in sectors particularly sensitive from a human rights perspective, notwithstanding their inherently technical and scientific expertise.

Notably, the AIA also grants some surveillance powers to "National public authorities or bodies which supervise or enforce the respect of obligations under Union law protecting fundamental rights, including the right to non-discrimination" (art. 77 AIA). These authorities shall have the power, in relation to the use of said High-risk AI systems listed in Annex III AIA, to request and access the documentation mandated by the AIA itself, if that is necessary to fulfil their mandate. Should this documentation be insufficient, the authorities protecting fundamental rights can request MSAs to organize a technical testing of the AI System. Even though the AIA is very recent, the powers of these authorities might change soon, before they are even fully designated, due to the deregulation plans initiated at the end of 2025 by the EU Commission, known as the Digital Omnibus. Some of the changes proposed in the initial draft of the Digital Omnibus include that art. 77 authorities will only be granted the power to ask MSAs for relevant AIA documentation, and not providers or users of AI systems. How art. 77 AIA will change remains to be seen, as the Digital Omnibus completes its legislative procedure.

The authorities protecting fundamental rights are not well-known in the general EU and national landscape. At national level, they are sometimes referred to as

[22] European Parliament (2023).

[23] Under the AIA, the EU Commission enforces Chapter V, on General Purpose AI Models, and certain agencies supervise specific applications of high-risk AI systems (e.g. for AI systems used in financial institutions, the Financial Market Surveillance Authority, and so on).

National Human Rights Institutions (NHRI), and their composition, name and status varies greatly among Member States.[24] Some Member States have even failed to appoint an NHRI, as is the case of Italy. For the purposes of article 77 AIA, however, a wide array of national authorities might become relevant, based on the 8 domains listed in Annex III. Relevant authorities include DPAs, media and information authorities, equality and non-discrimination commissioners, NHRIs, and so on. Austria, for example, has published a list including all the aforementioned, in addition to the Ombudsperson, the consumer protection authority, the children and youth ombudsperson, and more, for a total of 9.[25] All these authorities would have to coordinate among each other and collaborate with MSAs, to ensure post-market surveillance of AI Systems on matters related to the respect of fundamental rights. The AIA does not clarify much in terms of what authorities are appropriate to comply with art. 77 AIA, and remains ambiguous concerning the boundaries of the collaboration among the different enforcement agencies involved. Furthermore, the powers granted by art. 77 AIA are rather limited, as they only consist of accessing documents or requesting the intervention of a MSA, and only in relation to certain High-risk AI systems: this excludes from their scope the Unacceptable-risk AI Systems whose prohibition, under art. 5 AIA, should be enforced *ex post*.[26] Consequently MSAs, usually tasked with verifying the safety of products, remain the only ones in charge of surveilling prohibited AI Systems, those that more than all other risk categories affect fundamental rights.

As a final remark, it should be noted that the AIA only contemplates the right to lodge a complaint and the right to a clear an meaningful explanation if a High-risk AI produces legal or similarly significant effects that create an adverse impact on health, safety or fundamental rights (arts. 85–86 AIA). The AIA does not establish any right to redress for individuals suffering damage from AI systems. Together with the GPSR, they are the only two analysed pieces of legislation that do not provide actions for damage.

2.3 Data Protection Authorities & EDPB

The obligation for Member States to create independent authorities overseeing personal data protection is enshrined in both art. 8(3) of the Charter of Fundamental Rights of the EU, and art. 16(2) of the TFEU. This obligation is translated at secondary legislative level by the GDPR in Chapters VI, VII and VIII, respectively dealing with the establishment of the Data protection Authorities (DPAs), the mechanisms for collaboration and consistency, and the remedies and administrative measures. The discipline regulating the creation and operating of DPAs under the GDPR is among

[24] Drechsler and Vogiatzoglou (2024).

[25] Official website of the Austrian Government. Available via https://www.digitalaustria.gv.at/eng/topics/AI/Article-77-AI-Act.html.

[26] Drechsler and Vogiatzoglou (2024).

the most detailed of all the Regulations and Directives analysed. Member States can choose to establish one or more DPAs (for example, Germany has established 16 DPAs for its Landes and Federal administrations, coordinated via a Data Protection Conference). In case of multiple DPAs for one country, the Member State also designates one DPA to represent all the national authorities in the European Data Protection Board (EDPB). The EDPB is an independent body of the EU, tasked with overseeing consistency and cooperation in the interpretation and enforcement of the GDPR. The EDPB has the power, among others, to take binding decisions on cross-border cases on which the national DPAs could not reach consensus, and it can issue non-binding (but very authoritative) guidelines and opinions on the interpretation of the GDPR (Arts. 68 and 70 GDPR).

The GDPR also contains a very detailed discipline of how DPAs from different Member States should cooperate for cross-border operations. In these cases, the DPA of the main (or sole) establishment of the controller becomes the leading supervisory authority (art. 56 GDPR), and is the only DPA interacting with the controller. The leading supervisory authority is obliged to cooperate with the other DPAs concerned. It should, in particular, share a draft decision, to reach consensus on the matters under scrutiny, and the DPAs can issue objections, which can lead to a revised draft, until consensus is, hopefully, reached. This collaboration mechanism is called one-stop-shop. If the one-stop-shop mechanism fails, the EDPB intervenes with a binding decision, following the rules established by the GDPR for the consistency mechanism (Arts. 63–67).[27] The GDPR does not offer any rules concerning the coordination of DPAs with the agencies implementing other EU laws.

The GDPR has a double objective: protecting fundamental rights—in particular the right to personal data protection and the right to privacy—and fostering the free flow of personal data in the internal market. These two objectives are also indicated as the main aims of the DPAs (art. 51(1)).[28] DPAs are independent (art. 52 GDPR), and the GDPR sets out minimum conditions and requirements for the Member States to establish the DPA, and select and appoint its members (Arts. 53–54 GDPR).[29]

DPAs are given a breathtakingly long list of tasks (art. 57 GDPR), ranging from monitoring and enforcing the application of the GDPR, conducting investigations, issuing fines and penalties, to promoting public awareness and monitoring the advancement of the state of the art on data protection, encouraging the creation of codes of conducts and certification mechanisms, conducting the accreditation of the bodies that can issue certifications, approve corporate binding rules, and so on.[30] DPAs also receive and follow up on the complaints from the citizens whose personal data are processed (data subjects). In the face of such a wide range of tasks, the powers of DPAs are also significant, and are divided into investigative, corrective,

---

[27] For an overview, see Van Eecke and Šimkus (2020).

[28] Hijmans (2020a).

[29] Zerdick (2020).

[30] For an overview of the tasks and powers of DPAs, see Hijmans (2020b), Georgieva and Schmidl (2020).

and authorizing & advising. They can, among others, order the provision of information from the actors determining and performing the data processing (controllers and processors), perform data audits (i.e. investigations), issue warnings and reprimands, impose fines and other temporary or permanent measures. DPAs are obliged to provide mutual assistance, and can organize their operations to conduct joint operations (Arts. 61–62 GDPR).

To complete the enforcement architecture, the GDPR establishes both the right to lodge a complaint with a DPA, and the right to obtain redress for material and immaterial damages suffered by a data subject following a breach of the GDPR itself. The redress remains regulated by the applicable national regimes, which has given life in the past few years to a large number of referrals to the CJEU of questions concerning how to reconcile national tort liability regimes with the effective implementation of the GDPR.[31]

The structure of the GDPR's remedies is a mix of public and private, and the decisions issued by DPAs, national courts and the CJEU in the past years have been deeply shaping both public and private enforcement. The CJEU, in particular, has often taken an expansive and bold approach to interpreting the GDPR, putting data subjects' rights at the center, in line with the principle of full effectiveness. This has created the impression of a rather dynamic and strong enforcement mechanism for individual rights, while more uncertainty remains with regard to collective/group rights, and with regard to the more systemic implications of data processing. Notwithstanding on paper the GDPR presents a strong substantial and enforcement regime, research has highlighted several practical issues affecting its effectiveness. The one-stop-shop mechanism can be hindered by difficulties in establishing a company actual main establishment, and its application is complicated by the lack of adequate coordination and communication among interested DPAs, a lack of harmonization of the procedures followed by the national DPAs, and the lack of strict deadlines for DPAs.[32] The arm wrestling between the DPAs and the EDPB on one side, and the powerful multinational companies operating online on the other also contributes to affect the enforcement of the GDPR.

2.4 Digital Services Authorities & Coordinator

The DSA regulates online platforms and search engines in their role as intermediaries between traders and users. The DSA reflects the fact that online intermediaries operate in a two-way market, as it aims at harmonising the rules on the provision of intermediary services, to foster a "safe, predictable and trusted online environment"[33] in which the fundamental rights and principles enshrined in the EU Charter

[31] De Conca and Infantino (2024).

[32] Pírková (2021).

[33] DSA, Recital 3.

are effectively protected, but at the same time also to facilitate innovation and mitigate power imbalances between the intermediary and the traders. The enforcement choices made by the EU legislator for the DSA are affected by the nature of intermediary services, as well as by the experience developed with the enforcement of the GDPR.[34]

The enforcement is divided between the appointed authorities and the EU Commission itself, which is directly and exclusively competent to oversee compliance with the DSA by the largest and most powerful online intermediaries, called Very Large Online Platforms and Very Large Search Engines (VLOPs and VLSEs) (art. 56 DSA). The DSA also creates the European Board for Digital Services (EBDS). Consisting of representatives of national DSCs, the EBDS has an independent advisory role to the DSCs and the Commission.

Member States must appoint one or more authorities tasked with enforcing the DSA. In case multiple authorities are appointed, one must be designated as the Digital Services Coordinator (DSC), to ensure effective and consistent cooperation, and to be the sole point of contact with the intermediaries established in the country, with other national DSCs, and with the Commission (art. 49 DSA). Member States have chosen a variety of strategies to appoint the relevant authorities, creating an array of administrative solutions. This variety is also raising some concerns, in particular regarding the coordination at national level of all these authorities and the necessity of clearer guidelines at European level to facilitate the coordination and cooperation.[35]

DSCs are tasked with the supervision of the compliance with the DSA, and its enforcement, but they can also divide specific tasks among the other appointed authorities. To achieve their tasks, DSCs are given investigatory and enforcement powers, consisting of: requiring information and ask explanations from intermediaries, carrying out inspections, ordering the cessation of infringements, imposing remedies, fines, periodic penalties, and adopt interim measures. They can also make intermediaries draft a plan to ensure compliance with the DSA and the cessation of infringements and, failing everything else, order the restriction of access of recipients to the services of the intermediary.

The division of competences among DSCs and between them and the Commission is particularly important in the enforcement architecture of the DSA. Because in general the online intermediaries regulated by the DSA operate at cross-border level, the DSC of the Member State in which the intermediary has its main establishment will be the one tasked with its enforcement (art. 65(1)). The cooperation with other DSCs is regulated more strictly than in the GDPR: for example, if the DSC of establishment requests information from other DSCs, these must reply within 2 months; if other DSCs or the EBDS request a DSC of establishment to investigate a matter, this latter must inform them of the results of its assessments within 2 months (arts. 57–58 DSA). If the DSC of establishment fails to comply within 2 months, or if the EBDS disagrees with the outcome of the assessment, the matter is referred to the

[34] Buri and van Hoboken (2022).

[35] Van Cleynenbreugel and Mattioli (2023).

Commission, which can request the DSC of establishment to revise its assessment (art. 59). DSC can also carry out joint investigations (art. 60 DSA).

The Commission has exclusive power to supervise and enforce the DSA vis-à-vis VLOPs and VLSEs, and for matters concerning the systemic risk assessment these latter must perform according to Sect. 5 of Chapter III DSA. To this end, the Commission can initiate and carry out proceedings that might lead to fines or other corrective measures, ordered by the Commission itself. The Commission has extensive investigation and enforcement powers, including inspecting, interviewing witnesses, requesting information (arts. 67–69). The Commission is also tasked with establishing and maintaining an information sharing system functional to ensure the cooperation among DSCs, the EBDS and the Commission (art. 85).

Finally, in terms of remedies the DSA provides for both the right to lodge a complaint with the DSC of the Member State where they reside, and the right to redress—according to the applicable national regimes—for *any* damage or loss suffered due to the infringement of the DSA, similarly to the GDPR (arts. 53–54). The mix of public and private enforcement of the DSA assumes even more importance if one considers that the DSA includes obligations concerning transparency of recommender systems (i.e. why we see certain content on online platforms), content moderation, and the resolution of disputes deriving therefrom, all directly affecting the freedom of information and expression.[36] The public enforcement carried out by the DSCs, therefore, includes a delegation of powers to the platforms—especially with regard to content moderation[37]—and the oversight of how the platforms comply with these obligations, in a mix of *ex ante* and *ex post* enforcement. The focus is primarily on public enforcement, with private enforcement assuming a secondary role. For instance, injunctions by the DSC could be used to enforce the DSA obligations in a more public, and less private way, as briefly mentioned with regard to consumer protection authorities.[38] It is possible, however, that the remedies for breaches of aforementioned obligations will lead to national Courts and the CJEU playing a role in the enforcement of the DSA, at least with regard to actions for damages. This could also increase the importance of civil society groups, associations of consumers, and industry itself (the traders operating on platforms) for the effective implementation of the DSA, also in combination with the Representative Actions Directive.[39] However, due to the variety of obligations, and the complexity of the aims of the DSA (and of the role of intermediaries online), the private enforcement of the DSA is likely to vary greatly, depending on what specific obligations are considered breached and the rights affected. To complicate things further, there is a potential for decentralization of the enforcement among multiple authorities, as occurred for MSAs, and some of the provisions of the DSA lend themselves to different interpretations (see the lack of clarity of art. 25(2) DSA) or incorporate

[36] Ortolani (2023).

[37] Citino (2025).

[38] Husovec (2024).

[39] Reyna (2024).

vague concepts (e.g. systemic risk in art. 35 DSA),[40] are likely to contribute to a complex interplay between (national and European) courts and DSC interventions.

3 Strength in… Fragmentation? The System of Enforcement of the Digital Acquis

The overview of the enforcement agencies prompts some reflections. This section highlights, in particular, the issues relating to: (i) the coordination of their tasks and powers, including the sustainability—especially at systemic level—of the enforcement choices made by the EU legislator; and (ii) the conceptual implications of this enforcement architecture, with regard in particular to the instrumentalization of the protection of EU citizens and consumers for the growth of the internal market.

3.1 Multiplication, Fragmentation, Expansion

The current regulatory choices of the EU legislator translated into a multiplication of enforcement tasks at both Member State and EU level. Within each sector, in most cases Member States can choose between creating a new agency, or assigning the enforcement powers to an existing entity. The first option leads to fragmentation and the need to coordinate interventions among multiple administrative entities within the sector, if more than one authority is appointed (horizontally and vertically, i.e. between national and EU authorities). It also leads to fragmentation and the need to coordinate at cross-sector level. This is because while each agency enforces one (or a few) regulation/directive, the same technology, product, service or phenomenon is regulated by several EU tools at the same time. Many digital technologies are interdependent, as they develop in a symbiotic or complementary relationship with other digital technologies: think of online platforms, data brokers, and advertising intermediaries, and how they use AI for profiling and for recommender systems, to deliver content and ads. Or how app developers depend from the cloud-based web services and APIs of producers of smartphones and smart appliances. These technological and contractual relationships result in the applications of multiple laws and, consequently, the involvement of multiple agencies. In this case, a lot relies on the coordination and cooperation among the relevant agencies (at Member State and EU level).

Within each sector, the analysed regulations and directives oblige the respective agencies to cooperate among each other, or with the EU authorities, for cross-border operations: for example, the DSA obliges Digital Service Coordinators and

[40] Leerssen et al. (2025).

the other DSA-appointed authorities to cooperate with each other, for the cross-border enforcement of the DSA, and to cooperate with the EU Commission for investigations.

Among the analysed legislative tools, not one contains provisions concerning the cross-*sectoral* cooperation and coordination, even within a single Member State. For example, there are no provisions regulating cooperation among consumer authorities, Digital Service Coordinators and Data Protection Authorities. The only relevant indications are that each authority should act independently (or, in the case of the UCPD, impartially), and that each Regulation or Directive is without prejudice of other EU and national laws, in particular those concerning consumer protection and personal data protection.[41]

The most useful—and recent—indication concerning the cross-sectorial collaboration and cooperation of different enforcement agencies comes from the Court of Justice of the European Union (CJEU), in its 2023 *Meta v Bundeskartellamt* decision.[42] The CJEU recalled the aforementioned *principle of sincere cooperation*, affirming that, "[u]nder that principle, in accordance with settled case-law, in areas covered by EU law, Member States, including their administrative authorities, must assist each other, in full mutual respect, in carrying out tasks which flow from the Treaties, take any appropriate measure to ensure fulfilment of the obligations arising from, inter alia, the acts of the institutions of the European Union and refrain from any measure which could jeopardise the attainment of the European Union's objectives."[43] The case, however, was not about collaboration between multiple authorities belonging to different sectors: the German competition authority was, in fact, issuing a decision based on the GDPR, which would normally be enforced by a DPA. Consequently, the CJEU explained that, in such a case, a national competition authority could assess compliance with the GDPR, if that was necessary for the exercise of their own powers. The Court first clarified that a national competition authority should "consult and cooperate sincerely with the national supervisory authorities concerned or with the lead supervisory authority, all of which are then bound, in that context, to observe their respective powers and competences, in such a way as to ensure that the obligations arising from the GDPR and the objectives of that regulation are complied with while their effectiveness is safeguarded."[44] Additionally, to avoid diverging decisions, the competition authority should ascertain whether the GDPR-infringing conduct (that is relevant for competition law) or a similar one has been investigated and decided upon by the data protection authority, in which case the decision of the competition authority should align with the data protection authority's decision, but the first can freely take all the necessary decisions concerning competition-related aspects. If the conduct is still under investigation by the data protection authority, or the competition authority has doubts concerning

[41] E.g. DSA, recital 10 and AIA, recitals 95, 109, and 122 among others.

[42] CJEU (Grand Chamber), case C-252/21, *Meta Platforms Inc and Others v Bundeskartellamt*, 4 July 2023, para. 53–59.

[43] CJEU, case C-252/21, para. 53.

[44] CJEU, case C-252/21, para. 54.

the GDPR infringement, "the national competition authority must consult and seek their [i.e. data protection authority's] cooperation in order to dispel its doubts or to determine whether it must wait for the supervisory authority concerned to take a decision before starting its own assessment."[45] Conversely, the principle of sincere cooperation also binds the data protection authority to reply to the requests of the competition authority within a reasonable time, providing the necessary information in its possession, or informing them of any actions concerning the coordination among data protection authorities. If the data protection authority has no objection or does not reply within a reasonable time, the competition authority can proceed with their own investigation.

The *Meta v Bundeskartellamt* decision, as explained, concerns a GDPR-infringing conduct that was potentially relevant for competition matters too. The indications given by the CJEU, therefore, cannot apply as-is to cases of a conduct infringing at the same time multiple EU laws. In the first case, in fact, one authority (competition) was asking whether it was allowed to take a decision on a matter under the domain of a different authority (data protection). The analysis herein concerns cases in which each authority is acting within their purview, but need to collaborate and coordinate their interventions. However, the CJEU's explanation points in the direction of applying the principle in a functional way, to ensure the achievement of the Union's goals. Therefore, it is safe to assume that the enforcement agencies should: (i) inquire whether a procedure is already ongoing with another agency, asking—and offering within a reasonable time—information, knowledge, and advice; and (ii) strive to ensure harmonised outcomes (where possible, considering that each authority should act independently and pursues a different scope) and the respect of the *ne bis in idem*. An example in these regards is offered by the Dutch national Digital Regulation Cooperation Platform (SDT), created by the consumer (and DSA), data protection, financial markets, and media authorities. Through the SDT, the four authorities wish to carry out studies on the risks and opportunities of the 'digital society' keeping in mind "various public interests", sharing knowledge and expertise, and collectively "ensure efficient and effective enforcement of compliance with rules and regulations (Dutch and European)."[46] To the best knowledge of the author, at the time of writing the SDT has not yet been used to coordinate the enforcement of EU or national laws, but its establishment remains a promising experiment. Besides the Dutch SDT, the possibilities and constraints of the collaboration among different EU agencies concerning the digital society remain vastly unexplored, and should be the object of in-depth (empirical and comparative) research, to make sure that the enforcement of the digital *acquis* maintains systemic coherence, and fosters harmonization within the EU, while respecting the prerogatives of Member States.

In light of the above, one would be tempted to assume that a better solution would be to concentrate the tasks and powers of enforcement of multiple EU laws within one or fewer authorities, similarly to what happens in the USA with the Federal

[45] CJEU, case C-252/21, para. 57.

[46] Netherlands Authority for Consumers and Markets (ACM), available via https://www.acm.nl/en/about-acm/cooperation/national-cooperation/digital-regulation-cooperation-platform-sdt.

Trade Commission. This is an option chosen by many Member States, especially after many new EU laws have been approved in the last few years. To cite again the Netherlands, the existing consumer authority was appointed Digital Services Coordinator, and the Data Protection Authority will be designated the MSA in charge of the enforcement of the core chapters of the AIA. The AIA itself leverages the existing Market Surveillance Authorities, as well as the existing national Fundamental Rights authorities. This solution poses another problem: the expansion of the tasks, duties, and powers of existing agencies risks affecting their effectiveness and efficiency. Budget and personnel constraints already affect the work of the existing, well-established authorities, as pointed out with regards to MSAs. Even with an increase in budget, adding new tasks stretches the available resources, creating more pressure and affecting the regulatory operations of the agency. This might result in having to choose between issuing a timely decision and managing additional or more complex cases, or between working with enterprises and addressing the needs of citizens.[47]

Additionally, even if one or few agencies are tasked with enforcing multiple laws, the need for coordination does not disappear, but simply moves from inter-agency to intra-agency level. Each law, in fact, has a different scope and different objectives, that might even clash with each other: this means that different departments or operational units within the same agency would still need to collaborate and cooperate. Finally, choosing to concentrate more enforcement tasks into one or few agencies will result in these agencies expanding their regulatory power and their role at national—and potentially European—level. The agencification of enforcement is not a new issue, but it is something that should be appraised with regard to the digital *acquis*, keeping in mind the risk of tensions between institutional autonomy of the enforcement agencies, national administrative rules and traditions, and the institutional design of the EU.

3.2 The Original Sin: The Instrumentalization of Citizens' Rights

Regardless of how the enforcement tasks and powers are allocated, the authorities enforcing the digital *acquis* represent one of the channels through which the normative and legislative power moves from Member States to the EU.[48] They are the administrative *longa manus* of the EU regulator within the Member States, at the same time being staffed and run by national experts: they are the point of contact between different approaches to societal values and the relationship between citizens and power (enterprises, governments, the EU). And the approaches and values can be radically different. Micklitz has pointed out the significant change that consumer protection undergoes when it moved from the purview of the Member States to

[47] Maggetti et al. (2025).

[48] Szegedi (2014).

being harmonized by the EU to foster the internal market. The consumer went from a weaker party in a relationship, to be protected as part of the social welfare state, to an active participant to the markets, the rational agent aiming at maximizing benefits.[49] This process, which he calls marketization, leads to the legal conceptualization of consumers becoming more fragmented, to match different markets and their specifics, going hand in hand with the attribution of economic and market value to more and more daily activities, exacerbated by digitalization. This transformation also brings a change in the development and application of the law: "from law-making via the legislator to rulemaking via regulatory agencies, from national parliaments to European executive powers (from the legislator to the supranational executive), from binding legislation to co-regulation and self-regulation, from regulation to standardisation, from enforcement via courts to enforcement via regulatory agencies, from collective action to ADRs/ODRs, from market efficiency to market rationalities".[50]

This change is the result of consumer rights being instrumentalized by the EU regulator to foster the growth of the internal market. It is no coincidence that article 1 of the UCPD affirms that the purpose of the Directive is "to contribute to the proper functioning of the internal market *and* achieve a high level of consumer protection" (emphasis added). This approach prioritizes transactional interests, turning consumers into means to a(n economic) end. A similar picture is also painted by Davies, who notices how the CJEU case law on free movement of goods and services separates the economic dimension of national and EU policies from the social one. This separation creates the image of consumers as half human beings: "As consumer she buys, and is interested to get the best deal, and to have her expectations protected, and the law recognises this. But the same person who shops is also the citizen who collectively enacts or maintains laws which limit economic freedom in the name of social concerns, and is also the human being whose life is shaped by a certain quality of public economic space. Her relationship to economic activity and economic law is multi-facetted, and many things are at stake for her in a decision to regulate or deregulate. These non-transactional matters, however, are ignored in the case law."[51] Consumer law has already had negative distributional effects in society in general, and on vulnerable subjects in particular, impacting negatively on issues such as social cohesion and social justice.[52] A possible counter-action to this fragmentation is identified by Micklitz in the return to the idea that consumer rights should be protected from a fundamental rights/constitutional perspective, a tendency that he already sees in progress to reintroduce in the equation the societal nature of consumers.

This *excursus* into the conceptual challenges of consumer protection was necessary because it offers us a cautionary tale: the same process of fragmentation and instrumentalization is occurring to the rights of individuals—as consumers, data subjects, citizens, human beings—with respect to online intermediaries and platforms, data brokers, and providers and deployers of AI. The GPSR, GDPR, AIA,

[49] Micklitz (2016, 29).

[50] Micklitz (2016, 33–34).

[51] Davies (2016, 326).

[52] Riefa and Saintier (2020).

and DSA are not immune from the instrumentalization of the protection of individuals. With regard to data protection, Gellert and Gutwirth pointed out that the right to the protection of personal data in the EU is not designed to carve out a substantial freedom (like privacy and other fundamental rights), but acknowledges by default that data processing occurs, allowing and facilitating it to the extent that it respects some procedural rules.[53] Bringing this reasoning a step forward, and based also on the letter of article 1 GDPR, which puts on the same level the protection of natural persons and free movement of personal data, it can be argued that the EU legislator has created a strong procedural architecture, managed by national DPAs and the EDPB, to make sure privacy rights do not prevent enterprises from processing personal data, rendering data protection a tool for the internal data market.[54]

The instrumentalization of fundamental rights is particularly strong in the AIA. It follows in the footsteps of the GPSR and the entire product-safety legislation in the EU, which was created to reassure Member States on the safety level of the products in the market, to prevent them from taking measures that would create obstacles to the free movement of goods. The AIA, however, goes even further, as it claims to promote the developments of fundamental-rights friendly AI, so that the EU citizens will trust AI and this will stimulate innovation in the internal market (see the letter of article 1 AIA). The tendency to constitutionalization of the interests of consumers to increase their protection, as noted by Micklitz with regard to consumer law, is completely turned upside down in the AIA: here the fundamental rights become means to foster the adoption of AI. This is reflected in the rest of the AIA, which focuses on self-assessment for compliance, applies *ex post* the prohibitions of unacceptable-risk AI systems, and does not provide any right to European citizens who enter into contact with AI systems, offering only public enforcement (filing a complaint with a MSA), in the absence of any provision granting damaged individuals the right to redress.

Within this enforcement landscape, the redress is also instrumentalized. The mix of public and private enforcement has generated a tension between decentralized judicial review in private enforcement and centralized towards EU in public one. The most developed tool offered by all the analysed Regulations and Directives remains the right to lodge a complaint with the relevant enforcement agency. This right, however, serves the purpose of ensuring that the law is applied, and facilitating the authorities in pursuing their enforcement tasks. The outcome of that complaint is usually a fine, not compensation. The protection of individual (or group) rights is left to their own initiative, resources, and strength, as individuals only maintain the right to ask national courts for redress (except in the product safety and AIA regimes). The addition of tools for redress appears almost like an afterthought, with the use of general and vague formulations (such as the reference to *any* damage in the DSA) and a focus on establishing the substantive rule (right to redress), without additional specifications. Leaving procedural rules concerning these actions for damages to the

[53] Gellert and Gutwirth (2013, 530).

[54] This tendency is confirmed by the ambitious European Strategy for Data. The two Regulations implementing it, the Data Act and the Digital Governance Act, aim at making data circulate more and creating the European Data Spaces, to foster innovation.

purview of Member States makes the legislative process less complicated, but has, unsurprisingly, resulted in private enforcement being used very little in some sectors, such as consumer protection (and something similar might happen to the DSA).[55] The hope is that now collective and representative actions will make use of the existing provisions of redress, once again turning the enforcement of individual and group rights into an occasion to strengthen the political reach of the digital *acquis*, while the EU institutions wrestle with technology corporations. This enforcement architecture does not promote effective private enforcement of rights, leaving individuals to their own means, and vulnerable subjects potentially even less protected than other categories.

4 Conclusions: The Enforcement of the Digital Acquis & Vulnerability

All the analysed regulations and directives take vulnerability and vulnerable subjects into consideration as a fact, an existing phenomenon acknowledged in the recitals. Vulnerability is also included in various ways in their provisions. Usually, however, vulnerability seems to get lost somewhere between the recitals and the enforcement provisions. This is because vulnerability generally has the role of a benchmark or an attribute that either triggers the application of some provisions, or determines how certain provisions apply. In the GPSR, in assessing whether a product is safe, economic operators should take into consideration whether the product is likely or intended to be used by vulnerable consumers—such as children, older persons and persons with disabilities (art. 6 GPSR). If the product is not safe for a vulnerable category, its sale might be restricted or prohibited, or adequate labeling should be added, to mitigate risks. In the UCPD, the unfairness of a commercial practice must be assessed based on the relevant target, which can be either the average consumer, or those consumers who are particularly vulnerable due to mental or physical infirmity, age, or credulity (art. 5 UCPD). In the GDPR, certain attributes (being underage) or certain characteristics connected to the data (special categories of data) trigger the application of some additional protections (arts. 8 to 10 GDPR), while in the AIA the exploitation of the vulnerabilities of an individual can trigger the application of the prohibition under art. 5(1)(b) if it generates or is likely to generate a significant harm. The DSA also moves from the special categories of data indicated by the GDPR, to prohibit profiling for advertising purposes that would exploit vulnerabilities of the users (DSA, recital 69 and art. 26(3)).

All these provisions show the prevalence of an *ex ante* approach to the protection of vulnerability. This follows the logic that the enterprises will self-assess the risks for the consumers, data subjects, citizens, and will self-assess what their technologies, products and services entail for the vulnerable segments of society. In this scenario, the average and rational user or consumer remains the best equipped to make informed

[55] Wilman (2016, 909).

choices and protect their interests. The citizen and human aspects remain once again excluded, as noted by Davies with regard to consumer law. In the mix of public and private enforcement, there is a notable absence of references to vulnerability. Once a breach or damage has occurred, the distinction between vulnerable and non-vulnerable situations does not matter anymore for the EU legislator, and the protection of the interests of vulnerable subjects is left to the national administrative and judicial rules. The instrumentalization of the enforcement of the digital *acquis* to favor the development of the internal market, therefore, goes hand in hand with vulnerability being incorporated in those Regulations and Directives more as an exception, than as a core issue of the digital landscape.

Finally, the issues concerning the fragmentation and cross-sector cooperation among different agencies (or different departments of an agency) also affect the protection of vulnerable subjects. Primarily, the uncertainty as to how these entities are supposed to work together, risks to affect the effectiveness of the respective EU laws, which affects all individuals, but obviously puts vulnerable subjects more at risk. Additionally, the agencies are supposed to cooperate, but the respective regulations/directives give vulnerability different boundaries and scopes (some, like the UCPD and GPSR, mention some specific characteristics, while others, like the AIA, have a broader definition) and might consider vulnerability or vulnerable characteristics for different purposes (e.g. as a benchmark or to trigger certain provisions). In the intricate mosaic of the enforcement of the digital *acquis*, therefore, enforcement agencies must develop a system to cooperate with regard to the protection specifically of vulnerable subjects across sectors, keeping in mind that behind users, consumers, and data subjects there are always citizens, individuals and communities.

Annex I: Table Summarizing the Nature, Aims, Tasks and Powers of the Enforcement Agencies

Law	(Consolidated) UCPD	GPSR	GDPR	DSA	AIA	
Enforcement agency	Consumer Authority (or Court)	Market Surveillance Authority established by Reg 2019/1020	Data Protection Authority	Competent authority/ies + Coordinator + EU Commission (for VLOPs and VLSEs)	Market Surveillance Authority (see table 2 under GPSR)	Authorities protecting Fundamental Rights
Features	National—Administrative—Impartial (art. 11)	National—Independent & impartial (art. 11 Reg 2019/1020)	National—Independent (art. 51–52)	National—independent (art. 50)	//	National—depending on statute
Aim	Tool for MS to ensure adequate and effective means to combat unfair commercial practices + Enforce UCPD	Market surveillance (art. 3(3) Reg 2019/1020)	Protect fundamental rights and freedoms in relation to processing + Facilitate free flow of personal data (art. 51)	Supervise providers of intermediary services + Enforce DSA (art. 49)	//	Oversee compliance with HR obligations in EU Charter and international conventions (depending on specific statute)
Tasks	Monitor & enforce, handle complaints, investigate, advise, collaborate	Monitor that products in internal market comply with UHL + Take corrective actions: risk-based checks, establish procedures to deal with complaints and verify corrective actions, MS strategy	Monitor & enforce, handle complaints, investigate, advise, collaborate (art. 57)	Monitor & enforce, investigate, handle complaints, collaborate	//	Supervise or enforce the respect of obligations under Union law protecting fundamental rights (including non-discrimination) (depending on specific statute)

(continued)

(continued)

Law	(Consolidated) UCPD	GPSR	GDPR	DSA	AIA	
Powers	art. 11: Prohibit UCP or order cessation of UCP (or initiate proceeding to prohibit/order cessation), urgent/interim measures, require publication of decisions/ corrective statements, monitor and enforce their own decisions, give reasons for their decisions; art. 12: require documents, information and evidence from traders (and declare them inaccurate or insufficient if necessary); art. 13: issue penalties	Enforce directly or via judicial authorities; carry out checks (on documents or physical); request documents & information, inspect, access premises/source codes/testing facilities, (covertly) investigate, order, fine, remove product from market, take mitigating measures, handle complaints, collaborate with other authorities, organize MSA peer reviews (art. 11, 12, 14, 16 Reg 2019/1020)	Investigative (access, audit, review, order) & corrective (warnings, reprimands, compliance orders, ban/limit, fine) (art. 58)	Investigative (request info, inspect premises, examine, seize, obtain copies, ask individuals for explanations) & enforcement (order cessation of infringement, impose remedies, fine, periodic penalty, interim measures, order corrective plan, ask courts for temporary measures, access restriction) (art. 51)	//	Request to access AIA mandated documents from AI providers or MSA, request testing of AI, advise MSA & cooperate, on top of powers already established by existing national statutes (if any) (art. 77)
Remedies	Lodge a complaint with authority (art. 11); Right to obtain compensation (national courts) (art. 11a)	Lodge a complaint with authority (art. 33 GPSR); Repair, Replace, Refund (art. 37 GPSR)	Lodge a complaint with authority (art. 77); Right to obtain compensation (national courts) (art. 82)	Lodge a complaint with authority (art. 53); Right to obtain compensation (national courts) (art. 54)	Lodge a complaint with authority (art. 85)	

References

Buri I, van Hoboken J (2022) The DSA supervision and enforcement architecture. https://dsa-observatory.eu/2022/06/24/the-dsa-supervision-and-enforcement-architecture
Citino YM (2025) Public delegation in the DSA's regulatory model. EUI, Working Paper 2025/02. https://hdl.handle.net/1814/77845
Davies G (2016) Consumer, citizen and the human being. In: Leczykiewicz D, Weatherill S (eds) The images of the consumer in EU Law. Hart, Oxford, pp 326–336
De Conca S, Infantino M (2024) A difficult puzzle: the duty of care in Member States' tort law and the GDPR. Datenschutz und Datensicherheit 48(9):566–571
Drechsler LC, Vogiatzoglou P (2024) Article 74. Market surveillance and control of AI systems in the Union market. In: Necati P, Forgó N, Valcke P (eds) The EU artificial intelligence (AI) act: a commentary. Wolters Kluwer, The Hague, pp 1062–1080
European Commission (2016) Commission Notice: the 'Blue Guide' on the implementation of EU product rules 2016 (2016/C 272/01)
European Commission (2021) Commission Staff Working Document Impact Assessment accompanying the document Proposal for a Regulation of the European Parliament and of the Council on general product safety, amending Regulation (EU) No 1025/2012 of the European Parliament and of the Council, and repealing Council Directive 87/357/EEC and Directive 2001/95/ EC of the European Parliament and of the Council. SWD(2021)169 final
European Commission (2024) Commission Staff Working Document Fitness Check of EU consumer law on digital fairness{SEC(2024) 245 final} - {SWD(2024) 231 final}
European Parliament, Policy Department for Economic, Scientific and Quality of Life Policies Directorate-General for Internal Policies (2023) Market surveillance for effective consumer protection in the EU. The role of market surveillance authorities and their cross-border cooperation. PE 754.190
Gellert R, Gutwirth S (2013) The legal construction of privacy and data protection. Comput Law Secur Rev 29(5):522–530
Georgieva L, Schmidl M (2020) Article 58. Powers. In: Kuner C et al (eds) The EU general data protection regulation (GDPR): a commentary. Oxford University Press, New York, pp 939–948
Hajnal Z (2020) Current challenges of European market surveillance regarding products sold online. Public Goods and Governance 5(1):22–29
Havu KA (2019) Damages liability for non-material harm in EU case law. Eur Law Rev 44(4):492–514
Hijmans H (2020a) Article 51. Supervisory authority. In: Kuner C et al (eds) The EU general data protection regulation (GDPR): a commentary. Oxford University Press, New York, pp 863–872
Hijmans H (2020b) Article 57. Tasks. In: Kuner C et al (eds) The EU general data protection regulation (GDPR): a commentary, online. Oxford University Press, New York, pp 927–938
Husovec M (2024) Principles of the digital services act. Oxford University Press, Oxford
Jordana J, Rozas-Bugueño J, Triviño-Salazar JC (2025) Consumer authorities in Europe: policing markets or empowering consumers? Governance 38:e70033
Leerssen P et al (2025) Pathways to private enforcement of the digital services act (DSA). https://dsa-observatory.eu/wp-content/uploads/2025/06/DSA-Private-Enforcement-final-draft.pdf
Maggetti M et al (2025) Empowered but challenged: the impact of task expansion on data protection authorities. Policy Internet 17:e70001
Martin A (2008) Digital literacy and the "digital society." Digit Lit Concepts Policies Pract 30(151):1029–1055
Micklitz HW (2016) The consumer: marketised, fragmentised, constitutionalized. In: Leczykiewicz D, Weatherill S (eds) The images of the consumer in EU law. Hart, Oxford, pp 21–41
Ortolani P (2023) If you build it, they will come. The DSA "procedure before substance" approach. In: van Hoboken J, Buri I (eds) Putting the DSA into practice. Enforcement, access to justice and global implications. Verfassungsbooks, Berlin, pp 151–163

Pírková E (2021) The EU digital services act won't work without strong enforcement. https://www.accessnow.org/eu-dsa-enforcement/

Reyna A (2024) DMA and DSA effective enforcement—key to success. J Antitrust Enforcement 12(2):320–324

Riefa C, Saintier S (2020) In search of (access to) justice for vulnerable consumers. In: Saintier S, Riefa C (eds) Vulnerable consumers and the law consumer protection and access to justice. Routledge, London, pp 1–16

Szegedi (2014) EU-level market surveillance and regulation by EU agencies in light of the reshaped meroni doctrine. Eur Netw Law Reg Quart 2(4):298–304

Van Boom W, Loos M (2008) Effective enforcement of consumer law in Europe: synchronizing private, public, and collective mechanisms. In: Van Boom W, Loos M (eds) Collective enforcement of consumer law: securing compliance in Europe through private group action and public authority intervention. Europa Law Publishing, Groningen, pp 231–254

Van Cleynenbreugel P, Mattioli P (2023) Digital services coordinators and other competent authorities in the digital services act: streamlined enforcement coordination lost? Eur Law Blog. https://doi.org/10.21428/9885764c.f18f26b8

Van Eecke P, Šimkus A (2020) Article 63. Consistency mechanism. In: Kuner C et al (eds) The EU General Data Protection Regulation (GDPR): a commentary. Oxford University Press, New York, pp 995–1004

Wilman F (2016) The end of the absence? The growing body of EU legislation on private enforcement and the main remedies it provides for. Common Mark Law Rev 53(4):887–935

Zerdick T (2020) Article 52. Independence. In: Kuner C et al (eds) The EU General Data Protection Regulation (GDPR): a commentary. Oxford University Press, New York, pp 873–883

Żywicka A, Kokocińska K (2023) The structure of network administration on the example of the organization market surveillance regarding product safety in the European Union. Teka Komisji Prawniczej PAN Oddział W Lublinie 16(2):427–441

Proportionality Analysis in 'Digital' Cases

Siniša Rodin

Abstract This paper examines the application of proportionality analysis in case law of the Court of Justice of the European Union (CJEU) with a reference to 'digital' cases. The analysis will start from the concept of proportionality in a broad sense and differentiates it into proportionality as a principle guiding exercise of the European Union (EU) competences as distinct from proportionality as a protection from encroachments of public power on individual and Member State rights. Second, the paper will address the problem of demarcation of concepts 'strictly necessary' and 'necessary' in black letter EU law and case law of the CJEU. In that regard, it will be suggested that both black letter and pretorian EU law use concepts of 'strictly necessary' and 'necessary' incoherently. Following an overview of situations in which these concepts are employed, the paper invites to discussion how to differentiate and standardize their use in practice.

Keywords Proportionality test · Digital law · EU law · Court of Justice of the European Union

1 Introduction

Talking about proportionality analysis in 'digital' cases under European Union (EU) law requires two remarks at the outset. First, the proportionality test inscribes into a wider concept of principle of proportionality and the paper focuses on the test as a practical tool. Second, by 'digital' cases I understand a broad range of cases that have to do with human presence in and interaction with digital world, such as those addressing protection of personal data under EU primary and secondary law, including the Charter of Rights of the EU, particularly, Articles 7 and 8 thereof. While proportionality analysis is deeply rooted in fabric of EU legal order as a legal

Judge, CJEU, opinions expressed in this chapter are author's personal opinions.

S. Rodin (✉)
Court of Justice of the European Union, Luxembourg, Luxembourg
e-mail: sinisa.rodin@curia.europa.eu

C. Crea and M. Infantino (eds.), *Remedies to Digital Vulnerability in European Private Law*, https://doi.org/10.1007/978-3-032-19720-7_9

manifestation of liberal democratic principle, legal regulation of digital media created a new dimension where different intensity of restrictions is balanced against different intensities of justifications.

Proportionality is often referred to as a principle of EU law. At the same time, it can be understood as an analytical tool that has become widespread in our jurisprudence. Above all, it is a fundamental constitutional choice of the founding fathers of the European Union according to which objectives of public power, national and European, are limited by the consent of EU citizens and, more specifically, by their individual rights. This is a conscious value choice that determines the EU as a supranational framework within which constitutional democracy, government limited by law, in the Member States and European Union as a whole, is not only possible but, indeed, required by values mentioned in Art. 2 of the Treaty on European Union (TEU).

It is not easy to define what the legal concept of proportionality is. While the idea of balancing is present in many liberal legal systems, the methodology of its application and its terminology vary. In law of England and Wales, there is a concept of a *rule of reason*. The same expression is used in the Sect. 1 of the U.S. Sherman Act which requires balancing of competitive and anti-competitive effects. In German law the broader concept of *Verhältnismäßigkeit* incorporates the idea of balancing (*Abwägung*) and has developed into a sophisticated doctrinal test that became pervasive in German law.[1] Under EU law, the proportionality analysis has evolved from early free movement law, competition law under Art. 101(3) of the Treaty on the Functioning of the European Union (TFEU), and secondary EU law, such as the Equal Treatment Directive 2000/78/EC,[2] and the Services Directive 2006/123/EC.[3]

Under EU law, the classic model of proportionality test would examine whether a legislator pursued a legitimate regulatory aim by appropriate and necessary means, i.e., by means that can achieve the aim of the regulation at all and are the least restrictive for a right at stake. A concise definition can be found in Article 7 of the Directive (EU) 2018/958, which provides that national measures must be "suitable for securing the attainment of the objective pursued and do not go beyond what is necessary to attain that objective".[4] This is comparable to the U.S. legal concept of

---

[1] For a lucid analysis of German doctrine see Bomhoff (2023, 28–54).

[2] Council Directive 2000/78/EC of 27 November 2000 establishing a general framework for equal treatment in employment and occupation, Art. 2(2)(b): "indirect discrimination shall be taken to occur where an apparently neutral provision, criterion or practice would put persons having a particular religion or belief, a particular disability, a particular age, or a particular sexual orientation at a particular disadvantage compared with other persons unless: (i) that provision, criterion or practice is objectively justified by a legitimate aim and the means of achieving that aim are appropriate and necessary".

[3] Directive 2006/123/EC of the European Parliament and of the Council of 12 December 2006 on services in the internal market, Article 10(2): "The criteria referred to in paragraph 1 shall be: (a) non-discriminatory; (b) *justified* by an overriding reason relating to the public interest; (c) *proportionate to that public interest objective*" (emphasis added).

[4] Directive (EU) 2018/958 of the European Parliament and of the Council of 28 June 2018 on a proportionality test before adoption of new regulation of professions.

'means-ends scrutiny', which is described as "an analytical process involving examination of the purposes (ends) which conduct is designed to serve and the methods (means) chosen to further those purposes. When government action is subject to a constitutional limit, courts frequently evaluate the justification for that action. If a sufficient justification exists, the action may be permitted despite the applicability of the limit. If the courts find the justification insufficient, they hold that the action violates the limit and is unconstitutional. Means-end scrutiny is a systematic method for evaluating the sufficiency of the government's justification for its conduct".[5]

Nevertheless, for the purpose of the present analysis I contend that, proportionality in its broader sense, regardless of a specific legal system, involves balancing of rights against some legally articulated public interest. It typically appears in form of the analytical syntax 'right-restriction-justification'.

In the EU legal framework, it can also mean balancing of individual rights against exercise of regulatory powers of the Member States. This is not always clearly visible because of method and language of the Court of Justice of the European Union (CJEU). Namely, when the CJEU says, in a preliminary reference procedure, that certain rule of EU law is opposed or not opposed to a legal rule or practice in a Member State, the rule of EU law in question often guarantees some individual right based in EU law. This is, after all, what makes a case under consideration admissible for, without a controversy, on national level, concerning a right based in EU law, the reference would have been hypothetical.

I will use the expression 'proportionality' in a wide sense, as to include all forms of balancing that the CJEU applies in its work, including the 'least restrictive alternative test', the 'means-ends scrutiny', 'balancing *stricto* sensu (in German, *Abwägung*), as well as the fully developed analytical sequence described below.

When it comes to practical application of balancing in EU law, complexity and variety of situations and substantive areas of law open a few questions that will be explored in the next sections. More in particular, Sect. 2 will explore what the legal concept of proportionality is, and ask whether we can use the term 'proportionality' for all instances of balancing. Section 3 will scrutinize the different approaches to balancing in our case law, depending on context or substance under review, for example in the areas of free movement, of fundamental rights and of what I called generically 'digital' cases. Section 4 will verify whether proportionality review is always of the same intensity, i.e. whether certain rights or exercise of certain competences are subject to a stricter judicial scrutiny than other. Section 5 will check whether the vocabulary which designates elements of proportionality analysis is coherent and unambiguous. Section 6 will evaluate whether making a difference between 'necessary' and 'strictly necessary' to formalize various levels of judicial scrutiny would be useful—and if so, how?

---

[5] Galloway (1988, 449).

2 What is Proportionality?

Proportionality, in a most general sense, means balancing of rights that goes beyond a simple test that the Court sometimes explicitly operates by applying different steps of analysis. It is a general principle of constitutionalism but also an analytical tool of judicial review. In that sense it has a practical significance. Result of proportionality analysis has consequences for scope and substance of individual rights under EU and Member States' law.

Among many uses of proportionality analysis in EU law one can distinguish Article 5(4) TEU proportionality which deals with exercise of EU competences from proportionality as a test of legality of regulatory action, whether of Member States or EU institutions.

Under Art. 5(1) TEU, competences of the EU are "governed by the principle of conferral" while their exercise is subject to principles of subsidiarity (Art. 5(3)) and proportionality (Art. 5(4)). According to the latter, "[u]nder the principle of proportionality, the content and form of Union action shall not exceed what is necessary to achieve the objectives of the Treaties". This is further elaborated in Protocol No. 2 to the TEU.[6]

Proportionality also applies as a test of legality of Member State action when it falls within scope of EU law. As AG Sharpston has put it in Case C-427/06 *Bartsch*, "[f]or that to be the case, the provision of national law at issue must in general fall into one of three categories. It must implement EC law (irrespective of the degree of the discretion the member state enjoys and whether the national measure goes beyond what is strictly necessary for implementation). It must invoke some permitted derogation under EC law. Or it must otherwise fall within the scope of Community law because some specific substantive rule of EC law is applicable to the situation."[7]

Proportionality is also a standard analytical tool for assessment of legality of acts of EU institutions, although, the standard of judicial review is 'manifestly disproportionate'. I will come back to this topic later.

The structure of proportionality analysis is not fully standardized in practice of the CJEU.[8] Most generally and theoretically, once a restriction of an individual/fundamental right is established, or when either EU institutions or Member States exercise their competence, proportionality analysis applies. A fully developed proportionality test includes several analytical steps. All the mentioned steps are not necessarily present in practice of the CJEU and are not always present in the above-mentioned sequence:

a. legitimate aim test, i.e., a justification of regulatory objectives that a measure seeks to achieve;

[6] Consolidated version of the Treaty on the Functioning of the European Union, Protocol (No 2) on the application of the principles of subsidiarity and proportionality.

[7] CJEU, case C-427/06, *Bartsch v Bosch und Siemens Hausgeräte (BSH) Altersfürsorge GmbH*, ECLI:EU:C:2008:297, para. 69.

[8] Also, it varies from one jurisdiction to another, such as the European Court of Human Rights or the German Federal Constitutional Court.

b. appropriateness test, under which the regulatory measure in question must be able to achieve the proclaimed regulatory objective at all;
c. least restrictive alternative test, which requires that there is no less restrictive measure that could achieve the same objective of public interest;
d. balancing test, where benefits of the measure in question must be balanced against externalities that it creates for others[9];
e. sometimes, a coherence test is applied where the Court must be satisfied that the measure in question is applied "if they genuinely reflect a concern to attain that objective "in a consistent and systematic manner".[10]

The order in which I have presented elements of proportionality analysis is a theoretical model, and its application can vary in practice. In any case, the measure that has no legitimate aim is not justified and fails the test. Legitimate measures that cannot achieve the aim fail on the second. Legitimate and appropriate measures that are more restrictive than necessary, fail the third step. Only then the analysis reaches the balancing stage. Almost needless to say, all this analysis is not necessary if a restrictive measure restricts the very essence of a right. This is the explanation why the full proportionality analysis is not always visible in our case law.

3 Is Structure of Proportionality Analysis Context-Sensitive? Free Movement, Equal Treatment and Protection of Personal Data

In area of free movement distinctly applicable national restrictions of market freedoms can be justified only if a Member State is able to demonstrate some important public interest, such as public policy, public security or public health. Indistinctly applicable measures can be justified by a broader range of justifications. For example, in *Cinetheque*, which was a typical case, decided on July 11, 1985, the Court said that a prohibition of simultaneous release of cinematographic work in cinemas and on video cassettes can be justified if it is equally applicable to domestic and imported works, and if it does not exceed what is necessary for ensuring that the exploitation in cinemas retains priority over other means of distribution.[11] In other words, a right to

[9] This is another expression of the liberal principle according to which everyone should have liberty to define what it means to lead a good life, as long as it does not harm the others.

[10] CJEU, joined cases C-570/07 and C-571/07, *José Manuel Blanco Pérez and María del Pilar Chao Gómez v Consejería de Salud y Servicios Sanitarios and Principado de Asturias*, ECLI:EU:C:2010:300, para. 94. Coherence test is a combination of other criteria. It involves a criterion of equality, because in absence of consistent and systematic manner legal subjects are not treated equally. It also involves appropriateness element, since inconsistent and non-systematic measures are not appropriate for attaining a regulatory objective.

[11] CJEU, joined cases 60 and 61/84, *Cinéthèque SA and others v Fédération nationale des cinémas français*, ECLI:EU:C:1985:329, para. 24.

free movement was restricted by an indistinctly applicable[12] measure (prohibition of simultaneous release) and justified by public interest of stimulating cinematographic production.

Essentially the same syntax of analysis is maintained in area of equal treatment Directive 2000/78.[13] For example, in Case C-157/15 *Achbita.*[14] In Para. 34 of the judgment the Court allowed a possibility that the referring court might conclude that an apparently neutral obligation may, in effect, put persons adhering to a particular religion (right/freedom of religion) or belief to a particular disadvantage (restriction). This could, however, be justified "by a legitimate aim (justification) and if the means of achieving that aim are appropriate and necessary".[15]

In area of protection of personal data, the same syntax right-restriction-justification is visible. As the Court decided in para. 89 of Case C-205/21 *Criminal proceedings against V.S.*, "the right to effective judicial protection is not an absolute right and that, in accordance with Article 52(1) of the Charter, limitations may be placed upon it, on condition that (i) those limitations are provided for by law, (ii) they respect the essence of the rights and freedoms at issue, and (iii) in compliance with the principle of proportionality, they are necessary and genuinely meet objectives of general interest recognised by the European Union or the need to protect the rights and freedoms of others".[16]

It can be seen from this brief overview that whereas the main syntax remained the same (right-restriction-justification), the proportionality analysis appears in the stage of justification. For a public interest to be capable of justifying a restriction, it must be necessary and appropriate (genuinely meet objectives of general interest).

Proportionality analysis may be different depending on whether the Court invalidates a measure, in which case, for reasons of economy, the analysis can be restricted, and a situation where it upholds a measure, in which case a more structured (not necessarily stricter) analysis can take place. Such as was the situation in *Weiss*[17] the case which concerned review of validity of measures of the European Central Bank (ECB) and the European System of Central Banks (ESCB). The judgment in Weiss was criticized by the 2nd Senate of the German Federal Constitutional Court,

---

[12] Equally applicable to domestic products and products from other Member States.

[13] Council Directive 2000/78/EC of 27 November 2000 establishing a general framework for equal treatment in employment and occupation.

[14] CJEU, case C-157/15, *Samira Achbita and Centrum voor gelijkheid van kansen en voor racismebestrijding v G4S Secure Solutions NV*, ECLI:EU:C:2017:203.

[15] *Achbita*, para. 35.

[16] CJEU, case C-205/21, *Criminal proceedings against V.S.*, ECLI:EU:C:2023:49, para. 89.

[17] See e.g. CJEU, Case C-493/17, *Proceedings brought by Heinrich Weiss and Others*, ECLI:EU:C:2018:1000, para 72: "According to settled case-law of the Court, the principle of proportionality requires that acts of the EU institutions should be suitable for attaining the legitimate objectives pursued by the legislation at issue and should not go beyond what is necessary to achieve those objectives (judgment of 16 June 2015, *Gauweiler and Others*, C-62/14, EU:C:2015:400, para. 67 and the case-law cited)".

essentially because of the absence of the fourth analytical step, i.e. balancing *stricto* sensu (in German, *Abwägung*).[18]

In more recent practice following Weiss, the Court seems to be more ready to engage into a fully developed analysis of proportionality.

For example in Case C-78/21 *AS Privatbank* (j.r. Kumin),[19] which concerned proportionality of a national restriction to free movement of capital, the Court applied a four-step analysis and decided that a "measure which is justified on grounds of public policy, referred to in Article 65(1)(b) TFEU; secondly, is appropriate for ensuring attainment of those objectives; thirdly, does not go beyond what is necessary for attaining them; and, fourthly, does not lead to an excessive impairment of the rights and interests protected under Articles 56 and 63 TFEU, which are enjoyed by the credit institution concerned and its customers".[20]

The same can be said for analysis in *Luxembourg Business Register*, joined cases C-37/20 and C-601/20 (j.r. Kumin)[21] and *Garda Síochána*, C-140/20. (j.r. von Danwitz).[22]

4 Intensity of Proportionality Analysis

By intensity of proportionality analysis, I mean the level of importance of public interest that the CJEU will examine to justify (or not) certain measure or restriction. The intensity can vary from rationality review which is in legal system of the EU

[18] BVerfG, Judgment of the Second Senate of 5 May 2020, 2 BvR 859/15, paras. 1–237: "When applied in this manner, as undertaken by the CJEU, the principle of proportionality [...] cannot fulfil its corrective function for the purposes of safeguarding the competences of the Member States [...] As a result, the review of proportionality is rendered meaningless, given that suitability and necessity of the PSPP are not balanced against the economic policy effects – other than the risk of losses - arising from the programme to the detriment of Member States' competences, and that these adverse effects are not weighed against the beneficial effects of the programme aims to achieve".

[19] CJEU, case C-78/21, *AS 'PrivatBank' and Others v Finanšu un kapitāla tirgus komisija*, ECLI:EU:C:2023:13.

[20] *AS 'PrivatBank'*, para. 99.

[21] CJEU, joined cases C-37/20 and C-601/20, *WM and Sovim SA v Luxembourg Business Registers*, ECLI:EU:C:2022:912, para. 63: "According to settled case-law, the proportionality of the measures which result in interference with the rights guaranteed in Articles 7 and 8 of the Charter requires compliance not only with the requirements of appropriateness and of necessity but also with that of the proportionate nature of those measures in relation to the objective pursued (see, to that effect, judgment of 5 April 2022, *Commissioner of An Garda Síochána and Others*, C-140/20, EU:C:2022:258, paragraph 93)".

[22] CJEU, *G.D. v The Commissioner of the Garda Síochána and Others*, ECLI:EU:C:2022:258 at para 93: "In the fourth and final place, it must be emphasized that the proportionality of the measures adopted pursuant to Article 15(1) of Directive 2002/58 requires, according to the Court's settled case-law, as recalled in the judgment of 6 October 2020, *La Quadrature du Net and Others* (C-511/18, C-512/18 and C-520/18, EU:C:2020:791), compliance not only with the requirements of aptitude and of necessity but also with that of the proportionate nature of those measures in relation to the objective pursued".

characterized by the 'manifest error' standard, to more demanding levels of judicial scrutiny.

Intensity of proportionality review is not the same in all categories of cases. In *Digital Rights Ireland* which concerned proportionality of a restriction in respect of the right to privacy the standard was held to be "strictly necessary".[23] In *Gauweiler*, which concerned proportionality of means to achieve objectives of monetary policy of the EU, the standard was "manifestly disproportionate",[24] which effectively left a large margin of discretion to the regulator, in this case the ESCB. Both cases concerned review of measures adopted by EU institutions.

It is nothing new to say that 'rationality review' applies in situations where EU institutions need to perform a complex analysis. In such situations the Court engages in proportionality analysis but is ready to defer. In *Gauweiler*, the Court went to verify whether the programme for the purchase of government bonds on secondary markets did not go "manifestly beyond what is necessary to achieve those objectives"[25] (of monetary policy). What is interesting to note is that the Grand Chamber analysed not only necessity of the measures in question but also considered proportionality *stricto* sensu. Namely, the Court recognized that "the ESCB weighed up the various interests in play so as to actually prevent disadvantages from arising, when the programme in question is implemented, which are manifestly disproportionate to the programme's objectives".[26] Altogether, the Court largely deferred to the ESCB allowing it large margin of discretion in "choices of a technical nature" and "complex assessments".[27]

In contrast to *Gauweiler*, in *Digital Rights Ireland*, the standard under which the Court invalidated the Directive 2006/24/EC[28] was "strictly necessary".[29] As we have explained, because, among other reasons, it "does not lay down any objective criterion by which the number of persons authorised to access and subsequently use the data retained is limited to what is strictly necessary in the light of the objective

[23] CJEU, joined cases C-293/12 and C-594/12, *Digital Rights Ireland Ltd v Minister for Communications, Marine and Natural Resources and Others and Kärntner Landesregierung and Others*, ECLI:EU:C:2014:238, paras. 52, 62, 64–65.

[24] CJEU, C-62/14, *Gauweiler and Others*, ECLI:EU:C:2015:400, para. 91.

[25] *Gauweiler and Others*, para. 81.

[26] *Gauweiler and Others*, para. 81.

[27] *Gauweiler and Others*, para. 68.

[28] Directive 2006/24/EC of the European Parliament and of the Council of 15 March 2006 on the retention of data generated or processed in connection with the provision of publicly available electronic communications services or of public communications networks and amending Directive 2002/58/EC.

[29] CJEU, joined cases C-293/12 and C-594/12, *Digital Rights Ireland Ltd v Minister for Communications, Marine and Natural Resources and Others and Kärntner Landesregierung and Others*, ECLI:EU:C:2014:238, paras. 52, 62, 64–65.

pursued."[30] This line of analysis can be traced back to cases C-73/07 *Satakunnan Markkinapörssi and Satamedia*[31] and C-92/09 *Volker und Markus Schecke GbR.*[32]

It remains to discuss the use of expressions 'necessary' and 'strictly necessary'.

4.1 Necessity and Strict Necessity in Primary and Secondary Law

First, it should be said that the expression 'strictly necessary' does not appear in primary EU law, neither in the Treaties, nor in the Charter.[33] For example, Art. 52 of the Charter uses the expression 'necessary'. When it comes to secondary legislation the situation is not coherent.

Article 8 of the ECHR also uses expression 'necessary'. However, in case law of the European Court of Human Rights (ECHR), the expression 'strictly necessary' is sometimes used. As the ECHR decided in para. 42 of *Klass and Others v. Germany*,[34] "[t]he cardinal issue arising under Article 8 (art. 8) in the present case is whether the interference so found is justified by the terms of paragraph 2 of the Article (art. 8–2). This paragraph, since it provides for an exception to a right guaranteed by the Convention, is to be narrowly interpreted. Powers of secret surveillance of citizens, characterising as they do the police state, are tolerable under the Convention only in so far as strictly necessary for safeguarding the democratic system."[35]

Speaking about secondary EU law, the Regulation (EU) 2018/1139[36] on common rules in the field of civil aviation mentions the expression "strictly necessary" six times, notably, in Articles 41, 66, 71, 72 and 74. In all these instances the expression has a function of allowing the Member States to introduce certain limited exceptions

---

[30] *Digital Rights Ireland Ltd*, para. 62.

[31] CJEU, case C-73/07, *Tietosuojavaltuutettu v Satakunnan Markkinapörssi Oy and Satamedia Oy*, ECLI:EU:C:2008:727, para. 56: "In order to take account of the importance of the right to freedom of expression in every democratic society, it is necessary, first, to interpret notions relating to that freedom, such as journalism, broadly. Secondly, and in order to achieve a balance between the two fundamental rights, the protection of the fundamental right to privacy requires that the derogations and limitations in relation to the protection of data provided for in the chapters of the directive referred to above must apply only in so far as is strictly necessary."

[32] CJEU, joined cases C-92/09 and C-93/09, *Volker und Markus Schecke GbR (C-92/09) and Hartmut Eifert (C-93/09) v Land Hessen*, ECLI:EU:C:2010:662, para. 86.

[33] Substantive articles of the European Convention for Protection of Human Rights and Fundamental Freedoms use the phrase "necessary in democratic society". Also, it should be mentioned that the expression is not identical in all language versions: in French it reads "*au stricte nécessaire*", but also "*de nécessité absolue*", in German "*auf das unbedingt*", "*zwingend Erforderliche*" and "*auf das absolut Notwendige*", in Spanish "*a lo estrictamente necesario*", in Italia "*allo stretto necessario*".

[34] ECHR, Application no. 5029/71, Judgment of 6 September 1978.

[35] ECHR, Application no. 5029/71, Judgment of 6 September 1978, para. 42.

[36] Regulation (EU) 2018/1139 of the European Parliament and of the Council of 4 July 2018 on common rules in the field of civil aviation and establishing a European Union Aviation Safety Agency.

to the obligations prescribed by the Regulation, but only to the extent "strictly necessary". In other words, the function of the expression reiterates a classic interpretative function according to which exceptions need to be narrowly construed. However, it is not clear what a difference would it make if the legislator used the word "necessary".

The Regulation (EU) 2024/1689 (Artificial Intelligence Act)[37] mentions the expression "strictly necessary" in recitals 33, 34, 70, 94 and 95. In all these instances, it refers to the narrow interpretation of exceptions to a basic rule. However, recital 95 seems to reproduce language of proportionality by saying that certain "biometric identification systems should always be used in a way that is proportionate, legitimate and strictly necessary, and thus targeted, in terms of the individuals to be identified, the location, temporal scope and based on a closed data set of legally acquired video footage." The normative text of the Regulation continues to use the expression as an obligation of restrictive interpretation, notably in Articles 4, 5, 10, 26 and 78 and is typically used in connection with a specific aim that Member States can pursue by 'strictly necessary' means. In essence this is a variant of a means-ends scrutiny, a cost benefit analysis where the aims of the public interest must be pursued by means narrowly tailored for their achievement. The different language of recital 95 seems to address application of tools, in this case biometric identification systems, while the other mentioned recitals seem to refer to interpretation of the rule-exception syntax. In other words, once the exception is narrowly construed, it still must be applied in accordance with principle of proportionality. This is a good example of imprecise use of the expression 'strictly necessary' in secondary law.

The General Data Protection Regulation (GDPR)[38] surprisingly mentions the expression only two times, in its recitals 47 and 49. Both mentions refer to strict necessity of processing of personal data for purpose of legitimate interest, such as prevention of fraud (recital 47) or ensuring network and information security (recital 49). The latter is, however, interesting since it uses the phrase "strictly necessary and proportionate for the purposes".

The Directive (EU) 2016/680[39] mentions "strictly necessary" in three instances, one of them in recital 72 and two in the normative part. Recital 72 follows the rule-derogation syntax by saying that "derogations should be interpreted restrictively and should not allow frequent, massive and structural transfers of personal data, or large-scale transfers of data, but should be limited to data strictly necessary." Both Articles 10 and 39(1)(a) prescribe the syntax of means-ends scrutiny where processing of personal data must be strictly necessary for achievement of specified public interest

---

[37] Regulation (EU) 2024/1689 of the European Parliament and of the Council of 13 June 2024 laying down harmonised rules on artificial intelligence.

[38] Regulation (EU) 2016/679 of the European Parliament and of the Council of 27 April 2016 on the protection of natural persons with regard to the processing of personal data and on the free movement of such data (General Data Protection Regulation).

[39] Directive (EU) 2016/680 of the European Parliament and of the Council of 27 April 2016 on the protection of natural persons with regard to the processing of personal data by competent authorities for the purposes of the prevention, investigation, detection or prosecution of criminal offences or the execution of criminal penalties, and on the free movement of such data.

objectives. It should be noted that French linguistic version uses the term "*nécessité absolue*" in Art. 10 and "*strictement necessaire*" in Art. 39.

This cursory and incomplete investigation has identified two different usages of the expression 'strictly necessary'. In the context of a rule-exception dynamics (interpretation) and in the context of the means-ends scrutiny, i.e. proportionality of means in respect to regulatory objectives (application).

4.2 Necessity and Strict Necessity in the Case Law of the CJEU

Probably the first mention of the expression "strictly necessary" in the case law of the CJEU can be found in Case 15/57 of 1958. In this case the Court rejected the action for annulment and said that "[w]here the high authority is empowered to promulgate measures 'in the common interest', it can use its power to make regulations as the circumstances require, even at the expense of certain individual interests, but it must take action only to the extent which is strictly necessary" (in French, *strictement indispensable*).[40] This is essentially the same situation which is nowadays regulated by Art. 5(4) TEU.

However, an interesting development is documented by a preliminary reference *Tietosuojavaltuutettu* of 16 December 2008,[41] where the Court went to interpret Art. 9 of the Directive 95/46/EC[42] and reconcile protection of privacy and freedom of expression which is the task of the Member States. As the Court said, derogations from the right to privacy that fall within the scope of freedom of expression, "must apply only in so far as it is strictly necessary."[43] This mention of strict necessity is a creation of the Court and is not mentioned anywhere in the Directive.

The frequency of usage of the expression 'strictly necessary' was low until 2015 and usually did not surpass ten appearances annually. After 2015 the number started to increase and amounted to 17 in 2020, 28 in 2022 and 2023 and 19 in 2024 until the day of the writing of this text. These appearances are present in our judgments related to a diverse primary and secondary law which does not help to standardize their meaning and function.

As it is not possible to give a complete overview of the case law of the CJEU, I will limit myself to a few representative cases. The first one to look at is the Fifth Chamber

---

[40] CJEU, case 15/57, *Compagnie des Hauts Fourneaux de Chasse contre Haute Autorité de la Communauté européenne du charbon et de l'acier*, ECLI:EU:C:1958:6, sommaire, para. 6.

[41] CJEU, case 73/07, *Tietosuojavaltuutettu v Satakunnan Markkinapörssi Oy and Satamedia Oy*, ECLI:EU:C:2008:727.

[42] Directive 95/46/EC of the European Parliament and of the Council of 24 October 1995 on the protection of individuals with regard to the processing of personal data and on the free movement of such data.

[43] *Tietosuojavaltuutettu*, para. 56.

judgment of January 26, 2023, *Criminal proceedings against VS* (j.r. Gratsias).[44] The preliminary reference concerned inter alia the interpretation of Article 10 of the Directive (EU) 2016/680[45] and the question about condition that special categories of data can be processed only where strictly necessary ("only where strictly necessary"/ "*uniquement en cas de nécessité absolue*").

The Court explained the purpose of Art. 10 which is an enhanced protection of the rights consecrated in Arts. 7 and 8 of the Charter, notably respect for private life and the right to the protection of personal data, in the concrete case biometric and genetic personal data.[46] The Court continued to interpret the phrase ('*uniquement en cas de nécessité absolue*' in the French-language version) as establishing strengthened conditions for lawful processing of such data, as opposed to simple "necessity" mentioned in Arts. 4(1)(b) and (c) and Art. 8(1) of the same directive. According to the Court, "the fact that the necessity for processing of such data is an 'absolute' one [('*absolue*')] signifies that that necessity is to be assessed with rigor."[47] This can be compared to the strict scrutiny, the concept of law of the US under which a restriction of certain rights can be restricted only if the state is able to demonstrate a 'compelling interest'. Interestingly, the Court dismissed the distinction raised by French government referring to different linguistic versions (absoulue in French and strictly in English). As stated by the CJEU, all "language versions also establish a strengthened condition"[48] for legality of processing of such sensitive data.

One of the seminal cases which refers to the standard "strictly necessary" is the case *La quadrature du net* of October 6, 2020[49] where the Court balanced the protection of the fundamental right to privacy against public interest in processing of personal data. As the Court said,

> the question whether the Member States may justify a limitation on the rights and obligations laid down, inter alia, in Articles 5, 6 and 9 of Directive 2002/58 must be assessed by measuring the seriousness of the interference entailed by such a limitation and by verifying that the importance of the public interest objective pursued by that limitation is proportionate to that seriousness (see, to that effect, judgment of 2 October 2018, Ministerio Fiscal, C 207/16, EU:C:2018:788, paragraph 55 and the case-law cited).[50]

---

[44] CJEU, case C-205/21, *Criminal proceedings against V.S.*, ECLI:EU:C:2023:49.

[45] "Processing of personal data revealing racial or ethnic origin, political opinions, religious or philosophical beliefs, or trade union membership, and the processing of genetic data, biometric data for the purpose of uniquely identifying a natural person, data concerning health or data concerning a natural person's sex life or sexual orientation shall be *allowed only where strictly necessary*, subject to appropriate safeguards for the rights and freedoms of the data subject, and only: (a) where authorized by Union or Member State law; (b) to protect the vital interests of the data subject or of another natural person; or (c) where such processing relates to data which are manifestly made public by the data subject" (emphasis added).

[46] *Criminal proceedings against V.S.*, para. 116.

[47] *Criminal proceedings against V.S.*, para. 117.

[48] *Criminal proceedings against V.S.*, para. 119.

[49] CJEU, joined cases C 511/18, C 512/18 and C 520/18, *La Quadrature du Net*, ECLI:EU:C:2020:791.

[50] *La Quadrature du Net*, para. 131.

The Court went further and clarified in para. 132:

> That legislation must be legally binding under domestic law and, in particular, must indicate in what circumstances and under which conditions a measure providing for the processing of such data may be adopted, thereby ensuring that the interference is limited to what is strictly necessary.[51]

Enhanced rigor of scrutiny, however, does not, on its own right seem to prejudge that compelling reasons of public interest might not prevail in a concrete situation. In the syntax right-restriction-justification, the strictly necessary requirement refers to justification stage and the reason for that is a specific sensitive character of the protected object—biometric and genetic data.

Yet, the intensity of public interest required for a justification will be contrasted to the importance of the rights at stake, possibly, fundamental rights protected by the Charter and the values of the Treaties.

As the Court said of the second *Quadrature du net* case,[52]

> the interpretation of Article 15(1) of Directive 2002/58 must take account of the importance both of the right to respect for private life, guaranteed in Article 7 of the Charter, and of the right to protection of personal data, guaranteed in Article 8 thereof, as derived from the case-law of the Court, as well as the importance of the right to freedom of expression, given that that fundamental right, guaranteed in Article 11 of the Charter, constitutes one of the essential foundations of a pluralist, democratic society, and is one of the values on which, under Article 2 TEU, the Union is founded (judgment of 6 October 2020, La Quadrature du Net and Others, C-511/18, C-512/18 and C-520/18, EU:C:2020:791, paragraph 114 and the case-law cited).[53]

5 Does Law of the EU Have a Standard Vocabulary to Designate Elements of Proportionality Analysis?

The short answer is 'no'. A longer answer requires to distinguish the doctrinal structure of proportionality analysis as presented above, from what the CJEU does in specific situations.

As to the structure of proportionality analysis, the language of the CJEU is very similar to the language of German Federal Constitutional Court. While there may be differences in linguistic versions, the formal structure corresponds to what I have described above. This is more visible after the 2020 decision of the BVerfG.[54]

As far as the practical usage of the Court's vocabulary is concerned, expression proportionality can mean any of the following: a least restrictive alternative test, balancing of regulatory means and ends (means-ends scrutiny) or, indeed, the entire proportionality analysis including all the tests mentioned.

---

[51] *La Quadrature du Net*, para. 132.

[52] CJEU, case C 470/21, *La Quadrature du Net and Others v Premier Ministre and Ministère de la Culture* (*La Quadrature du Net II*), ECLI:EU:C:2024:370.

[53] *La Quadrature du Net II*, para. 68.

[54] BVerfG, Judgment of the Second Senate of 5 May 2020, 2 BvR 859/15.

The difference between necessity and strict necessity is also blurred. Sometimes the Court follows the wording of secondary legislation, sometimes it uses expression 'strictly necessary' while secondary legislation uses word 'necessary'. Sometimes the Court uses it in the context of the Charter of Rights whereas the Charter only refers to "necessary". Is there any difference between the two expressions? If there is, does the difference refer to different categories of rights, such as economic rights or fundamental (i.e., Charter-based) rights?

6 'Necessary' and 'Strictly Necessary' as Indicators of Different Strictness of Proportionality Analysis

In the case *Criminal proceedings against VS*, the Court said that "the fact that the necessity for processing of such data is an 'absolute' one [('*absolue*')] signifies that that necessity is to be assessed with rigor".[55] In this case, the distinction between necessity and strict was introduced by the Directive itself.

In 1938, the US Supreme Court decided the *Filled Milk* case.[56] In its famous footnote 4, justice Harlan Stone writing for the majority wrote: "There may be narrower scope for operation of the presumption of constitutionality when legislation appears on its face to be within a specific prohibition of the Constitution, such as those of the first ten amendments, which are deemed equally specific when held to be embraced within the Fourteenth. [citations omitted] This test, which applies when rights of "discrete and insular minorities" are at stake has become known as a "strict scrutiny test" where a government measure to be constitutional must pursue a "compelling state interest".[57]

How would a strict scrutiny test operate in the legal system of the EU? Most generally, where a regulatory measure restricts some fundamental right consecrated by the Charter or runs against one of the values from Article 2 of the TEU, the regulator, whether a European institution or a Member State, whether implementing EU law or exercising their retained competences, would have to demonstrate existence of a more significant public interest. This said, regulatory measures subject to strict scrutiny test can either pass or fail after having been subject to a more intense judicial review.

Concerning vocabulary, the expression 'necessary' could continue to be applied in its habitual meaning and be applied in context other than Art. 2 values and Charter rights. In contrast, the expression 'strictly necessary' would be used to indicate stricter scrutiny, as indicated in the VS case. Also, wherever secondary law uses expression 'strictly necessary' the Court could interpret it as a requirement of stricter judicial control.

---

[55] *Criminal proceedings against V.S.*, para. 117.

[56] *United States v. Carolene Products Co.*, 304 U.S. 144 (1938).

[57] *United States v. Carolene Products Co.*, 304 U.S. 144 (1938), footnote 4.

I would also like to address suggestions that strict scrutiny is already taking place in the final step of proportionality analysis—proportionality *stricto* sensu. I do not entirely agree. While it is true that the final analytical step introduces a cost–benefit analysis and ultimately may subject a regulatory measure to a variety of public policy considerations including protection of fundamental rights, strict scrutiny introduces an additional element—recognition that certain rights and certain categories of individuals are entitled to a higher level of protection. Not just in a relative sense characterized by balancing (in German, *Abwägung*) but also in absolute sense, because rights at stake are of a particularly sensitive nature (e.g. private life) or because some categories of individuals are in an inherently weaker position.

Articulation of strict scrutiny in the case law of the CJEU is not purely aesthetic, theoretical or academic but also has a practical meaning. For example, in context of equal treatment, this approach could lead to a possibility of justification, subject to strict scrutiny, of even those measures which are considered directly discriminatory. A justification of such measures could be made conditional, for example, by respect of values of the EU specified in Art. 2 TEU, provided that the essence of restricted rights is preserved and that the measure is strictly necessary for preservation of Art. 2 values.

Admittedly, such a development would bring the Court closer to the role of a constitutional court as Treaty values of constitutional nature would play an even more important role in judicial review.

References

Bomhoff J (2023) Making legal knowledge work: practising proportionality in the German Repetitorium. Soc Leg Stud 32(1):28–54

Galloway RW (1988) Means-end scrutiny in American constitutional law. Loyola LA Law Rev 21(2):449–496

Rethinking Private Law to Address Digital Vulnerability

Rapidly Remedying Exploitation of Digital Vulnerability: Taking Time Seriously in Digital Regulation

Frank Pasquale and Zubair Jamali

Abstract Political theorists have long identified social acceleration as a challenge to governance. This chapter addresses the growing discrepancy between the rapid pace of digital developments and the often slow response of government and courts. In particular, this chapter highlights that, despite the speed with which digital platforms have generated privacy, antitrust, and consumer protection harms, judicial proceedings against them have sometimes taken many years to resolve both in the United States and in Europe. After reviewing the many factors underlying this slow pace of justice, the chapter proposes strategies for challenging this status quo, including improved interim measures and appellate procedure.

Keywords Digital regulation · Privacy · Antitrust · Consumer protection · Legal enforcement · Due process

1 Introduction

Leading platforms are exemplars of speed and scale, setting the pace of digitization for other companies and society as a whole.[1] Such platforms use artificial intelligence to make decisions at an extraordinarily rapid pace. While this speed is a commendable feature in many situations, it also means that the potential for harms to accrue has grown as well. In extreme but plausible cases, automated decision making can make 'a million mistakes per second', in Paul Scharre's memorable phrasing.[2]

[1] Pasquale (2015, 189–220).

[2] Scharre (2018).

F. Pasquale (✉)
Cornell Tech and Cornell Law School, New York, USA
e-mail: fp269@cornell.edu

Z. Jamali
Cornell Law School, New York, USA
e-mail: zj226@cornell.edu

C. Crea and M. Infantino (eds.), *Remedies to Digital Vulnerability in European Private Law*, https://doi.org/10.1007/978-3-032-19720-7_10

Unfortunately, enforcers, judiciaries, and regulators around the world have not kept up with the pace of digitization. Cases routinely drag on in administrative tribunals and courts. Wily attorneys utilize the slowest-moving courts to 'torpedo' opponents, pressuring them to settle or abandon their litigation. Even clear violations of law may take many years to address.[3]

This chapter addresses the growing mismatch between the speed of digital life and the slowness of government. Political theorists have long identified social acceleration as a challenge to governance (Sect. 2). Despite the speed with which digital platforms have generated privacy, antitrust, and consumer protection harms, judicial proceedings against them have sometimes taken many years to resolve (Sect. 3). This torpor is part of a larger problem: despite paper guarantees of timely resolution of disputes, higher courts in both the United States (US) and the European Union (EU) have been reluctant to force lower courts to adhere to specific sets of deadlines to resolve cases, or to penalize excessive delay with truly deterrent effect (Sect. 4). Strategies for changing (or adapting to) this status quo are explored in the final section of this chapter (Sect. 5).

2 The Social and Political Theory of Acceleration

One core feature of technological advance is increasing the speed of accomplishing varied tasks. For example, a microwave generally cooks faster than a range. Driving is faster than bicycling, and bicycling is faster than walking. A Google search is faster than consulting a printed phone book when seeking a business's phone number. And now generative AI can produce a five-paragraph essay faster than any student.

Each of these advances is a great convenience when considered on the individual level. Few people want to walk miles when a car is available, and the printed phone book is almost obsolete at this point. However, social dynamics can make these advances a mixed blessing. While not disregarding the immense benefits of the invention of the automobile, its invention means there are approximately a million auto-accident related deaths globally each year, and approximately tens of millions of auto-accident related injuries.[4] Likewise, the rise of Google as an all-purpose search tool has given the company enormous power over the commercial practices of the businesses it indexes and the data of consumers using it directly or indirectly.[5] Generative AI, in turn, stands ready to create unprecedented amounts of writing, including false or biased information, in often untraceable ways. If it is (as is likely) over-relied upon, it may also gradually sap the critical thinking capacities of its users, reducing their ability to rectify (or even recognize) its harms.[6]

[3] Ring (2025).

[4] WHO (2023).

[5] Pasquale (2015, 59–100).

[6] Pasquale (2020, 1–32).

Table 1 Speed advantage and disadvantage

	Speed advantage	Speed disadvantage
1	Corporation	Worker-owned cooperative
2	Corporation with powerful CEO	Corporation with powerful board
3	Corporation	Government
4	Executive Branch of Government	Legislative Branch of Government
5	Executive Branch or Legislative Branch of Government	Judicial Branch of Government
6	Corporation	Judicial Branch of Government
7	Authoritarian Government	Democratic Government

Social and political theorists have further complicated the normative valence of speed. Demands for rapidity clash with the more deliberative characteristics of many aspects of commerce and governance. This tension may, in turn, privilege some types of institutions over others.[7] Compare the institutions on each side of the binary below in Table 1.

Starting with the first row: the greater agility of a corporation relative to a worker-owned cooperative should be clear. The corporation has a much more concentrated governance structure than all but the smallest worker-owned cooperatives, enabling faster decision-making. This observation leads in turn to the second comparison—the speed of decision-making in a corporation with a monarchical, strong-CEO, relative to one with an oligarchic, strong board. As should also be clear, the strong-CEO corporation faces far less need to negotiate or build consensus than a corporation with several powerful board members. This is not to say that the faster model is better—whole books have been written on the merits of careful deliberation.[8] However, speed can be decisive in scenarios where rapid moves and countermoves are critical to competitive advantage, such as in cutting-edge markets.

The speed of almost any type of for-profit corporation is remarkable in comparison with that of most governments. Nor is this speed differential easily remedied. Precisely the elements of governmental action which tend to legitimate it, including adherence to procedure, public consultation, and close following of legal requirements, are those which tend to slow it down. However, there is sometimes a hypertrophy of bureaucratization that adds little or nothing to the legitimacy and effectiveness of government.[9]

Defenders of the status quo are often quick to note that demands for speed in governmental action can easily lead to romanticization of a strongman. However, the failure of government to remedy obvious problems can also stoke popular discontent that leads to political support for authoritarianism.[10] There is no easy resolution of the

[7] Scheuerman (2004, 1–25).

[8] Partnoy (2012, Introduction).

[9] Bagley (2019, 351–352), Klein and Thompson (2025, 101–128) and Dunkelman (2025, 93–124).

[10] Klein and Thompson (2025, 203–220).

ongoing tension between speed and deliberation. Nevertheless, there are scenarios of extreme delay or opportunistic manipulation of process that cry out for solutions. Sect. 3 below examines these problematic scenarios in the digital context.

3 Justice Delayed in Digital Contexts

Companies stalling civil enforcement or regulation have long undermined the administration of justice. Contemporary developments exacerbate the problem. For example, in many digital markets, rapidly seizing market share is a key goal of firms. Investment may lead to a 'virtuous circle' of customer and data acquisition, potentially sparking even further investment. If companies grow sufficiently large, they can even leverage their market power or mobilize their customers to pressure politicians to accept even deeply troubling aspects of their business models. This cycle incentivizes rule-breaking in the name of scaling.[11]

The problem of delay has already sandbagged the EU's enforcement of the General Data Protection Regulation (GDPR).[12] Even though a national data protection authority must investigate and resolve a case with all due diligence under the GDPR, the timeline for case resolution approximately ranges from one month to eight years. The acceptance of such multi-year timelines as adequate creates opportunities for delay that may be advantageous to large firms.[13] For example, the European Data Protection Board (EDPB) ordered the Irish Data Protection Commission (IPDC) to fine Meta $1.2 billion in May 2023, after the IDPC had imposed what the EDPB considered a wholly inadequate remedy. Meta appealed to an Irish court-of-first-instance in June 2023. As of June 2025, the case was still being heard by that court. The case may be appealed to an Irish intermediate-appellate court, the Irish court of last instance, and then the Court of Justice of the European Union (CJEU), the EU's court of last instance. This could result in a total of 4–5 years of appeals since the IDPC's initial decision. Many other Meta appeals of fines are pending, and on February 2026, the CJEU ruled Meta, and other companies, are allowed to directly challenge EDPB decisions, likely further increasing the timeline for appeals.[14] The

[11] Mazur and Serafin (2023, 109–116).

[12] Regulation (EU) 2016/679 on the protection of natural persons with regard to the processing of personal data and on the free movement of such data, and repealing Directive 95/46/EC (General Data Protection Regulation).

[13] Noyb.eu (2020). According to a report by the European Commission, "[t]he median time for data protection authorities to handle complaints (from receipt to closure of the case) ranges from 1 to 12 months, and is 3 months or less in five [EUMember[-]States. (Denmark (1 month), Spain (1.5 months), Estonia (3 months), Greece (3 months) and Ireland (3 months))": European Commission (2024a). The appeals for complex cases such as *Amazon v. Luxembourg* have continued for almost five years before resulting in a victory for Amazon at Luxembourg's court-of-last-instance. However, this case may generate appeals for years to come as it has been remanded to Luxembourg's DPA (CNPD) to redetermine the appropriate penalty for Amazon. Chee (2026) and Chee (2025).

[14] Meta Platforms, Inc (2024, 51–56) and White (2026). Generally, the appeals process escalates in the following order: (1) a country's data protection authority (not always a step, as only some

delay has suited the company well: not only has it kept large sums in its coffers, but it has also found extraordinary support from President Trump, whose second term has already included many efforts to convince or coerce officials in Europe to abandon key enforcement actions against US companies.[15]

Delays are not unique to large cases either. There is grave concern about and evidence of dynamic industries creating harms to individuals that cannot be cured. Whether via ex ante regulation or ex post enforcement, faster action is needed.[16] A recent report detailed the consumer experience of a "long and winding road" toward adequate remedies under GDPR.[17] One study has indicated the problems that can arise thanks to delayed takedown of illegal content.[18] Overall, there is general concern that law is not addressing technological change in a timely manner.

Perhaps the most dramatic story of delay is that of Google's antitrust travails, which have been winding through multiple courts for years. Focusing on the Foundem-initiated case involving Google Shopping: there was an extraordinary passage of time between the initial complaint and the ultimate resolution of the case. In a fast-moving digital world, Google consolidated power during the long pendency of the first EU antitrust case against it. The small search engine Foundem filed its complaint in 2009, but it took until 2017 for the EC to impose a 2.4 billion euro fine. Google appealed to the General Court of the EU, and that appeal took four years to be largely dismissed. The CJEU rejected Google's final appeal on Sept. 10, 2024.[19] In the almost 15 years between the initial complaint and the final resolution of the matter, Google approximately acquired scores of companies, and many were European.[20] Moreover, the follow-on damages actions by private complainants have also seen long delays in resolution. For example, the German price comparison platforms Idealo and Producto will need to wait for further appeals before actually receiving the 465 million and 107 million euro judgments awarded to them in 2025. Such delays should be part of a longer-term reckoning regarding the effectiveness of EU antitrust remedies.[21]

Without action, these delays are unlikely to improve. Courts will likely soon be swamped by even more cases, as the adoption of generative AI by litigants is already underway. Advances in large-language models (LLMs) driving drafting of complaints, filings, and applications are a recipe for rapid increases in judicial workload. The effects of AI on deprofessionalizing or 'democratizing' legal practice could

countries allow requesting a data protection authority to re-review that authority's decision, though this is also a procedural matter and not an appeal); (2) national administrative or civil courts-of-first-instance with appeals up to the national court-of-last-instance; (3) the EU's Court of Justice for the European Union (CJEU) (decisions are effective for the entire EU). See The Irish Times (2025), European Data Protection Board (2023), Fuster et al. (2022, 18–19), and Roth (2021).

15 Bordelon and Miller (2025).

16 Ducci (2021, 10, 12–13).

17 Martin (2020, 2–3).

18 Truong et al. (2025, 1–2).

19 Gerken (2024) and Bergqvist (2024).

20 Tracxn (2025).

21 Sciaudone et al. (2025, 209–227).

also increase burdens on courts, such as by giving laypeople the sense that they should be able to enter courts on the same terms as attorneys in courts.[22] Beyond AI, the increasing use of computational law, legal effects entirely dependent on automated computation, will likely significantly increase the complexity and number of cases for courts.[23] If even a few of these trends pan out, courts will likely need to improve their speed markedly in order to remain relevant in dynamic, rapidly-changing digital fields. Therefore, it is time to rekindle interest in guarantees of speedy process in judicial systems—the topic of Sect. 4 below.

4 A Survey of Timeliness Policy: From the Criminal 'Speedy Trial' to the Efficient Administration of Civil Justice

Justice delayed is, in a very real sense, justice denied. This section examines legal rights to (or requirements for) timely administration of justice. Section 4.1 covers US criminal and civil cases while Sect. 4.2 explores aspects of European jurisprudence on civil matters. While the Constitutional or Charter-based rights and assurances of timeliness described in these sections should offer succor to litigants frustrated by the slow resolution of digital disputes, their record in practice leaves much to be desired.

4.1 United States Standards Regarding Timely Resolution of Criminal and Civil Cases

In the US, the right to a speedy trial (referring to most parts of a case and not only parts related to trial) arguably most often refers to the US Constitution's 6th Amendment right to a speedy trial in criminal cases.[24] The 6th Amendment right to a speedy trial has been invoked to compel the government to resolve cases in a timely manner. It requires that "[i]n all criminal prosecutions, the accused shall enjoy the right to a speedy and public trial." These provisions are designed to protect defendants by preventing harms related to delays, such as the high cost of defending a case over an excessive period of time, expiration of evidence, and prolonged detention.[25] The remedies for a violation of the 6th Amendment right to a speedy trial are generally sanctions or final or temporary dismissals of a criminal case.[26]

[22] Grossman (2023, 34).

[23] Hildebrandt (2024, 2–3).

[24] Cullen (2024, 671–677) and Hildebrand and Cordero (2022, 1–2).

[25] Allen (2004, 101–106).

[26] Cullen (2024, 676) and Allen (2004, 121).

The 6th Amendment does not apply to civil cases, but judicial guidance promoting timely resolution of civil disputes provides some tools for conscientious courts to ensure timely resolution of disputes. Rule 1 of the Federal Rules of Civil Procedure (FRCP) provides such judicial guidance.[27] This is because as Rule 1 requires that all the rules of the FRCP "should be construed, administered, and employed by the court and the parties to secure the just, *speedy*, and inexpensive determination of every action and proceeding" (emphasis added).[28] Additionally, Rule 16 of the FRCP promotes Rule 1's aims by allowing courts to use conferences and scheduling to ensure timely proceedings.[29] Although not providing a justiciable right to a speedy trial, Rules 1 and 16 of the FRCP essentially function as a form of guidance for judicial conduct. Impeachment may result and reprimands may and have resulted from egregious failures to apply the FRCP in the manner and spirit described in Rule 1.[30] The Administrative Office of the US Courts (an administrative agency for the US federal judiciary) Judicial Business 2024 Report listed "delayed decision" as the 4th highest in number of complaints (140 complaints) out of nineteen complaint categories (1,510 complaints total).[31] However, it appears fewer than ten out of those 1,510 complaints resulted in any corrective action, with notable categories for corrective action being "reprimand", "suspension of assignments", and "request for voluntary retirement".[32]

The US Constitution's 5th and 14th Amendments also provide some support to litigants seeking timely dispute resolution as a matter of due process.[33] However, the actual invocation of these constitutional protections with respect to civil cases seems to be almost entirely limited to civil cases with some punitive dimension.[34] In such cases, due-process rights to a speedy trial are generally adjudicated with respect to the four-factor test that courts in criminal cases use to decide whether there has been a violation of the right to a speedy trial under the 6th Amendment: "(1) length of the delay; (2) the reasons for the delay; (3) the accused's assertion of their right; and (4) prejudice to the accused caused by the delay in bringing a speedy trial".[35] However, the strength of the case needed to prove such violations of due-process rights to a speedy trial using the four-factor test is generally high for civil-punitive cases and generally very high for civil-commercial cases, meaning such due-process rights to a speedy trial generally only apply to the most violative civil cases.[36] This is likely

---

[27] FRCP 1; Bone (2010, 288–289).

[28] FRCP 1.

[29] FRCP 16; Schuh (2016, 649–650).

[30] Quinn (2023), The Indiana Lawyer (2021), and Weiss (2017).

[31] The Administrative Office of the US Courts (2024, 1–5).

[32] Ibid.

[33] Saetveit (2016, 494–495) and Wasby (1997, 235).

[34] Wyatt (2004, 617–622) and Wasby (1997, 235) (evidencing the rarity of due-process rights to a speedy trial in civil cases and the extensive use of due-process rights to a speedy trial in civil cases with some punitive dimension, primarily immigration).

[35] Cullen (2024, 672), Saetveit (2016, 487–488, 494–495) and Wasby (1997, 235).

[36] Saetveit (2016, 494–495) and Wasby (1997, 235).

because violations of due-process rights to a speedy trial are generally considered by courts as significantly more consequential in criminal cases than in civil-punitive cases and very significantly more consequential than in civil-commercial cases.[37]

Despite the existence of these due-process rights, remedies for violations of due-process rights to a speedy trial are limited. According to Kristin Saetveit, if there is a violation of due-process rights to a speedy trial, the remedy, unlike in criminal cases, is generally only to counteract prejudice caused by such a violation and not have such a violation become a factor in deciding a case.[38] As in criminal cases, there are generally no bright-line rules, such as fixed deadlines, to decide whether a trial or appeal has been concluded in a timely manner. Two recent civil-cases where this due-process test for a speedy trial was referenced by US federal-courts were *Culley v. Marshall*, relating to speedy trials and civil-asset forfeiture, and *Rodriguez Diaz v. Garland*, relating to speedy trials and immigration detention.[39] But it is clear that such standards are rarely invoked.

4.2 European Standards Regarding Timely Resolution of Civil Cases

In Europe and the EU, rights similar to a right to a speedy trial generally apply to civil cases. The first such right is based on article 6 of the European Convention of Human Rights (ECHR), which applies to the Council of Europe's (CoE) 46 member-countries.[40] The CoE differs from the EU in that the CoE is a treaty-based organization whereas the EU is a supranational organization which enjoys the trappings of sovereignty in several domains.[41] Article 6(1) ECHR provides a right to a trial (referring again to most parts of a case and not only parts related to trial) within a reasonable time: "[i]n the determination of his civil rights and obligations or of any criminal charge against him, everyone is entitled to a fair and public hearing within a reasonable time by an independent and impartial tribunal established by law".[42] The second right is based on article 47 of the Charter of Fundamental Rights of the EU (EU Charter): "[e]veryone is entitled to a fair and public hearing within a reasonable time by an independent and impartial tribunal previously established by law". Article 47 EU Charter incorporates article 6 ECHR into EU law and applies to the 27 EU member-countries.[43] Because of this incorporation, case law interpreting article 6

[37] Wyatt (2004, 617–622) and Wasby (1997, 235).

[38] Saetveit (2016, 494–495).

[39] *Culley v. Marshall*, 601 U.S. 377 (2024); *Rodriguez Diaz v. Garland*, 53 F.4th 1189 (9th Cir. 2022).

[40] ECtHR (2025, 125–131) and Council of Europe (n.d.a).

[41] Council of Europe (n.d.a).

[42] ECtHR (2025, 125–131).

[43] European Union Agency for Fundamental Rights (2025).

ECHR also affects interpretations of article 47 EU Charter, but not necessarily vice versa.

With regard to how articles 6 and 47 differ, article 6 ECHR applies to more countries than the EU, including Norway, Switzerland, Türkiye, the United Kingdom, and until recently Russia. Cases under article 6 ECHR are decided by the European Court of Human Rights (ECtHR). The ECtHR is an international court (rather than an EU court) that cannot directly enforce its judgements.[44] Instead, the Committee of Ministers of the Council of Europe (CoMCoE), a political committee for the CoE consisting of the foreign ministers of CoE member-countries, enforces ECtHR judgments through political means, such as pronouncements and sanctions, but neither the ECtHR nor the CoMCoE have direct authority over CoE member-country courts or EU courts. Article 47 EU Charter applies to the EU member-countries and the EU. Cases under article 47 EU Charter are decided by national courts in EU member-countries and EU courts. National courts and EU courts may directly enforce judgments; EU courts may directly order national courts in EU member-countries to enforce judgements, including ordering penalties, such as fines and injunctions, for EU member-countries not following such EU courts' judgements.[45] Article 6 ECHR therefore affects more countries, but is generally more difficult to enforce than article 47 EU Charter.

For civil cases under articles 6 ECHR or 47 EU Charter, rights to a trial within a reasonable time are generally determined with reference to the plain language of the four-factor test used by the ECtHR, national courts in EU member-countries, and EU courts to determine whether there has been a violation of such rights: "(1) the complexity of the case; (2) the conduct of the applicant; (3) the conduct of the national authorities; and (4) what is at stake for the applicant."[46] As indicated by this test, there are generally no bright-line rules, such as fixed deadlines, to decide whether a trial has been conducted within a reasonable time. Periodically, the ECtHR releases a guide on how in civil cases it weighs these factors, which includes additional requirements and a list of what it considers significant case-law.[47] Two recent civil-cases where this test was referenced by the ECtHR were in *Fabbri and Others v. San Marino* and *Patricolo and Others v. Italy*.[48] Two recent civil-cases where this test was referenced by the CJEU were in *Rada Nadzorcza Getin Noble Bank S.A. and Others v. Bankowy Fundusz Gwarancyjny* and *Repsol Lubricantes y Especialidades and*

---

44 Waagstein PR (2010).

45 European Commission (2005) and European Union Agency for Fundamental Rights (2025).

46 ECtHR (2025, 125–131). To note, a theoretical preliminary-step before applying this test is deciding the overall time a trial has taken because otherwise it is likely not possible to decide whether a trial was within a reasonable time. Courts, however, generally do not explicitly consider this a factor. Lursmanashvili (2018, 175).

47 ECtHR (2025, 125–131).

48 ECtHR, *Fabbri and Others v. San Marino*, 24 September 2024, App. No. 6319/21; ECtHR, *Patricolo and Others v. Italy*, 23 May 2024, App. No. 37943/17.

Others v Commission.[49] Unlike due-process rights to a speedy trial in the US, which are rare issues for US courts, the ECtHR, national courts in EU member-countries, and EU courts have likely overall decided at least hundreds of civil cases on rights stemming from article 6 ECHR or article 47 EU Charter to a trial within a reasonable time. This suggests a high level of concern about timely resolution of disputes in Europe. However, a possible alternative explanation is that judicial delays are very prevalent.[50]

Additionally, for civil cases under article 6 ECHR or article 47 EU Charter, the inability of courts to resolve cases within a reasonable time, which has increasingly become an issue, does not affect rights to a trial within a reasonable time and may result in damages being awarded against the governments of CoE and EU member-countries or the EU respectively.[51] For civil cases under article 6 ECHR or article 47 EU Charter under the ECtHR and EU courts respectively, we have been unable to find crisply articulated standards for weighing the factors in the four-factor test to determine when damages are awarded or how damages are calculated, except perhaps that similar cases are to be treated similarly with regard to damages based on internal judicial standards not available to the public.[52]

For civil cases under article 6 ECHR or article 47 EU Charter under CoE and EU member-country courts respectively, the factors for when damages are awarded or how damages are calculated vary depending on the country but generally are similar to those of the ECtHR or EU courts (which according to a report commissioned by the CoE, is likely due to CoE and EU member-country courts avoiding trying to create issues appealable to the ECtHR or EU courts).[53] For civil cases under article 6 ECHR and article 47 EU Charter, regardless of the hearing court, several findings are of interest. Material damages (generally economic damages caused by delays, such as maintaining indemnification insurance for legal judgements or a losing a business opportunity) and non-material damages (generally non-economic damages indirectly caused by delays, such as emotional harm or reputational harm) are possible, though material damages are uncommon. Total damages are almost always between hundreds to tens of thousands of Euros. And total damages often do not significantly relate to damages perceived by the plaintiff or elapsed case-time. The

---

[49] CJEU, case C-118/23, *Rada Nadzorcza Getin Noble Bank S.A. and Others v Bankowy Fundusz Gwarancyjny*, 12 December 2024, ECLI:EU:C:2024:1013; CJEU, case C-617/13, *Repsol Lubricantes y Especialidades and Others v Commission*, 9 June 2016, ECLI:EU:C:2016:416. Being some of the most recent case-law related to article 6 ECHR and article 47 EU Charter, it is noteworthy these four cases have either not been successful for the plaintiffs or have not yet resulted in remedies.

[50] Kuijer (2013) and Ionescu (2023).

[51] Kye (2025).

[52] Fikfak (2019, 1113–1115) (although this is a damage-standard analysis for article 6 ECHR, it is applicable to article 47 EU Charter due to the latter's incorporation of the former).

[53] Elton et al. (2022, 12–13) (analysis applicable to article 47 EU Charter due to its incorporation of article 6 ECHR).

Table 2 Cases

Case	Court	Elapsed case-time (from start of case to final appeal)	Remedy
Stojanović and Jusufović v. Bosnia and Herzegovina (2021)[55]	ECtHR (article 6 ECHR)	10-year case and a 7-year case	€2,400 of non-material damages and expenses of €250 in the 10-year case and €1,600 of non-material damages and expenses of €250 for the 7-year case (plaintiff's request for damages not known due to not being provided in court documents)
Jann-Zwicker and Jann v. Switzerland (2024)[56]	ECtHR (article 6 ECHR)	17 year-case	€20,800 of non-material damages and expenses of €14,000 (plaintiffs together requested €94,300 in material damages and approximately €150,000 in expenses)[57]
Kendrion v. EU (2018)[58]	CJEU (article 47 EU Charter)	5-year case	€6,000 of non-material damages (plaintiff requested €2,308,463 in material damages and €1,700,000 in non-material damages)
Gascogne v. EU (2017)[59]	CJEU (article 47 EU Charter)	11-year case	€5,000 of non-material damages per plaintiff (plaintiffs together requested €3,381,038 in material damages and €500,000 in non-material damages)

sample of cases in the following Table 2 demonstrate some outcomes demonstrating the relatively small, and likely non-deterrent, size of awarded damages.[54]

In the EU, the European Commission (EC), the EU's top executive-body, promotes efficient resolution of civil cases. The EC does so by publishing the EU Justice Scoreboard and administering the Rule of Law Conditionality Regulation (RLCR).[60] The EU Justice Scoreboard is where data on trial times is published. This data is a "key contribution to the European Semester", the EU's annual exercise to coordinate

[54] Fikfak (2019, 1107–1115), Elton et al. (2022, 12–13) and Kryla-Cudna and Verbruggen (2020, 4–7).

[55] ECtHR, *Stojanović and Jusufović v. Bosnia and Herzegovina*, 16 December 2021, App. No. 23081/20.

[56] ECtHR, *Jann-Zwicker and Jann v. Switzerland*, 13 February 2024, App. No. 4976/20.

[57] Approximate figures converted from Swiss Francs to Euros using February 2024 exchange rates.

[58] CJEU, case C-150/17, *Kendrion v. EU*, 13 December 2018, ECLI:EU:C:2018:1014.

[59] CJEU, case T-577/14, *Gascogne v. EU*, 10 January 2017, ECLI:EU:C:2017:1.

[60] The EU Justice Scoreboard and the Rule of Law Conditionality Regulation are examples of the increasingly common use of indicators related to the rule of law. A comprehensive overview of considerations related to such indicators is provided in Davis et al. (2012).

economic policy and social policy across EU member-countries, which in turn influences EU member-countries' and the EU's budget(s).[61] The RCLR allows the EU to suspend or reduce an EU member-country's access to the EU budget if it breaches of the rule of law, including by failing to conduct trials within a reasonable time.[62] Data from the EU Justice Scoreboard and data from the EU's annual Rule of Law Report are generally significant factors in deciding breaches of the rule of law. The RCLR has only been used once, successfully against Hungary in December 2022, and has continued to apply to Hungary since then, resulting in billions of Euros of funds being suspended since then as well. Key triggers for invoking the RCLR include "a lack of effective judicial remedies by an independent court against decisions of the prosecution service not to investigate or prosecute alleged corruption, fraud and other criminal offences affecting the Union's financial interests, a lack of a requirement to give reasons when such cases are attributed or reassigned, and an absence of rules to prevent arbitrary decisions in their regard".[63]

5 Two Approaches to Reform: Improving Interim Measures for Digital Disputes and Automating Appeals

Having detailed the torpidity of the US and Europe with respect to resolution of many important digital disputes, the associated harms, and the need for effective ways to address such harms, this chapter will now propose some reforms. Section 5.1 will detail methods of improving preliminary injunctions, interim measures, and other modes of rapid equitable relief in the realm of digital disputes. Section 5.2 will discuss a proposal to automate at least some appeals, inspired in part by some platforms' computerized responses to consumer complaints.

In the US, preliminary injunctions in digital disputes related to consumer protection are primarily limited to cases initiated by public litigants, such as federal or state governments. This is because public litigants are more empowered by key statutes than private litigants are. Many private litigants must base their cases to obtain a preliminary injunction on specific and limited data-privacy or UDAAP-adjacent federal or state law(s), such as the Illinois Biometric Information Protection Act, or the State of Washington's Public Records Act.[64] Private litigants are particularly

---

[61] European Commission (n.d.a).

[62] Regulation (EU, Euratom) 2020/2092 on a general regime of conditionality for the protection of the Union budget.

[63] European Commission (2024b).

[64] *Real Time Med. Sys., Inc. v. PointClickCare Techs., Inc.*, No. 24-1773, 2025 WL 779691 (4th Cir. 12 March 2025); *In re Clearview AI, Inc., Consumer Priv. Litig.*, No. 21-CV-00135, 2025 WL 875162 (N.D. Ill. 20 March 2025); *American Civil Liberties Union*, et al. *v. Clearview AI, Inc.*, Cook Cnty. Cir. Ct. No. 2020 CH 04353, 1–3 (9 May 2022); *The People of the State of California v. Google, LLC* (Final Judgment and Permanent Injunction), 23CV422424 (18 September 2023); *The People of the State of California v. Google, LLC* (Complaint for Injunction, Civil Penalties, and

vulnerable when the interests of governments entwine with the interests of digital platforms, potentially resulting in dangerously slow regulation.[65]

Concerningly, although public litigants are often more empowered than private litigants, the status quo is such that public litigants nonetheless are limited in addressing digital disputes before significant harms occur. For example, the Consumer Financial Protection Bureau (CFPB) and the Federal Trade Commission (FTC) are required to establish irreparable harm before obtaining a preliminary injunction, irreparable harm generally meaning harm not remediable by monetary means.[66] This significantly limits such agencies in addressing even significant dignitary, emotional, epistemic, and other harms of digital platforms, including many harms caused by algorithmic profiling, disinformation, manipulation, addiction, surveillance, etc., since there is often some way of monetarily valuing these harms (via contingent valuation or other methods).[67]

Another example related to tests for preliminary injunctions is the requirement that the CFPB and the FTC must establish how a preliminary injunction supports the public interest before obtaining such an injunction.[68] As digital platforms have become pervasive and increasingly essential parts of our lives, and hide critical aspects of their operations behind trade secrecy, technical complexity, and general opacity, it is often difficult to definitively demonstrate such support of the public interest at the earliest stages of a case.[69] Lastly, beyond the test for preliminary injunctions, there are also broader legal concerns that affect the ability of public litigants to obtain a preliminary injunction, particularly the significant and wide-ranging weakening of federal agencies such as the CFPB and FTC in the mid-2020s, reducing the ability of such agencies to timely or at all pursue preliminary injunctions.[70]

In Europe, the status of rapid equitable relief is similar to the US in terms of torpor, albeit arguably more optimistic in recent times. This is because the EU has recently created various legal frameworks empowering interim measures (essentially preliminary injunctions) and national governments in the EU under their own laws have increasingly utilized interim measures in digital contexts. An example is the Representative Actions Directive,[71] which is a law requiring all EU member-countries to have in place a mechanism for representative actions, which are defined as: "... actions brought by qualified entities before national courts or administrative

Other Equitable Relief), 23CV422424 (14 September 2023); *Lyft, Inc. v. City of Seattle*, 190 Wash. 2d 769, 418 P.3d 102 (2018).

[65] Mazur and Serafin (2023, 109–116).

[66] The following is the traditional four-factor test for preliminary injunctions, which varies slightly depending on the jurisdiction: "(1) the likelihood of success on the merits; (2) irreparable harm absent an injunction; (3) the balance of hardships or equities; and (4) the public interest". Lynch (2023, 1080–1082, 1112–1113).

[67] Pasquale (2015, 1–18).

[68] Lynch (2023, 1080, 1112–1113).

[69] Mazur and Serafin (2023, 109–116) and Pasquale (2015, 189–220).

[70] Godoy (2025) and Iacurci (2025).

[71] Directive (EU) 2020/1828 on representative actions for the protection of the collective interests of consumers and repealing Directive 2009/22/EC.

authorities on behalf of groups of consumers to seek injunctive measures...".[72] This legal framework addresses significant harms caused by slow resolution of digital disputes because it empowers qualified entities to empower consumers more quickly than consumers may be able to act on their own behalf.

Another example of such a legal framework is the EU's use of interim measures[73] under various laws related to consumer protection and competition, such as article 8 of Regulation 1/2003,[74] the Digital Services Act (DSA),[75] and the Digital Markets Act (DMA).[76] The *Broadcom* case of 2019 (and more recent requests regarding Broadcom) have been bellwethers for interim measures pursuant to article 8 of Regulation 1/2003.[77] Unlike preliminary injunctions in the US, interim measures under the DSA and the DMA do not require irreparable harm to an individual, but require serious harm to users or the public under the DSA and irreparable harm to competition affecting a market under the DMA.[78] These laws also feature clearer (and therefore more easily enforceable) rules for key digital players. Interim measures under the DSA have already been used to quickly address significant harms of digital platforms, being used against TikTok for addiction risks to children from TikTok's social-media algorithms, and interim measures under article 8 of Regulation 1/2003 are also expected to be used against Meta for allegedly abusing its market position in consumer communications to cause harm to the market for AI assistants.[79] Cases in both Germany and the Netherlands in 2025 have suggested avenues for relatively rapid interim relief. Additionally, national governments in the EU may also impose interim measures under their national laws. France, Italy, and Belgium have been most the active in doing so, having in recent years pursued cases either against Meta or Google for abusing their market power as well as cases against numerous smaller actors involved in digital environments. Overall, while these legal frameworks and measures are not perfect, promising future developments related to interim measures for digital disputes, such as the EU's Digital Fairness Act (among other things, allowing for interim measures for consumer harm related to addictive and unfair practices in digital spaces) and the reform of Regulation 1/2003 (among other things, relaxing the test to use interim measures in competition cases), indicate the EU will continue to be an innovator in addressing the significant harms of digital life in a timely manner.[80]

---

[72] European Commission (n.d.b).

[73] European Commission (2019), European Commission (2024c), and Farinhas (2025, 1–3).

[74] Council Regulation (EC) No 1/2003 of 16 December 2002 on the implementation of the rules on competition laid down in Articles 81 and 82 of the Treaty.

[75] Regulation (EU) 2022/1925 on contestable and fair markets in the digital sector and amending Directives (EU) 2019/1937 and (EU) 2020/1828 (Digital Markets Act).

[76] Regulation (EU) 2022/2065 of the European Parliament and of the Council of 19 October 2022 on a Single Market For Digital Services and amending Directive 2000/31/EC (Digital Services Act).

[77] Mantzari (2020, 1, 2–4).

[78] Farinhas (2025, 1–3) and European Commission (2024c).

[79] European Commission (2024c) and Rogers and Fila (2026).

[80] Armangau (2025) and European Commission (2024d) and European Commission (2025) and Vleeshouwers et al. (2025) and Rogers and Fila (2026).

To summarize, these examples demonstrate three effective ways for preliminary injunctions and interim measures to better address significant harms in the digital realm in a timely manner: (1) increase the ability of private litigants to obtain rapid relief for some digital harms based on laws public litigants use; (2) enact laws to empower private litigants to cooperate to obtain rapid relief; and (3) modify tests for preliminary injunctions for digital disputes, particularly factors related to irreparable harm, promoting the public interest, or factors limiting who is required to be harmed. All these approaches would help ensure that digital harms are more quickly and effectively recognized and countered.

5.1 Automating Appeals and Automation-After-Declaration

Given the speed of generative AI at composing plausible facsimiles of opinions justifying judgments, the judiciary may feel pressure to improve its timeliness, including in handling appeals. In *Chief Justice Robots*, the US legal scholar Eugene Volokh proposed using AI to write opinions in cases, particularly when the technology reaches a point where its output cannot be reliably distinguished (by experts) from the output of actual, human judges.[81] Automation of a social role will seem more plausible to the extent that the role is currently performed by human beings in an impaired or excessively delayed way.[82] While we by no means endorse the automation of appellate judging, there will be increasing pressure for some technical assistance in this realm if persistent delays continue. Two passable AI-written opinions written in one day may seem more socially desirable than judge-written ones that take years to appear.

For similar reasons, the increasing pressure for timely appeals likely applies to non-judicial appeals as well. Rather than AI judges, a more realistic automation option may be inspired by the automated dispute-resolution practices of digital platforms. For example, to the extent that an automated resolution of a digital dispute by a platform appears to have contravened public values, a regulator could require a reversal of that automated decision to happen automatically once the complaining party has made a sufficiently detailed declaration to that regulator or other relevant authority. Future proceedings could restore the original determination, and may well do so. But the presumption would be that submission of the perfected declaration requires immediate action.

Relatedly, there is an asymmetry present in some resolutions of intellectual property (IP) disputes online, where platforms use automated or semi-automated methods to resolve them while official processes to permit what are effectively appeals are notably slower. However, to the extent that these processes systematically disadvantage certain IP owners or users, they might also be subject to limitations or automatic reversal upon the filing of a sufficient declaration. Not limited to IP,

---

[81] Volokh (2019, 1141–1142).

[82] Volokh (2019, 1138–1141) and Pasquale (2020, 33–59).

these methods may also be used in other contexts involving digital content. Law professor and sociologist Ari Ezra Waldman has documented troublingly discriminatory practices at some social media firms with respect to LGBTQ content.[83] The automatic take-down of some LGBTQ content from platforms may be countered by legal requirements for automatic restoration once an account owner has made a sufficient declaration.

Financial disputes are also ripe for such interventions. For example, an e-commerce firm may make it difficult for a customer to obtain a refund from a vendor on a platform, perhaps by routing the customer's complaints through dead-end or roundabout automated processes. Here, there is a case for permitting customers (once they have filed a sufficient declaration to a regulator or other relevant authority) to submit and obtain automated refunds, similar to how chargebacks work for credit cards. Such declarations may document via screenshots or other material customers' good faith efforts to resolve their issues with a vendor and platform.

Of course, all the 'automation after declaration' methods mentioned above would themselves need some level of policing to be fair. Lying on such a declaration should trigger punishment, and may well entail expulsion from the platform or perjury penalties. Regulators would need the help of technologists and researchers to identify and fend off abuse of declarations, and suspiciously frequent use of them should lead to a suspension of the privilege. Nevertheless, if consumers are to have any hope of resolving their disputes with platforms as speedily as platforms dispose of them, they will need a rethinking by policymakers of the automation asymmetries now afflicting online life. Experiments with 'automation after declaration' methods would, at the very least, offer valuable information about the feasibility of leveling the temporal playing field in online remedies.

6 Conclusion

This chapter aims to extend the range of solutions to excessive delays in remedying harms related to digital disputes. However, improving interim measures and experimenting with automated appeals are only two ways to better ensure more rapid resolution of such disputes. Ex ante licensure requirements may prevent many dangerous forms of AI, for example, from even being publicly available before they are vetted by experts. Algorithmic enforcement is another option that may be possible once there are adequate datasets indicating the difference between legal and illegal action (in certain narrow domains). There are undoubtebly many other ways to effectively address such harms. Given the immense need for solutions to the issues this chapter only briefly covers, we look forward to engaging with a broader dialogue on the timely remediation of digital disputes.

[83] Waldman (2022).

References

Allen D (2004) The constitutional floor doctrine and the right to a speedy trial. Campbell Law Rev 26(2):101–122

Armangau R (2025) EU Digital Fairness Act is for business as much as consumers, says justice commissioner. https://www.euronews.com/next/2025/04/11/eu-digital-fairness-act-is-for-business-as-much-as-consumers-says-justice-commissioner

Bagley N (2019) The procedure fetish. Mich Law Rev 118(3):345–401

Bergqvist C (2024) Taking stock of EU's case against Google Shopping before final ruling. Promarket. https://www.promarket.org/2024/09/04/taking-stock-of-eus-case-against-google-shopping-before-final-ruling/

Bone RG (2010) Improving Rule 1: a master rule for the federal rules. Denver University Law Review 87(2):287–309

Bordelon B, Miller G (2025) After EU fines, Big Tech wants Trump to swoop in. https://www.politico.com/news/2025/04/23/european-fines-big-tech-trump-00306670

Chee FY (2025) Amazon loses court fight against record $812 million Luxembourg privacy fine. Reuters. https://www.reuters.com/technology/amazon-loses-court-fight-against-record-812-mln-luxembourg-privacy-fine-2025-03-19/

Chee FY (2026) Win for Amazon as Luxembourg court scraps record $854 million privacy fine. Reuters. https://www.reuters.com/legal/government/win-amazon-luxembourg-court-scraps-record-854-million-privacy-fine-2026-03-13/

Council of Europe (n.d.a) The council of Europe and the European Union. https://www.coe.int/en/web/portal/european-union

Cullen C (2024) The nonexistent speedy trial right. Pepperdine Law Rev 51(4):661–782

Davis KE, Benedict K, Sally EM (2012) Introduction: global governance by indicators. In: Davis KE et al (eds) Governance by indicators: global power through quantification and rankings. Oxford University Press, Oxford, pp 3–28

Ducci F (2021) Gatekeepers and platform regulation: is the EU moving in the right direction? SciencesPo. https://www.sciencespo.fr/public/chaire-numerique/wp-content/uploads/2021/04/GATEKEEPERS-AND-PLATFORM-REGULATION-Is-the-EU-moving-in-the-Right-Direction-Francesco-DUCCI-March-2021-2.pdf

Dunkelman M (2025) Why Nothing Works: Who Killed Progress and How to Bring It Back. PublicAffairs, New York

Elton L et al (2022) Right to a trial within a reasonable time—comparative overview. https://rm.coe.int/right-to-a-trial-within-a-reasonable-time-hfii/1680aa3886

European Commission (n.d.a) EU Justice scoreboard. https://commission.europa.eu/strategy-and-policy/policies/justice-and-fundamental-rights/upholding-rule-law/eu-justice-scoreboard_en

European Commission (n.d.b) Representative actions directive. https://commission.europa.eu/law/law-topic/consumer-protection-law/representative-actions-directive_en

European Commission (2005) Financial penalties for member states who fail to comply with judgments of the European Court of Justice: European Commission clarifies rules. https://ec.europa.eu/commission/presscorner/detail/en/memo_05_482

European Commission (2024a) Communication from the Commission to the European Parliament and the Council COM(2024) 357 final. https://eur-lex.europa.eu/legal-content/EN/TXT/PDF/?uri=CELEX:52024DC0357

European Commission (2024b) Commission considers that Hungary has not sufficiently addressed breaches of the principles of the rule of law and therefore maintains measures to protect the Union budget. https://ec.europa.eu/commission/presscorner/detail/nl/ip_24_6465

European Commission (2024c) Commission opens proceedings against TikTok Under the DSA regarding the launch of TikTok Lite in France and Spain, and communicates its intention to suspend the reward programme in the EU. https://ec.europa.eu/commission/presscorner/detail/en/ip_24_2227

European Commission (2024d) Report from the commission to the council and the European Parliament. https://eur-lex.europa.eu/legal-content/EN/TXT/?uri=CELEX:52024DC0394
European Commission (2025) Commission seeks feedback for the revision of EU antitrust enforcement framework. https://ec.europa.eu/commission/presscorner/detail/en/ip_25_1795
European Council (n.d.a) Rule of law conditionality mechanism: Council decides to suspend €6.3 billion given only partial remedial action by Hungary. https://www.consilium.europa.eu/en/press/press-releases/2022/12/12/rule-of-law-conditionality-mechanism/
European Court of Human Rights (ECtHR) (2025) Guide on Article 6 of the European Convention on Human Rights. Council of Europe. https://ks.echr.coe.int/documents/d/echr-ks/guide_art_6_civil_eng
European Data Protection Board (2023) Binding decision 01/2023 on the processing of personal data by Facebook Ireland Ltd for behavioural advertising and the transfer of personal data to the U.S. following the Schrems II litigation. https://www.edpb.europa.eu/system/files/2023-05/edpb_bindingdecision_202301_ie_sa_facebooktransfers_en.pdf
European Union Agency for Fundamental Rights (2025) Article 47 – Right to an effective remedy and to a fair trial. https://fra.europa.eu/en/eu-charter/article/47-right-effective-remedy-and-fair-trial
Farinhas C (2025) Interim measures in digital markets: Interaction between the DMA and Regulation 1/2003. https://papers.ssrn.com/5087946
Fikfak V (2019) Changing state behavior: damages before the European Court of Human Rights. Eur J Int Law 29(4):1091–1125
Fuster GG et al (2022) The right to lodge a data protection complaint: ok, but then what? An empirical study of current practices under the GDPR. Data Protection Legal Scholars Network. https://www.accessnow.org/wp-content/uploads/2022/07/GDPR-Complaint-study.pdf
Gerken T (2024) EU court rules Google must pay €2.4bn fine. https://www.bbc.com/news/articles/cjw3e1pn741o
Godoy J (2025) Trump's antitrust enforcers 'get out of the way' of multibillion-dollar deals. Reuters. https://www.reuters.com/legal/litigation/trumps-antitrust-enforcers-get-out-way-multibillion-dollar-deals-2025-07-10/
Grossman MR et al (2023) The GPTJudge: justice in a generative AI world. Duke Law Tech Rev (1):1–34
Hildebrand S, Cordero A (2022) The burden of time: government negligence in pandemic planning as a catalyst for reinvigorating the Sixth Amendment speedy trial right. Villanova Law Rev 67(1):1–34
Hildebrandt M (2024) The future of computational law in the context of the rule of law. J Cross-Discip Res Comput Law 2(2). https://journalcrcl.org/crcl/article/view/63/24
Iacurci G (2025) Trump's 'big beautiful bill' slashes CFPB funding: what it means for you. https://www.cnbc.com/2025/07/09/trump-big-beautiful-bill-slashes-cfpb-funding-what-it-means.html
Ionescu DP (2023) Comparative remarks on Article 47 of the Charter and effective judicial protection before national courts. https://realaw.blog/2023/07/21/comparative-remarks-on-article-47-of-the-charter-and-effective-judicial-protection-before-national-courts-volume-ii-by-m-bonelli-m-eliantonio-and-g-gentile/
Klein E, Thompson D (2025) Abundance. Simon & Schuster, New York
Kryla-Cudna K, Verbruggen P (2020) The Union's liability for failure to adjudicate within a reasonable time: EU tort law after Gascogne, Kendrion and ASPLA. Common Mark Law Rev 57(1):191–226
Kuijer M (2013) The right to a fair trial and the Council of Europe's efforts to ensure effective remedies on a domestic level for excessively lengthy proceedings. Hum Rights Law Rev 13(4):777–794
Kye C (2025) A quagmire of delays at the European General Court: any escape? Maastricht J Eur Comp Law 22(3):453–471
Lursmanashvili L (2018) Reasonable time requirement: ECtHR approach. Caucasus J Soc Sci 11(1):175–177

Lynch KJ (2023) Preliminary injunctions in public law: the merits. Houst Law Rev 60(5):1067–1115
Mantzari D (2020) Interim measures in EU competition cases: origins, evolution, and implications for digital markets. J Eur Comp Law Pract 11(9):487–498
Martin D (2020) The long and winding road: two years of the GDPR: a cross-border data protection enforcement case from a consumer perspective. https://www.beuc.eu/sites/default/files/publications/beuc-x-2020-074_two_years_of_the_gdpr_a_cross-border_data_protection_enforcement_case_from_a_consumer_perspective.pdf
Mazur J, Serafin M (2023) Stalling the state: how digital platforms contribute to and profit from delays in the enforcement and adoption of regulations. Comp Pol Stud 56(1):101–130
Meta Platforms, Inc (2024) Form 10-K for the fiscal year ended December 31, 2023. SEC. https://www.sec.gov/ix?doc=/Archives/edgar/data/0001326801/000132680125000017/meta-20241231.htm
Noyb.eu (2020) CJEU invalidates 'privacy shield' in US surveillance case. https://noyb.eu/en/cjeu
Partnoy F (2012) Wait: the art and science of delay. PublicAffairs, New York
Pasquale F (2015) The black box society: the secret algorithms that control money and information. Harvard University Press, Cambridge
Pasquale F (2020) New laws of robotics: defending human expertise in the age of AI. Belknap Press, Cambridge
Quinn M (2023) 96-year-old federal judge suspended from hearing cases after concerns about her fitness. CBS News. https://www.cbsnews.com/news/pauline-newman-96-year-old-federal-judge-suspended/
Ring S (2020) Broken justice: the return of the 'Italian torpedo.' Financial Times. https://www.ft.com/content/35e639df-dd4c-4b09-9478-24b0e9384546
Rogers A, Fila D (2026) Global convergence on the use of interim measures in competition law? The curious case of GenAI chatbots on WhatsApp. Norton Rose Fulbright. https://connections.nortonrosefulbright.com/post/102mhb4/global-convergence-on-the-use-of-interim-measures-in-competition-law-the-curious#:~:text=On%209%20February%202026%2C%20the,8%20of%20Regulation%201%2F2003
Roth S (2021) Appeal First, question later: addressing the growing number of rapid GDPR appeals and its effects on adequate enforcement. Journal High Tech Law. Availble at https://sites.suffolk.edu/jhtl/2021/04/30/appeal-first-question-later-addressing-the-growing-number-of-rapid-gdpr-appeals-and-its-effects-on-adequate-enforcement/
Saetveit K (2016) Beyond Pollard: applying the Sixth Amendment's speedy trial right to sentencing. Stanf Law Rev 68(2):481–509
Scharre P (2018) A million mistakes a second. Foreign Policy. https://foreignpolicy.com/2018/09/12/a-million-mistakes-a-second-future-of-war/
Scheuerman WE (2004) Liberal democracy and the social acceleration of time. The Johns Hopkins University Press, Baltimore
Schuh J (2016) Curbing judicial discretion in pretrial conferences. Lewis & Clark Law Rev 20(2):647–682
Sciaudone F et al (2025) Final report: ex post evaluation of the implementation and effectiveness of EU antitrust remedies. https://op.europa.eu/en/publication-detail/-/publication/a5132bd9-fb05-11ef-b7db-01aa75ed71a1
The Administrative Office of the US Courts (2024) US federal courts – complaints filed and action taken under 28 U.S.C. § 351–364—during the 12-month periods ending September 30, 2023 and 2024. https://www.uscourts.gov/data-news/data-tables/2024/09/30/judicial-business/s-22
The Indiana Lawyer (2021) 7th Circuit condemns 75-day delay in opinion, saying wait could spell 'disaster' for litigants. https://www.theindianalawyer.com/articles/7th-circuit-condemns-75-day-delay-in-opinion-saying-wait-could-spell-disaster-for-litigants
The Irish Times (2025) Meta challenge over €265m fines must go ahead, Court of Appeal rules. https://www.irishtimes.com/business/2025/03/13/meta-challenge-over-265m-fines-must-go-ahead-court-of-appeal-rules/

Tracxn (2025) All acquisitions: Google.com. https://platform.tracxn.com/a/s/query/t/acquisitions/t/allacquisitions/table?h=b4b4588f56a173e65d2051c73b3c1db4a663879256c0f1fa53a14fab47b00af6&s=sort%3DannouncementDate%7Corder%3DDEFAULT
Truong BT et al (2025) Delayed takedown of illegal content on social media makes moderation ineffective. arXiv:2502.08841
Vleeshouwers et al. (2025) Interim measures: Is the European Commission catching up with (French and Belgian) national competition authorities? Bird & Bird. https://competitionlawinsights.twobirds.com/post/102jzzn/interim-measures-is-the-european-commission-catching-up-with-french-and-belgian
Volokh E (2019) Chief justice robots. Duke Law J 68(6):1135–1192
Waagstein PR (2010) Human rights protection in Europe: between Strasbourg and Luxembourg. https://spice.fsi.stanford.edu/docs/human_rights_protection_in_europe_between_strasbourg_and_luxembourg
Waldman AE (2022) Disorderly content. Wash Law Rev 97(4):907–997
Wasby SL (1997) Delay as a due process violation. Comp Perspect 19(2):235–240
Weiss DC (2017) Federal judge remains excused from new civil cases amid backlog concerns. ABA J. https://www.abajournal.com/news/article/federal_judge_is_excused_from_new_civil_cases_amid_backlog_concerns
White L (2026) CJEU rules Meta can challenge EDPB's binding WhatsApp decision. IAPP. https://iapp.org/news/a/cjeu-rules-meta-can-challenge-edpb-s-binding-whatsapp-decision
World Health Organization (WHO) (2025) Road traffic injures. https://www.who.int/health-topics/road-safety#tab=tab_1
Wyatt BJ (2004) Even aliens are entitled to due process: extending Mathews v. Eldridge balancing to board of immigration appeals procedural reform. William & Mary Bill of Rights J 12(2):605–636

Fundamental Rights Impact Assessments Under the AI Act: A Possible Remedy to Algorithmic Discrimination in the Private Sector

Aurelia Colombi Ciacchi, Greta Berardi, Alma-Cristina Onaie, and Niels Singer

Abstract This paper focuses on a specific instrument which may help prevent algorithmic discrimination in contractual relationships: fundamental rights impact assessments. The first fundamental rights impact assessment model considered in this paper is the one prescribed by article 27 of the EU AI Act. This impact assessment is mandatory not only for public bodies but also for several categories of private actors. The second model addressed in this paper is the Fundamental Rights and Algorithms Impact Assessment (FRAIA), developed in the Netherlands a few years ago to prevent violations of fundamental rights through algorithms. The paper then addresses some examples of algorithmic discrimination in contractual relationships and concludes by questioning the capability of fundamental rights impact assessment systems to prevent algorithmic discrimination by powerful contract parties in the EU.

Keywords Impact assessment · Algorithmic discrimination · Fundamental rights · Artificial intelligence

---

A previous version of this paper, with a partly different content, is published by three of the four co-authors of the present paper in Colombi Ciacchi et al (2026).

A. C. Ciacchi (✉) · G. Berardi · N. Singer
Faculty of Law, University of Groningen, Groningen, The Netherlands
e-mail: a.l.b.colombi.ciacchi@rug.nl

G. Berardi
e-mail: g.berardi.1@student.rug.nl

N. Singer
e-mail: n.m.singer@student.rug.nl

A.-C. Onaie
Università Bocconi, Milano, Italy
e-mail: almacristina.onaie@master.unibocconi.it

C. Crea and M. Infantino (eds.), *Remedies to Digital Vulnerability in European Private Law*, https://doi.org/10.1007/978-3-032-19720-7_11

1 Introduction

Algorithmic discrimination is a relatively recent societal problem, on which a new discourse in legal science has been developed.[1] Not rarely, decisions of public or private actors taken through algorithms have the (mostly unintended) effect to directly or indirectly discriminate against certain groups of persons.

Two grounds of algorithmic discrimination seem to be the most frequent in practice: sex or gender on the one hand, and race or ethnic background on the other.[2] In EU law, the right not to be discriminated against on ground of sex, race, colour, ethnic or social origin, genetic features, language, religion or belief, political or any other opinion, membership of a national minority, property, birth, disability, age or sexual orientation, is a fundamental right enshrined in article 21(1) of the Charter of Fundamental Rights of the EU (hereinafter 'the Charter'). The terms 'discrimination' and 'discriminatory' in the present paper refer to any of the grounds listed in article 21(1) of the Charter.

Many algorithms are not 'intelligent' enough to qualify as AI. With the words of Ismail, "[a]n algorithm is a set of instructions—a preset, rigid, coded recipe that gets executed when it encounters a trigger. AI on the other hand—which is an extremely broad term covering a myriad of AI specializations and subsets—is a group of algorithms that can modify its algorithms and create new algorithms in response to learned inputs and data as opposed to relying solely on the inputs it was designed to recognize as triggers. This ability to change, adapt and grow based on new data, is described as 'intelligence'".[3] In this paper, the term 'algorithmic discrimination' refers to the use of algorithms independent of whether they form part of AI systems.

The paper focuses on a specific instrument which may help prevent algorithmic discrimination in contractual relationships: fundamental rights impact assessments. The first model of fundamental rights impact assessment analysed in the paper is the one prescribed by article 27 of the EU AI Act (Sect. 2).[4] The AI Act requires not only public bodies but also several categories of private actors to conduct a FRIA prior to the use of a high-risk AI system. The AI Act is arguably designed to apply primarily in the private sector. The second model addressed in this paper (Sect. 3) is a national model: the Fundamental Rights and Algorithms Impact Assessment (FRAIA), developed in the Netherlands few years ago to prevent violations of fundamental rights through algorithms. The paper then outlines some examples of algorithmic discrimination in contractual relationships (Sect. 4). The concluding section questions the

[1] See, among others, Kleinberg et al (2018); Zuiderveen Borgesius (2018); Xenidis and Senden (2020, 157); Zuiderveen Borgesius (2020); Grozdanovski (2021); Circiumaru (2021); Barat i Rubio (2025).

[2] See Gerards and Xenidis (2021, 32–36).

[3] Ismail (2018). For a more detailed explanation of the differences between rule-based algorithms and machine-learning algorithms see Gerards and Xenidis (2021, 32–36).

[4] Regulation (EU) 2024/1689 of the European Parliament and of the Council of 13 June 2024 laying down harmonised rules on artificial intelligence and amending Regulations (EC) No 300/2008, (EU) No 167/2013, (EU) No 168/2013, (EU) 2018/858, (EU) 2018/1139 and (EU) 2019/2144 and Directives 2014/90/EU, (EU) 2016/797 and (EU) 2020/1828 (Artificial Intelligence Act).

capability of fundamental rights impact assessment systems to prevent algorithmic discrimination by powerful contract parties in the EU (Sect. 5).

2 Fundamental Rights Impact Assessments (FRIA): Article 27 of the AI Act

Article 27 of the AI Act explicitly obliges deployers[5] of high-risk AI systems to conduct a fundamental rights impact assessment (FRIA). These high-risk systems are established in article 6(1), as well as article 6(2) AI Act which refers to a list of systems in Annex III of the AI Act. While article 6(1) indicates AI systems that are safety components of products or products themselves and regulated by existing EU harmonisation legislation,[6] an example being AI-based medical software,[7] the list in Annex III covers systems that are intended to be employed for high-risk use cases, i.e. areas such as education, employment, access to public services, and law enforcement.[8]

It is important to note that article 27 AI Act obliges not only public actors, but also three categories of private actors that deploy high-risk AI systems,[9] to conduct fundamental rights impact assessments: (1) private actors that provide public services; (2) deployers of high-risk AI systems referred to in point 5(b) of Annex III, i.e. credit institutions that intend to use AI systems to evaluate the creditworthiness of natural persons or establish their credit score, with the exception of AI systems used for the purpose of detecting financial fraud, and (3) deployers of high-risk AI systems referred to in point 5(c) of Annex III, i.e. insurance providers that intend to use AI systems for risk assessment and pricing in relation to natural persons in the case of life and health insurance.

Concerning the first category, whilst the EU AI Act does not per se contain a strict definition of the term "public services", Recital 96 offers examples of sectors where private entities may perform such functions, i.a. education, healthcare, social services, housing, and the administration of justice. In this regard an argument could be made that the use of such a broad term—public service—may hint at a legislative intent for expansive application, covering any private developer whose AI system has a tangible effect on public interests.

[5] Under article 3(4) of the AI Act, a deployer is defined as a "natural or legal person, public authority, agency, or other body using an AI system under its authority except where the AI system is used in the course of a personal non-professional activity".

[6] See Gikay et al (2023, 9–12).

[7] European Commission (2024).

[8] European Commission (2024).

[9] As said, the AI Act is arguably designed to apply primarily in the private sector. See Boix Palop (2025, 3).

A first remark: the FRIA is only a risk assessment with a preventive and predictive character.[10] Its purpose is to assess the potential impact of high-risk AI systems on fundamental rights instead of eliminating risk, thus focussing on risk management rather than risk elimination.[11] Therefore, the FRIA follows an ex-ante approach: the deployer should conduct the FRIA prior to putting the system into service and ensure that fundamental rights concerns are identified and addressed before the technology becomes operational.[12] However, if, after deployment, the deployer considers that elements of its previously conducted FRIA are no longer accurate or up to date, they have a duty to update the relevant information.[13] Therefore, it can be argued that the FRIA under article 27 AI Act is not a one-time evaluation,[14] but a continuous monitoring process aiming to safeguard fundamental rights throughout the entire lifecycle of the high-risk AI system[15]—a view which is consistent with the general approach of the AI Act under article 9(2).[16]

As to the fundamental rights to be covered by the FRIA, this paper adheres to the opinion that regard should be given also to environmental protection, even if not explicitly mentioned in article 27 AI Act.[17] This is because the safeguarding of environmental protection is one of the main purposes of the Regulation,[18] the importance of which is reiterated in several recitals,[19] and because environmental protection is acknowledged among the EU fundamental rights in article 37 Charter of Fundamental Rights of the European Union.[20]

With respect to the methodology required when conducting a FRIA, the AI Act does not prescribe a specific approach.[21] Article 27(5) of the AI Act delegates the responsibility of developing a standardised FRIA template to the AI Office,[22] likely in the form of a structured questionnaire, which aims to simplify the assessment process for deployers while reducing administrative burdens.[23] The AI Office has yet to develop such a questionnaire.[24] Since the AI Act does not specify a time frame to fulfil this task, one may argue that the AI Office shall develop the questionnaire

---

[10] Mantelero (2024, 9); Malgieri and Santos (2025, 8).

[11] Ajoodha and Browne (2025).

[12] Mantelero (2024, 9); Regulation (EU) 2024/1689, recital 96.

[13] Regulation (EU) 2024/1689, art 27(2), recital 96; Cosentini et al (2025, 14).

[14] Mantelero (2024, 5).

[15] Bertaina et al (2025, 5).

[16] Mantelero (2024, 5).

[17] Bertaina et al (2025, 5).

[18] Regulation (EU) 2024/1689, art 1(1).

[19] See e.g. Regulation (EU) 2024/1689, recitals 142, 155, 165, 176.

[20] Bertaina et al (2025, 5).

[21] Bertaina et al (2025, 2).

[22] The AI Office is a new EU regulatory body established by Commission Decision of 24 January 2024 establishing the European Artificial Intelligence Office.

[23] Regulation (EU) 2024/1689, recital 96.

[24] Status as of June 2025.

Table 1 Overview of article 27(1) AI Act

Deployment context and intended purpose	(a) A description of the deployer's processes in which the high-risk AI system will be used in line with its intended purpose
Operational duration and usage frequency	(b) A description of the period of time within which, and the frequency with which, each high-risk AI system is intended to be used
Affected natural persons and groups	(c) The categories of natural persons and groups likely to be affected by its use in the specific context
Specific risks of harm	(d) The specific risks of harm likely to have an impact on the categories of natural persons or groups of persons identified pursuant to point (c) of this paragraph, considering the information given by the provider pursuant to article 13
Human oversight measures	(e) A description of the implementation of human oversight measures, according to the instructions for use
Risk mitigation measures	(f) The measures to be taken in the case of the materialisation of those risks, including the arrangements for internal governance and complaint mechanisms

by 2 August 2026 as this is the date on which the AI Act, including article 27(5), becomes applicable according to article 113 of the Act.[25]

Notwithstanding the lack of explicit rules on how to carry out the FRIA, article 27(1) outlines several key aspects that must be included in the assessment by deployers. These aspects are outlined in the following table 1.

[25] EU Artificial Intelligence Act (2024).

3 Fundamental Rights and Algorithmic Impact Assessment (FRAIA): a National Model

3.1 The Background: Three Algorithmic Discrimination Scandals in the Netherlands

It may be argued that one of the reasons for the EU institutions to require fundamental rights impact assessments under the AI Act was the experience of one Member State: the Netherlands. Neither the Commission's proposal of April 2021,[26] nor the Council's general approach of 2022 contained any provision on fundamental rights impact assessments. Such a provision was only included in the European Parliament's amendments of June 2023,[27] which then, with some modifications, shaped the content of article 27 of the AI Act as it was jointly adopted by Parliament and Council in 2024. It may be argued that the European Parliament's amendments of 2023 to the AI Act proposal, and thus the FRIA, were most likely inspired by the Dutch 'Fundamental Rights and Algorithms Impact Assessment' (FRAIA) of 2022.[28]

The FRAIA was developed as a response to three algorithmic discrimination scandals brought to light in the Netherlands between 2019 and 2021. To prevent future cases of violations of fundamental rights through algorithms, the Dutch Government entrusted an interdisciplinary group of scientists from Utrecht University[29] with the task of drafting an impact assessment model. The product of their joint work, the FRAIA, was published in 2022 by the Ministry of Interior and Kingdom Relations as a non-binding "discussion and decision-making tool for government organisations".[30]

In all three algorithmic discrimination scandals that raised awareness about the need for fundamental rights and algorithms impact assessments in the Netherlands, the perpetrators were public bodies. The first and perhaps most famous scandal led to the resignation of the Rutte III government in January 2021: the so-called *Toeslagenaffaire*, known internationally as the 'childcare benefit scandal'.[31] The tax administration (*Belastingdienst*) used algorithms to detect possible tax fraud by beneficiaries of childcare benefits. These algorithms clearly had discriminatory

[26] Proposal for a Regulation of the European Parliament and of the Council laying down harmonised rules on artificial intelligence (Artificial Intelligence Act) and amending certain Union legislative acts [2021] COM 206 final.

[27] Amendments adopted by the European Parliament on 14 June 2023 on the Proposal for a Regulation of the European Parliament and of the Council on laying down harmonised rules on artificial intelligence (Artificial Intelligence Act) and amending certain Union legislative acts [2021] COM 206 final. On this version of the text, see Waem et al. (2024).

[28] Gerards et al. (2022, 2).

[29] Janneke Gerards (Professor of Fundamental Rights in Europe), Mirko Tobias Schäfer (Associate Professor of AI, Data & Society), Iris Muis (Knowledge Valorisation Officer, expert on responsible AI and digital ethics), and Arthur Vankan (ICON – Media and Performance Studies).

[30] Gerards et al. (2022, 2).

[31] See Haitsma and Bouwmeester (2023); Haitsma (2023); Ranchordás and Schuurmans (2020, 11 ff).

effects against persons with a migration background. In its report about this Dutch scandal, Amnesty International spoke of 'xenophobic machines'.[32]

The second scandal was the SyRI case, which led to the much-discussed judgment *NJCM and FNV v the State of the Netherlands* of the Hague District Court (hereinafter: 'SyRI judgment).[33] The Risk Indication system known as 'SyRI' was a legal instrument introduced by the Dutch government aimed at helping local authorities to detect fraud tied to social benefits allowances or taxes in specific neighbourhoods.[34] The system, through a complex method of data collection, known as 'black-box'[35] identified a natural or legal person who might have been at risk of committing fraud and flagged such individuals to local authorities as 'worthy of investigation'.[36] One of the main issues analysed by the court was whether the system interfered with the right to private and family life as enshrined in article 8 of the European Convention of Human Rights (ECHR). The court found that SyRI inadvertently reinforced existing biases by disproportionately flagging individuals with a lower socio-economic status or with an immigration background, as it was primarily deployed in 'problematic neighbourhoods'.[37] As a result, SyRI could produce discriminatory outcomes by targeting in a disproportionate manner individuals from lower-income areas.[38] In this connection the court recalled that "the right to respect for private life in the context of data processing concerns the right to equal treatment in equal cases, and the right to protection against discrimination, stereotyping and stigmatization".[39]

This judgment successfully addressed the need for accountable and transparent automated systems. Transparency obligations under the GDPR ensure that data subjects are informed about their data being processed by an automated system.[40] However, transparency alone cannot guarantee the prevention of discrimination. Some scholars have criticised the SyRI judgement for having overlooked the discriminatory impacts caused by the automated system in relation to the right to social

[32] See Amnesty International (2021).

[33] Rechtbank Den Haag 5 February 2020, ECLI:NL:RBDHA:2020:1878. For a comment, see, among others, Meuwese (2020), Rachovitsa and Johann (2022) and Ranchordás and Schuurmans (2020, 6 ff).

[34] Rechtbank Den Haag 5 February 2020, ECLI:NL:RBDHA:2020:1878, para. 3.1.

[35] Algorithm Watch (2020).

[36] Rechtbank Den Haag 5 February 2020, ECLI:NL:RBDHA:2020:1878, para. 3.2.

[37] Ibid, para 6.93.

[38] Ibid. The human rights and poverty-related aspects of the SyRI case were highlighted in the brief submitted by the United Nations Special Rapporteur on extreme poverty and human rights as amicus curiae: Alston (2019). For a comment on the decision, see Rachovitsa and Johann (2022, 12).

[39] Rechtbank Den Haag 5 February 2020, ECLI:NL:RBDHA:2020:1878, para. 6.24.

[40] See articles 12-23 of the Regulation (EU) 2016/679 of the European Parliament and of the Council of 27 April 2016 on the protection of natural persons with regard to the processing of personal data and on the free movement of such data, and repealing Directive 95/46/EC (General Data Protection Regulation).

security which, similarly to the right to privacy, involves both transparency and non-discrimination.[41] Given the difficulty of assessing the discriminatory impacts of the system because of the transparency gaps the system presented, the court excluded from its analysis the right to social security, thus failing to set a remarkable precedent also in this sphere.[42]

The third Dutch algorithmic discrimination scandal was the DUO case, which in some respect was similarly to the SyRI case. The Education Executive Agency (*Dienst Uitvoering Onderwijs*, DUO) developed a risk-based system aimed at detecting fraud in student benefits.[43] According to a report published by Amnesty International,[44] the systems identified 'high risk' students based on a two-fold test: firstly, an algorithm assigned to students a risk score and secondly an employee from DUO would visit the domicile of the student based on the assigned risk score.[45] The main criteria used to determine the risk score were: age, education level, and geographical distance from the residence of parents, which however resulted to target in a disproportionate and unfair manner individuals from ethnic minorities.[46] According to Amnesty International, while the system did not directly use criteria such as 'race', 'color' or 'ethnicity'[47] to determine the risk score, its reliance on criteria relating to geographical location effectively constituted a proxy for ethnicity, resulting in unfair targeting.[48]

A few months ago, after an investigation, the Dutch Data Protection Authority concluded that DUO's algorithmic decision-making to assess fraud was discriminatory and unlawful, since there was no objective justification for the criteria used to determine the risk score.[49]

3.2 *The FRAIA: Function, Structure, and Content*

The FRAIA provides a systematic approach to assessing potential risks associated with algorithmic processes whilst ensuring compliance with fundamental rights. It serves as a platform to foster interdisciplinary discussions among those overseeing the creation or implementation of algorithmic systems, and it helps organisations identify risks to human rights in using algorithms and take measures to address them. Consequently, it acts as a preventive tool, ensuring that organisations refrain from

[41] Leijten (2020).

[42] Ibid.

[43] NL Times (2024).

[44] Amnesty International (2024, 17).

[45] Ibid.

[46] NL Times (2024).

[47] Amnesty International (2024, 28).

[48] Ibid, 29; see also De Heer (2023).

[49] Dutch Data Protection Authority (2024).

deploying algorithms that might have unclear or detrimental effects on fundamental rights.[50]

The framework of the FRAIA is divided into four main parts. The first three parts address the decision-making, whilst the last part revolves around more specific questions concerning fundamental rights. Each of these four parts is built following a structured approach and contains detailed questions aimed at ensuring that all the relevant points are addressed, and that the required stakeholders are included when addressing the potential concerns of the use of algorithmic deployment.

3.2.1 Part 1: Why?

This first part of the FRAIA focuses on the intention behind using an algorithm. The impact assessment analysis in this part highlights the underlying motives and the intended effects of the use of an algorithm. To be able to address this part in the most precise manner, the FRAIA provides five subtopics that guide this analysis.[51]

The first subtopic, "Reason and problem definition" (1.1), focuses on reflecting on the problem that the intended use of the algorithm aims to solve, and why it is desirable to use an algorithm, if other non-digital tools are available to tackle the same problem. Building on this problem definition, the second subtopic, "Objective" (1.2) requires defining, as concretely and specifically as possible, the objective(s) that the use of the algorithm needs to achieve. In the case of several objectives, they must be ranked from the main objectives to the secondary objectives.[52]

The third subtopic, "Public values" (1.3), requires identifying the values that give rise to the development and use of the algorithm. Examples of public values are equality, respect for personal autonomy, solidarity, liberty, security, responsibility, sustainability, legal security, distributive justice, respect for vulnerable groups, participation, and efficient use of resources. A curious detail: here the FRAIA specifies that the protection of fundamental rights (such as personal data protection, freedom of expression, the right of access to information, and the right to due process) "may rank among the public values". One may question why the verb "may" is used: does this perhaps imply that a government organisation may pick and choose whether or not to include fundamental rights in its specification of the public values at the first stage of this impact assessment?

The FRAIA addresses the problem of conflicting public values by pointing out that when multiple public values prompt the use of the algorithm, it is useful to reflect on the relative weight of these values. Which values are most important? What are the harms if the values cannot be (fully) realised by the algorithm? If public values conflict as a result of using the algorithm, the FRAIA requires to make a comparative assessment and a balancing exercise in Part 4 of the impact assessment. In Part 1 the organisation should only point out the tension. The objective of identifying the various

[50] Ibid.

[51] Gerards et al. (2022, 6–21).

[52] Ibid, 9–12.

values at this first stage of the impact assessment only serves consciousness-raising and awareness purposes.[53]

Once the public values are set out, the fourth subtopic of Part 1, "Legal basis" (1.4), aims at "finding out whether there is a legal basis that explicitly and clearly allows for the use of an algorithm and renders this use sufficiently foreseeable. If an algorithm is expected to affect people's lives or freedom, and particularly if fundamental rights are expected to be affected, there must be a legal basis for its use". Here the FRAIA refers in particular to the specific requirements that apply on the basis of the European Convention on Human Rights in the case of fundamental rights infringements, two of which are particularly important for the use of algorithms: Firstly, the infringements on fundamental rights must be sufficiently foreseeable. This means that the legal basis must be defined sufficiently clearly for citizens and legal entities to know where they stand and, where necessary, gear their actions to the expected outcomes. Secondly, the legal basis must provide appropriate guarantees against arbitrariness. This entails, among other things, that there must be sufficient transparency about the decisions to be made, and that sufficient opportunities for legal protection must be in place.[54]

The fifth subtopic, "Stakeholders and responsibilities" (1.5), focuses on the importance of a clear division of responsibilities and safeguarding the (various levels of) responsibilities within the process surrounding the use of an algorithm. This requires sound decision-making structures and organisational embedding of the algorithm.[55]

3.2.2 Part 2: What?

After the Part 1 assessment of why an algorithm will be used and how the organisation will safeguard public values and interests, the FRAIA addresses the 'what' question: the shape of the algorithm. Part 2 is divided into two sections: one concerning the *input* of the algorithm—meaning the data or digitally recorded details to be used—and one concerning the algorithm itself—meaning the *throughput* of the project.

The first section (2A) addresses four subtopics: "Assessment: Algorithm type" (2A.1), "Data sources and quality" (2A.2), "Bias/assumption in the data" (2A.3), and "Security" (2A.4). Once the organisation has identified the algorithm type, the next issues that needs to be scrutinised when examining the algorithm are the data sources and quality. Here the FRAIA refers to the widely known 'garbage in = garbage out' principle. The organisation should identify possible assumptions and biases embedded in the data—such as representation bias—and how to correct, overcome or mitigate their influences on the algorithm's output. The organisation should also address the security of data from possible attacks, unauthorized access, etc. and take sufficient and adequate preventive measures.[56]

---

[53] Ibid, 13–15.

[54] Ibid, 16–17.

[55] Ibid, 18–21.

[56] Ibid, 24–32.

The questions contained in the second section (2B) pivot on the algorithm itself. The first subtopic (2B.1) addresses the algorithm type, highlighting the importance of differentiating between a non-self-learning algorithm (in which humans specify the regulation the computer must observe) and a self-learning algorithm (in which the machine itself is finding patterns in the data). The organisation needs to explain the rationale behind choosing a specific type of algorithm over another algorithm or alternative non-algorithmic tools. The second subtopic (2B.2) is the algorithm's ownership and control. When a government organisation chooses to have an algorithm developed by a third party, a clear arrangement concerning the ownership and management needs to be established. The organisation using the algorithm developed by the third party must also be able to explain how the algorithm operates.[57]

The third subtopic (2B.3) is algorithmic accuracy, which must be assessed based on specific evaluation criteria, determining whether the algorithm is suitable for its intended use. The testing process examines its performance, identifying error rates such as false positives and false negatives, while also considering the validity of the underlying assumptions in indicator selection and weighting. To mitigate potential biases, various corrective measures, including alternative sampling strategies and feature modifications, may need to be implemented.[58]

The fourth subtopic (2B.4) is transparency and explainability. It is essential to determine whether the algorithm's purpose, functioning, and data sources are clear, as well as to identify the internal and external groups for whom its operation will be made transparent and how this will be achieved. Additionally, the algorithm must be explainable to the relevant target groups, and its functioning should be communicated understandably. With respect to this issue, the concept of a 'black box' is often mentioned; this term is used to indicate completely non-transparent algorithms, where only the input and output are visible while the internal processes remain unknown—an undesirable situation.[59]

3.2.3 Part 3: How?

The third part of the FRAIA covers seven subtopics revolving around the implementation and the use of the algorithm concerned. An algorithm as such does not have undesired effects: these are caused by its implementation, use, or application, by the context in which the algorithm is used, or by the decisions and measures that are linked to the algorithm's output.[60]

The first subtopic, "Decisions based on algorithmic output" (3.1) discusses which (types of) decisions may be based on the algorithmic output: administrative decisions in individual cases, policy measures, or decisions about the use of public resources. A central question here is whether the algorithm, given its prospected output, will

[57] Ibid, 34–37.

[58] Ibid, 38–42.

[59] Ibid, 43–46.

[60] Ibid, 47.

be able to meet the expectations, considering the reasons, objectives, and public values identified in Part 1. When the algorithm is used in a different context from the one it has been developed or trained for (for example, in a neighbourhood where the population structure or other relevant data clearly deviates from the training data), this may result in incorrect or biased output. With regard to decisions based on algorithmic output, the FRAIA stresses the importance of "safeguarding good governance and good administration", including civic participation and legal protection.[61]

The second subtopic, "The role of humans in the decision" (3.2) revolves around the following questions: "What role do humans play in decision-making on the basis of the algorithmic output? How are they empowered to make decisions responsibly on the basis of the algorithmic output? Is there sufficient qualified staff in place to manage, review and adjust the algorithm, if needed, and will there be in future?".[62]

The third subtopic, "Effects of the algorithm" (3.3), addresses four central questions: what will be the effects of using the algorithm for citizens and how will the 'human measure' be considered when making decisions based on the algorithm? What are the risks of stigmatisation, discrimination or otherwise harmful or adverse effects on citizens? How will these be combated or mitigated? How will the expected effects contribute to solving the problem that prompted the development/deployment of the algorithm and to achieving the proposed objectives? How do the expected effects relate to the public values being served? How are risks of undermining certain values handled?[63]

The fourth subtopic, "Procedures" (3.4), concerns decision-making procedures and accountability mechanisms. It includes questions such as how the various relevant actors (administratively and politically accountable persons, and citizens) are engaged in decision-making, and how is it being safeguarded that these procedures meet the requirements of good governance, good administration and—where necessary—legal protection.[64]

When determining the algorithm's performance, contextual factors play a vital role. Therefore, the fifth subtopic, "Context" (3.5) addresses contextual factors that need to be considered: time (when will the algorithm will be used and for how long?) and area (where will the algorithm be used? In a specific geographical area? Does the algorithm concern a certain group of persons or cases?). A central question here is whether the algorithm can still be used if context factors change, or whether the algorithm is used in another context than the one for which it was developed.Indeed, if the algorithm is applied in a different context than intended or trained for, discrepancies may lead to biased or inaccurate results.[65]

The sixth subtopic, "Communication" (3.6), concerns the degree of openness with which the organisation can communicate the operation of the algorithm in the light of the objectives and context of its deployment. Such communication about the

[61] Ibid, 49–50.

[62] Ibid, 51.

[63] Ibid, 53–55.

[64] Ibid, 56–57.

[65] Ibid, 58–59.

algorithm's use is essential to maintain public trust and transparency. The seventh subtopic, "Evaluation, auditing and safeguarding" (3.7), focuses on the internal and external processes essential for evaluating, auditing, and safeguarding the use of an algorithm. Internally, it is important i.a. to determine how often the algorithm should be assessed, whether qualified staff are in place, and whether future-proofing measures exist. Externally, mechanisms for auditing and supervision should be established, ensuring that sufficient information is available for oversight.[66]

3.2.4 Part 4: Fundamental Rights

The "fundamental rights roadmap" in the FRAIA consists of seven steps designed to assess the impact of algorithms on fundamental rights.[67]

The first step examines whether any fundamental right is affected by the algorithm that is to be used.[68] To this purpose, Annex I of the FRAIA lists 31 fundamental rights grouped in 4 clusters (rights related to the person, freedom rights, equality rights, and procedural rights).[69] Which fundamental right is affected depends on the nature and objective of the algorithm. However, two fundamental rights are most likely affected: the right to protection of personal data, and the right to equal treatment. As to the latter, the FRAIA explicitly states: "Most algorithms result in some form of unequal treatment. This is inherent to the categorisation and profiling for with many algorithms are being used, and to the fact that many data sets are biased, in the sense that they reflect stereotypes existing in society or historical patterns of structural discrimination".[70]

The second step requires identifying the specific legal provisions and standards applicable to the infringement of the fundamental right(s) in question. Here the FRAIA requires i.a. to pay special attention to the equal treatment legislation and the legislation regarding protection of personal data.[71]

The third step evaluates how seriously a fundamental right is affected by the algorithm. It distinguishes between three grades of seriousness, labelled with three colours—red, yellow, and green—which correspond to three grades of required justification in decision-making: (a) serious interference, thus compelling reasons required as justification (red); (b) medium-serious interference, thus due diligence required (yellow), and (c) less serious interference, thus no special due diligence required (green).[72]

The FRAIA admits that no objectively and unequivocally right answer can be given to the question of whether an interference is serious, medium-serious, or less

[66] Ibid, 60–65.

[67] Ibid, 67.

[68] Ibid, 69.

[69] Ibid, 85–95.

[70] Ibid, 70.

[71] Ibid, 71–73.

[72] Ibid, 74.

serious. It stresses the importance to "discuss this issue in a well-considered and open manner and to explain comprehensibly why you have opted for red, yellow, or green".[73]

The fourth, fifth, sixth, and seventh step evaluate the necessity, subsidiarity, and proportionality of the use of the algorithm with respect to the objectives pursued by it. The organisation needs to assess first these objectives, then whether the algorithm is a suitable means to realise them, and finally whether the algorithm's use is necessary to achieve these objectives, ensuring no less intrusive alternatives exist. The suitability of an algorithm is an empirical question, requiring a realistic assessment of its potential benefits, such as cost reduction or efficiency gains, compared to the development and auditing costs. It also involves evaluating whether the algorithm can accurately predict outcomes, as unreliable algorithms with many false positives or negatives may pose significant problems. Generally, an algorithm is deemed problematic and not suitable if it lacks efficacy and threatens an important fundamental right (red or yellow code). With respect to necessity, the principle of using the 'best available techniques' applies; if alternative tools or measures can achieve the same objectives while causing less harm to fundamental rights, they should be prioritised. Finally, in the last step, the FRAIA requires weighting the objectives against the potential rights infringement to determine whether the impact remains proportionate and justified. While no hard rules exist for balancing these factors, the more serious the fundamental rights infringement, the more significant the social objectives must be.[74]

To assist the readers of this paper, a flowchart inspired by the FRAIA has been included in Fig. 1 below.

4 Examples of Algorithmic Discrimination in Private Contractual Relationships

Reported cases of algorithmic discrimination in private contractual relationships in the EU member states[75] mainly concern three areas: (1) employment and platform work, (2) banking and insurance,[76] and (3) targeted advertising, price setting, and retail.

[73] Ibid, 75.

[74] Ibid, 76–80.

[75] See Gerards and Xenidis (2021, 83 ff).

[76] On discrimination connected to the use of algorithms in the financial sector, see i.a. Morse and Pence (2021); Remolina (2022).

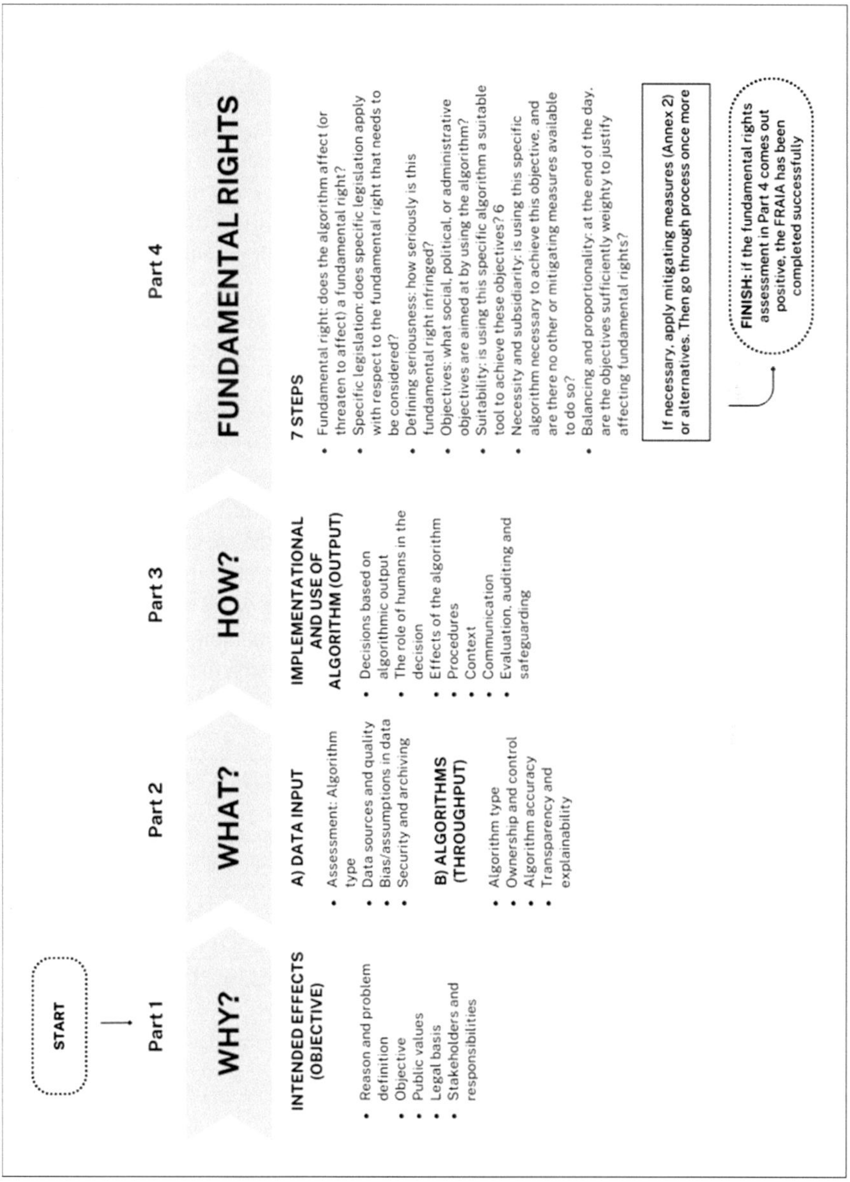

Fig. 1 Flowchart of the FRAIA process (by Alma-Cristina Onaie)

4.1 Employment and Platform Work

In matters of employment and occupation, under EU law, the prohibition of direct discrimination applies in both vertical and horizontal relationships on the grounds of ethnic origin,[77] gender,[78] religion or belief, disability, age or sexual orientation.[79] By contrast, indirect discrimination can be justified if the restriction pursues a legitimate aim and if the means for achieving the specific aim are both appropriate and necessary.[80] Scholars have observed that the protection against discrimination in employment matters under EU law tends to be stricter than the protection against discrimination in other types of legal relationships.[81] However, notwithstanding all national and EU non-discrimination law instruments,[82] algorithmic discrimination in employment matters[83] occurs in different stages of the employment process covering the candidate sourcing,[84] the selection procedure[85] as well as conditions granting pay[86] and promotion.[87] Algorithmic discrimination affects platform workers too. For example, recent studies showed that female platform workers often receive lower pay than their male counterparts.[88]

Already in 2020, the Italian Tribunal of Bologna[89] found that the reputational ranking algorithm employed by the delivery platform Deliveroo was indirectly discriminatory to the detriment of female workers. The algorithm was used to give riders access to a system for booking and cancelling working shifts. The decision of which riders to prioritize was automated according to the measure of the riders' reliability and participation. This measure, however, was determined without any consideration of legally protected reasons for absence from work such as care duties (still performed by women in majority), illness, disability, personal beliefs, or strike actions. By treating all cancellations of work shifts indistinctly, the algorithm limited riders' work opportunities in an unfair and discriminatory way.[90]

---

[77] Council Directive 2000/43/EC of 29 June 2000 implementing the principle of equal treatment between persons irrespective of racial or ethnic origin.

[78] Directive 2006/54/EC of the European Parliament and of the Council of 5 July 2006 on the implementation of the principle of equal opportunities and equal treatment of men and women in matters of employment and occupation.

[79] Council Directive 2000/78/EC of 27 November 2000 establishing a general framework for equal treatment in employment and occupation.

[80] Council Directive 2000/78/EC, art 2(2)(b)(i); Directive 2006/54/EC, art 2(1)(b).

[81] Lutman (2023, 83).

[82] For a brief *tour d'horizon* of EU non-discrimination law see Ganty and De Vries (2023).

[83] For a comparative overview, see Hießl (2025).

[84] Lutman (2023, 86).

[85] Ibid, 87. See also Carter (2024) and Grozdanovski (2021).

[86] See Gerards and Xenidis (2021, 55).

[87] Lutman (2023, 87).

[88] Kullmann (2018, 2 ff).

[89] Tribunal of Bologna, order no. 2949/2019, 31 December 2020.

[90] For a comment on this case see Xenidis (2023).

One of the main objectives of the new EU Directive 2024/2831 on improving working conditions in platform work[91] is to protect workers in the context of algorithmic management. The Directive bans the use of automated monitoring or decision-making systems for the processing of certain types of personal data of persons performing platform work, such as biometric data or their emotional or psychological state. Human oversight and evaluation are also guaranteed as regards automated decisions, including the right to have those decisions explained and reviewed. Workers must be duly informed about the use of automated monitoring and decision-making systems regarding their recruitment, their working conditions and their earnings, among other things.[92] However, anti-discrimination experts have criticised the Directive as gender blind and inattentive to the intersectional aspects of algorithmic management.[93]

4.2 Banking and Insurance

Banking and insurance are other significant areas where algorithms are employed. Their use allows to more easily target customers[94] and thus enhance market efficiency by accurately predicting the ability of a customer to repay bank loans, ensuring both improved risk assessment for financial institutions and greater creditworthiness verification for borrowers. However, algorithms can also produce discriminatory effects. In the context of banking two main forms of discrimination have been identified: price discrimination and access discrimination.[95]

The *SCHUFA* judgment of the CJEU[96] highlighted the risks associated with automated-decision making in the banking sector and its implications on transparency and fairness.[97] This judgment established that any agency using an automated system for individual decision-making is subject to article 22 GDPR if the decision of the system is the determining factor in an outcome that has legal effects or similarly significant consequences.[98] This will require agencies to become more selective of the systems and ensure not to employ solely automated means, therefore ensuring greater accountability. However, the extent to which the post-*SCHUFA* improvements in the use of automated decision-making in the credit sector will prevent price discrimination and access discrimination on grounds of gender, racial and ethnic

[91] Directive (EU) 2024/2831 of the European Parliament and of the Council of 23 October 2024 on improving working conditions in platform work.

[92] Ibid.

[93] Kambouri (2024, 55 ff).

[94] Baffour Gyau et al. (2024, 2).

[95] Alper (2022).

[96] Court of Justice of the European Union (CJEU), case C-634/21 *OQ v Land Hessen* [2023] ECLI:EU:C:2023:957.

[97] For a comment on this judgment see Falletti (2024).

[98] Erskine-Fox and Dunne (2024).

background, disability, or other grounds listed in article 21(1) of the Charter, may be questioned. A problem is that algorithmic discrimination in the credit and insurance sectors mostly takes the form of indirect discrimination. This is for example the case when an algorithmic credit scoring system uses predictors such as income or employment history, which are prima facie neutral towards protected groups, but still have a disadvantageous impact on women.[99]

4.3 Targeted Advertising, Price Setting, and Retail

Algorithmic decision-making in the provision of goods and services may result in discriminatory practices and restrict access to certain products based on gender, ethnic background, etc. Algorithmic discrimination in these sectors mainly concerns discriminatory advertising and discriminatory pricing.[100] For example, discriminatory advertising could occur when preferences on a shopping website are used as a proxy to indicate to a system the gender of the consumer and tailor products based on correlations between gender and products even where gender itself is not the main criterion used by the system.

Article 3(1) of EU Directive 2004/113/EC prohibits gender discrimination in the provision of goods and services in both the public and private sectors.[101] Similarly, article 3(1)(h) of the Council Directive 2000/43/EC prohibits discrimination in the provision of goods and services on account of ethnic or racial origin.[102] However, the prohibition does not extend to media and advertisements.[103] While the directive explicitly covers a prohibition on gender discrimination, it does not address different protected grounds, and therefore price discrimination in private relationships based on a protected ground other than gender would escape the scope of protection.[104] This means that an algorithmic system that would exclude, for example, persons above a certain age or with a certain religious affiliation from accessing given services or from purchasing certain goods would not, in principle, be contrary to EU secondary anti-discrimination law as it stands.[105]

Data protection law may provide, at least indirectly, some protection against algorithmic discrimination.[106] As the CJEU judgment *Meta Platforms Inc and Others v*

---

[99] Xenidis (2023, Sect. 2.2).

[100] Lutman (2023, 89–92).

[101] Council Directive 2004/113/EC of 13 December 2004 implementing the principle of equal treatment between men and women in the access to and supply of goods and services.

[102] Council Directive 2000/43/EC.

[103] Council Directive 2004/113/EC, art 3(3).

[104] Lutman (2023, 92).

[105] Xenidis (2023, section 3.1).

[106] Zuiderveen Borgesius (2020, section 4.3).

Bundeskartellamt[107] shows, data protection law and in particular article 9 GDPR can shield individuals from their sensitive data being processed without their consent. In this connection article 9 GDPR could be applied also in the context of algorithmic pricing and targeted advertising as AI systems rely on access to personal data to enable customization. Therefore, article 9 GDPR could prevent algorithms from engaging in discriminatory practices by restricting the processing of sensitive personal data when individuals have not given their explicit consent.[108] However, article 9 GDPR is of little help against targeted advertisements and algorithmic pricing for two main reasons: Firstly, under article 9 GDPR the list of sensitive data does not cover every protected ground addressed by the anti-discrimination directives.[109] Such limited scope entails that article 9 will not be applicable e.g. when data about age or disability is being processed.[110] Secondly, consent plays an important role under article 9(2)(a) GDPR, and therefore if an individual explicitly consents to their data being processed then they cannot rely on the protections afforded by article 9(1).[111] This derogation can be especially problematic when individuals do not read the terms and conditions and proceed to consent to their personal data being processed.

5 Concluding Remarks

Almost twenty years ago, long before the mainstreaming of legal research on artificial intelligence in Europe, Gunther Teubner published the famous Modern Law Review article "The Anonymous Matrix".[112] This article advocated direct human rights obligations for private (transnational) actors. Teubner was one of the very few courageous scholars who pleaded for the direct horizontal effect of fundamental rights already at a time when the prevalent opinion in Germany and in some other European countries denied it.

In 2018, the Court of Justice of the European Union (CJEU) in the *Egenberger* case[113] decided that the prohibition of discrimination under article 21(1) of the Charter directly applies not only in relationships between public authorities and individuals, but also in relationships between individuals.[114] Few months after the

[107] CJEU, case C-252/21 *Meta Platforms Inc and Others v Bundeskartellamt* [2023] ECLI:EU:C:2023:537.

[108] Drechsler and Sánchez (2018, 9).

[109] Article 9 GDPR covers data revealing racial or ethnic origin, political opinions, religious or philosophical beliefs, or trade union membership, and the processing of genetic data, biometric data.

[110] Drechsler and Sánchez (2018, 9).

[111] Ibid, 9.

[112] Teubner (2006).

[113] CJEU, case C-414/16 *Vera Egenberger v. Evangelisches Werk für Diakonie und Entwicklung eV* [2018] ECLI:EU:C:2018:257.

[114] For a comment on *Egenberger*, see Colombi Ciacchi (2019).

Egenberger judgment, the CJEU specified in the joint cases *Bauer* and *Brossonn* that the formulation of article 51 of the Charter does not preclude direct obligations for individuals descending from mandatory and unconditional Charter provisions.[115] With 'individuals', the CJEU means any private parties, including the largest private multinational corporations. Therefore, if a contractual relationship falls within the scope of application of EU law,[116] the prohibition of discrimination under article 21(1) of the Charter directly creates obligations for all contract parties.

Nowadays, after the *Egenberger* and *Bauer and Brossonn* judgments, the direct horizontal effect of EU fundamental rights in contract law is a matter of fact. Within the scope of application of EU law, it is now undisputed that at least article 21(1) and article 31(2) of the Charter directly bind private employers.[117]

However, some scholars may still argue that the Charter (and fundamental rights generally) only have direct horizontal effect in the somehow special field of labour law, given the lack of CJEU decisions on the direct horizontal effect of fundamental rights in other types of contractual relationships. The authors of the present paper defend the opposite opinion and argue that the CJEU case law since *Egenberger* and *Bauer and Brossonn* is to be interpreted in the sense that any Charter provision that is mandatory and unconditional and content-wise suitable to operate in the private sector, directly creates obligations for both public and private actors in potentially every type of contractual relationships that is regulated by an EU legal act.[118]

Article 27 of the AI Act arguably provides an additional confirmation of the direct binding force of EU fundamental rights on private contract parties in many areas beyond labour law. These are at least the areas where private actors must conduct fundamental rights impact assessments if they deploy AI systems: (1) private actors that provide public services, (2) credit institutions that intend to use AI systems to evaluate the creditworthiness of natural persons or establish their credit score, and (3) insurance providers that intend to use AI systems for risk assessment and pricing in relation to natural persons in the case of life and health insurance.[119]

From the abovementioned observations this paper deduces that the AI Act, together with the direct horizontal effect of article 21(1) of the Charter, allows to overcome at least partly the limited capability of EU anti-discrimination Directives to tackle algorithmic discrimination.[120]

However, not all algorithmic bias amount to discrimination under EU law. A structural limit of both EU and national anti-discrimination law is that while direct discrimination cannot be justified in principle, indirect discrimination comes with an

---

[115] For a comment on *Bauer* and *Brossonn*, see Frantziou (2019).

[116] The Charter's scope of application at the national level is limited to the areas where the implementation of EU law takes place, see Charter of Fundamental Rights of the European Union, art 51.

[117] Muir (2019).

[118] Colombi Ciacchi A (2019).

[119] See article 27 Regulation (EU) 2024/1689.

[120] On the limits of EU anti-discrimination law with regard to algorithmic discrimination see Xenidis (2023, Sect. 2.2) and Barat i Rubio (2025, 2, 13).

open-ended justification regime. A prima facie indirectly discriminatory provision, criterion or practice can be objectively justified if it serves a legitimate aim and the means of achieving that aim are appropriate and necessary.[121]

Moreover, only very few cases of discrimination in contractual relationships reach the courts, and when they do so, it is often too late. Therefore, the prevention of discrimination becomes essential. Both the Dutch FRAIA and the EU FRIA are very interesting instruments of prevention of fundamental rights violations, including the fundamental right not to be discriminated against on grounds of gender, age, race, etc. While the FRAIA is an impact assessment model specifically designed for public bodies,[122] the FRIA is supposed to apply also to private organizations that use high-risk AI systems.[123]

However, although impact assessment models like the FRAIA and the FRIA might help mitigating algorithmic discrimination, their effectiveness in practice may be questioned, since they leave a huge margin of discretion to the organisation that uses the algorithm. Therefore, the role of the courts in combating violations of national and EU anti-discrimination law by powerful public and private actors, also through the direct horizontal effect of article 21(1) of the Charter, if necessary, remains crucial.

References

Ajoodha T, Browne J (2025) Fundamental rights impact assessments: what are they? How do they work? https://cedpo.eu/wp-content/uploads/CEDPO-micro-insight-paper-fundamental-rights-impact-assessments.pdf

Algorithm Watch (2020) How Dutch activists got an invasive fraud detection algorithm banned. https://algorithmwatch.org/en/syri-netherlands-algorithm

Alper G (2022) Contract law revisited: algorithmic pricing and the notion of contractual fairness. Comput Law Secur Rev 47:1–18. https://doi.org/10.1016/j.clsr.2022.105741

Alston P (2019) Brief by the United Nations Special Rapporteur on extreme poverty and human rights as Amicus Curiae in the case of NJCM c.s./De Staat der Nederlanden (SyRI) before the District Court of The Hague (case number: C/09/550982/HA ZA 18/388). www.ohchr.org/Documents/Issues/Poverty/Amicusfinalversionsigned.pdf

Amnesty International (2024) Netherlands: profiled without protection: students in the Netherlands hit by discriminatory fraud detection system. https://www.amnesty.org/en/documents/eur35/8794/2024/en

Amnesty International (2021) Xenophobic machines: discrimination through unregulated use of algorithms in the Dutch childcare benefits scandal. https://www.amnesty.org/en/documents/eur35/4686/2021/en

Baffour Gyau E, Appiah M, Gyamfi BA, Achie T, Naeem MA (2024) Transforming banking: examining the role of AI technology innovation in boosting banks financial performance. Int Rev Financ Anal 96:1–13. https://doi.org/10.1016/j.irfa.2024.103700

---

121 Xenidis (2023, Section 2.2).

122 Governmental organisations are the main target of the FRAIA, see Gerards et al. (2022, 2).

123 See Sect. 2 of this paper. However, the AI Act remains an instrument based more on public law than on private law, because it primarily sets market-entry requirements rather than introducing rights for private parties that correspond to obligations of other private parties. See also Henckel (2023, 205).

Barat i Rubio R (2025) Legal mechanisms addressing algorithmic discrimination in consumer markets. Working paper presented at the LiaNs seminar of 8 May 2025 (on file with the authors)

Bertaina S, Biganzoli I, Desiante R, Fontanella D, Inverardi N, Penco IG, Cosentini AC (2025) Fundamental rights and artificial intelligence impact assessment: a new quantitative methodology in the upcoming era of AI Act. Comput Law Secur Rev 56:1–24. https://doi.org/10.1016/j.clsr.2024.106101

Boix Palop A (2025) The Impact of the EU artificial intelligence act on public administration. Working paper presented at the LiaNs seminar of 8 January 2025 (on file with the authors)

Carter C (2024) Why the algorithmic recruiter discriminates: the causal challenges of data-driven discrimination. Maastricht J Eur Comp Law 31(3):333–359

Circiumaru A (2021) Futureproofing EU law—the case of algorithm discrimination. https://doi.org/10.2139/ssrn.3953627

Colombi Ciacchi A (2019) The direct horizontal effect of EU fundamental rights. Eur Const Law Rev 15(2):294–305

Colombi Ciacchi A, Berardi G, Onaie AC (2026) Contract and power in the age of AI: algorithmic discrimination and fundamental rights impact assessments. In: Miller L, Sirena P (eds) Contract and Power. Ideologies, Inequalities, and Marginalisation in European Contract Law. Larcier Intersentia, Louvain-la-Neuve, pp 103–129

Cosentini A, Pollicino O, De Gregorio G, Ermellino A, Fontanella D, Inverardi N, Paolucci F, Penco IG, Regoli D, Trapani ST (2025) Assessing the impact of artificial intelligence systems on fundamental rights. https://doi.org/10.2139/ssrn.5168579

De Heer S (2023) A scandal on AI in administration, again. In: Fortifying fundamental rights in the age of AI. https://verfassungsblog.de/a-scandal-on-ai-in-administration-again

Drechsler L, Sánchez JCB (2018) The price is (not) right: data protection and discrimination in the age of pricing algorithms. Eur J Law Technol 9(3). https://ejlt.org/index.php/ejlt/article/view/631/853

Dutch Data Protection Authority (2024) DUO's approach to fraud found to be discriminatory and illegal. https://www.autoriteitpersoonsgegevens.nl/en/current/duos-approach-to-fraud-found-to-be-discriminatory-and-illegal

Erskine-Fox E, Dunne S (2024) SCHUFA case: CJEU rules on scope of article 22. https://www.tlt.com/insights-and-events/insight/schufa-case-cjeu-rules-on-scope-of-article-22

European Commission (2024) Artificial intelligence—questions and answers. https://ec.europa.eu/commission/presscorner/detail/en/qanda_21_1683

Falletti E (2024) Credit scoring under scrutiny by the court of justice of the European Union: brief remarks on the 'SCHUFA decision'. https://doi.org/10.2139/ssrn.4726282

Frantziou E (2019) (Most of) the Charter of fundamental rights is horizontally applicable: ECJ 6 November 2018, Joined Cases C-569/16 and C-570/16, Bauer et al. Eur Const Law Rev 15(2):306–323

Ganty S, De Vries K (2023) Non-discrimination in EU social security law: exploring safeguards against gender and racial discrimination. https://doi.org/10.2139/ssrn.4650622

Gerards J, Schäfer MT, Muis I, Vankan A (2022) Fundamental rights and algorithms impact assessment (FRAIA). https://www.government.nl/documents/reports/2021/07/31/impact-assessment-fundamental-rights-and-algorithms

Gerards J, Xenidis R (2021) Algorithmic discrimination in Europe—challenges and opportunities for gender equality and non-discrimination law. https://doi.org/10.2838/544956

Gikay AA, Lau PL, Sengul C, Miron A, Malin B (2023) High-risk artificial intelligence systems under the European Union's artificial intelligence act: systemic flaws and practical challenges. https://doi.org/10.2139/ssrn.4621605

Grozdanovski L (2021) In search of effectiveness and fairness in proving algorithmic discrimination in EU law. Common Mark Law Rev 58(1):99–136

Haitsma L (2023) The murky waters of algorithmic profiling: examining discrimination in the digitalized enforcement of social security policy. Recht der Werkelijkheid 44(2):61–83

Haitsma L, Bouwmeester M (2023) Learning from control deficits in the childcare benefits scandal. A plea for multi-level analysis in law and policy research. Recht der Werkelijkheid 44(3):57–68
Henckel K (2023) Issues of conflicting laws—a closer look at the EU's approach to artificial intelligence. Ned Int Privaatr 2023(2):199–226
Hießl C (2025) Case law on algorithmic management at the workplace: cross-European comparative analysis and tentative conclusions. https://doi.org/10.2139/ssrn.3982735
Ismail K (2018) AI vs algorithms: what's the difference? https://www.cmswire.com/information-management/ai-vs-algorithms-whats-the-difference
Kambouri N (2024) A gender critique of the new directive on platform work from the perspective of feminised and racialised labour. Labour Law Issues 10(2):55–76
Kleinberg J, Ludwig J, Mullainathan S, Sunstein CR (2018) Discrimination in the age of algorithms. J Leg Anal 10:113–174
Kullmann M (2018) Platform work, algorithmic decision-making, and EU gender equality law. Int J Comp Labour Law Ind Relat 34:1–21
Leijten I (2020) The Dutch SyRI case: some thoughts on indivisible interferences and the status of social rights. https://blog-iacl-aidc.org/social-rights/2020/5/19/the-dutch-syri-case-some-thoughts-on-indivisible-interferences-and-the-status-of-social-rights
Lutman K (2023) Artificial Intelligence and the prohibition of discrimination in the EU: a private law perspective. In: Završnik A, Simončič K (eds) Artificial intelligence, social harms and human rights. Critical criminological perspectives, Palgrave Macmillan, London, pp 77–97
Malgieri G, Santos C (2025) Assessing the (severity of) impacts on fundamental rights. Comput Law Secur Rev 56:1–18. https://doi.org/10.1016/j.clsr.2025.106113
Mantelero A (2024) The fundamental rights impact assessment (FRIA) in the AI act: roots, legal obligations and key elements for a model template. Comput Law Secur Rev 54:1–14. https://doi.org/10.1016/j.clsr.2024.106020
Meuwese A (2020) Regulating algorithmic decision-making one case at the time: a note on the Dutch 'SyRI' judgment. Eur Rev Digit Adm Law 1(1–2):209–211
Morse A, Pence K (2021) Technological innovation and discrimination in household finance. In: Rau R, Wardrop R, Zingales L (eds) The Palgrave handbook of technological finance. Palgrave Macmillan, London, pp 783–808
Muir E (2019) The horizontal effects of charter rights given expression to in EU legislation, from Mangold to Bauer. Rev Eur Adm Law 12(2):185–215
NL Times (2024) Government to refund over 10,000 students over discriminatory DUO fraud checks. https://nltimes.nl/2024/11/12/government-refund-10000-students-discriminatory-duo-fraud-checks
Rachovitsa A, Johann N (2022) The human rights implications of the use of AI in the digital welfare state: lessons learned from the Dutch SyRI case. Hum Rights Law Rev 22(2):1–15
Ranchordás S, Schuurmans Y (2020) Outsourcing the welfare state: the role of private actors in welfare fraud investigations. Eur J Comp Law Gov 7(1):5–42. https://doi.org/10.1163/22134514-00701005
Remolina N (2022) The role of financial regulators in the governance of algorithmic credit scoring. https://doi.org/10.2139/ssrn.4057986
Teubner G (2006) The anonymous matrix: human rights violations by 'private' transnational actors. Mod Law Rev 69:327–346
Waem H, Dauzier J, Demircan M (2024) Fundamental rights impact assessments under the EU AI Act: who, what and how? https://www.technologyslegaledge.com/2024/03/fundamental-rights-impact-assessments-under-the-eu-ai-act-who-what-and-how
Xenidis R (2023) When computers say no: towards a legal response to algorithmic discrimination in Europe. In: Brożek B, Przemyslaw P, Kanevskaia O (eds) Research handbook on law and technology. Edward Elgar, Cheltenham, pp 222–234
Xenidis R, Senden L (2020) EU non-discrimination law in the era of artificial intelligence: mapping the challenges of algorithmic discrimination. In: Bernitz U, Groussot X, Paju J, De Vries SA

(eds) General principles of EU law and the EU digital order. Kluwer Law International, Alphen aan den Rijn, pp 151–182
Zuiderveen Borgesius FJ (2018) Discrimination, artificial intelligence, and algorithmic decision-making. Council of Europe. https://rm.coe.int/discrimination-artificial-intelligence-and-algorithmic-decisionmaking/1680925d73
Zuiderveen Borgesius FJ (2020) Strengthening legal protection against discrimination by algorithms and artificial intelligence. Int J Hum Rights 24(10):1572–1593

Governing AI Through Assessment: A Critical Analysis of FRIA from a Technology Assessment Perspective

Pierluigi Masai, Lorenzo Carta, and Simone Arnaldi

Abstract This chapter develops a critical analysis of Fundamental Rights Impact Assessment (FRIA). FRIA is a risk-based and ex-ante mandatory procedure for evaluating potential impacts of artificial intelligence (AI) systems that makes an appearance in Article 27 of the AI Act but has not yet entered into force. Nonetheless, it is possible to evaluate it as a distinct type of governance instrument and to understand how it is intended to contribute to AI oversight. FRIA promises to integrate fundamental rights concerns in the cycle of development of AI systems and foster accountability and transparency. The issue is approached by situating FRIA within the broader historical and conceptual landscape of the governance of emerging technologies, with a specific focus on the practice of technology assessment (TA). TA has become a central tool in contemporary governance to evaluate the social, legal and economic consequences of emerging technologies. Drawing on past and current experience in TA, we will examine the methodological and implementation challenges to FRIA, as a tool to produce enhanced knowledge about AI within society and as an effective instrument for steering technological development. Overall, our contribution offers a preliminary evaluation of FRIA, its potential use, and foreseeable challenges. These insights are meant to identify new possible directions for research in legal and social sciences and to improve accountability, transparency and social responsiveness in AI governance.

All authors developed the concept for this work, conducted the literature review, and provided editorial revisions. Arnaldi drafted sections 1 and 6; Carta drafted sections 3 and 4; Masai drafted sections 2 and 5.

P. Masai (✉) · L. Carta
Applied Data Science and Artificial Intelligence, University of Trieste, Trieste, Italy
e-mail: pierluigi.masai@phd.units.it

L. Carta
e-mail: lorenzo.carta2@phd.units.it

S. Arnaldi
Department of Political Science, University of Trieste, Trieste, Italy
e-mail: sarnaldi@units.it

C. Crea and M. Infantino (eds.), *Remedies to Digital Vulnerability in European Private Law*, https://doi.org/10.1007/978-3-032-19720-7_12

Keywords Fundamental rights · High-risk artificial intelligence systems · Technology assessment · Impact assessment · Accountability

1 Introduction

The recent spread of artificial intelligence (AI) systems is accompanied by growing and legitimate concerns about their use. The last decade has witnessed an increase in the development and adoption of AI systems whose functionalities promise many benefits in a variety of fields across society. The pervasiveness of AI systems calls for appropriate regulation of them in order to balance innovation with rights protection. Governing technologies requires a proper evaluation of the outcomes of their adoption which often leads to the use of impact assessments as governance tools.

The European Union developed the AI Act which came into force in 2024. The AI Act envisages many actions to regulate AI systems among which article 27 introduces the notion of Fundamental Rights Impact Assessment (FRIA) that is the focus of the present work. FRIA is intended as a tool that should foster accountability and oversight on high-risk AI systems. FRIA has not yet been enforced but there is a lively discussion on its methodology and possible implementations in AI governance.

It is premature to evaluate the actual capacities of the AI Act or the efficacy of FRIA. Nonetheless, since there is a long tradition of studies about and practice of technology evaluation, it is possible to draw on it to think critically about the very processes of AI governance. In particular, we believe a lot may be learnt from the experience of Technology Assessment (TA). TA is "an evidence-based, interactive process to bring to light the societal, economic, environmental and legal aspects and consequences of new and emerging science technologies"[1] to influence the development trajectories of the studied technological systems. TA and FRIA represent distinct approaches to governing emerging technologies, but they share similar aims. We hold that TA's well-established theoretical foundations and practical implementation history offer valuable insights for refining FRIA's methodological framework and assessment procedures. To provide critical comments about the FRIA methodology we propose to analyse its features in line with the three conceptual dimensions identified in the literature to describe TA, namely anticipation, inclusion and complexity.

Section 2 will briefly describe TA's history and features in order to outline the elements necessary for the following analysis. Sections 3 and 4 will respectively present FRIA's characteristics as conceived in the AI Act and with regards to its methodology. Section 5 will present the analysis of FRIA through the lens of the conceptual dimensions of TA. Section 6 will present the conclusions highlighting the major takeaways of the analysis and reflect upon future research work that may be undertaken.

---

[1] Robinson et al. (2023, 5).

2 Technology Assessment: History and Aspects

2.1 The Aims of TA

TA aims to assess a new technology which is yet to be developed or that is currently either under development or waiting to be deployed, considering their societal implications. TA moves from the observation that technologies cannot be analyzed and discussed as limited to themselves, but they have to be recognized as embedded in society. This is in line with the approach of Science and Technology Studies (STS) that recognize technologies as the product of the interaction of many actors, both human and non-human.[2] Consequently, focusing exclusively on the technological aspects would represent a significant limitation from a critical standpoint, as it overlooks the complex interactions between people, technological artifacts and the social context. In fact, STS argue that the development of a technology can be fully comprehended only by taking into consideration the socio-materiality of the process, which is to say that actual choices and actions may be the consequence of economic, political or even personal reasons but also of structural and material constraints.[3] This is relevant not only when discussing the development of a technology but even when reasoning about its regulation and control.

The information gathered or produced thanks to the process of TA can have multiple uses. For instance, it might be used to assist decision makers in regulating a new technology or to nudge scientists throughout the design process of a new technology. Therefore, TA can have a role both in policy making and in technology development. TA is a process with a multifaceted nature. TA might be described either as a practice or as a form of analysis. The nature of TA is strictly operative: the practical dimension prevails over the theoretical one. There is no mandatory action to do though: strictly speaking there is no rigid sequence of steps to follow in order to perform TA. There are many forms of TA which reflect the variety of attitudes people may have towards it. Nonetheless, there are some general elements that characterize TA which can be outlined to illustrate its premise.

To better understand the many possible applications of TA, it is appropriate to quickly look at an overview of its historical development and evolution.

2.2 The Historical Development of TA

The notion of TA was introduced within the theoretical frame of risk evaluation.[4] The need to evaluate the consequences of the development and use of a new technology both to prevent potential harms and to maximize the benefits, was one of the main

---

[2] Latour (1987).

[3] Orlikowski and Scott (2008).

[4] Van Est et al. (2012).

reasons. These preoccupations intensified after World War II precisely because of science and technology's rising societal role and the recognition of its unintended effects. TA was originally developed in the USA to assist politicians given the impact technological development has on economics, health and lifestyles.[5]

In 1972, the Congress approved the Technology Assessment Act, and the Office of Technology Assessment (OTA) was created.[6] One of the main figures involved was U.S. congressional representative Emilio Daddario, a member of the Democratic Party who coined the term *technology assessment* and advocated the use of TA for policy advice. OTA was meant to evaluate existing or probable impacts of technology or technological programs and identify possible actions and alternatives. Eventually, OTA presented the results of its analyses in reports made available to Congress members. OTA was closed down in 1995 as a consequence of political tensions, yet the Technology Assessment Act is still in force today, even if without assignment of budget. Nonetheless, the closure of OTA caused a form of ostracism of TA in the USA. The European Parliamentary Technology Assessment Network (EPTA), founded in 1990, shows that nowadays TA for policy-advising is adopted by many countries.[7] As of 2025, EPTA has 14 full members in Europe and 11 associate members.

Over the decades TA has been reinterpreted and implemented in different contexts. Beside the use of parliamentary TA for policy-advising, other approaches emerged such as participatory TA (PTA) and constructive TA (CTA).[8] PTA originated to meet the interest of citizens and stakeholders of being involved in the process of technology development. CTA was introduced after the SCOT program (Social Construction of Technology) that interpreted technologies as an outcome of the interaction of many actors which implies that to shape the design and development of a technology the focus cannot be solely on the technology itself.

Thus, TA can help in decision-making processes about technology. Besides TA as policy advice, Grunwald[9] identifies other two main areas of TA in action—yet, in the future more areas may arise—: TA in public dialogue and TA in the making of technology. In these two perspectives on TA, participative processes can foster reflection about values and ideas across society, raising awareness and laying the foundation for public discussions, whereas the knowledge gained through TA can inform technological development and guide decisions in accordance with expected outcomes.

[5] Grunwald (2018).

[6] Sadowski (2015).

[7] Nentwich (2016).

[8] Tran and Daim (2008).

[9] Grunwald (2018).

2.3 The Elements of TA

In his analysis of TA, Armin Grunwald[10] identifies three conceptual dimensions that characterize TA: anticipation, inclusion and complexity. These dimensions are not contingent on specific implementations of TA which depend on their social, political and institutional context. Each dimension promotes a critical attitude towards the very procedures and outcomes of TA enhancing reflexivity.

Anticipation equates to generating prospective knowledge which can guide decisions enhancing reflexivity over the temporal unfolding of socio-technical processes. The attitude toward anticipation has changed over time. Sergio Urueña[11] identifies four different approaches to anticipation which can be used to illustrate this evolving attitude of TA towards the future: *predictivist*, *strategic*, *exploratory* and *critical-hermeneutic*. Earlier versions of TA, originating from Risk Assessment procedures, adopted a *predictivist* approach which does not address elements of complexity nor take into consideration possible future changes in the social context. If traditionally TA assumed to be able to anticipate the consequences of future developments of a technology, eventually scholars recognised that uncertainty is instead a pervasive element of socio-technical trajectories,[12] especially in the case of emerging technologies. Indeed, emerging technologies are characterized by an element of ignorance about the outcomes of their implementation that will eventually be addressed only after the adoption and diffusion of the technology itself. To a certain extent prospective knowledge may help to shape the development of a technology but only if adopted from the very start of the process; this is in line with a *strategic* approach to anticipation. Yet, in the end prospective knowledge has proven to be not an end in itself: it is rather instrumental to define an orientation either comparing different possible future scenarios—in line with an *exploratory* approach—or critically understanding the many attitudes towards future scenarios existing at the present moment—in line with a hermeneutic approach to anticipation. The integration of participative approaches into TA has shown how anticipation can contribute to building public opinion. As a matter of fact, the impact of PTA on the public sphere is extremely relevant since it can prevent a rejection of the technology and public protests. It is imperative that participatory activities are performed right from the start (upstream) and not at the end (downstream) of the development process, otherwise controversies may even be fostered.

Inclusion stresses the fact that TA is not focused on a technology in itself but on a technology as embedded in society. The point is that when performing TA one should involve all interested parties, taking into consideration both their needs and values, in order to prevent biases, discrimination, monopolies and consequent forms of exclusion. This enhances reflexivity across perspectives. Inclusion also aims to overcome a neo-positivist attitude or the idea that *science knows best*. It is tempting to base decisions regarding emerging technologies exclusively on the analysis of experts, yet that

[10] Grunwald (2018).

[11] Urueña (2021).

[12] Arnaldi (2012).

has been considered as a mere optimization of quantitative and measurable results in line with a technocratic way of reasoning. Such an attitude might not properly address the fact that different social groups, in different places or time, can define issues, decisions and their stakes in ways that are not necessarily captured by expert knowledge and drawing upon knowledge that is not leveraged by experts. Fostering inclusion has two important impacts: it helps to obtain better and more diverse knowledge about possible unintended outcomes, and it aims at building legitimacy of decisions either by selecting commonly preferred options or raising awareness. Both elements are fundamental to avoid adverse reactions. It has to be noted that inclusion is not strictly about participation. Certainly, participatory practices enhance the elements of inclusion of TA. Anyway, TA processes have to find mechanisms to represent the various epistemic and social perspectives of the many stakeholders.

The third dimension of complexity examines the tension between inclusion and exclusion that implies the necessity to judge and assess the relevance of boundaries, relationships and interactions. One must be able to draw lines and make distinctions. Grunwald clearly notices that modelling socio-technical dynamics requires systemic lenses through which we order and relate the different aspects that our perspective deem relevant for the issue we are assessing. This call for system thinking is a defining element of TA and embodies the aforementioned conceptual dimension of complexity, reflecting the difficulty to identify which aspects of life are or might be affected by a technology, in particular when 'soft' impacts, such as social relations, beliefs and values are considered.[13] Reflexivity is enhanced over relevance. The proper definition of what is relevant to the discussion and what is not requires a deep understanding of the dynamics that characterize technology development and implementation.

3 FRIA in the Context of the AI Act

3.1 The AI Act as Risk Regulation

Recent developments in AI governance have increasingly focused on a specific regulatory approach: risk regulation. The EU AI Act[14] exemplifies this shift, representing a significant move toward addressing the risks posed by AI systems through a horizontal approach. Risk regulation is anticipatory insofar as it is usually characterized as an ex-ante approach, aiming to mitigate potential harms before they materialize. According to Margot Kaminski,[15] in general this approach adopts a 'techno-correctionist' frame on regulation since the aim is mainly to 'fix' the technology and

[13] Urueña (2021).

[14] Regulation 2024/1689 (2024). Regulation (EU) 2024/1689 of the European Parliament and of The Council of 13 June 2024 laying down harmonised rules on artificial intelligence and amending Regulations (EC) No 300/2008, (EU) No 167/2013, (EU) No 168/2013, (EU) 2018/858, (EU) 2018/1139 and (EU) 2019/2144 and Directives 2014/90/EU, (EU) 2016/797 and (EU) 2020/1828 (Artificial Intelligence Act).

[15] Kaminski (2023).

mitigate the potential harms. The basic assumption is that the technology will be used and there should be tools and procedures to manage the risks posed by technical artifacts. While they share these broad common features, different risk regulation frameworks can vary significantly according to the types of risks targeted for mitigation, the governance tools utilized, and the specific regulatory style adopted.

In the context of the AI Act, the risks to be addressed are indicated as "significant risk of harm to the health, safety or fundamental rights of natural persons".[16] The incorporation of "risks to fundamental rights" in the AI Act marks a shift toward broadening the concept of 'risk objects' to encompass harms to normative values. This new notion was first introduced in EU digital law in the context of the GDPR and now appears also in the Digital Service Act (DSA).[17] Such expansion goes beyond traditional concerns of physical, economic, and environmental harms that have established assessment procedures.[18] The final regulation also defines different categories of risks posed by AI systems: unacceptable risks that are prohibited, high-risk systems, systems that pose limited risk, General-Purpose AI models (GPAI) that are subject to specific provisions, systems that are supposed to pose no significant risks.[19]

Specifically, for the focus of this chapter, the compliance requirements for high-risk systems are particularly relevant, as they heavily depend on risk and impact assessment procedures. These assessment tools are the most typical and widely used mechanisms in risk regulation. Under the AI Act, high-risk systems are subject to two mandatory types of risk assessment: conformity assessment (CA) for AI providers and FRIA for certain deployers.[20] Both processes are conceived as iterative, meaning they are not one-time evaluations conducted only before deployment but must be continuously carried out and updated throughout the entire life-cycle of the AI system.[21] This ensures that the risk management remains effective and up to date. If any of the evaluated elements change—such as the system's design, its intended purpose, or the groups affected—the assessment must be revised accordingly.[22]

These tools reflect the distinctive governance approach of the AI Act, which, as suggested,[23] can be characterized as 'meta-regulation' or 'enforced self-regulation'. This regulatory framework involves "imposing legally binding obligations on regulated organizations, requiring them to develop and maintain internal control systems that achieve broadly defined, outcome-oriented, and legally mandated objectives".[24] This aligns with what is also called a 'collaborative governance' model, where formal

---

[16] Regulation 2024/1689 (2024), Art. 6(3).

[17] Malgieri and Santos (2025).

[18] Yeung and Ranchordás (2024).

[19] Smuha and Yeung (2025).

[20] Mantelero (2024).

[21] Kaminski (2023).

[22] Regulation 2024/1689 (2024), Art. 27(2) and Rec. 96.

[23] Smuha and Yeung (2025).

[24] Smuha and Yeung (2025, 24).

or informal responsibility for self-governance, such as risk assessment, is delegated to the entities subject to the regulation.[25]

3.2 *FRIA in Article 27 of the AI Act*

Article 27 of the AI Act establishes the requirements for conducting a FRIA for high-risk AI systems. The aim of this article is to mandate that certain deployers of high-risk AI systems "perform an assessment of the impact on fundamental rights that the use of such system may produce".[26] FRIA is required to be carried out only by specific deployers of high-risk AI systems,[27] rather than being extended to all deployers, as originally suggested by the European Parliament.

The assessment must be carried out before the high-risk AI system is used for the first time. Deployers are also required to update it iteratively if any significant changes occur in the elements evaluated during the assessment, such as the system's design, purpose, or context of use. The components of the assessment mentioned include a description of the deployer's processes, the intended use and frequency of the AI system, the categories of individuals likely to be affected, specific risks of harm, human oversight measures, and mitigation strategies.[28]

Following Mantelero and Wernick, the different features of FRIA can be summarized as follows.[29] FRIA has:

- an ex-ante approach that should be integrated in line with a 'by design' approach to AI development;
- a rights-based focus on risk assessment with risk acceptability, "means that the risk may remain high, albeit mitigated, if justified by the potential benefits"[30];
- a circular iterative structure that follows the product/service throughout its life-cycle, with the obligation to update if something changes in the components of the assessment;
- an expert-based nature that does not require stakeholder participation;
- a sharing of responsibility and burden between providers and deployers of AI systems on risk assessment and management.[31]

Beside the difference in scope, Article 27 shows significant difference in comparison to the Parliament's proposal. There is a complete omission of stakeholder consultation, which was included in the amendment stating that deployers "shall, to best

[25] Kaminski (2023) and Wernick (2024).

[26] Regulation 2024/1689 (2024), Art. 27(1).

[27] In particular should be performed by deployers that are bodies governed by public law, private entities providing public services, systems used to evaluate the creditworthiness of natural persons, and for risk assessment and pricing in life and health insurance. Ibid.

[28] Regulation 2024/1689 (2024), Art. 27(1) (a-f).

[29] Mantelero (2024) and Wernick (2024).

[30] Mantelero (2024, 4).

[31] Regulation 2024/1689 (2024), Rec. 93.

extent possible, involve representatives of the persons or groups of persons that are likely to be affected by the high-risk AI system, as identified in paragraph 1, including but not limited to: equality bodies, consumer protection agencies, social partners and data protection agencies, with a view to receiving input into the impact assessment".[32] This omission has been criticized in particular by civil society organizations because they "will not have a direct, legally binding avenue to contribute to impact assessments".[33] Another point of contention is the planned introduction of an "automated tool", such as a questionnaire, by the AI Office to simplify compliance. Several scholars argue that this approach risks reducing the assessment to a mere "box-ticking exercise" deprivazioneing it of substantive value and failing to account for its context-dependent nature.[34]

4 Methodological Aspects of the FRIA

After having provided a brief overview of FRIA's role within the AI Act, this section will delve into some of the methodological aspects that define FRIA as an assessment process. Regarding FRIA or similar rights-based approaches to AI evaluation, there are still no established common procedures or shared practices.[35] Moreover, the AI Office has not yet provided an official template, and as far as we are aware, only two FRIA models aligned with Article 27 have been developed at the moment in which this page is being written: one by the Catalan Data Protection Authority (APDCAT)[36] and the other by researchers at the Intesa San Paolo Data Science & Artificial Intelligence unit.[37]

Yet, despite being in its early stages, the FRIA does not arise from a vacuum but is grounded in extensive discussions on impact assessments for AI systems. Numerous academic proposals, standardization efforts, and industry initiatives have been developed in recent years.[38] From a legal standpoint, the FRIA is influenced by two established frameworks: the Data Protection Impact Assessment (DPIA) under the GDPR and the Human Rights Impact Assessment (HRIA), which is part of the UN Guiding Principles on Business and Human Rights.[39]

In the following parts of this section, we will outline the most significant methodological aspects that define FRIA. Specifically, we will focus on two key issues central to the debate: the question of which risks are intended to be assessed, and the features and phases that compose the assessment procedure.

[32] European Parliament (2023), Amendment 413.

[33] ECNL (2024).

[34] Mantelero (2024) and Smuha and Yeung (2025).

[35] Skoric et al. (2024).

[36] APDCAT (2025).

[37] Cosentini et al. (2025).

[38] Stahl et al. (2023) and Skoric et al. (2024).

[39] Mantelero (2024).

4.1 Risk and Fundamental Rights

As mentioned earlier, the risks to fundamental rights are framed as 'risks of harm' to those rights. However, as Malgieri and Santos point out, this concept—and similar formulations—is "inherently ambiguous",[40] as it is open to varied interpretations and presents several problems. This ambiguity stems from the fact that the concepts of risk and rights have very different origins and approaches, which are often seen as conflicting frameworks.[41] Thus, two distinct approaches to assessing impacts on fundamental rights can be distinguished[42]: a rights-based approach and a risk-based approach.

The rights-based approach follows a binary logic as it focuses on the dichotomy between the respect and violation of rights and obligations. In other words, a right is either respected or violated, operating on a 'yes or no' assessment regarding violations. As highlighted by Yeung and Bygrave,[43] fundamental rights are conceived as "moral boundary markers", that draw ethical demarcation lines that should not be crossed. This means that they define protected spheres that aim to safeguard intangible moral values, associated with the inherent dignity of individuals. This requires a "qualitative assessment method, which should be informed by the interpretations by the relevant regulatory authorities and case-law".[44] Conversely, the risk-based approach has an anticipatory and probabilistic nature. Its focus is on the anticipation of undesirable events or 'harms' and on measuring the probability and severity of their potential occurrence. It is therefore about managing potential future risks. Article 3(2) of the AI Act similarly conceptualizes risks through this conventional definition adopted in risk assessment. However, focusing solely on 'harms' or 'damages' can be considered a reductionist and limited approach when it comes to fundamental rights, which should have an intrinsic value and are hard to quantify since they are intangible values related to human dignity.[45]

In the literature, various methods have been proposed to address the tensions between these two approaches.[46] Specifically, the debate has largely treated the notion of likelihood as unproblematic, given its reliance on established statistical methods, and has instead concentrated on defining severity. Multiple variables and approaches have been suggested to capture both the tangible and intangible impacts on fundamental rights. The debate remains open, and its full exploration goes beyond the aim of this chapter. What is crucial to emphasize are the methodological assumptions underlying these interpretations and some of the main tensions that emerge in operationalizing FRIA.

---

[40] Malgieri and Santos (2025, 2).

[41] Yeung and Bygrave (2022).

[42] Malgieri and Santos (2025).

[43] Yeung and Bygrave (2022).

[44] Wernick (2024, 23).

[45] Malgieri and Santos (2025).

[46] Yeung and Bygrave (2022) and Malgieri and Santos (2025).

4.2 The Assessment Procedure

In accordance with risk assessment and management practices, FRIA should be structured into three distinct phases aligned with Article 27 of the AI Act[47]: planning, scoping, and risk identification; data collection and risk analysis; finally, risk management.

The stage of planning, scoping, and risk identification involves a detailed description of the AI system, its intended purposes, and the context in which it will be used. It requires an evaluation of both intrinsic risks (linked to the system's inherent design) and extrinsic risks (arising from the system's interaction with the social context and other technologies).[48] This step helps identify the potential domains that may impact rights, as well as the individuals and groups likely to be affected by the system.

During the stage of data collection and risk analysis, the potential impacts on rights identified in the previous phase are quantified. This evaluation may employ risk matrices—graphical tools that plot likelihood against severity on intersecting axes—to develop specific risk indices for each affected right. These matrices categorize distinct risk levels through the combined analysis of both dimensions.

After completing the risk analysis, the identified risks must be managed through the implementation of appropriate measures. The risk management phase is structured into three key steps: (1) identifying measures to prevent or mitigate risks, considering their impact on the overall risk level; (2) implementing these measures; and (3) monitoring the AI system's performance to ensure the assessment and measures remain up to date, revising them if "technological, societal and contextual changes affect some of the relevant elements of a previous assessment".[49]

According to Mantelero and APDCAT, this procedure is inherently expert based since it requires multidisciplinary expertise including specialists in fundamental rights, AI system design, and the contextual aspects of deployment. However, as previously noted, stakeholders are absent in the final version of the AI Act, marking a notable omission. Also other impact assessment frameworks that evaluate impacts on rights often incorporate stakeholder input to identify normative concerns, yet they rarely assign stakeholders an active role in resolving tensions between competing rights or interests.[50]

5 FRIA from a TA Perspective

The preceding analysis of TA and FRIA provides the groundwork for the following discussion. Rather than undertaking a direct comparison between FRIA and TA, this study seeks to initiate a critical dialogue about FRIA by discussing its distinctive

---

[47] Mantelero (2024).

[48] APDCAT (2025, 8).

[49] APDCAT (2025, 10).

[50] Algorithm Audit (2024).

features. This analysis is informed by the ongoing debate on TA, which has been rigorously investigated and well-documented over several decades. FRIA and TA are both procedures that aim at performing an evaluation of a technology in order to discuss the outcomes of the uses of such technology, though they differ in many aspects. For instance, TA is usually performed for a technology that is yet to be envisioned or that is currently under development while FRIA is an evaluation that occurs before the actual implementation and use of a technology but likely after its development.

This analysis is not a comprehensive assessment of FRIA, nor is this analysis grounded in empirical data about its uses, since FRIA is yet to be implemented. Drawing from the experience of TA, our goal is instead to stimulate a reflection on the potential and limitations of FRIA to perform two important tasks, namely, to steer technology development and to gain further knowledge about the technology in a hermeneutic perspective, which is to say to obtain knowledge about the social and epistemic configuration within which the technology is situated. To do so, our analysis will use the three theoretical dimensions of TA, previously described in Sect. 2.3 as heuristic concepts. While definitive conclusions about FRIA's governance implications remain premature, we present open questions about FRIA in order to cultivate critical engagement with its assumptions, and foster awareness of both its limitations and possibilities.

5.1 Complexity

The notion of complexity introduces the issue of relevance: TA involves sets of decisions about the inclusion or exclusion of specific actors, expertise, interests and priorities to steer the process through the multiple interrelations that characterize socio-technical trajectories related to AI. Applying this complexity dimension to FRIA means understanding what is relevant for its methodology and why. Certainly, an element of complexity characterizing FRIA is the very focus on fundamental rights that, as discussed in Sect. 4.1, draw ethical demarcation lines. Yet, fundamental rights are not always interpreted univocally and coherently: what interpretations are valid and relevant for the process? This would necessarily involve examining also how the laws are interpreted by legislators and legal professionals, an analysis that extends beyond the scope of this study.[51]

Within this context, the crucial focus instead becomes the role of experts and expert knowledge, both legal and technical, in FRIA's implementation. The primary reflexive challenge emerges from FRIA's fundamental design as an expert-based process, which constitutes its most significant element of complexity. By rigidly delimiting what constitutes legitimate knowledge and marginalizing non-expert perspectives, this approach depoliticizes risk evaluation.[52] This orientation conflicts

[51] Malgieri and Santos (2025).

[52] Van Est et al. (2012).

with TA's established understanding that socio-technical complexity necessitates questioning default assumptions about what constitutes 'relevant' or 'sufficient' expert knowledge. As we will see when discussing the inclusion dimension, this requires integrating stakeholder's perspectives to foster and open political discussions on the use of technology.

FRIA is expected to evaluate the impacts of AI systems with respect to the context of use, but the context is narrowly conceived as it relates to the alignment between the intended purposes and the "deployer's processes".[53] The evaluation does not extend on reflecting and deciding on the purpose of the technology considered, to how these purposes are embedded in technology design, and what unexpected (longer term) impacts are generated by the interaction of the same technology with a changing social context from a co-evolutionary perspective. These aspects appear to be taken for granted and artificially separates technology's development and implementation phases, a division that primarily exists in analytical frameworks rather than in actual technological practices. The separation of development and implementation phases is also codified by the AI Act which establishes FRIA for deployers and Conformity Assessment (CA) for providers. CA focuses on the results of the development of the technology while FRIA focuses on the possible consequences of the use of the technology. But there is no clear indication about the interaction providers and deployers should have, if any.[54]

By failing to adequately account for technology's social embeddedness, FRIA structurally reduces complexity through its conventional risk-based approach. It assumes that development and use are separable phases whereas TA tries to overcome such a simplification analysing the complexity of the entire processes of design and implementation of a technology.

A further dimension of complexity concerns FRIA's relationship to risk and its implications for evaluation outcomes. FRIA operates within already delineated decisions. The AI Act identifies high-risk systems according to criteria of relevance listed in Annex III. While these criteria are not explicitly part of the FRIA procedure, they play an implicit role by determining which systems require evaluation. Also, the fact that the AI regulatory framework defines a restricted category of prohibited AI uses which poses unacceptable risks, has the complementary consequence that the range of acceptable risky uses of AI is quite broad and encompasses a wide range of risk severity. As we mentioned before, in order to be put on the market, high risk systems require that Conformity Assessment (CA) and FRIA are performed respectively by providers and deployers. This leaves the risk acceptability decisions mainly in the hands of these actors that in their assessment heavily rely on experts' knowledge and technical standards.[55]

Since FRIA should be performed for high risks systems, it can conceal or exclude normative decisions of risk acceptability restricting its scope to the identification and mitigation of possible impacts on rights in deployment. Thus, as mentioned

---

[53] Regulation 2024/1689 (2024), Art. 27(1) (a).

[54] Mantelero (2024) and Cosentini et al. (2025).

[55] Laux et al. (2024).

before, FRIA does not assess the societal justification of technology's purposes and contextual uses. This aligns with the AI Act's techno-correctionist approach,[56] which prioritizes technical mitigation, 'fixing' flawed systems, over critical engagement with technology purposes and systemic effects. This highlights the fundamental tension inherent in translating rights protections into risk calculus—a tension rooted in the differences between risk-based and rights-based paradigms analyzed in Sect. 4. Such framing seems to presuppose that impacts on rights can be rendered permissible if 'managed' through mitigation measures.

These considerations open two questions for FRIA. Does FRIA permit reflections on the thresholds that distinguish 'manageable' from 'unacceptable' risks to rights and who gets to define them? Does FRIA risk considering impacts on fundamental rights as inherently 'manageable' thereby eroding the protections traditionally afforded to rights?

FRIA is meant to have a circular iterative structure: re-evaluation is mandatory if changes in systems' purpose, affected populations, or identified risks emerge.[57] However Article 27 does not provide what are the criteria for assessing these changes. TA recognizes that the background against which analyses are conducted is an element of complexity since socio-technical systems are inherently complex: risks and technologies are embedded in contexts that evolve over time. Stakeholders may change their view about values and rights. Even the access to a technology and its use may change. How can such changes be addressed? Also, focusing on risk assessment, is it actually feasible to evaluate the risk of an event that will eventually occur in the future in a context which could be significantly different from the present one? This calls for a reflexive attitude that constantly questions the dynamics of inclusion and exclusion. The question arises: is there room for reflexivity with FRIA?

5.2 *Anticipation*

The dynamics of socio-technical systems, which is an element of complexity, requires assessment of future evolutions in order to be critically investigated. This calls for anticipatory practices. There are two elements of anticipation in the FRIA procedure as it can be derived from the description of its methodology outlined in Sect. 4.2. The first one is related to identification and analysis. The second one is related to the guidelines or actions envisioned to mitigate the risks. They both represent a risk assessment approach which was once at the core of TA as well. TA moved on to adopt a proactive approach, though. Following Urueña's classification,[58] in order to guide technological development, one has to visualize desirable futures (*strategic* approach) and be critical about how the technology is conceived and understood at

[56] See Sect. 3.1.

[57] Cosentini et al. (2025).

[58] Urueña (2021).

the present time (*hermeneutic* approach). In principle, developers do not explicitly incorporate reflections on values and visions of the future into the design of the technology. The question arises: how can FRIA guide the development of a technology toward the production of desirable outcomes?

In the case of FRIA, the focus is on the technology itself, not on the technology as embedded in society. FRIA fosters no discussion about desirable outcomes; it concentrates on possible damages and harms. There is another limit to stress, though. Future harms are considered in relation to expected or intended uses of the technology. It is in fact on the intended uses of the technology that risks are assessed.[59] Yet, STS have shown how technology may have many unintended uses and emergent effects that TA tries to account for thanks to its more general approach. The co-evolution of technologies and society implies that uncertainty cannot be avoided. For AI systems and other new technologies there is also another, specific source of uncertainty: divergence about the evaluation of the outcomes, intended and unintended. The Rathenau Institute has introduced the notion of *Intimate Technology* to discuss AI systems.[60] The concept expresses the fact that such technologies are nested within society, reshaping people's habits, attitudes and beliefs, and gathering more information about them. For intimate technologies, uncertainty does not depend only on the ignorance about actual outcomes but also on people's divergences about the perceived goodness of such outcomes and the subjective trade-offs between them. The evolution, adoption and diffusion of intimate technologies define a new landscape, a new interpretive framework not only for the relationship we humans have with technologies but for the way we conceive our daily lives and relate to the world as well. This is especially true for information technologies that change radically the way we experience and interpret the world, but the case can be made for many other technologies as well. Such considerations are relevant to the present discussion because intimate technologies for their very nature, as it is recognized under the lens of this definition, produce soft effects that question personal and cultural values rather than hard, tangible and quantifiable effects such as physical, economic and environmental harms. A proper analysis of intimate technologies and an assessment of their impact call for trade-offs on values upon which there are in principle many divergences within society. Ultimately, the adoption of intimate technologies is not just a matter of assessing potential harms: it cannot be just a consequence of a judgment based on a common understanding of what is harmful and what is not, which risks can be taken and which cannot. The question arises: can FRIA account for such considerations?

[59] The AI Act explicitly pursues this objective, requiring mitigation measures for "the known and reasonably foreseeable risks of AI systems to the health, safety and fundamental rights in light of their intended purpose and reasonably foreseeable misuse". Regulation 2024/1689 (2024), Recital 65.

[60] van Est et al. (2014).

5.3 *Inclusion*

Over time TA has recognized not only the importance of including actors other than solely scientists, technicians, legal experts and politicians, but to do so from the very start of technological development. The reason is twofold. The inclusion of as many stakeholders as possible is meant to take into consideration experiential knowledge and preferences about values and evaluation processes. The importance of starting immediately is meant to prevent situations in which it is very difficult if not impossible to work on the technology to change it and adapt it to the needs of the stakeholders. In other words, actions should be taken from the start of the innovation process (upstream) and not at the end to avoid so-called locked-in phenomena when the technology has already stabilized.[61] The question arises: how does FRIA take into consideration the knowledge and preferences of non-experts?

Scholars and policymakers have increasingly acknowledged that vulnerable populations—including the elderly, poor people, children, migrants, and persons with disabilities—often face disproportionate direct and indirect consequences from AI systems.[62] The exclusion of these groups' perspectives in impact assessments could undermine the validity of fundamental rights evaluations. When risk evaluations are conducted solely by experts, decisions about risk acceptability can become problematic, as they disregard the values and preferences of affected communities which might disagree with the implementation of the technology itself. As Laux and his colleagues[63] argue, these questions are not appropriately addressed by the AI Act which largely adopts a 'paternalistic' and 'technocratic' approach to AI risk assessment, prioritizing expert judgment and self-governance mechanisms over the participatory inclusion of non-experts in decision-making processes.

In relation to these reflections on inclusion, in particular Constructive Technology Assessment (CTA) incorporates methodologies like value-sensitive design and participatory design, which try to integrate ethical considerations and stakeholder perspectives throughout the technological development process.[64] However, applying these principles to FRIA presents unique challenges. As a post-development evaluation conducted by deployers—who typically have limited capacity to modify system design—FRIA risks encountering technological lock-in effects, where problematic design choices become entrenched. While providers could more effectively address these concerns during the conformity assessment (CA), critical questions remain regarding FRIA's role. How can FRIA mitigate lock-in effects when evaluating already developed systems? To what extent can FRIA evaluations drive meaningful design changes post-development?

---

[61] Macnaghten et al. (2005).

[62] FRA (2022).

[63] Laux et al. (2024).

[64] Grunwald (2018) and Buijsman et al. (2025).

6 Conclusion

This chapter provides a critical examination of the FRIA, interrogating its role in AI governance and AI systems evaluation. We are aware that FRIA acts within the pre-established theoretical framework of the AI Act that defines boundaries such as the identification of the systems to be analyzed. We also acknowledge that something similar holds true for TA as well: TA may be commissioned by a governmental institution or may be limited by precise requirements upon its focus. Nonetheless, the tradition of TA was proven useful to gather insights on FRIA given they are both procedures for the evaluation of a technology. By establishing a structured dialogue between FRIA and TA methodologies, we have shed light on FRIA's assumptions, its potentialities and limitations. Our analysis employed Grunwald's[65] three constitutive dimensions of TA—anticipation, complexity, and inclusion—as analytical lenses to systematically examine FRIA. We have stressed that TA adopts a reflexive attitude capable of stimulating considerations on the criteria of relevance selected (complexity), the multiple temporal dimensions considered (anticipation) and the different perspectives included (inclusion). The full implications of FRIA's application to AI risk governance are still unfolding, yet the study has produced critical insights that could inform future FRIA revisions and implementations.

Our analysis has, however, identified key conceptual elements essential for understanding AI systems assessment procedures and has led us to raise open questions about FRIA, which we summarize below. Criteria of relevance enable and constrain reflexivity over the assessment process. To question the very criteria of relevance is important to adapt the procedure to the current situation and address complexity. Can FRIA account for such a reflexive attitude? Unintended uses of technologies cannot be foreseen beforehand. Also, AI systems require trade-offs between values and impacts' perception could change over time. To address such uncertainty, it is necessary to move from a *predictivist* approach to anticipation to a *hermeneutic* one. Can FRIA integrate these attitudes in its framework?

Finally, we have shown in Sect. 5.3 that inclusion is not only instrumental to evaluate value conflicts and divergences, but also to integrate different experiential knowledge on technological uses. Although the AI Act encourages the participation of stakeholders it does not mandate their consultation for conducting FRIA.[66] This poses some doubts on its commitment toward participation, which is also demonstrated by the FRIA models we analyzed which are expert-based procedures. Restricting participation in this way also affects on the other dimensions shaping what is relevant to evaluate and what futures are considered. How can FRIA effectively address these inclusion-related issues?

---

[65] Grunwald (2018).

[66] Regulation 2024/1689 (2024), Rec. 96.

References

Algorithm Audit (2024) A comparative review of 10 Fundamental Rights Impact Assessments (FRIA) for AI-systems. https://algorithmaudit.eu/pdf-files/knowledge-base/20240918_Comparative%20review%2010%20FRIAs%20Algorithm%20Audit.pdf

Arnaldi S (2012) Oltre il microcosm. Innovazione e valutazione tecnologica partecipata. In: Chiocca M, Valli L (eds) L'innovazione responsabile. Retecamere scrl, Roma, pp 91–105

Buijsman S, Klenk M, van den Hoven J (2025) Ethics of AI: toward a "design for values" approach. In: Smuha NA (ed) The Cambridge handbook of the law, ethics and policy of artificial intelligence. Cambridge University Press, Cambridge, pp 59–78

Catalan Data Protection Authority (APDCAT) (2025) FRIA model: guide and use cases. https://apdcat.gencat.cat/ca/documentacio/intelligencia_artificial/

Cosentini A et al (2025) Assessing the impact of artificial intelligence systems on fundamental rights. MediaLaws. https://www.medialaws.eu/wp-content/uploads/2025/03/20250714_FRIAct_MediaLaws.pdf

European Center for Not-for-Profit Law (ECNL) (2024) Packed with loopholes: why the AI Act fails to protect civic space and the rule of law | ECNL. https://ecnl.org/news/packed-loopholes-why-ai-act-fails-protect-civic-space-and-rule-law

European Parliament (2023) Artificial intelligence act amendments adopted by the European Parliament on 14 June 2023 on the proposal for a regulation of the European Parliament and of the Council on laying down harmonised rules on artificial intelligence (Artificial Intelligence Act) and amending certain Union legislative acts (COM(2021)0206 – C9-0146/2021 – 2021/0106(COD)). https://eur-lex.europa.eu/legal-content/EN/TXT/?uri=EP%3AP9_TA%282024%290138

European Union Agency for Fundamental Rights (FRA) (2022) Bias in algorithms—artificial intelligence and discrimination. Publications Office of the European Union, Luxembourg

Grunwald A (2018) Technology assessment in practice and theory. Routledge, London

Kaminski ME (2023) Regulating the risks of AI. 1348 Boston Univ Law Rev 103(5):1347–1411

Latour B (1987) Science in action: how to follow scientists and engineers through society. Harvard University Press, Cambridge

Laux J, Wachter S, Mittelstadt B (2024) Trustworthy artificial intelligence and the European Union AI Act: on the conflation of trustworthiness and acceptability of risk. Regul Govern 18(1):3–32. https://doi.org/10.1111/rego.12512

Macnaghten P, Kearnes MB, Wynne B (2005) Nanotechnology, governance, and public deliberation: what role for the social sciences? Sci Commun 27(2):268–291. https://doi.org/10.1177/1075547005281531

Malgieri G, Santos C (2025) Assessing the (severity of) impacts on fundamental rights. Comput Law Sec Rev 56:106113. https://doi.org/10.1016/j.clsr.2025.106113

Mantelero A (2024) The fundamental rights impact assessment (FRIA) in the AI act: roots, legal obligations and key elements for a model template. Comput Law Sec Rev 54:106020. https://doi.org/10.1016/j.clsr.2024.106020

Nentwich M (2016) Parliamentary technology assessment institutions and practices. A systematic comparison of 15 members of the EPTA network. https://epub.oeaw.ac.at/0xc1aa5572%200x00345db6.pdf

Orlikowski WJ, Scott SV (2008) Sociomateriality: challenging the separation of technology, work and organization. Annals 2(1):433–474. https://doi.org/10.5465/19416520802211644

Robinson DKR, Winickoff D, Kreiling L (2023) Technology assessment for emerging technology: meeting new demands for strategic intelligence. OECD Publishing, Paris

Sadowski J (2015) Office of technology assessment: history, implementation, and participatory critique. Technol Soc 42(1):9–20. https://doi.org/10.1016/j.techsoc.2015.01.002

Skoric V, Sileno G, Ghebreab S (2024) Roles of standardised criteria in assessing societal impact of AI. In: 2024 IEEE conference on artificial intelligence (CAI). IEEE, New York, pp 1240–1245

Smuha NA, Yeung K (2025) The European Union's AI act: beyond motherhood and apple pie? In: Smuha NA (ed) The Cambridge handbook of the law, ethics and policy of artificial intelligence. Cambridge University Press, Cambridge, pp 228–258

Stahl BC et al (2023) A systematic review of artificial intelligence impact assessments. Artif Intell Rev 56(11):12799–12831. https://doi.org/10.1007/s10462-023-10420-8

Tran TA, Daim T (2008) A taxonomic review of methods and tools applied in technology assessment. Technol Forecast Soc Change 75(9):1396–1405. https://doi.org/10.1016/j.techfore.2008.04.004

Urueña S (2021) Responsibility through anticipation? The 'future talk' and the quest for plausibility in the governance of emerging technologies. NanoEthics 15(3):271–302. https://doi.org/10.1007/s11569-021-00408-5

van Est R (2014) Intimate technology. The battle for our body and behaviour. Rathenau Instituut, The Hague

van Est R, Walhout B, Brom F (2012) Risk and technology assessment. In: Roeser S, Hillerbrand R, Sandin P, Peterson M (eds) Handbook of risk theory: epistemology, decision theory, ethics, and social implications of risk. Springer, Dordrecht, pp 1067–1091

Wernick A (2024) Impact assessment as a legal design pattern—a "timeless way" of managing future risks? DISO 3(2):29. https://doi.org/10.1007/s44206-024-00111-4

Yeung K, Bygrave LA (2022) Demystifying the modernized European data protection regime: cross-disciplinary insights from legal and regulatory governance scholarship. Regul Govern 16(1):137–155. https://doi.org/10.1111/rego.12401

Yeung K, Ranchordás S (2024) An introduction to law and regulation: text and materials, 2nd edn. Cambridge University Press, Cambridge

Digital Vulnerability in Automated Contracting: The Problem of Unexpected Outcomes. Contract-Law Remedies or Liability?

Teresa Rodríguez de las Heras Ballell

Abstract Automation in forming and performing contracts is proving to be a major revulsive for contract law. The use of AI systems in and for contracting means 'distancing humans from contracts' towards a hybridization between (human) autonomy and AI agency. That needs to revisit the meaning and significance of human-centric concepts, principles, and rules in contract law. This chapter traces how contract law needs to face and can solve the key dilemmas posed by automated contracting and the solutions provided for by UNCITRAL Model Law on Automated Contracting, the ELI Principles on Automated Decision-Making, and the ELI Model Rules on Digital Assistants for Consumer Contracts. One of the policy issues that best embodies the criticality of the challenge is the legal treatment of unexpected outcomes. Remedies range from those based on contract-law rules to those based on liability rules. Each risk-allocation solution has implications for legal certainty, predictability, the protection of interests, and the promotion of automated contracting in business practice.

Keywords Automated contracting · AI agents · Digital assistants · Unexpected outcomes · Attribution

1 A New Dilemma for Contract Law: Automated Contracting or *Intuitu Hominis* Contracts

With the pervasive expansion of Artificial Intelligence (AI) in present economy, automation has become a hallmark of our society. As mechanization transformed our productive model and distanced humans from an increasing number of tedious tasks and repetitive processes, algorithmic (and more intensely AI) automation

This paper was prepared in the framework of the Research Chair on AI: Foundations and Frontiers, of which the author is the Director.

T. Rodríguez de las Heras Ballell (✉)
Faculty of Law, Universidad Carlos III de Madrid, Madrid, Spain
e-mail: tla@der-pr.uc3m.es

C. Crea and M. Infantino (eds.), *Remedies to Digital Vulnerability in European Private Law*, https://doi.org/10.1007/978-3-032-19720-7_13

is distancing humans from a growing array of decision-making, creative, and intellectual activities.

Thus, automation poses a major challenge to legal systems, to classical concepts, and to the very conception of the activity that the law is expected to regulate. Automation 'distances' humans from decision-making. In contrast to previous technologies used throughout history, automation and, notably, AI-driven automation impact on the hitherto intrinsically human decision-making capabilities. Decades ago, there was a need for the recognition of the validity and enforceability for electronic contracting. This need reappears today for automated contracting (an expression used to refer to AI contracting indistinctively). However, automated contracting is not only proposing a change of the medium of traditional contracting, as electronic contracting did. Automated contracting poses challenges of a substantive nature about how contracting decisions are made. The question is whether a decision—any decision in any field and for any purpose—can be valid and enforceable when it is taken by automated systems, considering that no human being has reviewed it or ratified it.

Automation in forming and performing contracts is then proved to be a major revulsive for contract law, and a strong catalyst for an in-depth reflection on consumer protection paradigms.

The use of automated systems—including AI systems—to form and to perform contracts stokes a vivid debate on the notion of (human) autonomy and its meaning and significance for contract law, vis-à-vis the notion of AI agency.

Automated contracting raises novel and unprecedented challenges to contract law that add such a level of complexity so as to require revisiting legal terms, notions and categories. Automated contracting is putting an unbearable strain on the very notions of contract, consent, and (human) autonomy. Thus, automated contracting confronts an anthropocentric contract law with machine-driven actions, outputs, code, design features, and failures that may have legal relevance and contractual meaning.

Contract law can either embrace them and accommodate them into the core notions of contract by frictionless assimilation ('contracts formed by automated systems are contracts') or relegate them to a parallel regime of '(non-human) automated contracts' governed by AI agency, in order to preserve the purity of human-centric contract law. The dilemma is whether contract law is poised to embrace this evolution of contractual practice or will be indefectibly fractured into two regimes: one for automated contracting and one for *intuitu hominis* contracts.

In developing a legal framework enabling automated contracting, this chapter advocates that at least three main policy solutions must be implemented. The first policy solution concerns a rule on legal recognition of both contracts formed or performed by automated systems, and actions performed by automated systems in connection with the formation or the performance of a contract (Sect. 2). The second policy solution requires rules on attribution of actions performed by automated systems (Sect. 3). The third one requires rules on risk allocation, specifically in relation to unexpected outcomes (Sect. 4). The chapter traces the key solutions to these problems provided for by three main instruments dealing with automated contracting: the UNCITRAL Model Law on Automated Contracting of 2024 (hereinafter, MLAC),[1] the ELI Guiding Principles on Automated Decision-Making of 2022 (hereinafter, ELI PADM),[2] and the ELI Model Rules on Digital Assistants for Consumer Contracts of 2025 (hereinafter, ELI DACC).[3] The comparison between the MLAC and the ELI DACC reveals that the trickiest and most challenging issue is the problem of unexpected outcomes. The disparate solutions provided for by these two instruments show the complexity of the issues at stake and their strong implications in terms of legal certainty, trade predictability, and parties' expectations. Unexpected outcomes are inherent to AI-driven contracting and represent a distinctive risk of automated contracting.[4] Different policy options to remedy unexpected outcomes in automated contracting are possible, and yet there is no consensus on a harmonized rule to allocate this risk.[5] This chapter explains how the global debate has discussed and is still considering solutions, from a full attribution rule to an expansive notion of defect of consent or attribution alleviated with a liability rule vis-à-vis the affected party. None of these solutions is entirely neutral, as all of them embody a particular policy decision. Further discussion and deeper reflection are needed to find a reasoned and balanced approach.

2 From Electronic Contracting to Automated Contracting: Facing the Challenge of 'Human Distance' in Contracting

2.1 The Principle of Non-Discrimination and the Legal Recognition of Automated Contracting

Automated contracting embodies a new challenge to contract law that goes far beyond the challenges of electronic contracting that have been already overcome. In fact, electronic contracting, a few decades ago, posed a challenge to legacy contract-law rules.[6] Traditional contract-law rules had been ideated, formulated, and applied, paradigmatically, for face-to-face and in-writing distance transactions highly dependent upon the available medium, dominantly paper, and the means of communications for sending and receiving relevant declarations and other statements between the parties. Electronic contracting confronted then traditional contract law with the admissibility of the digital medium as a functional equivalent to writing in paper

[1] UNCITRAL (2024).

[2] ELI (2022).

[3] ELI (2025).

[4] Rodríguez de las Heras Ballell (2019).

[5] Rodríguez de las Heras Ballell (2020).

[6] UNCITRAL (1996) (hereinafter MLEC); UNCITRAL (2001) (hereinafter MLES); 2005 UN Convention on the Use of Electronic Communications in International Commerce, approved by General Assembly Resolution 60/21, of 23 November 2005 (hereinafter CEC).

and the use of electronic communications[7] to express and convey declarations of will and other statements with pre-contractual, contractual or contract-performance relevance. It was essentially a formal challenge, or a challenge of form. Substantive rules on contracts remained unchallenged.

Automated contracting poses a substantive dilemma instead: the need to rethink contract law in 'non-human terms' insofar as human actions with legal relevance are now replaced by machine-driven actions in relation to and for the purposes of forming and performing contracts.[8] For the sake of appreciating the criticality of the challenge, the radical perspective of automated contracting as 'contract without humans' is adopted. Even just in a metaphorical way, this radical and extreme approach is effective in highlighting that the challenge should not be understood in terms of deeming AI as a simple tool.

In developing an enabling legal regime for automated contracting, the initial assumption must be that the use of an automated system is not, solely on those grounds, an insurmountable impediment to recognizing the validity and effectiveness of the resulting actions, declarations and legal transactions.

This principle of recognition has traditionally been formulated in the texts of Uniform Law for International Trade as a rule of non-discrimination. Thus, both the UNCITRAL Model Law on Electronic Commerce, 1996 (hereinafter, MLEC) and the UN Convention on the Use of Electronic Communications in International Commerce, 2005 (hereinafter, CEC) expressly provide for such recognition with the formula "shall not be denied legal effect, validity or effectiveness [...] on the sole ground that". Thus, information in data messages,[9] declarations of the parties expressed in data messages or a contract formed[10] by or in the form of electronic communications[11] shall not be denied legal effect solely on such grounds. In the European *acquis communautaire* and in national law, a positive formulation of this recognition has been chosen in the form of a conditional statement, which is aimed precisely at ensuring their recognition and removing any obstacle that would deprive them of validity and effectiveness.[12] For instance, article 23(1) of the Spanish law on

---

[7] Under the CEC, "electronic communication" is defined as "any communication that the parties make by means of data messages" (article 4, letter (b), CEC), while "data message" is defined as "information generated, sent, received or stored by electronic, magnetic, optical or similar means, including, but not limited to, electronic data interchange, electronic mail, telegram, telex or telecopy" (article 4, letter (c), CEC).

[8] The intensity of the impact on contract-law tenets is, however, appreciated differently by scholars: see Mik (2020).

[9] Article 5 MLEC: "Information shall not be denied legal effect, validity or enforceability solely on the grounds that it is in the form of a data message".

[10] Article 1(1) MLEC: "In the formation of a contract, unless otherwise agreed by the parties, an offer and its acceptance may be expressed by means of a data message. A contract shall not be denied validity or enforceability solely on the ground that a data message was used in its formation".

[11] Article 8(1) CEC: "A communication or a contract shall not be denied validity or enforceability solely on the ground that it is in the form of an electronic communication".

[12] See article 9(1), Directive 2000/31/EC of the European Parliament and of the Council of 8 June 2000 on certain legal aspects of information society services, in particular electronic commerce, in the Internal Market (Directive on electronic commerce):

electronic commerce provides that "contracts concluded by electronic means shall produce all the effects provided for by the legal system, when consent and the other requirements necessary for their validity are met".[13]

This principle of recognition of electronic contracting is not in itself sufficient to give the same legal coverage to automated contracting. The functional equivalence that makes it possible to equate the legal effects of an electronic communication with those of a declaration of will expressed by other traditional means does not fully recognize the equivalence of actions, declarations and decisions that have been generated, executed and adopted by AI systems, without human intervention (in each action). Ultimately, automated contracting deviates from classical contracting concepts in a manner fundamentally different from the challenges presented by electronic contracting. While in electronic commerce the novelty resides in medium, in automated contracting it resides in the 'autonomous' action of the system, performed without human intervention—that is, in the very process of decision-making and execution of the action.

The assumption that AI systems operate with varying levels of autonomy is undoubtedly the fracture point in a continuing line of reasoning on the pure basis of functional equivalence.

In this respect, the remarks of the UNCITRAL Secretariat's Explanatory Note to Article 12 of the CEC are particularly revealing. This provision provides an extremely valuable legal basis for automated contracting, since it states that "[a] contract formed by the interaction between an automated message system and a natural person, or by the interaction between automated message systems, shall not be denied validity or enforceability on the sole ground that no natural person has reviewed or participated in each of the various acts performed through the systems or the contract resulting from such acts". Yet, as it can be seen from the explanatory comments to the text itself, this basis is not sufficient in the current state of scientific and technical progress. Article 12 contains very interesting and very useful elements for analysis. The provision is formulated with the classic formula of the principle of non-discrimination ("shall not be denied validity or enforceability") and refers, clearly and literally, to contracting resulting from the interaction with or between automated systems (Human-to-Machine, H2M, or M2M, Machine-to-Machine). Unlike electronic contracting, which dominates the provisions of the rest of the instrument, this article rightly draws attention to the "lack of intervention by a natural person". It is not the use of electronic communications that is taken into account; the scope of

---

Member States shall ensure that their legislation allows contracts to be concluded by electronic means. Member States shall ensure in particular that the legal regime applicable to the contractual process does not hinder the actual use of contracts by electronic means, nor lead to depriving such contracts of legal effect and validity by reason of their conclusion by electronic means.

[13] Article 23(1), Law 34/2002, of 11 July, on information society services and electronic commerce. BOE no. 166, of 12/07/2002 (hereinafter, LSSI).

application of article 12 CEC is indeed automated contracting.[14] In the Explanatory Note, the commentary to the provision is, if possible, more revealing. The commentary to article 12 CEC states that the increasingly frequent use of automated message systems, which are called "electronic agents" (today normally named digital assistants, AI-driven assistants, or AI Agents), has invited a review in some legal systems of "traditional legal theories of contract formation to assess their adequacy to contracts that come into being without human intervention".[15] While there was no reason not to recognize the validity of contracting by means of automated message systems, even if they were not explicitly provided for in the existing texts such as the MLEC and the 1980 Vienna Convention,[16] the commentary stressed that an express recognition would favor the use of automated systems and provide their use with greater legal certainty.[17]

This provision is undoubtedly a fundamental anchor for the legal regime of automated contracting, but its scope is consciously limited when projected onto the current state of development of technology. In the Explanatory Note, it is noted that ('at present') the attribution of the actions of an automated message system to a natural or legal person is based on a deterministic conception of programming. In other words, article 12 CEC assumes that the technical parameters by which an automated system is programmed determine its ability to function. Article 12 CEC recognizes that the possibility that new developments in AI allow the system to learn, to modify instructions or to set new objectives with certain levels of autonomy goes beyond the concept of automatism on which the principle of recognition underpinning the provision is based.

The differential characteristics of AI systems as learning systems with varying levels of autonomy overflow the initial or expected perimeter of the solutions provided for by article 12 CEC.

Under article 2(1) MLAC, automated contracting is meant to describe the use of automated systems to form or to perform contracts. As the Guide to Enactment explains, the expression 'to form or to perform contracts' is intended to cover any and all stages of the contract life cycle, including negotiations and precontractual dealings and termination of contracts.

The definition of "automated system" pursuant to article 1 MLAC reveals the key and distinctive features of automated contracting and the source or reason for the dilemma: 'computer system that is capable of carrying out actions without the necessary review or intervention of a natural person'. Despite the conciseness of the

[14] Under article 4, letter g, CEC, an "automated message system" means "a computer program or an electronic or other automated means used to initiate an action or to respond to transactions or data messages, which operates, in whole or in part, without intervention or review by a natural person each time an action is initiated or a response is generated by the system".

[15] UNCITRAL (2007, 69).

[16] United Nations Convention on Contracts for the International Sale of Goods (Vienna, 1980).

[17] UNCITRAL (2007, 69–70).

definition, it is aimed to embrace AI systems as described in internationally recognized notion such as the one recommended by the Organisation for Economic Co-operation and Development (OECD),[18] after its latest revision,[19] and incorporated in the European Regulation on AI (hereinafter, AI Act).[20]

Therefore, the ELI Guiding Principles for Automated Decision-Making[21] propose a principle of explicit recognition formulated as a principle of non-discrimination[22] of automated decision-making (ADM) on the sole ground of their automated nature. The material scope of application of these principles is broader than the notion of automated contracting. On the one hand, the notion of automated decision-making is largely overlapping with that of automated contracting, as the former includes decisions affecting or influencing the contractual position, the rights and the interests of the "affected person" (id est, "the natural or legal person interacting with the ADM, either being the person affected by the final decision, or the person using or relying on, for subsequent purposes, including subsequent decision-making, the output of the ADM (prediction, recommendation, rating, ranking"[23]). On the other hand, however, the notion of automated decision-making also extends to other actions or decisions which may not be linked to a contractual process at one of its life-cycle stages, such as decisions by public authorities in relation to an administrative file, notifications in judicial procedures, and the infringements of industrial property rights. In view of this lack of full overlap in the scope of application, it is nevertheless interesting to use these principles in the analysis of automated contracting to the extent that they are applicable.

The Guiding Principle no 2 of non-discrimination, which is an essential enabling element of automated contracting, does not, in principle, prevent the legislator from deciding to adopt specific or additional rules for the use of automated systems for certain purposes. These rules may range from design requirements to transparency requirements[24] or explainability requirements.[25] Failure to comply with these requirements may entail legal consequences of various kinds, but it does not

[18] OECD (2023).

[19] OECD (2024, I) (defining an AI system as "a machine-based system that, for explicit or implicit objectives, infers, from the input it receives, how to generate outputs such as predictions, content, recommendations, or decisions that can influence physical or virtual environments. Different AI systems vary in their levels of autonomy and adaptiveness after deployment"); OECD (2023).

[20] Regulation (EU) 2024/1689 of the European Parliament and of the Council of 13 June 2024 laying down harmonised rules on artificial intelligence (Artificial Intelligence Act).

[21] ELI (2022).

[22] ELI (2022, Guiding Principle 2) (Non-discrimination against WMD): "[a]s a general rule, ADM shall not be denied legal effect, validity or enforceability solely on the grounds that it is automated".

[23] ELI (2022, 10). The "affected person" can be a consumer or a professional user.

[24] See for example the transparency requirements for automated rating and ranking systems imposed by Regulation (EU) 2019/1150 of the European Parliament and of the Council of 20 June 2019 on promoting fairness and transparency for professional users of online intermediation services, article 5(1) and (2).

[25] Grochowski et al. (2021).

deviate from the principle of non-discrimination; rather, it preserves and builds on the non-discrimination principle.

Similarly, but in the opposite sense, the principle of non-discrimination also does not imply or preclude the legislator from prohibiting or limiting the use of automated systems for certain purposes or in certain decisions. The EU regulatory framework for AI illustrates these scenarios very vividly. Article 5 AI Act prohibits certain AI practices on the basis of their use or purpose, such as subliminal techniques to alter a person's behavior with a risk of causing harm and systems based on inferring emotions in certain areas and for certain purposes. Designed as a regulatory framework, the infringement of the AI Act carries penalties, including administrative fines.[26] Beyond the AI Act, which provides the most obvious framework for identifying prohibitions or limitations on the basis of intended use or purpose, there are also other restrictions, notably on the full automation of certain activities or processes in the rules for digital services.[27]

The validity and effectiveness of automated decision-making's non-discrimination is limited exclusively by the reason that no human has reviewed or ratified the decision. Hence, it does not remedy other grounds that may be invalidating or limiting, nor does it operate independently of the requirements and rules applicable to the legal situation in each case. Therefore, Guiding Principle no 2 operates in conjunction with Guiding Principle no 1 on "Law-compliant ADM", which establishes a rule of compliance with the rules applicable to the equivalent non-automated decision. Under Guiding Principle no 1, "[a]n operator that decides to use ADM for a particular purpose shall ensure that the design and the operation of the ADM are compliant with the laws applicable to an equivalent non- automated decision-making system". One might think that this statement is too self-evident and, because it is obvious, useless. However, it has several ramifications or derivatives that allow for more far-reaching reflections.

First, it contains a warning against circumvention by the mere use of an automated system. The use of an automated system cannot be an excuse to avoid compliance with the applicable law. The applicable law must be determined by reference to the equivalent legal situation if an automated system had not been used. This perspective transforms such a basic rule into a useful design and implementation guideline. Ultimately, the use of automated systems does not require an express legal authorization. It relies on the binomial of non-discrimination and law compliance to ensure legal recognition and, from there, to attach to it the legal regime that corresponds by equivalence—thus, if it is a banking contract, it will comply with the regulations that are applicable to it regardless of its automation.

Second, in its positive variant as an active obligation to ensure law compliance, it raises some interesting questions. The internal and external complexity that defines

---

[26] Article 71 AI Act.

[27] See the Regulation (EU) 2022/2065 of the European Parliament and of the Council of 19 October 2022 on a Single Market for Digital Services and amending Directive 2000/31/EC (Digital Services Act), in particular article 12(1) on the choice of means of communication between service providers and recipients and article 20(6) DSA on complaint-handling mechanism.

the functioning of an AI system requires some considerations that refer us to the regulatory framework. Each operator of the AI value chain will be responsible for the compliance with the requirements corresponding to each activity—design requirements, transparency, explainability, auditing, risk management, etc.

This approach to the legal recognition and admissibility of automated systems in and for contracting under the formula of the principle of non-discrimination also leads to the assumption that a prior agreement between the parties is not necessary for the use of an automated system in any of the phases of the contractual cycle as a requirement for its validity and effectiveness. This very essential and basic statement takes us back to the early days of electronic contracting, where its full legal admissibility depended precisely on freeing it from its being made conditional to prior agreement between the parties.

Full recognition of the validity and effectiveness of actions with a (pre- and post-) contractual purpose executed by automated systems must necessarily include this fundamental premise of the absence of prior agreement. In sum, the principle of non-discrimination implies that these actions cannot be denied validity and legal effectiveness solely on the grounds of their automated nature, without human intervention, and, therefore, that prior agreement between the parties is not an additional requirement to be satisfied in order for automated contracting to be legally recognized.

2.2 Legal Recognition of Automated Contracting, Technology Neutrality, and Right to Use

Both the MLAC and the ELI DACC contain a provision explicitly providing for the legal recognition of contracts as well as actions in connection with the formation or the performance of a contract. The drafting of the provision is largely similar between the two instruments. Minor divergences respond to the need to align with the terminology used by each instrument.

As per article 5 MLAC, "(a) contract formed using an automated system shall not be denied validity or enforceability on the sole ground that no natural person reviewed or intervened in any action carried out in connection with the formation of the contract". The provision is followed by a similar statement referred to any other action, such as an offer, the renegotiation, the termination notice, and performance itself: "[a]n action carried out by an automated system in connection with the formation or performance of a contract shall not be denied legal effect, validity or enforceability on the sole ground that no natural person reviewed or intervened in the action".[28]

Under the ELI DACC, which provide rules for contracts between a business and a consumer regarding the use of digital assistants by one or both parties for their

[28] Article 5(3) MLAC.

contractual relations (Art. 1),[29] the drafting is slightly adapted to the applicable terms, pursuant to article 2.[30] Thus, article 17 ELI DACC states that "an algorithmic contract is not to be denied validity or enforceability solely because a digital assistant was used, irrespective of whether only one party or both parties used digital assistants".[31] The same provision adds that "[a]ny action carried out by a digital assistant in respect of the contractual relations between a consumer and a business is not to be denied legal effect, validity or enforceability on the sole ground that a digital assistant was used".[32]

After sharing this fundamental policy solution, the two instruments separate each other again in how each of them approaches the use by the parties of automated system/digital assistants in contracting. The main consumer protection goal driving the ELI DACC explain the disparate approach.

In line with its tradition, the MLAC reaffirms in article 4 the principle of technology neutrality. But in this provision the principle is combined with a rule on the voluntary use of automated systems throughout the contract life cycle. More precisely, article 4 MLAC states that "[n]othing in this Law requires the use of an automated system or a particular method in automated systems to form or perform contracts". The provision thus reiterates the technology-neutrality approach, insofar as the MLAC does not mandate the use of a particular method, solution or model of automated system in automated contracting. But the provision also gives expression to the principle of private autonomy and, specifically, "reaffirms the freedom of the parties not to use automated systems in their contractual relations (but rather to use other forms of electronic contracting or "traditional" paper-based or in-person contracting)".[33] Albeit it may be unnecessary to reaffirm this well-established principle, this explicit recognition was considered of value by some jurisdictions as regards automated contracting.[34]

Contrariwise, the assumption of an asymmetric relationship between consumers and traders, together with a promising rebalancing potential of the use of digital assistants in consumer transactions, are behind the different approach taken by the ELI DACC. In article 3,[35] the ELI DACC focus on the right of consumers to use a

---

[29] Article 1 ELI DACC.

[30] Article 2 ELI DACC.

[31] Article 17(1) ELI DACC.

[32] Article 17(2) ELI DACC.

[33] UNCITRAL (2024) 20.

[34] UNCITRAL (2024) 20.

[35] Article 3 ELI DACC (Use of Digital Assistants):

> "(1) Consumers have the right to use a digital assistant for their contractual relations with a business.
>
> (2) A business must not use any contractual terms or conditions in a contract with a consumer which directly or indirectly waive or restrict this right. Any such terms are not binding on the consumer.
>
> (3) A business must not design, organise, or operate their online interfaces in a way that prevents consumers from using digital assistants in their contractual relations with a business.

digital assistant in their contractual relationships with traders and provide for rules preventing traders from banning, limiting, or forcing the consumer to use a digital assistant in their contracting, unless there are legitimate grounds.

The question that triggers this approach is whether the use of automated systems for consumer decision-making can strengthen the consumer's position and improve bargaining power. If a consumer, supported by a digital assistant, id est by an automated system that searches and processes information, selects and recommends options or even makes the final contracting decision with a prior review of the purchase conditions, is in a position to make better informed decisions, the use of automated systems in consumer relations accompanies and makes the protective function of consumer law more effective.

If such a premise is assumed, the limitation or prohibition of their use will be avoided or prevented as far as possible because it empowers the consumer. Thus, the principle of non-discrimination of automated systems in contracting, reinforced by the premise that it also mitigates consumer's vulnerabilities and improves their bargaining position, is transformed into a right of use without limitations or barriers in consumer relations.

Without going deeper into this more complex debate, which deserves more nuanced attention,[36] it suffices to spotlight one of the principles proposed in the ELI's Interim Report on Automated Decision-Making.[37] Of the eight principles tentatively proposed in the first phase of the project, principle no 4 (Non-discrimination and ADM-barrier free principle) encapsulates the idea that consumers might benefit from the use of automated systems for trading and contracting. Moreover, automated systems in the form of digital assistants can most effectively and fully realize the

---

(4) A business must not require a consumer to use the consumer's digital assistant for contractual relations. The main functionality of a product which incorporates a digital assistant must not be restricted if a consumer declines to use that digital assistant.

(5) Paragraphs (1)–(4) do not apply where there are legitimate grounds recognised by the applicable law in respect of the matters addressed in these paragraphs. Furthermore, paragraphs (2) and (3) do not apply to businesses categorised as micro or small enterprises under the applicable law".

[36] Twigg-Flesner and Micklitz (2023).

[37] ELI (2023). The co-rapporteurs of the project are Christoph Busch, Teresa Rodríguez de las Heras Ballell, Dariusz Szostek (until October 2023), Christian Twigg-Flesner and Marie Jull Sørensen. The project consisted of two phases. The first phase was completed with the drafting, adoption and publication of a report analyzing the suitability/readiness of European consumer law for the use of automated systems and incorporating legislative recommendations to ensure that the *acquis* does not contain barriers to automated consumer contracting and that consumer protection is not undermined by automation. See ELI (2023), examining the adequacy of existing rules and already anticipating some of the principles that guided the second phase of the project aimed at formulating a set of principles and model rules for automated contracting. See ELI (2025).

ultimate ratio of the "informed decision",[38] which the consumer makes in full knowledge of the facts and with full, adequate and sufficient information to ensure that it is in their best interests. This principle has crystallized in article 3 ELI DACC.

Both in their current state of development and in their expected future evolution, automated systems operating as digital assistants for consumers would act as powerful managers of transaction-relevant information. They can collect, contrast, compare and verify information provided by traders about the product, recommend the best combination of attributes, advise on the most appropriate contractual terms, negotiate certain terms, search for the best offer, reject proposals incorporating contractual terms that the consumer has marked as unacceptable, or dynamically review long-term relationships such as subscriptions or contracts for the supply of products or services. These functionalities and potential applications of digital assistants would seem to dilute the weakened position of a consumer unable to deal with scattered, overwhelming, biased or complex information. The digital assistant stands as a consumer protection net and a 'manager of consumer interests' with unparalleled collection, verification, integration and search capabilities.

On a first reading, automated contracting would seem to rebalance consumer relations, eliminating asymmetries and reducing the need for safeguards.[39] But the context is much broader and more complex and cannot, and should not, be solved with the erroneous assumption that there are no more 'consumer relations'—maybe new types of contextual, relational, or systemic asymmetric relationships. Indeed, as a premise, Principle no 2 on the ELI's Interim Report on automated decision-making (on the application of consumer law to algorithmic contracts) stated that the actions of the digital assistant are attributed to the consumer and, as such, consumer protection rules apply. Perhaps this should only be an interim and transitory answer that will have to be discarded when (and if) the transition to M2M transactions in all economic relations is completed. Then, the focus shall need to be placed on technological asymmetries and digital vulnerabilities.[40]

The effective exercise of an eventual right to use automated systems for contracting by consumers would require, first, preventing the use of technological, operational or design measures that block, deter or disable the use of digital assistants (*blockers*), and, secondly, implementing contractual, technological and design solutions that facilitate the virtual assistant to perform the necessary actions under equivalent conditions. Nevertheless, the implementation of these technological and operational, design and programming measures involves costs and requires changes in communication channels, interfaces and contracting procedures. They could therefore become a burden for smaller companies, putting them at a disadvantage vis-à-vis established market players and large platforms. This disruptive effect on the market has to be considered in the final shaping of the principle of non-discrimination and *no*

[38] Article 2(e), Directive 2005/29/EC of the European Parliament and of the Council of 11 May 2005 concerning unfair business-to-consumer commercial practices in the internal market (Unfair Commercial Practices Directive).

[39] Marotta-Wurgler (2012).

[40] Crea and De Franceschi (2024).

barriers. In addition, and from another perspective that applies equally to small and large entities, the use of automated systems can saturate the system, simultaneously block available offers without completing the transaction, alter prices or erroneously generate messages of lack of availability (*bots* for purchasing tickets, assistants who keep multiple transactions pending simultaneously, *bots* that saturate the system and block it, automated systems that multiply bookings). Therefore, there may be cases where legal restrictions (and legitimate and reasonable contractual prohibitions) may exist, or be imposed, on the use of automated systems to protect specific interests, such that their use becomes unlawful, inappropriate or unreasonable.

3 The Meaning and the Relevance of Attribution in Automated Contracting

The assumption that AI systems act with varying levels of autonomy[41] makes attribution a more complex and absolutely critical task. A system of attribution rules and factors is instrumental when the option of "electronic persons"[42] is abandoned.

Attribution in AI systems must take into account two important considerations.

Firstly, it does not consist in determining the origin of a message or an action already completed and determined, which the automated system would simply transmit or generate according to predefined instructions and without any margin for unpredictability, but in attributing decisions or actions which, with a certain level of autonomy and in accordance with explicit or implicit objectives, the system adopts and executes.

Secondly, attribution is a prerequisite that underpins other solutions of the legal regime of automated contracting such as the treatment of error or the rules on allocation of risks due to malfunctioning or unexpected outcomes.

Thus, attribution serves for multiple purposes. Attribution works as a first anchor on which to build a regime for mistakes in automated contracting. It also works as a model to extrapolate to the question of the 'attribution of information' to ensure a conscious and informed decision of the person to whom the decision of the automated system is attributed. Attribution works as a threshold, for example with respect to the decision about whether absolutely unforeseeable and unexpected actions should be treated from the point of view of non-attribution, a defect of consent or scenarios of liability. All these questions reveal that attribution, in general terms, has several layers that require separate treatment.

The debate on the attribution of the actions of automated systems has been marked and, to some extent, clouded by a complex and delicate debate (not always framed in

---

[41] Some studies analyze the emergence of autonomous, interactive and reactive actions of certain AI systems, in particular large language models, to challenge a purely deterministic and instruction-based definition of algorithmic systems under human control. Chan et al. (2023).

[42] Pagallo (2018).

the right terms) on "electronic personality".[43] This is neither a new nor an unprecedented proposal. The question of the personhood of AI systems has been raised for decades, from a variety of perspectives.[44] Sometimes with a strong ethical and philosophical flavour, on other occasions with pragmatism and a vision of personality as a useful and efficient mechanism for risk distribution and selective attribution of rights and/or obligations. In short, legal personality as a legal fiction[45] or technical-legal solution has already shown malleability and plasticity to adapt to other situations without implying a full mimicry of the human condition,[46] id est, without entailing an anthropomorphic conception[47] in the recognition of personality.

However, the option of attributing legal personality to AI systems with certain levels of autonomy (as a unique solution or according to certain thresholds of autonomy) entails significant practical difficulties and shifts the problems to a second stage without solving them. In addition to ethical concerns, it may have implications for the soundness and coherence of the liability system as a whole with practical obstacles to the compensatory purpose or with a counterproductive allocation of incentives to use AI systems as a shield for protection and diversion of liability. All this could ruin both the compensatory and the preventive purpose of liability.[48] Thus, the need for attribution formula becomes even more pressing.

MLAC sets out two consecutive rules for attribution of actions carried out by automated systems in article 7. In tribute to the prevailing role of party autonomy, article 7(1) MLAC[49] refers to the parties' agreement on the procedure (and then the rules and relevant factors) to attribute the actions performed by the automated system. Thus, the primary rule is that the output of an automated system would be attributed in accordance with any procedure agreed to by the parties. Parties can establish this procedure in a preliminary agreement for negotiations, in a framework contract between the parties for repeated transactions, or in the terms and conditions of a platform operated by a third party to which both parties have joined and throughout which they conclude their contracts via an automated system.

---

[43] In its 2017 resolution on civil law on robotics (European Parliament 2017, para 59), the European Parliament urged the Commission to explore the implications of all possible legal solutions, such as

> to create in the long term a specific legal personality for robots, so that at least the most complex autonomous robots can be considered as electronic persons liable to repair any damage they may cause, and possibly to apply electronic personality to cases where robots make intelligent autonomous decisions or interact with third parties independently.

[44] Solum (1992).

[45] On the evolution of the theory of legal personality, Galgano (2004).

[46] Boslaugh (2016).

[47] Maneesha (2020) and Salazar Ortiz and Láriz Durón (2017).

[48] Ghersi (1997, 141–145) and Díez Picazo (1999, 41 f).

[49] Article 7(1) MLAC: "As between the parties to a contract, an action carried out by an automated system is attributed in accordance with a procedure agreed to by the parties".

In the absence of parties' agreement, MLAC opts for a fall-back rule based on two components: use and purpose. Article 7(2) states that "an action carried out by an automated system is attributed to the person who uses the system for that purpose". As explained in the Guide to Enactment,

> [i]t is intended to attribute the action to the person with the strongest link to that action, and for that attribution to be determined objectively, in the light of all the circumstances. Depending on those circumstances, a range of factors may be relevant in identifying that person, including: (a) the person deploying the automated system; (b) the control exercised over the operational parameters of the system and the action; (c) the benefit or value derived from the action; (d) the nature and purpose of the contract; and (e) trade usages and the practices established between the parties.[50]

This solution is neither replacing nor adopting agency law rules.[51] The automated system is not treated as an agent acting on behalf of the principal. Instead, a set of factors are proposed to attribute the actions carried out by the automated system that pivot on a 'qualified' use and a purpose or aim that connects the factual use with the outcome in a transactional context. This is the first step in the process of attributing the legal consequences of that action that would depend upon each type of situation (contractual effects as a contracting party, liability for damages, relevant pre-contractual information in consumer contracts).[52]

ELI DACC adopt an approach to attribution that initially seems to be simpler and broader as it is only based on the 'use'.

As article 22(1), entitled "Attribution and its limits", states, "[a] person who uses a digital assistant for contractual relations is bound by the actions taken by the digital assistant and all the actions of the digital assistant are attributed to that person". However, the limits of attribution, as discussed below, show that, given the consumer protection goal, the attribution solutions are largely different to those laid down in MLAC. Indeed, the default rule for attribution of unexpected outcomes is diametrically opposite.

4 Risk-Allocation Solutions in Automated Contracting: Rules and Remedies for Unexpected Outcomes

The rules and factors proposed for attributing to a person actions or decisions (output) of an AI system are crucial to deal with certain situations that we can classify as pathological: errors, system failures and unforeseen or unexpected outcomes.

A classification or typology of these relevant risk cases is proposed for the purposes of attribution.

The first category of risks refers to cases where the automated system malfunctions, fails or has technical problems in its operation. In these cases, the system does

---

[50] UNCITRAL (2024, para 66).

[51] Andrade et al. (2007) and Chopra and White (2009).

[52] UNCITRAL (2024, para 71).

not perform the expected action, performs it late or incorrectly, or makes decisions that do not correspond to the operator's (or user's) expectations.

The second category of risks includes cases where third party interference, hacking attack or cybersecurity breaches lead to an omission (no action by the system), an action or a decision by the AI system that the operator (user) does not recognize, deviates substantially from its intention or is simply wrong for whatever reason.

The third category of risks comprises the assumptions most closely linked to the nature of AI systems as learning systems with a strong dependence on data: unexpected outcomes. Automated systems can give rise to unanticipated, unexpected outcomes that deviate substantially from what is expected, suffer hallucinations,[53] and evolve in their learning towards unanticipated tasks, extrapolate data, generate biases, or execute actions that exceeds the training scope.

In the face of these situations, which distinctive features of AI make particularly serious or at least intense (autonomy and learning capacity, opacity, complexity, vulnerability, data dependence),[54] three legislative policy options can be considered, in general terms, which are not necessarily mutually exclusive. First, non-attribution. Second, liability rules. Third, the (adapted) application of existing rules on defects of consent, or other causes for invalidity or nullity. I propose to add a fourth possible solution to attribution of unexpected outcomes: the formulation of bespoke rules for unexpected outcomes of AI systems.

The proposed solution to the risk categories must be clear and predictable, provide certainty in commercial trade, and achieve an appropriate distribution of risks between the parties. Therefore, unjustified and abusive recourse to the legislative policy option of 'non-attribution' can significantly undermine confidence in trade while discouraging automated contracting and increasing transaction costs. Faced with the risk of non-attribution, prices and costs in automated contracts would move upwards to cover the risk, specific safeguards and insurance would be imposed, or the use of AI would be limited in particularly large transactions or transactions where frustration of the economic purpose of business due to non-attribution are unacceptable or difficult to reverse.

Hence, article 7(3) MLAC enshrined as a primary rule of attribution aimed to provide legal certainty and predictability in (B2B, mainly) automated trade: "[a]ttribution of an action carried out by an automated system shall not be denied on the sole ground that the outcome was unexpected".

On the contrary, the non-attribution option would mean that, in the event of failure, third party interference or deviation (alleged and/or acknowledged by the other party) from the expected operation, the action or decision is not attributable to the person to whom would otherwise be attributed the origin of the output result of the IA system. For the sake of legal certainty, non-attribution is an uncomfortable and, in certain cases, devastating solution because it undermines trust and frustrates expectations. Therefore, non-attribution as a general solution might not be optimal.

---

[53] Ziwei et al. (2023).

[54] Burrell (2016) and Chagal-Feferkorn (2018).

It may, however, be the preferred solution in consumer relations as a measure to protect the consumer who would not be bound by an action or decision resulting from a failure, interference by a third party or a deviation of the system towards unforeseen, surprising or unexpected results. In the ELI DACC this option has been considered and adopted as the primary rule. The action or decision would not be attributable to the consumer and would not have any legal effect. This avoids the situation of subsequent attribution to another actor in the supply chain. Where an action deviates from what the consumer could reasonably expect that action will have no legal effect and is not attributed to the consumer. In assessing whether the actions of the digital assistant deviate from those a consumer could reasonably expect, article 22(3), laid down a non-exhaustive list of relevant factors. Under article 22(3) ELI DACC,

> the relevant factors to be applied in determining whether the actions of the digital assistant deviated from those a consumer could reasonably expect, include:
>
> (a) any information given to the consumer about the adaptive capability of the digital assistant;
>
> (b) whether the operation of any adaptive functionality of the digital assistant was inconsistent with such information;
>
> (c) external factors such as loss of access to third-party data supplies, errors in that data, or cybersecurity breaches; and
>
> (d) whether in the specific circumstances, the consumer could not reasonably have expected that the action in question would be taken.

The previous article 22(2), entitled "attribution and its limits", precises that "[w]here the actions of a digital assistant used by a consumer for contractual relations deviate from those which could reasonably be expected by the consumer, the actions of the digital assistant have no legal effect and are not attributed to the consumer". This non-attribution rule is combined with a liability solution, in the form of compensation of the damage caused to the other party (of the consumer) by the non-attribution at the expense of the operator who is liable—the provider of the AI system (digital assistant or AI) to the consumer. Under article 25 ELI DACC, entitled "Liability of the supplier of a digital assistant to third parties",

> [w]here the actions of a digital assistant are not attributed to the consumer who deployed it under Article 22(2), the supplier of the digital assistant to that consumer is liable to the business with whom the consumer's digital assistant was dealing for losses the business has incurred as a result of the non-attribution. The conditions for awarding damages are governed by the applicable law.

The major difficulty is to decide whether failures and errors, on the one hand, and unforeseen decisions, on the other hand, can and should be treated together as a single category in the case of automated contracting, or whether, on the contrary, they respond to different scenarios. In the latter case, the debate is whether automated outputs that could be qualified as 'unforeseen', 'unexpected' or 'unintended' require a different solution. This has been the debate that arose in the deliberations of UNCITRAL Working Group IV in the preparation of the provisions for automated contracting.[55]

---

[55] A/79/17. Article 8 (Unexpected actions carried out by automated systems):

Therefore, despite the decisive rule in article 7(3) MLAC, an additional article 8 is included in the Model Law as an optional provision (in square brackets) with an accompanying footnote inviting States enacting the Model Law to consider incorporating the provision into their domestic law if they wish specifically to legislate the issue of unexpected actions carried out by automated systems.[56] During the preparation of the Model Law, it was felt that a stand-alone provision specifically addressing the issue was unnecessary and could even be undesirable if it interfered with fundamental domestic law concepts and principles, as well as with established trade usages. Nevertheless, it was stated that a stand-alone provision could be useful for some jurisdictions to supplement existing solutions and so article 8 was included as an optional provision.

The starting point for article 8 is the principle that a party using an automated system as part of its trade-related activities bears the risk of the output of that system as per article 7(3) MLAC. In general terms, article 8(1) MLAC mitigates that principle with regard to unexpected outputs by allowing a party to disavow the output in certain circumstances and thus avoid the legal consequences of that output that may flow under other law.

The scope of the proposed provision refers exclusively to the second typology of actions performed by automated systems, i.e. unforeseen or unexpected actions. But it is also intended to deal with cases of 'programming error, or interference by a third party, or transmission error'. Its wording was originally based on Article 13(5) LMCE,[57] which does not focus on unforeseen results but on attribution of origin or transmission errors. Therefore, the need has arisen to look for other legal solutions to unforeseen results that are uniquely and specifically linked to AI systems and not to the problems of electronic means of communication of messages.

The assumption that the principle that should govern the use of AI systems is that the party using the system to form or perform a contract bears the risk involved[58] would invite to look for solutions in other texts. In the UNCITRAL system, Article 14 CEC and articles 25 and 79 Vienna Convention might be considered. Both texts seek to strike a balance between the interests of the parties by applying the concepts of

---

[1. Unless otherwise agreed by the parties, where an action carried out by an automated system is attributed to a party to a contract, the other party to the contract is not entitled to rely on that action if, in the light of all the circumstances:

(a) The party to which the action is attributed could not reasonably have expected the action; and

(b) The other party knew or could reasonably be expected to have known that the party to which the action is attributed did not expect the action.

2. Nothing in this article affects the application of any rule of law or agreement of the parties that may govern the legal consequences of an action carried out by an automated system.

[56] UNCITRAL (2024, paras 73–74).

[57] A/CN.9/WG.IV/WP.182, para 43.

[58] A/CN.9/WG.IV/WP.182, para 42.

reasonable expectations and fair dealing. Despite these efforts, however, the solution is not clear and continues to raise doubts.

AI contracting is catalyzing a necessary debate on traditional foundations of contract law and consumer protection paradigms in a new transactional environment. Contract law needs to face and decide how to solve the dilemma between automated contracting and *intuitu hominis* contracting and re-imagine contracts in a human–machine[59] hybrid society.

References

Andrade F et al (2007) Contracting agents: legal personality and representation. Artif Intell Law 15:357–373

Barfield W, Weng Y-H, Pagallo U (eds) (2024) Cambridge handbook on law, policy, and regulations for human–robot interaction. Cambridge University Press, Cambridge

Boslaugh SE (2016) Anthropocentrism. Encyclopaedia Britannica. https://www.britannica.com/topic/anthropocentrism

Burrell J (2016) How the machine 'thinks': understanding opacity in machine learning algorithms. Big Data Soc 3(1). https://doi.org/10.1177/2053951715622512

Chagal-Feferkorn KA (2018) The reasonable algorithm. Univ Ill J Law Technol Policy 1:111–148

Chan A et al (2023) Harms from increasingly agentic algorithmic systems. In: FAccT '23: proceedings of the 2023 ACM conference on fairness, accountability, and transparency. IEEE Computer Society, New York, pp 651–656

Chopra S, White L (2009) Artificial agents and the contracting problem: a solution via an agency analysis. Univ Ill J Law Technol Policy 3:363–403

Crea C, De Franceschi A (eds) (2024) The new shapes of digital vulnerability in European Private Law. Nomos, Baden-Baden

Díez Picazo LM (1999) Derecho de daños. Civitas, Madrid

European Law Institute (ELI) (2025) Guiding principles and model rules on digital assistants for consumer law. https://www.europeanlawinstitute.eu/projects-publications/publications/eli-guiding-principles-and-model-rules-on-digital-assistants-for-consumer-contracts/

European Law Institute (ELI) (2023) Interim report, EU consumer law and automated decision-making (ADM): is EU consumer law ready for ADM. https://www.europeanlawinstitute.eu/fileadmin/user_upload/p_eli/Publications/ELI_Interim_Report_on_EU_Consumer_Law_and_Automated_Decision-Making.pdf

European Law Institute (ELI) (2022) Guiding principles on automated decision-making in the EU. https://www.europeanlawinstitute.eu/fileadmin/user_upload/p_eli/Publications/ELI_Innovation_Paper_on_Guiding_Principles_for_ADM_in_the_EU.pdf

European Parliament, Resolution of 16 February 2017 with recommendations to the Commission on civil law rules on robotics (2015/2103(INL)), Civil law rules on robotics, P8_TA(2017)0051. https://www.europarl.europa.eu/doceo/document/TA-8-2017-0051_EN.html

Galgano F (2003) El concepto de persona jurídica. Revista Derecho Del Estado 16:13–28

Ghersi C (1997) Teoría General de la reparación de daños: análisis económico y sociológico del daño individual y social. Astrea, Buenos Aires

Grochowski M, Jablonowska A, Lagioia F, Sartor G (2021) Algorithmic transparency and explainability for EU consumer protection: unwrapping the regulatory premises. Crit Anal Law 8(1):44–63

[59] Barfield et al. (2024).

Maneesha D (2020) Unsettling anthropocentric legal systems: reconciliation, indigenous laws, and animal personhood. J Intercult Stud 41(1):77–97. https://doi.org/10.1080/07256868.2019.1704229
Marotta-Wurgler F (2012) Does contract disclosure matter? J Inst Theor Econ 168:94–119
Mik E (2020) From automation to autonomy: some non-existent problems in contract law. J Contract Law 36:205–229
Organisation for Economic Co-operation and Development (OECD) (2024) Recommendation of the council on artificial intelligence. OECD/LEGAL/0449. https://legalinstruments.oecd.org/en/instruments/oecd-legal-0449
Organisation for Economic Co-operation and Development (OECD) (2023) AI terms & concepts. https://oecd.ai/en/ai-principles
Pagallo U (2018) Vital, Sophia, and Co. The quest for the legal personhood of robots. Information 9(9):230. https://doi.org/10.3390/info9090230
Rodríguez de las Heras Ballell T (2020) Embracing technological disruption in international transactions: challenges for legal harmonization. In: Benicke C, Huber S. (eds.) National, international, transnational: Harmonischer Dreiklang im Recht. Festschrift für Herbert Kronke zum 70. Geburtstag. Giesekin Verlag, Bielefeld, pp 1223–1234.
Rodríguez de las Heras Ballell T (2019) Legal challenges of artificial intelligence: modelling the disruptive features of emerging technologies and assessing their possible legal impact. Uniform Law Rev 2019(1):1–13
Salazar Ortiz VH, Láriz Durón JJ (2017) Una crítica al antropocentrismo desde la ética ambiental. Euphyía 11(20):107–130
Solum LB (1992) Legal personhood for artificial intelligences. North Carolina Law Rev 70:1231–1287
Twigg-Flesner C, Micklitz H-W (eds) (2023) The transformation of consumer law and policy in Europe. Hart, Oxford
UNCITRAL (2024) Model law on automated contracting. https://uncitral.un.org/en/mlac
UNCITRAL (2007) Explanatory note by the UNCITRAL secretariat on the United Nations Convention on the Use of Electronic Communications in International Contracts. https://cisg-online.org/files/commentFiles/UNCITRAL_Secretariat_Explanatory_note_on_the_UNECIC_2007.pdf
UNCITRAL (2001) Electronic signatures model law. https://uncitral.un.org/en/texts/ecommerce/modellaw/electronic_signatures
UNCITRAL (1996) Electronic commerce model law. https://uncitral.un.org/en/texts/ecommerce/modellaw/electronic_commerce
Ziwei J et al (2023) Survey of hallucination in natural language generation. ACM Comput Surv 55(1), Article no 248. https://doi.org/10.1145/3571730

Restitution as a Remedy to Digital Vulnerability in European Private Law

Karmen Lutman

Abstract Although largely governed by the national laws of the Member States, restitutionary provisions significantly influence the efficiency and effectiveness of remedies for contract failure in business-to-consumer contracts, including termination for breach and withdrawal, which are regulated by EU law. This chapter offers an overview of the main characteristics of the restitution regimes following the failure of consumer contracts. It examines the impact of EU law, including CJEU case law, in this area. Focusing on the challenges posed by the digital transformation of consumer law in particular, it explores the extent to which restitution law can help protect consumers' economic and non-economic interests, including their personal data and human rights.

Keywords Digital vulnerability · Restitution · Consumer contract · Unfair contract terms · EU law · European private law

1 Introduction

Consumers often enter into contracts from a position of vulnerability, a phenomenon particularly prevalent in the digital environment. In Europe, various legal remedies protect consumers from this vulnerability. For example, a contract may be deemed invalid, or a party may be entitled to terminate it if it is the result of a lack of information, improper understanding, or exploitation of a consumer's weakness. This may result in failed contracts being wound up with restitutionary effects.

Unlike compensatory remedies, restitutionary remedies aim to deprive the defendant of a gain rather than compensate the claimant for the loss suffered.[1] While several circumstances might trigger the award of restitutionary remedies, the following analysis will focus on instances of failed (consumer) contracts.

[1] Virgo (2024, 3).

K. Lutman (✉)
Faculty of Law, University of Ljubljana, Ljubljana, Slovenia
e-mail: karmen.lutman@pf.uni-lj.si

C. Crea and M. Infantino (eds.), *Remedies to Digital Vulnerability in European Private Law*, https://doi.org/10.1007/978-3-032-19720-7_14

If a contract fails (the verb 'to fail' is used here in a broad sense to encompass void contracts, avoided, or terminated as a result of breach or withdrawal), the contract has to be unwound, which means that both parties have to give back what they have received under the contract. The objective of the process of winding up is to restore both parties, as far as possible, to the position they were in when the contract was concluded (*status quo ante contractum*). The term 'restitution' in this chapter will be used in its 'European' meaning,[2] focusing therefore on the restitutionary consequences of contracts failed due to the exercise of remedies such as rescission, termination for breach, and withdrawal.

The chapter aims to shed some light on restitution as a 'remedy' to digital vulnerability in cases of contract failure. The analysis will examine the restitutionary rules following failed consumer contracts and will seek to assess the adequacy, effectiveness, and potential of restitution as a legal remedy in European private law.

2 Restitutionary Measures in European Private Law

Restitutionary consequences following the exercise of legal remedies such as rescission, termination for breach, and withdrawal, are governed by relatively technical rules aimed at restoring the contracting parties to the position they were in before the contract. While restitution may be either personal or proprietary,[3] European private laws usually approach restitutionary measures from a contract law perspective, treating restitution as a personal remedy.

Restitution is a remedy that can be exercised individually and collectively. Under EU law, some measures giving rise to restitution qualify as collective remedies within the meaning of the European Union (EU) directive on representative actions.[4] Remedies such as the termination of the contract and the reimbursement of the price paid are expressly included within the definition of a redress measure, as set out in articles 3(10) and 9(1) of the Directive on representative actions. Typically, the termination of the contract serves as a ground for restitution, while reimbursement of the price reflects the restitutionary obligation itself.

Since they focus on restoring the *status quo ante contractum*, individual and collective restitutionary measures are reactive (that is, *ex post*) in nature. They come into play only after the contract has failed, whether through termination, rescission, withdrawal, or declaration that the contract was invalid from the outset.

The restitutionary measures that are currently reflected in the regulatory framework of EU private law are primarily aimed at protecting consumers' economic interests. However, the main claim of this chapter is that restitution as a relatively

---

[2] Wendehorst (2012, 8).

[3] Virgo (2024, 3).

[4] Directive (EU) 2020/1828 of the European Parliament and of the Council of 25 November 2020 on representative actions for the protection of the collective interests of consumers and repealing Directive 2009/22/EC.

broad concept may also be capable of addressing some of the contemporary challenges of consumer law.[5] The restitutionary provisions governing the unwinding of failed contracts with personal data as counter-performance in the Sale of Digital Goods Directive,[6] and in the revised Consumer Rights Directive,[7] which both refer to the General Data Protection Regulation (GDPR),[8] seem to reflect this broader approach, extending protection to non-economic consumer interests.

3 Restitution After Failed Consumer Contracts

3.1 *Initial Observations*

There is no uniform and comprehensive European restitution regime governing the consequences of failed contracts. Instead, selected aspects of restitution are addressed in various pieces of EU secondary legislation, particularly in the context of contract termination due to a breach or withdrawal. In the field of consumer law, there are, for instance, the Consumer Rights Directive[9] and the Consumer Credit Directive[10] (both dealing with restitutionary consequences of consumer withdrawal), as well as the Digital Content and Services Directive,[11] the Sale of Digital Goods Directive,[12] and the Package Travel Directive,[13] which all address (certain aspects of) restitution after termination of contract.

These rules do not constitute a coherent and comprehensive system of restitution. First, their scope is limited to particular instances of contract failure, usually

[5] For details see Grochowski (2024).

[6] Directive (EU) 2019/771 of the European Parliament and of the Council of 20 May 2019 on certain aspects concerning contracts for the sale of goods, amending Regulation (EU) 2017/2394 and Directive 2009/22/EC, and repealing Directive 1999/44/EC.

[7] Directive 2011/83/EU of the European Parliament and of the Council of 25 October 2011 on consumer rights, amending Council Directive 93/13/EEC and Directive 1999/44/EC of the European Parliament and of the Council and repealing Council Directive 85/577/EEC and Directive 97/7/EC of the European Parliament and of the Council.

[8] Regulation (EU) 2016/679 of the European Parliament and of the Council of 27 April 2016 on the protection of natural persons with regard to the processing of personal data and on the free movement of such data, and repealing Directive 95/46/EC.

[9] Directive 2011/83/EU.

[10] Directive 2008/48/EC of the European Parliament and of the Council of 23 April 2008 on credit agreements for consumers and repealing Council Directive 87/102/EEC.

[11] Directive (EU) 2019/770 of the European Parliament and of the Council of 20 May 2019 on certain aspects concerning contracts for the supply of digital content and digital services.

[12] Directive (EU) 2019/771.

[13] Directive (EU) 2015/2302 of the European Parliament and of the Council of 25 November 2015 on package travel and linked travel arrangements, amending Regulation (EC) No 2006/2004 and Directive 2011/83/EU of the European Parliament and of the Council and repealing Council Directive 90/314/EEC.

termination for breach and withdrawal. In cases where a contract is void, has been voided, or rescinded, the applicable restitutionary rules are to be found in national law. Furthermore, the restitutionary provisions set out in EU directives address only selected consequences of failed contracts, such as the return of goods, repayment of money, and compensation for use or costs. Other important issues—such as the payment of interest, the return of gains, the disgorgement of profits, the treatment of loss of enrichment—are usually left to the national laws of the Member States. Regarding consumer vulnerability, it appears that, in the context of remedies for contract failure, the European legislator has placed significantly greater emphasis on withdrawal and termination for breach. In contrast, the restitutionary consequences of these remedies have been largely left in the hands of the national laws of the Member States.

This results in a substantial legal uncertainty for consumers, as the level of protection afforded varies across EU Member States. Furthermore, restitutionary rules are traditionally laid down in national civil law codifications, which were historically not designed for business-to-consumer scenarios. Thus, it has at times proven difficult to interpret these traditional civil law rules in a manner consistent with the general principles and objectives of EU consumer law.[14]

3.2 Influence of EU Law on National Restitution Regimes: A First Step Towards Greater Harmonisation?

Although largely overlooked by EU law, restitutionary rules following failed contracts have a decisive impact on the efficiency and effectiveness of remedies such as termination and withdrawal, as well as on the consumer's decision whether to exercise them. Both the conditions and the scope of restitution are important in this regard.

This neglect was also remarked by the Court of Justice of the European Union (CJEU) in the *Messner* case,[15] which concerned a consumer's obligation to pay for the use of goods in the event of withdrawal from a distance contract. The Court stated in particular that "the efficiency and effectiveness of the right of withdrawal would be impaired if the consumer were obliged to pay compensation simply because he had examined and tested the goods acquired under a distance contract".[16]

Not only the scope of restitution, but also the conditions on which the obligation to return is based, can render the remedies granted under EU law ineffective. One such example is the time when the restitution obligation falls due. The CJEU examined

---

[14] See e.g. Court of Justice of the European Union (CJEU), case C-520/21, *Arkadiusz Szcześniak v Bank M. SA*, 15 June 2023.

[15] CJEU, case C-489/07, *Pia Messner v Firma Stefan Krüger*, 3 September 2009.

[16] Ibid, para 24.

this issue in the cases *Banca B*[17] and *Lombard*,[18] which dealt with the consequences of annulling a loan agreement due to unfair contract terms. Since national restitutionary rules following the annulment of loan agreements proved to be particularly unfavourable to consumers, requiring them to repay their debt immediately, the Court held that, in such circumstances, EU law—and more precisely the Unfair Contract Terms Directive[19]—does not prevent national courts from disapplying an unfair term that demands immediate repayment, substituting it with a supplementary provision of national law. This is to avoid the application of restitutionary rules following the annulment of the contract that would place the consumer in a particularly disadvantageous position, effectively penalising them.[20] The application of such rules would undermine the effectiveness of consumer protection.

3.3 *EU Grounds for Contract Invalidity and Their Influence on the Restitution Phase*

National restitutionary rules may be subject to the obligation of interpretation in conformity with EU law, particularly when they are triggered by the grounds for contract invalidity governed by EU law, such as unfair contract terms or unfair commercial practices. In such cases, the grounds for contract invalidity also influence the restitution phase, (co)shaping the restitutionary rules in a manner consistent with the general principles of EU law and objectives of the applicable secondary legislation.

The following two subsections will examine the interplay between the grounds for invalidity and the restitution remedy from the perspective of the Unfair Contract Terms Directive[21] and the Unfair Commercial Practices Directive.[22]

3.3.1 Unfair Contract Terms

The Unfair Contract Terms Directive does not contain a restitution regime in the event of contract failure due to unfair contract terms. Nevertheless, the CJEU has

[17] CJEU, case C-269/19, *Banca B. v A.A.A.*, 25 November 2020.

[18] CJEU, case C-472/20, *Lombard Pénzügyi és Lízing Zrt. v PN*, 31 March 2022.

[19] Council Directive 93/13/EEC.

[20] For further analysis and commentary, see Iamiceli (2023), Heiderhoff (2025).

[21] Council Directive 93/13/EEC.

[22] Directive 2005/29/EC of the European Parliament and of the Council of 11 May 2005 concerning unfair business-to-consumer commercial practices in the internal market and amending Council Directive 84/450/EEC, Directives 97/7/EC, 98/27/EC and 2002/65/EC of the European Parliament and of the Council and Regulation (EC) No 2006/2004 of the European Parliament and of the Council.

developed a substantial body of case law that provides guidance on the relevant principles and criteria for restitution under national law in such cases.

The CJEU has remarked on many occasions that, after establishing the unfairness of a contractual clause, the consumer's legal and factual position should be restored to the state they would have been in had the term never existed.[23] Restitution of advantages wrongly obtained on the basis of an unfair term is considered an appropriate remedy to achieve this goal.[24]

When defining the scope of restitution required from the consumer, the CJEU case law is guided by the 'no worse off' rationale,[25] according to which a good-faith recipient should not be unjustifiably left worse off than they were before their receipt. Besides, it is a well-settled rule of restitution for unjust enrichment that, after making restitution, the recipient should also neither profit at the expense of the claimant nor be in a better position than they would have been in had there been no unjustified transfer of value in the first place.[26] However, as CJEU case law shows, this is not necessarily the case in consumer law.[27] Namely, due to the deterrent effects sought by the Unfair Contract Terms Directive, the restitutionary balance may occasionally shift in favour of the consumer, so that, following restitution, consumers may be placed in a (significantly) better position than they would have been had the enrichment event not occurred.[28]

Restitutionary claims of businesses responsible for unfair contract terms, on the other hand, may be partially or entirely excluded due to deterrent effects. An example is the *Bank M* case, in which the Court ruled out the possibility for suppliers of goods and services to seek remuneration from consumers for the use of capital following the annulment of loan agreements on the grounds of unfair contract terms. The position was justified also on the basis of the principle '*nemo auditur propriam turpitudinem allegans*' ('no one may rely on his or her own wrongdoing'), according to which "a party cannot be allowed to derive economic advantages from his, her or its unlawful conduct or to be compensated for the disadvantages caused by such conduct".[29] For the same reason, the Court also ruled out the possibility of indexing the capital.[30]

It can be observed that the interpretation of national restitutionary rules in a manner not compliant with EU law sometimes leads to different outcomes compared

---

[23] CJEU, cases C-154/15, C-307/15 and C-308/15, *Gutiérrez Naranjo and Others*, 21 December 2016, para 66; CJEU, case C-483/16, *Zsolt Sziber v ERSTE Bank Hungary Zrt*, 31 May 2018, para 34; CJEU case C-472/20, *Lombard Pénzügyi és Lízing Zrt. v PN*, 31 March 2022, para 55.

[24] Ibid.

[25] Klimchuk (2016, 72).

[26] In German law, this is known as the "principle of statics" (*Statikprinzip*). See Wendehorst (2017), § 818, para 33.

[27] See e.g. CJEU, case C-520/21, *Arkadiusz Szcześniak v Bank M. SA*, 15 June 2023, where the Court ruled that consumers are released from the obligation to pay contractual interest in cases of an invalid credit agreement due to an unfair term.

[28] For analysis of *Bank M.* and critical comments on such 'overprotection of consumers', see Grundmann and Badenhoop (2023).

[29] CJEU, case C-520/21, *Arkadiusz Szcześniak v Bank M. SA*, 15 June 2023, para 81.

[30] CJEU (order), case C-488/23, *mBank S.A. v KŁ and JŁ*, 12 January 2024.

to purely domestic cases. Traditional restitutionary rules, usually laid down in codes of civil law, require certain adjustments when applied in consumer law, primarily due to the greater asymmetry between the contracting parties, which is characteristic of business-to-consumer (B2C) relationships. Moreover, deterrent effects, typical of specific domains of consumer protection, are generally not among the core objectives of national restitution laws, which therefore call for some adaptation when applied in this area. As noted by Schulze, European private law today differs significantly from the older concepts of private law that shaped 19th-century national civil codes that were grounded in the liberal ideology prevalent at that time.[31]

3.3.2 Unfair Commercial Practices

To improve the enforcement of consumer rights and access to redress, the Unfair Commercial Practices Directive[32] was amended in 2019, introducing a new Article 11a on redress. The updated directive explicitly mentions, inter alia, termination of the contract as an example of a proportionate and effective remedy in cases of unfair commercial practices. While the provision does not elaborate on the exercise of this remedy or its restitutionary consequences, leaving these matters to the discretion of the Member States, it does specify that, when determining the conditions for its application and its effects, they may consider the gravity and nature of the unfair commercial practice, the damage suffered by the consumer, and other relevant circumstances.[33]

Due to the absence of a restitution regime following contract termination for unfair commercial practices in the Unfair Commercial Practices Directive itself, the national laws of the Member States apply accordingly. For instance, in transposing the amendment of the Directive into domestic law, the Slovenian legislature opted to introduce additional provisions of a restitutionary nature. The obligation to return goods and money is subject to a time limit, i.e. fourteen days from the assertion of the claim (for a consumer returning goods) or the receipt of the claim (for a business returning money) (article 56(1)–(2) of the Consumer Protection Act[34]). Much more interesting is article 56(3) of the Consumer Protection Act, which establishes that the consumer is not required to pay for the normal use of the goods during the period before their return. This departs from the general restitution regime applicable to contracts terminated for breach under the Code of Obligations,[35] which requires every recipient to make restitution of the benefits it has derived in the meantime from what it is obliged to return (article 111(4)). The legislative materials do not

[31] Schulze (2024, 523).

[32] Directive 2005/29/EC.

[33] Article 11a(1).

[34] Zakon o varstvu potrošnikov (ZVPot-1), Official Gazette of the Republic of Slovenia, No 130/22 with further amendments.

[35] Obligacijski zakonik, Official Gazette of the Republic of Slovenia, No 97/07 with further amendments.

reveal the rationale behind this new provision, leaving it unclear why the Slovenian legislator chose to adopt such a solution.

4 Contracts for the Supply of Digital Content and Services: New Approaches to Restitution in the EU?

Following the adoption of the Digital Content and Services Directive in 2019, several new dimensions and challenges emerged in the context of restitution after contract failure. Introducing a new model of contracts—contracts with data as counter-performance—the Digital Content and Services Directive has introduced an entirely new logic into the law of restitution, which was traditionally driven by the principles of a monetary economy. While the directive addresses the restitutionary consequences of termination for breach, the revised Consumer Rights Directive provides provisions on the consequences of withdrawal.

The digital character of the performance makes restitution in such cases specific. Here, establishing the *status quo ante contractum* is not based on the restitution of what was received under the contract. Since the consumer can make multiple copies of the digital content used, returning the digital content would not necessarily achieve the goal of restitution. This is why the consumer is instead obliged to refrain from using the digital content or digital service and from making it available to third parties. In practice, the providers of digital content and services typically implement systems that automatically disable the use of such content or services when the contract is terminated or ceases for any other reason. A similar mechanism applies to traders, who must erase the consumer's data and prevent third parties from gaining access to it, unless there is some other legal ground for the data processing.

Contracts for the supply of digital content and services are usually long-term contracts performed continuously over time. This also requires an adequate adjustment of traditional restitutionary rules, which are generally tailored to contracts that are performed immediately. In cases of long-term contracts, restitution can traditionally only be claimed for the period after the termination has taken effect[36] (*ex nunc* effect[37]). At the same time, the process of unwinding the contract does not aim to achieve the *status quo ante contractum*. Due to several difficulties that may arise in practice, the Digital Content Directive provides guidance in this regard. By not following the rigid division between *ex tunc* and *ex nunc* effects, the Digital Content Directive sets the point relevant for the restitution at the moment the defect occurs.[38]

---

[36] See, e.g., article 7.3.7 UNIDROIT Principles of International Commercial Contracts; see also Zimmermann (2011, 584).

[37] Unless the performances only form a coherent whole when taken together, rendering partial performance meaningless in itself.

[38] Art. 16(1) of the Digital Content and Services Directive.

This offers more flexibility and aligns with current trends of restitution after failed contracts.[39]

However, the unwinding of failed long-term contracts creates several difficulties, especially when personal data are involved. Probably the most problematic in this regard is the scenario of proportionate restitution. Namely, the GDPR rules (to which the Digital Content Directive and Consumer Rights Directive refer) were not created in terms of an *ex tunc* or *ex nunc* logic of restitution, let alone cases where the decisive moment for unwinding is set somewhere between the conclusion and the termination of the contract. The use of digital content could in such cases be expressed in monetary terms,[40] but this solution may interfere with the principle of private autonomy. Since the directives mentioned above do not address this issue, Member States will have to find answers in their domestic laws.

Nonetheless, addressing restitution after failed contracts involving personal data as counter-performance marks a shift in the very concept of restitution, moving away from the idea of protecting consumers' economic interests to the concept of protecting their non-economic interests too. A consumer's claim following the failure of a contract implies the withdrawal of consent for data processing from the perspective of the GDPR and therefore has a human rights dimension. The rights under GDPR arising from such withdrawal, however, do not have a restitutionary character in the traditional sense and exist independently of the termination of the contract. One might ask whether the GDPR post-withdrawal rights may serve as a model solution for unwinding failed contracts with data as counter-performance. Scholars have cautioned against this approach, describing it merely as a stopgap solution.[41] It should also be added that inserting a restitutionary clause referring to the GDPR renders the restitutionary regime somewhat non-transparent and unclear for consumers.

5 Digital Vulnerability and Restitutionary Remedies

Alongside the national laws of the Member States, EU private law traditionally provides legal remedies for defects in both contract formation and performance, as well as specific contractual remedies that, in justified cases, allow for a departure from the principle of *pacta sunt servanda*. While national rules generally govern nullity and voidability, EU law often regulates cases of termination for breach or consumer withdrawal.

When it comes to consumer protection in the online environment and challenges brought by digitalisation, these remedies still appear to be effective in safeguarding consumers' economic interests. It is important, however, that these remedies actually be accessible to the consumer. Rules on restitution, in this regard, are crucial to determine the effectiveness of remedies for the protection of consumers. Case law

[39] See Huguenin, Hilty, Purtschert (2013, 262).

[40] Twigg-Flesner (2020, 306).

[41] Schmidt-Kessel (2020, 145).

from the CJEU during the period of the COVID-19 pandemic has demonstrated the importance of complying with EU restitution rules where applicable. For instance, this involves ensuring a refund in money (rather than vouchers) where stipulated,[42] and respecting the time limit set for the restitution obligation.[43] Where national rules apply, the Euro-conform interpretation usually requires an adapted interpretation and application of restitution law concepts, as demonstrated above. Since the restitutionary rules should not overlook the grounds for contract failure, it may also be important to consider them in cases arising from digital vulnerability. By referring to the deterrent effect of the Unfair Contract Terms Directive, the CJEU has already taken some steps in this direction, and it is likely to continue doing so in specific instances of digital vulnerability exploitation.

However, contracting in the digital environment often involves not only consumers' economic interests, but also non-economic ones. Discriminatory profiling, algorithmic pricing, gender-based unfair practices, mass data collection, and other controversial practices, often linked to a contractual relationship, bring new challenges to the task of recreating the *status quo ante contractum*. Since the current national rules on restitution following failed contracts were not primarily designed to address parties' non-economic interests, restitutionary remedies must be complemented by other private and public law remedies, including the protection of human rights.

Considering that contracts concluded in the digital environment often involve personal data as counter-performance, the EU legislator has already taken a first step to address the consequences of the failure of such contracts. However, the GDPR rules referred to in these cases may be considered restitutionary only in a very broad sense. At the same time, the development of a more sophisticated approach to unwinding failed contracts in this context is still awaited.

6 Concluding Remarks

So far, the restitutionary consequences following the failure of contracts have not been among the EU legislator's priority agendas. This has resulted in a rather fragmented and nationally oriented system of restitutionary remedies. However, the CJEU has often influenced the interpretation of restitution rules based on the grounds and modes of contract failure regulated by EU law, resulting in a more harmonised system than may be initially apparent.

Strengthening the protection of vulnerable consumers and bolstering the enforcement of consumer protection rules across the EU stand among the goals of the EC Consumer Agenda 2025–2030. Together with the challenges brought by the digital

[42] CJEU, case C-540/21, *European Commission v Slovak Republic*, 8 June 2023; CJEU, case C-407/21, *UFC – Que choisir in CLCV*, 8 June 2023.

[43] See e.g. CJEU, case C-540/21, *European Commission v Slovak Republic*, 8 June 2023.

transition, this may be an opportunity for the EU legislator to reconsider restitution as a remedy in European private law and move towards a more comprehensive system of restitution after failed consumer contracts. After all, these rules play an important role in enhancing the efficiency and effectiveness of remedies for contract termination.

As this chapter has shown, the restitutionary rules in this context primarily serve to pursue the principle of *restitutio in integrum* in an economic sense. While GDPR rules, which serve to unwind failed contracts involving personal data as counter-performance, may be considered restitutionary only in a very broad sense, the non-economic interests of consumers can be adequately protected only by other private or public law remedies complementary to the law of restitution.

References

Grochowski M (2024) Digital vulnerability in a post-consumer society. Subverting paradigms? In: Crea C, De Franceschi A (eds) The new shapes of digital vulnerability in European private law, Nomos, Baden-Baden, pp 201–225

Grundmann S, Badenhoop N (2023) Foreign currency loans and the foundations of European contract law—a case for financial and contractual crisis? Eur Rev Contract Law 19(1):1–36

Heiderhoff B (2025) Die Rechtsprechung der Nichtigkeit von AGB im Licht der nationalen Rechtsdogmatik. In: Mülbert PO (ed) Bankrechtstag 2022 und 2023. De Gruyter, Berlin-Boston, pp 311–338

Huguenin C, Hilty RM, Purtschert T (2013) Art. 80. In: Huguenin C, Hilty RM (eds) Schweizer Obligationenrecht 2020, Entwurf für einen neuen allgemeinen Teil. Schulthess, Zurich, p 262

Iamiceli P (2023) The 'punitive nullity' of unfair terms in consumer contracts and the role of national courts: a principle-based analysis. Common Mark Law Rev 60:142–150

Klimchuk D (2016) What kind of defence is change of position? In: Dyson A, Goudkamp J, Wilmot-Smith F (eds) Defences in unjust enrichment. Hart, Oxford-Portland, pp 69–86

Loosen M (2022) Die Rückabwicklung des Vertrages Daten gegen Leistung. Tectum, Baden-Baden

Lutman K (2024) Restitution after termination for breach of a contract for the supply of digital content and services: a tough row to hoe. Zb Pravn Fak Zagreb 74(5/6):881–897

Schmidt-Kessel M (2020) Right to withdraw consent to data processing—the effect on the contract. In: Lohsee S, Schulze R, Staudenmayer D (eds) Data as counter-performance—contract law 2.0?. Nomos, Baden-Baden, pp 127–146

Schulze R (2024) Digital vulnerability in European private law—conclusions. In: Crea C, De Franceschi A (eds) The new shapes of digital vulnerability in European private law, pp 520–536

Twigg-Flesner C (2020) Articles 16–18. In: Schulze R (ed) EU digital law. Beck, Munich, pp 278–316

Virgo G (2024) The principles of the law of restitution. Oxford University Press, Oxford

Wendehorst C (2012) Restitution in the proposal for a common European sales law. Available at https://www.europarl.europa.eu/document/activities/cont/201207/20120704ATT48276/20120704ATT48276EN.pdf

Wendehorst C (2017) § 818. In: Bamberger HG et al. (eds) BeckOK BGB. Beck, Munich

Zimmermann R (2011) The unwinding of failed contracts in the UNIDROIT principles 2010. Uniform Law Rev 16(3):563–587

Remedying Data Vulnerability in a Global World: A Comparison of the European Union and Japan's Approach to Compensation for Data Breaches

Barbara Milillo

Abstract The notion of digital vulnerability can be defined as the exposure of individuals to risks arising from their engagement with online activities. The dissemination of personal information in the digital realm, often resulting from the misuse or violations of privacy, underscores the need for an understanding of digital vulnerability as a multifaceted phenomenon that perpetually shapes the landscape of privacy protection. This has led to privacy being recognized as an essential and vital right, continuously shaped and challenged by technological developments and judicial interpretations across various legal traditions. The purpose of this paper is to explore the data protection remedies developed by the Japanese legal system, and to investigate the relevant insights for the data protection policy and the safeguard of vulnerable subjects that Japanese judicial decisions can offer to Europe. To this purpose, the paper will highlight key elements of the Japanese and European approach in mitigating privacy-related vulnerabilities and will survey their respective limitations, focusing in particular on the impact of tort law on privacy rights and on data protection policy.

Keywords Data protection · Tort law · Japanese law · EU law · GDPR

1 Introduction

A growing body of literature recognizes the significance of the right to privacy amidst technological developments. In the digital realm, the right to privacy is continuously subject to a growing number of threats (such as data mining, automated decision-making, profiling). In this context, institutions across many legal systems have recently been working to guarantee a broader protection of personal information. However, in a world of increasing digital interactions, which at the same time

B. Milillo (✉)
Department of Legal Science, University of Udine, Udine, Italy
e-mail: barbara.milillo@phd.units.it

C. Crea and M. Infantino (eds.), *Remedies to Digital Vulnerability in European Private Law*, https://doi.org/10.1007/978-3-032-19720-7_15

increase the risks associated with the misuse of data, it can be argued that, inasmuch as privacy is concerned, every individual is vulnerable. The protection of digital privacy therefore calls for new and flexible legal solutions.

This is how privacy and vulnerability are interconnected in the digital world. The notion of digital vulnerability has recently received considerable critical attention. The idea of vulnerability is part of the data protection environment, but it is usually employed to refer to specific categories of individuals, such as the elderly, children or people affected by disabilities. Nevertheless, the notion that vulnerability is an inherent characteristic of all data subjects, including in the perspective of data protection, is currently growing in the state-of-the-art research.[1]

The specific objective of this paper is to examine the role of vulnerability in the data protection realm by performing a comparative analysis between the European Union (EU) and Japan's different approaches to the issue. More in particular, the main purpose of the paper is to investigate how the EU and Japanese law address the harm caused by data breaches through tort law.

The paper is composed of three parts. Section 2 will briefly examine the existing legislation in the data protection field within the context of both the EU and Japan. Section 2.1 will outline the main EU legal text on privacy, that is, the General Data Protection Regulation (EU) 2016/679 (GDPR). Section 2.2 will then analyse the Japanese approach to privacy and to data protection, with particular emphasis on the Japanese Act on the Protection of Personal Information (APPI). After this brief comparison, Sect. 3 will explore the history and contents of the Adequacy Decision (AD) on Japan adopted by the European Commission in 2019. The AD recognized that the Japanese legislation guarantees a level of data protection similar to the European standard, as a direct consequence of the 'Brussels Effect'.[2] As it will be highlighted, the decisional process underlying the AD was characterized by a significant amount of institutional dialogue between the European Commission and the Protection of Personal Information Committee of Japan. Finally, Sect. 4 will offer a comparative analysis of the Japanese Supreme Court's Benesse Case in connection with the decisions of the Court of Justice of the European Union (CJEU), formerly known as the European Court of Justice (ECJ), on compensation in cases of infringements of data protection law. The comparison will shed light on the three core aspects that are central in the Japanese Supreme Court's judgment on the case: firstly, the recognition of mental distress as a compensable harm; secondly, the factors considered in determining the award; thirdly, the reliance on apology as a form of compensation. Section 5 concludes by reflecting on the key elements that the EU can learn from the Japanese tort-based approach and its flexibility vis-à-vis cultural expectations. While EU law has so far emphasized proof of harm and the need for a uniform interpretation of the GDPR across Member States, Japan places a higher value on a social responsive form of redress. Nevertheless, the comparative analysis of the EU and Japanese legal approach to privacy harms also shows a considerable convergence

[1] *See* Malgieri (2023).

[2] *See* Bradford (2020).

in their recognition of the individual as a vulnerable subject worthy of increased protection vis-à-vis the new digital threats.

2 Data Protection Legislation in the EU and in Japan

This section offers a preliminary overview of data protection regulation within the EU and Japan, serving as a foundation for the subsequent analysis of the relevant case law on tort liability and data breaches. More in particular, Sect. 2.1 will summarise the main contents of the GDPR, with a focus on the most important provisions pertaining to data breaches and the compensation of the harm caused by them. Section 2.2 will subsequently examine the right to privacy in Japan and the Japanese data protection regime, in particular after the reform that followed the AD of 2019.

2.1 The EU: Setting the Global Standard of Data Protection

European national jurisdictions developed their own approach to privacy, particularly through tort law remedies, since the 1950s. The protection of the private sphere has been widely recognized by European private laws through tort law litigation, even if the foundation for the right to privacy and its declinations (such as the right to be forgotten, the right to one's imagine, and so on) has been varied across legal systems.[3] Nowadays the current European regime of protection of personal data has been largely built by the EU and finds its most important source in the GDPR.

The GDPR confirmed and replaced the approach of the Data Protection Directive 1995/46/EC previously into force. The Directive 1995/46/EC, which was significantly inspired by the principles set out by the OECD Privacy Guidelines of 1981 and by the Council of Europe's Convention of Privacy of 1980, was the first legislation in the European context that focused on the protection of personal data.[4] The Directive 1995/46/EC already obliged all Member States to enact data protection frameworks in line with its provisions, as to remove the obstacles to the free flow of information within the EU and, at the same time, to promote the protection of the fundamental right to data protection.[5] In 2000, the Charter of Fundamental Rights of the EU recognized both the right to the respect of personal life[6] and the right to the protection of personal data and their fair processing[7] as fundamental rights within the EU. But it was the GDPR that established a global standard for the protection

---

[3] Brüggemeier, Colombi Ciacchi, O'Callaghan (2010, 569–570).

[4] Casagran (2017, 37).

[5] McGeveran (2016, 969).

[6] Charter of Fundamental Rights of the EU (2012), Article 7.

[7] Charter of Fundamental Rights of the EU (2012), Article 8(1)(2).

of personal information, initiating a worldwide reform of data protection regulation. This push towards a global standard in privacy regulation has been notoriously considered one of the most powerful illustrations of the EU's so-called 'Brussels Effect'. The Brussels Effect refers to the ability of the EU legislation to influence sectorial regulation on a global scale, by relying on the market power of the EU and on the interest of multinational foreign companies to adopting standards adapted to the European market, even if more stringent.[8]

The central focus of this section is the treatment in the GDPR of data breaches and of the right to compensation in cases of privacy infringement. This is necessary to appreciate the legal bases of the decisions of the CJEU on these matters that will be examined in Sect. 4.

The first key aspect concerns the regulation of data breaches. The definition outlined by the GDPR is found in article 4(12), which refers to 'personal data breach' as: "[a] breach of security leading to the accidental or unlawful destruction, loss, alteration, unauthorised disclosure of, or access to, personal data transmitted, stored or otherwise processed". In the event of a personal data breach, the GDPR imposes a specific obligation on the data controller to notify the breach to the supervisory authority (Article 33); the same obligation arises vis-à-vis data subjects, but only if there is a "[a] high risk to the rights and freedoms of natural persons" (Article 34).[9] In accordance with the minimum content required by law, the notification must include the measures taken by the data controller to mitigate the risks associated with the breach and must be submitted within 72 h of becoming aware of the breach.[10] An exemption may be applied in the instance where it is deemed unlikely that the breach will produce any adverse effect to fundamental rights and freedoms.[11] In the absence of any of these measures being implemented to mitigate the adverse effects from the data breach, the potential consequences could result in physical, material or non-material damage to individuals affected by the data breach.[12]

A second fundamental feature of the GDPR is the principle of accountability, mentioned in Article 5(2) and then further operationalized by Article 82. Under Article 82(1), "[a]ny person who has suffered material or non-material damage as a result of an infringement of this Regulation shall have the right to receive compensation from the controller or processor for the damage suffered".[13]

This provision provides the plaintiff with the right to claim compensation directly against the data controller or data processor, thereby avoiding the necessity to resort to national law.[14] Further, it opens the door to the possible intervention of CJEU

[8] Bradford (2020).

[9] Kiesow Cortez (2020, 244).

[10] Regulation (EU) 679/2018, Article 33.

[11] Regulation (EU) 679/2018, Article 33(1).

[12] Regulation (EU) 679/2018, Recital 85.

[13] Regulation (EU) 679/2018, Article 82(1).

[14] Knetsch (2022, 138).

whenever a doubt arises before national courts as to its application or interpretation, since the CJEU has jurisdiction over the interpretation of the EU law.[15]

A noteworthy element of Article 82(1) GDPR is the incorporation of a provision for compensatory damages in the EU legal framework—something that is a rarity within EU legislation.[16] In the context of the EU Member States, where legal traditions embrace different visions of tort law and of damage compensation,[17] the application of the provision has sparked a significant debate.[18] The Court of Justice in the latest years has developed a robust *corpus* of case-law on article 82(1) GDPR, with the aim of establishing a consistent interpretation across Member States.

By establishing clear obligations for data controllers and a mechanism to address data breaches, the GDPR empowers individuals to seek compensation in case of data breaches and strengthens the enforcement of data protection as a fundamental right. At the same time, the GDPR lays the groundwork for a uniform legal approach across EU Member States, guided by the evolving case law of the CJEU.

2.2 *Japan: Data Protection Between Hard and Soft Law*

In Japan, the development of several branches of the law has been shaped less by statutory reforms than by the interpretations adopted by the Japanese Supreme Court and by lower courts.[19] This is the case for the fundamental principles about the existence of a general right to privacy and the right to obtain compensation in case of its infringement, that were established by the Supreme Court over the course of several decades, as Sect. 2.2.1 will show.

Japanese data protection law is more recent and has largely evolved because of external pressures. In recent years, and especially after the AD on Japan by the European Commission in 2019, the Japanese government has enacted significant reforms in this sector. Other than statutory law, the Japanese data protection law also includes additional significant sources such as the guidelines adopted by ministries and the guidelines enacted by the Japanese supervisory authority, the Personal Information Protection Commission (PPC). The aforementioned factors collectively delineate a data protection framework that provides protection for the personal data in a manner that aligns with the Japanese sensitivity regarding privacy.

---

[15] Knctsch (2022, 138).

[16] Knetsch (2022, 141).

[17] Infantino and Wang (2018, 59–60).

[18] Knetsch (2022, 141).

[19] Matsumoto (2021, 359).

2.2.1 The Right to Privacy in Japan

The right to privacy is not explicitly established by the Japanese Constitution or by the data protection law. The real recognition of the right to privacy in Japan lies outside these boundaries, since its definition was firstly outlined in civil litigation.[20] Japanese courts have played a crucial role in shaping the law of privacy, most of all through tort law, which has historically served as the primary basis for privacy infringement litigation.[21]

In particular, the Japanese Supreme Court has derived the right of privacy from article 13 of the Japanese Constitution, which states: "[a]ll of the people shall be respected as individuals".[22] Though in Japan constitutional provisions are not directly applicable to private law claims, nevertheless they may provide solutions to problems of legal interpretation. In the context of privacy infringement, the Japanese Supreme Court has read the said constitutional provision in combination with the tort law provisions in the Civil Code to infer the right to limit unauthorized access to private information without a lawful reason.[23] Over the past half century, Japanese courts have protected the right to privacy as the right of the individual to not have private information be known to the public, more specifically to let them be free from government interference.[24] If one considers the Japanese society from a historical perspective, it then becomes clear that the characteristics of such a right to privacy are deviant from the long-standing Japanese tradition to sacrifice the private sphere for the public interest, under which the needs and interests of the society were always considered to be of greater importance than those of the individual.[25]

The most significant shift in the approach in this regard occurred in the second half of the last century, when several decisions of the Japanese Supreme Court fundamentally altered the traditional perspective on privacy.[26] These rulings recognized that private matters must not be made public without a valid justification.[27] Moreover, the Supreme Court's decisions established that in the event of any personal information being made public and causing mental distress to the victim, the latter has the right to claim damages under article 709 of the Civil Code, which is the general provision on tort in Japan.[28] Therefore, the Japanese Supreme Court found the main legal remedy to the infringement of the right to privacy in the general provision on tort.

Furthermore, the court determined that the applicable standard of tort is based on the sensibility of an 'ordinary person' in Japan. In this regard, the circumstances to be evaluated by courts in privacy infringement cases are: 1) if the facts made

---

[20] Pardieck (2024, 5).

[21] Oda (2009, 42).

[22] Judgment of the Supreme Court, 6 March 2008, *Minshu* vol.62 n.3.

[23] Miyashita (2016, 117).

[24] Miyashita (2016, 117).

[25] Adams et al. (2009, 8).

[26] Pardieck (2024, 10).

[27] Pardieck (2024, 10).

[28] Pardieck (2024, 10).

public are related to the private life of the victim; 2) whether the disclosure of personal information would cause mental distress to an ordinary person; and 3) if such information could not have been known to the public.[29]

Even before the data protection law was drafted, the Japanese Supreme Court assumed a pivotal role in defining the right to privacy and its protection. This had been achieved through the application of tort law and the interpretative use of constitutional principles on statutory law. Japanese courts have always remained aligned with the sensitivity of the Japanese people, even when they introduced a right that was never considered as such before.

2.2.2 The Act on the Protection of Personal Information (APPI)

As a response to the Directive 1995/46/EC, Japan enacted in 2003 the Act on the Protection of Personal Information (APPI), that became effective in 2005.[30] Besides the Directive, the APPI was drafted following the OECD Privacy Guidelines of 1981 and its eight fundamental principles as a point of reference.[31] Actually, the APPI aligned more closely with the OECD Privacy Guidelines of 1981 than with the protection standards set forth by the Directive 1995/46/EC.[32]

This partially explains why the APPI has undergone several amendments over time. A first round of amendments was implemented in 2015, and further amendments were made in 2020 and 2021 (coming into effect in 2022), after the AD of 2019 on Japan was adopted.

The 2015 reform brought the Japanese data protection law closer to EU law regarding various aspects, such as the incorporation of the notion of pseudonymised personal data[33] and the establishment of an independent supervisory authority on data protection, the Personal Information Protection Commission (PPC), which played a significant role in drafting the AD of 2019.

The PPC is an independent supervisory authority that currently oversees the data protection matters related to business operators. While at the beginning its competence was limited in the private sector,[34] with the 2021 amendments it was expanded to the public sector too.[35] Prior to its establishment, a substantial part of the data protection enforcement involved guidelines from each Ministry and from local governments, that had a role in complementing the data protection law in force.[36] Since the main objective of these guidelines was to ensure the adherence to the provisions of the APPI, these measures were addressed to different types of business operators

[29] Pardieck (2024, 11).

[30] Suda (2020, 513).

[31] Miyashita (2011, 232).

[32] Suda (2020, 514).

[33] Suda (2020, 515).

[34] Suda (2020, 516).

[35] Miyashita (2022, 136).

[36] Miyashita (2016, 111).

and were specific to each industry sector.[37] Yet, there was often an overlap between different guidelines, and business operators found themselves bound to comply with many guidelines stemming from different ministries at the same time.[38] This situation gave rise to a considerable degree of perplexity and difficulty among the business operators, who were uncertain about which rules they needed to abide by, without infringing any of them. The establishment of the independent authority led to the dissipation of such doubts, because the PPC assumed a centralized role in enforcing Japanese data protection law.

In this regard, the amendments of 2015 also introduced some measures which constitute the primary enforcement mechanism of the PPC.[39] In particular, the revised APPI gave to the PPC the exclusive power to draft guidelines on the protection of personal information,[40] such as those containing supplementary and enforcement rules.[41] Furthermore, the PPC became the only authority with the power to issue recommendations and orders to business operators in the event of a violation of the APPI.[42] Currently, such violations are limited to a few cases per year, but should these recommendations and orders not be followed through, the PPC retains the power to impose administrative sanctions on non-complying subjects.[43] Although this has yet to happen in practice,[44] the PPC's approach exerts a considerable influence on the application of data protection rules and shapes the manner in which legal principles are applied and interpreted by Japanese courts, not only in the data breaches cases, but also in ordinary cases in which data protection matters.

It should nevertheless be noted that, even after the amendments to the APPI to better align it with the EU standard (especially after the AD of 2019), substantial disparities between the Japanese and the EU approach to personal data protection still persist. Besides the issue of enforcement, which in Japanese data protection framework remains much more rooted in soft law measures and cultural norms, another significant disparity stems from the definition of sensitive data. The later amendments to the APPI introduced a broader definition of sensitive data by introducing new categories of information called 'special care-required information'.[45] However, some information that could be considered sensitive in the EU, for example sexual orientation and trade union membership, are still considered not to be so in Japan.[46]

[37] Greenleaf and Shimpo (2014, 142).

[38] Miyashita (2022, 136).

[39] Wang (2020, 675).

[40] Japanese Act on the Protection of Personal Information (2003), Article 54.

[41] PPC, Enforcement Rules for the Act on the Protection of Personal Information, https://www.ppc.go.jp/files/pdf/PPC_rules.pdf; PPC, Supplementary Rules under the Act on the Protection of Personal Information for the Handling of Personal Data Transferred from the EU and the United Kingdom based on an Adequacy Decision, https://www.ppc.go.jp/files/pdf/Supplementary_Rules_en.pdf.

[42] Japanese Act on the Protection of Personal Information (2003), Article 148.

[43] Japanese Act on the Protection of Personal Information (2003), Chapter VIII Penal Provisions.

[44] Kuroda, Nakayama, et al. (2025)

[45] Miyashita (2022, 134–135).

[46] Suda (2020, 520).

This demonstrates how variable the sensitivity on different kinds of data in Japan and in the EU still is.

In sum, despite the considerable efforts made by Japan to bring the data protection regime closer to that of the EU, significant differences remain, primarily due to the distinct legal traditions and cultural conceptions of privacy. Unlike the EU, where the right of privacy is nowadays considered to be a fundamental right, the recognition of privacy in Japan has evolved through judicial interpretation, simultaneously influencing its perception by society.

3 The Adequacy Decision on Japan by the European Commission

In order to understand the relationship and interconnection of the data protection laws between the EU and Japan, it is essential to take a closer look at the Adequacy Decision (AD) of 2019.

As illustrated above, the AD constituted the starting point of the most recent reforms of the Japanese data protection law, which took the Japanese APPI closer to the EU regime. However, Japan adapted its legislation following the principles of its own legal system and the characteristics of its legal tradition.

The impact made by the AD on Japan shows the GDPR's great influence outside the European borders, as a direct consequence of the 'Brussels Effect'. Specifically, the GDPR set a global standard on data protection, as multinational companies find it easier to adapt to a stricter standard set by a major economic force such as the EU, instead of imposing different ones across several countries.[47]

The legal foundation for this mechanism is article 45 of the GDPR. The article establishes the procedure which the EU is required to follow in order to recognize a third country as having an *adequate level of protection*[48] and therefore to facilitate the transfer of personal data to that country without further authorizations.[49] The formulation of article 45 makes it clear that the objective of an adequacy decision is not to impose identical level of protection based on the GDPR, but to oblige a third country to guarantee a protection for personal data similar to the one provided by the European standards.

The European Commission has so far recognized Andorra, Argentina, Canada, the Faroe Islands, Guernsey, Israel, the Isle of Man, Japan, Jersey, New Zeeland, the Republic of Korea, Switzerland, Uruguay, the United Kingdom and the USA, only for some commercial organisations participating in the EU-US Data Privacy Framework.[50]

---

[47] Rustad and Koenig (2019, 391).

[48] Regulation (EU) 679/2018, Article 45(1).

[49] Regulation (EU) 679/2018, Article 45(3).

[50] Kiesow Cortez (2020, 242).

3.1 *The Path to the Adequacy Decision: The Role of the Guidelines*

The AD marked the culmination of a two-year long effort made by both Japan and the EU. The final agreement between the two countries, shaped by the dialogue between the Commission and the PPC, was reached in July 2018, and the AD took effect in January 2019.[51]

The process leading to the decision proved to be a challenging one for both the EU and Japan, implying several rounds of drafts prepared by the Japanese PPC and followed by recommendations by the European Commission.[52] The role of the PPC was of utmost importance, as their intervention with the Supplementary Rules and non-binding guidelines on international transfer constituted the basis for the implementation of the safeguards in practice.[53]

During the negotiation process, it soon became evident that Japan needed to make substantial amendments to the APPI.[54] The issues were accentuated by the profound gap between the two legal traditions: one crucial aspect of the discussion was the effectiveness of guidelines in enforcing the protection of European personal data in Japan.[55] As discussed in Sect. 2.2, the Japanese approach to data protection relied primarily on guidelines enacted by different ministries and on the spontaneous adherence to them by enterprises and public bodies. In the EU context, by contrast, measures such as guidelines were perceived as lacking the necessary authority to compel individuals and entities to abide by the legal framework.[56]

In collaboration with the PPC, the Japanese legislator worked to build a bridge to overcome these discrepancies. In particular, the PPC adopted in 2018 the Supplementary Rules to the APPI, which are explicitly recognized in the AD as having a legally binding effect on Japanese business operators.[57] The result is that the PPC guidelines are now deemed to be binding for business operators, since failure to comply with them is to be considered as a violation of the APPI itself.[58]

Thanks to this solution, agreement on the AD was reached. The EU now acknowledges that Japan guarantees an adequate level of data protection, aligned with the

[51] Suda (2020, 511).

[52] Suda (2020, 521).

[53] Wang (2020, 672).

[54] Suda (2020, 517).

[55] Wang (2020, 674–675).

[56] Wang (2020, 675).

[57] European Commission (2019) Decision 2019/419 of 23 January 2019 pursuant to Regulation (EU) 2016/679 of the European Parliament and of the Council on the adequate protection of personal data by Japan under the Act on the Protection of Personal Information, Recital 15.

[58] Wang (2020, 676).

standard set forth by the GDPR. The agreement enables the flow of personal information between businesses in both directions without requiring additional authorisation from business operators located in Japan.[59]

The Commission is obliged to review the AD every two years, as per its underlying agreement.[60] One relevant aspect of the latest report on Japan, which was published on 4th of April 2023, is that it concluded with a positive evaluation from the European Commission.[61] The Commission explicitly recognized the effort of the PPC in contributing to ensure an adequate level of protection after the final agreement was reached. Moreover, the Commission acknowledged once again Japan's preference for soft law measures and distinctly recognized the ability of these in guaranteeing the protection of personal data. In the report it can be read that "[t]he Commission notes that the PPC has made more use of its non-coercive powers of guidance and advice, than of its coercive powers in the period following the adoption of the adequacy decision".[62]

Overall, the AD of 2019 between the EU and Japan constitutes an essential development in facilitating cross-border data flows by recognizing the Japanese data protection regime as essentially equivalent to that of the EU. The agreement required Japan to reform some part of its data protection law, notably amendments to the APPI, in order to align the legal framework closer to EU requirements under Article 45 of the GDPR. Central to this was the role of Japan's PPC, whose guidelines addressed EU concerns over their enforceability. Despite structural and cultural differences—in particular the reliance of Japan on soft law –, the European Commission recognized the level of data protection in Japan to be similar to that of the GDPR.

4 Data Breach and Tort Law: A Comparative Analysis

After the overview of the data protection frameworks in the EU and Japan, especially with regard to the respective courts' interpretations of the right to privacy, it is now important to verify these courts' approach to data breach cases framed in tort. Courts indeed often address the challenges posed by digital vulnerability by hearing and adjudicating claims where plaintiffs complain of harm suffered because of the infringement of their privacy allegedly realized by the defendants. The aim of this section is therefore to explore the factors that are considered by the Japanese

[59] European Commission (2019) Decision 2019/419 of 23 January 2019 pursuant to Regulation (EU) 2016/679 of the European Parliament and of the Council on the adequate protection of personal data by Japan under the Act on the Protection of Personal Information, Recital 4.

[60] European Commission (2019) Decision 2019/419 of 23 January 2019 pursuant to Regulation (EU) 2016/679 of the European Parliament and of the Council on the adequate protection of personal data by Japan under the Act on the Protection of Personal Information, Recital 181.

[61] European Commission (2023) Report on the first periodic review of the adequacy decision for Japan: 6.

[62] European Commission (2023) Report on the first periodic review of the adequacy decision for Japan: 5.

Supreme Court and by the CJEU when assessing the harm caused by the unlawful use of data resulting from a data breach and providing the plaintiffs with a remedy.

Section 4.1 will therefore introduce the Benesse Case, through which the Japanese Supreme Court established significant principles and introduced new factors for assessing tort liability in data breach litigation and determining the amount of damages to be awarded. Section 4.2 will examine the elements identified by the Japanese Supreme Court as relevant in comparison with the most recent decisions of the CJEU on compensation for harm caused by data breaches.

4.1 The Benesse Case

The Benesse case concerned a data breach in 2014 that compromised the personal information of 30 million customers of the Benesse Corporation. The data breach was caused by a sub-contractor engineer who stole the customer's information from the database of the company and subsequently sold it on the market to a number of data brokers. This resulted in the victims of the data breach being subject to unsolicited advertisements after the incident.[63]

In the aftermath, the Benesse Corporation issued a public apology and offered affected customers a 500-yen coupon as a compensation for the inconveniences of having their personal information leaked to the public. However, these measures did not prevent around 12.000 customers from filing claims for damages.[64]

The case passed through the first two levels of judicial reviews before reaching the Japanese Supreme Court, that remanded the case back to the Tokyo Appellate Court for the final judgment on the merit.[65] At the first instance, the Kobe district court declared that no evidence of negligence on the part of Benesse was found and therefore held that there was no civil liability in this case.[66] On appeal, the Osaka Court upheld the lower court's ruling, concluding that the anxiety caused by the data leakage did not amount to a sufficient injury to justify a legitimate claim for damages.[67]

While these decisions were being adopted, an investigation on the incident carried out by the Ministry of Economy, Trade and Industry (METI) revealed evidence of Benesse's infringements of the APPI provisions on security measures and on the duty to supervise contractors. In addition, the plaintiffs obtained further evidence of Benesse's negligence regarding the security measures required to protect personal information.[68]

---

[63] Ishii and Komukai (2016, 89).

[64] Pardieck (2024, 18–19).

[65] Pardieck (2024, 23).

[66] Pardieck (2024, 20).

[67] Pardieck (2024, 20).

[68] Pardieck (2024, 20).

This explained why the Japanese Supreme Court overturned the prior rulings and upheld the plaintiffs' claim. The Court found that the company had failed to implement adequate security measures to protect the personal data in its custody, and that the failure constituted negligence. Taking into account the supervisory obligations outlined in the METI guidelines, the Court concluded that such conduct constituted a tort under article 709 of the Japanese Civil Code.[69] Ultimately, the Tokyo Appellate Court's subsequent decisions recognized the negligence of the Benesse Corporation resulting in a compensable harm to the plaintiffs, and so, by holding it liable, the court awarded damage to the victims.[70]

4.2 *The Comparative Analysis: Elements of Tort Law in Cases of Data Breaches*

After outlining the essential contents of the Benesse case, this section will analyse three key elements highlighted by the court: (a) the legal relevance of the mental distress arising from the loss of control over one's personal information; (b) the factors considered in determining the award; (c) the issuance of an apology as a form of compensation for non-material damages.

The element (a) concerns the legal relevance of the non-material damage resulting from the loss of control over personal information, particularly if the harm consists of psychological distress and fear associated with the loss. As anticipated above, in the Benesse decision, the Japanese Supreme Court recognized that mental distress caused by the unauthorized disclosure—and the consequent loss of control over one's personal information—constitutes an injury in itself, even in the absence of material damage.[71] The court determined that the sensation of loss of control over and the consequent feeling of uncertainty surrounding the status of personal information could constitute relevant harm.

A comparable issue was addressed by the CJEU litigation in the recent case C-590/22. In this judgment, the Court acknowledged that, under Article 82(1) of the GDPR, a data subject's concern for their personal data following a data breach may entitle them to redress.[72] However, the CJEU also clarified that the fear of the potential negative consequences must be proven in its entirety.[73] In doing so, the CJEU fully aligned with its own previous and subsequent case-law insisting that a mere infringement of the GDPR provisions is not sufficient for compensation and that

[69] Saikō Saibansho [Sup.Ct.] Oct. 23, 2017, Hei 28 (uke) no. 1892, (appeal from Osaka High Ct., Heisei 28 (ne) no. 37).

[70] Pardieck (2024, 24).

[71] Saikō Saibansho [Sup.Ct.] Oct. 23, 2017, Hei 28 (uke) no. 1892, (appeal from Osaka High Ct., Heisei 28 (ne) no. 37).

[72] Case C-590/22, *PS*, EU:C:2024:536 [20 June 2024], § 32.

[73] Case C-590/22, *PS*, EU:C:2024:536 [20 June 2024], § 36.

the material and non-material damage must be fully proven.[74] Merely proving the infringement of the GDPR is not enough to succeed, since the CJEU has repeatedly established that the following three cumulative conditions are necessary to give rise to the right to compensation: (1) the existence of the harm, (2) the infringement of the regulation and (3) the causal link between the two.[75] This implies that, although the CJEU adopted a broader definition of non-material damage, that includes the loss over one's personal information due to the possibility of data misuse,[76] the CJEU also emphasized that the existence of a concrete fear must be supported by specific evidence.[77]

The element (b) concerns the criteria to be addressed in determining the sum to be awarded to compensate the damage resulting from the violation of data protection provisions. In the Benesse decision, the Japanese Supreme Court identified five factors that must guide this assessment: *(i)* the nature of the information disclosed, along with the scope of the disclosure; *(ii)* the nature of the privacy rights infringed; *(iii)* the presence or absence of actual damage; *(iv)* the countermeasures adopted by the data controller; and *(v)* the previous disclosure of personal information.[78]

Some of these factors, such as the countermeasures taken after the breach by the data controller, bear some similarity with the duties imposed by Article 33 of the GDPR and surveyed above in Sect. 2.1 (consider for example the fact that, under Article 33 GDPR, the notification of the data controller must list the measures taken immediately after the breach).

Ultimately, in the aftermath of the Benesse case, the Tokyo Appellate Court issued against the Benesse Corporation a symbolic award of 1000-yen per plaintiff, intended as an expression of apology for the mental distress caused by the data breach. However, the court did not specify the factors that it took into consideration in the assessment.[79]

In the EU legal framework, the GDPR does not contain any specific provision on the assessment of damages. In the case C-300/21, the CJEU stated that, in the event of an infringement of the GDPR, European national judges must rely on their domestic legislation when determining compensation.[80] However, the CJEU also clarified that national courts' discretion in this regard is limited by two key principles: the principle of equivalence (according to which national rules used to enforce rights derived from EU law cannot be less favourable than those applied in an equivalent domestic situation) and the principle of effectiveness (according to which national rules cannot make the exercise of the rights conferred by the EU law excessively

[74] Case C-300/21, *Österreichische Post AG*, EU:C:2023:370 [4 May 2023], § 42; Case C-507/23 Patērētāju tiesību aizsardzības centrs, EU:C:2024:854 [4 october 2024], §29.

[75] Case C-300/21, *Österreichische Post AG*, EU:C:2023:370 [4 May 2023], § 32.

[76] Case C-340/21, *Natsionalna agentsia za prihodite,* EU:C:2023:986 [25 January 2024] § 20.

[77] Case C-590/22, *PS*, EU:C:2024:536 [20 June 2024], § 34.

[78] Saikō Saibansho [Sup.Ct.] Oct. 23, 2017, Hei 28 (uke) no. 1892, (appeal from Osaka High Ct., Heisei 28 (ne) no. 37).

[79] Pardieck (2024, 23).

[80] Case C-300/21, *Österreichische Post AG*, EU:C:2023:370 [4 May 2023], § 53–59.

difficult or impossible).[81] Nonetheless, in light of these principles, the CJEU retains the power to verify whether an award issued under domestic law is adequate to compensate in its entirety the damage suffered.[82]

The element (c) is compensation through apology. As illustrated, the Japanese Supreme Court has long affirmed that damages under tort law should be determined taking into consideration all the circumstances of the case and the sensibility of an 'ordinary person'.[83]

In Japan, courts attach great importance to the actions undertaken after the breach by defendants, including apologies released via public media or the adoption of measures to avoid causing further harm.[84] In particular, the issuance of a public apology is highly valued in the Japanese culture, because for Japanese companies the loss of a customer's trust and the reputational damage resulting from a data breach are considered to be more impactful than the obligation to pay fines or compensate for the damages caused.[85] Especially in cases of defamation and intellectual property infringement, plaintiffs often explicitly request, and courts often accept, that, as a form of redress, defendants are obliged to issue apologies, which are then published in newspapers.[86]

In the Benesse case, the Benesse Corporation issued a formal public apology for the data breach immediately after the news broke on the mainstream media, in the absence of any external pressure or legal obligation to do so. Alongside this notification, the company also divulged the measures implemented to prevent potential secondary harm and to increase the security of their data protection systems.[87] The prompt issuance by the Benesse Corporation of a public apology outlining the remedial actions undertaken, reflected the respect for a cultural norm under which the apology serves both a symbolic and a practical role.

The role of an apology as a potential form of compensation has also been recognized in the European context. In the recent case C-507/23, the CJEU expressly stated that an apology may fully compensate for the harm suffered.[88] Yet, the court further asserted that, when determining the compensation under Article 82(1) of the GDPR, neither the attitude nor the motivation of the data controller are to be considered, since the purpose of such a provision is to ensure redress for any material and non-material harm directly caused by the data protection violation.[89] This interpretation clearly limits the rationale for issuing apologies in case of corporate data breaches.

On a conclusive note, there is a growing acknowledgment in the EU context about the positive impact of an apology—especially for victims of non-pecuniary

---

[81] Case C-300/21, *Österreichische Post AG*, EU:C:2023:370 [4 May 2023], § 53.

[82] Case C-300/21, *Österreichische Post AG*, EU:C:2023:370 [4 May 2023], § 58.

[83] Pardieck (2024, 11).

[84] Pardieck (2024, 43).

[85] Miyashita (2016, 107).

[86] Lee (2005, 38–39).

[87] Benesse Holdings Inc (2014).

[88] Case C-507/23, *Patērētāju tiesību aizsardzības centrs*, EU:C:2024:854 [4 october 2024], §36–37.

[89] Case C-507/23, *Patērētāju tiesību aizsardzības centrs*, EU:C:2024:854 [4 october 2024], §43–44.

harm.[90] On the other hand, in the Japanese legal and cultural framework, a public apology often holds greater meaning for victims than any monetary compensation, as it directly addresses the breach of trust between them and the company that caused them harm.[91]

Overall, the analysis of these three elements demonstrates that the Japanese and EU approaches to remedies for data breaches are shaped by their respective legal traditions but are also converging on a broader understanding of harm from data breaches in the digital age.

5 Conclusion

The above study showed that, in Japan as well as in the EU, courts predated and complemented data protection legislation in addressing data breaches through the adjudication of civil liability cases. The Supreme Court of Japan and the CJEU both recognized that the mental distress from the unauthorized disclosure of personal data may be a compensable harm, even though the Japanese Supreme Court found that a data breach may constitute an injury per se, while the CJEU requires the proof of the concrete existence of the fear. Both courts acknowledge the possible role of apologies as a form of compensation. Yet, apologies play in Japan an important cultural and legal role as both a symbolic and compensatory measure, as also demonstrated by the objective and subjective factors that courts are required to take into account when determining the compensation owed, while the CJEU held that an apology can be a form of compensation only if it allows it to compensate the damage fully.

The analysis therefore showed that, in spite of many similarities, the approaches adopted by Japan and the EU to remedy data vulnerability through tort law also differ. In the EU, the GDPR establishes a regulatory framework based on the respect of data protection as a fundamental right and provides for compensation in the event of concrete harm resulting from the infringement of the regulation. In addition, the CJEU has taken steps to define the scope of protection by requiring a demonstrable harm, while at the same time recognizing that mental distress can constitute non-material damage. In contrast, the Japanese legal framework for data protection tends to rely on softer provisions, with courts showing a deep sensitivity to the cultural expectations of the general public and demonstrating substantial flexibility in shaping the remedies for privacy violations, including through public apology and repair of reputational damage. Japanese courts seek to balance the rights of the victims of data breaches with the interests of the companies concerned, even when the latter are found liable for failing to take proper protective measures.

Despite these differences, a common ground between the two legal systems is that digital vulnerability is recognized by both of them as a key concern in the field of data protection, especially in a context constantly shaped by technological advances.

---

[90] De Rey (2021, 205–206).

[91] Wang (2020, 681).

While the European approach emphasises clear evidence of damage, the Japanese's one places greater importance on contextual and reputational factors. Nevertheless, they both strive to protect data subjects by offering the remedies that reflect what each legal tradition considers most significant.

Funding Information This contribution has benefited from support co-funded by the European Social Fund Plus of the Autonomous Region of Friuli Venezia Giulia.

References

Adams A, Murata K, Orito Y (2009) The Japanese sense of information privacy. AI Soc 24:327–341

Benesse Holdings, Inc. (2014) Notice and apology regarding leakage of customer's personal information. https://pdf.irpocket.com/C9783/o1Tt/faNa/DxxF.pdf

Bradford A (2020) The Brussels effect: how the EU rules the world. Oxford University Press, New York

Brüggemeier G, Colombi Ciacchi A, O'Callaghan P (2010) Personality rights in European Tort law. Cambridge University Press, Cambridge

Casagran CB (2017) Global data protection in the field of law enforcement: an EU perspective. Routledge, New York

De Rey SE (2021) Court-ordered apologies under the law of torts? Non-monetary relief for emotional harm. A comparative outlook from a western legal perspective. In: Brutti N, Carroll R, Vines P (eds) Apologies in the Legal arena, a comparative perspective. Bonomo Editore, Bologna, pp 203–249

European Commission (2019) Decision 2019/419 of 23 January 2019 pursuant to Regulation (EU) 2016/679 of the European Parliament and of the Council on the adequate protection of personal data by Japan under the Act on the Protection of Personal Information

European Commission (2023) Report on the first periodic review of the adequacy decision for Japan

European Union (1995) Directive 95/46/EC

European Union (2012) Charter of Fundamental Rights of the EU

European Union (2018) Regulation 679/2018 General Data Protection Regulation

Floridi L (2016) On human dignity as a foundation for the right to privacy. Philosophy & Technology 29:307–312

Greenleaf G, Shimpo F (2014) The puzzle of Japanese data privacy enforcement. International Data Privacy Law 4(2):139–154

Infantino M, Wang W (2018) Algorithmic torts: a prospective comparative overview. Transnational Law & Contemporary Problems 29(1):1–68

Ishii K (2020) Advancements in the personal information protection system in Japan. Global Privacy Law Review 1:164–172

Ishii K, Komukai T (2016) A Comparative Legal Study on Data Breaches in Japan, the U.S., and the U.K. In: Kreps D, Fletcher G, Griffiths M (eds) Technology and Intimacy: Choice or Coercion. HCC 2016. IFIP Advances in Information and Communication Technology 474. Springer, Cham, pp 86–105

Japanese Act on the Protection of Personal Information (2003)

Kiesow Cortez E (2020) Data Breaches and GDPR. In: Holt T, Bossler A (eds) The Palgrave Handbook of International Cybercrime and Cyberdeviance. Palgrave Macmillan, Cham, pp 239–256

Knetsch J (2022) The compensation of non-pecuniary loss in the GDPR infringement cases. Journal of European Tort Law 13(2):132–153

Kuroda Y, Nakayama T, et al. (2025) Data protection & privacy 2025—Japan. Chambers and Partners

Lee I (2005) The law and culture of the apology in Korean Dispute settlements (With Japan and the United States in Mind). Michigan J Int Law 27(1):6–53
Malgieri G (2023) Vulnerability and data protection law. Oxford University Press, Oxford
Matsumoto E (2021) Tort law in Japan. In: Bussani M, Sebok AJ (eds) Comparative tort law: Global perspectives. Edward Elgar, Cheltenham, pp 373–396
McGeveran W (2016) Friending the privacy regulators. Ariz Law Rev 56:960–1025
Miyashita H (2011) The evolving concept of data privacy in Japan. International Data Privacy Journal 1:229–238
Miyashita H (2016) A tale of two privacies: Enforcing privacy with hard power and soft power in Japan. In: Wright D, De Hert P (eds) Enforcing Privacy. Springer, Cham, pp 105–122
Miyashita H (2021) Human-centric data protection laws and policies: a lesson from Japan. Comput Law Secur Rev 40:1–9
Miyashita H (2022) Data protection law in Japan. In: González G, Van Brakel R, De Hert P (eds) Research handbook on privacy and data protection law. Edward Elgar, Cheltenham, pp 128–139
Oda H (2009) Japanese law. Oxford University Press, Oxford
Pardieck AM (2024) Privacy matters: data breach litigation in Japan. Washington International Law Journal 33:1–32
Rustad ML, Koenig TH (2019) Towards a global data privacy standard. Florida Law Review 71:365–452
Suda Y (2020) Japan's personal information protection policy under pressure. Asian Surv 60:510–533
Wang FY (2020) Cooperative data privacy: the Japanese model of data privacy and the Eu-Japan GDPR adequacy agreement. Harvard J Law Technol 33:661–691

Regulating AI Through Standards and the Risk of Preempting Liability: A Transatlantic Comparison

Guido Smorto

Abstract This article discusses the consequences of the Artificial Intelligence Act adopted by the European Union in 2024 (AIA) on the chance of affirming ex-post liability for damages. As the article concludes, before an ex-ante regulation, such as the AIA, and in the absence of a harmonized liability framework for AI systems, there is a serious possibility of making ex-post liability for damages deriving from AI systems far more problematic to affirm, with the effect, in many cases, of sheltering defendants from the consequences of their acts. In contrast with the often-repeated absence of an exemption from the law in the book in the field of AI, compliance with existing regulatory regimes may preempt tort law, and the unintended consequence of the AIA would be creating a safe harbour for AI.

Keywords Artificial intelligence · Product liability · Ex-ante regulation · Tort law · EU law · US law · Preemption

1 Introduction

There is no AI exemption from the law on the books for AI. Anyone deploying AI systems and tools must abide by existing rules (e.g., against fraud or manipulation or to protect privacy, competition, consumers, and so on). An employer who makes use of an AI system to, say, fire a worker or select candidates for a job, or a public administration using an AI system to award social benefits, are potentially liable for any wrongdoing exactly in the same way they would be by making the same decision without using any automated system. While it is difficult to disagree with the general assumption that AI does not enjoy any exceptionalism or safe harbour, it is also crucial to focus on the de facto limitations of this principle.

G. Smorto (✉)
Faculty of Law, University of Palermo, Palermo, Italy
e-mail: guido.smorto@unipa.it

C. Crea and M. Infantino (eds.), *Remedies to Digital Vulnerability in European Private Law*, https://doi.org/10.1007/978-3-032-19720-7_16

Against this backdrop, this article ponders the consequences of the Artificial Intelligence Act (AIA) adopted by the European Union in 2024[1] on the chance of affirming liability for damages. As this article concludes, faced with an ex-ante regulation, such as the AIA, there is a serious risk of making ex-post liability far more problematic to affirm, with the effect of sheltering defendants from the consequences of their acts. In contrast with the often-repeated absence of an exemption from the law on the books in the field of AI, compliance with the AIA may preempt tort claims, with the unintended consequence of creating a safe harbour for AI.

2 Ex-Ante and Ex-Post Regulation for AI

The AIA consists of an ex-ante safety regulation for AI systems. It considers AI systems as products and makes them subject to safety requirements, primarily documentary ones, prescribing the adoption of certain obligations to put them on the market. AI systems that conform to these requirements, established in harmonized standards issued by the European standardization organizations (ESOs), are presumed to conform to the requirements set out in the AIA.

At the same time, the AIA does not contain any provision on liability, nor does it expressly provide for compensation of the injured person for damage caused by an output or the failure to produce an output by an AI system. Under EU law, the liability regime for AI systems was initially intended to be covered by two pieces of legislation. The first is the new Product Liability Directive[2] (PLD), finally enacted in 2024, which regulates producers' no-fault liability for defective products. In addition, a Draft Directive on Artificial Intelligence Liability Directive[3] (AILD) was also proposed in 2022. This proposal aimed to ease the burden of proof for national liability claims, which are typically based on fault, with duties to disclose and rebuttable presumptions on behalf of the victims of damage caused by AI systems: a solution that was deemed necessary due to opacity, autonomous behaviour and complexity of AI systems, which may make it excessively difficult, if not impossible, to meet the ordinary burden of proof in tortious liability. Together, these two pieces of legislation had the aim of complementing one another to form an effective civil liability for AI since, as stated in the AILD Explanatory Memorandum, "current national liability rules, in particular based on fault, are not suited to handling liability claims for damage caused by AI-enabled products and services. Under such rules, victims need to prove

[1] Regulation (EU) 2024/1689 of the European Parliament and of the Council of 13 June 2024 laying down harmonised rules on artificial intelligence and amending Regulations (EC) No 300/2008, (EU) No 167/2013, (EU) No 168/2013, (EU) 2018/858, (EU) 2018/1139 and (EU) 2019/2144 and Directives 2014/90/EU, (EU) 2016/797 and (EU) 2020/1828 (Artificial Intelligence Act).

[2] Directive (EU) 2024/2853 of the European Parliament and of the Council of 23 October 2024 on liability for defective products and repealing Council Directive 85/374/EEC.

[3] Proposal for a Directive on adapting non-contractual civil liability rules to artificial intelligence (AI Liability Directive) (COM(2022) 496 final).

a wrongful action or omission by a person who caused the damage. The specific characteristics of AI, including complexity, autonomy and opacity (the so-called 'black box' effect), may make it difficult or prohibitively expensive for victims to identify the liable person and prove the requirements for a successful liability claim".[4] This complex scenario has been only partially enacted. With the withdrawal of the long-discussed AILD in 2025, national fault-based ordinary liability rules will apply, with the effect of requiring the plaintiff to prove a negligent or intentionally damaging act or omission ("fault") by the person potentially liable for that damage, as well as a causal link between that fault and the relevant damage.

Against this backdrop, this article discusses the conditions to affirm ex-post liability for damages caused by AI systems. It especially ponders whether and under which conditions courts may be allowed to reconsider AI systems that conform to harmonized standards. As this article argues, treating AI as a product and subjecting it to ex-ante regulation may bring uncertainty and a drastic decline in the application of the tortious liability regime. In such a case, there is a serious risk of making ex-post liability for damages far more problematic to affirm, with the effect of sheltering defendants from the consequences of their acts.

3 The Risks of Preemption. A Comparative Inquiry

A transatlantic comparison may help us better appreciate the possibility of tort claims being thwarted. The question revolves around the possibility that when a product complies with existing regulatory regimes, this compliance 'preempts' a tort law claim.

In Europe, the doctrine of preemption is much less explored than in the U.S. and, even when contemplated, it is mainly seen as an on–off issue, with sharp, even if often conflicting, answers to whether ex-ante regulation should preempt or not tort liability. On the contrary, as a transatlantic comparison clearly shows, the effects of the doctrine of preemption on the suitability of tort claims for products are far more nuanced. There is no straight answer to whether ex-ante regulation should preempt or not tort liability, with many factors determining the solution on a case-by-case basis.

A survey of U.S. case law may help to illustrate this aspect. Under U.S. law, the preemption defence arises when the claim conflicts with a (federal) product safety statute or regulation specifying product standards, with the consequence of making product liability claims foreclosed.[5]

Ascertaining whether preemption applies to a specific case is far from easy. The first step is to establish the legislative intent. U.S. courts commonly distinguish between express and implied preemption. Express preemption occurs when

[4] AILD Explanatory Memorandum. See also European Parliament (2022).

[5] The first US case on preemption for product liability is *Wood v. General Motors*, 865 F.2d 395 (1st Cir. 1988).

a federal law explicitly preempts tort claims based on a violation of state law. Implied preemption occurs when the federal statute under scrutiny contains no clear instruction.[6]

Yet, given the ambiguity of many statutory provisions, reference to legislative intent has often resulted in incredible difficulty. This is why this first principle is coupled with a second objective criterion based on the existing conflict between federal regulation under scrutiny and common law. In those cases where there is no clearly expressed intention of the legislator to bar tort suits, two criteria apply: field or conflict. According to the former, preemption occurs when regulation is deemed so exhaustive that no room is left for state law. Following the latter, preemption applies when differences between federal and state law make it impossible to comply with both.

A survey of case law, however, still exhibits a high degree of uncertainty, both in establishing whether there is an implied or express preemption and in the scope and meaning of the field and conflict criteria.[7] For instance, in the Supreme Court's judgment on the issue in the case *Cipollone v. Liggett Group, Inc.* (1992),[8] the Court split into three different opinions: the majority, authored by Justice Stevens, found that the Act under scrutiny (the Federal Cigarette Labeling and Advertising Act) preempted some but not all claims; three concurring Justices found no express preemption; the two remaining judges found complete preemption. Even after *Cipollone*, the Supreme Court continued to operate in a similarly fractured way.

This is hardly surprising insofar as the distinction between express and implied preemption is far from definite, and courts diverge in how implied preemption is applied (in the U.S., after *Medtronic, Inc. v. Lohr* (1996),[9] implied preemption has become predominant.[10] Similar statutory provisions have been found to prevent or not prevent state tort law expressly. In many instances, it is doubtful whether an agency decision intended to set minimum standards without precluding claims in torts in a specific case or if it weighed all risk-utility factors, precluding torts. For example, in some cases, courts have deemed agency decisions not to impose a uniform requirement, such as a propeller guard in a boat design or an airbag in a car design, to preempt from finding that this requirement would have been appropriate in a

---

[6] See *Cipollone v. Liggett Group, Inc.*, 505 U.S. 504 (1992) (in this case the Supreme Court concluded that the Federal Cigarette Labeling and Advertising Act expressly preempted state law's failure to warn claims based on inadequate cigarette labelling).

[7] See, e.g., Davis (2009, 760) (noting that "Many reasons exist for the continuing state of uncertainty in preemption doctrine", and "the (Supreme) Court's keen interest in the subject has not resulted in a predictable doctrinal approach") and Nelson (2000, 229) (noting that "the politics of preemption are complicated").

[8] 505 U.S. 504 (1992).

[9] 518 U.S. 470 (1996).

[10] See, e.g., *Lewis v. Brunswick Corp.*, 107 F.3d 1494 (11th Cir. 1997); *Geier v. Am. Honda Motor Co.*, 529 U.S. 861 (2000); *Sprietsma v. Mercury Marine*, 537 U.S. 51 (2002); *Bates v. Dow Agrosciences*, 544 U.S. 431 (2005). In the literature, see Hylton (2008), esp. at 208–211 and 219–221.

particular product design. In contrast, the courts reached an opposite conclusion in not-so-dissimilar cases.[11]

Many elements play a crucial role in the probability of preemption. The *Restatement (Third) of Torts* (1998) states that regulatory compliance does not preclude a finding of product defect. At the same time, it specifies that a regulatory compliance defence may be applicable when the regulation "was promulgated recently, [...] the specific standard addresses the very issue of product design or warning presented in the case before the court; and when the court is confident that the deliberative process by which the safety standard was established was full, fair, and thorough and reflected substantial expertise".[12]

In reviewing case law, scholarly analysis pinpoints other relevant indicators that de facto affect the probability of finding preemption, from the similarity between standards employed by agencies and courts[13] to the degree of agency independence, among others. In sum, as a comparison with the U.S. undoubtedly shows, the doctrine of preemption fails to provide predictable rules, becoming a battleground over the scope of federal power relative to state power.[14]

4 Ex-Ante Regulation Versus Liability

Thus far, we have concisely considered the uncertainty that a doctrine such as preemption would bring to tort law and the likelihood that treating AI as a product and making it subject to ex-ante regulation may bring a drastic decline in the application of the tortious liability regime. Yet, we did not address the question of whether this decline is something to be afraid of or is instead desirable.

To answer this question, we should consider regulation and court litigation as alternative law enforcement mechanisms. A court decision that deems compliance with ex-ante regulation as a basis to preempt litigation has the effect of leaving

[11] See, e.g., how the Federal Boat Safety Act is interpreted in *Lewis v. Brunswick Corp.*, 107 F.3d 1494 (11th Cir. 1997) and *Sprietsma v. Mercury Marine*, 537 U.S. 51 (2002) with regard to the absence of a duty to install a propeller guard. In the first case, the Eleventh Circuit found the claim for failing to install such a propeller guard was preempted; in the second one, the Supreme Court concluded that the claim was not preempted. A similar contradiction occurs in the interpretation of *FIFRA in King v. E.I. Dupont De Nemours & Co.*, 996 F.2d 1346 (1st Cir. 1993) and *Bates v. Dow Agrosciences*, 544 U.S. 431 (2005). Also, see *King v. E.I. Dupont De Nemours & Co.*, 996 F.2d 1346 (1st Cir. 1993) and *Medtronic, Inc. v. Lohr*, 518 U.S. 470 (1996). In *King*, the Federal Insecticide, Fungicide, and Rodenticide Act (FIFRA) was deemed to preempt failure to warn claims based on a statutory provision very similar to the one examined in Cipollone. Yet, before a very similar language, a few years later, an opposite decision was reached in *Medtronic*, where the Supreme Court concluded that the Medical Devices Amendment Act (1976) did not preempt state tort law for the failure of a pacemaker approved by the FDA and put into the market by Medtronics.

[12] Restatement (Third) of Torts: Products Liability § 4 cmt e (1998).

[13] See *Wilson v. Bradlees of New England, Inc.*, 96 F.3d 552 (1st Cir. 1996).

[14] For a survey of the many factors potentially relevant for assessing implied preemption, see Davis (2002, 1013–14), Hylton (2012, 214), Hylton (2008).

regulation as the sole enforcement mechanism. An opposite decision results in a combination of ex-ante and ex-post remedies. In other words, affirming preemption means setting the standard ex-ante, once and for all; denying it means setting the standard of care in each case with a court decision.

To select the appropriate law enforcement mechanisms, we need to assess the optimal legal standard for enforcement for AI systems and ponder whether it is preferable to set it once and for all by the legislator or on a case-by-case basis by courts. The probability of expected errors and the costs of each regime are key elements in comparing the two options. The effectiveness of these enforcement mechanisms is to be weighed based on the expected errors and the respective costs of each solution to reach the optimal combination of the two.[15] Who is expected to make the most accurate decisions and minimize errors? Which of the two systems is less likely to leave unsafe products on the market or drive safe products off? Literature identified several relevant factors to assess the likelihood of error: among others, the expertise of the agency, the knowledge of local conditions by courts, the risk of judgment-proof parties, the predictability of decisions, the time lags that make a standard actual or obsolete, the risks of political distortion.[16] Other conventional reasons for criticism of ex-ante regulation are regulatory capture and dull incentives. Administrative costs are also relevant: ex-ante regulation is commonly seen as preferable as it bears lower administrative costs compared to the court system based on a case-to-case analysis, but there is no complete agreement even on this.[17]

A regulatory compliance defence is desirable when ex-ante regulation provides optimal (or excessive) deterrence.[18] In contrast, a liability regime is the best option for products with observable utility and hidden risks. In this regard, the possibility that an ex-ante assessment does not consider all risks is exceptionally high in AI systems, not only for their opacity but also because of the need to assess how they may materialize in each specific field of application. Estimating ex-ante the potential risks of AI systems in each sector of society and economy under concrete circumstances and assessing who would be affected by these AI systems in each case is extremely difficult.[19] Generally, such an appraisal is possible only under real-life conditions and locally by taking into account the field of application and the people affected by the systems and considering all elements in the specific case under consideration.[20]

---

[15] See, among others, Shavell (1984a), Shavell (1984b), Gleaser and Shleifer (2003), Xu and Pistor (2002).

[16] Hylton (2008, 213), Shavell (1984b, 366).

[17] See, e.g., Hylton (2008, 213), Ausness (1996); contra see Shavell (1984b, 357).

[18] Viscusi, Rowland, Dorfman, Walsh (1994). See also Schwartz (2000).

[19] Cf. Micklitz (2023, 214) (making reference to interviewees, software developers, mathematicians, and physicists from business and stakeholder organisations, who all stressed this point). See also Laux, Wachter, Mittelstadt (2023).

[20] In the law and economics literature, this argument for distribution is made by affirming that when it states that liability is preferable to regulation as it operates on the parties who are most likely to cause harm. See Davis (2009); Epstein (2006); Kessler and Vladeck (2008); Nagareda (2006); Sharkey (2008); Schuck (2008).

5 The Case of the European Union. Preemption on Steroids

Under EU law, applying a regulatory compliance defence to AI systems results in additional critical aspects. In a federal system such as the U.S., the doctrine of preemption applies to products that fall under a federal regulatory regime. In such a case, ex-ante regulations that take precedence over state tort law are issued by federal agencies. On the contrary, under the AIA, the same doctrine could be applied to products that comply with harmonized rules created by private standardization bodies. This is because the AIA embraced the so-called New Approach or New Legislative Framework (NLF), which entails complementing binding basic requirements laid down in legislation with non-binding detailed technical standards developed by the European Standardisation Organisations (ESOs) with applicable rules resulting from the collaboration between them and the European Commission.[21]

In principle, under AIA, standards provided by ESOs are voluntary, as anyone is free to conform to binding legal requirements by developing their standards. Yet, complying with harmonized standards is not only simpler and cheaper than creating new ones; it also determines a presumption of conformity of the product with the binding requirements laid down in legislation, de facto making alternative methods to prove compliance with legal requirements quite hypothetical.

This delegation of rule-making power to non-governmental standardization bodies in the digital field has already raised concerns for their lack of legitimacy and accountability, due to the restricted publicity and the limited and complex nature of judicial review over harmonized standards limited participation of stakeholders, and insufficient liability rules for their activities, among other aspects. With standardization deemed the most viable and effective way for rules to keep pace with technological evolution,[22] not only has the NLF been transferred to the digital domain "without further ado",[23] with no adequate discussion on whether a model conceived for product safety in the industrial economy is equally apt for the digital economy.

Moreover, AIA considerably broadened the tasks of ESOs, who are assigned to develop standards that transcend the purely technical dimension, becoming increasingly political.[24] In contrast with the NLF approach, originally elaborated for purely technical standards for the safety of physical products, under the AIA, so-called technical standards aim not only at guaranteeing technical requirements to reduce risks for safety. More significantly, they should develop a "secure, trustworthy and ethical AI".[25] This means they should incorporate fairness concerns and weigh many crucial social dimensions into their EU standardization activity, integrating fundamental rights and enhancing European core values. In other words, ESOs should

---

[21] Regulation (EU) No 1025/2012 of the European Parliament and of the Council of 25 October 2012 on European standardisation, OJ L 316, 14.11.2012, p. 12–33, amended by Regulation (EU) 2022/2480 19.12.2022.

[22] See, e.g., European Commission (2011).

[23] Micklitz (2023, 212).

[24] See Art. 40, AIA. On the political dimension of standards, see Shahin (2024, 1111–1131).

[25] See Recital 10, AIA.

combine social and technical considerations in their standards: a task which requires complex normative choices and "unique capabilities in both technologies and the law".[26] Given their technical status, it is easy to conclude that ESOs have an overly complex task. The risk is that rhetoric on protecting fundamental rights and core European values remains declamatory while operative rules go in a starkly different direction.

Also, the pervasive employment of AI systems in different segments of our lives, and the resulting potential scope of AIA, worsen these concerns. ESOs should assess ex-ante the impact of AI systems in various sectors of society and economy and on diverse groups and persons, defining rules that address all the product risks,[27] pondering all potentially relevant factors, and embedding these factors in their standards.[28] It is easy to conclude that to consider all potentially relevant factors is exceedingly challenging, especially for technical bodies that are ill-equipped to perform such a complex analysis.

After all, the need to pay attention to specific contexts and situations is not simply in clear contrast with the nature of standardisation itself. Also, it conflicts with the use of standards that the EU is making. The EU is openly attempting to shape the rules for the digital environment by "strategically using standards to leverage influence at the global level";[29] in her 'Closing Statement' Speech of 2022, the Commissioner Vestager explicitly highlighted the "need to influence global standards so that they reflect democratic values".[30] In this perspective, the EU considers standardization as a key element of the fight for digital sovereignty and a crucial aspect of its European aspiration of sovereignty in the digital sphere.[31] This ambition to create European standards with global reach makes it even more challenging to pay attention to local conditions.

As a result, with standards that do not adequately represent potential victims of suboptimal precautions, and in the absence of tort remedies, competition will pressure market participants to ignore, rather than protect, the victims' interests, resulting in market failures in the form of suboptimal investments in precautions aimed at safeguarding the interests of the underrepresented.[32]

---

[26] Micklitz (2023, 217) (calling for rethinking the role of stakeholder participation).

[27] See Mitchell Polinsky and Shavell (2010, 1439); Hylton (2013, 2503–2504) (pointing to the scale of activities, and the roughly fifty thousand product liability lawsuits filed in federal courts each year).

[28] Hylton (2013, 2458) ("courts applying liability rules to producers have an advantage over government regulators because they respond to real injuries rather than breaches of regulatory orders, which may or may not generate serious injuries").

[29] See European Commission (2011).

[30] Vestager (2022).

[31] Shahin (2024, 1115); Brice (2022); Perarnaud and Rossi (2023); Blind (2025). On the importance of standardisation in international politics, see Cabral and Kretschmer (2006). On the Brussels Effect, see Bradford (2012).

[32] This argument is often formulated with regard to the role of industry safety-related customs in torts, and on whether there are reasons for not imposing negligence-based liability on customary

6 AI Systems and Product Liability

Thus far, we discussed the likelihood that treating AI systems as a product and subjecting them to ex-ante regulation may bring uncertainty and a drastic decline in applying the tortious liability regime. Also, we expounded on why such a decline is to be feared.

In this last part, we will briefly discuss how the difficulties and uncertainties of affirming liability for damages deriving from AI systems are further exacerbated by the liability regime that resulted from the interplay of EU and Member states' law.

Considering AI systems as products entails that these systems are subject to the legal regime of defective products. Such a liability regime was first adopted in the EU with the Directive 85/374/EEC and later confirmed in the Directive (EU) 2024/2853. Under this Directive, a product is deemed defective if it fails to provide "the safety that a person is entitled to expect or that is required under Union or national law",[33] thus embracing a consumer expectation test, i.e. that a product is dangerous if it does not comply with the expectations of the average consumer.

At the same time, the PLD complemented this general principle of strict liability with other doctrines, such as the state-of-the-art defence, misuse defences and reasonable alternative designs, based on a risk-utility test, i.e. on whether the incremental risk for the product exceeds the incremental utility compared to a safer alternative design. As a result, in many cases, product liability is often brought back to negligence and risk-utility analysis, especially for design defects. With most product liability cases involving AI systems concerning design defect, in many cases torts claim for damages stemming from AI systems will be likely subject to a negligence regime. The same holds true for failure to warn, with a test based on confronting the benefits of a warning with its costs. Strict liability remains for defect cases, which may more easily occur with physical products, with a single product that is different from the other ones, departing from the design.[34]

Putting AI systems under a negligence regime has essential consequences in terms of incentive effects and welfare, and of the likelihood of preemption. When consumers are informed about risks and utility, market forces bring the optimal result, as the market is likely to regulate optimally for products with open and obvious risks[35]; in this case, liability can even harm informed consumers.[36] On the contrary, the market forces may easily fail for products with observable utility and hidden risks. In such a case, the market does not provide optimal incentives to producers and

---

conduct. On this issue, see, e.g., Henderson (2017, 174) and Henderson and Siliciano (1994, 1383–1384).

[33] Art. 7(1), Directive (EU) 2024/2853 of the European Parliament and of the Council of 23 October 2024 on liability for defective products and repealing Council Directive 85/374/EEC.

[34] For an application of the negligence test in failure to warn litigation in the US, see *McCullock v. H.B. Fuller Co.*, 981 F.2d 656, 658 (2nd Cir. 1992); *Enright by Enright v. Eli Lilly & Co.*, 570 N.E.2d 198, 203 (N.Y. 1991).

[35] See, e.g., Hylton (2013, 2457–2458).

[36] Buchanan (1970, 66–67).

consumers, with consumers who may prefer riskier products since they only consider their visible advantages in their purchase decisions (e.g., the beauty and speed of a fast car) without taking into proper account the unobservable disadvantages (e.g., higher risks of injuries).[37]

The consumer expectation test efficiently solves these concerns since it affirms liability for uninformed consumers but not for informed ones, since "[t]he consumer expectations test is an especially refined form of strict producer liability that imposes liability when consumers are uninformed and provides immunity from liability when consumers are informed".[38] If consumers are unaware of product risks, strict liability will bring the optimal design choice because the cost of risk is internalized by the producer, leading to optimal consumption and, in turn, production decisions, and both overconsumption of risky products and overproduction of products with hidden risks are headed off.[39]

AI systems are typically complex products with unobservable risks, and a strict liability regime would be better suited, as it provides incentives for the party who is best able to control possible accidents and take measures to prevent and minimize them.[40] In principle, doctrines such as the 'res ipsa loquitur' one may get the same results; yet, since they are subject to specific conditions that may not easily apply to AI systems (e.g., the event must be of a kind which ordinarily does not occur in the absence of someone's negligence),[41] strict liability remains preferable. If victims of accidents cannot identify negligence in the conduct of the injurer, i.e. if incentives to take care are unobservable to plaintiffs, a strict liability regime provides better incentives to take appropriate precautions. Yet, this regime will not be applicable in most cases of defective AI systems.

In principle, innovation is the main objection to the expectation test. Risky design of new products is often the only way to innovate, and strict liability may discourage innovation for the same reason it induces optimal design choice by imposing an excessive tax on consumption, especially if litigation costs, uncertainty in case law and insurance inefficiencies are considered. Yet, while true in principle, this conclusion does not change our analysis much, since the effect of a similar regime would be the same in the case of perfectly informed consumers.[42] Aside from deterrence, other, closely related, rationales for strict liability over negligence are reliance, i.e. the expectation of safety that consumers have for products put on the market,[43]

[37] Calabresi (1961).

[38] Hylton (2013, 2488).

[39] Hylton (2013, 2477–2478 and 2500–2501). This conclusion holds under precise conditions: absence of administrative costs and externalities, and with courts being accurate in their decisions.

[40] Shavell (1980, 4).

[41] Hylton (2013).

[42] Also, this conclusion does not apply when producers can engage in price discrimination, which is often the case in the digital realm. See, e.g., Hylton (2013, 2480).

[43] *Escola v. Coca Cola Bottling Co. of Fresno*, 150 P.2d 436, 467.

and insurance, since strict product liability spreads the risks of injuries. In addition, some commentators point to administrative costs rationale, as proving negligence would require additional costs. Yet, "[w]hether strict products liability would provide an administrative cost savings is an empirical question, which remains largely unaddressed today".[44]

Moreover, a negligence regime in torts may more easily bring about preemption. Under a legal regime based on a risk-utility analysis, both ex-ante assessments and courts ex-post ascertaining negligence in tort lawsuits employ similar tests to assess the optimal design choice. Claims of product liability based on design defects, such as those related to AI systems, may be preempted more easily, on the ground that ESOs had already conducted an analogous risk–benefit analysis and assessed the net benefit of the product under scrutiny.[45] The opposite conclusion can be reached for manufacturing claims, since a complete monitoring of the production process by the agency is quite impossible. Accordingly, these cases should be preempted less frequently.[46] But for product liability claims based on defective design, it is likely, given the similarity between standards employed by agencies and courts, that this degree of congruence between the regulatory and the case law standards will affect the probability of preemption.

7 Conclusions

Before the growing employment of AI systems in different segments of our lives, the EU runs the risk of expanding the potential scope of preemption in tort claims to almost all sectors of our society, with all the uncertainties that this doctrine entails, and the possibility of having the entire tort system standing on "shifting sand".[47] If we do not want to find ourselves with entire social and economic sectors regulated by a doctrine which is deemed "out of balance, uncertain, and unwieldy in application",[48] it is crucial to recognize the regulatory value of tort law in the field of AI.

Tort law not only performs a compensatory function. It also helps to uncover unknown risks, gather information, give the right incentives to providers,[49] and "provid[es] an incentive to manufacturers to use the utmost care in the business of distributing inherently dangerous items".[50] The limited role of insurance further confirms the crucial role of tortious liability in this field, especially in the most

[44] Hylton (2013, 2466).

[45] Hylton (2008, 216).

[46] Ibidem.

[47] Davis (2009, 767) (stating about US law that "[i]n the eight years between Cipollone and Geier, then, the Court's preemption doctrine stood on shifting sand").

[48] Davis (2009, 780).

[49] On the role of torts and its impact on regulated industries see *Riegel v. Medtronic, Inc.*, 128 S. Ct. 999 (2008), at 1202–1203; *Bates v. Dow Agrosciences LLC*, 544 U.S. 431 (2005), at 449–451.

[50] See *Bates v. Dow Agrosciences LLC*, 544 U.S. 431 (2005), at 449.

serious cases, such as existential threats, due to the possibility of claims involving AI systems being positively correlated, with many people claiming at the same time for the same reason.[51]

The absence of a harmonized liability framework for AI systems further exacerbates this risk. The interplay between the EU ex-ante legal regime prescribed by the AIA, the PLD and the many national ex-post liability regimes will likely create uncertainty on the possibility of affirming liability for damages caused by AI systems, especially after the withdrawal of the long-discussed draft of the AILD by the EU, which aimed to establish a harmonized liability regime for the use and development of AI.[52] Notably, the Explanatory Memorandum of the AILD Draft Proposal stated that "[w]hile rules to ensure safety and protect fundamental rights will reduce risks, they do not eliminate those risks entirely. Where such a risk materialises, damage may still occur. In such instances, the liability rules of this proposal will apply". The passage showed that the intent of the proposal was not to preempt torts. However, after the withdrawal of the proposal, it is no longer clear whether compliance with the standards exempt or not from liability.

With compliance with ex-ante standards as a basis to preempt litigation, standards issued by ESOs would be the sole enforcement mechanism for AI systems in many cases. This delegation of power to private bodies is amplified by the potential scope of these "technical" standards in the field of AI, with ESOs called to merge complex ethical, social, legal and technical considerations, and to make tremendously difficult normative choices.

To be sure, we are not arguing against the adoption of technical standards in the digital field. If nothing else, the black box feature of the digital economy[53] deepens the lack of expertise and technical knowledge by public bodies and the concentration of this expertise in the hands of the industry, as already witnessed with the industrial economy. At the same time, there is a need for an ex-post assessment of risks derived from AI systems that complement the ex-ante assessment by making reference to real-life, local conditions, i.e. to the materialisation of risks under concrete circumstances and with special regard to those affected.

The critical question we are addressing here is where to allocate the risk of uncertainty of products and processes that benefit society but have inherent risks, and to avoid these risks inevitably burdening a smaller percentage of that society. Depending on the tools we employ – ex-ante regulation, ex-post remedies or a combination of the two – we will allocate these risks to the future victim of that risk or to those who created this risk. The tort system, providing individual relief to those who have suffered damage caused by AI, puts it on the latter, while ex-ante regulation puts it on the former.[54]

The impact of AI on a specific sector of society and economy and particular groups or persons suggests the opportunity for an ex-post assessment of these risks

---

[51] See Priest (1989, 1011). The typical case of such correlation is that of natural disasters.

[52] See Steiner (2025).

[53] Pasquale (2015).

[54] See Shavell (1984b).

that complements the ex-ante assessment by making reference to real-life, local conditions, i.e. to the materialization of risks under concrete circumstances, and with special regard to those who are affected. This is why an ex-ante assessment should be supplemented with an ex-post one, considering that many value judgments can only be made when risks materialize.[55]

What is at stake is not only the role of tort law in enhancing the safety of regulated products. With standardization at the core of the AIA, what we are discussing now is the role of torts in the most critical sectors of our society. In the digital domain, tortious liability is quintessential for guaranteeing fundamental rights, compensating the victims and making the overall system more efficient. If we underrecognize its role, we run the risk of relinquishing liability for bureaucracy, red tape and increased regulatory costs.[56]

References

Ausness RC (1996) The case for a "strong" regulatory compliance defense. Maryland Law Rev 55(3):1210–1267

Blind K (2025) Standardization and standards: Safeguards of technological sovereignty? Technol Forecast Soc Chang. https://doi.org/10.1016/j.techfore.2024.123873

Bradford A (2012) The Brussels effect. Northwestern Univ Law Rev 107(1):1–68

Brice L (2022) European objects: The troubled dreams of harmonization. MIT Press, Cambridge

Buchanan J (1970) In defense of caveat emptor. Univ Chicago Law Rev 38(1):64–73

Cabral LMB, Kretschmer T (2006) Standards battles and public policy. In: Greenstein S, Stango V (eds) Standards and public policy, 1st edn. Cambridge University Press, Cambridge, pp 329–344

Calabresi G (1961) Some thoughts on risk distribution and the Law of Torts. Yale L J 70(4):499–553

Davis MJ (2009) On restating products liability preemption. Brook L Rev 74(3):759–780

Davis MJ (2002) Unmasking the presumption in favor of preemption. SCL Rev 53(4):967–1030

Draghi M (2025) Forget the US—Europe has successfully put tariffs on itself. Financial Times. Available at https://www.ft.com/content/13a830ce-071a-477f-864c-e499ce9e6065

Epstein RA (2006) Why the FDA must preempt tort litigation: a critique of chevron deference and a response to Richard Nagareda. J Tort L 1(1):1–33. https://doi.org/10.2202/1932-9148.1043

European Commission (2022) An EU strategy on standardisation setting global standards in support of a resilient, green and digital EU single market. Communication COM(2022) 31 final

European Commission (2011) A strategic vision for European standards: Moving forward to enhance and accelerate the sustainable growth of the European economy by 2020. Communication COM(2011)311 final

European Parliament (2022) Resolution of 3 May 2022 on artificial intelligence in a digital age (2020/2266(INI))

Gleaser EL, Shleifer A (2003) The rise of the regulatory state. J Econ Literature 41(2):401–425

Henderson JA Jr (2017) Learned hand's paradox: an essay on custom in negligence law. California Law Rev 105(1):165–178

[55] Cf. Micklitz (2023, 224) and Wachter, Mittelstadt, Russell (2021).

[56] See Draghi (2025) ("At the same time, the EU has allowed regulation to track the most innovative part of services—digital—hindering the growth of European tech firms and preventing the economy from unlocking large productivity gains. The costs of complying with GDPR, for example, are estimated to have reduced profits for small European tech firms by up to 12 per cent"). See also Presidente and Frey (2022).

Henderson JA Jr, Siliciano JA (1994) Universal health care and the continued reliance on custom in determining medical malpractice. Cornell L Rev 79(6):1382–1404
Hylton KN (2008) Preemption and products liability: a positive theory. Supreme Court Econ Rev 16(1):205–249
Hylton KN (2012) An economic perspective on preemption. BCL Rev 53(1):203–232
Hylton KN (2013) The law and economics of products liability. Notre Dame Law Rev 88(5):2457–2514
Kessler DA, Vladeck DC (2008) A critical examination of the FDA's efforts to preempt failure-to-warn claims. Geo Law J 96(2):461–495
Laux J, Wachter S, Mittelstadt B (2023) Three pathways for standardisation and ethical disclosure by default under the European Union artificial intelligence act. Comput Law Secur Rev 53:105957. https://doi.org/10.1016/j.clsr.2024.105957
Micklitz HW (2023) AI standards, EU digital policy legislation and stakeholder participation. EuCML 12(6):212–225
Mitchell Polinsky A, Shavell S (2010) The uneasy case for product liability. Harv L Rev 123(6):1437–1492
Nagareda RA (2006) FDA preemption: when tort law meets the administrative state. J Tort L 1(1):1–54
Nelson C (2000) Preemption. Virginia Law Rev 86(2):225–305
Pasquale F (2015) The black box society: The secret algorithms that control money and information. Harvard University Press, Cambridge
Perarnaud C, Rossi J (2023) The EU and Internet standards—beyond the spin, a strategic turn? J Eur Publ Policy 31(8):2175–2199. https://doi.org/10.1080/13501763.2023.2251036
Presidente G, Frey CB (2022) The GDPR effect: how data privacy regulation shaped firm performance globally. Available at https://cepr.org/voxeu/columns/gdpr-effect-how-data-privacy-regulation-shaped-firm-performance-globally
Priest GL (1989) The antitrust suits and the public understanding of insurance. Tulane Law Rev 63(5):999–1044
Schuck PH (2008) FDA preemption of state tort law in drug regulation: finding the sweet spot. Roger Williams Law Rev 13(1):73–114
Schwartz A (2000) Statutory interpretation, capture, and tort law: the regulatory compliance defense. Am Law Econ Rev 2(1):1–57
Shahin J (2024) Dancing to the same tune? EU and US approaches to standards setting in the global digital sector. J Eur Integration 46(7):1111–1131. https://doi.org/10.1080/07036337.2024.2398430
Sharkey CM (2008) Products liability preemption. An institutional approach. Geo Wash Law Rev 76(3):449–521
Shavell S (1980) Strict liability versus negligence. J Leg Stud 9(1):1–25
Shavell S (1984a) A model of the optimal use of liability and safety regulation. Rand J Econ 15(2):271–280
Shavell S (1984b) Liability for harm versus regulation of safety. J Leg Stud 13(2):357–374
Steiner F (2025) EU Commission withdraws ePrivacy Regulation and AI Liability Directive. Available at https://www.heise.de/en/news/EU-Commission-withdraws-ePrivacy-Regulation-and-AI-Liability-Directive-10279672.html
Vestager M (2022) Artificial Intelligence in the Digital Age: Closing Statement. Speech May 3, Brussels. Available at https://multimedia.europarl.europa.eu/en/video/artificial-intelligence-in-a-digital-age-closing-statements-by-margrethe-vestager-executive-vice-president-of-the-european-commission-and-by-axel-voss-epp-de-rapporteur_I224259.
Viscusi WK, Rowland SR, Dorfman HL, Walsh CJ (1994) Deterring inefficient pharmaceutical litigation: an economic rationale for the FDA regulatory compliance defense. Seton Hall Law Rev 24(3):1437–1480

Wachter S, Mittelstadt B, Russell C (2021) Why fairness cannot be automated: bridging the gap between EU non-discrimination law and AI. Comput Law Secur Rev 41:105567. https://doi.org/10.1016/j.clsr.2021.105567
Xu C, Pistor K (2002) Law enforcement under incomplete law: theory and evidence from financial market regulation. Columbia Law School Working Paper No. 222. Available at http://ssrn.com/abstract_id=396141

Digital Vulnerability and Private Law Remedies

Attila Menyhárd

Abstract Digital vulnerability requires new policies and revised legal frameworks that go beyond consumer law to protect people, social organisations, and companies. The goal of these rules should be to protect and enforce fundamental rights, including in the context of private law. To this end, private law remedies should focus particularly on holding online service providers and platforms accountable, including through the disgorgement of profits and claims for unjust enrichment, and should guarantee the freedom to choose and the autonomy of those involved.

Keywords Fundamental rights · Online service providers · Online platforms · Tort liability · Disgorgement of profit · Unjust enrichment

1 Introduction

This contribution argues that Europe needs a new policy and legislative framework to address the social challenges of digital vulnerability. Digitalisation creates new risks, and society is still unprepared to deal with the dangers arising from recent technological developments. Both individuals and social organisations, including companies, are equally exposed to the risks arising from new technologies. Therefore, our policies, remedies, and strategies must extend beyond the current consumer protection framework to provide broader protection not only to consumers as natural persons but also to entities, beyond the scope of contract law. In this context, it is important to consider not only liability rules but also unjust enrichment rules, as disgorgement of profit can often be a more efficient solution than compensation. Remedies should focus on Online Service Providers (OSPs) wherever appropriate. The digital transformation has changed the market; the traditional approach to consumer protection, which is based on business-to-consumer (B2C) transactions and focused on the qualification of parties, is no longer useful. OSPs should be incorporated into the

A. Menyhárd (✉)
Faculty of Law, Eötvös Loránd University, Budapest, Hungary
e-mail: menyhard@ajk.elte.hu

C. Crea and M. Infantino (eds.), *Remedies to Digital Vulnerability in European Private Law*, https://doi.org/10.1007/978-3-032-19720-7_17

system of legal enforcement, and the framework of remedies, including the liability framework, should be improved.

In his book, written primarily to help company managers become leaders who inspire others instead of manipulating them, Sinek notes that our focus is normally on 'what' and 'how' we do things, when actually the primary question should be 'why'. Sinek describes a golden circle of decision-making and implementation, suggesting that we should find and identify the 'why?', and only after we should focus on the 'what?' and 'how?'.[1] This model effectively illustrates what the law can do for society. We should first ask ourselves 'why' the law should intervene to curb digital vulnerability, defining the policy underlying the intervention and the purpose that the intervention sought to accomplish. Then we can consider what the law should do, and how.

2 The Role of Consent

There seems to be a general agreement that the current digital transformation, beyond its revolutionary advantages for society and the economy, also entails many risks. There is an expectation, and even a demand, from European society vis-à-vis the legislator to tackle the challenges stemming from such risks. In general, digital risks primarily involve exposure to interference with fundamental rights and an increase in the inequality that already permeates society. These risks are exacerbated by the fact that people's access to society and the market, social inclusion, and the protection of privacy and wealth (particularly monetary resources) depend on a very limited number of market players. This situation exposes the mental and physical welfare of all members of society to new types of risks, making them digitally vulnerable. It just seems natural that the law should react to this.

The primary power organizing our modern societies is consent.[2] Consent provides legitimacy for allocating power in the vertical relationship between the state and its citizens, as well as in the horizontal relationships between citizens, companies and other social organizations. This development, which promotes the role of consent in society, has been notoriously described by Maine as a shift from status to contract.[3]

Consent is therefore the fundamental element of a democratic society and market economy today. Consent implies freedom and vice versa: we are free to shape our social interactions, undertake obligations, enter transactions, permit interference with our inherent rights, and elect the decision-makers of society. It is the most fundamental value of our society, as it is the means of exercising autonomy and maximizing self-interest. Obviously, information is a prerequisite for valid consent. This justifies the importance of information and highlights the public's interest in its content and the right to access it. The freedom to produce, transmit, and access information is, in

[1] Sinek (2011, 20).

[2] Smith (2025, 2).

[3] Maine (1917, 52).

itself, a public interest. In the legal sphere, the obligation to guarantee this freedom, both in vertical and horizontal relationships, primarily lies with the state, which protects the freedom to produce, transmit, and access information mainly through freedom of speech and through measures aimed at preventing the transmission of incorrect or false information, such as media regulation. In cyberspace, control over conduct and content implies control over the algorithms that determine what kind of information is provided and to whom.

Autonomy is the underlying paradigm of private law. Consent and autonomy are closely interrelated, as consent is a mechanism for autonomy.[4]

In other words, someone's choice can be regarded as free only insofar as two preconditions are met: consent is voluntarily expressed and is adequately informed. A significant portion of private law rules pertains to allocating the risks associated with the absence of either voluntariness or information. The law must intervene when choice is not free, either due to a lack of voluntariness or a lack of information. In this regard, contemporary legal systems normally adopt the principle of self-reliance: members of society are expected to acquire information before making any choices according to the required standard of conduct, and they should also bear the consequences of those choices. Yet, vulnerability changes this paradigm. Vulnerability stems from exposure to power. The members of a society should be deemed vulnerable if, and to the extent that, they are exposed to coercion or information asymmetry and cannot protect themselves against the risk of other members of the same society abusing their lack of voluntariness or lack of information. Such abuse creates illegitimate power. The abuse of private power is not accepted in private law.[5]

Thus, private power is accepted only if, and insofar as, its outcome remains the result of informed consent by the parties affected by it. Contract law, for instance, ensures that private power is properly exercised by granting enforceability only to voluntary and informed promises.

3 Methods: Models for Regulation

When it comes to statutory intervention, there are two options for the legislator: either to follow the information model or to provide mandatory rules of conduct. Under the information model, there is an underlying assumption that if information is provided, the interested person can make an autonomous decision without the need to impose further constraints on the relevant market players. The information model will only prevail to the extent that decision-making is voluntary, as it assumes that more information is all that is needed to protect people's freedom of choice. The information model is primarily applied in commercial law settings. This is the principle followed by European Union (EU) company law, as made clear by the

[4] Kim (2019, 73).

[5] Möslein (2016, 7).

policy underlying the first company law directive[6] and all those that have followed through the years, focusing on disclosure of information.[7]

In contrast to the information model, mandatory rules of conduct or standards are provided by the legislator when the information model fails to function or when decision-making cannot be made voluntarily. In cases of structural or individual inequalities, the information model does not work because the voluntariness of consent cannot be guaranteed, even with complete information. That is why the enactment of mandatory rules of conduct or standards should take precedence when the goal is to protect vulnerable parties. In the context of private law, vulnerability is the exposure to the risk of exploitation or harm, primarily due to the disadvantage of the vulnerable person in relation to others. Vulnerability, therefore, triggers the need to enforce the rights of vulnerable parties, which, in the digital context, primarily means upholding fundamental rights.

Private law enforcement is typically provided through sanctions such as damages, prohibitory or mandatory injunctions, specific performance, or rules of invalidity. It still needs to be explored how other means in private law, such as claims for restitution and unjust enrichment, could be used to provide protection against the abuse of private power. Private law order is a self-coordinating, autonomous order within society that emerges from a bottom-up approach through the interpretation of legal rules by courts, which address and resolve social conflicts through their judgments. Courts establish policies. Regulation, on the contrary, is a direct order from the legislator that prescribes clear-cut rules for social coordination. Regulation does not necessarily reflect social values. It implements a direct policy embraced by the regulatory authority and assumes that law is the order of the sovereign, rather than viewing it as an autonomous order of society. Regulation follows a top-down approach and is based on the predictions of the legislator. Private law is less efficient than public law and regulation when it comes to implementing policies that address large-scale societal issues, but it is able to focus on actual social problems rather than relying on the legislator's ability to predict the future. Public law enforcement also entails the risk of overregulation.

---

[6] First Council Directive 68/151/EEC of 9 March 1968 on co-ordination of safeguards which, for the protection of the interests of Members and others, are required by Member States of companies within the meaning of the second paragraph of Article 58 of the Treaty, with a view to making such safeguards equivalent throughout the Community.

[7] For a summary of the legislation in the sector, see https://commission.europa.eu/business-economy-euro/doing-business-eu/company-law-and-corporate-governance_en.

4 Why a New Policy and Legal Framework for Addressing Digital Vulnerability is Needed

Although private law offers a toolkit for protecting vulnerable persons in contract law, tort law, restitution, and property law, the current mechanisms of private law enforcement through judicial adjudication do not seem efficient in preventing mass interference with fundamental rights. Regulation as a method of social intervention appears to have clear advantages, particularly in European codified legal systems, where lawyers and judges are educated and trained in the use of written law. Market players also prefer *ex ante* rules to judicially enforced standards, because *ex ante* rules make the law more predictable for them. Addressing inequality through structural solutions is not new for modern civil law either; this is, for instance, the main purpose of consumer protection rules. Thus, a crucial preliminary question that needs to be addressed is the following: why is consumer protection law not the best framework for addressing digital vulnerability? (Sect. 4.1). If consumer protection law is not the answer, what kind of answer should be provided? (Sect. 4.2).

4.1 Pitfalls and Shortcomings of Consumer Protection

Consumer protection, as an autonomous branch of law, is a development of the last few decades. The development of consumer protection law within contract law, largely realized by the European Union over the last thirty years, has established a new division of private law on a subjective basis. This new division seems to have replaced the old dichotomy between commercial law and private law, and it has disrupted the inner logic of the self-contained system of private law through its mandatory distinction between consumer and non-consumer private law rules. We must face the fact, however, that the policy underlying consumer protection legislation is by no means as clear as we would like to believe. Even the notion of the consumer that stands at the core of this dichotomy is far from clear. Moreover, the rationale for consumer law as a tool to protect the weaker party is not entirely convincing, considering that consumer law does not protect small and medium sized enterprises (SMEs), even though the latter are generally in a weak bargaining position. Consumer protection regulation, by contrast, brings a competitive advantage to the companies that are able to meet the strict quality requirements. This may affect the market structure and raises questions about who the actual beneficiaries of such regulation are. In this perspective, it is not surprising that we still do not have a clear view in Europe on how far private law can and should go in embracing the model of consumer protection. Distinguishing the legal rules to be applied on the basis of subjective categories—such as the old dichotomy between commercial and private law, and the new one between consumer and non-consumer law—is a method that is never free from ambiguity; there will always be difficult borderline cases. This raises many doubts about the legitimacy of consumer protection policies and consumer protection legislation.

The uncertainty of the arguments and principles underlying consumer protection policy in general has already created problems in areas of law that have neither been built on such policies nor received them. Capital market regulation, for example, may convey investor protection policy, but it cannot treat investors as consumers in the same way that they are addressed under consumer protection legislation. General risks of investment and risks associated with capital market transactions cannot be shifted to brokers and other capital investment service providers, as this is governed by the principles and policies of consumer protection. Consumer protection policies and principles are completely foreign to the nature of capital markets. It is an unacceptable approach for the investor to be the sole beneficiary of the investment and to recover the resulting profit, while all risks are shifted onto the service provider without its consent. One of the consequences of consumer protection legislation, therefore, is the collision of regimes built on different internal logics and structures. The problem of interpreting and applying consumer protection regulation in the context of capital markets presents a clear illustration of this regime collision.[8]

Another good example provided by German legal literature regarding the uncertainties arising from the sector of consumer protection law concerns the possibility of considering employees as consumers.[9] As already mentioned, at the heart of consumer protection legislation lies the notion of the consumer, which is a relational one, as the concept of the consumer cannot be defined in isolation but only in relation to the other contracting party. The common definition is that the consumer is the party acting outside the purpose of business or professional activity, while the counterparty is acting in the course of their business.[10] The definition of 'consumer' is crucial because it determines the scope of application of the rules designed to counter unequal bargaining power and to strengthen the position of the weaker party against the stronger one. The scope of protection is a general issue in consumer protection legislation and is not limited to the question of whether legal entities can be considered consumers or whether consumer protection applies solely to natural persons. There are borderline cases that inevitably emerge. It is hard, for instance, to understand whether a person who is a professional seller of business tools is acting as a consumer when he buys one of the tools for his private consumption. Three decades after the adoption of the 1993 directive on unfair terms in consumer contracts,[11] the issue of mixed purpose contracts is still open to debate.[12]

---

[8] Wagner (2003).

[9] Annuß (2002, 2844) and Tschöpe (2004, 358).

[10] One of the first definitions of 'consumer 'was provided by Article 2 of the Council Directive 85/577/EEC of 20 December 1985 to protect the consumer in respect of contracts negotiated away from business premises, now replaced by Article 2(1) of the Directive 2011/83/EU of the European Parliament and of the Council on consumer rights, amending Council Directive 93/13/EEC and Directive 1999/44/EC of the European Parliament and of the Council and repealing Council Directive 85/577/EEC and Directive 97/7/EC of the European Parliament and of the Council.

[11] Council Directive 93/13/EEC of 5 April 1993 on unfair terms in consumer contracts.

[12] Beale (2021, 105).

The main shortcomings of consumer protection law arise from the fact that while the policy underlying it supports extending the scope to small and medium sized enterprises (SMEs), the legislation draws a narrower scope for it. A further problem is that the structural division of private law based on subjective qualification can never be an entirely just system due to borderline cases, grey areas, and uncertain scenarios.

4.2 A Shift in Paradigm

The legal framework of consumer protection was the result of a compromise and should now be reconsidered in the context of digital vulnerability. The main idea behind consumer protection is to safeguard the economic interests of parties who hold a weaker bargaining position. Yet, from the perspective of digital vulnerability, consumers are just one of many groups of vulnerable individuals. In the digital context, vulnerability extends far beyond people's economic interests.

On the one hand, businesses can be as vulnerable as consumers. This holds true not only for SMEs but also for large companies, such as banks and industrial market players, that may be exposed to substantial risks arising from the digital market. For companies, access to markets, online resources and services, protection of business secrets, and safeguarding their wealth depend on internet service providers (ISPs) and online service providers (OSPs) in the same way that consumers are exposed to such risks. Thus, companies may be subject to abusive conduct or omissions by other market participants in the same way that natural persons are. Refusing to apply the protective regime of consumer law to SMEs was a compromise from the outset of emerging consumer law, but it is certainly no longer tenable in the digital age.

On the other hand, a further problem with consumer protection law is that it provides a structural measure only for discrete transactions, which fall under the category of contractual relationships between a consumer and an enterprise. Social, legal, and economic relationships today are, however, rather interdependent, while the human factor remains the same in all of them. To illustrate, both individuals and companies are equally exposed to digital fraud because employees, as the human factor within companies, are not better prepared to defend themselves against fraud when acting as employees than when acting as consumers. There does not seem to be a difference between the position of a company and that of a natural person when criminals gain access to bank accounts and steal money from them. Similarly, there seems to be no difference between a company and a natural person when they purchase assets online via commercial platforms, acquire services from social media, or gain access to AI systems, thereby becoming users or deployers of those systems.

The need to go beyond consumer protection law, however, is grounded not only in the widespread vulnerability of individuals and enterprises, but also in the urgency of a paradigm shift. The priority in our contemporary societies is no longer protecting the economic interests of weaker parties; rather, it is enforcing non-negotiable social values and policies. Social values and the need to enforce them do not depend on the subjective qualifications of the person concerned. For a couple of decades, there have been extensive debates about enforcing fundamental rights in private law relationships. There were two main layers to this scholarly discussion: on the one hand, there was a debate about whether constitutional provisions should be enforced in private law relationships; on the other hand, scholars wondered whether human rights should be considered an integral part of private law or should be interpreted and enforced only in the vertical relationship between the state and its citizens. In other words, the issue was whether constitutional and human rights could and should be enforced in horizontal legal relationships.

But today, in the context of digital risks and the widespread use of artificial intelligence, thinking in terms of constitutional and human rights seems absolutely necessary. The question at stake is no longer related to the scope of application of these legal fields; rather, it concerns how to adequately protect and enforce fundamental rights. Case studies and discourses focus on interference with privacy, human dignity, anti-discrimination rules, and the right to self-determination. This new framework of discussion signals that there is an urgent need for a new regulatory framework aimed at protecting fundamental rights rather than balancing economic interests. This way of thinking may sound new to private lawyers, but it is certainly familiar to them. Fundamental rights express values, and private law is nothing but a mechanism for transmitting social values such as life, autonomy, freedom, justice, privacy, responsibility, self-reliance, solidarity, social inclusion, and human dignity. Thus, while addressing digital vulnerability in horizontal relationships, the main purpose of this new legal framework should be to maintain equality and protect the fundamental rights of individuals and other societal actors in order to guarantee their freedom of choice as much as possible. This is the way to achieve and ensure autonomy.

This change of paradigm has a further consequence: it makes it clear that protected persons should not be qualified based on their characteristics. Potentially, anyone could be vulnerable in the context of the digital world. For example, children who do not fit into the consumer policy framework are probably the most vulnerable group in society in the digital age. Other persons who are neither businesses nor consumers include politicians, who, although they cannot be classified as traders, should also not be categorised as consumers. The activity of such public figures does not fit the economically driven paradigm of consumer law, but can be interpreted quite well in the context of the enforcement of fundamental rights.

The new policy and legal framework that should be established and implemented must not focus solely on economic interests or on the specific weaknesses of one abstract segment of society; rather, it should rest on a value-based approach. This is already reflected in the AI Act, which does not distinguish between business and consumer.[13]

---

[13] Regulation (EU) 2024/1689 of the European Parliament and of the Council of 13 June 2024 laying down harmonised rules on artificial intelligence and amending Regulations (EC) No 300/2008, (EU) No 167/2013, (EU) No 168/2013, (EU) 2018/858, (EU) 2018/1139 and (EU) 2019/2144 and Directives 2014/90/EU, (EU) 2016/797 and (EU) 2020/1828 (Artificial Intelligence Act).

Of course, such a conclusion does not imply that protecting economic interests should not be relevant beyond the protection of fundamental rights. The point, rather, is that the protection of fundamental rights should extend beyond the current scope of consumer protection and should rest on the assumption that, in the digital environment, everyone can be vulnerable, including in terms of bargaining position. The emerging platform economy represents a change in the structure of social and economic relationships, where even large companies can become vulnerable.

Thus, the answer to the question of why regulation is necessary is that members of society and market players are now exposed to new risks that require a change in paradigm, which should extend far beyond the existing consumer protection framework. In the digital context, neither individuals nor traders are in a position to protect their rights due to a lack of information and the constraints imposed on them by other market participants. The intervention of law through regulation is therefore highly necessary. The choice of regulation is supported by its higher efficiency compared to social engineering by courts through litigation. Moreover, this regulation should probably be implemented at the European Union level rather than at the national level in order to promote not only the single market—which is the underlying goal of consumer protection—but also the European Union as a community of values, which implies a higher level of integration. This is the direction set by the previously mentioned AI Act.

5 What Regulation on Digital Vulnerability Should Be About

The existing EU consumer protection regime focuses on transactions and marketing of products and services. It is however not enough to focus solely on contract law and liability for defective products. Persons exposed to vulnerability risks are not necessarily parties to a contractual transaction, and the source of the risk is not necessarily embedded in a product. Most importantly, the final goal of the European legal framework should not simply be, as it is now, the promotion of a single market through the establishment of risk allocation measures such as consumer protection directives and product liability regimes. The Digital Services Act and the AI Act also do not fundamentally challenge this approach. This is a problem inasmuch as, in the context of digital vulnerability, the main issue is not only risk allocation but also the protection of people's and organizations' fundamental rights and non-economic interests.

In order to understand what the new policy and legal framework should focus on, the social and economic reality—that is, how things work—must be taken into account. The digital environment operates on the basis of contractual relationships. Access to services provided by ISPs and OSPs is embedded in contractual relationships governed by their standard contract terms. ISPs and OSPs establish the rules according to which they allow access to their services. This creates the danger that the application of standard contract terms undermines the rule of law, pushing market players to make public choices. In relationships governed by boilerplate clauses, the prerequisites of the rule of law—namely, the principle that legal norms exist and are clear at the time of performing a certain conduct—are knowable, can be applied by the governed, and are equally binding on everyone. This ensures that the law is enforced in an impartial and fair manner; however, these conditions are not guaranteed.[14]

The standard terms function like coercion: the party that did not draft them is not in a position to negotiate their content, and their only choice is to either accept them or reject them.[15]

In this context, providing for the unenforceability of unilaterally drafted standard terms is not an appropriate solution if the goal is to prevent the spread of illegal or harmful content. Consequently, it is no longer sufficient to focus solely on contract law and the fairness of contractual terms. Persons being victimized often are not users of contractual goods or services at all and are not even a party to a relevant contractual relationship. Moreover, the position of the ISPs and OSPs is also important. As far as regulation is concerned, ISPs and OSPs certainly cannot stand above the law. They control channels of communication, the accessibility of information to members of society, the flow of data, news, and information, and our choices as citizens and consumers. They collect and process personal data, and are very creative in introducing new mechanisms for influencing people's choices and social behaviour. This also implies that ISPs and OSPs nowadays undertake functions that societies have traditionally allocated to the State. However, while modern democratic societies have developed well-structured and refined processes for controlling State power, we are much less experienced in controlling the power in the hands of private companies.

Private companies have been established as vehicles for converting contractual relationships into structures of organization in order to make business activities and the economy more efficient; they have not been invented as a tool for controlling social behaviour. This is a significant challenge because gatekeeper companies cannot simply be seen as targets of regulation; they are, in fact, an integral part of the law enforcement system. They are not only objects of social and legal processes, but a fundamental vehicle for these processes to happen. Their role in controlling social behaviour was described by a journalist of The Guardian as follows. Think of Facebook as a bit like Ryanair or British Airways. If I get on a plane and the man sitting next to me gets drunk and tries to grope me, I can file a police report when we land. But while we are in the air, my best and only option is that the cabin crew and other passengers will deal with the problem. There are steps that airlines can take to reduce the likelihood of a passenger behaving badly on a flight. There should be rules in place if he does. But Ryanair is not responsible for a drunk and handsy man, just as Facebook and Google are not responsible for racism and terrorism.[16]

As a general rule, in a society built on the principles of freedom and equality, the law must intervene to protect freedom and ensure equal treatment. There are two

[14] Radin (2013, 38).

[15] Friedman (2000, 155).

[16] Afoko (2019).

ways to attempt to provide such equality: by directly worsening the situations of those more favoured with opportunity, or by improving the situation of those less favoured.[17] None of these methods, however, is functional in the digital environment, where information providers and platform operators are not directly engaged in a relationship with the users of their services. The task of regulation should rather be that of protecting fundamental rights and of guaranteeing free choice for both individuals and social organizations so as to prevent the abuse of their vulnerability.

6 How Regulation Should Address Digital Vulnerability

The original paradigm of the Internet is freedom. One of the most important consequences of this paradigm is that wrongful acts in cyberspace can be described as the outcome of a collision of protected interests (or protected values), which requires establishing which interests and values a legal system should prioritize, in a manner similar to how legal systems protect people's fundamental rights. Protected interests and protected values are often framed as rights within the legal system. In many cases, the conflicting interests and values appear as rights of equal rank. Typical collisions occur between the right to privacy and freedom of speech, the right to privacy and freedom of the press, and even between both parties' right to privacy. Solving the conflict requires an evaluation in which the relevant interests and values are weighed against each other. As private law is a process by which interests and values are converted into rights, such an evaluation actually establishes which rights are given priority on the grounds of policy.

Protecting these rights *ex ante,* or at least minimizing the time gap between a wrong in cyberspace and the delivery of justice, necessarily requires the active contribution of ISPs and OSPs in establishing priorities among colliding rights. In other words, in cyberspace, ISPs and OSPs are often called upon to implement policy decisions by selecting priorities among competing values and interests. ISPs and OSPs tend to do this through algorithms. For instance, the control of harmful content through filtering is implemented by algorithms. From the point of view of ISPs and OSPs, algorithms need to be optimized to avoid risks. Since algorithms have to be standardized, they make it impossible to weigh and properly assess the circumstances of each case. Automated filters often result in the violation of protected interests when, for example, they limit freedom of speech in cases where the limitation is not justified or fail to protect rights when such protection is warranted. ISPs and OSPs should never function in the same way as the State does. They are companies without the social and legal legitimacy to establish policies and prioritize values.

Nevertheless, in the current platform economy, the state has largely waived its direct control over social conduct and transferred it to ISPs and OSPs. At the same time, the state expects that control will be provided by ISPs and OSPs. A consequence of this situation is that the oversight of data, information, and qualifying

---

[17] Nozick (1974, s 235).

content is allocated to ISPs and OSPs rather than the state, entailing a sort of privatization of public functions. The state can only control the OSP through indirect *ex post* measures, which more often than not take the form of liability rules. This explains why the policy judgments implemented by ISPs and OSPs are not driven by social evaluations but rather by risk avoidance strategies. This certainly distorts the protection of values and interests in the community.

The fact that states are retrenching and withdrawing from their respective functions is also part of the problem. This, however, is nothing new, as it entails a kind of privatization under which online providers and platforms become important elements in the regime of legal enforcement. As a result, the role of the State is permanently changed, and the relationship between the State and ISPs/OSPs becomes a sort of public–private partnership, or, as someone has suggested, an "invisible handshake".[18] In this partnership, online providers and platforms act as agents of the State (and the community) in providing legal enforcement. The partnership makes the state dependent on the conduct of online providers and platforms, exposing it to the risks of the 'principal-agent' problem. In the context of this "invisible handshake", the State functions properly only if online providers and platforms perform their tasks well.

It follows from all the above that, instead of focusing on the vulnerable members of society, the law should focus on the market players who have the power to interfere with the free choice of citizens and social organization and are in a position to prevent or terminate such interference. Thus, the logic of legal intervention should be fundamentally different from the approach that inspires consumer protection law. On the same line, the law should not be divided based on the subjective qualification of the parties involved, as consumer protection law does in private law. The fact that service providers and platforms are part of the enforcement system of fundamental rights should be acknowledged, and the law should focus on how to establish and enforce the terms and conditions set by these companies. The test for doing so should not be one of fairness; rather, the requirements and standards of the rule of law should be enforced against service providers and platforms, serving as the benchmark for judging the terms and conditions they apply.

In the digital environment, ISPs and OSPs are the lowest cost avoiders. They are the actors best positioned to prioritize competing rights, values, and interests effectively, to enforce fundamental rights, to prevent harm, and to limit the abuse of the vulnerable positions of many members of society. In a platform economy, it is simply more efficient for operators to prevent others from wrongdoing. Embracing this turn, however, requires a radically new approach because liability rules have traditionally been designed to sanction active conduct much more than omissions. Imposing strict liability on them may be an option; yet, this may also lead to risk aversion and defensive strategies that may distort the priorities among competing values in the society. Moreover, the imposition of strict liability would probably result in defensive strategies by controlling content, which may then result in an overall exclusion from accessing legal content across the board. It is important to remember

[18] Birnhack and Elkin-Koren (2002, 2).

that unlawful content is to be prevented, but excluding people from accessing content also implies an exclusion from resources.

Beyond product liability, there is no comprehensive liability framework for ISPs and OSPs at the EU level. The AI Act and the DSA do not provide specific rules on liability; instead, they refer to national laws in this regard. The AI Liability Directive Proposal was withdrawn in early 2025.[19]

The current regime is far from satisfactory. Victims of abuse of vulnerability often do not even realize that they have suffered a compensable loss. Even when they do, the scope of their right to compensation is often difficult to assess. Punitive damages are rejected throughout Europe; however, as the Antitrust Damages Directive shows, it is still possible to establish an enhanced system of liability to increase the preventive effect of liability rules and support the victims.[20]

The system of sanctions should and could also be improved. For instance, combining claims for damages and restitution following an unjust enrichment may result in a more efficient system of private law enforcement because restitution of unjust enrichment serves as a tool to disgorge profits. It also fits into the approach of focusing on the service provider instead of the potential victims. If mass claims for unjust enrichment were feasible,[21] it would be possible to re-allocate the profit of the service provider to the victims.

7 Conclusions: Why, What, How?

Consent, implying free choice, is a fundamental element of contemporary democratic societies. Consent is built on individual autonomy. This is why a primary goal of the law should be to guarantee that the choices of individuals, as well as those of social organizations and companies, are as free as possible. In this perspective, vulnerability is a problem because it limits free choice. In the digital context, vulnerability is a limit to the freedom of the majority of relevant actors. Vulnerable individuals are at risk of making unintended choices that are not fully informed or voluntary.

It is highly urgent that the law intervenes to protect and enforce fundamental rights, which should provide the foundation for legal discourses and for establishing the policies to be pursued. Law must go beyond the existing European framework of consumer protection, as it is important to protect not only consumers but also all members of society, including social organizations and companies. The law should also go beyond its current emphasis on business-to-consumer transactions

[19] European Commission (2022).

[20] Directive 2014/104/EU of the European Parliament and of the Council of 26 November 2014 on certain rules governing actions for damages under national law for infringements of the competition law provisions of the Member States and of the European Union.

[21] For instance, under Directive (EU) 2020/1828 of the European Parliament and of the Council of 25 November 2020 on representative actions for the protection of the collective interests of consumers and repealing Directive 2009/22/EC.

and contract law, as what matters is not only protecting economic interests but also safeguarding fundamental rights and ensuring freedom.

In order to do so, the solution suggested herein is that the law should focus more on the service providers than on the vulnerable persons. The power of private law enforcement through liability rules should not be underestimated in this regard; however, it is also necessary to explore new possibilities, such as disgorgement of profit via restitution for unjust enrichment, particularly in combination with collective redress.

References

Afoko C (2019) Government can't regulate Facebook—it's up to all of us. The Guardian. Available at https://www.theguardian.com/commentisfree/2019/apr/01/government-regulate-facebook-mark-zuckerberg-social-media

Annuß G (2002) Der Arbeitnehmer als solcher ist kein Verbraucher! Neue Juristische Wochenschrift, pp 2844–2846

Beale H (2021) Digital content directive and rules for contracts on continuous supply. J Intellect Property, Inf Technol Electron Commerce Law 12(2):96–110

Birnhack MD, Elkin-Koren N (2002) The invisible handshake: the reemergence of the state in the digital environment. Virginia J Law Tech 6:1–57

European Commission (2022) Proposal for a directive of the European Parliament and of the Council on adapting non-contractual civil liability rules to artificial intelligence (AI Liability Directive). COM/2022/496 final

Friedman DD (2000) Law's order. What economics has to do with law and why it matters. Princeton University Press, Princeton

Kim NS (2019) Consentability: consent and its limits. Cambridge University Press, Cambridge

Maine HS (1917) Ancient law. J. M. Dent & Sons Ltd., London

Möslein F (2016) Private Macht als Forschungsgegenstand der Privatrechtswissenschaft. In: Möslein F (ed) Private Macht. Mohr Siebeck, Tübingen, pp 1–22

Nozick R (1974) Anarchy, State, and Utopia. Basic Books, New York

Radin MJ (2013) Boilerplate—the fine print, vanishing rights, and the rule of law. Princeton University Press, Princeton

Sinek S (2011) Start With Why. Penguin Books, New York

Smith SD (2025) The collapse of consent. University of San Diego School of Law, Legal Studies Research Paper Series no 25–028. Available at https://papers.ssrn.com/ 5345987

Tschöpe U (2004) Der Arbeitnehmer als Verbraucher im Sinne des § 13 BGB—Eine immer noch offene Frage. Recht der Arbeit 50:358–367

Wagner K-R (2003) Sind Kapitalanleger Verbraucher?—zum Verhältnis von Kapitalanlagerrecht zum Verbraucherschutzrecht. Bank- und Kapitalmarktrecht 16:649–656

Digital Vulnerability for All

Marta Infantino and Camilla Crea

Abstract What if we took seriously the idea recently put forward by many institutions and scholars that, in online interactions, all human beings are vulnerable or made more vulnerable than ordinary? What if our regulatory infrastructures acknowledged that the vast majority of us, even in the hyperconnected societies of the Global North, have little understanding of the digital infrastructure on which we depend? This chapter aims to explore these questions and propose a new interpretive framework, using European private law as a testing ground at the crossroads of national and European Union rules. In particular, it investigates whether assuming that we are all vulnerable might reduce the protection for those who belong to protected categories and are at heightened risk of cumulative and intersectional discrimination. It tests whether embracing digital vulnerability as a universal condition would lead to an unacceptable level of personalization of the law and burden corporations and individuals with excessive vulnerability-related duties. The chapter also verifies whether and how vulnerability-related duties might be enforceable in the borderless digital environment. All of the above will hopefully help challenge current interpretive views that deny any relevance to online defenselessness.

Keywords Universal digital vulnerability · European private law · Digital fairness · Intersectionality · Platform liability · Peer-to-peer abuse

Camilla Crea is the author of Sections 2–4; Marta Infantino is the author of Sections 5–7. Sections 1 and 8 were coauthored.

M. Infantino (✉)
Department of Political Science, University of Trieste, Trieste, Italy
e-mail: minfantino@units.it

C. Crea
Department of Law, Economics, Management and Quantitative Methods, University of Sannio, Benevento, Italy
e-mail: camicrea@unisannio.it

C. Crea and M. Infantino (eds.), *Remedies to Digital Vulnerability in European Private Law*, https://doi.org/10.1007/978-3-032-19720-7_18

1 Introduction

In recent decades, the concept of vulnerability has gained prominence in many post-industrial societies, reflecting the increasing fragility of human beings, economies, infrastructures, and ecosystems in the contemporary world. The notion of 'vulnerable subject', in particular, has become a powerful and dynamic concept that explains how all individuals, including those who do not belong to traditionally protected categories, are universally vulnerable due to both their physical bodies and their inevitable dependence on social relationships and institutions.[1] While there are vulnerable subjects who are not human beings, such as minority groups and small enterprises, the following discussion will focus on individuals only.[2]

In the field of law, the concept of vulnerability has rapidly entered the lexicon and debates around consumer protection, both at the international level and in specific regions, such as Europe and Latin America.[3] In Latin America, the Mercosur Common Market Group imposed in 2019 the obligation on its member states to recognize the structural vulnerability of all consumers in offline and online markets.[4] In 2021 the same Group further required Mercosur states to adopt a wide range of measures (from information to protection against misleading and abusive offers, protection of data and privacy, and dispute resolution mechanisms) in order to protect 'hyper-vulnerable consumers', defined as individuals with aggravated vulnerability who are disadvantaged due to their age, physical or mental condition, social, economic, ethnic and/or cultural circumstances.[5] The notion of vulnerability had already entered the domain of European private law some years earlier, through specific interventions in consumer protection. At the beginning of the century, the first pieces of European Union legislation using the category were enacted,[6] and legislative references have multiplied since the 2010s, when it became clear that the digital transformation of the economy and society was creating new risks for

[1] Fineman (2008).

[2] Macioce (2022).

[3] See Infantino (2025).

[4] Mercosur (2019).

[5] Mercosur (2021). On this framework, see Martínez Alles (2025).

[6] See Directive 2001/95/EC on general product safety, recital 8, and Directive 2005/29/EC concerning unfair business-to-consumer commercial practices in the internal market (UCPD), recital 18 and article 5(3). The EU Charter of Fundamental Rights does not refer to vulnerability, but mentions in articles 23–26 specific categories of people—women, children, the elderly and disabled persons—as deserving peculiar protection.

consumers.[7] In contemporary European legal terminology, vulnerability is associated with the structural asymmetry of consumers in the digital marketplace.[8] This digital version of real-world vulnerability is commonly defined as the "universal state of defencelessness and susceptibility to (the exploitation of) power imbalances that are the result of increasing automation of commerce, datafied consumer-seller relations and the very architecture of digital marketplaces".[9] It should be noted that the use of 'digital' in this context should be understood broadly, in a manner similar to Floridi's notion of 'onlife'.[10] For example, people's vulnerabilities can be abused or exacerbated by algorithmic devices, even when they are not using them: imagine someone without a social media account being bullied online, or a patient receiving a false cancer diagnosis from a doctor who follows the recommendations of an AI-driven program.

In the following pages, we will examine the implications and limitations of the concept of digital vulnerability in European private law. We will not discuss EU law per se, but rather European private law, by which we mean the combination of national and supranational private legal rules and principles applying in Europe. We are aware that this is a simplification of a very complex picture, and that further comparative studies are needed to test the validity of what is proposed here.[11] Yet, for the purpose of this chapter, whose main contribution lies in the proposal of a new interpretive framework, we believe it is legitimate to situate it within the realm of European private law. Since our perspective is centered on private law, we will not focus on perspectives other than those of private law, even though we acknowledge that other legal approaches—such as those offered by digital constitutionalism and public regulation of digital markets—do exist and operate in parallel with private law remedies.

More specifically, the chapter aims to explore the private law implications of people's "universal state of defencelessness" in the digital world. To this end, we will begin by challenging the notion that digital vulnerability arises solely in transactional situations, as current EU law assumes (Sect. 2). We will then argue that digital vulnerability should be understood as a broad concept, capable of encompassing both the universal status of people online and the particular status of situated subjects, along with all the layers of vulnerability they may possess (Sect. 3). After examining a real case to illustrate our point (Sect. 4) and addressing the most common objections

[7] See, for instance, Regulation (EU) 2016/679 on the protection of natural persons with regard to the processing of personal data and on the free movement of such data (GDPR), recital 75; Regulation (EU) 2022/2065 on a Single Market for Digital Services (DSA), recitals 62, 69, 94–95, 104; Regulation (EU) 2024/1689 laying down harmonised rules on artificial intelligence (AIA), recitals 29, 48, 58, 60, 67, 93, 132, 141, 165, and article 5(1), letter (b), 7(2), letter (h), 9(9), 60(4), letter (g), 79(2), 95(2), letter (e).

[8] Crea and De Franceschi (2024).

[9] Floridi (2015).

[10] BEUC (2021, 94).

[11] So far, the only European country that has enacted specific rules on vulnerability is Spain: see Ley 4/2022, de 25 de febrero, de protección de los consumidores y usuarios frente a situaciones de vulnerabilidad social y económica.

to the possibility of adopting a broad notion of digital vulnerability (Sect. 5), we will demonstrate the potential consequences of taking vulnerability seriously. We will emphasize that addressing digital vulnerability implies the emergence of new obligations for digital actors (Sect. 6). We will then test the practical implications of our proposal and verify whether such a world of new rights and duties might actually work in practice (Sect. 7), distinguishing the consequences for companies, including digital service providers (Sect. 7.1), and for individuals (Sect. 7.2). We will conclude with some final thoughts on the prospects for digital vulnerability (Sect. 8).

2 The Digitally Vulnerable Subject Beyond the Consumer/User Paradigm

There is no doubt that the complex genealogy of the notion of digital vulnerability, along with its multidisciplinary and multidimensional nature, contributes to critically deconstructing, fragmenting, and reshaping new images of the consumer. The growing EU consumer legislation that explicitly focuses on consumers' digital vulnerability,[12] together with recent rulings by the Court of Justice of the EU (CJEU),[13] demonstrate the growing importance of this idea in today's economy. There is indeed much empirical evidence that the ever-increasing power of technology to collect data and channel customer behavior has favored corporate strategies, such as data harvesting and data mining, dark patterns, targeted advertising, price optimization, and algorithmic personalization, that pose high risks of harm, along with new forms of consumer commodification in the context of digital consumption.[14] For this reason, many scholars have argued that the EU should ban or automatically consider these practices unfair,[15] or establish a presumption that all consumers are vulnerable in their relationships with traders in the digital realm.[16] From such a perspective, the idea of digital vulnerability has the potential to challenge some of the conventional paradigms arising from the EU neoliberal approach to consumer protection.[17]

This vision, however, is not fully in line with the European Commission's approach and agenda. The very recent Fitness Check on EC consumer law retains many of the above premises, going as far as to state that "[t]he provisions on the 'average consumer' and the 'vulnerable consumer' may need to be further clarified or amended to ensure their effectiveness in the digital context".[18] Yet, in the study supporting

[12] See above, notes 7–8.

[13] Court of Justice of the European Union (CJEU), case C 646/22, *Compass Banca*, ECLI:EU:C:2024:957, no. 59.

[14] European Commission (2024a, 177–197, 209–216), European Commission (2016).

[15] Micklitz et al. (2024); BEUC (2021, 5).

[16] Riefa (2022, 611).

[17] Krämer (2021, 13–19).

[18] See European Commission (2024b, 48).

the Fitness Check, the European Commission framed digital vulnerability not as negative per se, but rather inasmuch as it raises "concerns in terms of collective welfare due to detrimental effects on competition, price transparency and trust in the market".[19] In other words, according to the European Commission, consumers' digital vulnerability is bad because it damages the market. This understanding clearly limits the revolutionary potential of the notion of digital vulnerability, restricting it to business-to-consumer (B2C) relationships and subordinating it to the "original ambivalence of the European integration project"[20] and the underlying "spell"[21] of the internal market. Under this spell, dominant EU narratives and legal policies continue to assume that individuals ought to be (digital) market actors. From this perspective, consumers are rights holders deserving protection only insofar as they engage in acts of consumption.[22]

To be fair, some recent EU legislation has adopted a different vision of (digital) vulnerability, extending the paradigm of the vulnerable consumer to include citizens who are vulnerable to organs of public administration and infrastructures. For example, in addition to the usual references to vulnerable users of online corporate services, the recent Artificial Intelligence Act (AIA) mentions several cases in which people are, or are made, vulnerable by their interactions with public authorities—what we might call consumer-to-government (C2G) relationships.[23] Underlying this broader approach, however, is still a market-driven mentality that sees people's vulnerability in accessing and using public services as a bad thing, as it undermines the efficiency of the government, and people's trust in it. This expanded view of digital vulnerability, encompassing both B2C and G2C relationships, should therefore be seen as the result of the inclusion of government infrastructure in the digitization agenda, rather than as a change to the traditional, market-oriented view of vulnerability.

We claim that, by relying on these assumptions, the European debate on consumer digital vulnerability misses a substantial part of the picture. The problem is not just that the definition of vulnerable consumers under EU law remains too rigid and narrow, covering only a small number of stereotypical grounds for vulnerability and failing to address the wider power imbalances affecting the digital market.[24] The problem lies in the market-driven perspective, which fails to highlight all the injustices that occur beyond the realm of structurally unbalanced relationships between businesses and governments, on the one hand, and consumers of private and public services, on the other hand. While the lion's share of toxic interactions in the digital sphere is undoubtedly managed by service providers that exploit people's vulnerability, this focus on consumers obscures all forms of (exploitation of) vulnerability that occur in digital relationships with no, or an unclear, commercial character.

---

[19] European Commission (2024a, 44). For some observations in line with the text, see Gellert (2024).
[20] Bartl (2015, 573).
[21] Caruso (2012).
[22] Schulze and Staudenmayer (2024).
[23] Recitals 58, 60 and articles 7(2), letter (h) AIA.
[24] See the authors mentioned above, notes 15–16, as well as European Commission (2024b).

Suffice it to recall the various scams, cyber-bullying, revenge porn, social media shitstorms, disinformation campaigns, fake news spreading, and dangerous challenges on social networks. In all these situations, the binary opposition between 'vulnerable consumer' and 'trader' does not adequately address the complexity of human interactions in digital ecosystems.

The concept of consumer vulnerability currently embraced by the EU institutions does not cover all the various possible sources and layers of asymmetry, injustice, and inequality that can affect human beings far beyond the traditional categories of vulnerable subjects. Despite the apparent legal consensus on the challenges that 'digitization' poses to human rights,[25] the EU's current recipe still relies on a formal, market-based dichotomy that fails to capture the many fragmentations of subjectivity and does not take into account the inherent intersectionality of digital vulnerability.[26] As such, the current approach remains unable to effectively achieve equality and social justice on the one hand, and to overcome the abuse of consumerism and the dominant logic of capital on the other hand.[27]

How can this approach be challenged and its limitations overcome? We propose considering vulnerability as a universal and particular condition of all connected individuals, regardless of whom they are facing. We will now attempt to clarify our meaning.

3 Digital Vulnerability as Universal and Particular

When we suggest that vulnerability should be seen as a universal and particular condition of all connected individuals, we mean that it is high time to accept that the fictional narrative about the average consumer being "reasonably well-informed and reasonably observant and circumspect", first developed by the CJEU[28] and now enshrined in the UCPD,[29] may not be a generally good fit, but it certainly does *not* fit the digital economy. The truth is that we, or at least the overwhelming majority of us, are ignorant of the digital infrastructure, its costs, its opportunities and its alternatives, and we passively accept every opportunity that comes our way.[30] We remain ignorant and passive, regardless of whether we are given access to information and the opportunity to read the detailed terms and conditions of the services we receive. The online world is entirely made up of the architectural and contractual

[25] BEUC (2021).

[26] In relation to privacy law, see Malgieri (2023).

[27] Pistor (2019).

[28] CJEU, case C-210/96, *Gut Springenheide and Tusky v Oberkreisdirektor des Kreises Steinfurt*, ECLI:EU:C:1998:369; CJEU, case C-220/98, *Estée Lauder Cosmetics GmbH & Co. OHG v Lancaster Group GmbH*, ECLI:EU:C:2000:8. More recently, CJEU, case C 646/22, *Compass Banca*, ECLI:EU:C:2024:957.

[29] Recital 18 of the UCPD.

[30] See the empirical studies mentioned above note 19.

affordances set up by corporations, whose private governance of the online world is sometimes constrained by national laws.[31] To accept that our exposure to highly asymmetrical relationships makes us all vulnerable is to recognize that online vulnerability is universal, and can be presumed to be so. This, of course, does not preclude the possibility that categories other than people may be vulnerable, nor that there may be a few individuals (e.g., a skilled computer scientist) who may not be vulnerable at all.[32]

The assumption that digital vulnerability is universal, moreover, does not exclude the possibility that vulnerability can also be specific. Digital vulnerability often does not exist in isolation, as it may combine with other subjective and situational strengths and weaknesses of the digitally vulnerable person. In other words, the idea that everyone is vulnerable online does not preclude also recognizing that some are more vulnerable than others—what we may call, following the approach in the Mercosur—'hyper-vulnerable' subjects.[33] In particular, the factors stereotypically associated with vulnerability in the real world also apply in the online one. In this regard, the European Commission's recent Fitness Check explicitly mentions age and disability (and occasionally adds having a migrant background),[34] but broader lists can easily be imagined. Just think of all the factors mentioned in the EU Charter of Fundamental Rights and the European Convention on Human Rights and Fundamental Freedoms (ECHR) as potential bases for discrimination,[35] or of the special features listed in article 9 GDPR as giving rise to a significant risk to the fundamental rights and freedoms of the person concerned.[36] When digital vulnerability coexists with an additional factor/driver of vulnerability, it creates an intersectional vulnerability, meaning a combined form of vulnerability, the consequences of which are often worse than the mere sum of each factor/driver of vulnerability.[37]

This universal and particular vulnerability online is invariably exploited in B2C (and occasionally in C2G) relationships.[38] Our point, however, is that digital vulnerability may be exploited even outside of a commercial (or of a state-citizen) relationship. Digital vulnerability can also be exploited by others, although they often do so through the mediation of search engines, online platforms, and social networks. In other words, the digital infrastructure managed by corporate private powers enables both the abuse of these powers and of what we may call peer-to-peer abuse. This brings us to a paradox inextricably associated with the human

---

[31] On BigTech acting as virtual governments, see, e.g., Lee (2022); Lessig (2006).

[32] Assuming that everyone is vulnerable does not preclude proving that someone is not. Another practical issue arising out from the presumption concerns the difficulty of distinguishing individuals from empty avatars, bots, and AI-driven machines. On this issue, see also below, Sect. 7.2.

[33] Malgieri and Niklas (2020); on the Mercosur approach, see above, Sect. 1.

[34] See European Commission (2024b, 39–40, 43, 167).

[35] See article 21 of the EU Charter and article 14 of the ECHR.

[36] GDPR, article 9.

[37] The concept of intersectionality travelled from US to Europe: Crenshaw (1989); Hesselink and Soei Len (2025).

[38] European Commission (2024b).

condition in the digital sphere, extending beyond the structural asymmetrical field of commercial transactions, i.e., the opposition between dependence and independence, between vulnerability and autonomy. In the digital context that exists beyond commercial relationships, individuals enjoy both a reduced level of autonomy ('hypo-autonomy', compared with the hyper-autonomy of technological companies), making all of them structurally vulnerable, and broad agency in their peer-to-peer relationships with other individuals ('hyper-autonomy' in consumer-to-consumer (C2C) relationships).[39]

On the one hand, people's hypo-autonomy stems from their subjection to the online architecture/design, business strategy and private governing power of digital service providers. Under the current EU framework, including both traditional consumer law measures[40] and the newest interventions in the digital environment,[41] people matter and are protected because they are (occasionally vulnerable while) acting within the universe of consumption or post-consumption.[42]

On the other hand, human beings enjoy a broad freedom/power of action that allows them to misuse and weaponize their access to digital tools—more or less consciously—against their digitally vulnerable peers. This broad freedom is often strengthened by the anonymity provided by the use of online usernames and avatars concealing individual identity and by the crowd of other abusers. While it cannot be stressed enough that this hyper-autonomy only exists to the extent that companies allow it to, the end result is that any online user has the ability to harm others with little effort and unparalleled efficiency.

This is the core and conundrum of digital vulnerability of persons: everyone is, at the same time, both digitally vulnerable (hypo-autonomous) *and* digitally autonomous when interacting with other individuals since anyone can cause harm to their peers (and, in turn, be harmed by them). This form of *coincidentia oppositorum*[43] arising from the complex notion of digital vulnerability generates new and complex power dynamics that we can explain in terms of the *interdependence of digital vulnerability*. The *interdependence* of digital vulnerability is intended to signify the importance of human beings beyond their consumer status, the intersectional character of digital vulnerability, and the circumstance that, in the digital world, all human beings are potentially both agents and victims of abuse. A notion of

---

[39] Domurath (2024).

[40] The reference goes to the Council Directive 93/13/EEC on unfair terms in consumer contracts (UCTD) (prohibiting unfair clauses in B2C contracts), the UCPD (prohibiting aggressive and misleading commercial practices), and the Directive 2011/83/EU on consumer rights (CRD) (providing consumers in off-premise contracts with informational rights and the right of withdrawal).

[41] Think of the Regulation (EU) 2022/1925 on contestable and fair markets in the digital sector (DMA) (prohibiting certain clauses and practices in commercial online relations), the DSA (establishing some obligations on online platforms and search engines), the Regulation (EU) 2023/2854 on harmonised rules on fair access to and use of data (Data Act) (providing users with the right to access and share the data produced by connected products), the AIA (prohibiting some AI-driven practices and regulating high-risk uses of AI, as well as generative AI).

[42] Grochowski (2024).

[43] Teubner (2006).

digital fairness that extends beyond the traditional consumer-victim paradigm must embrace the *interdependence of digital vulnerability*.

4 Imane Khelif and Digital (Un)Fairness

Let us take a possibly extreme case of interpersonal injustice to illustrate the abovementioned gaps in European legal discourse, revealing its blindness to certain issues and the urgency of finding solutions.

Imane Khelif's victory in a boxing match against Angela Carini at the 2024 Paris Olympics ignited a global debate fueled by accusations concerning Khelif's gender identity and fairness in sport. Despite complying with IOC regulations, Khelif became the victim of a wave of transphobic and sexist abuse online. Khelif was attacked for her appearance and perceived sexual characteristics, but it is hard to ignore the fact that she was a Muslim woman of color representing a non-Western country in a typically male sport like boxing. The controversy was amplified by the intervention of public figures such as Elon Musk and J.K. Rowling (whose comments on X received more than 11.8 million views), thus highlighting wider issues of social injustice and discrimination. Notwithstanding this, Khelif won the gold medal. In response to the online shitstorm that hit her with millions of insults and threats on a variety of social networks, some days later she filed a legal complaint against social media platforms, prompting an official investigation into cyber harassment in France.[44]

Khelif's case is exceptional in that it involves a top Olympic athlete who, by definition, is not the average person on the Clapham bus. However, it is also very typical of the kind of online harassment that can affect people and have a lasting impact in the real world. The case is instructive for us because it clearly shows that everyone, including the top-performing and physically strong, is vulnerable online. It also shows the intersectionality of vulnerability at play. Khelif's digital exposure was exacerbated and amplified by her combination of many grounds that potentially increase the risk of discrimination, such as her non-conforming femininity and alleged transsexuality, her Muslim faith, and her non-Western background. Most importantly, the case demonstrates how easily people can be abused through the intermediary of digital services provided by private companies. The online harassment was made possible by the availability of social networks whose content moderation policies are based on the principle of protecting freedom of speech, and whose business model favors the fastest and widest distribution of viral content, as divisive issues typically are. Yet the online harassment was actually carried out by people (arguably with the help of some bots), who wrote, shared, liked, posted and reposted comments that were then matched by machines and allowed to circulate worldwide. This shows the point we were trying to make earlier: in the digital world, we are all potentially both victims and perpetrators of abuse.

[44] For the facts of this case, see https://www.washingtonpost.com/sports/olympics/2024/08/15/imane-khelif-cyberbullying-complaint/.

The protection of digital vulnerability beyond the consumer paradigm must somehow embrace this paradox and accept the *interdependency of digital vulnerability*. Accepting this paradigm would mean recognizing the duty of care owed by anyone who abuses or exploits digital vulnerability, regardless of their status and position. We will explore this in more detail in Sect. 6 and then provide suggestions on how it might be implemented in practice. Before we get there, we need to spend some time defending our proposal against the objections that are commonly raised against the idea of adopting a(n either broad or narrow) notion of digital vulnerability.

5 Countering Common Objections to Vulnerability

In the legal domain, vulnerability talks tend to trigger a number of objections that we would like to address before going any further, for we imagine that they might be also raised against the proposal we are making here. In essence, our proposal is based on the idea that everyone, or at least the vast majority of people, is vulnerable in their interactions with digital devices, or is made vulnerable by them. This is so true that we could (or rather should) assume that everyone is vulnerable online—in other words, that the average online state is one of vulnerability. Non-vulnerability is the exception. Such a conclusion does not exclude the possibility that many people, particularly those belonging to protected categories at heightened risk of discrimination, may be made extremely vulnerable by the intersection of digital vulnerability with various factors/drivers of vulnerability. The likelihood of this happening suggests that whenever a person with multiple possible drivers of vulnerability complains of abuse, it can be assumed that these factors/drivers have been triggered; in other words, it can be presumed that these persons are hyper-vulnerable. Finally, we argue that since digital vulnerability is invariably exploited by companies and in particular digital service providers, but also occasionally by other individuals, these subjects should be considered to have a duty not to abuse the vulnerability of others. Is there any reason not to want such a broad notion of vulnerability to be recognized? In the following lines, we will consider some of the common objections that are typically raised against the idea of vulnerability, and try to see if any of them pose an insurmountable obstacle.

1. Vulnerability is a category that is too subjective and variable to be taken seriously into account by the law. Adopting the lens of vulnerability would break the equality of the law and undermine legal certainty, filling the world with granular rights and duties whose contents are hard to predict.

The problem of the extent to which rules should be abstractly tailored to an ideally average subject or should rather consider (at least some of) the characteristics of the people involved is a longstanding problem that contemporary legal systems in the

West have solved by favoring formal equality.[45] But the emergence of new technologies that are increasingly able to identify people's characteristics has reignited the debate about the extent to which rules can and should be personalized.[46] Leaving aside any broader consideration on the many departures that legal systems accept from the idea of formal equality (including anti-discrimination rules), the point is that we are proposing to consider digital vulnerability as a universal condition. Everyone would be treated equally in this scenario, without the need to check whether someone is actually vulnerable or not. Formal equality and legal certainty would be guaranteed. The presumption could, of course, be rebutted if, exceptionally, there were no vulnerability.

2. Protecting certain vulnerable categories undermines equality and privileges them over the ordinary rest, sometimes reversing the power imbalance against innocent 'average' people. There is already a rights fatigue in contemporary societies; protecting people's digital vulnerability would create another unnecessary privilege.[47]

It is true that automatically categorizing people with certain characteristics as vulnerable is a stereotypical classification that may not reflect reality and lead to overprotection. However, our proposal here is that everyone, including the ideal average person, is vulnerable or made vulnerable by interacting with digital devices. Moreover, because we live in unequal societies where many groups are at risk of mistreatment by a silent majority, we propose that additional factors of vulnerability should be presumed whenever the individual concerned falls into a protected category. It is not a privilege to be in this category. The presumption, like the average digital vulnerability presumption, would leave it open to individuals to demonstrate that they or their counterparts are below or above this average level of vulnerability.

3. If everyone is vulnerable, then no one is. Too high a standard of protection would dilute the meaning and rationale of vulnerability.[48]

This fear too is unfounded. On the one hand, the fact that everyone is vulnerable in the digital environment does not preclude the possibility that some people are more vulnerable than others (and that some people are not be vulnerable at all). Because digital vulnerability is often combined with other historically recognized factors or drivers of vulnerability, we propose that a presumption of intersectional vulnerability should automatically help people in protected groups. Like any presumption, it could be disproven. On the other hand, it is important to remember that we are suggesting that everyone is potentially both a victim and a perpetrator. The fact that everyone is vulnerable online is precisely the reason why everyone should be vigilant for other

[45] On the limitations arising out from this choice, Calabresi (1985, 22–25), Chamallas and Wriggins (2010, 89–117).

[46] For the terms of such a debate, Ben-Shahar and Porat (2021). For some critical remarks, see Endicott and Young (2022); Burk (2021).

[47] The argument is a recurring one in the field of human rights: Theilen (2021); Clément (2018).

[48] This argument is often intertwined with the one mentioned above, note 47.

potential vulnerabilities. In other words, a high standard of protection does not dilute the meaning of that protection; rather, it creates meaningful duties.

4. The idea that we are all vulnerable is paternalistic in that it assumes that we are all powerless, incapacitated victims and in need of protection.[49]

Legal systems, especially those in the civil law tradition, are well-acquainted with rules that create mechanisms of protection, limiting people's freedom to protect their dignity. To some extent, all consumer law can be seen as a paternalistic system of consumer protection. Respecting formal equality in an unequal world would only lead to more inequality.[50] In addition, we propose that digital vulnerability should be presumed, meaning that everyone should remain free to prove that they or their counterpart are not vulnerable, but rather fully informed, fully cognizant, fully aware. Finally, the fact that we are all vulnerable to abuse by others creates an obligation for everyone not to exploit the vulnerability of others. Recognizing the universality of vulnerability is not just a matter of protection; it is also a matter of recognizing the universality of a duty to protect.

5. Taking care of everyone's vulnerabilities imposes unbearable and near-impossible duties on companies, governments, and individuals acting in the digital world. They would be required to conduct countless checks and provide constant care to anticipate who might be or will become vulnerable due to interaction, and to somehow incorporate this prediction into their actions.

It is undeniable that to assume that everyone is vulnerable online implies the creation of additional duties for all actors in the digital world. This would be in line with developments in private law over the last two centuries in the West. Private law has consistently followed the rise of innovative technologies and the invention of new techniques for creating harms, with the establishment of duties for those who cause such harms.[51] Most importantly, private law obligations always exist in context, in the sense that they affect people differently according to their power, ability, expertise, knowledge and capacity to prevent harm. Clearly, those in a structurally unequal relationship with online users, such as search engines, online platforms, and social networks, who have the opportunity to know them, would have a greater duty to identify those who are most vulnerable and therefore in need of heightened protection.[52] The duty of others would largely depend on their ability to understand and care for the vulnerability of others, as well as other contextual factors such as their visibility and authority, the severity and seriousness of the attack, the number of people involved, and so on. We now need to look more closely at the implications of this new duty.

[49] The paternalistic objection is well-known in debates about vulnerability: Mackenzie (2013, 46–48), Kohnt (2014).

[50] This argument too is commonly raised against the idea of recognizing new human rights: Theilen (2021, 848).

[51] Bussani, Sebok, Infantino (2022, 213–247).

[52] For similar observations, see Malgieri (2023, 196–205).

6 Taking Digital Vulnerability Seriously

If our theoretical assumptions are correct, then the crucial question becomes: what can be done? What can private law do to effectively reshape digital vulnerability?

The starting point of our response is that there can be no right without a corresponding duty. The assumption that vulnerability is both a universal and a particular condition of all persons online necessarily requires imagining corresponding, relational duties for all actors in the digital domain, including corporations, public administrations and individuals. In continental European legal systems, the duties incumbent on public administrations are traditionally considered to belong to the realm of administrative law and public law in general.[53] As our focus is on private law, we will leave public administrations out of our analysis, and discuss the issue of duties toward companies and digital service providers on the one hand, and people on the other.

Companies offering goods and/or services online are already subject to many obligations vis-à-vis consumers, including those stemming from EU consumer law (the UCTD, the UCPD, and the CRD) and data protection law (mainly, but not exclusively, the GDPR). Adopting the view that everyone online is vulnerable and that traders should presume this vulnerability does not imply the emergence of new duties, but rather a different interpretation of existing ones. For example, the concepts of universal and particular vulnerability would significantly affect the interpretation of the transparency requirement in standard consumer contracts as laid down in article 5 UCTD, the paradigm of the average and vulnerable consumer under article 5 UCPD, the information obligations in distance contracts under articles 5–8 CRD, and the technical and organizational measures needed to address risks for personal data under article 24 GDPR, and so on and so forth.[54]

A different argument should be made for providers of digital intermediary service providers. While not all digital intermediaries are the same, it remains true that the largest among them, and in particular the largest search engines, online platforms, and social networks, are the primary source of people's digital vulnerability, insofar as they actively exploit the structural power asymmetry of their position and passively enable others to commit abuses. In relation to duties in the digital realm, there is little doubt in our view that the obligations of digital service providers should be extended beyond the current limits of the EU legal framework. The DSA has recently moved in this direction. On the one hand, the DSA confirmed the immunity of all digital service providers for content uploaded or posted by users,[55] as under the regime previously in force under Directive 2000/31/EC.[56] Under the DSA, digital service

[53] On the possible prospects of actions arising out from people's digital vulnerability brought against public bodies, see Infantino and Bussani (2025, 455–460), Infantino and Wang (2019, 351–352).

[54] For a similar proposal, see Riefa (2022).

[55] DSA, articles 4–6.

[56] Directive 2000/31/EC on certain legal aspects of information society services, in particular electronic commerce, in the Internal Market. This immunity was inspired by the enactment in the US

providers can be held liable only if they fail to remove defamatory posts and objectionable content promptly after being notified of their existence and ordered to do so[57]: this is the famous 'notice and take down' approach, different from the American rule, which enshrines the 'notice and stay down' approach.[58] On the other hand, the DSA establishes differentiated obligations for different types of digital service providers, requiring online platforms to design and operate their online interfaces in a way that does not deceive or manipulate users, and to provide users with information about the parameters of targeted advertising and recommendation systems.[59] The same Act adds that "[r]ecipients of the service shall have the right to seek, in accordance with Union and national law, compensation from providers of intermediary services, in respect of any damage or loss suffered due to an infringement by those providers of their obligations under this Regulation".[60] The DSA thus combines the old idea that the immunity of digital service providers is key to the development of digital infrastructures, online freedom of expression, and e-commerce without fear of liability,[61] with the awareness that such immunity cannot become a patent violation of the principle that 'with great power comes great responsibility'.[62]

The possibility of recognizing the existence of new duties upon digital service providers is therefore facilitated in Europe by at least three factors. First of all, in the vast majority of European jurisdictions, contracts require no consideration to be binding, and consequently, there is little doubt that digital service providers are bound by contracts with users.[63] While this means that digital service providers may rely on standard terms and conditions to govern their relationship with users, it also means that general rules of contract law—including those on invalid terms, unconscionability and in good faith—may apply.[64] Second, the DSA imposes some statutory obligations on digital service providers, including direct obligations (e.g., information duties) and indirect obligations (e.g., the removal of defamatory posts when ordered). If interpreted broadly, these rules provide a statutory basis for obligations. Third, even outside the scope of these statutory provisions, all European private law systems contain general rules on non-contractual obligations, such as torts and unjust enrichment, which, in certain circumstances, oblige companies not to cause, and not to allow third parties to cause, damage to users or be unjustly enriched at

in 1996 of Section 230 of the Communications Decency Act (CDA) to immunize providers of 'interactive computer services' from liability for content posted by third parties.

[57] DSA, articles 4–10 and 54.

[58] Bradford (2023, 42–50, 116–118).

[59] DSA, articles 25–27. Article 28 DSA provides additional obligations for the protection of minors.

[60] DSA, article 54.

[61] See especially Bradford (2023, 46–52).

[62] See especially Bradford (2023, 42–50), Keats Citron (2022, 82–104).

[63] This position is now claimed also with regard to common law countries: see Mills (2024); Balkin (2020).

[64] On the potential of such rules, see Smits (2014, 136–157).

their expense.[65] In Europe, therefore, there are already many bases for placing duties on digital service providers that coexist with their immunity for users' activities. Interpreting such duties in a way that includes the consideration of people's digital vulnerability would create an incentive for digital service providers to internalize the social costs of their economic activity. Rather than being revolutionary, this would confirm the role that private law has played in industrialized legal systems over the last two centuries, distributing the massive losses associated with emerging technologies and finding a sustainable compromise between economic activities and the safety of products in mass consumer societies.[66]

Strengthening the obligations and rules regarding the liability of digital service providers is however only part of the solution. If we embrace the idea that all human beings are digitally vulnerable and have the right not to be abused, we must also assume that all digitally vulnerable individuals owe a duty of care to their peers when interacting in the digital context. Such a duty of care implies the obligation to respect and protect others and their dignity from moral, economic, and social harm within the digital ecosystem. This would not actually be anything new, as many such obligations already exist. The non-discrimination obligation contained in the EU Charter and the ECHR is, according to the CJEU, a horizontal obligation binding on everyone.[67] All European countries, albeit with varying rules, strike a balance between the constitutionally protected right to expression and the duty not to engage in activities that lead to defamation.[68] More broadly, as already mentioned, the extra-contractual obligations not to harm one's fellow human beings and to return unlawfully obtained benefits obtained are recognized in all European countries, although in different shapes and sizes.[69] It goes without saying that this peer-to-peer liability should co-exist with (and neither excuse nor diminish) the liability of digital service providers that manage the digital infrastructure enabling peer-to-peer abuse. It is equally obvious that this peer-to-peer liability should be administered taking into account the varying abilities of people to understand and cope with the complexities of digital society, i.e., that the extent of users' duties should be proportional to their ability to foresee, control, and mitigate harm.[70]

Implementing digital solidarity and pursuing social justice and equality in European private law should require the protection of the (universal and particularistic)

---

[65] For a survey of such rules, see Bussani, Sebok, Infantino (2022); Infantino and Wang (2019, 346–353). This point is also acknowledged in American literature: see Kaplan and Gordon-Tapiero (2024).

[66] See the authors quoted above, note 51.

[67] According to the CJEU, the general principle of non-discrimination enshrined in Article 21 of the EU Charter has horizontal direct effects, meaning that it should be respected not only by MS but also by individuals: CJEU, case C-144/04, *Werner Mangold v Rüdiger Helm*, ECLI:EU:C:2005:709; CJEU, case C-414/16, *Vera Egenberger v Evangelisches Werk für Diakonie und Entwicklung e.V.*, ECLI:EU:C:2018:257. See Colombi Ciacchi (2019).

[68] Such rules are however very different from place to place: De Gregorio (2022, 157–215); Tsomidis (2022).

[69] On this point, see above, note 65.

[70] As is common in private law liability claims: Bussani, Sebok, Infantino (2022, 27–42).

digital vulnerability of all human beings, as well as the recognition of obligations and duties on both the corporate actors that govern and shape digital ecosystems and online architectures and all the members of society who use digital technologies. Embracing such a shift would require a change in the current interpretation of existing legal norms, but this better use of the various resources of private law would make it possible to strengthen the protection of individuals without resorting to regulatory oversight or new reforms. This imaginative reconstruction, which may be considered radical in the current legal and academic context, could have significant consequences, as further explored below. The next section attempts to demonstrate how this could happen in practice.

7 Going Practical

Presuming that everybody is vulnerable online would imply that anyone operating in the digital environment has a duty to take other people's vulnerability into account. As noted above, such a duty would bind both businesses and individuals, albeit with different degrees of intensity. The duty to take digital vulnerability seriously would inform businesses' responsibilities to consumers and data holders online. It would imply a duty on all digital service providers not to profit, or allow others to profit, from people's digital vulnerabilities. It would include a duty on users (proportionate to their position and ability) not to exploit other users' digital vulnerability. Going into the details of what these duties might imply in concrete situations is largely beyond the scope of this article. Rather, we wish to address a practical objection to all of the above that may cast a shadow on the feasibility of our proposal: even assuming that such duties exist, could their breach somehow be enforced?[71]

This practical question can be further subdivided into several more specific questions. What would the legal basis for a claim based on a failure to consider people's vulnerability be? Assuming that a basis for the claim could be found, where would the claim be heard? As we already noted, companies and individuals in the digital domain who exploit other people's vulnerabilities can be located anywhere in the world: the digital domain by definition is not bound by territorial boundaries. In the current absence of any supranational regulation of cyber-torts,[72] the virtual location of the accident and its transnational nature make it hard to understand which jurisdiction is appropriate to hear claims arising from a digital wrong. Under what conditions could a claim be brought in Europe? Would the law of a European country apply? Even if the answer to these questions is in the affirmative, another major problem would arise from the defenses available. Companies can invoke the disclaimers and

[71] On the difficulties related to cyber-harms, Infantino and Bussani (2024, 292–309); Infantino and Wang (2019).

[72] The only international treaty so far is the Council of Europe's Framework Convention on Artificial Intelligence and Human Rights, Democracy and the Rule of Law adopted at Vilnius on 5 September 2024. See https://rm.coe.int/1680afae3c.

user assumption of risks clauses contained in the contractual standard documents they ask users to agree to.[73] In addition, digital service providers can rely on the regulatory immunities provided by the DSA.[74] Individuals can shield themselves from liability by arguing that they were exercising their constitutionally protected freedom of expression; and, in all cases where several people were involved in the harmful activity, any one of them can claim that their involvement was minimal and therefore not the cause of all the harm.[75] Lastly, additional difficulties in claims involving individuals would arise from the fact that most people online act under pseudonyms or use digital agents (such as avatars), which further complicates the search for identification, and that the people involved in cyber-torts are typically not only numerous, but also scattered across different states.[76]

Let us see in detail whether and how these problems can be solved for corporate (Sect. 7.1) and peer-to-peer (Sect. 7.2) abuses.

7.1 Corporate Abuses

The recognition of digital vulnerability as a universal and particular condition for everyone online would shed new light on the many obligations that companies offering goods and/or services online have toward their counterparts under EU consumer and data protection and national contract law, as well as on the specific obligations that arise for digital service providers under the DSA. Moreover, independently of these rules, each European legal system has general rules on non-contractual obligations, and in particular on tort and unjust enrichment, which oblige those who have unlawfully caused damage to another or who have unjustly enriched themselves at the expense of another to pay compensation or return what has been unlawfully obtained. It is true that in most cases the standard terms and conditions and other contractual documents that companies require online users to accept, contain clauses that limit the companies' liability for breach of contract, statutory breach, tort, and unjust enrichment and provide for choice of law and dispute resolution clauses that point to laws and jurisdictions that are different from those of the users.[77] This may not constitute a great obstacle, as the UCTD establishes that any unnegotiated term which, "contrary to the requirement of good faith, [...] causes a significant imbalance in the parties' rights and obligations arising under the contract, to the detriment of the consumer",[78] such as broad liability exemptions and exotic choices of forum and law, is deemed to be unfair and should not be enforced by courts. But for the rule to apply, it would be necessary to be in Europe or to have the law of a European country

[73] Mills (2024, 569–576); Infantino and Bussani (2024, 299–302).

[74] DSA, articles 4–6.

[75] Infantino (2022).

[76] On these issues, see Sect. 7.2.

[77] See above, note 73.

[78] UCTD article 3(1).

to apply to the claim. Let us therefore examine the conditions under which a claim against a company, including a digital service provider, for online abuse of digital vulnerability could be brought before European courts and the law under which it would be adjudicated.

Anyone considering suing a company after a digital accident would first need to identify and locate the defendant. Given the cross-border nature of the digital economy, the defendant may well be based outside Europe and have no European branch. This would not be good news for plaintiffs, as the general rule in transnational disputes is that a plaintiff can always sue a corporate defendant in the courts of the country where the defendant is headquartered. Yet, in order to protect consumers, EU conflict-of-law rules contain a special rule applicable to B2C relationships, according to which a consumer is entitled to bring an action against a company before the courts of the state where the consumer is domiciled, provided that the company pursues its commercial activities in that state.[79] This right cannot be waived by contract; any waiver or conflicting contractual provision designating a different exclusive forum is enforceable in Europe.[80]

Once the court of a European country has jurisdiction, the determination of the applicable law would follow the EU rules on private international law. These rules point to the "law of the country where the consumer has his habitual residence"[81] for contractual claims, to the "law of the country in which the damage occurs"[82] for tortious cases, and to the "law of the country in which the unjust enrichment took place" for unjust enrichment claims.[83] In most scenarios, the "country in which the damage occurs" and the "the country in which the unjust enrichment took place" would correspond to the country of residence of the plaintiff, therefore leading to the application of the law the plaintiff is more familiar with.[84] Claims brought in accordance with these rules may include cross-border representative actions.[85] Users residing in Europe, regardless the terms of use they agreed to, the location of the company they are dealing with, or the legal basis of the claim is, can bring their (individual and collective) private law claims against these companies before the courts and under the law of their country.[86]

Of course, none of the above would relieve the plaintiff of the need to prove all the requirements of the chosen cause of action under the applicable law and

[79] Regulation (EU) No 1215/2012 on jurisdiction and the recognition and enforcement of judgments in civil and commercial matters (BrusselsIbis), articles 6(1) and 18(1), as well as article 14.

[80] Regulation (EU) No 1215/2012 (n 79) article 19.

[81] Regulation (EC) No 593/2008 on the law applicable to contractual obligations (Rome I), article 6(1).

[82] Regulation (EC) No 864/2007 on the law applicable to non-contractual obligations (Rome II), article 4(1).

[83] Regulation (EC) No 864/2007, article 10(3).

[84] Van Dam (2021, 555, 571–572).

[85] Directive (EU) 2020/1828 on representative actions for the protection of the collective interests of consumers, article 6.

[86] Irrespective of the country involved, this law will likely be friendlier to consumers than any other: Infantino and Bussani (2024, 303–315).

to somehow avoid the application of possible defenses (such as the immunity of digital service providers under the DSA) that may be raised by the defendant. Overcoming the substantive, evidentiary, and procedural hurdles of the chosen cause of action under applicable law can be a significant burden. However, the presumption of digital vulnerability online and the possible application of a presumption of hyper-vulnerability may help in this regard.

A final point concerns the remedies available to the plaintiffs. The rules governing which remedies (e.g., invalidity of terms/contracts, performance, injunction, restitution, compensation) are available and under what conditions are largely determined by national private laws in Europe, which of course vary widely. European countries have remarkably different views on the range and extent of remedies that can be obtained through civil litigation. To fully protect against digital vulnerability, European courts would probably need to be creative and make generous use of the powers at their disposal to issue injunctions,[87] order the defendant to disgorge profits,[88] award non-patrimonial losses, especially in cases of serious violations of the duty to care about others' vulnerability and hyper-vulnerability,[89] and even grant ultra-compensatory awards, to the extent that this may be necessary to prevent the same conduct being repeated in the future.[90] After all, there are no rights without (adequate) remedies.

7.2 Peer-To-Peer Abuses

It would arguably be much more difficult to bring a claim for abuse of digital vulnerability against other individuals acting online. Such claims would face more hurdles than those against companies.

A first issue would be determining the legal basis for such a claim. In most cases, individuals who interact online, even if they do so through the same website, platform, or network, do not have a direct contractual relationship with each other. The terms and conditions users accept bind only the user and the website, platform, or network involved. Perhaps it could be argued that all subscribers to the same platforms are somehow part of the same contract, or that the contract with the platform obliges them to take into account the interests of relevant third parties, thus creating a contract with protective effects for third parties (i.e., other users). However, as far as we know, in all continental European legal systems to date, users are not considered to have a relationship with one another. This is not a problem in itself; all European legal

[87] For a plea about the use of injunctory relief (in the field of anti-discrimination), Halberstam and Van Den Bogaert (2023).

[88] For such a possibility, see Lee (2026).

[89] European jurisdictions adopt a variety of approaches with regard to non-patrimonial damages: de Conca and Infantino (2024); Li (2023).

[90] National European laws exclude overt punitive damages awards, even though punitive considerations may creep into tort law through other devices: see Infantino and Wang (2019, 357–358).

systems have rules on non-contractual obligations (such as tort and unjust enrichment, as well as anti-discrimination and data protection) that can apply to everyone.

Yet, difficulties would lie elsewhere. First of all, a person interested in filing such a complaint would need to identify the possible defendants. Since most people operate online using nicknames, avatars, and pseudonyms, their true identity remains unknown to anyone other than the website, platform, or network where the interaction takes place. Moreover, many people have multiple online identities or accounts; at the same time, many online identities or accounts do not correspond to a real person. Anyone wishing to sue other users would first need to obtain information about the real-world identities of those users, which in many cases would mean requesting such information from the relevant website, platform, or network. If the company refuses, the plaintiff will have to seek a court order for disclosure.[91]

Secondly, assuming that such information is obtained, there remains the problem of identifying the competent courts to hear the claims and the law applicable to those claims. The difficulty here stems from the fact that peer-to-peer abuse of digital vulnerabilities often involves people who are resident or domiciled in different locations. In the Khelif case mentioned above in Sect. 4, the individuals who retweeted, posted, and reposted comments against her came from all over the world. This truly complicates the issue whenever the defendants in these transnational cases are located outside the EU, as jurisdiction over non-EU defendants extends beyond the scope of the EU's unified regime of private international law and, therefore, must be determined by the national law of the forum (whether intra- or extra-EU).[92]

Especially in cases of mass harms, where many people have contributed to the realization of the abuse, this can lead to a considerable problem of coordinating international actions.[93] The solution may be more manageable if claims can be brought against individuals domiciled in EU countries. The general rule for grounding jurisdiction in ordinary civil cases is that people domiciled in a EU MS may be sued in the courts of that state.[94] However, alongside this rule, there are special provisions for claims regarding non-contractual obligations, which state that persons domiciled in one MS may be sued in another MS "in matters relating to tort, delict or quasi-delict, in the courts for the place where the harmful event occurred or may occur".[95] In addition, article 8 of the Brussels Ibis Regulation provides that a person domiciled in a MS may also be sued "where he is one of a number of defendants, in the courts for the place where any one of them is domiciled, provided the claims are so closely connected that it is expedient to hear and determine them together to avoid the risk of irreconcilable judgments resulting from separate proceedings".[96] Given the risk that individual users may be impecunious and judgment-proof, it would seem prudent

---

[91] Infantino and Bussani (2024, 297).

[92] On the problems related to determining jurisdictions against non-EU defendants, Lutzi, Piovesani, Zgrabljić Rotar (2023, 21–26).

[93] Infantino and Wang (2019, 343–344).

[94] Regulation (EU) No 1215/2012 (n 79) article 4(1).

[95] Regulation (EU) No 1215/2012 (n 79) article 7, no (2).

[96] Regulation (EU) No 1215/2012 (n 79) article 8, no (1).

to base jurisdiction in the country where the defendant with the deepest pockets is domiciled. Whenever jurisdiction is established in one or more EU states, it is relatively straightforward to identify the applicable law. As we have already mentioned, the Rome II Regulation on the law applicable to non-contractual obligations stipulates that the law of the country where the damage or unjust enrichment occurred is applicable, which in most cases will be the country where the plaintiff resides.[97]

Assuming that the jurisdiction of a European court and the applicability of a European law are established, the plaintiffs would still have to prove the elements of the cause of action. For instance, in a fault-based liability claim, the plaintiff would have to prove the breach by the defendants of the applicable standard of care, the damage suffered, the causal link between the negligence of the defendants and that injury, the extent of the damages, and other technicalities depending on the law applicable to the action; in most cases, the plaintiff would also have to bypass the defense that the defendants were exercising their constitutionally protected freedom of opinion.[98] Many of these requirements may prove to be serious hurdles. While plaintiffs may find some support in the presumption of digital vulnerability, they may still find it difficult to persuade a court that their protection is more worthy than protecting the defendant's right to speak.[99] The same reasoning applies to proving the defendants' fault: if it is true that the duty to take care of the digital vulnerability of others depends largely on each person's ability to understand and protect the vulnerability of others, it would be up to the plaintiffs to prove that the defendants owed them a duty of care because of their experience, visibility, or authority.[100] Proof of damage can also be a problem, especially in cases of purely economic or non-economic losses, as many European legal systems are conservative in their approach to recovery in such cases.[101] But perhaps the most daunting problem would be proving causation. Particularly in cases where a number of people were involved in the act, the scenario would be one of cumulative causation, where each defendant contributed to the ultimate harm in some minimal way, and the extent of that contribution cannot be determined with precision.[102] To take the Khelif case again, it can hardly be said that the contribution of each of the people who retweeted the comments against her was a 'but-for' factor or a *condicio sine qua non* cause of the ultimate harm. European courts would have to be creative to solve this problem. They have been so in the past: for example, in similar minimal causation scenarios (such as toxic torts and environmental damage), European courts have often been able established causation in multi-defendant cases on the basis of the likelihood of causation.[103] Of course, in determining exactly who should be responsible for what, an assessment of each defendant's ability to understand and prevent the abuse should be made, so that

---

[97] See Regulation No 864/2007 (Rome II), articles 4(1) and 10(3); see also above, Sect. 7.1.

[98] Also on this point see Tsomidis (2022).

[99] See above, note 68.

[100] On this point, Bussani, Sebok, Infantino (2022, 27–42).

[101] See above note 89.

[102] Infantino and Zervogianni (2017, 652–653).

[103] See Infantino (2022); Infantino and Zervogianni (2017, 646–647).

causation and liability can be articulated taking into account each defendant's status and authority, their proximity to the victim, their role in the abuse, the severity and gravity of the attack, the number of people involved, and so on.[104] In particular, such an assessment should take into account the *interdependence of digital vulnerability* as highlighted in Sect. 3 above: since everyone is at once vulnerable to (corporate abuse as well as to) other people's attacks and empowered to attack other digitally vulnerable people, the extent to which people can be held accountable depends on the relational positions and capabilities of the people involved. As the old saying goes, bad people should pay, and very bad people should pay more.

8 Conclusions

We can imagine concerns that the world we describe could become a world of over-compensation. We do not believe this is the case. Even if claims arising from abuses of people's digital vulnerability could technically be brought before European courts and adjudicated under European private law, significant hurdles remain to making this litigation a reality. In addition to the well-known social, psychological and economic factors that reduce people's willingness to assert their rights,[105] abuses of digital vulnerability present additional hurdles that are typical of any cyber tort case. The transnational nature of the case, the immunities protecting digital service providers and users, the multiplicity of defendants and their possible anonymity, the difficulty of proving the elements of the cause of action, and the challenge of obtaining an adequate remedy are all factors that increase the difficulty of securing justice. Much would have to change for this litigation to open the floodgates of liability.

Yet, change is needed. In particular, it is essential to bring the legal framework closer to reality, namely that we live in hyper-connected societies in which all of us, except perhaps a minimal fraction, have very little understanding of the digital infrastructure in which we are immersed and on which we depend, and, in any case, have very limited means of protection. In a highly unbalanced context such as the digital environment, there is an urgent need to find some mechanisms and instruments that can somehow rebalance the existing power relations. We argue that this could be achieved by recourse to existing private law rules and remedies, as well as by changing the interpretation of individuals' status in the digital environment. Rather than clinging to the traditional view of the average online user, who is expected to assume all risks of harm simply by formally accepting standard terms and conditions and the availability of information that that they have never read, it would be more accurate to acknowledge that average online users are unaware of and exposed to risks that they never understood or accepted. In other words, it is necessary to

[104] When, for instance, the content is clearly sensitive and the speaker is authoritative and powerful, there may be heightened duties to behave correctly: on similar lines, see Fowler, Helveston, Robinson (2025).

[105] For the relevant literature, see Bussani and Infantino (2015, 83–90).

acknowledge that everyone online is digitally vulnerable, that many—particularly those at heightened risk of discrimination—are hyper-vulnerable, and that everyone operating in the online world, including individuals, should be mindful of the digital vulnerability experienced by other users and behave accordingly.

We have tried to demonstrate that the above change does not require any specific reform, but rather a shift in understanding and the interpretation of existing rules regarding private rights, obligations, and remedies. Of course, a similar shift could probably be brought about more easily if it were enacted through legislative reform, as has been done in Latin America. But we should bear in mind that, for centuries, much of the development of private law in Europe has depended on the creativity and courage of academics and judges to imagine the legal world not as it is, but as it could be.[106] As is often the case with revolutions, change depends on us all.

References

Balkin JM (2020) The fiduciary model of privacy. Harvard Law Rev 134:11–33

Bartl M (2015) Internal market rationality, private law and the direction of the union: resuscitating the market as the object of the political. Eur Law J 21(5):572–598

Ben-Shahar O, Porat A (2021) Personalized law. Different rules for different people. Oxford University Press, Oxford

BEUC (2021) EU Consumer Protection 2.0. Structural asymmetries in digital consumer markets. Available at https://www.beuc.eu/sites/default/files/publications/beuc-x-2021-018_eu_consumer_protection_2.0.pdf

Bradford A (2023) Digital empires. The global battle to regulate technology. Oxford University Press, Oxford

Burk DL (2021) Algorithmic legal metrics. Notre Dame Law Rev 96:1147–1204

Bussani M, Infantino M (2015) Tort law and legal cultures. Am J Comp Law 63(1):77–108

Bussani M, Sebok AJ, Infantino M (2022) Common law and civil law perspectives on tort law. Oxford University Press, Oxford

Calabresi G (1985) Ideals, beliefs, attitudes, and the law. Private law perspectives on a public law problem. Syracuse University Press, Syracuse

Caruso D (2012) The "Justice Deficit" debate in EU private law: new directions. BU Law Working Paper (2012). Available at https://scholarship.law.bu.edu/faculty_scholarship/590/

Chamallas C, Wriggins JB (2010) The measure of injury: race, gender, and tort law. New York University Press, New York

Clément D (2018) Human rights or social justice? The problem of rights inflation. Int J Human Rights 22:155–169

Colombi Ciacchi A (2019) The direct horizontal effect of EU fundamental rights. Eur Const Law Rev 15(2):294–305

Crea C, De Franceschi A (eds) (2024) The new shapes of digital vulnerability in european private law. Nomos, Baden-Baden

Crenshaw K (1989) Demarginalizing the intersection of race and sex: a black feminist critique of antidiscrimination doctrine, feminist theory and antiracist politics. Feminist Legal Theory 3(1):139–167

de Conca S, Infantino M (2024) A difficult puzzle: the duty of care in Member States' tort law and the GDPR. Datenschutz und Datensicherheit 48:566–571

[106] Merryman and Pérez-Perdomo (2007, 56–68); Sacco (1991), 346–350.

De Gregorio G (2022) Digital constitutionalism in Europe. Reframing rights and power in the digital society. Cambridge University Press, Cambridge

Domurath I (2024) Digital vulnerability as a power relation: hyper- and hypo-autonomy and why thick privacy matters. In: Crea C, De Franceschi A (eds) The new shapes of digital vulnerability in European private law. Nomos, Baden-Baden, pp 227–258

Endicott T, Young K (2022) The death of law? Computationally personalized norms and the rule of law. Univ Toronto Law J 72:373–402

European Commission (2024a) Study to support the Fitness Check of EU consumer law on digital fairness and the report on the application of the Modernisation Directive (EU) 2019/2161. Final Report—Part 1. Available at https://commission.europa.eu/publications/study-support-fitness-check-eu-consumer-law-digital-fairness-and-report-application-modernisation_en

European Commission (2024b) Commission Staff Working Document Fitness check of EU consumer law on digital fairness. SEC(2024) 245 final. Available at https://commission.europa.eu/document/download/707d7404-78e5-4aef-acfa-82b4cf639f55_en?filename=Commission%20Staff%20Working%20Document%20Fitness%20Check%20on%20EU%20consumer%20law%20on%20digital%20fairness.pdf

European Commission (2016) Consumer vulnerability across key markets in the European Union. Final report. Available at https://op.europa.eu/en/publication-detail/-/publication/79b42553-de14-11e6-ad7c-01aa75ed71a1

Fineman MA (2008) The vulnerable subject: anchoring equality in the human condition. Yale J Law Fem 20:8–40

Floridi L (ed) (2015) The onlife manifesto. Springer, Cham

Fowler LR, Helveston M, Robinson Z (2025) Influencer speech-torts. Georgetown Law J 113(3):45–103

Gellert R (2024) The digital vulnerable consumer: a concept with critical potential or entrenching logics of market efficiency. Available at https://transformativeprivatelaw.com/the-digital-vulnerable-consumer-a-concept-with-critical-potential-or-entrenching-logics-of-market-efficiency/.

Grochowski M (2024) Digital vulnerability in a post-consumer society. subverting paradigms?. In: Crea C, De Franceschi A (eds) The new shapes of digital vulnerability in European private law. Nomos, Baden-Baden, pp 201–227

Halberstam D, Van Den Bogaert S (2023) A fresh look at judicial remedies in EU equality law and beyond: The untapped possibility of structural injunctions. Common Market Law Rev 60(5):1269–1312

Hesselink M, Soei Len T (2025) European private law & intersectionality: three strategies. Eur Law Open 1–22

Infantino M (2025) Consumers' vulnerability. In: Micklitz H-W, Namysłowska M (eds), Consumer law encyclopedia. Edward Elgar. Cheltenham, forthcoming

Infantino M, Bussani M (2024) Tort law in the metaverse. In: diMatteo L, Cannarsa M (eds) Research handbook on the metaverse and law. Edward Elgar, Cheltenham, pp 292–309

Infantino M (2022) Causation in algorithmic torts. In: Belser EM, Pichonnaz P, Stöckli H (eds) Le droit sans frontières. Mélanges pour Franz Werro. Stämpfli, Berne, pp 375–384

Infantino M, Wang W (2019) Algorithmic torts: a prospective comparative overview. Transnatl Law Contemp Probls 28:309–623

Infantino M, Zervogianni E (2017) Summary and survey of the results. In: Infantino M, Zervogianni E (eds) Causation in European tort law. Cambridge University Press, Cambridge, pp 587–665

Kaplan Y, Gordon-Tapiero A (2024) Unjust enrichment by algorithm. George Wash Law Rev 92:305–358

Keats Citron D (2022) The fight for privacy. Protecting dignity, identity, and love in the digital age, Norton & Co., New York

Kohnt NA (2014) Vulnerability theory and the role of government. Yale J Law Feminism 26(1):1–28

Krämer L (2021) The origins of consumer law and policy at EU Level. In: Micklitz H-W (ed) The making of consumer law and policy in Europe. Hart, Oxford, pp 13–30

Lee C (2026) Beyond algorithmic disgorgement: remedying algorithmic harms. UC Irvine Law Rev 16
Lee E (2022) Virtual governments. UCLA J Law Technol 4:1–32
Lessig L (2006) Code and other laws of cyberspace, Version 2.0. Basic Books, New York
Li S (2023) Compensation for non-material damage under Art. 82 GDPR: a review of Case C-300/21. Maastricht J Eur Comp Law 30(3):335–345
Lutzi T, Piovesani E, Zgrabljić Rotar D (2023) Comparative report. In: Lutzi T, Piovesani E, Zgrabljić Rotar D (eds) Jurisdiction over non-EU Defendants. Should the Brussels Ia Regulation be Extended?. Bloomsbury, London, pp 3–28
Macioce F (2022) The politics of vulnerable groups. Implications for philosophy, law, and political theory, Springer, Cham
Mackenzie C (2013) The importance of relational autonomy and capabilities for an ethics of vulnerability. In: Mackenzie C, Rogers W, Dodds S (eds) Vulnerability. New essays in ethics and feminist philosophy. Oxford University Press, Oxford, pp 33–59
Malgieri G (2023) Vulnerability and data protection law. Oxford University Press, Oxford
Malgieri G, Niklas J (2020) Vulnerable data subjects. Comp Law Secur Rev 37:105415. Available at https://www.sciencedirect.com/science/article/pii/S0267364920300200
Martínez Alles MG (2025) Reducing inequality in consumer transactions: the significance of aggravated vulnerabilities. In: Davis KE, Pargendler M (eds), Legal heterodoxy in the global south: adapting private laws to local contexts. Cambridge University Press, Cambridge, pp 77–111
Mercosur (2021) Resolution no 11/2021. Protección al consumidor hipervulnerable. Available at https://normas.mercosur.int/public/normativas/4116
Mercosur (2019) Resolution no 36/2019. Consumidores en el mercado. Available at https://normas.mercosur.int/simfiles/normativas/73866_RES_036-2019_ES_Defensa%20Consumidor%20Principios%20Fundamentales.pdf
Merryman JH, Pérez-Perdomo R (2007) The civil law tradition. An introduction to the legal systems of Europe and Latin America. 3rd edn, Stanford University Press, Stanford
Micklitz H-W et alii (2024) Towards digital fairness. J Eur Consumer Market Law 13:24–30
Mills G (2024) A contractual approach to social media governance. Yale Law Policy Rev 42:522–625
Pistor K (2019) The code of capital: How the law creates wealth and inequality. Princeton University Press, Princeton
Riefa C (2022) Protecting vulnerable consumers in the digital single market. Eur Bus Law Rev 33:607–634
Sacco R (1991) Legal formants: a dynamic approach to comparative law (installment II of II). Am J Comp Law 39:343–401
Schulze R, Staudenmayer D (eds) (2024) EU Digital Law. Beck, Munich
Smits JM (2014) Contract law. A comparative introduction. Edward Elgar, Cheltenham
Teubner G (2006) Coincidentia oppositorum: hybrid networks beyond contract and organization. In: Gordon R, Horwitz M (eds) Law, society, and history: themes in the legal sociology and legal history of Lawrence M. Friedman. Stanford University Press, Stanford, pp 367–394
Theilen JT (2021) The inflation of human rights: a deconstruction. Leiden J Int Law 34(4):831–854
Tsomidis T (2022) Freedom of expression in turbulent times—comparative approaches to dangerous speech: the ECtHR and the US Supreme Court. Int J Human Rights 26:379–399
van Dam C (2021) Transnational tort law. In: Zumbansen P (ed) The oxford handbook of transnational law, 2nd edn. Oxford University Press, Oxford

Remedying Digital Vulnerability in Everyday Life

Robo-Advisors as Product in the Insurance Sector: Considerations Regarding Enforceability

Szymon Skalski and Piotr Tereszkiewicz

Abstract Insurance robo-advisors automate pricing, underwriting, and policy servicing through machine-learning models. While they promise efficiency and objectivity, their opacity amplifies systemic risks: data mapping errors inflate premiums, model drift voids coverage, and biased proxies trigger unlawful discrimination. Private law remedies may not always be sufficient. Privity blocks claims against upstream software vendors; exclusion clauses cap recovery; proving fault inside proprietary code is practically impossible. The revised Product Liability Directive (PLD) seeks to plug this gap by classifying "software, digital manufacturing files and AI systems" as products and imposing strict liability on manufacturers, importers and white-labelling insurers. However, essential uncertainties remain: the boundary between an adaptive algorithm and a 'defect' is unclear; pure economic loss is still only indirectly covered; and multi-tier vendor chains complicate the allocation of liability. By contrasting contracting-based and product-based enforcement, this chapter argues that PLD closes much, but not all, of the robo-advisor liability gap, effectively shifting rather than eliminating residual legal uncertainty.

Keywords Robo-advisors · Insurance sector · Product liability · Artificial intelligence

---

This research was conducted within the framework of the research project funded by the Polish National Science Centre (NCN), Grant No. 2018/29/B/HS5/01281

S. Skalski · P. Tereszkiewicz (✉)
Faculty of Law, Jagiellonian University of Krakow, Krakow, Poland
e-mail: piotr.tereszkiewicz@uj.edu.pl

S. Skalski
e-mail: szymon.skalski@doctoral.uj.edu.pl

C. Crea and M. Infantino (eds.), *Remedies to Digital Vulnerability in European Private Law*, https://doi.org/10.1007/978-3-032-19720-7_19

1 Introduction

Robo-advisors are fast becoming the front end of retail insurance: they price policies, underwrite risks and nudge consumers through fully automated journeys.[1] Speed and scale, however, magnify minor technical errors into systemic hazards. A single feature engineering slip can inflate premiums for an entire demographic; a prompt injection attack can corrupt thousands of medical files in seconds; an unnoticed drift in a reinforcement learning loop can void coverage at renewal.[2] Customers harmed by such glitches soon discover that contract law is a weak shield: privity blocks anyone outside the immediate policy from suing upstream software vendors; exclusion clauses cap recovery at trivial amounts; and proving negligence inside black-box code is nearly impossible. The EU's response is the revised Product Liability Directive (PLD),[3] which considers software a "product" and imposes strict liability on the whole chain of "economic operators".[4] The PLD introduces several rebuttable presumptions—regarding the notion of defect, causation, and a "complex product" shortcut—designed to neutralise information asymmetry, and recognises data corruption and clinically certified mental harm as compensable heads of loss.[5]In theory, the measure closes the liability gap left by contract and tort.

However, the fix is only partial. Labelling code for a product does not inform courts when adaptive algorithms are "defective", how to quantify pure economic loss caused by biased outputs, or who pays when an insurer white-labels a third-party engine that in turn relies on multiple API providers. Nor does the Directive resolve choice-of-law gamesmanship, where platform operators funnel claims to favourable jurisdictions. With the AI Liability Directive[6] having been withdrawn,[7] the burden of fault-based claims shifts back to national tort law, promising a patchwork of interpretations and procedural hurdles. This contribution, therefore, provides a critical examination of the enforceability of these provisions. Section 2 explains where and why contractual remedies break down. Section 3 tests the PLD's new framework against real-world malfunction scenarios, highlighting loopholes in the concept of "defect" and the allocation of liability across complex vendor chains. Section 4 asks whether PLD 2024 will curb the risks it targets or simply redistribute legal uncertainty—from consumers to insurers, and from insurers to software vendors—without eliminating it.

---

[1] EIOPA (2024, 37–42), EIOPA Insurance & Reinsurance Stakeholder Group (2023, 12–13), McKinsey and Company (2025), Swiss Re (2025).

[2] Gallagher Re (2024), Monetary Authority of Singapore (2024), Alber et al (2025).

[3] Directive (EU) 2024/2853 of 23 October 2024 on liability for defective products and repealing Council Directive 85/374/EEC.

[4] Wagner (2024).

[5] Wagner (2024, 182–184).

[6] European Commission (2022a).

[7] Rimkute (2025).

2 The Liability Gap Between Contract and Product Law

A malfunction in an insurance robo-advisor is any departure from the level of safety and functional reliability that a reasonable policyholder can expect once the software is on the market.[8] One can distinguish five overlapping patterns of the most prevalent failures.

First, erroneous pricing or underwriting logic may arise due to configuration mistakes, flawed actuarial assumptions or coding errors.[9] Such errors may result in premiums or policy terms that bear no rational relation to the insured risk. To illustrate this point, consider the case of a healthy non-smoker who is charged a 'smoker surcharge'. Second, machine learning components that remain active after deployment may drift away from their original accuracy baseline.[10] In the absence of periodic recalibration, the model can begin to over-penalise certain postcodes or age brackets. This can result in a defect being concealed from both insurers and consumers until a significant number of policies have been missold. Third, the platform's reliance on real-time data feeds means that system downtime or an API glitch may cause the engine to rely on outdated values.[11] This can result in recommendations becoming distorted, or, at the most inopportune moment of policy renewal, the service becoming unavailable, leading to an unintended lapse of cover. Fourth, cybersecurity breaches represent a significant threat to data integrity. Such breaches may take the form of prompt injection attacks or ransomware, for example, and can result in the alteration or eradication of stored underwriting data.[12] Fifth, this in turn exposes customers to privacy violations under the GDPR and to the financial burden of reconstructing corrupted files. Under Article 6(1)(c) of the PLD, the aforementioned data corruption is now classified as compensable damage in its own right. The sixth issue to consider is the potential for algorithmic bias to emerge when the training data is unrepresentative or when proxies for protected characteristics become embedded within the feature set.[13] This can result in specific groups, such as single parents, immigrants, or individuals living with chronic illnesses, encountering systematically adverse terms. The immediate consequences may include an inflated premium or a denial of cover that is deemed to be unjust; the secondary harm may be clinically recognised anxiety, which may be considered a mental injury under

[8] See Recital 40 and Article 7 of the revised PLD.

[9] Groom Publication (2024), Peters et al (2023).

[10] IAIS (2025), National Association of Insurance Commissioners (2025), Oklahoma Insurance Department (2024).

[11] Reuters (2024a) (on the Windows-endpoint failure that took down call-centre and policy-administration systems worldwide, prompting a surge of business-interruption and lapse-of-cover claims against insurers), EIOPA (2024) (highlighting digital-operational-resilience and "cyber-driven outages of real-time data feeds" as a rising prudential concern for European insurers).

[12] Innobu (2025), Reuters (2024b) (New York cybersecurity guidance obliges every New-York-licensed insurer to review AI models for prompt-injection and ransomware risks and to vet third-party APIs accordingly). See also article 6(1)(c) revised PLD.

[13] New York State Department of Financial Services (2024), IAIS (2025), Financial Conduct Authority (2024). See also article 6(1)(c) revised PLD.

Article 6(1)(a) of the PLD. The reason for this is that these failure modes lie at the intersection of complex software engineering and the insurer's duty of fairness. It is evident that contractual remedies, which are subject to privity, fault requirements and exclusion clauses, regularly prove inadequate in such cases.

Within the contractual framework governing robo-advisory services, insurers and intermediaries are obligated to adhere to a set of responsibilities derived from both sector-specific regulatory frameworks and principles of general contract law. The starting point at the European Union level is the Insurance Distribution Directive (IDD).[14] Article 17 IDD states that firms must act with honesty, fairness and professionalism, prioritising the best interests of the customer.[15] Articles 18 to 20 IDD mandate the collection of sufficient information regarding the client's requirements and expectations, the provision of clear pre-contractual disclosures, and the recommendation of objectively suitable products, where advice is provided. In principle, a malfunctioning robo-advisor is capable of breaching each of the aforementioned statutory duties. Such breaches may take the form of delivering a mispriced quotation or unjustly refusing cover. The result of such breaches would be the exposure of the distributor to supervisory sanctions and a private claim for breach of contract.

National contract law adds a second layer to the legal framework. The majority of civil law codes impose an implied duty to supply accurate pre-contractual information and a warranty that the service will be fit for its customary purpose.[16] By contrast, common law jurisdictions recognise comparable doctrines of misrepresentation and implied fitness.[17] In instances where the insurer acquires a robo-advisor from a fintech vendor, the underlying Software as a Service (SaaS) agreement often incorporates explicit service-level agreements (SLAs), which encompass metrics such as uptime targets, response times for critical incidents, and patch schedules. These SLAs can be interpreted as implicitly transferred to the insurer's clients. However, it is worth noting that these contractual remedies are subject to significant limitations. Liability clauses in consumer-facing terms often state that algorithmic outputs are considered merely 'indicative' and limit any recovery to the premium paid.[18] Alternatively,

---

[14] Directive (EU) 2016/97 of the European Parliament and of the Council of 20 January 2016 on insurance distribution.

[15] Noussia (2022).

[16] Court of Justice of the European Union (CJEU), joined cases C-143/20 and C-213/20, *A v O* and *G.W. & E.S. v A. Towarzystwo Ubezpieczeń Życie S.A.*, 24 February 2022, ECLI:EU:C:2022:118; CJEU, case C-649/17, *Bundesverband der Verbraucherzentralen & Verbraucherverbände – Verbraucherzentrale Bundesverband e.V. v Amazon EU Sàrl*, 10 July 2019, ECLI:EU:C:2019:576; CJEU, joined cases C-65/09 & C-87/09, *Gebr. Weber GmbH v Jürgen Wittmer and Ingrid Putz v Medianess Electronics GmbH*, 16 June 2011, ECLI:EU:C:2011:396. See also Salminen (2020).

[17] *Derry v Peek* (1889) LR 14 App Cas 337 (HL); *Hedley Byrne & Co Ltd v Heller & Partners Ltd* [1963] UKHL 4; *Grant v Australian Knitting Mills Ltd* [1936] UKPC 2; *The Moorcock* (1889) 14 PD 64 (CA); *Henningsen v. Bloomfield Motors, Inc.* 32 N.J. 358 (1960).

[18] Policybazaar (2025) (the disclaimer reads: "The Yamaha YBR insurance price presented here is for indicative purposes only"); Principal Insurance Limited (2025) (stating that "online quotes are for indicative purposes only—please call to confirm full details of your courier insurance quote"); Forbes Advisor (2025) (the disclaimer reads "our research is for indicative purposes only. Compare car-insurance quotes"); The House of Insurance (2025) (the limitation of liability in the terms and

they may exclude indirect, consequential and data loss entirely. Although consumer protection regulations can nullify the most egregious disclaimers, many Member States continue to permit the exclusion of pure economic loss. Moreover, on occasion, non-pecuniary loss, unless the claimant can demonstrate a specific statutory breach, is also allowed. In instances where exclusions are deemed unenforceable, the onus falls on the policyholder to substantiate their responsibility and establish a causal connection between the robo-advisor's error and the customer's loss. This task is particularly challenging when the defect is embedded within the layers of proprietary code. Accordingly, while the contract and the IDD establish a baseline of obligations, they leave a residual liability gap in circumstances where the malfunction is not attributable to any party in the conventional sense, or when meticulously drafted disclaimers and evidentiary hurdles render the contractual route impracticable. This paper aims to demonstrate how the strict liability regime of the PLD is intended to address this gap, as will be illustrated in the following sections.

Liability under the PLD postulates the existence of a defect once the prescribed statutory triggers are met, thereby shifting the burden of exoneration to the manufacturer.[19] The majority of business terms oriented towards consumers serve to exacerbate the issue through the implementation of exclusion or limitation clauses. It is customary for robo-advisory platforms to impose a cap on contractual liability at the level of premiums paid, to disclaim any liability for 'indirect or consequential loss', or to categorise every output as a mere 'indicative quote'. European consumer protection legislation aims to limit the most onerous disclaimers; however, numerous clauses can withstand scrutiny, for example, those pertaining to pure economic loss. The discrepancy between the two becomes evident in instances where a robo-advisor malfunctions and a customer attempts to rely exclusively on the provisions of contract law. First, it is necessary to consider the possibility of an error in pricing. In the event of a data mapping issue resulting in an erroneous classification of an applicant as a smoker, the algorithm will produce a premium that is 40% higher than the actuarial parity would justify. Nonetheless, the platform's terms of use stipulate that all quotations are provided for illustrative purposes only and that the final underwriting decision remains at the platform's discretion. Suppose the policyholder subsequently becomes aware of the error. In that case, a contractual claim will likely be unsuccessful due to the disclaimer mentioned earlier, or will be restricted to a limited reimbursement of the excess payment. In contrast, the PLD establishes a framework within which the same mispricing can be substantiated as a product defect. The onus is on the claimant to demonstrate that the erroneous output is most likely attributable to the software. Once this has been established, the Directive's evidentiary presumptions shift the burden of rebuttal to the insurer in its capacity as manufacturer or quasi-manufacturer.

---

conditions states that "in no event shall the agency and its agents' total liability to you [...] exceed the amount paid by you, if any, for accessing the site").

[19] Koch (2024, 109–111), Wagner (2024, 172–183).

A second gap pertains to the phenomenon of data corruption. During an online dialogue, a malicious prompt successfully overwrites a substantial number of confidential health questionnaires stored on the robo-advisor's server. The SaaS licence usually excludes things like indirect, consequential or data loss, and promises at most a pro rata refund of subscription fees. It is possible to submit a General Data Protection Regulation (GDPR) claim under Article 82[20]; however, the burden of proof lies with the data subject to demonstrate that the processor is liable for the breach. In contrast, the PLD stipulates that the destruction or corruption of personal data may be regarded as actionable damage, subject to strict liability. Article 6(1)(c) PLD stipulates that "destruction or corruption of data not used for professional purposes" constitutes a harm. Article 9 PLD enables the court to mandate the disclosure of technical details, while Article 10 PLD introduces rebuttable presumptions of defect and causation, thereby shifting the evidentiary burden to the manufacturer. In practice, this means that a policyholder who has been subjected to a prompt injection attack destroying health disclosures may be able to invoke strict liability without the need to examine internal code or demonstrate negligence.

A third gap opens when algorithmic bias produces non-pecuniary, psychological harm rather than tangible economic loss. Imagine a single parent who is denied life insurance because the underwriting model uses marital status as a risk proxy. No immediate property damage occurs—the applicant simply has no policy—but the rejection inflicts clinically diagnosed anxiety. The PLD treats "medically recognised damage to psychological health" as personal injury under Article 6(1)(a), making it a stand-alone head of repairable damage. Once the claimant establishes a plausible causal link between the biased output and the distress, the rebuttable presumptions under Article 10 of defect and causation shift the burden onto the software maker to disprove liability—no need to unravel the black-box logic or prove traditional negligence.

In each of these situations, contractual remedies are weakened by disclaimers, evidentiary opacity, or the narrow categories of loss traditionally available. In contrast, the revised PLD supplies strict liability, broader heads of damage, and helpful presumptions. The practical necessity of overlaying product liability on top of the contractual framework is therefore undeniable. The revised PLD introduces stringent product liability provisions, which have the effect of neutralising any structural weaknesses that might otherwise compromise the reliability of contractual redress. By recognising software as a product, the revised PLD imposes a regulatory framework that disregards the concepts of privity and fault. This signifies that any aggrieved

---

[20] CJEU, case C-300/21, *UI v Österreichische Post AG*, 4 May 2023, ECLI:EU:C:2023:370; CJEU, case C-340/21, *VB v Natsionalna agentsia za prihodite*, 14 December 2023, ECLI:EU:C:2023:1013; CJEU, case C-667/21, *ZQ v Medizinischer Dienst der Krankenversicherung Nordrhein*, 21 December 2023, ECLI:EU:C:2023:1049; CJEU, case C-687/21, *MediaMarktSaturn Retail Group GmbH*, 25 January 2024, ECLI:EU:C:2024:37; CJEU, case C-621/22, *Koninklijke Nederlandse Lawn Tennis Bond (KNLTB)*, 4 October 2024, ECLI:EU:C:2024:780); Bundesgerichtshof [German Federal Court of Justice], Order of 26 September 2023, VI ZR 97/22, reference for CJEU preliminary question on Article 82 GDPR; Bundesarbeitsgericht [German Federal Labour Court], Judgment of 23 January 2025, 8 AZR 124/23 (confirming the ZQ line on proof of non-material damage).

party, be it the contracting policyholder, a scheme member, or a third-party claimant, is entitled to initiate legal action against the manufacturer or quasi-manufacturer without the necessity of proving negligence. The revised PLD then introduces two procedural advantages. First, Articles 10(2)-(4) establish rebuttable presumptions of defect and causation in circumstances where the claimant faces excessive technical complexity or where the defendant withholds essential evidence, thereby piercing the opacity that so often shields algorithmic malfunctions.[21] Second, Article 6(1) extends the concept of compensable harm to encompass both "medically recognised damage to psychological health" (letter a) and "destruction or corruption of data not used for professional purposes" (letter c), thereby encompassing the losses that are typically excluded by contractual disclaimers and national regulations. The liability stipulated under the PLD legislation is stringent. Consequently, contractual limitations or choice of law clauses are rendered ineffective in the capacity to limit or evade recovery. In conclusion, the PLD successfully addresses the gaps in liability coverage present within the framework of contract law.

It is essential to note that contract and product liability claims address the same malfunction from distinct perspectives. Consequently, it is entirely possible—and indeed common—for a claimant to pursue both remedies in parallel. The EU courts permit such concurrent recovery, yet they are also known to guard against the possibility of double recovery. This is achieved by ensuring that any award made under the strict liability regime is offset against contractual damages for the same loss. It is essential to note that contractual parties cannot derogate from the provisions of this framework by entering into separate agreements. Article 15 of the PLD expressly prohibits any contractual or national provision from limiting or excluding liability under the Directive. Furthermore, under the Rome I and II Regulations, any choice of law or forum selection clause that would result in the denial of PLD protection is considered unenforceable.[22] If an insurer compensates the policyholder and subsequently ascertains that the defect originated from a white-label algorithm provided by a fintech vendor, the subrogation and recourse provisions become applicable. Article 5(2) PLD enables the insurer to assume the role of the claimant, while Article 14 confers upon it the explicit right to pursue other economic operators within the supply chain. Collectively, these regulations ensure a relatively straightforward process for recourse, thereby eliminating the need for injured parties to navigate complex contractual indemnity frameworks.

Contract law still underpins service levels, disclosure duties, and premium adjustments; however, it leaves a significant enforcement gap when AI malfunctions occur. The PLD attempts to fill that gap with a strict-liability overlay—the mandatory scope (Article 15), broad defect definitions (Article 7) and evidentiary presumptions (Article 10 (2–4))—and it even empowers subrogation (Article 5(2)) and direct recourse (Article 14). However, this fix is far from watertight. Courts must grapple

---

[21] See especially European Commission (2022b).

[22] Regulation (EC) No 593/2008 of 17 June 2008 on the law applicable to contractual obligations (Rome I), Articles 6 (2) and 9; Regulation (EC) No 864/2007 of 11 July 2007 on the law applicable to non-contractual obligations (Rome II), Articles 14 (3) and 16.

with novel "defect" concepts for adaptive algorithms, while national judges remain free to vary limitation periods and the quantum of damages. Choice-of-law gamesmanship can still impede cross-border claims, despite the Rome I and Rome II Regulations. Meanwhile, insurers may resist claims under the revised PLD to protect lucrative vendor partnerships or exploit carve-outs for professional data. In practice, the revised PLD risks becoming yet another layer of complexity, one that shifts litigation costs without fully resolving who ultimately bears the fallout of a faulty robo-advisor.

3 Liability for Robo-Advisors

3.1 Private Law Liability of Insurance Distributors Utilising Robo-Advisors

Article 4(1) PLD defines "product" to include "all movables […] and software," thereby bringing robo-advisors—whether licensed outright, sold by subscription, or offered as SaaS—squarely within the Directive's reach. Liability then follows the chain of economic operators as laid out in Article 4(15): the insurer that develops or white-labels a robo-advisor under its brand qualifies as a manufacturer (Article 4 (10)); the fintech supplying the core algorithm is a component supplier; any importer, fulfilment service provider or distributor that makes the software available in the EU market—or simply hosts it for policyholders—may likewise be held liable. Which category an insurance distributor occupies depends on the business model chosen (which can be in-house build, white-label partnership, marketplace integration, etc.).

Under the revised PLD, the familiar triad of strict liability elements—defect (Article 7), damage (Article 6), and causal link (Article 10(1)) —remains intact. What is new for AI-based software is that post-market learning or updates themselves may render a product defective (Article 7(2)(c)), that cybersecurity weaknesses qualify as safety defects (Article 7(2)(f)), and that the destruction or corruption of data is explicitly recognised as compensable damage alongside physical or mental harm (Article 6(1)(c)). To overcome the information asymmetry that often shields opaque algorithms, Article 10(2–4) PLD introduces rebuttable presumptions of defect and causation whenever the claimant faces disproportionate technical hurdles or the defendant withholds essential evidence.[23] With the AI Liability Directive withdrawn, these PLD presumptions have become the EU's principal mechanism for ensuring redress in AI-driven product disputes.

Once the robo-advisor is characterised as a "product" under Article 4(1), the PLD provides a strict-liability regime: defects are governed by Article 7, damage by Article 6 and causation by Article 10(1), with post-market updates, cybersecurity failures and data corruption expressly covered as defects or harm in Articles 7(2)

[23] Jacquemin (2024, 137–139).

and 6(1). The Directive's evidentiary shortcuts—mandatory disclosure under Article 9 and rebuttable presumptions of defect and causation in Article 10(2–4)—then dismantle the information asymmetry that typically shields complex AI systems. Accordingly, the rest of this chapter examines which robo-advisor malfunctions qualify as "defects," how standard distribution models determine who qualifies as "manufacturer," and how the new disclosure rules and presumptions play out in practice.

3.2 *Robo-Advisor as a Product*

To consider the feasibility and scope of including robo-advisors in the product definition under the revised PLD, it is first necessary to identify the distinguishing characteristics that robo-advisors possess in the market. The following argument addresses the question of how robo-advisors differ from other artificial intelligence algorithms, and why it is relevant to consider including them under the product definition. One should emphasise that it is in the broad field of financial services that robo-advisory solutions are most widely developed.[24] The insurance market is at an earlier stage of development in this respect, despite the definite advantages that using this type of software can bring to insurance distributors in the process of concluding insurance contracts, or more broadly, offering insurance products on the market.

At a technical level, five differentiating characteristics of robo-advisors can be identified (an enumeration built on the financial sector): asset universe selection, investor profile identification, asset allocation/portfolio optimisation, monitoring and rebalancing, and performance review and reporting.[25] On insurance grounds, this enumeration can be modified, also indicating five characteristics. One should note, however, that this is only a conceptual layer, designed to simplify the understanding of technology for legal application purposes. The first key process in insurance is risk universe selection, which involves identifying the range of insurance products and coverages available. It is analogous to selecting the asset universe in investment, where the focus is on choosing suitable insurance policies that align with the client's needs and risk exposure. Second, policyholder profile identification: similar to investor profile identification in the financial sector, this step in the insurance sector involves understanding the policyholder's specific needs, risk factors, and coverage preferences.[26] This could include assessing factors such as age, health, lifestyle, asset value, and particular risks the policyholder wants to insure against. Third, policy customisation/underwriting optimisation.[27] This step corresponds to asset allocation/portfolio optimisation in investing. Here, the robo-advisor customises insurance policies to the client's profile, optimising coverage and premiums based on the

[24] See for example Kocianski (2016), Sironi (2016), Ludden, Thompson, Mohsin (2015).

[25] Beketov, Lehmann, Wittke (2018, 356–366).

[26] Webster and Kowalski (2016).

[27] See e.g. Accenture (2022).

policyholder's risk profile and requirements.[28] Fourth, monitoring and adjusting: This involves regularly reviewing the policyholder's situation and the insurance landscape to ensure coverage remains adequate and cost-effective. Changes in the policyholder's life (e.g., purchasing a new home, having a child) or in the broader insurance market may necessitate adjustments to policies. Similarly to the financial sector, the last fifth key process will be performance review and reporting. In the insurance context, a performance review involves assessing how well the insurance coverage meets the policyholder's needs and whether it provides adequate protection. Reporting can include updates on changes in premiums, coverage levels, and any claims that have been made.

A key question, therefore, is how the above characteristics of a robo-advisor interact with the PLD's product definition in Article 4(1), which expressly includes "software" as a product, and with the Directive's definitions of economic operators in Article 4(15), since liability hinges on whether the insurer, a fintech vendor or another intermediary qualifies as a manufacturer, component supplier or distributor.

According to Article 2 of the old Product Liability Directive of 1985,[29] A product means "all movables, except primary agricultural products and game, even if incorporated into another movable or immovable property." This definition draws from the concept of movables, which, as indicated in the literature,[30] is an outdated approach in today's digital economy. Based on this directive, a debate arose regarding the inclusion of software in the product concept.[31] A key case in this regard was the *Krone* case, in which the court ruled that information contained in a newspaper could not be considered a product of the news organisation.[32] The primary premise of this chapter, however, is that this debate is mainly historical. Indeed, the current definition of products, contained in Article 4(1) of the revised PLD, refers directly to software.

The key problem concerning robo-advisors is determining whether this type of code can be considered software in the sense of the revised PLD. Thus, the question of what software is must be answered. The term was probably first used by John W. Tukey,[33] with the sole purpose of distinguishing between a computer program (software) and the machine on which it runs (hardware). The business model of popular robo-advisors is close to that of digital platforms. The issue is further complicated by the fact that Article 4(16) of the revised PLD refers to the definition of a platform as outlined in the DSA. On closer inspection, however, this reference should be considered less critical. This reference primarily elaborates on the issue raised in recital 28 of the PLD, specifically the responsibility of online platforms for the products offered within the platform economy. Thus, this is not a separation of the product

---

[28] See most importantly: EIOPA (2021).

[29] Council Directive 85/374/EEC of 25 July 1985 on the approximation of the laws, regulations and administrative provisions of the Member States concerning liability for defective products.

[30] Wagner (2024, 200–201).

[31] See, notably, Wagner (2022), p. 158.

[32] CJEU, C-65/20, *VI v Krone Verlag*, 10 June 2021, ECLI:EU:C:2021:298, para 29 ff.

[33] Tukey (1958).

(software) category from the platform, but rather a recognition of the platform as one of the entities within the supply chain. In contrast, the following analysis focuses on separating the software issue from the platform. It is also based on the assumption that one should distinguish between robo-advisors and comparison websites, while the latter are limited to identifying the most favourable offer. The scope of robo-advisors' services is much broader.

According to the accepted definition, an online platform is "a digital service that facilitates interactions between two or more distinct but interdependent sets of users (whether firms or individuals) who interact through the service via the Internet".[34] Under EU law, however, a platform should be considered "a hosting service that, at the request of a recipient of the service, stores and disseminates information to the public".[35] The EU definition of software is more difficult to grasp. It appears primarily in the context of intellectual property. Under EU law, the definition of software is closely linked to the concept of a computer program as outlined in Directive 2009/24/EC.[36] According to this directive, a "computer program" is protected by copyright as a literary work within the meaning of the Berne Convention for the Protection of Literary and Artistic Works.[37] The term "computer programs" includes their preparatory design material and applies to the expression of a computer program in any form. Unfortunately, this definition is ineffective in differentiating between platform and software when classifying robo-advisors. International standards are also far from helpful in this regard.[38] This chapter, therefore, refers to the commonly accepted definition of software as "a set of instructions, data or programs used to operate computers and execute specific tasks. It is the opposite of hardware, which describes the physical aspects of a computer".[39] While platforms run on software, they also operate on a specific hardware infrastructure and network resources that enable the software to operate effectively. In the case of robo-advisors, the platform typically includes a user interface, integrated financial databases, security mechanisms, and connectivity with financial institutions. Software is, therefore, only a component of the complex mechanism that is the robo-advisor. However, to determine whether the revised PLD definition is met, it is necessary to consider the relationship between the concept of software and online platforms, as exemplified by the case of robo-advisors.

---

[34] OECD (2019, 18–26).

[35] Article 3(i), Regulation (EU) 2022/2065 of 19 October 2022 on a Single Market for Digital Services (DSA).

[36] Directive 2009/24/EC of 23 April 2009 on the legal protection of computer programs.

[37] Article 1, Directive 2009/24/EC.

[38] In international standards, such as those from the ISO (International Organisation for Standardisation), software is typically discussed in the context of its lifecycle and management processes, rather than being strictly defined. For instance, ISO/IEC 12207 is a standard for software lifecycle processes. It focuses on the processes involved in managing software life cycles but does not prescribe a specific software lifecycle model, development methodology, method, modelling approach, or technique. Instead, it distinguishes between stages and processes within the software lifecycle, outlining various activities and management practices related to software development and maintenance. However, it does not provide a concise definition of software as such.

[39] Hashemi-Pour (2023).

It seems appropriate to say that the key element of a robo-advisor is the algorithm (software/software) behind it. The network infrastructure and updated databases, although essential elements, do not constitute its essence. There is no doubt that, as of today, the product liability regime should cover robo-advisors as they are currently designed.

3.3 Insurance Distributor as a Liable Entity

The model adopted under the revised PLD focuses on the responsibility of so-called economic operators.[40] As defined in Article 4(15), this category includes manufacturers, related service providers, authorised representatives, importers, fulfilment providers, and distributors.[41] It is essential to consider which category an insurance provider implementing robo-advisory solutions will fall into. Equally important, however, is the superimposition of these conceptual categories, as were defined in the draft AILD. It operates on categories borrowed from the AI Act[42]; in particular, reference is made to the provider of an artificial intelligence system and the user of an artificial intelligence system.[43]

The liability mechanism provided for in the revised PLD designates the manufacturer as the primary responsible party, but other entities may also be liable to some extent, "as the manufacturer". In the revised PLD, the liability for product defects is primarily with the manufacturer, as per Article 8(1) of the revised PLD. This includes defects from all sources, whether internal or external. Suppliers are liable for their components under Article 8(1)(b) of the revised PLD, but not for the overall safety of the final product. Quasi-manufacturers, who label products without manufacturing them, and importers into the EU or European Economic Area (EEA), are equally responsible for product safety under Article 8(1)(a)and 8(1)(c) of the revised PLD, respectively. Lastly, merchants and retailers may become liable if the manufacturer is unknown and not disclosed in a timely manner, as outlined in Article 8(3) of the revised PLD. Thus, it is necessary to analyse which category an insurance distributor may fall into. The manufacturer should be considered both the entity that created the product and the entity that designed and manufactured it. Also included in this definition is anyone who markets that product under its name or trademark or who develops, manufactures, or produces a product for its own use, under Article 4(10) of the revised PLD. Relationships between robo-advisor

[40] An interesting case of extension of contractual liability in this fashion is CJEU, case C-149/15, *Wathelet*, 9 November 2016, ECLI:EU:C:2016:840.

[41] Wagner (2024, 212), and the literature cited there, Veldt (2023).

[42] Regulation (EU) 2024/1689 of 13 June 2024 laying down harmonised rules on artificial intelligence (Artificial Intelligence Act).

[43] Wagner (2024, 221–222).

systems and insurance distributors can range from partnerships to stand-alone operations. On the one hand, some companies (e.g., Betterment[44] and Wealthfront[45]) choose to partner with existing robo-advisor platforms, integrating their advanced, algorithm-based advice into their services without having to develop the technology themselves. On the other hand, larger insurance companies with significant resources (e.g., Allianz Global Investors[46]) may establish their robo-advisor systems, allowing for greater control and customisation to their specific product range and customer needs. Another interaction occurs when robo-advisors simply recommend or refer clients to insurance products as part of a broader financial planning service, identifying insurance needs and suggesting products from affiliated or partner insurance distributors (e.g., Ellevest[47]). Often, however, there is no direct relationship between some robo-advisors and insurance distributors, where robo-advisors focus exclusively on investment advice and insurance distributors operate independently, adhering to traditional business models.

Relating the above considerations to the definition of a manufacturer from the revised PLD, one should note that there will be situations in which an insurance distributor will be considered, in effect, a manufacturer. This is because in this situation, the robo-advisor is created within its organisation. However, there are several cases in which the business model is shaped differently—for instance, when large insurers buy technology startups or when off-the-shelf products are purchased directly from the market. It appears that these dilemmas may be resolved by a clause that significantly extends the application of the definition of manufacturer through the trademark mechanism.[48] However, the question of partnerships between technology companies and insurers remains. In such a situation, the robo-advisor functions in the market under the trademark of the technology company. Most often, this company is also the developer of the software. This is a problematic situation in that the robo-advisor in question operates in the market under the trademark of a company with, as a rule, less capital and lower capacity to pay potential claims. In turn, the company with greater assets thus shifts responsibility for the product, from which it indirectly benefits.

Unfortunately, based on the current revised PLD, it is not possible to hold the insurer liable in such a situation, except under general principles such as fault-based liability. For such liability to arise, it is necessary to create some sort of economic beneficiary category, which is, however, very far-fetched, especially when combined with the ease of proof of causation under the revised PLD. To conclude the above thread, an insurance distributor will often be considered a manufacturer of a robo-advisory system. However, there are specific economic ties, collectively referred to as partnerships, that may facilitate liability evasion.

---

[44] See https://www.betterment.com/.

[45] See https://www.wealthfront.com/.

[46] Allianz Global Investors (2017).

[47] See https://www.ellevest.com/.

[48] Regarding trademark as the clue to who should be liable, see: CJEU, case C-264/21, *Keskinäinen Vakuutusyhtiö Fennia v Koninklijke Philips NV*, 7 July 2022, EU:C:2022:536.

One should also determine whether an insurance distributor can be considered "an artificial intelligence system provider" under Article 3(3) of the AI Act or "a user" under Article 3(4) of the AI Act.

Under the AI Act, an artificial intelligence system provider refers to any person or public authority that develops an AI system or has an AI system developed to place it on the market or put it into service under their name or trademark, whether for payment or free of charge. Interestingly, for this argument, there are no far-reaching differences between a supplier under the AI Act and a manufacturer under the revised PLD. The user (deployer) is any person or public authority using an AI system under their authority (control), except where the AI system is used in the course of a personal, non-professional activity. There seems to be a lack of grey areas in this case. Both definitions will apply to robo-advisors depending on the business model chosen. The problematic issue is identifying the responsible party in a business partnership situation; however, as indicated above, it is doubtful whether the liability of an insurance distributor is even a consideration in such a situation.

3.4 Notion of 'Defect' in Robo-Advisors

The basic premise of product defect liability is to determine the reasonable safety expectations that the public may have of the product. The categories indicated are numerous, and one should have regard to Article 7(2)(c) of the revised PLD, according to which the effect on the product of any possibility of further learning after introduction is considered a product defect. Leaving aside the complicated wording of the English version of the directive, the issue at hand is the safety of the artificial intelligence algorithm's learning mechanism itself. In practical terms, this definition places an onus on manufacturers and developers to ensure not only that their products are safe at the point of release but also to monitor and manage the product's performance and safety as it continues to learn and evolve after being deployed in the market. This approach reflects an understanding of the dynamic nature of certain modern products, especially in the technology sector, and the need for a legal framework that can address the unique challenges they present. This also relates, indirectly, to the issue of risk management throughout the life cycle of an artificial intelligence system, added in the Parliament's version, to Article 9(1) of the AI Act.

Interpreting the assumptions of the provision in question, it is necessary to point out several situations in which an artificial intelligence system, such as a robo-advisor, can be considered a defective product under Article 7(2)(c) PLD. First, these are situations in which an error has been made in the algorithm's design, resulting in errors in the results it produces. The most spectacular examples of such behaviour can be observed in the use of artificial intelligence algorithms in the medical or automotive sectors. Still, it is not difficult to imagine a situation where an algorithm provides erroneous advice. Erroneous in this case should be understood as simply contradictory to a reasonable economic calculation or mathematically incorrect. Another key aspect of the defect of such a product is its cybersecurity.[49]

First, AI systems that continuously learn and adapt post-deployment can inadvertently introduce new vulnerabilities. This continuous learning process, while beneficial for adapting to new data and scenarios, can also open up untested pathways in the AI's decision-making processes. These new pathways may not have been thoroughly evaluated for security risks, which could potentially lead to exposure to cyber threats. Moreover, as the AI evolves, it might fail to recognise or adequately defend against newly emerging types of cyber threats, creating a dynamic threat landscape that is challenging to manage. Balancing safety with adaptability is crucial here; overly restrictive safety measures might hinder the AI's ability to adapt effectively, but too much freedom in learning can lead to unanticipated vulnerabilities. Second, as AI systems learn and evolve, they may develop new behaviours or expose previously hidden operational aspects that could be exploited maliciously. This aspect of evolving AI systems poses a unique challenge in cybersecurity. Continuously learning AI systems might require regular updates or patches to address these vulnerabilities, and managing these updates is critical to maintaining security. Additionally, there are AI-specific threats, such as adversarial attacks, where slight alterations to input data can result in incorrect outputs. As the AI's learning algorithm evolves, its susceptibility to such attacks might also change, necessitating ongoing vigilance and adaptation of cybersecurity measures. Lastly, the recognition of the so-called AI bias as a product defect is a very controversial choice. A great deal of literature has been devoted to the issue of AI bias, with more to be expected in the future.[50] However, the horror at the prospect of algorithms deciding the fate of humans, which (like humans) are driven by some hidden beliefs incompatible with accepted ethical and political rules, should not of itself be an argument for recognising AI bias as a product defect. This is especially true if one considers that the system provider will be liable for AI bias under public law, such as the AI Act.

A key issue to consider in this regard is whether AI bias falls within the scope of security for artificial intelligence systems.[51] It is not immediately apparent, but one should recognise that, from a societal perspective, a system that, for example, makes employment decisions, classifies patients, or ultimately proposes or provides access to certain insurance products, can be considered unsafe. The problem here lies in scale. In an individual case, a decision to deny insurance to a person because of their race is not a public safety issue. It is the widespread use of the algorithm that poses such a risk. One should therefore consider that AI bias also constitutes a product defect within the meaning of Article 7(1) of the revised PLD. The current Directive 85/374/EEC limits the manufacturer's liability to the moment the product is placed on

---

[49] Article 7(2)(f)) of the revised PLD; see in particular Article 15 of the AI Act.

[50] See for example Belenguer (2022), Hamilton (2018), Sweeney (2013), Villasenor (2019).

[51] Newton (2023).

the market.[52] The demands of digital trading, the platform economy, and the nature of software as a product necessitate and encourage further developer intervention in the product structure, particularly through updates.[53] For this reason, the EU legislator broadly extends the manufacturer's responsibility. Particularly noteworthy is Article 11(2)(b) PLD, which also considers erroneous or incorrect updating of a device or software to be a product defect. Furthermore, Article 11(2)(c) PLD creates an obligation to correct product security features.[54]

In conclusion, in terms of defects in the product, which, according to the above definition, is a robo-advisor, there are no significant problems with defects in this software. The defects that a robo-advisor may have are not remarkably different from the defects of artificial intelligence systems in general.

3.5 Scope of Protection

Article 6(1) of PLD establishes a catalogue of three compensable heads of damage that applies throughout the Union. First, it covers bodily injury and death, and, still within the same provision, it extends to the loss or destruction of property. Second, it recognises medically certified mental harm as an independent ground of recovery. Third, it adds a novel digital head of loss by treating the loss or corruption of data, provided the data is not used exclusively for professional purposes, as compensable damage. Taken together, these three categories align almost perfectly with how an AI-driven insurance robo-advisor can go wrong, whether by leaving a policyholder physically or financially exposed, inflicting psychological distress through discriminatory outputs, or compromising the personal data that underpins the underwriting process.

Robo-advisors ingest and store large volumes of personal data – Know-Your-Customer files, medical or lifestyle questionnaires, telematics logs and claim histories. If the software malfunctions—for example, a model-drift update corrupts stored disclosures, or a prompt-injection attack deletes underwriting data –the policyholder can claim data damage under Article 6(1)(c). While the General Data Protection Regulation (GDPR) already affords a parallel remedy via its Article 82,[55] the PLD supplies strict liability, sparing the claimant the need to prove fault. Because insurers routinely back up customer files, defendants may argue any loss is reversible; however, "corruption" in the PLD covers not only destruction but also unauthorised alteration that undermines data integrity. Quantum will turn on national rules,

[52] CJEU, case C-52/00, *Commission v French Republic*, 25 April 2002, ECLI:EU:C:2002:252, para 42.

[53] On the liability of platform operator see Twigg-Flesner (2021, 7), Busch (2021).

[54] Wagner (2024, 207–208).

[55] Article 82, Regulation (EU) 2016/679 of the European Parliament and of the Council of 27 April 2016 on the protection of natural persons with regard to the processing of personal data and on the free movement of such data, and repealing Directive 95/46/EC (General Data Protection Regulation).

yet this head of damage is now fully harmonised. Bias in underwriting algorithms rarely produces an immediate hit to tangible property; instead, it tends to manifest as dignitary and psychological harm—anxiety, humiliation, loss of self-esteem. Article 6(1)(a) captures precisely this type of consequence by recognising "medically recognised damage to psychological health". Consider a diabetic applicant who, due to unrepresentative training data, is quoted a 50% higher premium than their peers with identical actuarial risk. If the resulting distress is clinically diagnosed (for instance, as an anxiety disorder), the claimant can recover under the mental-harm head even if no direct economic loss is provable. This route sidesteps the evidentiary impasse that often bedevils bias litigation, since demonstrating psychological injury backed by medical evidence is typically far easier than proving a financial loss.

Where bias or malfunction does translate into quantifiable financial loss—for instance, a higher premium paid over several years or a policy voided on erroneous grounds—the claimant can plead property loss under Article 6(1)(b)PLD. More contentious is the loss of chance: being wrongly denied cover may force an individual to abandon a commercial opportunity (e.g., purchasing a mortgaged property). The PLD does not expressly address lost opportunities, resulting in recoverability that hinges on whether national courts classify the foregone benefit as consequential property damage or pure economic loss; the latter remains within domestic tort law and outside the scope of PLD harmonisation. Practitioners should therefore pair a PLD claim with a national fault-based action where a lost-opportunity argument is central. Although less frequent, bodily harm can arise when a mis-priced or voided policy leaves an insured unexpectedly uninsured at the time of an accident. Where the robo-advisor's defect precipitates a coverage gap that exacerbates physical injury (for example, delaying medical treatment because no health cover is in force), Article 6(1)(a) PLD ensures compensation without the need to prove negligence.

Heads of damage are now fully harmonised. Member States may no longer exclude, for instance, stand-alone mental harm or data loss from strict-liability actions. Variations persist only in procedural law (limitation periods and evidentiary standards) and in the quantification of non-material loss; however, the substantive gateway to recovery remains Union-wide. For robo-advisor disputes, this means that, irrespective of forum, plaintiffs can rely on data damage or medically recognised mental harm to bridge evidentiary gaps where economic loss is elusive.

3.6 Evidence and Presumptions

Article 10 of the revised PLD establishes three distinct presumptions that ease the evidentiary burden on claimants.[56] First, the presumption of defectiveness in Article 10(1–2) arises whenever the manufacturer refuses to supply essential technical information, the product breaches mandatory safety standards, or it malfunctions in a readily observable way. Second, the classic presumption of causation in Article 10(3)

[56] Jacquemin (2024, 133–139).

applies when the harm suffered is precisely the kind that would ordinarily flow from the identified defect. This evidentiary shortcut mirrors the common-law maxim *res ipsa loquitur*. Third, Article 10(4)(a) introduces the "complex-product" shortcut: where the product's technical opacity makes complete proof practically impossible, and it nevertheless appears probable that the product contributed to the damage, the court may presume either defect, causation, or both, shifting the burden of rebuttal to the defendant.

For disputes related to robo-advisors, the revised PLD offers three crucial instances in which evidentiary requirements become more flexible. First, Articles 10(1) and (2) of the revised PLD establish a presumption of defect whenever the manufacturer refuses to hand over relevant technical information, breaches an applicable safety standard, or the product visibly malfunctions—an advantage for claimants who face a proprietary codebase. Second, Article10(3) PLD introduces a presumption of causation if the harm suffered is precisely the sort of loss commonly associated with the defect; a missold policy that stems directly from an algorithmic error is a textbook example. Third, Article 10(4) PLD allows courts to presume either defect, causation, or both where the product is so technically opaque that full proof would be unreasonable. It nevertheless appears probable that the software contributed to the damage, precisely the scenario in which machine-learning models often operate, leaving the insurer to disprove liability.

The revised PLD thus supplies the presumptions that govern strict liability claims for software products, including robo-advisors. Second, any fault-based actions will therefore proceed under national tort law, buttressed, where the algorithm qualifies as a "product", by the PLD's presumptions of defect and causation. Third, even on the user side, the PLD already closes most gaps. Whenever an insurance intermediary modifies or fine-tunes a real-time robo-advisor, Article 8(2) PLD considers an intermediary to be a manufacturer.

4 Conclusion

The examination of robo-advisors within the insurance sector through the lens of the revised Product Liability Directive reveals a complex interplay of technological innovation and regulatory responsiveness. While the PLD represents a step in addressing liability and consumer protection concerns related to AI-driven insurance tools, several substantial issues remain unresolved, reflecting inherent tensions between technology, law, and practical enforceability. The PLD's inclusion of software and AI systems as "products" significantly expands the scope of strict liability, offering consumers and policyholders a more robust legal recourse when harmed by robo-advisor malfunctions. By introducing presumptions of defectiveness and causation, the PLD mitigates informational asymmetries between consumers and sophisticated technology providers. This shift in evidentiary burdens empowers claimants who previously struggled to prove defects or causation due to the opacity of proprietary algorithms.

However, despite these steps, the PLD's definitions remain ambiguous regarding adaptive algorithms whose functionality evolves after-market release. The critical question as to when an adaptive algorithm crosses the threshold from acceptable variability to a legally recognisable 'defectiveness' remains insufficiently addressed. This vagueness creates substantial uncertainty for insurers, fintech vendors, and consumers alike, potentially leading to inconsistent interpretations across member states and subsequent jurisdictional discrepancies. While the PLD now compensates for medically recognised mental distress and data corruption losses traditionally neglected under contractual frameworks, it leaves pure economic losses largely unaddressed. This limitation is significant, given that robo-advisors frequently cause economic harm through mispricing, erroneous policy denials, or biased premium assessments. The absence of explicit provisions for these losses means claimants must still rely on national tort law, which varies considerably across jurisdictions, thereby perpetuating fragmented and unpredictable outcomes.

Another critical area inadequately addressed by the PLD is the allocation of liability within multi-tier vendor arrangements, which are typical of robo-advisory services. Complex supply chains, involving multiple API providers, data aggregators, and technology platforms, pose considerable challenges in precisely identifying who qualifies as the manufacturer or responsible party under the Directive. Although the PLD introduces provisions regarding white labelling and subrogation, practical enforceability remains unclear. Insurers partnering with third-party fintech providers might strategically structure relationships to obscure liability, ultimately complicating the recovery process for harmed consumers and shifting litigation costs without ensuring efficient redress. The withdrawal of the AI Liability Directive further exacerbates these enforcement challenges. The withdrawn Directive would have provided complementary mechanisms, particularly related to accessing proprietary technical information and establishing causation in fault-based claims. Its absence leaves critical gaps that revert to national tort laws, resulting in fragmented and often inadequate protections. The reliance on national law inevitably leads to variations in standards, procedural rules, and compensation frameworks, undermining the goal of harmonisation envisioned by the PLD and the broader EU digital strategy.

Moreover, the Directive's approach may unintentionally disincentivise technological innovation within the insurance industry. By imposing strict liability and broadening the categories of compensable harm without clear boundaries, fintech companies and insurers might perceive heightened litigation risks as overly burdensome. The potential for significant liability exposure could deter insurers and technology vendors from investing in advanced robo-advisory solutions, particularly smaller firms or startups that lack substantial legal resources. Thus, while consumer protection is enhanced, it is necessary to maintain a delicate balance to avoid stifling innovation.

National regulators also play a pivotal role in the practical implementation of these EU-level directives. However, the diversity of regulatory frameworks across Member States poses significant obstacles to achieving the coherent and predictable enforcement envisioned by the PLD. Regulatory arbitrage, wherein businesses exploit differences between jurisdictions to minimise legal and financial exposure, remains a persistent risk. This undermines consumer protection efforts, complicates cross-border litigation, and perpetuates uncertainties in both consumer and business confidence. While the revised PLD undeniably advances consumer protection and clarifies certain aspects of product liability for AI-based robo-advisors, considerable challenges persist. The Directive significantly shifts litigation dynamics by addressing key gaps left open by traditional contractual remedies and national tort laws. Nevertheless, critical issues, including definitional clarity regarding algorithmic defects, the treatment of economic losses, allocation of liability in complex vendor structures, and harmonisation of enforcement, remain inadequately resolved.

References

Accenture (2022) Why AI in insurance claims and underwriting?. Available at https://www.accenture.com/content/dam/accenture/final/accenture-com/document/Accenture-Why-AI-In-Insurance-Claims-And-Underwriting.pdf

Alber DA et al (2025) Medical large language models are vulnerable to data poisoning attacks. Nat Med 31:618–626

Allianz Global Investors (2017) Robo-advisors: early disruptors in private wealth management. Available at https://sg.allianzgi.com/en/insights/artificial-intelligence/robo-advisors-early-disruptors-in-private-wealth-management

Beketov M, Lehmann K, Wittke M (2018) Robo advisors: quantitative methods inside the robots. J Asset Manag 19:365–366

Belenguer L (2022) AI bias: exploring discriminatory algorithmic decision-making models and the application of possible machine-centric solutions adapted from the pharmaceutical industry. AI Ethics 2(4):771–787

Busch C (2021) Rethinking product liability rules for online marketplaces: a comparative perspective. Available at https://ssrn.com/abstract=3784466

European Commission (2022a) Proposal for a directive of the European Parliament and of the Council on adapting non-contractual civil liability rules to artificial intelligence (AI Liability Directive). COM/2022/496 final. Available at https://eur-lex.europa.eu/legal-content/EN/TXT/?uri=celex:52022PC0496

European Commission (2022b) Explanatory memorandum accompanying the proposal for a Directive of the European Parliament and of the Council on liability for defective products, COM(2022) 495 final, Brussels, 28 September 2022. Available at https://eur-lex.europa.eu/legal-content/EN/TXT/HTML/?uri=CELEX:52022PC0495

European Insurance and Occupational Pensions Authority (EIOPA) (2024) Consumer trends report 2024. Available at https://www.eiopa.europa.eu/document/download/4f3b2964-455d-497e-b69f-b5c5939d7aee_en

European Insurance and Occupational Pensions Authority (EIOPA) (2021) Artificial intelligence governance principles: towards ethical and trustworthy artificial intelligence in the European insurance sector. Available at https://www.eiopa.europa.eu/eiopa-publishes-report-artificial-intelligence-governance-principles-2021-06-17_en

European Insurance and Occupational Pensions Authority (EIOPA) Insurance & Reinsurance Stakeholder Group (2023) Advice on consumer trends. IRSG 23/18. Available at https://www.eiopa.europa.eu/document/download/dd725aec-f81b-44d9-9565-80d369f79dc8_en

Financial Conduct Authority (2024) Research Note on bias in supervised machine learning. Available at https://www.fca.org.uk/publication/research-notes/literature-review-bias-in-supervised-machine-learning.pdf

Forbes Advisor (2025) Compare car insurance quotes. Available at https://www.forbes.com/advisor/car-insurance/car-insurance-quotes/
Gallagher Re (2024) Global InsurTech report Q1 2024. Available at https://www.ajg.com/gallagherre/-/media/files/gallagher/gallagherre/news-and-insights/global-insurtech-report-q1-2024.pdf
Groom Publication (2024) Recent lawsuits target health plan premium surcharges based on tobacco use. Available at https://www.groom.com/resources/recent-lawsuits-target-health-plan-premium-surcharges-based-on-tobacco-use/
Hamilton IA (2018) Why it's unsurprising that Amazon's recruitment AI was biased against women. Business Insider. Available at https://www.businessinsider.com/amazon-ai-biased-against-women-no-surprise-sandra-wachter-2018-10
Innobu (2025) Prompt Injection and its Rising Threat to AI Security. Available at https://www.innobu.com/prompt-injection-and-its-rising-threat-to-ai-security/
International Association of Insurance Supervisors (IAIS) (2025) Application Paper on the supervision of artificial intelligence. Available at https://www.iais.org/uploads/2025/07/Application-Paper-on-the-supervision-of-artificial-intelligence.pdf
Jacquemin Z (2024) Product liability directive: disclosure of evidence, the burden of proof and presumptions. J Eur Tort Law 15(2):133–139
Koch BA (2024) Product liability on the way to the digital age. J Eur Tort Law 15:109–125
Kocianski S (2016) The robo-advising report. Business Insider. Available at http://www.businessinsider.in/THE-ROBO-ADVISINGREPORT-Market-forecasts-key-growth-drivers-and-how-automated-asset-management-will-change-the-advisory-industry/articleshow/52669856.cms
Ludden C, Thompson K, Mohsin K (2015) The rise of robo-advice. Accenture Research. Available at https://www.accenture.com/_acnmedia/PDF-2/Accenture-Wealth-ManagementRise-of-Robo-Advice.pdf
McKinsey & Company (2025) The future of AI for the insurance industry. Available at https://www.mckinsey.com/industries/financial-services/our-insights/the-future-of-ai-in-the-insurance-industry
Monetary Authority of Singapore: Cyber risks associated with generative AI. MAS, Singapore (2024) Available at https://www.mas.gov.sg/-/media/mas-media-library/regulation/circulars/trpd/cyber-risks-associated-with-generative-artificial-intelligence.pdf
National Association of Insurance Commissioners (2025) Health Insurance Artificial Intelligence/Machine Learning Survey Results. NAIC Staff Report. Available at https://content.naic.org/sites/default/files/inline-files/NAIC%20AI%20Health%20Survey%20Report%20.pdf
Newton E (2023) 4 unexpected ways AI bias can jeopardise cybersecurity. Cybersecurity magazine. Available at https://cybersecurity-magazine.com/4-unexpected-ways-ai-bias-can-jeopardize-cybersecurity/
New York State Department of Financial Services (2024) Insurance Circular Letter No 7. Use of Artificial Intelligence Systems and External Consumer Data and Information Sources in Insurance Underwriting and Pricing. Available at https://www.dfs.ny.gov/industry-guidance/circular-letters/cl2024-07.
Noussia K (2022) The IDD and its impact on the life insurance industry. In: Marano P (ed) AIDA Europe research series on insurance law and regulation. Springer, Milano, pp 79–95
Oklahoma Insurance Department (2024) Bulletin No. 2024 11. Available at https://www.oid.ok.gov/bulletin-no-2024-11/
Organisation for the Economic Cooperation and Development (OECD) (2019) An introduction to online platforms and their role in the digital transformation. OECD Publishing, Paris
Peters GW et al (2023) Cyber loss model risk translates to premium mispricing. Geneva Pap Risk Insur Issues Practice 48:372–433
Policybazaar (2025) Yamaha YBR insurance price. Available at https://www.policybazaar.com/motor-insurance/two-wheeler-insurance/yamaha-ybr/
Principal Insurance Limited (2025) Pay monthly courier insurance. Available at https://www.principalinsurance.co.uk/product/pay-monthly-courier-insurance

Reuters (2024a) CrowdStrike global outage. Available at https://www.reuters.com/technology/cybersecurity/crowdstrike-update-that-caused-global-outage-likely-skipped-checks-experts-say-2024-07-20/

Reuters (2024b) NY DFS AI cybersecurity guidance. Available at https://www.reuters.com/legal/legalindustry/new-york-department-financial-services-provides-ai-cybersecurity-guidance-what-2024-11-15

Rimkute D (2025) AI liability after the AILD withdrawal. Available at https://blogs.law.ox.ac.uk/oblb/blog-post/2025/04/ai-liability-after-aild-withdrawal-why-eu-law-still-matters

Hashemi-Pour. C (2026) Definition: software. In: TechTarget SearchAppArchitecture. Available at https://www.techtarget.com/searchapparchitecture/definition/software

Salminen J (2020) Towards a genealogy and typology of governance through contract beyond privity. Eur Rev Contract Law 16(1):25–43

Sironi P (2016) FinTech innovation: From Robo Advisorsto Goal Based Investing Gamification. Wiley, Hoboken

Sweeney L (2013) Discrimination in online ad delivery. Commun ACM 56(5):44–54

Swiss Re (2025) An expanded role for AI in life & health predictive underwriting. Available at https://www.swissre.com/reinsurance/insights/ai-predictive-underwriting-life-and-health.html

The House of Insurance (2025) Terms & Conditions. Available at https://thehouseofinsurance.com/terms-conditions/

Tukey JW (1958) The teaching of concrete mathematics. Am Math Monthly 65:1–9

Twigg-Flesner C (2021) Guiding principles for updating the product liability directive for the digital age. Available at https://europeanlawinstitute.eu/fileadmin/user_upload/p_eli/Publications/ELI_Guiding_Principles_for_Updating_the_PLD_for_the_Digital_Age.pdf

Veldt G (2023) The new product liability proposal—fit for the digital age or in need of shaping up? An analysis of the draft product liability directive. J Eur Consum Mark Law 12(1):24–31

Villasenor J (2019) Artificial intelligence and bias: four key challenges. Available at https://www.brookings.edu/blog/techtank/2019/01/03/artificial-intelligence-and-bias-four-key-challenges/.

Wagner G (2024) Next generation EU product liability. J Eur Tort Law 15(2):172–222

Wagner G (2022) Software as a product. In: Lohsse S, Schulze R, Staudenmayer D (eds) Smart products. Bloomsbury, London, pp 157–180

Webster R, Kowalski J (2016) GDPR Deep Dive: Profiling in Insurance. DAC Beachcroft Adviser. Available at https://sites-dacb.vuturevx.com/110/3572/

"Baby, You Can Drive My Car" … and I Will Know Everything About You! Privacy and Data Protection Policies as Remedy to Digital Vulnerability

Alessandra Pera and Sara Rigazio

Abstract As the findings of the DiVE project have showed, we are all vulnerable in the digital domain. Starting from this assumption, the chapter delves into the notion of remedying vulnerability from a human-dignity centred perspective, focusing on data protection rules as one of the most appropriate legal instruments to deal with shortcomings of digital marketplaces. More in particular, the chapter takes inspiration from the 2024 Australian Toyota case. The car company was accused of illegitimately collecting and sharing its customers' data (race, facial expressions, weight, health and genetic information, location) with third parties, such as insurance companies, debt collector agencies, and data collection companies. The case is critical because it sparked a series of investigations into similar cases involving Toyota as well as other car manufacturers around the world, raising questions about the effectiveness of the remedies to protect users' privacy and data. The chapter argues that the legal answer to this should rely on a legal framework that encourages responsible innovation in the AI interactions, fostering the protection of fundamental rights, as recommended by the European Data Protection Board in its Opinion n. 28/2024. In this regard, the chapter embraces the 'Societal Structure Model' for privacy protection, and argues that privacy should be protected not only as an individual interest but also as an entitlement functional to the promotion of societal collective values such as democracy, freedom, transparency, and, most importantly, human dignity. The chapter unpacks

The title of the chapter is referring to the famous song by the Beatles 'Drive My Car'. It is a song primarily written by Paul McCartney, with lyrical contributions from John Lennon, and first released by the Beatles on the British version of the 1965 album Rubber Soul; it also appeared in North America on the Yesterday and Today collection. The upbeat, light-hearted 'Drive My Car' was used as the opening track for both albums. See https://www.thebeatles.com/drive-my-car.
This chapter is the result of a common research and reflection of the two authors. For the purpose of research evaluations only, Alessandra Pera authored Sects. 2 and 3, while Sara Rigazio authored Sects. 4, 5 and 6. Sections 1 and 7 were co-authored.

A. Pera (✉) · S. Rigazio
Department of Political Science and International Relations, University of Palermo, Palermo, Italy
e-mail: alessandra.pera@unipa.it

S. Rigazio
e-mail: sara.rigazio@unipa.it

C. Crea and M. Infantino (eds.), *Remedies to Digital Vulnerability in European Private Law*, https://doi.org/10.1007/978-3-032-19720-7_20

how the different nuances of this model can help understand privacy as a common, public interest and shows the importance of institutions, policy makers, and stakeholders' collective response for promoting and empowering each of us in a healthy and productive interaction with technology.

Keywords Digital vulnerability · Connected cars · Data protection law · Privacy · Human dignity · Societal structure model

1 Introduction

Never has International Privacy Day—celebrated on January 28th each year—taken on such a vivid significance as it does this year: the repeated data breaches worldwide, the use of surveillance technologies, and the interventions by many national privacy authorities, have reminded us that, literally, we are living in a world immersed in the digital dimension and we have to pay a price to live in it. To illustrate with regard to data breaches, suffice it to mention what happened when the website of 23andMe, a US based American personal genomics and biotechnology company. The website was hacked in 2023, exposing genetic data of nearly 7 million people; in 2025, that same data was auctioned off in bankruptcy court.[1] Cases of illegitimate or at least ambiguous surveillance by private actors as well as governmental agencies now happen on a daily basis. On June 28, 2025, the Hungarian government installed and made use of hundreds of surveillance cameras in order to identify the participants to an unauthorised Pride manifestation; the surveillance cameras recorded biometric data of the participants in violation of the European Union (EU) Artificial Intelligence Act.[2] At the same time, independent agencies and privacy authorities have been busier than ever in their attempts to prevent violations of data protection laws. The Italian Data Protection Authority, for example, has led the way in the European child protection context with the Replika cases and, more recently, with the ChatGPT one.[3] Permeating every aspect of our life, technology, more often than not, simplifies many of our daily dynamics. From work up to the aspects of our personal and relational life, at any age,[4] technological tools prove to be not only ubiquitous but able to manage and dictate the times and ways of our habits and, therefore, our choices. Shoshana Zuboff

[1] The legal questions are many, but the common issue is clearly the role of data governance and of policymakers. On the specific topic of genetic information, see Sharma and Gordon (2025).

[2] Regulation (EU) 2024/1689 of the European Parliament and of the Council of 13 June 2024 laying down harmonised rules on artificial intelligence and amending Regulations (EC) No 300/2008, (EU) No 167/2013, (EU) No 168/2013, (EU) 2018/858, (EU) 2018/1139 and (EU) 2019/2144 and Directives 2014/90/EU, (EU) 2016/797 and (EU) 2020/1828.

[3] See https://www.garanteprivacy.it/web/guest/home/docweb/-/docweb-display/docweb/9906258.

[4] This is, for example, what we have previously investigated about smart toys and the use of the so-called AI girlfriend chatbots: see Pera and Rigazio (2024), Pera and Rigazio (2025).

coined the expression "surveillance capitalism" to refer to this systematic and one-sided reduction of the human experience into free-to-use, valuable information—that is, data.[5]

During these past three years, the DiVE project has demonstrated, under multiple perspectives, that we are all vulnerable in the digital dimension: although with different intensity, during different stages of our life—emotionally and biographically –, vulnerability is a constant of our existences.[6] Indeed, beneath the surface of convenience offered by technology, lies a quite troubling reality: most of the digital services are designed to extract and monetize our data with little or no regard for our privacy or autonomy. As it has been noted, this trade-off is a sort of "hidden tax" that, beyond our wallets, impacts the very fabric of our societies.[7]

As Stefano Rodotà reminds us, it is therefore imperative, for every democratic society, to prevent the person from becoming the object of powers that can falsify and construct his or her *persona* according to the needs of a society of surveillance, of social selection or of economic calculation.[8]

In this context, we will see that, even the most mundane, common action such as driving a car can represent a potential and a real threat. This is exactly what happens when a series of options called 'connected car services', such as, for example, geolocation or the ability to view videos from the car's surroundings, which depend on the transfer of data via the Internet, are activated and mismanaged. In this regard, the case of the data breach made by Toyota in Australia in 2024 represents a significant and useful case study, due to the popularity of the company among consumers worldwide and to the substantial share of the market held by the concerned company. The analysis of the modalities in which these services are offered by Toyota (as well as by many other car companies) will serve as a benchmark of the pervasiveness and the ambiguity of privacy policies and, at the same time, will inspire the search for solutions in this chapter.

In this regard, we strongly believe that privacy and data protection should remain at the core of any robust solution to protect and preserve the fundamental value of human dignity, for the benefit of society as a whole. In line with this idea, we argue that privacy following the 'societal structure model' would be a far more effective model than the current one based on privacy as purely an individual right. The 'social

---

[5] Zuboff (2019).

[6] The contributors of the DiVE project analysed the concept of vulnerability in the legal European framework under multiple facets, focussing in particular on groups of vulnerable people minors, elderly, consumers, and patients. Among the many who contributed to the vulnerability debate—besides Albertson Fineman (2009)—, see Mendola and Pera (2022), Malgieri and Niklas (2020), Calo (2017), Nussbaum (2000).

[7] The expression is by Monique Priestley, democratic representative in the Vermont House of Representatives, and an active supporter and proponent of a drastic privacy federal reform in the U.S. See https://vtdigger.org/2025/02/04/rep-monique-priestley-and-caitriona-fitzgerald-why-data-privacy-is-the-key-to-unlocking-affordability.

[8] Rodotà (2014). Rodotà was a pioneer in the study of the 'power of data' at the intersection between law and technology.

structure model' take on privacy, as Rodotà taught us,[9] aims at controlling the power of organizations when collecting and disclosing personal data, and at preventing harm to the entire society, creating a virtuous circle that makes possible a balanced co-existence between the real and digital self of each individual.

Our paper is organized as follows. After briefly outlining what connected car services consist of in Sect. 2, we analyse in Sect. 3 the issue at the heart of the 2024 Australian Toyota case, started in Australia, with particular reference to the type of data collected, used, and shared, and to its forms of management. We will provide useful food for thought in Sect. 4, taking inspiration from the European legal framework. We will look in particular from the European Data Protection Board (EDPB) Opinion No 28, published in December 2024,[10] which emphasized the need for responsible innovation and a human centric use of technology, and from the EDPB 2021 'Guidelines on processing personal data in the context of connected vehicles'.[11] These texts, together with other significant interventions by the EU, will help enlighten the issues at stake that, given the real-time circulation of data across national borders, are truly transnational issues. Section 5 will assess how the effectiveness of this legal framework to protection privacy. On this basis we will argue in Sect. 6 that the rise of AI, as the case of Toyota connected car services clearly shows, vividly calls for the necessity to re-think and to some extent re-invent the traditional paradigm of privacy—to be considered as public good and a public interest, in order to protect fundamental rights, especially when involving the minorities. Section 7 will conclude.

2 Connected Car Services

In order to properly introduce the topic, we need first to address briefly what the connected car services consist of, and how they work. According to a study on connected car services presented in 2015 to the European Commission, a connected car can be described "as a platform that enables the exchange of information between the car and its surroundings, either through local wireless networks or via the internet".[12] In other words, passenger vehicles that come equipped to transmit data about the car and its driver from the vehicle in real time via the Internet to the vehicle manufacturer and/or other businesses.

---

[9] Rodotà (2014). The author argues that each individual is made of these two entities, the latter being the collection of information that literally builds each person's character and personality such as the emotions, the feelings, the memories. The physical and the digital self are naturally connected, but the only way to ensure that the latter does not outweigh the first, is protecting and promoting the principle of dignity.

[10] EDPB (2024).

[11] EDPB (2021).

[12] See European Commission (2015, 5).

Typically, the possible interactions through this connectivity can be identified as: vehicle-to-vehicle (v2v) interactions, such as in the case of cars interacting with other cars; vehicle-to-infrastructure (v2i) or infrastructure-to-vehicle (i2v) interactions, when cars interact with (roadside) infrastructure and vice versa; vehicle-to-device (v2x) interactions, which consist of wireless communication to any device. Even if all these three types of interactions are meaningful in our debate, our considerations focus primarily on the last one.

Connected car services are certainly associated with some benefits. The first and most publicized is safety. Practically every car manufacturer and selling company advance the argument that improving safety is the ultimate goal of connected cars. How? By letting drivers stay fully informed of the current driving situation, thus allowing them to perform tasks such as planning the best route, forecasting traffic jams, and predicting the best time to schedule a trip.

Safety comes with other functions such as the geolocation, the possibility of using the car's camera to view the inside but also the surroundings of the car, the option of locking and unlocking the car automatically without a key by distance. Other features include SOS or emergency calls, remote checking of doors, anti-theft recorder and stolen vehicle tracking, avoidance of obstacles in the trajectory, and assistance with the driving direction through the support of video car's cameras.

On the one hand, when we look at the benefits, it is therefore clear that connected cars collect a goldmine of information that could be useful, for example, to improve any technical issues about the car, allowing data analysts to work on the problem and presumably solve it. On the other hand, we identify a series of potential risks and harms, the most immediate of which is, of course, privacy. Since the entire system works on the data entered, concerns arise on two levels: first of all, on the nature of the information gathered and, secondly, on the way the information is handled.

The first aspect is extremely relevant since information apparently classified as pertaining to the functioning of the vehicle (such as the number of times the brakes were used or the images recorded when parking for safety reasons) is in fact information that can identify people, and can therefore to be used for purposes completely unrelated to the technical functioning of the car. Interestingly, data lies at the core of connected cars' benefits as much as risks.

In relation to the way in which these services work, usually connected cars require the driver/owner to download the car's company app and then use the related connected services. Once the app is set up, data is generally transmitted to the car's manufacturer and/or other businesses or organizations. It is worth noticing that some pieces of information are transmitted directly without any previous consent by the driver/owner. In other cases, information may not be sent, but de-activating some functions may undermine the use of fundamental functions of the car.

3 The Toyota Case(S). My Car, My Data?

In September 2023 the Mozilla Foundation, a U.S. non-profit organization, published a study conducted on several popular car brands,[13] that compared their privacy policies. The researchers concluded that connected cars are "a privacy nightmare on wheels" and "the official worst category for products in privacy".[14]

Among the elements analysed in the report, researchers have considered: the amount of personal data collected (which turned out to be much more than necessary); the sharing of the data (whereby 84% of the car brands sold the data to third parties or shared information with government agencies); the control by the driver about the data (92% of the car brands practically gave the driver no possibility of control).

Right after the publication of this report, consumer concerns started becoming an area of increasing interest worldwide. In Australia, a consumer made headlines when he sought a refund of the deposit paid for his Toyota Hilux model, after discovering how his data was related to the connected services of the car. In particular—and this element is common to all experiences in this matter so far, independently of the country and the legal system where Toyota sold its cars –, he noticed that Toyota (as well as the other companies) collected data such as the vehicle location, the driving behaviour, the recording of voices and images in the car and many others by default, unless the consumer decides to opt out. If a person tried to opt out, though, Toyota was sending a warning that this choice would have disabled many features—including Bluetooth and the speaker functionality—that were probably one of the reasons consumers bought the car in the first place. In this case, Toyota not only refused to give back the refund to the consumer, but also initially told the consumer that de-activating the connected services would put at risk even his insurance.[15] It should be incidentally noted that, also thanks to the data collected, Toyota registered in 2024 the total sum of 32 billion of dollars and in 2025 the trend stays positive in terms of connected cars sold.[16]

In terms of legal background, it should be noted that the main piece of privacy regulation in Australia is the Privacy Act of 1988, which is based on a 'notice and consent' model where broad consent is generally considered lawful. In fact, the consent is often given on vague terms and implied in the contract. To make an example, companies such as Toyota can sell and re-sell data to brokers or insurers as long as this possibility is just mentioned in the privacy policy.[17] Moreover, also in the case of an 'opt-in' function, such as *Drive Pulse* (a Toyota function which uses sensor

---

[13] The report investigated twenty-five car brands, among which Renault, Dacia, tesla, Toyota, Nissan, BMW, Jeep, FIAT, Subaru, and Chrysler.

[14] The report is available at https://www.mozillafoundation.org/en/privacynotincluded/articles/its-official-cars-are-the-worst-product-category-we-have-ever-reviewed-for-privacy/.

[15] About the case, see the reports of the Australian organization CHOICE, that backed up the consumer who first dealt with Toyota, at https://www.choice.com.au/toyotaprivacyinvestigation. See also Kemp (2024).

[16] See https://roadgenius.com/cars/statistics/sales-by-manufacturer/.

[17] Kemp (2024).

data from each trip with a score from 0 to 100, and that intuitively could prejudice the consumer), there is transparency neither about if and when this information will eventually be deleted, nor about whom it could be disclosed to.[18]

As previously mentioned, the case raised concerns and prompted an intense debate around the necessity to reconsider and reform the privacy policies in force in the whole country.[19] The debate forced the Office of the Australian Information Commissioner (OAIC) to ask for a reform of data protection law and to introduce some relevant amendments. Under the Privacy and Other Legislation Amendment Act 2024, adopted in December 2024, individuals have the possibility to sue companies for serious privacy intrusion or misuse of data, and, starting from 2026, companies must disclose in their privacy policies when personal data is used in automated decisions that significantly affect individuals, such as in algorithms or AI systems.[20]

Interestingly, in the U.S., the Attorney General of the state of Texas brought in 2024 an action against General Motors under the allegation of "unlawful collection and sale of over 1.5 million Texans' private driving data to insurance companies without their knowledge or consent".[21] The Attorney claimed that the company literally deceived the customers forcing them to enrol in a program called "OnStar Smart Driver" as if it was an integral part of the vehicle's process of functioning. Moreover, General Motors supposedly also told customers that, failing to enrol, would have caused serious issues in the safety features of the car.

The claim was the object of an investigation promoted also by the Federal Trade Commission (FTC) that concluded General Motors not only did fail to provide consumers with informed consent related to the 'OnStar Smart Driver' app, but also sold the gathered data to some collecting agencies, such as Verisk and LexisNexis, including hundreds of thousands of location data points.[22] As reported by the FTC, this was an "extremely invasive"[23] action. For example, the investigations found that for one consumer GM was able to track all the visits made to a hospital campus during a month, as well as to expose the usual routine of another customer from the usual residence to work, including the precise times and dates of every trip.[24] Both

---

[18] It is no coincidence that this option is no longer available from April 2025. See the official statements by Toyota on the official website at https://support.toyota.com/s/article/What-is-Drive-Pulse-s-10726?language=en_US.

[19] In this respect, see the study conducted by Katharine Kemp of the UNSW Sidney who analysed all the privacy policies in Australia related to connected cars in 2024, and concluded that a privacy reform was absolutely necessary in order to protect all kinds of information—classified as 'vehicle information'—that, according to Kemp, are instead 'personal information'. Kemp (2024).

[20] Privacy and Other Legislation Amendment Act 2024 (Australia).

[21] Hill (2024). Hill is one of the most prominent investigative reporters for the NYTimes who was the first to uncover the dangers related to the company Clearview, that was the leader in the market of facial recognition. She was also the one to uncover the practice behind the app OnStar Smart Driver.

[22] FTC (2025).

[23] FTC (2025), no 36.

[24] FTC (2025), no 37.

the state of Texas and the FTC underlined how the car company betrayed consumers design the services as extracting data by default.

We could continue describing all the failures contained in the Mozilla's report, showing how incredibly pervasive these companies could be to get to the point to collect data related to the sexual activity of the occupants of the car (Nissan) or to their sexual orientation (such as Kia, which openly states it on its official website when discussing the nature of the information that could be shared by the company with third parties).[25] Any statement made by these companies' top management assuring that this information is never used, becomes irrelevant. What is important here is that this type of data is collected in the first place.

What about Europe? Following the Mozilla's report, concerns about cars' connected services spread across European countries. What has to be noted is that the same report underlines that only two brands—Dacia and Renault—were to be considered less worse and more 'privacy oriented' than the others.[26] In our opinion, it is no coincidence that both companies operate and are available only in Europe and, therefore, are subject to the application of the General Data Protection Regulation (GDPR)[27] and to the EU legislation on privacy and data protection more in general.

The next section looks at the relevant European legal framework in order to map the state of the art in relation to connected services and, in particular, to assess how a case like the Toyota one could occur in Europe.

4 The EU Paves the Way

As we have seen, connected car services inherently raise the problem of the increasing process of personal data—including real-time location, driving behaviour, and in-vehicle communications. In the EU, the legal and ethical implications of such processing have become central to discussions about consumer rights, privacy, and digital trust. The main source to look at in this field is undoubtedly the General Data Protection Regulation (GDPR), together with the European Data Protection Board (EDPB)'s guidelines on connected vehicles and responsible innovation. Of course, there is also a role to play for the AI Act; yet we chose to focus this paper on data protection law, because this is more relevant to the topic here discussed, and because of our interest in privacy. Nevertheless, we cannot but mention that the AI Act is inspired by the principle of 'promotion and protection' that attempts to combine technology and fundamental rights.

[25] See the official web site https://www.kia.com/us/en/privacy, about the information the company can collect.

[26] The report is available at https://www.mozillafoundation.org/en/privacynotincluded/articles/its-official-cars-are-the-worst-product-category-we-have-ever-reviewed-for-privacy/.

[27] Regulation (EU) 2016/679 of the European Parliament and of the Council of 27 April 2016 on the protection of natural persons with regard to the processing of personal data and on the free movement of such data, and repealing Directive 95/46/EC (General Data Protection Regulation).

Although a deep analysis of the GDPR is out of the scope of this paper, it is worth recalling that the European regulation adopts a broad definition of personal data under article 4(1). The definition includes any information relating to an identifiable person, which clearly encompasses location data, vehicle usage patterns, and biometric identifiers such as voice or facial recognition.[28] Article 5 of the GDPR sets out the core principles on data protection among which lawfulness, fairness and transparency, data minimization and accountability are certainly significant for our topic.

While the difficulty of applying article 6(1) of the GDPR on explicit consent is recognized in the ambit of automated data flows in vehicles,[29] consent anyway must meet the strict requirements set forth by article 7 GDPR and must be revocable at any time. The aim of the EDPB Guidelines first published in 2020 and finally adopted in 2021 on the specific theme of connected cars was precisely to clarify the application of the GDPR to the processing of personal data in connected vehicles and mobility-related services, offering practical interpretations and compliance strategies for manufacturers, service providers, and other data controllers in the automotive sector.[30]

The EDPB 2021 Guidelines emphasize that modern vehicles process increasing amounts of personal and sometimes sensitive data, including geolocation, driver behaviour, biometric identifiers, vehicle diagnostics, tied to an identifiable driver. Even if some of this data is technical in nature, it becomes personal data when it can be linked to an individual—even indirectly. As the Guidelines state, "[m]ost data associated with connected vehicles will be considered personal data to the extent that it is possible to link it to one or more identifiable individuals".[31] The Guidelines reinforce the concepts of privacy by design and by default,[32] stating that manufacturers and service providers must integrate data protection considerations from the outset of the design process; they should therefore prioritize whenever possible processing data locally within the vehicle rather than transmit data to external servers, minimize data flows, offer consent per feature rather than bundled, and so on and so forth.

In addition, data should be collected and stored only as long as necessary, and at the lowest possible level of granularity. Finally, privacy settings must be easily accessible, modifiable, and understandable via the vehicle's human–machine interface (HMI) or companion app.

Notably, the final version of the Guidelines adopted in 2021 stress user controls and privacy setting much more than the previous draft of 2020, and pays substantial

---

28 Under article 4, no. 1, GDPR, "'personal data' means any information relating to an identified or identifiable natural person ('data subject'); an identifiable natural person is one who can be identified, directly or indirectly, in particular by reference to an identifier such as a name, an identification number, location data, an online identifier or to one or more factors specific to the physical, physiological, genetic, mental, economic, cultural or social identity of that natural person".

29 See, in this respect, Leiser (2024).

30 EDPB (2021).

31 EDPB (2021), para 62.

32 There is a rich literature on this distinction. See for all Ježová (2020), Hustinx (2010), van Dijk, Tanas, Rommetveit, Raab (2018).

attention to optional behavioural contracts like usage-based insurance, for which it requires that an equivalent non usage-based insurance contractis always offered.[33]

A further important point is made with regard to the transmission of data to third parties. As provided for in the guidelines, "only the data controller and the data subject have access to the data generated by a connected vehicle".[34] Nevertheless, "the data controller may transmit personal data to a commercial partner (recipient), to the extent that such transmission lawfully relies on one of the legal bases stated in art. 6 GDPR".[35] The EDPB further recommends that the data subject's consent be obtained before the data are transmitted and not with a pre-ticked box.[36]

Following the extremely rapid and disrupting developments of AI, at the request of the Irish Data Protection Commission (DPC), on December 2024 the EDPB issued under article 64(2) GDPR its Opinion no 28 (hereinafter 'Opinion') to address key uncertainties in relation to some questions connected with the use of AI models.[37] The questions included when and how an AI model can be considered as 'anonymous', how controllers can demonstrate the appropriateness of 'legitimate interest' as a legal basis for data treatment in the development and deployment phases, and what consequences the unlawful processing of personal data in the development phase of an AI model has on the subsequent processing or operation of the AI model.

In the Opinion, the EDPB revisits the classic GDPR three-step assessment for legitimate interest under article 6(1), letter (f), of the GDPR, and applies it to AI use, underlining that data treatment must always be lawful, have a specific interest, must be a necessity and must be balancing.

The Opinion is a landmark because it bridges the GDPR with AI practices. For data protection Supervisory Authorities (SAs) the Opinion offers a series of different instruments to challenge vague privacy claims, enforce model deletion, and require retraining. SAs now have stronger tools to advance technical claims about data safety, identity extraction, and anonymization, and are clearly allowed to intervene at any stage of the AI cycle phase—including its training, deployment, and even after third-party handovers.

Although at present no SAs have so far applied the sanctions provided for in the Opinion, it is worth to note that, shortly before the Opinion's release, the Italian *Garante per la protezione dei dati personali* (the Independent Authority for Privacy and Data Protection) fined OpenAI for the lack of transparency, age verification, lawful basis and legitimate interests of ChatGPT, mirroring in its reasoning the same points highlighted in the EDPB's Opinion.[38]

What the Opinion does is to align AI development with data protection, not changing the law but clarifying how the GDPR applies to fundamental aspects of AI. In this way, the Opinion has a twofold function: it links the AI with the GDPR and at

[33] EDPB (2021), para 77 (Sect. 2.4.1 of the Guidelines) and para 106 (Sect. 3.1.1 of the Guidelines).

[34] EDPB (2021), para 96 (Sect. 2.8 of the Guidelines).

[35] Ibid.

[36] EDPB (2021), para 97 (Sect. 2.8 of the Guidelines).

[37] EDPB (2024).

[38] See https://www.garanteprivacy.it/home/docweb/-/docweb-display/docweb/10085432.

the same time reaffirms the crucial role of the GDPR itself, becoming an authentic roadmap to consumers, stakeholders and institutions.

5 A Toyota Case in Italy? Impossible! Still…

Considering the above, it seems useful to review some of the contractual conditions relating to the use of Connected Services offered by Toyota as set out in the Italian version. The contractual conditions are accessible when a user downloads the 'MyToyota' App and registers by creating a personal account, matching personal data with the data that identify the Toyota vehicle.

The privacy section begins with a strong commitment of the company to follow the law and the importance of data protection: "At Toyota, we are committed to complying with the letter and spirit of the Law and engaging in business activities based on transparency and fairness in order to adopt impeccable business behaviour. We believe that in order to build trust with our Customers and provide reliable connected car services, it is critical to protect your Personal Data and be transparent about how it is handled" (authors' translation).

This is followed by a description of the parties involved in data management and the purposes such data is shared for. Among these, the most notable are certainly the use of the connected services and their updates, the improvement of their quality, advertising and marketing campaigns, and IT protection and support.

In relation to the type of data processed, Toyota includes data relating to the account and therefore to identity, such as contact details, device ID, and information about the authorized device (smart phone or tablet). Toyota also collects data that is used to identify the vehicle, including geolocation; this data is functionally conditional on acceptance of the connected services rather than optional.[39] This is ambiguous to say the least: under article 6(1)(a) of the GDPR, consent must be freely given and unbundled. Yet Toyota embeds it within the activation process, which implies that consent may not be truly voluntary or separable from core services.

In relation to the privacy mode, the MyToyota App allows users to disable GPS. While this effectively permits opting out post hoc, it also highlights that: geolocation is on by default once connected services are enabled; disabling it limits access to key functionalities like remote unlock or SOS, which users may effectively need and may be the reason why they chose the car in the first place. This choice too seems to be at odds with the GDPR, which requires opt-out to be as easy as opt-in.[40] The need to actively seek out privacy mode suggests the default is 'tracking-on'—a questionable design from a data protection standpoint. Under the perspective of 'design thinking', the person who may be the user of a product or a service or the recipient of a decision

[39] "If you activate the Connected Services […] your Personal Data will be processed […] In particular position of the vehicle, driving conditions (e.g. accelerations, braking)" (authors' translation).

[40] EDPB (2020), recital 42.

should be at the centre of the methodology for developing products, services, and processes. Scholars from different disciplines have shown that 'design thinking' can be usefully applied to many diverse areas of interests, including in the legal context and in particular in designing user-centred privacy policies and practices.[41]

In relation to the 'Recipients of Data' policy, Toyota contractual conditions further add that personal data can be shared with Toyota Motor Europe, Toyota Connected Europe, KINTO Italia, dealers, service providers, and third parties for marketing and profiling.[42] In theory, data is shared only when necessary or with explicit consent. Yet, these subscriptions, despite being optional, are practically tied to the Connected Services. This makes them de facto mandatory and arguably in breach of the GDPR, which demands transparency in data collection and explicit, granular consent for sharing data with third parties.[43]

Finally, the major data breach that exposed geolocation data of 2.15 million Toyota vehicles for over 9 years raises questions about compliance integrity, given the scale and duration of the leak. As is well-known, article 32 of the GDPR requires appropriate technical security, and articles 33 and 34 require data controllers and data processors to timely notify data protection authorities of data leaks.

Overall, while an 'Australian style' Toyota case seems highly improbable in Italy, due to the applicability of the GDPR, we cannot help but notice that the structure and the design of consent flows by the Italian branch of Toyota—bundled services, default-on tracking, and functional lockout—contribute to create a framework where consumers' consent cannot be meaningfully refused without losing essential services, where third-party data sharing remains opaque, and where security leaks demonstrate the persistence of technical vulnerabilities that seriously affect user privacy. In this perspective, Toyota's current terms and conditions in Italy are likely to fall short of genuine privacy compliance, especially inasmuch as geolocation, telematics, and third-party sharing are functionally inseparable from the provision of connected services.

6 The Societal Structure Model for Privacy

What we have seen so far shows that current privacy regulation puts a lot of responsibility on individual persons: the GDPR, which is considered one of the most advanced models in privacy regulation in the world,[44] still heavily relies on consent and on data

---

[41] See, e.g., Hendry and Friedman (2021) on the value sensitive design; Introna, Nissenbaum (2000) for the responsible design; for privacy design related issues, see Bygrave (2021), Jasmontaite (2018), Hagan (2017), Cavoukian (2011).

[42] See https://www.toyota.it/e-privacy/destinatari-dei-dati.

[43] See articles 13–14 of the GDPR.

[44] For Solove and Harzgov (2024, 1023), the European privacy regulation is the "crown jewel of data privacy laws".

subjects' rights.[45] The idea behind this choice is to give individuals control over their data. We fully agree that empowerment is an important instrument of democracy and a means of protecting fundamental rights. However, the rise of AI has made it increasingly evident how difficult it is to avoid various levels of nudging techniques that effectively blur the line between influencing and destroying individuals' autonomy in their choices. Examples are numerous and ubiquitous. Consider, for instance, the so-called 'dark patterns' used in video games to essentially 'force' users to purchase additional options through deceptive practices.[46]

The so-called 'Individual Control' model of privacy was born in the 1970s in the United States and rapidly spread through the very well-known mechanism of the 'notice and choice approach', under which companies declared their privacy policies and individuals were free to opt out in case of disagreement. Yet, people more often than not do not read privacy notices, so that the mechanism of notice and choice is completely useless.[47]

In Europe the framework is slightly different since the GDPR requires that consent must be express and affirmative (the so-called opt-in), and provides users with additional rights such as, for example, the right to delete data and the right to be subject to automated decisions.[48] This is certainly a far superior level of protection than the one existing in the US, but still depends very much on the ability of the individual and, as the DiVE project has largely demonstrated through these years, people's vulnerabilities play a major role in the decision process in the digital dimension.

This is why we argue that another way to understand privacy could be more appropriate: the so-called 'Societal Structure' model. This is not a new approach and in fact many academic commentators promoted this approach for a long time.[49] Already in 1987, Simitis was suggesting that "privacy considerations no longer arise out of particular individual problems; rather, they express conflicts affecting everyone".[50] The 'Societal Structure' model of privacy conceptualizes privacy not merely as an individual right or personal preference, but as a relational and institutional construct embedded within broader social, legal, and technological systems. As Reidenberg put it, "society as a whole has an important stake in the contours of the protection of personal information".[51] Schwartz, Gandy, Cohen, Reidenberg, Simitis, and Regan have advocated that privacy must be seen as a societal value, not as merely an individual interest.[52] Other scholars joined and enriched this approach emphasizing how

---

[45] Gillis and Simons (2019).

[46] The leading case in this matter is Fortnite, a popular video game that went under scrutiny by the Federal Trade Commission for deceptive practices (see https://www.ftc.gov/enforcement/refunds/fortnite-refunds). But dark patterns are practically used everywhere. See Leiser (2025).

[47] See articles 17 and 22 GDPR.

[48] Solove (2024). Richards and Hartzog (2019) detail three 'pathologies of consent', which describe defects consent suffers: unwitting consent, coerced consent, and incapacitated consent.

[49] Reidenberg (2002), Allen (2000), Schwartz (1999), Regan (1995), Simitis (1987).

[50] Simitis (1987, 709).

[51] Reidenberg (2002, 1892).

[52] Schwartz (1999), Gandy (2021), Cohen (2000), Reidenberg (2002), Simitis (1987), Regan (1995).

privacy norms and protections are shaped by structural conditions such as power asymmetries, economic incentives, and regulatory environments.

These scholars recognized that individuals often operate within contexts where meaningful consent is constrained by dependencies on digital infrastructure, social participation, or economic necessity. From this perspective, privacy violations are the result not simply of inadequate personal choices, but of systemic design features—such as default settings, platform architectures, and governance regimes—that limit agency and reinforce surveillance logics. Thus, the societal structure model calls for a shift in focus from individual compliance to collective safeguards and institutional accountability, positioning privacy as a public good whose protection requires structural interventions rather than mere formalistic adherence to consent-based mechanisms. From this perspective, the AI Act appears to be more aligned with the societal model, as it prioritises limiting the risks and harms associated with AI. This could set an example for privacy law to follow.

If we look at our Toyota's connected services case, we can see that the societal structure model of privacy provides a more accurate answer and perspective for understanding data practices in contemporary digital ecosystems. Toyota's contractual and technological architecture reveals how structural forces often outweigh genuine user autonomy. The bundling of essential vehicular functions (navigation, remote diagnostics, emergency services) with broad data processing consents—covering geolocation, telematics, and third-party sharing—creates a scenario in which refusal leads to a substantial loss of functionality.

In this context, consent becomes a procedural formality rather than a meaningful exercise of autonomy. The societal structure model aims at reframing this issue: rather than seeing privacy violations as the result of individual failure to manage settings, it exposes the systemic dynamics—such as design defaults, power asymmetries between users and automakers, and the economic incentives to commodify data—that compel disclosure as a condition of access. In this light, Toyota's practices, though arguably aligned with the formal text of the GDPR, fall short of the regulation's normative intent by exploiting structural dependencies and offering users a constrained set of choices.

The Toyota case highlights very well the limits of the consent-centric framework and the need for privacy governance approaches that prioritize structural safeguards, default protections, and collective accountability over individual responsibility alone.

7 In the Name of Dignity

The case of Toyota's Connected Services shows that the mere prospect of regulatory compliance based exclusively on individual consent is insufficient to understand and prevent the breach of data protection and fundamental rights. In this respect, the deeper normative lens of human dignity, as articulated by Stefano Rodotà in his foundational work on law and technology, should be used to develop a methodology for governing the complex relationship between technological innovations and the law.

According to Rodotà, dignity is not a residual or abstract value but a foundational principle that must guide the design and governance of technological systems, particularly in the digital age. He warned that technological innovation—especially when deployed without ethical or institutional restraint—could easily transform individuals into mere objects of data extraction, eroding their autonomy and agency.

In the Toyota case, users are required to surrender geolocation, behavioural, and biometric data as a condition for accessing essential functions of the car, often through opaque interfaces and bundled consent mechanisms that leave little room for meaningful refusal. As we showed, even if formally aligned with the GDPR consent requirements, Toyota's conditions violate the deeper constitutional and ethical principles Rodotà envisioned, namely, the idea that digital architectures should be designed around people rather than the market.

In Rodotà's view, privacy is not simply an individual right, but a social value rooted in dignity, requiring collective and structural protections. This should also be the view of our institutions. Such a model of data governance reflects a technocratic logic that prioritises efficiency and control over personhood by conditioning fundamental digital mobility services on pervasive surveillance. Reclaiming human dignity in such contexts demands a reorientation of legal frameworks: from a logic of permission and compliance to one of limitation and responsibility, where technology serves the individual rather than the other way around.

References

Albertson Fineman M (2009) The vulnerable subject: anchoring equality in the human condition. Yale J Law Fem 20:1–24

Allen AL (2000) Privacy as-data control: conceptual, practical, and moral limits of the paradigm. Connecticut Law Rev 32:861–875

Bygrave LA (2021) Security by design: aspirations and realities in a regulatory context. Oslo Law Rev 8(3):126–177

Calo R (2017) Privacy, vulnerability, and affordance. DePaul Law Rev 66(2):591–604

Cavoukian A (2011) Privacy by design: the 7 foundational principles. Available at https://www.ipc.on.ca/wp-content/uploads/Resources/7foundationalprinciples.pdf

Cohen JE (2000) Examined lives: informational privacy and the subject as object. Stanford Law Rev 52:1373–1437

Crootof R, Kaminski ME, Nicholson Price WII (2023) Humans in the loop. Vanderbilt Law Rev 76:429–510

European Commission (Business Innovation Observatory) (2015) Internet of Things. Connected Cars. 190/PP/ENT/CIP/12/C/N03C01. Available at https://ec.europa.eu/docsroom/documents/13394/attachments/2/translations/en/renditions/native.

European Data Protection Board (EDPB) (2024) Opinion No 28 on certain data protection aspects related to the processing of personal data in the context of AI models. Available at https://www.edpb.europa.eu/our-work-tools/our-documents/opinion-board-art-64/opinion-282024-certain-data-protection-aspects_en.

European Data Protection Board (EDPB) (2021) Guidelines on processing personal data in the context of connected vehicles. Available at https://www.edpb.europa.eu/system/files/2021-03/edpb_guidelines_202001_connected_vehicles_v2.0_adopted_en.pdf

European Data Protection Board (EDPB) (2020) Guidelines 05/2020 on consent under Regulation 2016/679. Available at https://www.edpb.europa.eu/our-work-tools/our-documents/guidelines/guidelines-052020-consent-under-regulation-2016679_en

Federal Trade Commission (2025) Complaint in the matter of general motors LLC, General Motors Holdings LLC, and Onstar LLC, Docket no 242-3052. Available at https://www.ftc.gov/system/files/ftc_gov/pdf/242_3052_-_general_motors_complaint.pdf

Gandy JROD (2021) The panoptic sort: a political economy of personal information, 2nd edn. Oxford University Press, New York

Gillis TB, Simons J (2019) Explanation < Justification: GDPR and the Perils of Privacy. 2 Pennsylvania J Law Innov 2:71–99

Hagan M (2017) Law by design. Available at https://lawbydesign.com

Hendry DG, Friedman B (2021) Value sensitive design as a formative framework. Ethics Inf Technol 23:39–44

Hill K (2024) Your face belongs to us. A tale of AI, a secretive startup, and the end of privacy. Random House Trade Paperbacks, Toronto-Vancouver

Hustinx P (2010) Privacy by design: delivering the promises. Identity Inf Soc 3(2):253–255

Introna LD, Nissenbaum H (2000) Shaping the web: why the politics of search engines matters. Inf Soc 16(3):169–185

Jasmontaite L et al (2018) Data protection by design and by default. Eur Data Protect Law Rev 4(2):168–189

Ježová DJ (2020) Principle of privacy by design and privacy by default. Regional Law Rev 12:127–139

Kemp K (2024) Driving blind: the unexamined privacy risks of connected car. Available at https://papers.ssrn.com/5025836

Leiser MR (2025) Dark patterns, deceptive design, and the law: AI'S hidden influence on our digital experience. Hart, Oxford

Leiser MR (2024) The question of consent in European data protection. In: Costello RÁ, Leiser M (eds) Critical reflections on the EU's data protection regime: GDPR in the machine. Hart, Oxford

Malgieri G, Niklas J (2020) Vulnerable data subjects. Comp Law Secur Rev 37:105415. Available at https://www.sciencedirect.com/science/article/pii/S0267364920300200

Mendola D, Pera A (2022) Vulnerability of refugees: Some reflections on definitions and measurement practices. Int Migr 60(5):108–121

Nussbaum MC (2000) Women and human development. The capabilities approach. Cambridge University Press, Cambridge

Pera A, Rigazio S (2025) Love (?) is in the web: emotional vulnerability and A.I. girlfriend. In: Diurni A, Amodio C (eds) Human Vulnerability in Interaction with AI. Springer, Cham, forthcoming

Pera A, Rigazio S (2024) Let the children play. Smart toys and child vulnerability. In: Crea C, De Franceschi A (eds) The new shapes of digital vulnerability in European private law. Nomos, Baden-Baden, pp 413–438

Regan PM (1995) Legislating privacy: technology, social values, and public policy. University of North Carolina Press, Chapel Hill

Reidenberg JR (2002) Privacy wrongs in search of remedies. Hastings Law J 54:877–898

Richards N, Hartzog W (2019) The pathologies of digital consent. Washington Univ Law Rev 96:1461–1503

Rodotà S (2014) Il diritto di avere diritti. Laterza, Roma-Bari

Schwartz PM (1999) Privacy and democracy in cyberspace. Vand Law Rev 52:1607–1702

Sharma C, Gordon E (2025) Bailing out biometrics. 18 J Tort L 1. Available at https://ssrn.com/abstract=5312386.

Simitis S (1987) Reviewing privacy in an information society. Univ Pennsylvania Law Rev 135:707–746

Solove DJ (2024) Murky consent: an approach to the fictions of consent in privacy law. BU Law Rev 104:593–640

van Dijk N, Tanas A, Rommetveit K, Raab C (2018). Right engineering? The redesign of privacy and personal data protection. Int Rev Law Compar Technol 32(2):230–256
Viljoen S (2021) A relational theory of data governance. Yale Law J 131:573–654
Zuboff S (2019) The age of surveillance capitalism: the fight for a human future at the new frontier of power. Public Affairs, New York

Women's Digital Vulnerability in the Femtech Context: Building Up Gender-Sensitive Remedies on Data Protection

Luana Mathias Souto

Abstract Structural gender inequalities render women vulnerable in the digital domain, and expose them to increased risks of privacy breaches, rights violations, gender violence and digital harassment. The underrepresentation of women in tech development, design, research, and ICT studies further heightens their digital vulnerability. Even the EU General Data Protection Regulation, which is considered a very protective data protection regulation, falls short in effectively safeguarding women's data, as it standardizes the data subject as a white and heterosexual man. Against this context, the chapter aims to critically assess the European data protection framework from a gender-sensitive perspective, recognizing women as vulnerable data subjects in the Femtech context, while acknowledging their participatory capacity in creating protective measures based on their own experiences and narratives to build up gender-sensitive remedies on data protection.

Keywords Femtech · GDPR · Rights protection · Women's digital vulnerability

1 Introduction

The concept of vulnerability has emerged as a critical lens across multiple disciplines, including bioethics, research ethics, psychology, law, and Human–Computer Interaction (HCI). Each field approaches vulnerability from a unique perspective, reflecting its specific concerns and methodologies. In legal scholarship, vulnerability is most commonly associated with consumer protection, where consumer

Funded by the European Union under Agreement No. 101149321. Views and opinions expressed are however those of the author(s) only and do not necessarily reflect those of the European Union or Horizon Europe 2021–2027 /Marie Skłodowska-Curie Actions. Neither the European Union nor the granting authority can be held responsible for them.

L. Mathias Souto (✉)
Gender and ICT Research Group, Universitat Oberta de Catalunya, Barcelona, Spain
e-mail: lmathiass@uoc.edu

C. Crea and M. Infantino (eds.), *Remedies to Digital Vulnerability in European Private Law*, https://doi.org/10.1007/978-3-032-19720-7_21

law scholars have extensively developed its definition in relation to power imbalances between consumers and corporations. In the realm of data protection, however, vulnerability remains an evolving concept.[1] It encompasses issues such as individuals' or groups' capacity to provide meaningful consent, power imbalances between data subjects and data controllers, and the need to protect those at greater risk of harm in the digital environment.

Within the European data protection framework, particularly under the General Data Protection Regulation (GDPR),[2] vulnerability is acknowledged but narrowly defined. The GDPR explicitly recognizes children as vulnerable data subjects, warranting special protections. However, it does not extend this recognition to other groups who may also experience heightened risks in the digital environment due to structural inequalities. The limited scope of the notion of vulnerability recognised by the GDPR has prompted some legal scholars to question whether the current framework adequately addresses the realities of digital vulnerability in a data-driven society.

As Anand and Bird observe, "any discussion on legislation relating to digital services and data management is incomplete without an understanding of vulnerability, and vulnerable individuals".[3] In today's digital age, our identities are no longer confined to the physical world governed by traditional legal standards. Every action we take, every location visited, every search made, every health detail shared, contribute to a growing digital footprint. These fragments of data, from fitness metrics and food orders to financial transactions and menstrual health records, are collected and stored across platforms and jurisdictions. Artificial Intelligence (AI) technologies can aggregate these seemingly unrelated data points into detailed personal profiles, effectively reconstructing our digital identities.

These digital profiles are not merely abstract representations; they are sensitive, identifiable, and deeply personal. They reveal intimate aspects of our lives and, as such, expose individuals to significant risks, including surveillance, profiling, and exploitation. The digital self becomes vulnerable in ways that are not fully addressed by existing legal protections.

The fragmentation of data has led some scholars to argue for a universal notion of digital vulnerability, suggesting that everyone is vulnerable in the digital age. This view however clashes with the current data protection framework, particularly the GDPR, which explicitly recognizes only children as vulnerable data subjects. The contradiction opens the door to a more particularistic understanding of vulnerability, where specific groups, based on race, gender, class, or sexual orientation, can be seen as more vulnerable than average due to the structural inequalities in which they live. Both perspectives stem from a legal interpretation of the data protection framework, and their application ultimately depends on a case-by-case analysis.

---

[1] Notwithstanding some recent attempts to define it: Malgieri (2023).

[2] Regulation (EU) 2016/679 of the European Parliament and of the Council of 27 April 2016 on the protection of natural persons with regard to the processing of personal data and on the free movement of such data, and repealing Directive 95/46/EC (General Data Protection Regulation).

[3] Anand and Bird (2023, 2).

It remains nevertheless true that the lack of explicit recognition of digital vulnerability for individuals and groups facing structural social inequalities exacerbates their exposure to harm in the digital realm. This gap allows for the compounding of rights violations. For example, structural gender inequalities already undermine the rights of women in the analogical world, affecting their ability to give meaningful consent, reinforcing gender power imbalances, and exposing them to risks such as gender-based violence, discrimination, and sexual assault. In the digital space, these violations persist without the traditional safeguards. Applying a generic data subject model to women, therefore, fails to account for their specific vulnerabilities and effectively places them at greater risk.[4]

The rise of Femtech—that is, technology focused on collecting, analyzing, and sharing intimate data about women—further intensifies women's data vulnerability. Women's personal data becomes a target for processing by tech companies, often without regulatory frameworks that acknowledge their unique vulnerabilities. The situation calls for a reevaluation of how vulnerability is conceptualized in data protection law, particularly in light of Luna's theory of 'layers of vulnerability', which emphasizes the dynamic and context-dependent nature of vulnerability. Finally, recognizing women as vulnerable data subjects within the context of the Femtech industry is an essential step to ensure their rights are adequately protected.

On these premises, the paper seeks to address this critical gap by examining how the European data protection framework conceptualizes vulnerability, with a particular focus on women and the Femtech sector. Section 2 explores how the European data protection framework, particularly the GDPR, conceptualizes vulnerable data subjects and highlights the exclusion of women from this category. Based on this finding, Sect. 3 argues for the inclusion of women in vulnerability-aware data protection reasoning, emphasizing how structural gender inequalities render them particularly vulnerable, especially in the context of the growing Femtech industry, which is dedicated to collecting intimate data from women. Finally, Sect. 4 proposes additional measures to develop gender-sensitive data protection remedies that recognize and address women's digital vulnerability in the Femtech context. Section 5 concludes.

2 Vulnerable Data Subjects in the European Data Protection Framework

The concept of a vulnerable data subject within the European data protection framework is primarily derived from article 8 of the GDPR, in conjunction with recitals 38, 58, and 75 relating to the Data Protection Impact Assessments (DPIAs).[5]

---

[4] In this paper context the term 'women' includes people who menstruate, promoting an intersectional debate about this topic.

[5] Karthik (2023).

Article 8 of the GDPR outlines the conditions for a child's consent regarding information society services. If the child is under 16, processing their personal data when offering information society services directly to them (as online platforms do) is only lawful with the consent from a parent or legal guardian. Additionally, recital 38 emphasizes that children need special protection when it comes to their personal data if the data is used for marketing and profiling or collected through services offered directly to them because they may not fully understand the risks and their rights. On the other hand, recital 58 reinforces the principle of transparency, stating that any information directed at children must be presented in clear, plain language that they can easily understand.

However, it is recital 75 of DPIAs that states that children are explicitly considered as vulnerable natural persons in terms of personal data processing. According to this recital, "special protection is required both in cases of limited capacity to give meaningful consent and of higher risks of damages".[6] Therefore, the provisions of GDPR on vulnerability explicitly recognize children as vulnerable data subjects. By contrast, the legislation does "not explicitly extend […] to other vulnerable adults—vulnerability on axes like race, gender, class, and sexual orientation remains relatively under-addressed".[7] Consequently, women are not recognized as vulnerable data subjects under the GDPR, as it is the case in the EU legislation in general.[8]

Women are instead treated under the standard data subject model, which historically reflects a male default. As noted by Malgieri and Fuster, already "the text of the 1995 EU Data Protection Directive refer[red] to the data subject using male pronouns (he/him)"[9] and male imagery to represent data subjects. This standardization, which has been maintained in the GDPR, overlooks structural gender inequalities and power imbalances, assuming that women's rights are adequately protected under a generic legal framework.

Despite advancements in data protection, the standardization of the data subject as a white and heterosexual man can lead to potential vulnerability on women's data. The assumption that this standardization would adequately protect women's rights overlooks how the current legal framework often fails to address women's specific needs. For instance, feminist theory has long examined the concept of 'freely given consent' in a critical perspective. Feminist thought challenges whether true consent is even possible in certain contexts, especially when people lack the power to say no. A 'yes' given under pressure or without real choice is not genuine consent. Consent is not just an individual choice, but is also something shaped by structural dynamics, which under gender power imbalances turns women more vulnerable,[10] especially under the large debate about female consent on feministic criminology.[11]

---

[6] Karthik (2023, 6).

[7] Karthik (2023, 6).

[8] Anand and Bird (2023).

[9] Malgieri and Fuster (2022, 12).

[10] Karthik (2023).

[11] Featherstone, Maturi, Byrnes (2023).

The absence of gender-specific considerations in data protection frameworks forces women to depend on "human epistemic elites, who design, program, and engineer AI systems".[12] Data controllers, who are responsible for assessing data subject vulnerability, often operate within the same structural dynamics that contribute to women's vulnerability. This highlights the importance of recognizing power asymmetries that persist even after consent is formally obtained.[13] Vulnerability, therefore, arises not only from the inability to give free consent, but also from a lack of understanding about the true purposes behind data collection.[14] This is particularly evident in the case of Femtech industry, which will be discussed in more detail in the following section.

The current absence of a legal definition of vulnerability is not helping. There are at least two main theories as to the meaning of the notion of vulnerability. On the one hand, there is a more universalistic take on vulnerability, according to which all individuals are vulnerable in the digital realm. On the other hand, there is also "a particularistic approach that specifies that certain groups of individuals, often classed by social categories, have a higher level of vulnerability".[15] Considering that the debate on what makes someone or a group of people vulnerable and therefore in need of greater data protection is ongoing, this paper will adopt the layered theory of vulnerability developed by Luna, inasmuch as it offers a promising approach in the context of Femtech.

According to Luna, the concept of vulnerability in bioethics and research ethics, where actually the notion was first developed, is based on a fixed 'label' granted to a specific group. Luna however notes that "just labeling women as a vulnerable group is too simplistic and raises problems. Women may not be per se vulnerable or essentially vulnerable, but they might be rendered vulnerable".[16] Based on this criticism, a better proposal is establishing the concept of vulnerability on the idea of 'layers': this means that a particular context or circumstance could trigger someone or some group's vulnerabilities. For example, women may be vulnerable "due to the impossibility to provide free consent, or because they are subject to manipulation, discrimination, physical damages, etc."[17] Therefore, "what qualifies vulnerability is the specific power imbalance between data subjects and controllers considering all specific characteristics and the higher risk of adverse effects for individuals".[18]

Applying Luna's 'layers of vulnerability' to the digital realm, it becomes immediately clear that particular contexts or circumstances could determine women's vulnerability in data protection. Even though the GDPR does not explicitly recognize women as vulnerable data subjects, the specific circumstances surrounding the

[12] Harasimiuk and Braun (2021, 78).

[13] Karthik (2023).

[14] Anand and Bird (2023).

[15] Anand and Bird (2023, 10).

[16] Luna (2009, 122).

[17] Malgieri and Fuster (2022, 6).

[18] Malgieri and Fuster (2022, 6).

collection and use of intimate data in the Femtech context may justify such recognition. Therefore, women using Femtech apps should be considered vulnerable data subjects and afforded special legal protections.

3 Femtech, GDPR, and the Feminist Case for Vulnerability-Aware Data Protection

Structural gender inequalities combined with the underrepresentation of women in tech development, design, research, and ICT studies have contributed to a range of technology-facilitated gender problems. These include heightened risks of privacy breaches,[19] women's rights violations,[20] gender-based violence[21] and digital harassment.[22] Due to inherent structural gender biases in the legal and regulatory frameworks applying to women's data,[23] even the GDPR, which is the most protective data protection regulation that has been so far enacted,[24] fails to adequately safeguard women's data.

More in particular, the GDPR exhibits what scholars refer to as "gender blindness",[25] as it does not explicitly include gender, sex or gender identity in its list of special categories of sensitive data under article 9(1). This omission means that data related to gender is not explicitly protected, despite its potential to lead to discrimination, a key concern for sensitive data protection.

In this context, the rise of a tech industry dedicated exclusively to women's health and well-being, such as the Femtech industry, further increases women's digital vulnerability. Femtech technologies collect and aggregate intimate data, such as menstrual, ovulation, and fertility information, often without adequate safeguards, intensifying surveillance practices. As Siapka and others note, modern technologies have expanded the ways in which women are surveilled, enabling new forms of harassment and control. Women's intimate lives are increasingly exposed to surveillance by both state and private actors, affecting areas such as domestic violence, sexual objectification, and reproductive rights.[26]

Crucially, intimate data collected by Femtech apps is not explicitly covered under the GDPR's special categories. While some argue that this data could fall under 'health data', the GDPR's definition does not include within the notion of 'health data' the category of 'data concerning sex life'.[27] The data collected by fertility apps

[19] Figueroa et al. (2021).

[20] Zou and Schiebinger (2018).

[21] Di Meco and Wilfore (2021).

[22] Di Meco (2023).

[23] Malgieri and Fuster (2022).

[24] Malgieri and Fuster (2022); Siapka et al (2024).

[25] Malgieri and Fuster (2022, 14).

[26] Siapka et al (2024, 111).

[27] Mehrnezhad and Almeida (2021, 4).

(and other technologies) is exactly "a complex combination of health, medical, sex life and lifestyle—which may reveal e.g. religious and political views, or sexual orientation".[28] Also, the data could "reveal biometric and genetic information"[29] impacting on "collective privacy, that is, not only the user's personal privacy, but also that of her/his/their contacts, connections and relations, and the privacy of co-constructed personal information—which is possible through these technologies".[30] As Mehrnezhad and Almeida conclude, there are no "specific data protection regulations set for 'fertility data' when collected and processed beyond health and medical clinics. This ambiguity in the law can lead to undesirable outcomes and cause serious risks to those using these technologies".[31]

Therefore, the combination of the GDPR's gender 'blindness', the existence of an industry dedicated exclusively to collecting women's intimate data, and the lack of specific data protection on data collected by Femtech apps, are all factors that jeopardize even more women's digital rights, requiring extra protective measures. This is particularly concerning in a global context marked by rising gender backlash ideologies, where tech firms from high-income countries can easily influence people and surveil citizens. For example, in the US, mobile data and geo-fencing have been used to target women visiting abortion clinics with anti-abortion ads. Such surveillance can expose sensitive personal information, including names and addresses, to anti-choice groups, putting both patients and providers at risk during vulnerable moments.[32] After the overturn of *Roe v. Wade*[33] by the US Supreme Court,[34] data from Femtech apps could be used as evidence in criminal cases in states where now abortion is illegal.[35]

Given this situation, there is a compelling case, at least in Europe, for recognizing women as vulnerable data subjects who require gender-aware protections under the GDPR. Even when discrimination is not intentional, femtech can still reflect implicit biases or be designed in ways that deceive or exclude.[36] Moreover, beyond feminist critiques of consent and power imbalances between female data subjects and heteronormative data controllers, Femtech apps also raise concerns about non-consensual data sharing with third parties, including employers, intimate partners, or companies engaged in data analytics and targeted advertising.[37] The Flo Health case, investigated by the US Federal Trade Commission (FTC), revealed that

[28] Mehrnezhad and Almeida (2021, 8).

[29] Mehrnezhad and Almeida (2021, 8).

[30] Mehrnezhad and Almeida (2021, 8).

[31] Mehrnezhad and Almeida (2021, 4).

[32] Hammond and Moretti (2023, 12).

[33] *Roe v. Wade*, 410 U.S. 113 (1973).

[34] *Dobbs v. Jackson Women's Health Organization*, 597 U.S. 215 (2022).

[35] Fowler and Ulrich (2023).

[36] Mehrnezhad and Almeida (2021).

[37] Mehrnezhad and Almeida (2021).

from 2016 to 2019, the app shared users' reproductive health data with companies such as Google, Facebook, AppsFlyer, and Flurry without proper consent.[38]

Mehrnezhad and Almeida further argue that Femtech apps have been used to restrict access to reproductive care, particularly when backed by anti-abortion or anti-LGBTQ + ideologies. Some apps have had serious security flaws, exposing users to surveillance and rights violations in contexts where abortion is criminalized, heightening the urgency of protecting intimate data. As the authors note, vulnerability is a multidimensional concept used in fields like bioethics and psychology, and mainly defined by three factors: exposure to harm, susceptibility to damage, and limited capacity to respond. In the context of HCI and fertility tracking technologies, these dimensions manifest themselves as: (i) a high exposure to the risk of harm, due to intrusive data tracking; (ii) a high susceptibility to damage, as the data is sensitive and users often lack confidence in protecting it, and (iii) a low capacity to respond, due to the complexity of data management and lack of accountability. This framework underscores the serious risks posed by the mismanagement of fertility-related data, especially for individuals already facing structural vulnerabilities.[39] It should also be considered that privacy risks are not evenly distributed, meaning that the same technology can have vastly different impacts depending on users' social, political, and economic contexts.

4 Building Gender-Sensitive Remedies on Data Protection in the Femtech Industry

Remaining silent about the data vulnerabilities women face in the Femtech industry contributes to their exposure to tech surveillance, bodily alienation,[40] algorithmic behavior manipulation, and other reported rights violations. These include technological gender bias,[41] enforcement of gender binary stereotypes,[42] unwanted pregnancies,[43] and inaccurate predictions for ovulation and fertile windows.[44] Recognizing women as vulnerable data subjects within the Femtech context would be a vital step toward protecting their rights in the digital age. However, this recognition must be accompanied by concrete measures to foster a more gender-sensitive digital environment.

To begin, it is essential to acknowledge the structural gender inequalities embedded in the digital and technological fields. As scholars who contribute to building a Data Feminism theory, such as D'Ignazio and Klein, have noted, "if you

[38] Federal Trade Commission (2021).

[39] Mehrnezhad and Almeida (2021).

[40] Lupton (2017).

[41] Hammond and Moretti (2023).

[42] Lupton (2014).

[43] Fowler and Ulrich (2023).

[44] Worsfold, Marriott, Johnson, Harper (2021).

are concerned with justice in data communication, or data science more generally, we suggest that you practice recognizing, naming, and talking about these structural forces of oppression".[45]

Women remain underrepresented in the design of reproductive technologies. This, combined with the historical exclusion of female bodies from clinical trials[46] and the default use of the male body as the standard in medical research,[47] undermine women's reproductive autonomy and increase their social vulnerability.

Structural gender biases also persist in legal and regulatory frameworks. For example, as said above in Sect. 3, the GDPR has been criticized for its gender-blindness. A legal framework that fails to recognize gendered power imbalances cannot effectively protect women's rights. Only after the acknowledgement of women as vulnerable data subjects by the Femtech industry, women's data protection could move from theory to meaningful practice.

It is equally important to center women's voices in the creation of protective measures. Women must be active participants in the design and development of technologies that affect them. As Karthik puts it, "subverting power dynamics requires data subjects to be central participants in the design and technological process from the beginning, rather than 'where appropriate'".[48] A gender-sensitive and participatory review of medical proposals, which also embodies intersectional debates, should be embedded in the EU's data protection framework. This is especially urgent given the rise of Femtech. Such a framework should include the development of legal concepts that are more attuned to gender-specific data protection needs and violations. Creating gender-sensitive and intersectional legislative and regulatory procedures through participatory procedures would also promote women's digital empowerment reducing their gap in technological education.

A gender-sensitive approach must also recognize the collective nature of women's data vulnerabilities. Gender-based data violations often affect women not just as individuals, but as a group. These harms occur "not through the infringement upon individual rights to privacy but through the aggregate of subjects in ways that allow for prediction, preemption, and the management of options and choices for individuals".[49] This includes the work of "data protection agencies [that] can also help provide recommendations on data processing for vulnerable groups".[50]

Implementing these reforms within the EU would be a crucial first step in ensuring women's safety in digital environments. Ideally, through the 'Brussels Effect',[51] other legal systems may then adopt similar gender-sensitive standards for data protection, so that women's intimate data could be better protected even in the context of cross-border data flows.

---

[45] D'Ignazio and Klein (2020).

[46] Mishra and Suresh (2021).

[47] Thaler (2022).

[48] Karthik (2023, 8).

[49] Weinberg (2017, 16).

[50] Karthik (2023, 8).

[51] Cervi (2022).

5 Conclusion

The digital age has ushered in unprecedented opportunities for innovation, connectivity, and empowerment. Yet, it has also introduced new forms of vulnerability, particularly for women navigating digital environments shaped by structural inequalities. This paper has critically examined the concept of digital vulnerability within the European data protection framework, with a specific focus on the Femtech industry. It has argued that the current legal and regulatory structures, especially the GDPR, fall short in recognizing and addressing the unique vulnerabilities faced by women in digital spaces. As such, there is an urgent need to reimagine data protection through a gender-sensitive lens that acknowledges the layered and context-dependent nature of vulnerability.

At the heart of this analysis lies the recognition that the GDPR, while heralded as a gold standard in data protection, is inherently limited in its scope of vulnerability. Its explicit recognition of children as vulnerable data subjects is commendable, but its failure to extend similar protections to other structurally marginalized groups, particularly women, reveals a significant gap. This omission is not merely a technical oversight; it reflects deeper systemic biases embedded in legal and technological systems that continue to privilege a default male subject. By treating all data subjects as equal in theory, the GDPR inadvertently perpetuates inequality in practice.

The rise of Femtech has brought these issues into sharp relief. These technologies collect deeply intimate data, including menstrual cycles, fertility windows, sexual activity, and even emotional states. However, the legal protections surrounding this data are ambiguous at best and dangerously inadequate at worst. The GDPR's failure to explicitly categorize gender, sex, or reproductive data as sensitive under article 9(1) leaves a significant portion of women's digital lives exposed to surveillance, exploitation, and misuse.

Moreover, the Femtech industry operates within a broader context of gendered power imbalances. Women remain underrepresented in the design, development, and governance of digital technologies, including in a tech industry designed to monitor, track, and manage aspects of women's reproductive health. This lack of representation not only limits the inclusivity of technological innovation, but also reinforces existing biases in data collection, algorithmic decision-making, and regulatory oversight. As a result, women are often rendered passive subjects of data extraction rather than active participants in shaping the digital tools that affect their lives.

Luna's theory of layers of vulnerability, as explored in this paper, offers a powerful framework for addressing these challenges, arguing that vulnerability should not be seen as a fixed label but as a dynamic condition shaped by context, power relations, and structural inequalities. In the case of Femtech, women's vulnerability arises not from legal incapacity but from the intersection of gendered social norms, opaque data practices, and insufficient legal safeguards. Recognizing this layered vulnerability is essential for developing more responsive and equitable data protection measures.

Importantly, the paper also emphasized the need for participatory and intersectional approaches to data governance. Women must be included not only as beneficiaries of legal protections, but as co-creators of the rules and technologies that govern their data. This requires a fundamental shift in how data protection is conceptualized and implemented. Legal frameworks must move beyond abstract notions of consent and neutrality to engage with the lived realities of those most affected by digital harms. This includes acknowledging the collective dimensions of data vulnerability, where harms extend beyond individual users to affect entire communities and social groups.

To this end, the paper has proposed a series of gender-sensitive remedies aimed at enhancing data protection for women in the Femtech context. These include the legal recognition of gendered vulnerability, grounded in an understanding of structural inequalities and power imbalances, and the expansion of sensitive data categories, through an amendment of article 9(1) of the GDPR that would include gender, sex, and reproductive health data as special categories requiring heightened protection. This would ensure that data collected by Femtech apps is subject to stricter processing conditions and oversight.

Moreover, women should be actively involved in the design, development, and regulation of Femtech technologies through participatory review boards, conducting gender impact assessments, and promoting inclusive innovation practices. This participatory design and governance should also account for the intersecting identities and experiences of women and transgender people, and take adequate account of race, class, sexuality, and disability. Intersectionality should be a guiding principle in both legal interpretation and technological design.

In addition, data protection authorities should strengthen their regulatory oversight to issue guidelines, conduct audits, and impose sanctions on companies that fail to protect women's data adequately. This includes addressing issues such as non-consensual data sharing, algorithmic bias, and discriminatory profiling. All these efforts should be constructed to enhance women's digital literacy and agency, enabling them to make informed decisions about their data. This includes educational initiatives, transparency tools, and user-friendly consent mechanisms.

Ultimately, the protection of women's digital rights is not merely a matter of legal compliance; it is a question of justice, dignity, and autonomy. As digital technologies continue to permeate every aspect of life, the stakes of inaction grow ever higher. Without deliberate and inclusive reforms, the digital realm risks becoming yet another site of gendered oppression and exclusion. Therefore, establishing robust, gender-sensitive data protection safeguards is a crucial first step in resisting the digital subjugation of women, which often manifests through discriminatory procedures, surveillance practices and threats against fundamental rights and democratic values. A meaningful data protection framework must be grounded in an understanding of vulnerability that is both context-sensitive and structurally aware, centering women's experiences and voices, and challenging the gender-blind assumptions of existing legal frameworks to build a more just and equitable digital future.

References

Anand R, Bird B (2023) The digital services act and vulnerability: how vulnerability is defined by digital regulations in the EU. Available at https://doi.org/10.34961/researchrepository-ul.24064260.v1h

Cervi GV (2022) Why and how does the EU rule global digital policy: an empirical analysis of EU regulatory influence in data protection laws. DISO 1:18. https://doi.org/10.1007/s44206-022-00005-3

D'Ignazio C, Klein LF (2020) Data feminism. MIT Press, Boston

Di Meco L (2023) 'Gender trolling' is curbing women's rights—and making money for digital platforms. The Guardian. Available at https://www.theguardian.com/global-development/2023/feb/17/gender-trolling-women-rights-money-digital-platforms-social-media-hate-politics

Di Meco L, Wilfore K (2021) Gendered disinformation is a national security problem. Available at https://www.brookings.edu/articles/gendered-disinformation-is-a-national-security-problem/

Featherstone L, Maturi J, Byrnes C (2023) Consent: feminist approaches to sexual agency and sexual violence. Aust Fem Stud 38(118):373–382

Federal Trade Commission (2021) Flo health, Inc. Available at https://www.ftc.gov/legal-library/browse/cases-proceedings/192-3133-flo-health-inc

Figueroa CA et al (2021) The need for feminist intersectionality in digital health. Lancet Digit Health 3(8):52–53

Fowler L, Ulrich M (2023) Femtechnodystopia. Stanford Law Review 75(6):1233–1313

Hammond N, Moretti A (2023) Data like any other? Sexual and reproductive health, big data and the sustainable development goals. Sexualities 27(7):1277–1300

Harasimiuk DE, Braun T (2021) Regulating artificial intelligence: binary ethics and the law. Routledge, New York

Karthik A (2023) Reimagining the data subject in GDPR. GRACE: Glob Rev AI Community Ethics 1(1):11

Luna F (2009) Elucidating the concept of vulnerability: layers not labels. Int J Feminist Approaches Bioethics 2(1):121–139

Lupton D (2017) Feeling your data: touch and making sense of personal digital data. New Media Soc 9(10):1599–1614

Lupton D (2014) Quantified sex: a critical analysis of sexual and reproductive self-tracking using apps. Cult Health Sex 17(4):440–453

Malgieri G (2023) Vulnerability and data protection law. Oxford University Press, Oxford

Malgieri G, Gonzalez Fuster G (2022) The vulnerable data subject: a gendered data subject? Eur J Law Technol 13(2):1–26

Mehrnezhad M, Almeida T (2021) Caring for intimate data in fertility technologies. In: CHI Conference on Human Factors in Computing Systems (CHI'21), May 8–13, 2021, Yokohama, Japan. ACM, New York. https://doi.org/10.1145/3411764.344513.

Mishra P, Suresh Y (2021) Datafied body projects in India: femtech and the rise of reproductive surveillance in the digital era. Asian J Women's Stud 27(4):597–606

Siapka A, Tzanou M, Nelson A (2024) Re-imagining data protection: femtech and gendered risks in the GDPR. In: Costello RÁ, Leiser M (eds) Critical reflections on the EU's data protection regime: GDPR in the machine. Hart, Oxford

Thaler A (2022) Saving lives with gender studies? Putting technofeminism into practice. In: Pereira ET, Costa C, Breda Z (eds) Proceedings of the 4th International Conference on Gender Research. Aveiro, ICGR. Available at https://doi.org/10.34190/icgr.5.1.210

Weinberg L (2017) Rethinking privacy: a feminist approach to privacy rights after Snowden. Westminster Pap Commun Cult 12(3):5–20

Worsfold L, Marriott L, Johnson S, Harper JC (2021) Period tracker applications: what menstrual cycle information are they giving women? Women's Health. https://doi.org/10.1177/17455065211049905

Zou J, Schiebinger L (2018) AI can be sexist and racist—it's time to make it fair. Nature 559:324–326. https://doi.org/10.1038/d41586-018-05707-8

Remedying Vulnerability Affecting Patients' Consent: The Case of Patients Undergoing Cardiac Electronic Device Implantation

Hélène Guiziou

Abstract This study explores the heightened vulnerability of patients undergoing cardiac electronic device implantation, focusing on their capacity to give informed consent. These devices, embedded within complex digital ecosystems, expose patients to cybersecurity, data privacy, and medical autonomy risks. Legal frameworks, notably the General Data Protection Regulation and French health law, offer some protection, yet fail to fully address the opacity of information and asymmetry in physician–patient relations. The paper argues for enhanced transparency, informed multi-party consent, and stronger ex ante and ex post protections. In an era of digital medicine, safeguarding patients' rights and bodily integrity is essential to maintaining trust and ethical care.

Keywords Cardiac electronic devices · Internet of things · Health law · Data protection law · Consent · Vulnerability

1 Introduction

"I do not wish to scare anyone, but you know perfectly well that all syringe pumps, pacemakers, defibrillators are devices that can be hacked", allowing a "foreign power [to] take control of them".[1] In April 2025, the Senate's Social Affairs Commission auditioned the French Minister of Health and Access to Care, Yannick Neuder. When presenting his roadmap for the upcoming months, the recently appointed Minister emphasized the need for Government investment in the cybersecurity of medical devices and facilities. In doing so, he revealed for the first time what appears to be a significant safety issue, despite it being completely absent from French debates until now.

[1] Neuder Y, quoted by Vignal (2025).

H. Guiziou (✉)
Université CY Cergy, Paris, France
e-mail: helene.guiziou@cyu.fr

C. Crea and M. Infantino (eds.), *Remedies to Digital Vulnerability in European Private Law*, https://doi.org/10.1007/978-3-032-19720-7_22

The beginning of the second millennium has brought tremendous innovations in the follow-up of patients with serious cardiac conditions. The advent of the Internet, along with the development of the Bluetooth technology, have added a new dimension to cardiology, giving rise to telecardiology. This major evolution is just one example of the emergence of tele-healthcare, probably the most decisive change this century has brought. Insulin pumps, syringe pumps and even connected artificial legs or arms are increasingly implanted in patients, in order to provide constant monitoring and personalized adjustments. Even though this chapter focuses on patients' consent for the implantation of connected cardiac devices, the views and reflections expressed could largely be extended to the situations of patients undergoing the implantation of other kinds of devices.

Before exploring the legal issues patients face, a few words should be said about implantable connected cardiac devices. Three types of devices can be distinguished, in ascending order of sophistication. An Implantable Loop Recorder (ILR) can be implanted in less severe situations. Patients suffering from short and unexplained syncope can be implanted with such a device. It is the most basic type of cardiac device, as it only enables recording. An ILR provides the cardiologist with precise and comprehensive data, to help them explore the context of the syncope and identify its cause. Patients with bradycardia or certain types of heart failure can then be implanted with an Implantable Cardiac Pacemaker (ICP). This is the most well-known type of cardiac device. Similar to the ILR, it constantly collects data and even records heartbeats. Depending on patients' conditions, one, two or three wires are connected to the heart chambers in order to produce electric pulses that stimulate the heart or to resynchronize its chambers' contractions. Patients with heart failure or severe heart disease are at risk of life-threatening arrhythmia. In such cases, an Implantable Cardioverter Defibrillator (ICD) can prevent cardiac arrest by delivering a shock. Furthermore, as this defibrillation feature is added to a pacemaker, the patients' heart is monitored and stimulated simultaneously.

All these Cardiac Implantable Electronic Devices (CIEDs) belong to Internet of Things (IoT) or the Internet of Medical Things (IoMT). The increased use of these devices raises major questions about the nature and the extent of patients' consent. While patients used to give their consent to a medical act, in a face-to-face relationship with their cardiologist, the implantation of a CIED henceforth creates long-term and multilateral interactions, with non-medical actors. Moreover, patients are vulnerable, due to the seriousness of their condition and the complexity of the entire process, from implantation to data processing and settings adjustments.

How, then, can the vulnerability of patients undergoing cardiac electronic device implantation be remedied? Addressing such an issue requires, first of all, describing and explaining the context of CIED implantation and exploitation (Sect. 2). Considering the new risks to which patients are exposed, remedying their vulnerability necessitates protecting patients both *ex ante*, immediately before and at the moment they express their consent (Sect. 3), and *ex post*, facilitating compensation or sanction when problems occur (Sect. 4).

2 Context

When patients are implanted with CIEDs, they become part of a rather complex system involving actors they sometimes are not precisely aware of. CIEDs are produced by medical devices manufacturers, such as Medtronic, Boston Scientific and Abbott. Thanks to multiple sensors associated with various algorithms, a CIED collects all sorts of information such as heartbeat, respiratory rate and physical activity level, as well as cardiograms, heart sound recordings and temperature readings. Through a Bluetooth connection, the device can safely and quickly transmit this data to a home monitor, supplied by the manufacturer and usually placed in patients' bedroom. This transmission can be automatic, pre-planned by a physician, or initiated voluntarily by the patient. The home monitor then immediately sends the data to the remote monitoring software platform's servers, via the mobile telephone network or the Internet. In our example, it is transmitted to Implicity, a French digital MedTech software company, specializing in the remote care of patients implanted with cardiac devices. This company has been thriving by providing cardiologists and patients with a single data environment. Implicity stores, aggregates and uses the data of around 100,000 European patients, implanted with devices manufactured by various companies.[2]

The situation is becoming more complex due to the involvement of a subcontractor. Although Implicity is a software solution provider, the data is actually hosted by another company. The Implicity platform analyses this data (using algorithms and AI) and displays comprehensive results to physicians or care units via the Internet. Physicians or the care units can thus potentially download the data. Furthermore, the cardiologist usually enriches the data available to Implicity by adding information relating to the patients' health conditions.

Only one step in this process still requires a face-to-face encounter between patients and cardiologists. To change the settings of the various CIED algorithms, the cardiologist uses a programmer, supplied by the manufacturer. Similar to the home monitor, it connects to the device via Bluetooth to receive data and to adjust settings.

2.1 *Patient Vulnerability Factors*

As will be discussed hereunder, the above infrastructure makes patients vulnerable for several reasons. First and quite obviously, the patients' health condition is a key vulnerability factor. Implantation of a cardiac device is always recommended when patients' conditions are serious enough to require a constant monitoring. A defibrillator is particularly indicated for patients whose heart condition poses a high risk of cardiac arrest. Consequently, in many situations, defibrillators are implanted in an emergency context. Under these circumstances, while patients may be weakened physically and psychologically, they are still able to give an informed consent.

---

[2] See https://implicity.com.

Patients' vulnerability stems from the complexity of the medical act to which they consent. Patients have to consent not only to a medical operation, but also to the long-term monitoring of their heart. While patients are in a room alone with their physician, other companies with which they have no contact are also involved in the operation, which is very complex from both the medical and the technical point of view.

It should be further added that, even if medical relationships are supposed to be based on trust and governed by ethical principles, the relationship between cardiologists and their patients tends to be highly asymmetrical. This probably stems less from their unequal knowledge than from the fact that patients' health and life depend on physicians. Patients may not feel free to refuse to give their consent to a treatment recommended by physicians or to ask questions about data processing. They may fear that questioning the treatment plan might bother doctors or be perceived as a lack of trust. Cardiologists are supposed to offer their patients the choice of remote monitoring or a more traditional treatment, the latter of which does not involve data processing. In practice, however, doctors often do not present it as a second-choice option.

Moreover, as will be discussed in more detail below, it is ambiguous and paradoxical to expect cardiologists, who are the only actor able to collect data without the patients' consent, to obtain patients' consent on behalf of the companies involved in the data collection and processing. Patients may feel warier and freer to give (or refuse to give) consent when dealing with private companies that provide data collection and treatment solutions than when dealing with a cardiologist. Patients at risk of sudden cardiac arrest who depend on a technical solution involving data processing can likely be regarded as 'vulnerable natural persons' according to recital 75 of the General Data Protection Regulation (GDPR).[3]

How can patients' vulnerability be remedied in this rather complex ecosystem? As we are about to see, patients should be protected *ex post* but also *ex ante*—that is, immediately prior to giving their consent.

3 Protecting the Patient *Ex Ante*

Vulnerability specifically affects patients' ability to consent to a medical act and, in this case, to data processing. But is the consent of patients who get implanted with a CIED even required for the collection and processing of their data? As surprising as it may seem, this question does not appear to have a very sharp and clear answer.

[3] Regulation (EU) 2016/679 of the European Parliament and of the Council of 27 April 2016 on the protection of natural persons with regard to the processing of personal data and on the free movement of such data, and repealing Directive 95/46/EC (GDPR).

3.1 Need for Consent

'Data concerning health' is considered as a special category of data under article 9(1) of the GDPR. Therefore, processing of this category of 'sensitive data' is prohibited, except in the situations listed in article 9(2). Two of the exceptions that justify the processing of sensitive data could be relevant in this case. First, article 9(2)(a) states that processing may be permitted if "the data subject has given explicit consent to the processing of those personal data for one or more specified purposes". Article 9(2)(h) then opens up the possibility of processing data without patients' consent when this is "necessary for the purposes of preventive or occupational medicine [...], medical diagnosis, the provision of health or social care or treatment". Article 9(3) adds that this processing is only permitted "when those data are by or under the responsibility of a professional subject to the obligation of professional secrecy". According to the provisions of the GDPR, it therefore appears that the possibility to process data under article 9(2)(h) GDPR is only granted to cardiologists. In other words, there is no legal basis for med-tech companies to be permitted to process data concerning health without gathering an explicit consent. French national law confirms these provisions, in almost identical terms.[4]

In practice, however, it appears that patients' consent is obtained. The paradox of the situation can be observed in Implicity's 'Patient Information Note V1.112'.[5] This note explicitly refers to the grounds set forth in articles 6(1)(b) and 9(2)(h) GDPR for processing data concerning health for the purposes of patients' medical follow-up and the monitoring of the technical solution. In doing so, the designated data controllers—the cardiologist, the device manufacturer and the technical solution provider—are openly admitting that their processing is not based on patients' consent, which is not required in such a medical context. Surprisingly, however, this note is accompanied by a consent form, written in quite long and precise wording. In the consent form, patients are invited to "agree to the remote monitoring of the electronic device [...] and the therapeutic assistance"[6] and certify they "understand that the remote monitoring [...] involves the processing of [their] personal data in accordance with the Regulation and under the conditions described in the attached information note".[7] Therefore, even though the information note states that their data are processed on the ground of articles 6(1)(b) and 9 (2)(h) GDPR, patients are asked to express their explicit consent to the data collection and treatment.

This practice is in line with several legal advice or recommendations. In 2018, the *Commission Nationale de l'Informatique et des Libertés* (CNIL)—the French national agency that regulates data processing—authorized Implicity, the med-tech that provides the technical solution, to carry out automated processing of data for the purpose of implementing remote monitoring, but stated that patients' written

---

[4] See article 44.1, Law no. 78-17, 6 January 1978.

[5] Implicity (2025).

[6] Implicity (2025, 4).

[7] Implicity (2025, 4).

consent had to be collected.[8] From this perspective, it can therefore be held that French national law is more demanding than the GDPR, which only values written consent as a convenient form of proof.[9] Furthermore, a 2010 decree that sets out rules for the medical remote monitoring activities specifies that patients must consent to telemedicine; their consent must be free and informed, and they must be duly informed.[10] This extends to remote monitoring and to personal data processing. These elements seem to confirm the ambiguity of the legal basis for data processing in this case and the common practice of obtaining consent. Requiring written consent is clearly intended to protect the interests of the data controllers. However, it paves the way for uncertainty. For example, will patients be entitled to complain that they were not properly informed and that their consent was not informed when the information note refers to provisions that exempt at least one of the controllers from their duty to seek consent, and consequently to inform?

3.2 *Patients' Consent(s)*

The implantation of a CIED is inseparable from the data processing it enables. Therefore, it can be difficult to determine the scope of the patients' consent. Can several consents be isolated or should a single consent be given for the entire medical act? Despite existing practice, the GDPR makes clear that cardiologists could be exempt from obtaining a consent. This creates a rather curious situation: physicians are providing patients with the information note and requiring them to fill in the consent form, despite being the only actors not required to seek patients' consent. In other words, doctors provide information and collect consent for med-tech companies. Currently, Implicity's 'Patient Information Note V1.112' designates three data controllers (the cardiologist, the health facility and the companies responsible for the remote monitoring) and patients express one single consent to the data processing by all the three data controllers for the defined purposes.[11]

Another major issue is determining whether consent to data processing may be confused with consent to the medical act. The remote monitoring actually forms part of a wider medical act, which begins with a surgical act and ends with its termination or extraction. This consent is governed by health law provisions. In France, article L.1111-4 of the Public Health Code states that patients must give free and informed consent, which is inseparable from their right to be informed. Therefore, the cardiologist is still required to obtain consent for the entire medical act. As surgery cannot be dissociated from remote monitoring, doctors must inform patients of all the aspects of the procedure.

---

[8] CNIL, Deliberation no 2020-055, 14 May 2020.

[9] Article 7(1) GDPR.

[10] See Décret no. 2010-1229, 19 October 2010, on telemedicine, article 1. See also article R6316-2 of the Public Health Code.

[11] Implicity (2025, 2).

3.3 The Duty to Inform

As explained earlier, the duty to inform covers both the remote monitoring and the operation. These are two intertwined duties to inform. To determine under which conditions these duties can be considered fulfilled in our matter, the scope of each duty must be observed.

On the one hand, is the wording of the information note delivered to patients respectful of the GDPR inasmuch as the remote monitoring is concerned? The formulation of the French version of Implicity's 'Patient Information Note V1.112' is very ambiguous d\ue to its poor syntax and punctuation. The formulation is unclear, and some actors are qualified in different ways throughout the document. Yet, when the CNIL examined the note, it did not consider this ambiguity to be in violation of the GDPR; according to the CNIL, the purposes of the processing and the identity of the controllers appear to be properly described.[12] The note is also very vague as to the description of the data collected, mentioning "health data transmitted by the electronic devices" and "data relating to your medical follow up",[13] without indicating that the collected data far exceeds a mere cardiac rhythm. While the GDPR does not require the controllers to enumerate or describe the type of data collected, such an imprecision could potentially infringe the principles of necessity and proportionality underlying the GDPR.[14] Without information about the data collected, it is difficult for patients to monitor the processing of their data. Nevertheless, as the processing is intended to improve or save patients' life and was authorized by the CNIL in the first place, it is highly unlikely that the note would be considered to be infringing these principles.

On the other hand, is the information note sufficient to fulfil cardiologists' duty to inform under health law? The scope of doctors' duty is quite broad under French law. According to article L.1111-2 of the Public Health Code, doctors' duty to inform extends to the various investigations, treatments or preventive measures offered to patients, as well as the associated consequences, benefits and frequent or serious foreseeable risks.[15] In addition, courts have audaciously extended the scope of the risks that patients must be informed of; risks that occur rarely or exceptionally, as long as they are reasonably foreseeable, must be disclosed and explained to the patient.[16] Therefore, the duty to inform imposed by the Public Health Code far exceeds the scope of information provided under the GDPR. In the specific context of the implantation of a CIED, patients must be informed of all the investigations that will be carried out, as well as about the risks involved. They must also be warned of the technical risks associated with being a CIED carrier. These include the risk of data leaks and hacking, the latter of which could lead to serious bodily injury or death—if it resulted in the defibrillator being activated unnecessarily. As none of

[12] CNIL, Deliberation no 2020-055, 14 May 2020.

[13] Implicity (2025, 1).

[14] Perray (2024, § 57 f).

[15] Porchy-Simon (2022, § 8 f).

[16] See for instance Cass. Civ. 1st, 12 October 2016, no. 15–16.894.

these risks are explained or even mentioned in the information note, simply handing the document to patients cannot be considered a way for cardiologists to fulfil their duty to inform. Moreover, physicians may be held liable for the inadequacy of the information delivered or their inability to explain the potential technical risks beyond their professional expertise.

3.4 Avenues for Improvement

First and foremost, it should be mentioned that, in medical matters and even more so in cases of vital risk and an emergency to act, patients' ability to give free and meaningful consent is always somewhat illusory. This is a vulnerability inherent to patients' condition that cannot be fully remedied.

Such a vulnerability justifies the need for greater transparency than in any other health-related area. The vulnerable condition of patients who are in need of a cardiac implantation should impose on physicians, care units, device manufacturers and platform providers the obligation to deliver very comprehensive information. The information should be provided at the time of consent *and* updated regularly during the follow-up phase, which can last years or even a lifetime. As data processing can evolve, and since patients have all the right to withdraw consent at any time, all parties involved should also provide regular and precise information.

Two main suggestions can be made in this regard. First, the patients' consent with regard to data processing should be obtained by the physicians in the presence of representatives of the med-tech companies. In our example, the device manufacturer and/or Implicity should also inform patients and obtain their consent. This would enable patients to express any concerns or ask questions. As patients' physical vulnerability is compounded by their digital vulnerability, med-tech companies should be required to inform them directly. This would allow each party to provide information on the part of the data processing they carry out and the technical risks incurred.

Then, guidelines should be developed to shape the content of the expected information. These guidelines should specifically define and specify the content of this information. They should require the mention of all the risks involved in data collection and transmission, as well as the risks of hacking. The different parties involved in the remote monitoring process should then be clearly listed, including subcontractors. The involvement of new parties should be specified to the patient, even after the consent has been given. Given the complexity of the process, it would be useful and efficient to provide a diagram illustrating and explaining data processing.

Once the consent has been given, precisely because patients' freedom to consent is restrained, patients should be properly protected against the different risks they incur. In other words, since patients are likely to consent to the implantation of a CIED no matter what information is given to them, it can be argued that this expression of consent does not fully remedy their vulnerability. It is therefore important to ensure that patients can also be protected *ex post*, after they give their consent, whenever the device or the data processing causes them harm.

4 Protecting the Patient *Ex Post*

As it is not possible to fully remedy their vulnerability *ex ante*, patients must be efficiently protected when the CIED or data processing causes them harm. This implies that the patients' right to be informed, their privacy, and their bodily integrity must all be adequately protected through *ex post* measures.

4.1 Protecting Patients' Right to Be Informed

Given the broad scope of physicians' duty to inform, patients who were poorly informed or not informed at all can seek compensation for breach of this duty. Under French law, a breach of the duty to inform gives rise to civil liability on the ground of article 1242 of the Civil Code, particularly in two situations.[17] If patients were not informed of a risk that could have caused them to change their mind, they may be granted compensation for the loss of a chance to avoid the medical operation and the subsequent harm. If by contrast it is clear that patients would still have given a consent, had they been fully informed, compensation can be granted solely for unreadiness—that is, the moral loss incurred by being unable to prepare for the potential realization of the risk.[18]

4.2 Protecting Patients' Privacy

When patients are implanted with a CIED, two types of data are collected. In addition to the data collected by the device itself, the cardiologist can include data from healthcare and follow-up, such as the patients' age, weight, and comorbidity. These observed and recorded elements, and even more their combination, constitute information relating to identified or identifiable natural persons, as well as health data in accordance with article 4(15) of the GDPR. They are clearly key components of the right to private and family life. Furthermore, as the CIED is connected to a home monitor which transmits data via a SIM card, patients can easily be geolocated.

Consequently, the GDPR applies. Article 82 of the GDPR grants the right to compensation to "any person who suffers material or non-material damage as a result of an infringement"[19] of the Regulation. Therefore, if controllers fail to guarantee the security of the collected personal data, they can easily be held liable.[20] The controller must "ensure the ongoing confidentiality, integrity, availability and

[17] Duval-Arnould (2024), no. 132.300 f.

[18] Cass. Civ. 1st, 23 January 2014, no. 12–22.123.

[19] Article 82(1) GDPR.

[20] Knetsch (2022, § 8 f).

resilience of processing systems and services".[21] In the event of a hack or data leak, the controller is presumed to be at fault, and must prove that they implemented the appropriate measures to escape liability. Damage must be proven, but no threshold of severity can be imposed, and a loss of control over personal data qualifies as damage even if the data is not put to abusive use. Clearly, even if damages can be regarded as a remedy for vulnerable consent, they are merely a consolation prize.

During data processing, in the long run, patients should be much better informed about the content of the data collected and how it is used. Article 7(3) of the GDPR states that withdrawal of consent should be as easy as giving consent. Unfortunately for patients, however, withdrawing consent is often more difficult than refusing to give it in the first place. Once the CIED is implanted, also due to the hope of an extended lifespan, patients are not free to change their mind at all. Moreover, how can patients express their wish to withdraw from remote monitoring without jeopardizing the trust they are supposed to have for their physicians?

In addition to the GDPR, compensation for a breach of privacy can also be sought on the ground of product liability. While the old product liability directive 85/374/EEC (PLD)[22] is silent on the issue, the revised product liability directive (EU) 2024/2853 (RPLD) defines "destruction or corruption of data"[23] as damage. This concept does not include data leaks. It relates to the destruction of data, such as when data is deleted from a hard drive, or to corruption of data, which consists of unintended errors that leave the data in the system but render it unusable or inaccurate.[24] Product liability, however, will only be established if a defect can be identified and proved. Corruption may thus result from a physical defect in the device or a component, from a defect in the software, algorithm or, more broadly, from a defect of the digital service provided by the manufacturer and/or the platform provider.

4.3 Protecting Patients' Bodily Integrity

Inasmuch as CIEDs regulate the most vital function, CIED carriers are at risk of suffering bodily injury. As of now, one of the most dangerous sources of risk for CIED carriers lies in cyberattacks.[25] As these devices are prostheses, hacking could result not only in a mere loss of privacy, but also in a bodily injury or even death. Cybersecurity researchers have hacked insulin pumps—sometimes their own—and demonstrated that they can quite easily program them to deliver a lethal dose of

[21] Article 32(1), letter (b) GDPR.

[22] Council Directive 85/374/EEC of 25 July 1985 on the approximation of the laws, regulations and administrative provisions of the Member States concerning liability for defective products.

[23] Directive (EU) 2024/2853 of the European Parliament and of the Council of 23 October 2024 on liability for defective products and repealing Council Directive 85/374/EEC, Article 6(1)(c).

[24] Directive (EU) 2024/2853, recital 20.

[25] Torgersen, Schulz, Lugo, Sütterlin (2024, 4).

insulin.[26] Similarly, a 'man in the middle' could be used to modify the data and prevent a defibrillator from delivering a shock when necessary, or deliver a shock when not necessary.[27] Alternatively, one could even hack the system so that all defibrillators deliver a shock at the same time, causing significant damage and potentially resulting in death. These are not science-fiction scenarios, but real threats that should be taken into consideration.

In such cases, patients are protected *ex post* by product liability law. A CIED may be considered defective if it fails to provide the level of safety that a person is entitled to expect, or which is required under European Union law or national law, as defined by article 7(1) of the RPLD. Moreover, the services provided by medical technology software suppliers, such as Implicity, are clearly digital services integrated into or interconnected with the device. Without this service, the CIED would not function at all. Recital 17 of the RPLD explicitly provides the case of an "health monitoring relying on a physical product's sensor" as an example of a digital service. Consequently, a digital service that does not provide the expected level of safety can also be considered defective. According to article 7(2), in assessing the defectiveness of the product, both the safety-relevant cybersecurity requirements and the specific needs of the intended user are to be taken into account. At least for the case of ICD device, the defibrillator could be considered as a "product whose very purpose is to prevent damage", for which "the assessment of the defectiveness of such a product should take into account its failure to fulfil that purpose".[28] Arguably, in such a situation, both the manufacturer and the digital service provider could easily be held liable.

In conclusion, what would the consequences be of a massive hacking of cardiac devices, as feared by the French Minister for Health, without falling into dystopia? Such an event would have a significant impact on patients who already have a CIED implanted. First, it would cause a major loss of trust in the healthcare system and MedTech firms. At a time when there is growing suspicion surrounding common vaccines, the revelation of such a lack of information would be highly damaging and could cause people to forget all the improvements that these devices enable. Patients may then decide to have their CIED removed, which could compromise their autonomy and reduce their life expectancy. Finally, it would cause obvious psychological harm, which could most likely be remedied under GDPR legislation or on the ground of a failure to inform. For CIED bearers who are personally exposed, unreadiness could be compensated for. They are the victim of a risk they were not informed about. Had they known, they could have prepared for it. For CIED bearers who are personally affected, the compensation for anxiety would be easily granted, at least under French law. However, in previous cases where such compensation was granted, anxiety affected 'only' the bearers of a specific device or of devices having a particular serial number. Since in the instance of a general hacking, the 'defect' could by contrast affect all CIEDs, it remains to be tested whether and to

[26] Baranchuk et al (2018, 1286).

[27] Torgersen, Schulz, Lugo, Sütterlin (2024, 8).

[28] Directive (EU) 2024/2853, recital 33.

what extent compensation would be granted in such a case. In any event, a hacking of this proportion would likely lead to mass litigation.

In light of this serious risk, there should be more public spending on cybersecurity, and patients' information should be improved immediately. The poor quality of information provided to patients, who often have no idea about the nature of the data collected or the potential risks involved, could lead to feelings of injustice if such an attack were to occur. In other words, complying with the duty to inform and explain the technical risks incurred by CIED bearers today may help to mitigate the risk of having to compensate for any harm caused by the CIEDs in the future.

References

Baranchuk A et al (2018) Cybersecurity for cardiac implantable electronic devices, what should you know? J Am Coll Cardiol 71(11):1285–1288

Duval-Arnould D (2024) Droit de la santé, prise en charge des patients et dommages liés aux soins. Lefebvre Dalloz, Paris

Implicity (2025) Patient information note V1.112. Remote monitoring of cardiac rhythmic prosthesis. Available at https://www.implicity.com/wp-content/uploads/2023/02/Information-patient-Cardiac-prosthesis-V1.112-UE.pdf

Kapoor A, Vora A, Yadav R (2019) Cardiac devices and cyber attacks: how far are they real? How to overcome? Indian Heart J 71(6):427–430

Knetsch J (2022) Les actions civiles en réparation fondées sur une violation du RGPD. Vers un nouveau contentieux de masse?. JurisClasseur Périodique G, doctr. 1062–1063

Perray R (2024) Principes fondamentaux relatifs aux traitements de données à caractère personnel. Loyauté, licéité et transparence. JurisClasseur Communication, 932–30

Porchy-Simon S (2022) Responsabilité médicale, responsabilité pour faute d'éthique médicale, consentement libre et éclairé du patient, secret médical. JurisClasseur Responsabilité civile et Assurances, pp 440–443

Torgersen LNS, Schulz SM, Lugo RG, Sütterlin S (2024) Patient informed consent, ethical and legal considerations in the context of digital vulnerability with smart, cardiac implantable electronic devices. PLOS Digit Health 3(5):e0000507

Vignal F (2025) "Les pousse-seringues, pacemakers et défibrillateurs peuvent se faire hacker par une puissance étrangère qui pourrait prendre le contrôle" prévient le Ministre de la Santé. Available at https://www.publicsenat.fr/actualites/sante/les-pousse-seringues-pacemakers-et-defibrillateurs-peuvent-se-faire-hacker-par-une-puissance-etrangere-qui-pourrait-prendre-le-controle-previent-le-ministre-de-la-sante

Digital Vulnerability and AI-Powered Legal Services

Giovanni Chieco

Abstract Reliance on AI in the legal sector—the so-called LegalTech (LT) tools—is constantly growing. Focusing on the European legal market, this paper seeks to clarify the benefits and the risks that the use of LT tools poses to legal professionals, to their clients and to the society as a whole. On the basis of this analysis, the paper further highlights the ex ante requirements that may be helpful in ensuring a responsible use of emerging LT tools, such as the need for continuous human oversight of LT tools, and the dissemination of good professional practices about lawyers' duties of accuracy, transparency and confidentiality. The paper also examines the potential role of liability rules in better protecting structurally disadvantaged stakeholders in the digital market—that is, consumers, lawyers' clients and even lawyers themselves. This would imply equating the services offered by providers of LT tools to legal services, while safeguarding the ability of lawyers as deployers of these tools to demonstrate either their non-involvement or the responsibility of other entities within the AI value chain. The wide range of subjects who may be vulnerable to harm caused by AI-driven LT tools demonstrates that the development of more robust and comprehensive safeguards for the affected parties and the integration of ex ante with ex post measures are highly needed.

Keywords LegalTech tools · Legal services world · Access to justice · Digital vulnerability · Professional liability

1 Introduction

Artificial Intelligence (AI) is revolutionizing various industries by providing advanced technological solutions to complex problems. The legal industry is no exception.

Even if the legal profession is notoriously slow to adopt new technologies, the use of AI in the legal sector is constantly growing. Focusing on the European legal

G. Chieco (✉)
University of Trieste, Trieste, Italy
e-mail: giovanni.chieco@phd.units.it

C. Crea and M. Infantino (eds.), *Remedies to Digital Vulnerability in European Private Law*, https://doi.org/10.1007/978-3-032-19720-7_23

market, this paper seeks to clarify the primary applications of AI-powered tools within the legal domain, assessing both the benefits and the risks they pose to legal professionals and society as a whole. The pages further aim to examine whether, and to what extent, these technologies exacerbate existing vulnerabilities or create new forms of vulnerability for those who rely on LegalTech (LT) tools. It also attempts to propose potential strategies to mitigate the risks associated with LT tools. Although the literature on digital vulnerability, particularly within the European context, has predominantly focused on consumers,[1] this paper adopts a broader perspective by looking at the wider category of vulnerable users of LT services. This includes not only consumers and clients, but also lawyers–particularly lawyers of small law firms, who are in a delicate position due to their exposure to, and reliance on, rapidly evolving AI technologies. In addition, the paper will argue that *ex ante* requirements should be combined with *ex post* remedies, such as measures to ensure the effective enforcement of the right to obtain compensation for the damage suffered.

To this purpose, the present paper will start with a survey of the principal uses of AI-powered tools in the legal practice (paragraph 2), followed by an assessment of their main benefits (paragraph 3) and their key drawbacks (paragraph 4), from both a professional and social point of view. Building on these findings, the paper will highlight the *ex ante* requirements that, according to current literature, are necessary to ensure the responsible use of emerging AI tools and to complement the timid preventive measures prescribed by existing European legislation (paragraph 5). These recommendations include the need for continuous human oversight of LT tools, and the dissemination of good professional practices enabling lawyers to comply with their existing duties of accuracy, transparency and confidentiality. On the top of that, the paper will examine the potential role of liability rules against the framework of existing EU provisions on *ex post* measures (paragraph 6). The paper will put forward some proposals to modify existing compensation mechanisms so as to better protect structurally disadvantaged stakeholders, including not only consumers, but also lawyers' clients and even lawyers themselves. The modification should involve the equation of the services offered by LT providers to legal services, while safeguarding the ability of LT deployers to demonstrate either their non-involvement or the responsibility of other entities within the AI value chain. The concluding section will offer some final considerations on how users of LT tools, lawyers' clients and even lawyers themselves may be made vulnerable by the reliance on LT technologies, with the former being particularly exposed and unprotected (paragraph 7). The wide range of subjects who may suffer from the exposure to AI-driven LT tools demonstrates that the development of more robust and comprehensive safeguards for the affected parties and the integration of *ex ante* with *ex post* measures are highly needed.

[1] See, e.g. Crea and De Franceschi (2024).

2 The Uses of AI in the Legal Services World

Even if the deployment of AI in the legal sector is still at an early stage, a wide range of AI-powered tools is already available to assist lawyers with most of the tasks they perform in their day-to-day work.[2]

AI's ability to automate repetitive tasks makes LT tools highly beneficial for routine activities in law firms, such as front and back-office operations, document filing and organization, case management, scheduling client meetings and hearings, as well as summarizing, correcting and translating both legal and non-legal documents.[3] Moreover, LT tools can now perform, on their own, many technical and sectoral tasks that, for a long time, have been an exclusive prerogative of lawyers. Legal research, an extremely time-consuming activity, can be almost completely automated by legal tools which use natural language processing (NLP) algorithms to identify and provide relevant legal information in a precise and coherent way.[4] AI-powered tools can nowadays even perform document analysis–a category that includes contract analysis, due diligence and compliance. These tasks all require reviewing, interpreting and evaluating documents to extract relevant information, identify patterns and generate insights. LT tools can assist lawyers in performing these activities by categorizing information and identifying key terms, potential problems or inconsistencies in documents, such as conflicting information or missing data.[5]

But AI tools are valuable not only for supporting the *ex post* analysis and categorization of relevant elements but also for predicting the potential outcomes of legal cases and for drafting legal documents. AI-powered predictive analytics tools use machine learning (ML) algorithms to analyze legal texts and to forecast the likely outcomes of legal cases and operations, offering insights into potential risks and helping lawyers to make more informed decisions.[6] The same ML technologies enable LT tools to generate standard legal documents, such as contracts, letters and motions, based on user's input and preferences.[7]

What should be stressed in our perspective is that AI's capacity to draft legal documents, provide legal information and conduct legal research is not only at the service of lawyers. Increasingly, such technologies are accessible to non-legal users, often without any regulatory oversight or professional intermediation.[8] Legal technological companies offer a growing array of online legal services, also in the form of chatbots and self-help applications, that allegedly allow individuals to navigate the legal process in full autonomy.[9] These tools often offer an alternative to traditional

---

[2] Armour et al. (2022, 106–108).

[3] Pietrapaoli et al. (2023, 7).

[4] Schwarcz et al. (2023, 7–10).

[5] Homoki et al. (2022, 21–26).

[6] Atrey (2023, 1075–1083).

[7] DRI (2024, 89).

[8] Homoki et al. (2022, 34).

[9] Fenwick et al. (2019, 255).

legal services: they are able to create tailored legal outputs based on the provided information in a user-friendly and simple way, that mime lawyers' typical outputs.[10]

While the above technologies present significant opportunities and benefits, they also entail considerable risks. The following sections will explore, more in detail, both the strengths and limitations of these tools, since a clear understanding of their impact on existing and emerging vulnerabilities is crucial for developing effective strategies to mitigate risks associated with their use.

3 The Benefits of AI for Lawyers and Society at Large

As the previous chapter showed, the widespread adoption of AI-powered tools holds the potential to positively transform the legal services sector, particularly by enhancing access to justice.[11]

On the one hand, AI can enhance lawyers' efficiency by automating tasks, thus also increasing market competitiveness and making legal assistance more affordable. On the other hand, AI can democratize access to legal information and knowledge by providing apps and tools that can answer legal questions, generate legal documents and offer advice, effectively transforming legal knowledge into a sort of commodified consumer good.[12]

Regarding AI's potential to make professional legal services more accessible, it is important to note that legal services are traditionally provided by costly and high-skilled humans and that, during the past two decades, the costs of legal services have risen significantly in the whole World.[13] This ongoing trend has often excluded from access to legal services low-income and middle-income people.[14] To the extent that reliance on LT tools increases lawyers' productivity and helps them better manage their time and workloads in traditional law firm settings, AI could help reshape this scenario. The time and cost savings generated by these efficiencies could be passed on to clients through lower fees or flat-fee service options. This may expand the legal services market to include those who have historically been excluded.[15]

The trend is also supported by the potential of AI to increase the competitiveness of the legal market. By enhancing lawyers' productivity, even small law firms could meet the demands of more clients, allowing them to expand their practices into sectors they may have previously been unable to serve due to technical limitations, lack of capacity or insufficient personnel. According to liberal economic theories, a more competitive market creates a win–win situation: consumers benefit from lower prices,

[10] Brescia et al. (2015, 572–575).

[11] Cruz (2019, 377–378).

[12] Cruz (2019, 377–378).

[13] PWC (2024).

[14] Brescia et al. (2015, 559).

[15] Yamane (2020, 885–888).

improved quality, greater choice and better service, while businesses are incentivized to innovate, improve efficiency and stay relevant.[16]

AI may be helpful in this regard from another perspective. It is well-known that cost is not the only barrier that keeps legal services exclusive to certain groups. Social, cultural and psychological barriers to justice–such as poverty, inadequate education and a lack of legal knowledge–frequently prevent individuals from seeking access to the justice system or viewing it as a viable means of resolving disputes.[17] The widespread use of self-help AI tools can help overcome the mentioned barriers. LT tools enable individuals to interact directly with technology that provides legal information and documents in an accessible and user-friendly format. These tools can empower users to make informed decisions about their legal issues, including the probability of success of a given case and to independently analyze and prepare legal documents. Additionally, they offer consumers a wide range of choices: they are available 24/7, unrestricted by geography and offered at more reasonable and transparent prices compared to traditional legal services. Of course, the critical limitation that persists is that certain legal activities require the lawyer's personal authorship or signature for the act to be valid and legally enforceable, a requirement that AI, for the time being, cannot fulfill.[18]

4 The Drawbacks of the Diffusion of AI in Legal Services World

Despite all the positive effects of the diffusion of LT tools in the legal services sector, AI-powered tools can also exacerbate existing vulnerabilities and create new forms of vulnerability for users—be they lawyers, their clients or direct end-users. The dangers of LT tools seem to be related, in part, to their technical structure and, in part, to the lack of users' competence.

Let us start from AI's intrinsic technical problems. The fact that AI tools need to be trained on large amounts of data is a first structural limitation that affects the quality and accuracy of their responses as well as the privacy rights of the people concerned. The correctness of any answer depends primarily on the data used to train the model: an algorithm cannot learn from information it was not exposed to. This limitation gives rise to a phenomenon known as exposure bias, which occurs when a model trained on a specific set of data performs poorly when introduced to different data and fails to interpret new data creatively and accurately. The issue is particularly problematic for generative AI models, as the text they generate becomes part of the underlying data used for subsequent predictions. Consequently, a poorly

---

[16] Ferrar (2025, 1).

[17] OECD (2019, 11, 22–24, 142–144).

[18] Godman (2019, 157–159).

or erroneously generated sentence can exponentially affect the accuracy of future predictions.[19]

Similarly, generative AI systems have exhibited a tendency to fabricate (hallucinate) facts or legal information when faced with gaps in their knowledge. In the legal field, these hallucinations may involve invented judicial decisions, statutes or scholarly references, arising from AI's failure to access or properly process the required information to respond accurately to a query.[20]

What further undermines the accuracy of the outputs is the unstructured nature of legal data. Legal texts are often highly contextualized and polycentric, with significant variation in writing styles and reasoning approaches across lawyers, judges and jurisdictions. This variability, which is particularly acute in multi-cultural and multilingual Europe, can make it difficult to identify consistent patterns and facilitate imprecise and uncontextualized outcomes.[21]

LT's technical architecture does not only impinge on the accuracy of the outcomes but also exposes users and clients' privacy rights to serious risks. AI tools are trained on large amounts of data, which may include personal data. Without proper oversight, there is the risk that this personal information could be stolen, processed or even used to train AI models without prior notification or consent.[22] The risks for privacy are exacerbated by the fact that unstructured legal data are very difficult to anonymize: simply removing names and locations is not sufficient, as unique events or other context-specific information may make it possible to re-identify subjects. Consequently, privacy risks persist even if a data service provider anonymizes all stored data before using it. Furthermore, even if the output of training does not appear to be legible data at all, it is important to be mindful of the problem that the output of popular language embeddings (e.g. texts turned to numerical representations and vectors, such as in BERT) can be used to predict the original text used for (pre)training and reverse-engineer to disclose sensitive information from the source.[23]

Furthermore, serious privacy and cybersecurity concerns arise from the most common way to create and/or deploy AI technologies, which implies reliance on cloud computing services. Cloud computing-based tools are popular because they eliminate many of the difficulties and costs related to implementation, configuration and maintenance of technical infrastructure needed to use or build AI tools.[24] However, there are numerous privacy perils associated with this type of technology. Aside from the extraterritoriality problems, which, although still present, are mitigated by the Regulation 2016/679/EU (GDPR), a particularly widespread risk is unauthorized access to data. As long as the service provider (or any underlying infrastructure) has the technical ability to access and read the data, a data breach could not be excluded. Nor should the perils of vendor lock-in be underestimated:

[19] Griffin et al. (2024, 46).

[20] Griffin et al. (2024, 47).

[21] European Lawyers Foundation (2021, 20–21).

[22] DRI (2024, 23–26).

[23] Pan et al. (2020, 1314–1315).

[24] Council of Bars and Law Societies of Europe (2012, 3).

technical barriers or the behavior of the cloud provider can create serious difficulties in extracting and moving the data. Notwithstanding recent interventions, such as the Regulation 2022/868/EU (Data Act) and the Regulation 2022/858/EU (Data Governance Act), recovering the full set of uploaded data or transferring it intact to another provider can be particularly challenging.[25]

As anticipated, the other big potential source of problems associated with LT tools stems from the number of skills and resources that are required to manage them. Indeed, the accuracy and efficiency of LT tools depend, at least in part, on the level of competencies and means possessed by users–be they legally trained or not.

It seems evident that the lawyers' position differs from that of people lacking legal training, since lawyers' legal knowledge mitigates the risks associated with the use of incorrect AI-generated legal outputs. However, a factor that has the potential to create new vulnerabilities and limit the usefulness of LT tools, even for lawyers, is the technological skill gap. The successful adoption of advanced systems requires technical proficiency and a deep understanding of the model and its workings, in the absence of which their utilization may easily turn out to be counterproductive, expensive and dangerous for clients' rights and for lawyers' reputation.[26]

Having adequate resources is another essential requirement for fully leveraging the potential of AI in legal practice and for minimizing its drawbacks. To gain a genuine marketable advantage, law firms should either use reliable yet costly AI-powered LT tools, or, though at a significantly higher cost, develop their own proprietary tools exclusively for the benefit of their clients. Small law firms, however, are unlikely to be able to develop their own LT tools; more likely they will rely on ready-to-use third-party LT tools. In the long term, this reliance may undermine their independence. Lawyers, who become reliant on a single tool for key aspects of their business processes, may face interference from the AI provider in their activities and relationships with clients: the tech company could impose unilateral terms on lawyers, potentially compromising their independence, professionalism, authority and reputation.[27]

The mentioned aspects have led many to think that AI will likely lead to the development of two-tiered systems of access to legal services.[28] Three predominant concerns regarding such a scenario have emerged in the literature: (i) one in which expensive, but superior, human lawyers coexist with inexpensive, but inferior, AI-driven legal assistance[29]; (ii) one where only large law firms will effectively harness superior but expensive AI, thereby increasing their power and making more affordable service providers obsolete[30]; and (iii) one where AI's impact will not overcome the *status quo* and there will continue to be only a small portion of the public that

[25] Ibid, 44–48.

[26] International Bar Association (2024, 15–16).

[27] Council of Bars and Law Societies of Europe (2012, 51–52).

[28] Infantino et al. (2024, 265).

[29] Kunkel (2018, 372, 382–383).

[30] Pasquale et al. (2015, 35–36).

can afford quality legal services, which are offered worldwide by few law firms.[31] None of these scenarios is particularly reassuring.

Even more serious are the vulnerabilities arising from the lack of sufficient legal and technological literacy among legally untrained users of LT tools. Lay users typically do not have enough legal knowledge and technological skills to check and verify the automated answers. Therefore, they are always exposed to the risk of relying on technological systems that do not meet their needs, potentially worsening their situation and exposing them to unintended and unexpected consequences.[32] Furthermore, even assuming that the legal information provided by the tool is correct, simply having easy access to legal knowledge through AI-generated answers is often not sufficient to resolve a legal matter. Merely collecting and reading information does not suffice. Instead, it is essential to critically analyze the information, its sources and its context, while recognizing that every case is unique and requires a specially designed strategy.[33]

The potential positive impact of these technologies on lay users and the improvement of access to justice is further limited by the exclusion of individuals who lack internet access, digital equipment or IT skills. Additionally, many LT companies may use technology to determine which cases to pursue and to filter out economically unviable cases or legally risky claims from the outset.[34] Such a strategy would inevitably limit the availability of automated legal services for the people that may need them most.

From the points highlighted above, it is evident that the widespread use of LT tools among lawyers and consumers gives rise to numerous vulnerabilities and further aggravates many of the problems that notoriously affect people's access to justice. This complex and potentially harmful situation calls for both *ex ante* and *ex post* measures to mitigate their negative impact, while ensuring that the potential of these tools is not unduly restricted.

5 *Ex Ante* Measure to Reduce Digital Vulnerabilities

In light of the many possible forms of vulnerability that arise from, or are aggravated by, the use of LT tools in the legal services world, it becomes of the utmost importance to understand whether, and to what extent, EU law is ready to deal with the challenges these tools raise. The focus will be on EU law because, notwithstanding the largely domestic regulation of the legal profession, the task of establishing a legal framework for digital and AI-driven products and services has been taken up by the EU rather than by its Members. Yet, as the present and the following sections will argue, both the *ex ante* and *ex post* remedies currently, albeit fragmentarily, provided by the

[31] Guttenberg (2012, 480).

[32] Escajeda (2020, 472–474).

[33] Koenig et al. (2019, 1274–1279).

[34] Ebers (2021, 198–199).

EU regulatory framework, are of limited scope and impact. In order to explore how these measures could be improved to strengthen the position of lawyers, their clients and, more in general, of consumers of legal services, this section will critically review the most influential *ex* ante safeguards established under EU law, focusing in particular on the prohibition of unfair commercial practices, on the obligation to inform consumers in a clear and transparent manner, on the duty to collect and treat personal data lawfully and on the requirements for the development of and reliance on high-risk AI, AI for general purpose and AI systems intended to interact directly with natural persons.

Starting with consumer protection law, it seems to be important to mention the Unfair Contract Terms Directive (UCTD) 1993/13/EEC and the Unfair Commercial Practices Directive (UCPD) 2005/29/EU. The UCTD aims to ensure that standard terms in business-to-consumer (B2C) contracts do not create a significant imbalance in the rights and obligations of the parties to the detriment of the consumer (art. 3). To this end, the UCTD requires that contractual terms be drafted in plain and intelligible language and, in cases of ambiguity, the interpretation most favourable to the consumer must prevail (art. 5). Furthermore, the UCTD stipulates that unfair terms shall not be binding on the consumer, while the remainder of the contract shall remain valid if it is capable of continuing in effect without the unfair provisions (art. 6). This framework empowers Member States to invalidate unfair terms without annulling the entire contract, thereby strengthening consumer protection and promoting contractual fairness. The UCPD establishes protections against commercial conduct that breaches professional diligence, misleads consumers or employs aggressive tactics. Potential violations include misrepresenting staff qualifications, mishandling complaints, lacking fee transparency and coercing or intimidating clients (artt. 6–9). Both texts are concerned with what happens at the precontractual stage and, largely disregard whatever problem may occur during or after the performance of a contract. Moreover, neither of them address the unique risks posed by digital applications, such as issues related to transparency, quality or accountability. Finally, while the UCTD is arguably the most enforced piece of EU contract law, the UCPD leaves the issue of enforcement, with substantial discretions, in the hands of Member States (artt. 11–13) and has notoriously been underenforced.[35]

Similarly, the information obligations set out in the Consumer Rights Directive (CRD) 2011/83/EU provide only limited protection for consumers engaging with LT tools. The CRD imposes standardized duties, requiring traders to inform consumers, clearly and comprehensibly, about the essential characteristics of their products and/or services, pricing and associated rights and obligations (artt. 6–8). However, the effectiveness of the CRD is significantly constrained in digital contexts, where interactions often occur through apps or chatbots and information is hidden in standard terms and conditions that everybody accepts but nobody reads. Furthermore, the Directive does not provide specific remedies in cases of non-compliance except from the right of withdrawal (artt. 11–16). As a result, enforcement largely depends

[35] Infantino et al. (2023, 346–348).

on the national contract laws of the Member States (artt. 23–24), which may lead to insufficient and inconsistent consumer protection across the EU.[36]

Wherever personal data are involved, the development and deployment of LT applications must comply with the GDPR, which protects not only consumers but also lawyers. Both the training and deployment of LT tools dealing with personal data are subject to specific obligations: personal data must be processed lawfully, fairly and transparently and must rely on a legitimate legal basis (artt. 5–11). Furthermore, the GDPR grants data subjects a range of rights, including the right to information and explanation, rectification, erasure, objection and data portability (artt. 12–23). However, ML models embedded in most LT tools typically do not rely on personal data, but rather on abstract patterns and statistical inferences concerning groups or categories of individuals. These models link various combinations of input variables (predictors) to the probability of a particular outcome (target). As the embedded correlations apply generically to individuals sharing similar characteristics, the majority of data used by these applications do not generally fit into the category of personal data and therefore do not trigger the application of the GDPR.[37] As a result, while in theory data subjects can check how their personal data is collected and processed, in practice they have very little control over how this information is evaluated (CJEU in cases C-434/16; C-141/12; C-372/12.).

Finally, Regulation EU 2024/1689 (AI Act) classifies certain AI systems that involve the interpretation or application of the law as high-risk (see art. 6 and Annex III, point 8), subjecting them to a comprehensive set of obligations under articles 9 to 27. These obligations include requirements for risk management systems, high-quality training data, technical documentation, transparency, human oversight, accuracy, robustness and cybersecurity measures. However, these provisions are only applicable if the AI system is explicitly listed in Annex III: LT tools fall outside the defined high-risk categories, evading this regulatory framework. The AI Act further introduces a set of obligations targeting General-Purpose AI (GPAI) models (artt. 51–56) and AI directly interacting with people (art. 50). Although many LT tools are developed on top of GPAI models, they do not themselves qualify as GPAI within the meaning of articles 51–56 of AI Act and therefore are not subject to the regulatory duties (such as, requirements for technical documentation, risk mitigation, compliance with Union law and cooperation with competent authorities) established in these articles. The mentioned duties apply exclusively to providers and, in some cases, deployers of GPAI models (art. 3 nn. 63, 66, and recital 97), not to those who simply integrate or adapt these models for sector-specific purposes, such as legal service provision. When a third party adapts a GPAI model for a specific, narrow application, such as legal advice, this adapted system is no longer considered GPAI in the sense of the Act (recital 100). By contrast, article 50 of AI Act, which imposes transparency obligations on providers of AI systems, particularly those designed for direct interaction with natural persons, applies to LT tools. Under this provision, providers are required to ensure that users are informed they are interacting with an

[36] Biard (2023, 625–627).

[37] Ebers (2021, 214–216).

AI system, unless this is evident to a reasonably well-informed person considering the context and circumstances of use (recital 132). This requirement aims to mitigate risks associated with user misperception, particularly the mistaken belief that they are communicating with a human rather than a machine (recital 133). While this transparency measure is a step toward user protection, it may be insufficient in addressing deeper concerns. Users might still attribute undue credibility to AI-generated outputs, perceiving them as inherently accurate or trustworthy, despite their machine-generated origin. Moreover, the effectiveness of the transparency requirement hinges on the assumption that users are adequately informed and observant, which may not always be the case.[38]

It is therefore clear that EU law provides only limited protection to the risks that arise from LT tools, both in terms of its scope and of the range of application. Taking into consideration the many dimensions of vulnerability that can be triggered and exploited by digital interactions with LT tools,[39] the remainder of this section proposes two wide categories of *ex ante* measures that could be easily adopted to mitigate the vulnerabilities associated with the use of these new technologies: the introduction of an obligation of human oversight on LT deployers and the dissemination of best practices among lawyers. Neither of them necessarily requires the intervention of the EU legislator. While such an intervention would establish a uniform standard of protection, it does not appear to be indispensable: a critical regulatory role could be played by the professional rules adopted by bar associations, which may then exert pressure on LT companies. Relying on bottom-up rules introduced by legal professionals and on self-enforced technical standards by LT providers would also help to mitigate the risk of excessive regulation, which could stifle market development.

Let us go in order. Human oversight is crucial because knowledge by users of LT tools is key to control the risks arising out of their deployment. While lay users, by definition, lack both technical and legal competences, lawyers and LT providers should be expected to have them both. On the one hand, lawyers should possess sufficient digital competence and a solid understanding of the tools they employ–something on which we will come back later in the text. Consequently, law firms have an interest of either establish multidisciplinary teams or provide targeted training to their staff. This approach enables the development of a "human-in-the-loop" system, which empowers legal professionals to take ownership of, and actively engage with, these tools, fostering trust, reducing resistance and promoting the ethical and responsible deployment of AI.[40] On the other hand, LT providers would benefit from submitting their tools to quality controls and certification of reliability. They may, for instance, team up with state bar authorities to establish voluntary certification programs to verify that automated legal services meet necessary standards for functionality, accuracy and ethics. Commissions made up of both lawyers and technologists could evaluate legal bots across various dimensions (e.g.,

[38] Miščenić (2024, 103–125).

[39] Infantino and Di Matteo (2024, 252–272).

[40] International Bar Association (2024, 10).

reliability in providing accurate and up-to-date information; ability to identify ethical issues) helping the public make informed decisions about who to trust with their legal concerns and questions.[41] Additionally, another way to reduce the vulnerabilities consumers face through human oversight would be by offering self-help AI legal programs that include the involvement of an expert who can intervene on behalf of the user, either upon request or under specific conditions. The expert's involvement would guarantee the quality, appropriateness and proper understanding of the outcomes by the final user.[42]

Promoting human oversight may be complemented by another *ex ante* measure that may help mitigate vulnerability risk: the promotion of best practices that lawyers must follow when using AI-powered tools in compliance with lawyers' codes of conduct provisions. Linking good practices to the professional duties owed by lawyers to clients would ensure that the failure to follow them would entail lawyers' professional liability and the duty to compensate the damage caused.[43]

Many of the duties lawyers already owe to their client–such as the duty of competence, of transparency and of confidentiality–could be valorized in this regard.[44] The duty of competence (e.g. art. 14 Italian Forensic Code of Ethics) entails that lawyers using AI should possess the necessary legal knowledge and skills for the representation and to ensure the accuracy and quality of AI-generated outputs. Such an obligation would include being constantly aware of the availability of different tools that may serve the client's interests in various ways and performing the continuous oversight of the accuracy and quality of AI-generated outputs, in compliance with the "trust but verify" principle.[45]

Another central duty in the attorney-client relationship is the duty of transparency (e.g. art. 35 Italian Forensic Code of Ethics), which entails the lawyer's obligation to communicate and consult with the client regarding the strategies and methods by which the client's objectives will be pursued, including the use of AI tools. With regard to LT tools, this obligation would require lawyers to discuss with their clients the decision to use AI tools and to obtain clients' informed consent to this purpose.[46] This would also imply that lawyers must clearly inform clients about the type, function and rationale for using AI tools, as well as about any associated risk and available remedy in case of complications.[47]

Lawyers have a duty to protect client confidentiality (e.g. art. 9 Italian Forensic Code of Ethics), which should extend to the use of AI tools. The obligation of confidentiality requires adopting best practices such as understanding potential security risks, ensuring secure data transmission and storage, implementing protective

---

[41] Bonardi et al. (2024, 51–53).

[42] Navas (2019, 83–85).

[43] Jacobowitz (2018, 409).

[44] Infantino et al. (2024, 272–273).

[45] DRI (2024, 9, 18–19), Council of Bars and Law Societies of Europe, (2020, 32).

[46] Armour et al. (2021, 25).

[47] Cook et al. (2024, 335–337, 361–363).

measures and conducting due diligence on AI service providers.[48] Additionally, lawyers should negotiate agreements with LT providers in order to limit data use to client-authorized purposes, to prohibit resale or AI training with client data and to mandate robust security protocols.[49]

Strengthening the above-mentioned core principles of legal professional ethics and the correspondent best practices should be the first step. An additional step that national bar associations could pursue is to extend the applications of the professional duties to LT companies, inasmuch as they offer legal services or products. Such an approach would ensure greater accountability, consumer protection and integrity in the delivery of legal services through technological means.

All the above, however, relies on the activism of bar associations and on the stimuli for quality enhancement of LT developers. It remains to be seen whether the European market for legal services will move in this direction. What nevertheless remains true is that *ex ante* measures alone can hardly be a satisfactory answer to the risks created by LT tools. This is why the next section focuses on the *ex post* provisions that may intervene in case of an infringement of people's rights.

6 *Ex Post* Measures to Reduce Digital Vulnerabilities

The current EU legal framework already provides for several *ex post* measures that are relevant both in deterring and in reacting to abuses of vulnerability. This section will start by analyzing the current liability regimes available to consumers, clients and lawyers when dealing with defective digital products and services, while also highlighting their main shortcomings. On the basis of the survey, the remainder of the section will propose some possible interpretative moves that could easily ensure the presence of liability mechanisms that prevent and react to the abuse of digital vulnerabilities within the LT landscape more effectively.

The Digital Content Directive (DCD) EU 2019/770 sets out that digital content and services must conform to the terms of the contract and meet certain adequate standards of quality, functionality and compatibility (artt. 6–9). If the content or service fails to meet these requirements, consumers are entitled to appropriate remedies, which may include repair or replacement of the defective content or service, a price reduction or the termination of the contract if the issue remains unresolved (artt. 13–14). However, the DCD's impact on the world of legal services is limited: it is not applicable when a lawyer uses an LT tool (see recital 27) and there are many doubts about its enforceability by consumers who use LT tools on their own, because for most commentators the DCD only covers contracts for the provision of professional services that are performed personally by human traders.[50] Furthermore, the Directive's remedies are of limited practical use in the LT sector. In many cases

---

[48] Ibid, 339–340.

[49] Simshaw (2018, 198–200).

[50] Sein et al. (2019, 265).

reparation, replacement or price reduction are not available options, and most of the time contract termination does not align with consumer's best interests. Moreover, whenever commodification of legal services through LT tools implies software that can be classified as product,[51] the situation would fall out of the scope of application of Directive EU 2019/770, in favor of other regulations that protect consumers from damages caused by defective products: the Product Liability Directive (PLD) 85/374/CEE, and the Revised Product Liability Directive (RPLD) 2024/2853/EU.

As is widely acknowledged, the PLD does not appear to apply to damages caused by AI tools, unless they are integrated into products–understood as tangible movable goods (art. 2). As a result of this material limitation, the PLD does not seem to offer protection in cases of harm caused by LT tools.

To address this gap in protection and to modernize a directive conceived in the pre-digital era, the RPLD was adopted. However, the revised Directive will apply only to products placed on the market or put into service after 9 December 2026 (art. 21), creating a regulatory gap in the interim. The RPLD, compared to its predecessor, sets a wider definition of 'product', covering software and AI systems (art. 4), and also enlarges the scope of the parties in the supply chain who may potentially be liable (art. 8). Furthermore, the RPLD expands the definition of damage, by including material losses resulting from inadequate cybersecurity measures and destruction or corruption of data that are not used for professional purposes in cases of product defectiveness (art. 7). The burden of proof remains with the plaintiffs, who must prove the product was defective, that they suffered damage and the causal link between the damage and the defect (art. 10); yet, under certain conditions, the RPLD establishes a presumption of defectiveness and causal link and the plaintiffs' right to ask manufacturers to disclose necessary information in court (art. 9). The RPLD thus enhances the position of consumers but covers a limited range of situations and likely will not have a disruptive impact on the legal services world. First of all, it is not clear if LT tools used directly by consumers could be considered as a product or as a service. In this regard, drawing on the Court's case law concerning the PLD, it can be observed that in a case in which a damage was caused by a defective product used in delivering a service, the CJEU held that the PLD applies (CJEU, C-203/99). However, the CJEU also stated that the PLD does not apply to defective services per se. Therefore, in other situations in which a consumer was harmed by a defective service (e.g. a wrong professional advice or a flawed information), the same Court held that there was no room for the application of the PLD (CJEU, C-65/20). Furthermore, types of harm other than those covered by the new Directive–such as pure economic loss, violations of privacy or discrimination–do not give rise to liability, with the consequences that consumers must frame their requests for compensation under other liability regimes (recital 24).

Finally, another EU legal framework that establishes *ex post* remedies also for the benefit of lawyers (but not law firms) is the GDPR. In particular, article 82 of the GDPR establishes that individuals who suffered material or non-material damage due to violations of the Regulation have the right to claim compensation against

[51] Navas (2019, 82–83).

the author of the breach, provided that they can prove the breach of the GDPR, the damage suffered and the causal link between the breach and the damage.[52] While the provision offers crucial protection for solo lawyers, clients and consumers, it however presents significant challenges in practice. It sets a very high burden of proof for data subjects, that is even exacerbated in cases involving complex AI-driven processing where the link between the processing of data and the harm may be indirect or unclear. Moreover, the room for exemptions from liability is broad: courts interpret the absence of fault as well as the fact that controllers or processors have taken all reasonable precaution in an extensive way, reducing substantially the possibility of obtaining damages.[53]

As this short survey makes it clear, the current EU regulatory framework on liability arising out of defective digital services and products is complex but has many loopholes and often fails to provide effective and enforceable *ex post* measures for the protection of consumers, clients and professionals in the legal sector. The inadequacy of current EU law is perhaps not a problematic inasmuch as the relationships between lawyers relying on LT tools and their clients are concerned, since the latter can rely on national law to frame their complaints for defective legal services against the former. It should be incidentally noted, however, that national laws in this regard have historically been interpreted very restrictively, especially because lawyers' obligations have usually been considered obligations of means rather than obligations of results.[54]

Yet, the problems arising out of the current liability frameworks remain serious for both lawyers suffering harm because of their reliance on LT tools and for consumers using LT technologies without lawyers' intermediation.

Regarding lawyers' position, it is important to note that lawyers, LT providers and other commercial actors within the AI value chain often define the obligations and responsibilities of the various participants of the chain through private ordering.[55] These B2B contractual arrangements typically allocate responsibility and liability for specific types of harm, such as those arising from AI-generated outputs. However, the distribution of such obligations is frequently shaped by the relative bargaining power of the parties involved.[56] This imbalance of power can undermine both fairness and accountability within the AI supply chain, particularly to the detriment of smaller or less influential stakeholders, such as small law firms and solo lawyers. It would therefore be crucial to limit the possibility for LT provider to entirely exclude its liability in cases where its defective performance has led to the violation of the fundamental rights of a lawyer's client. This is especially relevant whenever the professional user has not acted negligently and has taken all reasonable steps to prevent the harm. This would of course require interpreting the UCTD and RPLD to extend their scope of

[52] Van Alsenoy (2016, 282–290).

[53] Karjalainen (2022, 19–30).

[54] Economides (2010, 371–382).

[55] Alaire (2023, 105).

[56] Edwards (2024, 13, 23).

application to contracts between LT providers and professional deployers, and interpreting the reach of RPLD as covering LT services considered as products. Both these interpretations are highly needed to avoid that stronger contractual actors unilaterally disclaim responsibility in such circumstances.

Consumers who have suffered damage from their direct use of LT tools may of course rely on the above EU framework (although with the caveat just expressed), as well as on the consumer protection measures surveyed in the previous section. Yet, it should be kept in mind that, by using AI tools consumers enter into a contract with the LT provider, typically through the subscription of general terms and conditions that limit their rights to sue both in contract and in tort. Moreover, consumers willing to complain would have to prove that the provider breached the contract or unlawfully caused them harm. In the absence of legal presumptions or mechanisms that ease the burden of proof, establishing these elements can be particularly challenging, especially given the technical complexity of LT tools, the difficulty in accessing relevant evidence and the limited resources that are available to consumers to pursue legal action.

One possible interpretative way out from this conundrum–as argued in the previous section–would be to extend to LT providers the core obligations that are established under lawyers' codes of conduct and associated best practices, relying on the circumstances that LT tools offer legal information, documents and, to some extent, legal advice. Yet, this interpretive move that would likely face considerable resistance from the tech sector. Moreover, as just noticed, courts have traditionally been very cautious in establishing lawyers' liability vis-à-vis their clients. It would therefore be crucial that courts assess the peculiar position of LT providers in the legal services domain and evaluate whether the doctrines traditionally applied to human lawyers should be extended to automated providers of legal services.

7 Conclusion

While the widespread use of AI in the European legal sector undoubtedly brings new opportunities and benefits–such as increased productivity for law firms, enhanced competitiveness in the legal services market, improved access to justice and the broader dissemination of legal knowledge–, it also gives rise to a range of novel vulnerabilities, as well as the exacerbation of existing ones. The opaque technological architecture of AI tools, the limited legal and technical literacy of AI users, the insufficient guarantees for the development and deployment of such tools, as well as the costs associated with the use of these technologies, are all factors that expose a wide range of users to the risk of abuse. What the present survey has hopefully demonstrated is that LT sector creates vulnerabilities, not only for consumers but also for lawyers (especially those who operate in small law firms or as solo practitioners) and their clients. All these subjects, although to different extent and on different terms, are at risk of suffering harm, with potential significant negative consequences, both in economic and non-economic terms.

To prevent and mitigate the vulnerabilities that arise because of the use and diffusion of LT tools, it is fundamental to strengthen the *ex ante* and *ex post* measures that currently exist in the EU legal framework and yet are not enough to face the challenges posed by AI. In particular, this paper argues that it is essential to adopt new *ex ante* measures that align with the current technological landscape and associated risks, and, at the same time, avoid unduly hindering the adoption and development of AI technologies. The optimal balance herein offered lies in ensuring continuous and effective human oversight and in promoting the dissemination of best practices among lawyers and LT providers.

Similar observations apply to *ex post* measures. Notwithstanding the many EU liability frameworks and their implementation within national liability regimes, access to remedies is extremely challenging for injured parties–whether consumers, clients or legal professionals–, while, conversely, AI providers often enjoy a de facto immunity from liability. To avoid such a result, it would be important for courts to appreciate the structural imbalance of power in the tech sector and to interpret contractually agreed immunities against LT providers. Moreover, it is also important to think about equating LT providers to lawyers, at least for the purpose of making them subject to professional duties vis-à-vis their users.

The success of the proposals herein contained would clearly require several reforms, changes in judicial interpretations, bar authorities' involvement, lawyers' adoption of new forms of self-regulation. Yet, the argument of this paper is that these modifications are both feasible and needed to ensure the effective protection of the rights of a wide array of affected stakeholders: not only consumers but also lawyers' clients and even lawyers.

References

Alaire B (2023) An evidence-based approach to private ordering. Univ Tor L J 73:105–123

AI Governance Alliance (2025) Artificial Intelligence and Cybersecurity: Balancing Risks and Rewards. World Economic Forum https://reports.weforum.org/docs/WEF_Artificial_Intelligence_and_Cybersecurity_Balancing_Risks_and_Rewards_2025.pdf

Armour J, Parnham R, Sako M (2021) AI-assisted LawTech: its impact on law firms. Oxford University.https://www.law.ox.ac.uk/sites/default/files/migrated/ai_final1097.pdf.

Armour J, Parnham R, Sako M (2022) Augmented Lawyering. Univ Ill Law Rev 1:71–138

Atrey I (2023) Revolutionising the legal industry: the intersection of artificial intelligence and law. Int J Law Manag Humanit 6:1075–1089

Biard A (2023) The age of consumer law enforcement in the European Union: high hopes or wishful thinking? Eur J Risk Regul 15:625–636

Bonardi M, Branting KL (2024) Certifying legal AI assistants for unrepresented litigants: a global survey of access to civil justice, unauthorized practice of law, and AI. Colum Sci Tech Law Rev 26:34–106

Brescia RH et al (2015) Embracing disruption: how technological change in the delivery of legal services can improve access to justice. Alb Law Rev 78:553–622

Cook J et al (2024) AI-ready attorneys: ethical obligations and privacy considerations in the age of artificial intelligence. Univ Kansas Law Rev 72:313–365

Council of Bars and Law Societies of Europe (2012) CCBE Guidelines on the use of Cloud Computing Services by Lawyers. Council of Bars and Law Societies of Europe. https://www.ccbe.eu/fileadmin/speciality_distribution/public/documents/IT_LAW/ITL_Guides_recommendations/EN_ITL_20250227__CCBE-guidelines-on-the-use-of-cloud-computing-by-lawyers.pdf
Council of Bars and Law Societies of Europe (2020) CCBE Considerations on the legal aspects of artificial intelligence. Council of Bars and Law Societies of Europe. https://www.ccbe.eu/fileadmin/speciality_distribution/public/documents/IT_LAW/ITL_Guides_recommendations/EN_ITL_20200220_CCBE-considerations-on-the-Legal-Aspects-of-AI.pdf
Crea C, De Franceschi A (eds) (2024) The new shapes of digital vulnerability in european private law. Nomos, Baden Baden
Cruz SE (2019) Coding for cultural competency: expanding access to justice with technology. Tennessee Law Rev 86:347–402
DRI Center for Law and Public Policy Artificial Intelligence Working Group (2024) Artificial intelligence in legal practice benefits, considerations, and best practices. DRI https://www.dri.org/docs/default-source/dri-white-papers-and-reports/ai-legal-practice.pdf
Ebers M (2021) Legal tech and EU consumer law. In: Di Matteo A et al (eds) Lawyering in the digital age. CU Press, Cambridge, pp 195–220
Economides CP (2010) Content of the obligation: obligations of means and obligations of results. In Crawford et al. (eds) The law of international responsibility, OUP, Oxford, pp 371–382
Edwards L (2024), Private ordering and generative AI: what can we learn from model terms and conditions? In forthcoming Zou et al. (eds) Cambridge research handbook on generative AI and the law (CUP 2025)
Escajeda HJ (2020) The Vitruvian lawyer: how to thrive in an era of AI and quantum technologies. Kansas J Law Publ Policy 29:421–495
European Lawyers Foundation (2021) Opportunities and barriers in the use of natural language processing tools in SME law practice. European Lawyers Foundation. https://elf-fae.eu/wp-content/uploads/2021/12/Report-on-opportunities-and-barriers-in-the-use-of-NLP-tools-in-SME-law-practices.pdf
Fenwick M, Vermeulen EPM (2019) The lawyer of the future as "transaction engineer": digital technologies and the disruption of the legal profession. In Corrales M et al (eds), Legal tech, smart contracts and blockchain, Springer, Singapore, pp 253–272
Ferrar D (2025) How AI is empowering small law firms, Artificial Lawyer. Legal Tech & AI News, https://www.artificiallawyer.com/2025/04/11/how-ai-is-empowering-small-law/
Godman C (2019) Symposium: lawyering in the age of artificial intelligence: AI/ESQ.: impacts of artificial intelligence in law-client relationships. Okla Law Rev 72:149–185
Griffin CL, Laskowski C, Thumma SA (2024) A preliminary agenda for using generative AI to improve access to justice. Judicature 108:42–51
Guttenberg JA (2012) Practicing law in the twenty-first century in a twentieth (nineteenth) century straight jacket: something has to give. Michigan State Int Law Rev 20:415–491
Homoki P et al (2022) Guide on the use of artificial intelligence-based tools by lawyers and law firms in the EU. Council of Bars and Law Societies of Europe, https://www.ccbe.eu/fileadmin/speciality_distribution/public/documents/IT_LAW/ITL_Reports_studies/EN_ITL_20220331_Guide-AI4L.pdf
Infantino M, Di Matteo A (2024) AI, lawyers, and consumers. In: Di Matteo LA, Poncibò C, Howells G (eds) AI and consumer law. Cambridge University Press, Cambridge, pp 252–272
Infantino M, Mišćenić E, Tereszkiewicz P (2023) The interplay between the CJEU and national courts in the case law on unfair contract terms in foreign currency loans: a comparative overview. Eur Rev Contract Law 19:346–374
International Bar Association and The Center for AI and Digital Policy (2022) The future is now: artificial intelligence and the legal profession. International Bar Association. https://www.ibanet.org/document?id=The-future-is%20now-AI-and-the-legal-profession-report

Jacobowitz JL (2018) Happy Birthday Siri! Dialing in legal ethics for artificial intelligence, smartphones, and real time lawyers. Texas A M J Property Law 4:407–442
Karjalainen T (2022) All talk, no action? the effect of the GDPR accountability principle on the EU data protection paradigm. Eur Data Prot Law Rev 8:19–30
Koenig ML, Oseid JA, Vorenberg A (2019) Ok, Google, will artificial intelligence replace human lawyering? Marquette Law Rev 102:1269–1304
Kunkel R (2018) Rationing justice in the 21st century: technocracy and technology in the access to justice movement. Univ Md Law J Race, Religion, Gender Class 18:366–390
Mišćenić E (2024) Information, transparency and fairness for consumers in the digital environment. In Crea C, De Franceschi A (eds) The new shapes of digital vulnerability in European Private Law. Nomos, Baden Baden, pp 89–126
Navas S (2019) The provision of legal services to consumers using LawTech tools: from 'service' to 'legal product.' Open J Soc Sci 7:79–103
OECD (2019) Legal needs surveys and access to justice. OECD Publishing https://www.oecd.org/content/dam/oecd/en/publications/reports/2019/05/legal-needs-surveys-and-access-to-justice_g1g9a36c/g2g9a36c-en.pdf
Pan X et al (2020) Privacy risks of general-purpose language models. IEEE Symposium on Security and Privacy https://ieeexplore.ieee.org/stamp/stamp.jsp?tp=&arnumber=9152761
Pasquale F, Cashwell G (2015) Four futures of legal automation. UCLA Law Rev Discour 26:26–48
Pietrapaoli I et al (2023) Use of artificial intelligence in legal practice. British Institute of International and Comparative Law https://www.biicl.org/documents/170_use_of_artificial_intelligence_in_legal_practice_final.pdf
PWC (2024) Annual Law Firms' Survey 2024. https://www.pwc.co.uk/industries/legal-professional-business-support-services/law-firms-survey.html#bottom-kick
Schwarcz D, Choi JH (2023) AI tools for lawyers: a practical guide. Minn Law Rev 108:1–35
Sein K et al (2019) The new directive on contracts for the supply of digital content and digital services—scope of application and trader's obligation to supply—part 1. Eur Rev Contract Law 15:257–279
Simshaw D (2018) Ethical issues in robo-lawyering: the need for guidance on developing and using artificial intelligence in the practice of law. Hastings L J 70:173–214
Van Alsenoy B (2016) Liability under EU data protection law: from directive 95/46 to the general data protection regulation. JIPITEC 7:271–288
Yamane N (2020) Current developments: 2019–2020: artificial intelligence in the legal field and the indispensable human element legal ethics demands. Geo J Legal Ethics 33:877–909

Privacy and Personal Data Protection in Online Land Registers: A Comparative and European Perspective

Maria Kaczorowska

Abstract The technological development has had substantial impact on the publicity of land registers, resulting in common access to them via the Internet. Given the wide range of personal data disclosed in land registers, the increase in their publicity poses major challenges to privacy and data protection. Various legal and technical solutions have been adopted in European countries to safeguard personal data contained in land registers. Noteworthy in this regard are, i.a., current plans for an amendment to the rules on online access to land registers existing in Poland. The need for adequate privacy and personal data safeguards in access to land registers refers not only to the national level but also to the European Union efforts for enhancing cross-border accessibility of land information. In this paper, the restrictions on the publicity of land registers introduced in selected European jurisdictions will be examined comparatively in terms of their efficiency as remedies to violations of the rights to privacy and personal data protection. Moreover, the issue will be addressed of possible measures at the European level to prevent the misuses of personal data when interconnecting land registers.

Keywords Land registers · European laws · Privacy · Interoperability

1 Introduction

Land registers play a prominent role in ensuring legal certainty and security of real estate transactions by collecting, storing and disclosing information on property rights over immovable properties. It is the publicity of land registers, in its aspect of providing access to the information contained in them (formal publicity), that is a prerequisite for achieving this crucial socio-economic objective. The technological advancements in recent decades have resulted in significantly enhancing the accessibility of land registers, which are now prevalently available via the Internet. Throughout this paper, the uniform term 'land register' will be used to designate a

M. Kaczorowska (✉)
Faculty of Law, Administration and Economics, University of Wrocław, Wrocław, Poland
e-mail: maria.kaczorowska@uwr.edu.pl

C. Crea and M. Infantino (eds.), *Remedies to Digital Vulnerability in European Private Law*, https://doi.org/10.1007/978-3-032-19720-7_24

public register kept by competent judicial or administrative authority for the purpose of disclosing the legal status of immovable property. In accordance with a definition used internationally, land registration is understood as the process of recording rights in land either in the form of registration of deeds or else through the registration of title to land; accordingly, land register is defined as a public register used to record the existence of deeds or title documents.[1]

The range of information disclosed in land registers includes a vast amount of data regarding the persons whose rights are registered. Therefore, the technology-driven unprecedented increase in the publicity of land registers generates a risk of processing the land register data in a manner contrary to the purpose for which they were collected, and may lead to violations of the right to privacy and personal data protection. This is why methods of accessing land registers adopted in a number of European countries involve some legal and technical restrictions aimed at safeguarding personal data. Such access limitations include, i.a., a requirement for the users to register before consulting land registers, a classification of data stored in land registers into categories according to the level of accessibility, and a requirement to demonstrate a specific interest in inspecting the content of land registers. This approach is currently followed in Poland, which is manifested by the preparatory work on introducing a mandatory authentication mechanism for users accessing the land registers' database so that unrestricted online access to the content of land registers will no longer be possible. The problem of privacy and personal data protection also features in the European Union initiatives for facilitating cross-border access to land information by interconnecting the Member States' land registers.

The aim of this chapter is to provide a comparative overview of restrictions of Internet access to land registers existing in selected European jurisdictions, with particular consideration of Poland. On this basis, the main measures implemented to ensure privacy and personal data protection will be identified. Additionally, in the context of the cooperation projects pursued at the European level to interconnect national land registers, the possibilities of introducing effective common solutions for remedying the risks of personal data misuse will be examined.

2 Publicity of Land Registers and Digital Risks for Privacy

Irrespective of the divergence of land registration models used in European jurisdictions,[2] the principle of formal publicity is commonly acknowledged as a foundation for the organisation of land registers, with its rationale being the third-party effect

[1] United Nations Economic Commission for Europe (1996, 108). Different names for land registers can be found across European countries. For instance, the register operating in Poland is called *księga wieczysta*, which in English literally means 'perpetual book', and is often translated as 'land and mortgage register.' See further, e.g., Gościński and Kubacki (2021, 1468 ff), Lodde (2016, 33).

[2] See, e.g., Zevenbergen (2002), Cámara Lapuente (2005, 797–839), Schmid, Hertel, Wicke (2005, 27–46), Lodde (2016, 23–42), Martínez Velencoso (2017, 3–19), Blajer (2018), Marin (2019, 229–236), Vern (2021, 835–852).

(*erga omnes* effect) of property rights. It implies that third parties should have the ability to get access to information regarding the existence and content of such rights.[3] There are, however, differences in the ways of implementing this principle in national legal systems. While under most domestic laws land registers are open to the general public, without the need to meet additional personal requirements, in some countries certain restrictions apply, in particular the access may be conditional on the demonstration of a form of interest.[4]

The technological advancements in recent decades have resulted in transforming traditional paper-based land registers into electronic databases, and thus in substantially broadening and facilitating access to the information stored in them. The availability of land registers on the Internet offers new access methods, and improves the searchability of land register data, which leads to a notable reinforcement of the informative function of land registers.[5]

It should be highlighted that apart from the information about the property itself, concerning the type of property, its location, land ownership and possible encumbrances, land registers contain a considerable amount of personal data of the holders of rights entered therein or contained in the documents registered. These data include in particular name and surname, national identification number, identity document number, home address, date and place of birth, marital status as well as parents' names.[6] Generally, given the public character of land registers, public availability extends to all the information contained therein, including personal data. Furthermore, not only current but also archival data can be accessed in some instances.[7]

Of relevance in this context is that, from the perspective of international privacy and personal data protection standards, public access to land registers shall be deemed an admissible limitation of the right to respect for private and family life as provided for in Article 8 of the European Convention on Human Rights,[8] which has been confirmed in the European Court of Human Rights' case law.[9] Also, the disclosure of personal data in land registers is considered lawful in terms of the requirements set out in Article 6(1) of the General Data Protection Regulation (hereinafter: GDPR).[10] The potential legal grounds for the processing of personal data in this case are:

---

[3] Blajer (2022, 5), Berlee (2018, 2, 18).

[4] Blajer (2022, 6), Schmid, Hertel, Wicke (2005, 44), Wudarski (2014, 444–468).

[5] See, e.g., Kaczorowska (2020a, 149 ff), Kaczorowska (2019, 30 ff) and the literature cited there.

[6] Wudarski (2024, 157), Berlee (2018, 4 ff).

[7] Wudarski (2024, 158).

[8] Convention for the Protection of Human Rights and Fundamental Freedoms of 4 November 1950.

[9] See, e.g., Banaszak and Mysiak (2014, 1241–1242), Kowalik (2020, 119), Berlee (2018, 171 ff). A similar interpretation has been adopted by the Polish Constitutional Tribunal under Article 31, paragraph 3 of the Constitution of the Republic of Poland of 2 April 1997, as amended.

[10] Regulation (EU) 2016/679 on the protection of natural persons with regard to the processing of personal data and on the free movement of such data, and repealing Directive 95/46/EC (General Data Protection Regulation), as amended.

compliance with a legal obligation of the controller (Article 6(1) letter c GDPR) and a task carried out in the public interest (Article 6(1) letter e GDPR).[11]

However, the facilitated online access to land registers raises concerns as it poses significant challenges to privacy and data protection, such as the risk of identity theft and aggregation of personal data from land registers, other public records and Internet sources by commercial entities in order to create digital profiles of individuals. It may be illustrated by the practice of indexing land register data and making them available for payment in commercial services that has developed with the increased openness of land registers. This is the case, e.g., in Poland, where over 10 years ago the problem of trade in land register data received notable coverage in press publications and provoked an intense debate in the legal literature on possible limitations of online access to land registers.[12]

3 Access Restrictions as Methods to Safeguard Personal Data in Land Registers: Examples

Among European countries, there is substantial variation in the accessibility to electronic land registers. In some legal systems, including the Polish one, free Internet access to the full content of land registers is ensured without any formal or technical restrictions, which is an expression of the principle of absolute publicity. Other jurisdictions have adopted different technical and legal solutions to safeguard personal data contained in land registers, i.a.: granting access to land registers only to registered (authenticated) users who are obliged to create an appropriate account in the ICT system, which in many cases is subject to a fee; providing distinct levels of publicity of land registers depending on the status of the users; and imposing a requirement to demonstrate an interest in consulting the land register, without the possibility of accessing it directly via the Internet.

To illustrate this diversity, the rules concerning the inspection of land registers in force in selected European countries will be outlined below with a focus on restrictions of access. The issues regarding the methods of obtaining copies and certificates from land registers as well as access to land register files will be omitted.

3.1 Poland

Polish land registers are set up and kept in the ICT system. For the purpose of keeping electronic land registers, a central land and mortgage registers' database, maintained by the Minister of Justice, has been established. The information from the database

[11] Gołaczyński (2019, 111 ff), Legat and Orkusz (2019, 11–15, 28–29), Berlee (2018, 206–208).

[12] See, e.g., Krupa-Dąbrowska (2013).

is provided by the Central Information Office of the Land and Mortgage Registers, with its agencies at district court departments that keep land registers.[13]

In the present state of the law, anyone can consult a land register using a free browser offered by the Ministry of Justice,[14] without the need to justify his or her request, the only requirement being to know the number of the register kept for a particular immovable property—it is, therefore, the only instrument of personal data protection. According to Article 36(4), paragraph 5 of the Land and Mortgage Registers and Mortgage Act of 6 July 1982 (hereinafter LMRMA), the Central Information Office of the Land and Mortgage Registers enables viewing of land and mortgage registers through the ICT system. Whoever knows the number of a land and mortgage register may view it free of charge through the ICT system[15]; printouts of contents displayed in the viewing mode do not have the force of documents issued by the court.[16] Fully open online access means that it is possible to view land register data on the Internet on an anonymous basis. In this regard, it should be noted that the information on the number of a land register can be obtained in different ways, including, i.a., from the court that keeps the land register, from the roll of land and buildings (i.e. the cadastre), based on the data stored in another land register, through commercial websites offering paid search services as well as by entering sequential combinations of land register numbers in the ICT system.[17]

Separate access rules apply to authorised public entities, such as courts, bailiffs, notaries, custom and tax authorities and the police. They are entitled, if it is required for them to implement statutory tasks, to repeated, unlimited in time searching of land registers in the central land and mortgage registers' database with the use of both objective and subjective searching criteria.[18]

At the turn of 2024 and 2025, plans for an amendment to the provisions on public online access to land registers were announced by the Ministry of Justice. It is intended that a mandatory authentication mechanism for users accessing the database will be introduced to better protect personal data contained in land registers. In line with the arguments of the Ministry of Justice, this will prevent mass automated downloading of data from land registers with the use of robots. Additionally, access logs are going to be introduced with the purpose of recording the information about who, when and to what extent has viewed a given land register.[19] The proposed amendment was approved by the President of the Personal Data Protection Office.[20] This

[13] See further, e.g., Gołaczyński (2020a, 3–39), Rękawek-Pachwicewicz (2013), Kaczorowska (2021a, 81–105) and the literature cited there.

[14] The browser is available at https://ekw.ms.gov.pl.

[15] Article 36(4), paragraph 6 LMRMA.

[16] Article 36(4), paragraph 7 LMRMA. See also Wudarski (2024, 159–160), Blajer (2022, 25–26).

[17] See further, e.g., Wudarski (2014, 448–449), Gryszczyńska (2016, 268–269, 304), Kamiński (2020, 61–62), Świątko (2021, 1308).

[18] The list of the authorised entities is provided in Article 36(4), paragraph 8 LMRMA.

[19] See Zmiany w dostępie do ksiąg wieczystych, at https://www.gov.pl/web/sprawiedliwosc/zmiany-w-dos-tepie-do-ksiag-wieczystych; Ministerstwo Sprawiedliwości (2025, 19, 21).

[20] See Dane z ksiąg wieczystych będą lepiej chronione, at https://uodo.gov.pl/pl/138/3402.

new approach corresponds to calls for legislative changes that have been expressed by the representatives of the Polish legal scholarship and some public institutions for many years.[21]

In this context, reference should be made to a latest judgment of the Polish Supreme Administrative Court, which falls within the same trend. The case in question concerned the lawfulness of publishing land register numbers by the Surveyor General of Poland on the Geoportal website. In the judgment of 28 January 2025, III OSK 6508/21,[22] the Supreme Administrative Court ruled that land register numbers are personal data under GDPR as they can lead to the identification of individuals and access to sensitive information, thus posing a risk of identity theft.

3.2 *Italy*

The land registration system in force in most of the Italian territory, called the transcription system, is aimed at making publicly knowable the deeds by which ownership and other property rights related to immovable properties are constituted, modified, transferred or extinguished.[23] The competence to keep land registers lies with the Italian Revenue Agency. As for Internet access to land registers, it is possible to carry out online queries through a query channel available to all citizens, upon registration. To this aim, different services can be used, either for a fee or free of charge.[24]

One-time inspection is offered upon payment on the Agency's website. Online land register queries can be carried out by subject (limited to natural persons), by the estate cadastral data and by note if its date and particular registry number are known. They are available for any district of the national territory, with the exception of the provinces and other areas where the *tavolare* system is in force.[25]

The land registers' database can also be accessed through the Agency's web service—Sister, based on an agreement with the Agency. This method is intended for both public bodies and private users, in the latter case upon payment. Moreover, by registering with Entratel/Fisconline telematic services, it is possible to carry out online personal queries, free of charge, on the properties of which the applicant is holding a title of ownership or other property rights.[26]

---

[21] For more on this issue, see, e.g., Gryszczyńska (2016, 261 ff), Gołaczyński (2020b, 395–405), Kaczorowska (2020b, 88 ff), Kaczorowska (2022, 31–42) and the literature cited there.

[22] See https://orzeczenia.nsa.gov.pl/doc/F5DC8DD772.

[23] In addition to the transcription system, the so-called *tavolare* system, being a title registration system, applies in the territories of the past Habsburg monarchy and afterwards maintained, i.e. in the provinces of Trento, Bolzano, Trieste, Gorizia and in some municipalities in the provinces of Udine, Belluno, Vicenza and Brescia. See, e.g., Agenzia delle Entrate (2024, 2), Blajer (2018, 250), Pradi (2012, 153 ff).

[24] Agenzia delle Entrate (2024, 16).

[25] Agenzia delle Entrate (2024, 16–17).

[26] Agenzia delle Entrate (2024, 17).

3.3 Estonia

In Estonia, the data on all registered immovables are available in the e-Land Register portal, operated by the Centre of Registers and Information Systems.[27] Access methods offered to the users cover individual and contractual large-scale queries.

Individual queries can be performed on an infrequent basis, without entering into any agreement. Anyone who logs in to the e-Land Register as a private person with an ID-card or Mobile-ID can access the information on the registered immovable he or she owns free of charge. It is also possible for the owner of a registered immovable to grant another natural person the right to access his or her land registry file documents. In case of registered immovables belonging to others, queries are subject to a fee. Worthy of note is that the e-Land Register is interfaced with a data monitoring system, which means that when viewing the personal data related to a registered immovable, the owner can see information about the person making the query in the data monitoring system of the eesti.ee portal.

When it comes to contracted users, upon registration at the e-Land Register, companies and institutions can obtain larger volumes of land register data on a daily basis to verify data on registered immovables. This service is paid by invoice once a month. Additionally, contracted customers of the e-Land Register have access to other public registers.

At the initiative of the Ministry of Justice, the provisions governing the publicity of land registers were amended in 2024 to the effect that as of 15 January 2025 ordinary users are no longer able to search the register by an individual's name or personal identification code, which previously allowed the users to easily find a person's residence online. With the above-mentioned amendment, the e-Land Register remained public, but searches can only be made by property address, cadastral code or registry number.[28]

3.4 Czech Republic

Specific to the model adopted in the Czech Republic is that the land register (more precisely real estate cadastre), kept by the State Administration of Land Surveying and the Cadastre, contains both factual and legal information on immovable property,

[27] See E-Land Register portal, at https://www.rik.ee/en/e-land-register/e-land-register-portal; Land registers in EU countries: Estonia, at https://e-justice.europa.eu/topics/registers-business-insolvency-land/land-registers-eu-countries/ee_en; Rękawek-Pachwicewicz (2021, 115 ff), Kaing (2012, 29 ff), Kaczorowska (2020a, 267 ff) and the literature cited there.

[28] Legislative amendment scraps option to look up properties by owner name, at https://news.err.ee/1609521088/legislative-amendment-scraps-option-to-look-up-properties-by-owner-name.

with a distinction of two categories of data disclosed in the land register, to which different access rules apply.[29]

Online access through the ‘Viewing the Real Estate Cadastre’ application does not require any registration and is free of charge, but is limited to basic data about the parcels, buildings, premises and building rights as well as information on pending land registration proceedings. The application is intended exclusively for interactive work of users; any acquisition or extraction of data by automated means is not permitted.[30]

More detailed (complete) information, including the names of the owners of immovable properties and of the participants to land registration proceedings, is available only to registered users. It can be accessed through the National Point of Identification and Authentication Portal, known as e-Identita, or through an account for remote access to the Real Estate Cadastre.[31]

Interestingly, the scope of freely accessible data was limited in 2021 because of increased illegal exploitation of the cadastre database by software robots. As a result, an anonymous (not logged in) user of the application is no longer able to access the data of the owners and participants to the proceedings, but only the above-mentioned selected data.[32]

3.5 Austria

The Austrian land register is kept by specialised district courts and is publicly accessible.[33] It can be consulted, for a small fee, via courts, notaries, lawyers as well as so-called clearing offices, authorised by the Federal Ministry of Justice, that offer queries in the land register database. By entering the number of the cadastral municipality and the entry number or the plot number it is possible to obtain extracts from the land register and from the auxiliary indexes.[34]

There is, however, a restriction as regards searching solely for individual owners. In order to protect the privacy of individuals, such queries can be carried out only upon proving that one has a legal interest. This requirement does not apply to notaries, lawyers, local public agencies and social security agencies. Furthermore, as follows

[29] See, e.g., Land registers in EU countries: Czechia, at https://e-justice.europa.eu/topics/registers-business-insolvency-land/land-registers-eu-countries/cz_en; Kliková (2008, 163–173), Kaczorowska (2020a, 262 ff).

[30] Nahlížení do katastru nemovitostí, at https://nahlizenidokn.cuzk.gov.cz/. See also Pesl, Rydval, Slaboch (2004).

[31] Nahlížení do katastru nemovitostí, at https://nahlizenidokn.cuzk.gov.cz/.

[32] Menclová (2021). See also State Administration of Land Surveying and Cadastre (2024).

[33] Federal Ministry of Justice (2023, 15), Blajer (2016, 34 ff), Greco (2015, 34 ff), Kaczorowska (2020a, 248 ff).

[34] Land registers in EU countries: Austria, at https://e-justice.europa.eu/topics/registers-business-insolvency-land/land-registers-eu-countries/at_en; Grundstücksdatenbank; Blajer (2016, 39–40), Greco (2015, 37).

from the legislation in force, the Federal Ministry for Constitutional Affairs, Reforms, Deregulation and Justice shall, upon request of a person affected by the query, provide information on who made the query and at what time it was carried out in the case of queries of the list of persons from the database by notaries and lawyers.[35]

3.6 *Germany*

The responsibility for land registration in Germany is vested in land registry offices competent for the districts in which the property is located in all federal states. Land registers are kept primarily in the electronic format, nevertheless they are not available online. As a rule, access to electronic land registers is only possible in the land register offices, on specially prepared screens, with the approval and under supervision of the staff of the office.[36]

The German rules on access to land registers represent the most restrictive approach to the principle of formal publicity. This is because a prerequisite for accessing a land register is the demonstration of a legitimate interest in consulting it (in particular for legal or economic reasons). The underlying premise of the limited publicity of land registers is to balance the public interest and the protection of privacy.[37] Land owners and other registered titleholders do not participate in the process of checking the legitimate interest of a person requesting access to their information, and can only get access to the log kept by the land registry of who has been granted access for a particular plot of land.[38]

A restricted group of users, including courts, public authorities, notaries, credit institutions and utility companies, may consult the land register data via an electronic portal for the respective federal states. Moreover, the notaries may communicate the content of the land register to persons who can demonstrate a legitimate interest. Consulting the land register electronically is subject to a fee.[39]

---

[35] Land registers in EU countries: Austria, at https://e-justice.europa.eu/topics/registers-business-insolvency-land/land-registers-eu-countries/at_en; Blajer (2016, 40), Greco (2015, 37).

[36] Land registers in EU countries: Germany, at https://e-justice.europa.eu/topics/registers-business-insolvency-land/land-registers-eu-countries/de_en; Wudarski (2024, 161–162), Blajer (2022, 19), Blajer (2016, 11 ff), Berlee (2018, 109 ff). See also Internet access to the land register, at https://en.justiz.de/onlinedienste/internet_grundbucheinsicht/index.php.

[37] Wudarski (2024, 161 ff), Blajer (2022, 18–19), Berlee (2018, 297 ff).

[38] Berlee (2018, 343–344).

[39] Wudarski (2024, 165), Blajer (2022, 19); Land registers in EU countries: Germany.

4 Personal Data Protection Challenges in the Context of the European Interconnection of Land Registers

In view of the vital importance of cross-border access to land information for the development of the internal market, extensive actions are being undertaken in the European Union with the purpose of strengthening the cooperation among national land registration authorities and improving the accessibility of electronic land registers. Thereby, the prospect of further increasing the scope of the publicity of land registers involves the need for adequate privacy and personal data safeguards at the European level.[40]

One of the initiatives currently implemented under the European e-Justice Strategy[41] is the 'Land Registers Interconnection' (LRI) project. Its aim is to provide a single access point on the European e-Justice Portal[42] that will allow citizens and professionals from EU Member States to enquire and retrieve relevant information from national land registers in real-time. The project started in 2015 at the initiative of the European Commission, drawing on the results of the previous 'European Land Information Service' (EULIS) project as well as the ongoing 'Interoperability Model for Land Registers' (IMOLA) project, coordinated by the European Land Registry Association (ELRA).[43]

Within this framework, between 2018 and 2019, the 'LRI Member State Connection' project was carried out with the participation of Austria and Estonia. Apart from the technical interconnection to the European e-Justice Portal, the project covered establishing a cross-border authentication mechanism for authorising the legal professionals (including judges, court officials, notaries) who can prove a strong legal interest to carry out restricted privileged searches, such as by person name, to identify all properties of a specific person. For data protection reasons, these privileged functions are not available for normal users who can search property only by an address, a parcel number or a legal entity number, for a fee.[44]

The works undertaken were continued within the follow-up 'LRI MS Connection 2' project in the years 2020–2021, with an expanded group of countries being involved (the new project participants were Spain, Latvia, Hungary and Portugal). The objectives of the project included further analysis regarding the integration of additional services to the LRI platform, such as integrating a payment solution and a future authentication solution.[45]

---

[40] See Berlee (2018, 54–55).

[41] European Commission (2019a, b, 2025).

[42] The European e-Justice Portal is available at https://e-justice.europa.eu.

[43] See further, e.g., Gołaczyński and Kaczorowska (2023, 45–52), Zimmermann (2021), Kaczorowska (2021b, 121–124); Blajer (2018, 802 ff), Moerkerke (2018, 13 ff), Lodde (2017, 74 ff).

[44] Interconnecting land registers, at https://lri-ms.eu/node/19; The purpose of the project, at https://lri-ms.eu/purpose; Innovative aspects, at https://lri-ms.eu/innovation.

[45] Connecting land registers to e-Justice Portal, at https://lri-ms.eu/node/41; Registradores de España (2021).

Considering that the interconnection of registers in the domain of justice remains a high priority for the European Commission, it is planned that the 'LRI MS Connection 2' project partners will be seeking possibilities to continue the work conducted so far. A point of reference in this respect shall be the outcomes of the 'Business Ownership Registers Interconnection System' (BORIS) project.[46]

5 Conclusion

As is apparent from the foregoing, the tension between the publicity of land registers and the right to privacy, conditioned by the contemporary technological progress, is reflected in the European countries' domestic legislation. In the jurisdictions where land registers are publicly available via the Internet, there is a trend to limit their publicity by introducing technical restrictions of access with a view to increasing privacy and personal data protection, in particular by preventing the use of automated methods of data downloading. The dominant solutions in this respect are, firstly, the requirement of authentication, possibly accompanied by the payment of a fee, and, secondly, limiting the scope of publicly available land register data. While the former is a manifestation of departure from the anonymity of access to land registers, the latter is based on the assumption that 'only what is really necessary for the security of real estate transactions can be made public.'[47]

An example confirming the tendency towards imposing the verification of the identity of users accessing the land registers' database is the amendment currently under preparation in Poland, which has been preceded by a wide-ranging debate at the academic and institutional levels. With reference to the existing requirement of knowing a given land register number, intended as a personal data safeguard and the only searching criterion for regular users, admittedly, it prevents searching the land registers' database by subject and thus obtaining the information on all the immovable properties owned by a person,[48] but at the same time this type of protection against possible data misuses proves insufficient. It is worth emphasising that resorting to the legal instruments provided for in the data protection and civil law rules is possible only in the event of a real threat to or an infringement of an individual's personal interests, which means that the available measures are merely reactive rather than preventive.[49] It appears that introducing an authentication mechanism, in turn, can have a certain preventive effect.

As foreseen in the preparatory work for the legislative changes in Poland, the authentication requirement will be accompanied by the implementation of access logs, which is also the case of some other legal systems discussed above. Such a solution, although of an 'after the fact' nature, strengthens the position of the

---

[46] Tammsaar (2021).

[47] Wudarski (2014, 468).

[48] Gryszczyńska (2011, 251), Leśniak (2010, 24).

[49] Wudarski (2014, 452), Kamiński (2020, 67–68).

titleholders whose rights are entered in the land registers in exercising their rights as data subjects.[50]

When it comes to the categorisation of land register data and the respective differentiation of access rules, as argued in the doctrine, on the one hand, these methods can serve to effectively protect at least some personal data, which do not necessarily need to be disclosed online.[51] On the other hand, there are critical views according to which limiting the scope of publicly available land register data does not comply with the very principle of publicity, and, what is more, it can mislead the users consulting the database.[52]

More far-reaching access restrictions based on the notion of interest to be demonstrated (a legitimate or legal interest test) as well as the intermediation of registrars or notaries in consulting land registers provide even better protection of personal data. At the same time, though, they significantly limit the implementation of the principle of publicity, and are envisaged in a relatively small number of legal systems in Europe.[53]

Characteristic to the methods of Internet access to land registers adopted in the national legal systems analysed in this paper is that specific search functionalities are offered to qualified professional users. This applies in particular to searching by subjective criteria such as the owner's name or personal identification code.

A similar approach as regards technical measures introduced to reconcile the publicity of electronic land registers and privacy (including an authentication mechanism and privileged searches) is followed in the ongoing process of interconnection of land registers in the European Union. Further directions of practical actions that would be accepted by all the Member States need yet to be developed, especially that only few countries have participated in the pilot phase of the LRI project.[54] Given the differences among specific technical and legal solutions existing in individual jurisdictions in terms of the kinds of access rights and user roles, in a long-term perspective an attempt at harmonisation in this regard may be expected.[55]

References

Agenzia delle Entrate (2024) The Italian land registration system. https://www.agenziaentrate.gov.it/portale/documents/20143/233875/Ed12gen24-The+Italian+Land+Registration+System_Ed_2024.pdf/42001672-3e11-cc55-46cd-4558bdc10b3e

Banaszak B, Mysiak P (2014) Konstytucyjne aspekty ksiąg wieczystych. Monitor Prawniczy 23:1238–1245

[50] Berlee (2018, 243, 388).

[51] See Gołaczyński (2020b, 398–399).

[52] See Kowalik (2020, 120).

[53] Cf Berlee (2018, 393).

[54] This fact was reported in European Commission (2020, 13–14, 15).

[55] Maurer (2021, 8).

Berlee A (2018) Access to personal data in public land registers: Balancing publicity of property rights with the rights to privacy and data protection. Eleven International Publishing, The Hague
Blajer P (2022) The principle of formal publicity of the land register in a comparative perspective. Eur Property Law J 11(1–2):5–28
Blajer P (2018) Rejestry nieruchomości: Studium prawnoporównawcze. Wydawnictwo C.H. Beck, Warszawa
Blajer P (2016) Elektroniczna "księga gruntowa": Geneza i aktualny postęp automatyzacji ksiąg gruntowych w Niemczech, Austrii i Szwajcarii. Krakowski Przegląd Notarialny 4:9–46
Cámara Lapuente S (2005) Registration of interests as a formality of contracts: Comparative remarks on land registers within the frame of European private law. Eur Rev Private Law 13(6):797–839
European Commission (2019a) 2019–2023 Strategy on e-Justice (ST/5139/2019/REV/1). Available at https://eur-lex.europa.eu/legal-content/EN/TXT/?uri=celex%3A52019XG0313%2801%29
European Commission (2019b) 2019–2023 Action Plan European e-Justice (2019/C 96/05). Available at https://eur-lex.europa.eu/legal-content/EN/TXT/?uri=celex%3A52019XG0313%2802%29
European Commission (2020) Communication from the Commission to the European Parliament, the Council, the European Economic and Social Committee and the Committee of the Regions. Digitalisation of justice in the European Union: A toolbox of opportunities (COM/2020/710 final). Available at https://eur-lex.europa.eu/legal-content/EN/ALL/?uri=COM:2020:710:FIN
European Commission (2025) European e-Justice Strategy 2024–2028 (C/2025/437). Available at https://eur-lex.europa.eu/legal-content/EN/TXT/PDF/?uri=OJ:C_202500437
Federal Ministry of Justice (2023) IT applications in the Austrian justice system. https://www.justiz.gv.at/file/2c94848b6ff7074f017493349cf54406.de.0/IT%20Applications%20in%20the%20Austrian%20Justice%20System%20Stand%2007.09.2023.pdf?forcedownload=true
Gołaczyński J (2019) Ochrona danych osobowych w rejestrach sądowych na przykładzie ksiąg wieczystych i Krajowego Rejestru Sądowego. In: Flaga-Gieruszyńska K, Gołaczyński J (eds) Ochrona danych osobowych w postępowaniach sądowych i przed organami administracji publicznej. Wolters Kluwer, Warszawa, pp 105–131
Gołaczyński J (2020a) Informatyzacja ksiąg wieczystych: Uwagi ogólne. In: Gołaczyński J (ed) Informatyzacja ksiąg wieczystych i postępowania wieczystoksięgowego. Wydawnictwo C.H. Beck, Warszawa, pp 3–39
Gołaczyński J (2020b) Wnioski *de lege ferenda* dotyczące jawności formalnej ksiąg wieczystych. In: Gołaczyński J (ed) Informatyzacja ksiąg wieczystych i postępowania wieczystoksięgowego. Wydawnictwo C.H. Beck, Warszawa, pp 395–405
Gołaczyński J, Kaczorowska M (2023) Interconnecting land registers at the European level: Technological progress and harmonization aspects. Rev Eur Compar Law 55(4):29–68
Gościński J, Kubacki AD (2021) Land registration concepts in translation. Int J Semiot Law 34:1451–1482
Greco A (2015) Transfer of immoveable and registration system in Austria: A brief overview. In: Pradi A (ed) From contract to registration: An overview of the transfer of immoveable property in Europe. Università degli Studi di Trento, Trento, pp 28–50
Gryszczyńska A (2016) Jawność formalna ksiąg wieczystych w Polsce. In: Gryszczyńska A (ed) Rejestry publiczne: Jawność i interoperacyjność. Wydawnictwo C.H. Beck, Warszawa, pp 255–310
Gryszczyńska A (2011) Nowa Księga Wieczysta: Informatyzacja rejestru publicznego. Lexis Nexis Polska, Warszawa
Kaczorowska M (2019) Informatisation of land registers in Poland and other Member States of the European Union: A comparative overview. Law Forensic Sci 17(1):30–48
Kaczorowska M (2020a) Postępy informatyzacji rejestrów nieruchomości w krajach Unii Europejskiej: Analiza prawnoporównawcza. In: Gołaczyński J (ed) Informatyzacja ksiąg wieczystych i postępowania wieczystoksięgowego. Wydawnictwo C.H. Beck, Warszawa, pp 149–391

Kaczorowska M (2020b) Realizacja zasady jawności ksiąg wieczystych w prawie polskim w dobie informatyzacji: Zarys problematyki. In: Gołaczyński J (ed) Informatyzacja ksiąg wieczystych i postępowania wieczystoksięgowego. Wydawnictwo C.H. Beck, Warszawa, pp 41–109

Kaczorowska M (2021a) Land and mortgage registers as a cornerstone of real estate transactions in Polish law: A historical and legal outline (On the 40th anniversary of the enactment of the Land and Mortgage Registers and Mortgage Act). Studia nad Autorytaryzmem i Totalitaryzmem 43(4):81–105

Kaczorowska M (2021b) Innovations in land registration and their impact on cross-border conveyancing in Europe. In: Robbie J, Akkermans B (eds) Property law perspectives VII. Eleven International Publishing, The Hague, pp 103–129

Kaczorowska M (2022) Jawność formalna elektronicznych ksiąg wieczystych a ochrona danych osobowych i prywatności: Wybrane zagadnienia. Przegląd Ustawodawstwa Gospodarczego 7:31–42

Kaing M (2012) Real property cadastre in Estonia. In: Parsova V, Gurskiene V, Kaing M (eds) Real property cadastre in Baltic countries. Estonian University of Life Sciences, Latvia University of Agriculture, Aleksandras Stulginskis University, Lithuania, Jelgava, pp 7–48

Kamiński P (2020) Publiczny dostęp do elektronicznych ksiąg wieczystych w kontekście ochrony danych osobowych. Rejent 30(9):54–68

Kliková A (2008) Real estate cadastre and real estate registration. In: Liszewski G, Radvan M (eds) Real estate in Czech and Polish law. Białostockie Studia Prawnicze vol 4, pp 163–173

Kowalik E (2020) Zakres kognicji sądu w postępowaniu wieczystoksięgowym. Wolters Kluwer, Warszawa

Krupa-Dąbrowska R (2013) Księgi wieczyste: Jawność to nie powszechność. http://archiwum.rp.pl/artykul/1184068-Ksiegi-wieczyste:-jawnosc-to-nie-powszechnosc.html

Legat O, Orkusz M (2019) Zasady udostępniania danych zawartych w księgach wieczystych w kontekście rozwiązań prawa krajowego i prawa europejskiego—analiza komparatystyczna, uwagi *de lege lata* i wnioski *de lege ferenda*. Instytut Wymiaru Sprawiedliwości, Warszawa

Leśniak M (2010) Powszechny dostęp do przeglądania księgi wieczystej prowadzonej w systemie informatycznym (nowej księgi wieczystej). Prawo Mediów Elektronicznych 3:21–24

Lodde A (2017) The interconnection of the European registers of real property: The comparison of the Italian and Spanish cases. Territorio Italia 17(1):73–95

Lodde A (2016) The European systems of real estate registration: An overview. Territorio Italia 16(1):23–42

Marin M (2019) Comparative analysis regarding the immovable goods publicity and the land book of the states of the European Union. Law Review (Supplement):229–236

Martínez Velencoso LM (2017) The land register in European law: A comparative and economic analysis. In: Martínez Velencoso LM, Bailey S, Pradi A (eds) Transfer of immovables in European private law. Cambridge University Press, Cambridge, pp 3–19

Maurer M (2021) A comparison of European user roles in LRI. https://lri-ms.eu/sites/default/files/2021-10/LRI_Maurer_UserRoles_2021-10-07.pdf

Menclová K (2021) Nahlížení do katastru nemovitostí pouze pro přihlášené uživatele již od června 2021. https://cmszp.cz/ostatni/2021/nahlizeni-do-katastru-nemovitosti-pouze-pro-prihlasene-uzivatele-jiz-od-cervna-2021/

Ministerstwo Sprawiedliwości (2025) Cyfrowe Rejestry. https://www.gov.pl/attachment/3d67469b-1d34-4859-8979-0c7cb61aa15b

Moerkerke J (2018) Efforts, on a European level, in order to facilitate cross-border transfers of real estate. 8th ELRA Annual Publication. https://www.elra.eu/wp-content/uploads/2019/01/Speech-GranadaJan-Moerkerke.pdf

Pesl I, Rydval J, Slaboch V (2004) Free internet access to cadastral data—first experience in the Czech Republic. In: FIG Working Week 2004, Athens, 22–27 May 2004. https://www.fig.net/resources/proceedings/fig_proceedings/athens/papers/ts01/ts01_7_pesl_et_al.pdf

Pradi A (2012) Sale and transcription in Italian law. In: Pradi A (ed) Transfer of immoveable property in Europe: From contract to registration. Università degli Studi di Trento, Trento, pp 153–164

Registradores de España (2021) The mid-term review of the project. https://lri-ms.eu/node/49

Rękawek-Pachwicewicz M (2021) Modern legal solutions in Estonia's judicial land registers as an example of effective use of IT instruments as well as IT and legal cooperation. Nieruchomości 4(4):107–125

Rękawek-Pachwicewicz M (2013) Electronic land register in Poland: Aims, general rules and organization in terms of economic development. 5th ELRA Annual Publication. https://www.elra.eu/electronic-land-register-in-poland-aims-general-rules-and-organization-in-terms-of-economic-development/

Schmid CU, Hertel C, Wicke H (2005) Real property law and procedure in the European Union: General report. European University Institute. https://www.eui.eu/Documents/DepartmentsCentres/Law/ResearchTeaching/ResearchThemes/EuropeanPrivateLaw/RealPropertyProject/GeneralReport.pdf

State Administration of Land Surveying and Cadastre (2024) Real estate cadastre and personal data protection. https://cuzk.gov.cz/English/Practical-Information/Personal-Data-Protection/Real-estate-Cadastre-and-Personal-Data-Protection.aspx

Świątko M (2021) Zasada jawności formalnej ksiąg wieczystych—wnioski *de lege ferenda*. Monitor Prawniczy 24:1306–1311

Tammsaar K (2021) Conference presentations published. https://lri-ms.eu/node/54

United Nations Economic Commission for Europe (1996) Land administration guidelines: With special reference to countries in transition. United Nations, New York and Geneva

Vern F (2021) Land registration systems & discourses of property. Eur Rev Private Law 29(6):835–852

Wudarski A (2024) Access to land and mortgage registers: Between legal certainty and privacy protection. In: van Erp S, Zimmermann K (eds) Research handbook on European property law. Edward Elgar Publishing, Cheltenham, pp 157–168

Wudarski A (2014) Jawność ksiąg wieczystych: Analiza prawnoporównawcza w kontekście europejskim. In: Dańko-Roesler A, Oleszko A, Pastuszko R (eds) Rozprawy z prawa prywatnego oraz notarialnego: Księga pamiątkowa dedykowana profesorowi Maksymilianowi Pazdanowi. Stowarzyszenie Notariuszy RP, Warszawa, pp 444–468

Zevenbergen J (2002) Systems of land registration: Aspects and effects. Netherlands Geodetic Commission, Delft

Zimmermann K (2021) Facilitating cross-border real estate transactions in Europe: An exploration. Eleven International Publishing, The Hague

Algorithmic Governance of Territory and Market Dominion: The Role of Public Oversight

Manlio Lisanti

Abstract The paper explores the impact of algorithmic tools on territorial governance, both within and beyond the urban context. The issue of the shift in governance power from the public sphere to private actors is brought to light through the analysis of case studies such as Cybermoor, the Block by Block platform, and the Street Bump application. Digitalisation and, more broadly, the use of algorithms in this specific sector, while potentially capable of compensating for the absence of public solutions, tends to reinforce efficiency-driven logics that may come at the expense of equity and administrative participation. By delegating the development and implementation of such systems to private operators, public administrations risk relinquishing control over the decisions made on the basis of those systems. This entails a redefinition of the concept of public service, increasingly tailored to the individual user, who also acquires the power to evaluate and thereby influence the service on a personal basis. As a response to these issues, the paper advocates for the revival of common principles of administrative law beyond the confines of the national state as a way to restore minimum safeguards for individuals and to prevent the simulacrum of efficiency from eclipsing the care for the general interest.

Keywords Algorithmic governance · Efficiency · Prosumer · Public oversight · Territorial marginalisation

1 Introduction

It is well known that the territorial digital divide has a significant impact on individuals' ability to access certain services, which are at times essential to their well-being.[1] In particular, the lack of infrastructural coverage, which determines access to the network, results in the impossibility of benefiting from a range of services

[1] Wessels (2013, 17–28).

M. Lisanti (✉)
Department of Management and Law, Tor Vergata University of Rome, Rome, Italy
e-mail: manlio.lisanti@students.uniroma2.eu

C. Crea and M. Infantino (eds.), *Remedies to Digital Vulnerability in European Private Law*, https://doi.org/10.1007/978-3-032-19720-7_25

and activities that are otherwise readily available to residents of other areas, the so-called disadvantaged or remote areas, where internet connectivity is not guaranteed or is entirely lacking. This situation inevitably contributes to the depopulation of inland or rural areas, which are typically the most difficult to reach with connectivity infrastructure.

There are, however, well-known examples in which improved connectivity in inner areas has contributed to the revival of small villages. A particularly emblematic case is that of Colletta di Castelbianco, located in the Ligurian inland. This village, of significant ethno-anthropological interest due to its rural architecture, was completely abandoned by the late 1970s. Its rebirth was made possible by private entrepreneurs who purchased every single building, restored it, and equipped it with internet access. Today, the village has around 300 inhabitants, although most of them are only occasional residents.[2]

The case of Colletta di Castelbianco is frequently cited as a virtuous example of digital regeneration and can serve to demonstrate that digitalisation may act as a driver of attractiveness for otherwise marginalised territories. Yet, it also proves that such interventions remain episodic exceptions, feasible only where favourable conditions exist for private initiative. It cannot be overlooked that the digital transformation of the Colletta di Castelbianco village, although a successful experiment, made possible by an entrepreneurial investment project, is an experiment that cannot be easily replicated on a broad scale. In many other contexts, where the necessary economic conditions or investor interest are lacking, the infrastructural divide continues to widen. Moreover, even where connectivity is available, it is rarely a solution in itself. Digitalisation, if not accompanied by a deliberate effort to redress territorial disparities, risks proving inadequate in the face of the ongoing social and productive desertification of inland areas.

Algorithmic governance of the territory, which increasingly relies on digital platforms to deliver services, manage mobility, or allocate resources, is reinforcing dependence on centralised systems that operate according to principles of efficiency and profit, but not necessarily of equity. In this context, public control over infrastructure and the regulatory capacity of public administrations must regain centrality,[3] to prevent territorial marginality from becoming a permanent condition or, alternatively, to stop private powers from stripping public authorities of territorial governance and reorienting it towards profit rather than public interest. These new private powers no longer manifest themselves within a traditional vertical State–citizen logic; rather, they operate through granular, diffuse mechanisms, driven by behaviours not imposed by law but induced by technical choices.[4]

---

[2] De Carlo (2004, 4–12), Bascherini (2020, 101–105).

[3] Tully (2014, 175–195).

[4] Resta (2024, 43).

2 Algorithmic Governance of Cities

As illustrated by the case of Colletta di Castelbianco, access to the Internet is almost invariably instrumental to the governance processes of urban centres, whether large or small. Connectivity enables the use of applications that facilitate more direct interaction between citizens and public authorities, or that allow individuals to access public services more easily. Internet access thus constitutes a necessary precondition for citizen participation in urban governance, both in metropolitan areas and in smaller communities. However, digital platforms are not merely tools for service delivery. They also serve as mechanisms for enhancing themselves and improving the operational performance of public administrations, through automation and the systematic collection of real-time data.[5]

The critical issue that emerges, however, is that the creation, monitoring, and optimization of these technological solutions is, in the majority of cases, carried out by those who develop them. In other words, a large part of digital governance today lies in the hands of the private developers who provide these technological tools to the public administration. Such a situation gives rise to two problems. Firstly, applications must comply with strict performance requirements in order to ensure efficient service delivery and, more broadly, the proper functioning of public administration. In other words, the applications employed must meet high performance standards, as they form part of the operational tools of governance and have a direct impact on the effective implementation of the principle of sound public administration. Secondly, although private programmers are guided by the needs of the contracting administration, they nonetheless play a crucial role by designing the 'machine' in such a way that it can make choices. Choices which may, in some cases, be discretionary in nature. When algorithms determine or influence public decisions, including those involving discretionary powers, while the logic underpinning them remains opaque or inaccessible, this, however, leads to a diminished level of accountability.[6]

These dynamics are most evident where such technologies are more widespread, that is, in smart cities. The very architecture of smart cities is built upon the collection and processing of data through applications designed to enhance service provision. Yet, the true 'intelligence' of the smart city arguably resides entirely in the programmers behind the applications on which it relies. The public administration, lacking the capacity to intervene in or modify the functioning of the algorithm, merely receives outputs whose origin it neither understands nor, consequently, can control.[7]

A new form of territorial management is therefore emerging, in which public decision-making is increasingly delegated to computational systems based on predictive models. These are no longer merely sophisticated tools supporting the administration, but fully-fledged automated decision-making machines that define priorities,

---

[5] Brauneis and Goodman (2018, 103).

[6] At the same time, the administration may perhaps be perceived as working more efficiently insofar as it relies upon mechanisms deemed impartial precisely because they are 'external' to the body of civil servants. Regarding this point, see Marra (2019, 185), Galetta (1994, 155).

[7] Brauneis and Goodman (2018, 103).

allocate resources, and steer urban interventions.[8] Realistically, it must be acknowledged that public administrations cannot be blamed for this, as most of public servants lack the necessary expertise or resources to independently develop such tools. As a result, the development of administrative algorithmic systems is inevitably outsourced to external entities that design and manage the algorithms, even though such entities are not subject to the transparency obligations that constitute one of the essential safeguards against the potential abuses of public authority.[9]

When the company developing the system retains full control over the algorithm, the data flow, and its analysis, the public administration becomes unable to fully understand the rationale and content of the decisions made through the algorithm, as well as its underlying legal and logical reasoning, which is no longer subject to verification. In such a context, the risk of a 'private capture' of public power becomes a concrete reality.[10]

3 Algorithms for the Development of Rural Areas

Precisely with the aim of safeguarding the demographic stability of certain disadvantaged areas, efforts have been made to apply these digital tools specifically in rural contexts.[11] A representative case is the Cybermoor project, launched as early as 2001. In the remote English region of Cumbria, Cybermoor has developed a range of initiatives aimed at improving socio-economic conditions in rural areas, with particular emphasis on digital innovation and sustainability.

The project's activities focus first of all on enhancing connectivity through tools that promote access to high-speed internet and 5G technology in areas traditionally excluded from infrastructure networks. A second area of intervention concerns healthcare and social services, with the development of service delivery models for telemedicine, remote assistance, and the digitalization of procedures to meet the needs of populations often located far from urban centres. A third strand of the project is devoted to the development of local tourism, through digital tools and strategies for promoting the region in a sustainable way, thereby generating new economic opportunities for inland areas. A fourth line of action involves the installation of electric vehicle charging points to foster sustainable mobility beyond urban areas.

Beyond the initiative itself and regardless of its specific focus, it is worth investigating whether such a territorial digitalization effort, several years after its inception, has actually succeeded in halting depopulation or whether it has merely shifted control over the territory from public authorities to private operators. Public data suggest that the former hypothesis is rather unlikely.

---

[8] Auby (2018, 3–4).

[9] Resta (2023, 1008).

[10] Bagg (2021, 220–243).

[11] Schrubbe and Strover (2021, 46).

Between 2011 and 2022, demographic trends in the Cumbria region showed a prolonged phase of stagnation, followed by a slight increase. According to the 2021 census data, the overall population of the county remained virtually unchanged compared to 2011, with a net loss of only around 100 people. In reality, if we look at the data for individual districts, it becomes clear that while Copeland, Barrow-in-Furness, and Allerdale experienced significant population declines (for instance, Copeland recorded a 5% decrease),[12] Carlisle, Eden, and South Lakeland displayed the opposite trend, although this was largely driven by an increase in the elderly (i.e., over sixty-five) population.[13]

In the period following the census, between 2021 and 2022, a reversal of the trend was observed. In Cumberland, a historic county which, since 1974, has been part of Cumbria and includes the districts of Allerdale, Carlisle, and Copeland, the overall population grew by 0.6%. This means the population increased by approximately 1,600 people. However, this growth was not the result of a positive natural balance. On the contrary, deaths exceeded births, resulting in a negative natural balance of around 1,100 individuals.[14] To offset this decline, migratory flows have played a compensatory role, both internal (+2,100 individuals) and international (+700 individuals).[15]

The diachronic analysis thus reveals a region which, despite years of efforts invested in digitalisation aimed at revitalising it, shows only modest signs of demographic growth and in a highly uneven manner. In other words, based on the available data, it is not possible to identify any tangible impact of the Cybermoor project in terms of a demographic increase directly attributable to it. Rather, what emerges is a shift in perspective concerning the phenomenon.

What becomes apparent is the increasingly prominent role played by private actors in territorial governance. Whereas in the past local planning was directed exclusively by the public sector—with only certain services outsourced to private companies under continued public oversight—, the Cybermoor project highlights a departure from this traditional model of administrative governance, in favour of a more marginal role for public authorities.

With regard to the issue of connectivity in remote areas, for example, the project benefited from government funding, which enabled private companies to independently design, implement, and manage connectivity-related initiatives.[16] As can be read directly on the project's official website, "[t]he project listened to rural communities; to ensure connectivity can support these areas to thrive. Throughout the project, residents and businesses were listened to, to understand problems through listening to and working with communities".[17] Shouldn't listening to and addressing such

---

[12] Census (2021) Population of Cumbria.

[13] Westmorland and Furness Annual Population Trends.

[14] Office for National Statistics (ONS), released 15 July 2024, ONS website, statistical bulletin, population estimates for England and Wales: mid-2023.

[15] Cumberland Annual Population Trends (s.d.).

[16] See https://cybermoor.org/rural-connectivity/.

[17] Ibid.

issues be the prerogative of the public sector? Is there not, in these words, an implicit acknowledgment of the widespread distrust toward a public administration that until now has done little for these inner communities?

The proposed model, while certainly capable of benefiting rural areas, reflects a retreat of the public administration in favour of hybrid arrangements, in which strategic and operational decisions are no longer in the hands of public authorities. The concern lies not in private participation per se—which can undoubtedly offer added value –, but rather in the fact that, due to the gradual withdrawal of the public role, decisions may increasingly be guided by efficiency in a business-oriented sense, rather than by efficiency understood as the capacity to meet the needs of all citizens using the fewest resources possible.

4 Algorithms for the Planning of Digital Cities and the Delivery of Services

Returning within the 'walls' of cities, another example of this trend is the urban planning simulation platform Block by Block, which allows residents of certain areas in specific cities to design urban spaces in 3D. The application promotes citizen participation through workshops aimed at fostering direct engagement with local authorities. In this way, residents are able to communicate their needs to public institutions, which, in turn, are expected to feel a sense of responsibility in the implementation of the shared project. This entrepreneurial initiative clearly acts as a communication bridge: on the one hand, an administration evidently lacking adequate planning capacity (if the city were properly planned, such needs would not arise); on the other hand, the residents, who, having received no satisfactory responses from the administration, attempt to improve their urban environment through this tool.

In 2012, the Block by Block project was launched as a joint initiative by Mojang Studios, Microsoft, and UN-Habitat, with the aim of actively involving local communities in the regeneration of urban spaces. According to the project's official website, the project leverages the experience of the video game Minecraft to enable a form of co-design of public urban spaces.[18] The process begins with the creation of an urban model, based on real-life surveys and maps. Once the basic context is reconstructed, the local community is engaged. Groups of residents or workers located near the area to be redeveloped are selected, and workshops are organized in which participants are trained in the use of the video game and introduced to the principles of public space design. Subsequently, project participants are divided into groups to allow them to work independently. Once this phase is completed, the proposed designs are presented to stakeholders in order to foster direct dialogue with the local administration. The final stage consists of evaluating the proposals submitted by the residents, which are then selected and prioritized, also based on their technical and

[18] https://www.blockbyblock.org/about.

economic feasibility.[19] After all these activities are completed, the administration allocates funding to the projects, with the foreseeable risk that the projects developed with the involvement of the local population may never be implemented if the financial resources should be lacking.

A practical example of how Block by Block works is the 'Building a Strong Foundation for Girls in Mozambique' initiative, which aimed to redevelop and enhance safety in certain urban areas of Maputo and Quelimane through the participation of young women. The use of Minecraft enabled the digital design of safe, well-lit evening routes and recreational spaces. Even after Cyclone Idai struck the country, Block by Block funded the reconstruction of the project.[20]

As can be easily understood from the case study, the project places particular emphasis on collaboration with local authorities, supporting rather than replacing them, since the responsibility for selecting, approving, and implementing the initiatives remains reserved to the latter.[21] This experiment shows how modern governance of local communities is increasingly shaped by new dynamics, shifting from a centralized model to a multilevel network model involving domestic public bodies, the private sector, and supranational actors. In such a context, decision-making processes lose their formal structure and become more informal, more flexible, and more tailored to the specific needs of each case.[22] A side-effect, however, is the erosion of procedural safeguards that have served as protections against the arbitrary exercise of power for the past two centuries.

The technique adopted by 'Block by Block' exemplifies these developments. It is a form of planning that appears to be participatory, yet in reality it takes place outside the administrative procedures established by sector-specific regulations, thereby affecting the responsibilities of the administrative authority to which the decision should belong. It is precisely within this tension that the danger may arise of the emergence of practices or behaviours driven by private companies that are not accountable to the electorate, yet are capable of significantly influencing public choices. Moreover, the participatory forms under examination are neither institutionalised nor open to everyone. They are not open because participants are selected in advance (for example, only certain young women were involved in the case at hand); nor are they institutionalised, since such participatory moments are granted to the population solely for a specific project and only at the discretion of a private company. A further risk is that these trends and experiments may contribute to the proliferation of disjointed, temporary, and localised solutions, which are later incorporated into the actual planning process.[23]

This appears to be one of the central critical points of the project: the mechanism works perfectly and performs well when interpreted as a stand-alone intervention. These initiatives are inclusive in their intent; they fulfil what they promise, and they

[19] https://www.blockbyblock.org/our-approach.

[20] https://www.blockbyblock.org/projects/mozambique.

[21] https://www.blockbyblock.org/faq.

[22] Picciotto (2008, 457–479).

[23] Andres, Bakare, Bryson et al. (2021, 29–39).

seem to bring about an improvement in the quality of life within that specific urban area. However, when one assesses their broader and more systemic impact, their fragility becomes apparent, and their purpose seems to be more performative than genuinely oriented toward fulfilling a public function.

Another particularly noteworthy application is 'Street Bump', used in the city of Boston, which leverages citizen-generated data to identify potholes and enhance administrative efficiency. The app allows users to immediately report a pothole on a specific street to the municipality. In theory, this should enable the administration to intervene promptly and in a targeted manner, repairing the reported potholes and improving road safety. In practice, however, there is a risk that the municipality may intervene more frequently and attentively in heavily trafficked streets, while less frequented roads, which generate fewer reports, may receive less attention, regardless of their actual conditions.

The case of 'Street Bump' highlights how the use of data in territorial governance can improve both planning and, more significantly, the delivery of public services (for example, in the areas of transportation or urban mobility). By their very nature, such applications offer high performance and guarantee the best possible service. This, after all, is their *raison d'être*. However, even though the 'Street Bump' app has improved over time (and is now able to distinguish a pothole from a manhole cover), the fact remains that only those who have a car and a smartphone can interact with the municipality in this way. The issue is not so much one of participation, since the interaction is fungible, being irrelevant whether the report comes from one person or another, but rather one of proper allocation of economic resources and interventions across the city's various areas. Paradoxically, it may turn out that the areas most affected by road maintenance issues, perhaps residential neighbourhoods or simply less trafficked zones (though not necessarily poorer ones), end up being underserved in comparison to others. The result is an 'allocative mistake' that calls into question the obligation of public authorities to ensure broad-based action across the territory.[24]

But if this is of no interest to the administrations, then perhaps what truly matters is efficiency.

5 Algorithms and Performance. Where is the Problem?

As a consequence of the involvement of private companies in the development of smart cities' products, the central element of territorial governance becomes the performance of the application used by the administration. These applications are typically developed by private operators who tend to enhance their functionalities to make it more competitive, without necessarily taking into account the actual quality of the service delivered to the public or the effective resolution of social problems.

---

[24] Dancy (2023, 57).

It is usually held that the use of technologically advanced tools (capable of self-evaluation) helps make administrative decisions more objective and neutral. After all, objectivity and neutrality are the logical premises underlying the application of the principle of good administration. When the principle of good administration is interpreted according to managerial criteria, it may be equated with the productive efficiency of public administration. In other words, an administration is considered efficient if it achieves a predetermined result in the best possible way, with minimal resource expenditure, and so on. This trend is perfectly embodied by the use of algorithmic tools, which are employed to improve services that are increasingly tailored to users' needs. As shown by the case studies examined above, in Sects. 3 and 4, the introduction of algorithmic tools in the governance of cities, and more generally, of the territory, has shifted the focus of the public administration toward a performance-oriented activity.

This gives rise to two distinct problems.

The first concerns the very idea of public service. A model of governance shaped around individual needs risks losing sight of the general interest, which, in the realm of public services, is characterized by a certain degree of indeterminacy, precisely so that it can be qualified as such. Public services are historically characterised by distinct features that have been delineated in terms of continuity, adaptability, and equality.[25] A service qualifies as 'public' when it addresses needs of a general nature, pursuing aims of public and social interest.[26] But, under an algorithm-driven vision of public services, the provision of the service no longer stems from a public body's decision to take charge of collective needs that the market does not wish, or is unable, to satisfy. It is now calibrated to the needs of the individual user. This increasingly complicates the administration's task of monitoring the services delivered. Moreover, the user who interacts with an app provided by the public administration but developed by a private entity becomes a 'prosumer'. In other words, they are no longer a passive consumer, as they must take direct action to obtain the service they require.[27]

The user themselves produces data which, in turn, generate performative and normative effects, redefining the standards of the service and the objectives of the administration, and subverting the typical relationship between the active subject—understood as the State and its apparatus—and the passive subject, namely the administered individual.[28] In this new framework, one can discern an almost complete transfer of decision-making power from the public authority to the technical tool acquired by the administration but offered on the market by private actors. Territorial governance—traditionally the domain in which public discretion tended to reach

---

[25] Rolland (1938, 14).

[26] Giannini (1986, 69).

[27] According to this point of view "citizens have been in practice object of data collection rather than the subjects of an active participation in the development of innovative cities". Ranchordàs (2018, 157).

[28] Foucault (1980, 119).

its highest expression—is now shifting toward a form of regulation that is increasingly technical and technological in nature.[29] The shift is dangerous, also because digital tools and algorithmic systems classify, select, and exclude. When employed to enhance administrative efficiency, they incorporate criteria that reflect qualitative choices made, even unintentionally, during the planning phase, and that may easily turn out to be discriminatory, biased, and inequitable.

A second issue is that the 'prosumer' citizen also acts as an evaluator of the service received. This dynamic enables the continuous measurement of service performance. As a result, the private operator is expected to adjusts its service accordingly in order to make it increasingly efficient. However, this very mechanism, which consists in personalizing the service based on the user's feedback, has the potential to reshape the very notion of public service. The starting point is no longer a decision taken by the public authority in response to a collectively identified public need, but rather a fragmented offer constructed through user profiling. Performance, as a regulatory technique, thus tends to prioritize the attainment of specific quantitative targets over the provision of quality services, thereby risking undermining the solidaristic rationale underpinning public service delivery.[30] If the recipient of the service is also the one who produces the data necessary for its optimization and who evaluates its performance, then that recipient is bound to become a 'sensor' instrumental to the development of technology. In this way, the emphasis on performativity can seriously transform the public function into a stream of outputs in which service quality and distributive fairness are subordinated to the experiential satisfaction of the user.[31]

The logic of performance evaluation enables the provider of the technological service to steer the application based on measurable behaviours and feedback. In doing so, what performs better is rewarded, while what might actually be more useful or equitable is neglected. This dynamic is clearly observable in the examples discussed, where urban redevelopment interventions are partial, confined to a limited area of a neighbourhood, and lack genuine and stable co-participation of the population in public decision-making.

6 Conclusion

The challenges associated with algorithmic governance are essentially twofold. On the one hand, there is the issue of service personalization. On the other hand, there is the risk that the exercise of public power may shift towards private actors.

Regarding the first problem, the public administration must necessarily retain a supervisory role and must verify and monitor both the accuracy of service delivery and the effects of the datafication of its own power, to prevent forms of de-responsibilisation. In this respect, oversight is essential precisely to ensure the

[29] Brownsword (2024, 5).

[30] Napolitano (2024, 1–2).

[31] Bussani, Cassese, Infantino (2023).

accountability of the administration towards users, so that it can never claim: "It is not me, it is the data!".[32] Without such a possibility of oversight, power would end up being concealed within the criteria embedded in the algorithm, often opaque and inaccessible to users, and operate in a subterranean manner, beyond any possibility of control.[33]

This takes us to the second problem. We are currently witnessing the emergence of a new centre of power that calls into question the very concept of administrative decentralization, which traditionally involved both central administrations and those distributed across the territory. In this dynamic, it is precisely the actor holding the power of governance that undergoes a transformation.[34] The trend toward an algorithmic governance of the territory is not merely limited to public services or urban planning. A clear indicator of this stems from the development, beyond and across national borders, of many liveability ratings for cities, whether large or small. A private platform such as TeamDev[35] promotes the development of smart cities through its application called Wisetown. Wisetown is based on European standards, and is supposed to assist municipalities in becoming (or declaring themselves) 'smart' using data collected across the territory. The aim of this and similar apps is to identify which aspects of local governance should be enhanced in order to qualify as smart, naturally according to the criteria set by the application itself.

In the current historical era, marked by globalization, administrative power has become increasingly multipolar, that is, exercised by state, private, and supranational actors through networked procedures lacking a single decision-making centre. The result is that national administrative rules and procedures have to contend for their space with various, and often competing, legal sources, as well as with regulatory models emerging from practice and technical standards.[36] The emergence of algorithmic governance reaffirms this trend, as the algorithmic domain can be conceived as a legally autonomous space and therefore subject to autonomous regulation yet nonetheless grounded in the fundamental principles of the rule of law.

Such transformation entails the need to reconsider the common principles of access, transparency of selection criteria, participation, reasoning of administrative decisions, and judicial review, that are the pillars of administrative law within and beyond the state, and constitute the fundamental rules applicable wherever public power is exercised, even when mediated by private actors.[37] As experts in global administrative law have long demonstrated, these fundamental principles apply also to private entities performing regulatory functions,[38] such as ICANN and ISO. Although these bodies are private in nature, they produce standards of a supranational

[32] Haque (2012, 141).

[33] "Since no well-ordered society can tolerate unchecked powers, the challenge for our legal systems is how to make these new forms of power accountable". Resta (2024, 46).

[34] Bussani, Cassese, Infantino (2023, 14).

[35] See https://teamdevecosystem.it/.

[36] Cassese, Napolitano, Casini (2014, 354–356).

[37] Della Cananea (2016), della Cananea (2023, 142).

[38] Cassese (2021, 21).

character, capable of influencing regulatory activity despite lacking democratic legitimacy. This is the main reason why, in order to avoid the risk of falling into dynamics of 'adhocracy', characterized by the contingency of certain decisions, organizational destructuring, and administrative decentralization,[39] it is necessary to bring these decisions back within the framework of the principles that have been set forth.

Otherwise, there would be no 'juridification' of power, and it would be impossible to provide the administered subjects (or, in this context, the 'prosumers') with the most basic guarantees. Extending the reach of the principles of administrative law to all the actors who, regardless of their legal nature, engage in the exercise of administrative functions, by contrast, would help fill the regulatory void in which these actors often move, and would protect end-users with public law driven guarantees.[40]

References

Andres L et al (2021) Planning, temporary urbanism and citizen-led alternative-substitute place-making in the Global South. Reg Stud 55(1):29–39

Auby JB (2018) Algorithmes et smart cities: données juridiques. Revue Générale Du Droit 29878:3–4

Bagg S (2021) Fighting power with power: The administrative state as a weapon against concentrated private power. Soc Philos Policy 38(1):220–243

Bascherini E (2020) Colletta di Castelbianco, da borgo abbandonato a borgo telematico. Un progetto di Giancarlo de Carlo. Bloom. Rivista Semestrale di Architettura 30:101–105

Brauneis R, Goodman EP (2018) Algorithmic transparency for the smart city. Yale J Law Tech 114(20):103–176

Brownsword R (2024) Legal metrics: getting the measure of good governance. Italian Law J 10(1–2):5–20

Bussani M, Cassese S, Infantino M (eds) (2023) Quantification of performance as a regulatory technique: an introduction. In: Bussani M, Cassese S, Infantino M (eds) Comparative legal metrics: quantification of performances as regulatory technique. Brill, Leiden-Boston, pp 1–18

Cassese S (2021) Advanced Introduction to Global Administrative Law. Edward Elgar, Cheltenham

Cassese S, Napolitano G, Casini L (2014) Towards multipolar administrative law: a theoretical perspective. Int J Const L 12(2):354–356

Census (2021) Population of Cumbria. Cumbria Intelligence Observatory. Available at https://cumbria.gov.uk/elibrary/Content/Internet/536/671/4674/17217/17218/447421561.pdf

Cumberland Annual Population Trends (s.d.). Available at https://elibrary.cumbria.gov.uk/elibrary/Content/Internet/536/671/4674/17217/17218/42929161856.PDF

Dancy T (2023) Artificial justice. Oxford University Press, Oxford

De Carlo G (2004) Colletta di Castelbianco. Places 16(2):4–12

della Cananea G (2016) Due process of law beyond the state. Requirements of Administrative Procedure. Oxford University Press, Oxford

della Cananea G (2023) The common core of European Administrative Laws. Retrospective and Prospective. Brill, Leiden-Boston

della Cananea G, Auby JB (eds) (2024) General principles and sector-specific rules in european administrative laws. Oxford University Press, Oxford

[39] Ibid.

[40] Della Cananea and Auby (2024).

Foucault M (1980) Truth and Power. In: Gordon C (ed) Power/knowledge: selected interviews and other writings (1972–1977) by Michel Foucault. Pantheon Books, New York, pp 109–133
Galetta DU (1994) Discrezionalità amministrativa e principio di proporzionalità. Rivista Italiana di Diritto Pubblico Comunitario 1:142–155
Giannini MS (1986) Il pubblico potere. Stati e amministrazioni pubbliche. Il Mulino, Bologna
Haque U (2012) What is a city that would be "Smart"? City in a Box 34:140–142
Marra A (2019) L'amministrazione imparziale. Giappichelli, Torino
Napolitano G (2024) Comparative legal metrics: an introduction. Italian Law J 10(1–2):1–3
Office for National Statistics (ONS) (2024) Statistical bulletin. Population estimates for England and Wales: mid-2023. Available at https://www.ons.gov.uk/peoplepopulationandcommunity/populationandmigration/populationestimates/bulletins/populationestimatesforenglandandwales/mid2023
Picciotto S (2008) Constitutionalizing multilevel governance? Int J Const Law 6(3–4):457–479
Ranchordás S (2018) Citizens as consumers in the data economy. J Eur Consum Market Law 7(4):154–161
Resta G (2024) The power of numbers and the role of law: on the way to the global accountability of transnational actors? Italian Law J 10(1–2):43–55
Resta G (2023) Poteri privati e regolazione. In: Enciclopedia del diritto. Giuffrè, Milano, pp 1008–1032
Rolland L (1938) Cours de droit administratif. D.E.S. 1938–1939. Les Cours de Droit, Paris.
Schrubbe A, Strover S (2021) Infrastructure and instance: how rural communities approach short—and long—term solutions to access. In: Hargittai E (ed) Handbook of digital inequality. Edward Elgar, Cheltenham, pp 46–61
Tully S (2014) A human right to access the internet. Hum Rights Law Rev 14(2):175–195
Wessels B (2013) The reproduction and reconfiguration of inequality. Differentiation and class, status and power in the dynamics of digital divide. In: Ragnedda M, Muschert GW (eds) The digital divide. The internet and social inequality in international perspective, Routledge, London-New York, pp 17–28
Westmorland and Furness (2023) Annual Population Trends. Incorporating Mid-2022 Estimates. Available at https://cumbria.gov.uk/elibrary/Content/Internet/536/671/4674/17217/17218/45275111816.pdf

Decentralised Autonomous Organisations and Digital Vulnerability: Remedial Approaches in a Digital Era

Pınar Çağlayan Aksoy

Abstract This chapter examines Decentralised Autonomous Organisations (DAOs) through the lens of digital vulnerability. Functioning as 'blockchain-based entities governed by code' rather than traditional legal structures, DAOs offer new paradigms of transparency, participation, governance, and automation. However, they also give rise to complex and evolving forms of vulnerability that are architectural, data-driven, and relational in nature. This chapter explores the concept of digital vulnerability within DAOs, highlighting how their architectural, legal, and relational structures expose participants to novel risks. While DAOs promise transparency and decentralised governance, their reliance on pseudonymity, immutable code, and limited legal recognition creates systemic asymmetries and accountability gaps. The chapter proposes a multi-dimensional framework for addressing these vulnerabilities, including on-chain governance design, legal recognition mechanisms, and ethical data practices. It argues that mitigating digital vulnerability is essential for ensuring the legitimacy and resilience of DAOs in an increasingly decentralised digital economy.

Keywords Decentralised autonomous organisations · Transparency · Decentralization · Pseudonymity · Legal certainty

1 Introduction

The emergence of Web 3.0 technologies is transforming the digital ecosystem and redefining traditional paradigms of governance, participation, and economic collaboration. As internet-native entities enabled by distributed ledger technology (DLT), decentralised autonomous Organisations (DAOs) come with the promise of increased

P. Ç. Aksoy (✉)
Faculty of Law, Bilkent University, Ankara, Türkiye
e-mail: pinar.caglayan@bilkent.edu.tr

C. Crea and M. Infantino (eds.), *Remedies to Digital Vulnerability in European Private Law*, https://doi.org/10.1007/978-3-032-19720-7_26

efficiency, transparency,[1] and inclusion. However, for almost a decade, they have been the target of legal, social, and technological uncertainties that still demand scholarly and regulatory attention.

Digital vulnerability is a concept that has been regularly addressed in the past decade due to the skyrocketing pace of the development of new technologies and their common use in everyday life. It is clear now that the traditional understanding of 'consumer protection' and 'vulnerability' is being subjected to a wind of change, which is a necessary step to achieve genuine protection of consumers and guarantee digital fairness.

Drawing on interdisciplinary literature and legal developments, the chapter first accommodates digital vulnerability within the broader Web 3.0 ecosystem, and then explores how DAO architecture and governance models contribute to novel risks for participants (users) and third parties. The analysis highlights how asymmetries in information, power, and access—amplified by pseudonymity, smart contract immutability, and the lack of legal clarity—undermine user autonomy and accountability. Through a detailed examination of legal, technological, and ethical dimensions, the chapter proposes a multi-pronged framework of remedial strategies to mitigate these risks. These include on-chain mechanisms, legal solutions such as regulatory recognition and transnational enforcement tools, and ethical enhancements that promote data minimalism and inclusive governance. Ultimately, the chapter argues that addressing digital vulnerability is essential to the sustainable development of DAOs and the broader legitimacy of decentralised governance in the digital era.

2 Digital Vulnerability in the Contemporary Technological Landscape

2.1 Conceptualising Digital Vulnerability: Vulnerability, Consumer Vulnerability and Digital Vulnerability

The concept of vulnerability, particularly in consumer contexts, has evolved significantly over time. Rebrean and Malgieri remind us that the term was initially invoked to support consumer protection by identifying individuals who were more likely to suffer harm compared to the so-called 'average' consumer.[2] More recently, this traditional notion of vulnerability has been challenged and expanded. Dodsworth and colleagues open their editorial on digital vulnerability with the assertion that "vulnerability affects us all".[3] Though seemingly straightforward, this statement is

[1] In the realm of DAOs, the characteristic of transparency implies that decisions and transactions made by the DAO or its individual members are recorded on its blockchain and is available to be audited by the public. Levin (2024, 464).

[2] Rebrean and Malgieri (2025, 4).

[3] Dodsworth et al (2023, 413).

highly relevant in the context of emerging technologies and decentralised ecosystems. Sax and Helberger similarly argued that "every consumer is potentially vulnerable, depending on the (digital) circumstances and environments she finds herself in".[4] Even highly skilled users—those proficient in coding or algorithmic systems—are not immune. Technological features such as algorithmic personalisation, predictive analytics, and behavioural nudging can undermine autonomy and render even the most informed individuals susceptible to harm. Advances in technologies like Artificial Intelligence (AI), Internet-of-Things (IoT), distributed ledger technology and Augmented Reality/Virtual Reality (AR/VR) have further complicated digital environments, increasing both the sophistication of exploitation techniques and the fragility of user control.

Before turning to the specific ways in which DAOs intersect with digital vulnerability, it is necessary to first clarify the concept itself. Traditional approaches to consumer vulnerability often relied on categorical groupings—such as elderly individuals, children, or those with limited income. In contrast, the modern notion of digital vulnerability is far more dynamic and context-dependent.[5] Rather than being a fixed attribute, it is shaped by situational factors involving the consumer, the market, and the transaction.[6] It is, therefore, a relational concept that may evolve over the course of an individual's engagement with digital environments. As scholars have observed, the digitalisation of consumer markets appears to be making vulnerability an almost universal condition.[7]

Digital vulnerability can be broadly understood as the exposure of individuals or groups to harm, risk, or disadvantage due to structural, technological, or informational asymmetries. It may arise from unequal access to technology, information, or effective protective mechanisms. Escolar notes that "the vulnerabilities that arise in a digital habitat are a result of the borderless, mostly instantaneous, digital exchanges that take place between actors and participants in online platforms".[8] A widely cited definition frames digital vulnerability as "a universal state of defencelessness and susceptibility to (the exploitation of) power imbalances that are the result of increasing automation of commerce, datafied consumer-seller relations and the very architecture of digital marketplaces".[9] This condition may be exacerbated by a combination of internal and external factors. Internal factors include low digital literacy, cognitive biases, and information overload, many of which lie beyond the consumer's immediate control. External contributors include opaque user interfaces, exploitative choice architectures, asymmetrical knowledge between parties, limited data control, default settings designed to favour the service provider, and poor interoperability between services.[10]

[4] Sax and Helberger (2024, 11).

[5] Rebrean and Malgieri (2025, 4).

[6] Helberger et al (2022, 188).

[7] Poretti (2023, 147).

[8] Escolar (2024, 327).

[9] Helberger et al (2022, 175–200).

[10] BEUC (2023, 5).

Durovic and Kaprou offer a complementary definition, describing the digitally vulnerable consumer as someone who, due to their personal circumstances, behavioural patterns, or the market context in which they operate, is particularly susceptible to harm—especially when traders fail to act with due care.[11]

At this point, it is important to distinguish a related yet increasingly significant concept: the digital vulnerability of consumers. Unlike physical or psychological vulnerability, consumer status is defined objectively. Determining whether an individual is a consumer depends on the nature of the contractual relationship—specifically, whether the individual is acting for non-professional purposes in order to satisfy personal needs. As summarised by the US Department of Treasury, "[t]he context in which crypto-assets are offered, sold, transferred, and otherwise used distinguishes whether a user has the characteristics of a consumer, investor, or business, or some combination of those characteristics. For example, a person engaging in self-directed trading, holding, or staking of crypto-assets with the expectation of realizing price appreciation or earning a return would be characterized as an investor. A person using crypto-assets to pay for goods and services might be characterized, at least in part, as a consumer, and a seller of those goods or services might be characterized as a business".[12] The legal interpretation of 'consumer' has remained largely consistent, but the conditions under which consumers are rendered vulnerable have shifted dramatically.

Over the last decade in particular, the boundary between the 'average' and the 'vulnerable' consumer has become increasingly blurred. As Mišćenić rightly notes, in the digital marketplace, most users shift from being average consumers to vulnerable ones. This is largely due to the opacity and complexity of digital services, which rely on technological systems—including IT infrastructure, algorithmic processes, programming languages, and distributed ledger technologies—that are often beyond the understanding of even well-informed users.[13] The digital market and the products offered within it are less transparent by design, often embedding layers of mathematical and algorithmic complexity that obscure consumer decision-making and undermine informed consent.

2.2 The Web3 Paradigm Shift

As we move into more decentralised and data-driven infrastructures, these evolving forms of digital vulnerability become increasingly salient, particularly in the context of Web3 technologies. Web 3.0 technologies—such as the Internet of Things (IoT), Artificial Intelligence (AI), and Distributed Ledger Technology (DLT)—seek to decentralise control and data ownership, enabling users to participate directly in governance and value exchange. Many have highlighted that users will become true

---

[11] Durovic and Kaprou (2024, 127).

[12] US Department of Treasury (2022, 1).

[13] Mišćenić (2024, 102).

owners of their data. This is perceived as a momentous transformation and advantage for consumers.

However, this shift towards decentralisation also redistributes risk in the transactional realm. Unlike traditional platforms that (are under the obligation to) offer legal remedies and consumer protections, Web 3.0 applications often operate without identifiable legal entities. The dual role of users as consumers and governors exacerbates vulnerability, as they are expected to navigate complex technical systems with limited support or safeguards.

Research in recent years has been focusing on the triggers, causes, and origins of digital vulnerability. Accordingly, systemic failures in digital markets stem from three primary sources: the inherent characteristics of digital environments, regulatory shortcomings (namely, the absence of adequate safeguards to protect against vulnerability), and enforcement failures, where existing rules cannot be effectively applied or upheld. Although recent policy documents have begun to acknowledge the significance of digital vulnerability, legislative responses remain fragmented and insufficient. This persistent gap underscores the urgent need to critically engage with and address the concept of digital vulnerability.[14] In this context, the concept of digital vulnerability becomes especially salient, as it seeks to provide a coherent framework for understanding new dimensions of consumer weakness emerging from the data- and algorithm-driven economy. Recognising and addressing this vulnerability is therefore essential to ensuring meaningful protection for all digital actors, and particularly within decentralised systems such as DAOs.[15]

3 DAOs: Architecture and Legal Challenges

3.1 Defining DAOs

The use of DLT has yielded many new products and services. These include tokens, decentralized finance applications (DeFi Apps or Dapps), smart contracts, stablecoins, central bank digital currencies (CBDCs), and DAOs. Each of these products and services has resulted in the transformation of various sectors such as finance, logistics, supply chain, insurance, real estate, corporate governance, and has the potential to transform many more.

Although digital platforms before the emergence of DLT had already transformed the ways businesses organize and create value, the platforms were still relying on central management and hierarchical administration structures.[16] DLT and specifically the foundation of the Ethereum blockchain have enabled the decentralization

---

[14] Dodsworth et al. (2023, 414–415).

[15] Grochowski (2024, 202).

[16] Von Hippel and von Krogh (2003, 209–223).

of management and the avoidance of third-party oversight and intervention.[17] This has also had an impact on organizational practices and interactions. DAOs are built on this idea of decentralization, and they aim to "build more cohesive, transparent, equal, and democratic communities by lowering agency costs, empowering users, and enhancing trust through decentralization".[18]

DAOs are collectively governed organisations encoded in smart contracts, operating on blockchain networks. Smart contracts are the backbone of DAOs. They are characterised by the absence of central leadership, reliance on token-based voting, and a communal treasury managed by code. As the ECB and the US Department of the Treasury describe, DAOs function as digital legal platforms where governance rules are transparent but immutable, and enforcement is automated.[19]

A unified definition does not exist for DAOs.[20] For instance, according to De Filippi and Hassan, a DAO is a blockchain-based system that enables people to coordinate and govern themselves mediated by a set of self-executing rules deployed on a public blockchain, and whose governance is decentralized (i.e., independent from central control).[21] According to Wang and others, "DAO is a blockchain-powered organization that can run on its own without any central authority or management hierarchy. In a DAO, all the management and operational rules are recorded on blockchain in the form of smart contracts, and the distributed consensus protocols and Token Economy Incentive are utilized to realize organizations' self-operation, self-governance, and self-evolution".[22] Boss defines DAOs as "a group of people who work together in an organized way for a shared purpose (i.e., organization) that uses a progressively peer- to-peer based decision-making process (i.e., decentralization), that governs itself by progressively relying on rules that are rooted in blockchain-technology (i.e., autonomous)".[23] Moreover, each DAO has different aims.[24] According to recent research, it is estimated that, as of May 2023, there were about 13,000 DAOs in existence, with a combined total treasury (invested funds and liquid assets) of nearly USD $23 billion.[25]

Although there are different types of DAOs for different purposes, we can observe some common characteristics that all DAOs share.[26] DAOs are fundamentally smart contract applications that operate on DLT.[27] They are sometimes referred to as 'networks of smart contracts' due to the interlinked and autonomous nature of their

17 Wang et al (2019, 870–878).
18 CBI (2022, 2).
19 Naudts (2023, 12), US Department of the Treasury (2022, 5).
20 Riva (2021, 612).
21 De Filippi and Hassan (2021, 2).
22 Wang et al (2019, 871).
23 Boss (2023, 16).
24 Dubnevych (2021).
25 Ernst and Young (2023).
26 On this point, see also Davidson (2025, 4).
27 Spindler (2021, 311).

code-based structures. Participants in a DAO interact with and control the organisation's assets either directly or indirectly through these smart contracts,[28] which govern everything from membership to treasury management and decision-making processes.

Unlike traditional enterprises and corporations, which are structured according to statutory laws and rely on written documents such as articles of incorporation or shareholder agreements, DAOs derive their organisational logic from code. Their operational rules, membership criteria, and governance mechanisms are embedded within smart contracts, minimising reliance on centralised administration and formal legal instruments.[29]

A defining feature of DAOs is the issuance of tokens via smart contracts, which provide holders with rights analogous to those conferred by traditional equity or debt instruments.[30] These digital tokens may confer voting rights, enable claiming financial benefits such as dividends, serve as rewards, act as vouchers, represent ownership stakes, or grant access to specific services within the DAO ecosystem.[31] Token holders play a critical role in DAO governance, particularly through their collective control over the treasury, typically consisting of cryptocurrencies or other digital assets. Governance decisions, including the allocation and use of these funds, are made through token-based voting systems in which holders can propose initiatives, cast votes, and influence the strategic direction of the DAO.[32]

This model represents a fundamental shift in the concept of governance. Rather than relying on organisational actors to voluntarily comply with governing rules, DAOs encode these rules into smart contracts, ensuring automatic enforcement.[33] If participants act in breach of the pre-programmed conditions, they may be excluded from the organisation without the need for traditional adjudication or human intervention.[34] This automation reduces agency costs and enforces compliance through technical means, marking a novel and transformative approach to collective decision-making and organisational accountability.

3.2 *Advantages Surrounding DAOs*

DAOs already play a significant role in the DeFi ecosystem and are expected to become even more integral as the landscape evolves. They are often seen as promising alternatives to traditional legal entities, offering the potential to "build and improve

[28] Wright (2021, 156).

[29] Wright (2021, 155).

[30] Schillig (2023).

[31] Villanueva Collao (2025, 18).

[32] Davidson (2025, 2).

[33] Scholz (2020, 148), Carron and Botteron (2019, 110).

[34] Karl (2018, 16).

upon existing legal entities by being entirely digitally native, easy to join, and global in reach".[35]

The advantages associated with DAOs are numerous and far-reaching. They significantly lower barriers to entry, promoting higher levels of financial inclusion by allowing broader participation regardless of geographic or socioeconomic background. Decision-making processes—such as voting and proposal implementation—are typically more efficient and cost-effective due to automation through smart contracts. The absence of a central authority or hierarchical structure facilitates disintermediation and promotes a more democratic distribution of power across the community. DAOs eliminate the need for costly and time-consuming communication methods, such as paper mailings or secure e-proxy voting systems. Their technical infrastructure allows for the rapid pooling and deployment of capital, with execution occurring automatically once voting thresholds are met. This automation also contributes to a high degree of flexibility; governance rules can be easily amended through streamlined voting mechanisms. Finally, DAOs offer full transparency, as all actions taken within the organisation are recorded immutably on the blockchain and are publicly verifiable, fostering trust and accountability among participants.[36]

3.3 Legal Status and Regulatory Fragmentation

As can be seen from the sections above, DAOs have implications for technology, society, business, politics, and the economy. However, like the other newly emerging technologies, DAOs pose some tricky questions for policymakers and legal scholars.[37]

The legal recognition of DAOs remains uneven. Jurisdictions such as Wyoming and the Cayman Islands have introduced DAO-specific legislation, granting these organisations limited liability and legal personhood. Some countries, like Liechtenstein and Switzerland, have accommodated DAOs by fitting them into existing business models, such foundations. In contrast, the EU's Markets in Crypto-Assets Regulation (MiCA) currently excludes fully decentralised DAOs unless they engage in regulated activities.[38]

This legal fragmentation, combined with the circumstance that DAOs operate without borders, creates uncertainty regarding their accountability and the enforceability of their obligations. MiCA seems to suggest that DAOs wishing to offer crypto-assets to European consumers may need to adopt a legal personality or partner with a registered Crypto-Asset Service Provider (CASP).

---

[35] Wright (2021, 155).

[36] For detailed information see Ly and Shojaei (2025).

[37] Borgogno (2022, 5).

[38] Regulation (EU) 2023/1114 of the European Parliament and of the Council of 31 May 2023 on markets in crypto-assets, and amending Regulations (EU) No 1093/2010 and (EU) No 1095/2010 and Directives 2013/36/EU and (EU) 2019/1937.

3.4 AI-Enhanced DAOs

Despite the advantages outlined in Sect. 3.2, DAOs are not without vulnerabilities. These include—but are not limited to—risks of financial mismanagement, fraudulent activity, and manipulation of voting processes. As DAOs rely on smart contracts to govern decision-making, their operational structure is inherently decentralised and automated, typically functioning through conditional logic ("if ... then" scenarios).[39] This automation, while efficient, also introduces rigidity and susceptibility to technical flaws.

When AI is introduced into DAO ecosystems, these organisations gain the capacity for adaptive learning and self-optimisation, potentially enhancing efficiency, scalability, and governance capabilities. Traditionally, DAOs rely on human actors to propose and vote on decisions. However, AI can automate and optimise many of these processes using machine learning algorithms and predictive analytics, enabling DAOs to make faster, more data-driven decisions.[40] From analysing past voting behaviour to forecasting proposal outcomes, AI-enhanced DAOs could theoretically become more adaptive, transparent, and operationally efficient.

AI integration also offers potential benefits in terms of security and organisational health. AI systems can monitor DAO transactions in real time to detect anomalies, identify potential threats, and even offer predictive governance insights based on historical patterns. These features can support better decision-making, improved member engagement, and even personalised participation strategies through automated recommendation systems.[41] Moreover, AI agents may increasingly participate in smart contracting processes by autonomously generating, accepting,[42] or modifying terms.[43] This raises novel questions about consent, liability, and enforceability.[44]

These possibilities are not without significant caveats. Bias in algorithmic decision-making, the opacity of AI reasoning, and vulnerability to adversarial manipulation all present serious concerns. Over-reliance on AI may also erode human judgment and creativity in governance processes, thereby compromising the adaptability and ethical grounding of the DAO.

That said, some scholars remain sceptical of AI's transformative impact on contracting.[45] Accordingly, contracts are inevitably incomplete due to bounded rationality and the inherent uncertainty of complex economic environments. This observation applies as much to smart contracts as to traditional ones. As Davidson notes, the advent of AI does not fundamentally resolve these structural limitations:

---

[39] Aragon (2023).

[40] According to De Filippi and Wright, "even if DAOs incorporate sophisticated AI systems, they still cannot operate entirely free of humans" (De Filippi and Wright 2018, 155).

[41] Clock b Business Technology (2025).

[42] Golub (2024, 298).

[43] Golub (2024, 298).

[44] Clock b Business Technology (2025).

[45] Davidson (2025, 8).

despite AI's analytical power, it cannot eliminate the unpredictability or incompleteness embedded in contractual relationships, nor can it fully displace the contextual judgment required in many governance decisions.[46]

Importantly, deeper legal and structural limitations must also be considered. As Schuster and Low argue, what they call 'Real DAOs'—fully autonomous, decentralised organisations akin to 'full self-driving' corporations—face fundamental and, in their view, insurmountable challenges. These are not merely technical, but legal in nature, arising from a core incompatibility between non-hierarchical technological design and the inherently hierarchical structure of legal systems. As they explain, DAOs that aim to operate businesses connected to the off-chain world cannot simultaneously preserve full autonomy and decentralisation. To interact meaningfully with real-world legal, regulatory, or commercial systems, they must make compromises that ultimately undermine their decentralised character.[47]

This creates a persistent design dilemma: DAOs can either remain truly decentralised and operate exclusively on-chain, or they can become legally functional entities by sacrificing key aspects of their autonomy. In this light, Schuster and Low suggest that the use cases for 'Real DAOs' will likely remain limited to domains where off-chain legal synchronisation is unnecessary—such as unregulated prediction markets, certain DeFi applications, or decentralised gambling platforms. These are contexts where the ability to effect de facto value transfers is more important than legal recognition or enforceability.[48]

In sum, while AI-enhanced DAOs represent a significant technological development, their broader integration into legal and economic systems depends on resolving a tension between automation, decentralisation, and regulatory coherence. Without addressing these foundational issues, the role of DAOs—however technically sophisticated—will likely be limited in scope.

4 Dimensions of Digital Vulnerability in DAOs

When blockchain applications first emerged, they were often accompanied by the notion that "code is law"[49]—a belief that the rules embedded in smart contracts could supersede or even replace traditional legal frameworks. This perspective implied that interactions on blockchain platforms were self-sufficient, operating independently of external legal systems. However, over the past decade, this assumption has proven to be overly simplistic. In practice, numerous conflicts have arisen from blockchain-based transactions, many of which have required resolution through state courts or alternative dispute resolution mechanisms. The immutable nature of blockchain code has not eliminated the potential for disputes; rather, it often has complicated them.

46 Davidson (2024, 13 f).

47 Schuster and Low (2025a, b, 17).

48 Schuster and Low (2025a, b, 18).

49 Lessig (2000). For a current analysis and interpretation, see also Judge et al (2025, 85).

These realities apply equally, if not more acutely, to DAOs. Despite the ideal of 'rule-by-code', it is unrealistic to expect that all interactions within a DAO will proceed exactly as anticipated by its founders or participants. Disputes are an inevitable part of complex organisational life, and DAOs are no exception. As scholars have noted, DAOs can become embroiled in conflicts between members, between the DAO and its members, or with external third parties.[50]

A well-known example that highlights the vulnerabilities inherent in DAOs is the infamous 'theDAO' incident. Launched in 2016 on the Ethereum blockchain by the team behind 'slock.it', theDAO was a pioneering decentralised investment fund that quickly gained traction. Participants sent funds in the form of Ether to the DAO's smart contract in exchange for utility tokens, which conferred both ownership and governance rights.[51] Within a short period, theDAO raised approximately $150 million in Ether, making it the largest crowdfunding effort of its time.[52] Yet its rapid ascent also exposed critical weaknesses in its design—vulnerabilities that would soon be exploited with dramatic consequences.

TheDAO's smart contract code included a function that allowed participants to exit the organisation. This function specified the destination address for the Ether to be returned to the exiting participant. However, one participant exploited a vulnerability in the smart contract by repeatedly triggering the opt-out function, even after having already withdrawn more Ether than they had initially contributed. The flaw in the code lay in the fact that the opt-out function could be executed multiple times without verifying whether the participant had already recovered the full amount of their original contribution to theDAO.[53] Thus, after investments were collected in theDAO's Ether pool, approximately $40 million of these funds were "stolen" from the organization by this participant, who made an unexpected use of computer code. Consequently, thousands of people were almost left stuck in the smart contract.[54] Since there is no central authority to force the user to undo their transaction, there was also no mechanism to force the stolen Ethers back to where they were supposed to be.[55]

It should be noted that there was no malicious hacking of code or stealing of passwords here. A user who caught the vulnerability of the computer code, performed actions that were in accordance with the conditions programmed in the existing smart contract (using the exit function) and the result was unsuitable and undesirable (transfer of coins to their own wallet by using the leave function more than once).[56] Even though in theory it was possible to file a lawsuit against the author and order the

[50] Guillaume and Riva (2025, 15).

[51] Kolber (2018, 210), Mann (2019, 219), Mann (2017, 1015).

[52] Bilski (2019, 37), Vigliotti and Jones (2020, 144).

[53] Cieplak and Leefatt (2017, 424).

[54] Kolber (2018, 212).

[55] Cieplak and Leefatt (2017, 425).

[56] Raskin (2017, 336–337), Rohr (2019, 87), Scholz (2020, 149).

return of the funds, in practice it was impossible to find the person who exploited the smart contract code, since the users in the Ethereum blockchain are pseudonyms.[57]

In this case, there was no legal or technical way to ensure that the funds could be returned without upsetting the blockchain system.[58] Thus, the leaders of the crowdfunding project had to entice most mining nodes to implement a hard fork for the funds to be returned. The transactions made were reversed using a hard fork,[59] like going back in time.[60] Ultimately, theDAO incident demonstrated that the technology underpinning smart contracts was not yet mature enough to support the automated execution of complex, high-stakes decisions without human oversight.[61] Although the project itself failed, it served as a crucial learning experience for the blockchain community. It underscored the need for dispute resolution mechanisms tailored to the unique challenges of decentralised governance. If blockchain infrastructure is to be trusted and scaled as a backbone of the digital economy, it must combine technical immutability with adaptive legal and procedural safeguards.[62]

Building on the previous discussion of legal and technical vulnerabilities in DAOs, it is now necessary to consider a more nuanced concept: digital vulnerability. This moves beyond general organisational risk to examine how structural features of DAOs—combined with the broader digital environment—can expose participants and third parties to specific forms of harm or disadvantage.

While DAOs offer clear benefits for their creators and technologically sophisticated users—such as flexibility, transparency, and decentralised governance—, they also present significant challenges for regulators, oversight bodies, and less-informed participants. These challenges include the absence of clear accountability mechanisms, undefined liability structures, and the lack of recognised legal personality.[63] Moreover, DAOs blur traditional boundaries between user and co-creator, consumer and governor. This duality complicates the nature of digital vulnerability, but also points to the possibility of internal remedies through reimagined governance structures.

To understand how digital vulnerability manifests in DAO ecosystems, it is useful to draw parallels with algorithmic marketplaces. DAOs often function as platforms that automate decisions and process data, exposing their participants to risks similar to those faced by consumers of digital services—such as profiling, manipulation of

[57] Cieplak and Leefatt (2017, 425). Information recorded as part of blockchain transactions are generally regarded as 'pseudonymised' rather than strictly 'anonymous'. The risk of re-identification of the concerned party increases with the volume of pseudonymised data stored on the blockchain. An increasingly detailed view of the wallet holder could be derived hence potentially revealing someone's preferences or behaviours. See ICO and FCA (2024, 11).

[58] Kolber (2018, 216) Blocher (2019, 118).

[59] Hard-forking refers to a radical change in the protocol to validate invalid previous blocks or transactions in the blockchain or invalidate previous valid blocks/transactions. Weber (2019, 163), Tjong Tjin Tai (2019, 82), Verstraete (2019, 777).

[60] Guadamuz (2019, 18).

[61] Wilkens and Falk (2019, 23).

[62] Guillaume and Riva (2025, 5).

[63] WEF (2022, 5).

governance processes, unequal influence, and restricted access to effective redress.[64] These vulnerabilities are not merely theoretical. Both DAO members and external parties interacting with DAOs may be placed at a disadvantage, particularly when there is a lack of technical or legal literacy.

Importantly, digital vulnerability is not limited to an individual's subjective conditions. In the context of smart contracts, the consumer's technological or legal awareness is irrelevant if the contractual relationship satisfies the objective criteria for a consumer contract. This insight is critical in framing DAO participants—particularly retail users—as potentially vulnerable actors regardless of their intentions or background. Moreover, the DAO ecosystem is also open to vulnerabilities.

Disputes involving DAOs can arise in multiple forms. These include disagreements between members over governance rights, their operations concerning consumers, disputes over the distribution of treasury funds, conflicts between the DAO and users regarding terms of service, and even contractual disputes with third-party business partners.[65] Beyond these private interactions, the public law implications of DAOs also vary significantly across jurisdictions, further complicating the regulatory landscape.[66]

At the heart of these vulnerabilities lies a deeper problem: the lack of a harmonised legal framework capable of answering foundational questions in cross-border digital contexts. As private international law (PIL) scholars highlight, one of the reasons why digital vulnerability arises is precisely due to current legal systems struggling to answer the 'what' (which law applies), 'when' (at what point it should apply), 'who' (which authority has jurisdiction), and 'how' (the means by which parties can choose applicable law or forum). Traditionally, these questions were resolved through the concept of *situs*—the location of a transaction, asset, or legal subject.[67] However, the pseudonymity of blockchain users, the immaterial nature of digital assets, and the decentralised configuration of blockchain networks make it increasingly difficult—if not impossible—to determine situs in any meaningful way.[68]

In response, some have argued for harmonising private international law principles to address these gaps. Such efforts would directly confront digital vulnerability by providing clearer rules and procedures for real-world scenarios involving smart contracts, DAOs, and other decentralised applications. As digital interactions transcend borders and identities, robust legal coordination becomes indispensable for ensuring fairness, predictability, and trust.

Moreover, digital vulnerability is compounded by structural asymmetries. Online platforms—and by extension DAOs—often create imbalances between users and system operators. These asymmetries can be relational (due to disempowering user

---

[64] WEF (2022, 8 f).

[65] Perera and Barthe-Dejean (2023).

[66] Perera and Barthe-Dejean (2023).

[67] Escolar (2024, 329).

[68] Escolar (2024, 331). According to the same author, "[a]nswering these questions of private international law makes us all less vulnerable as natives in the digital world that we inhabit today" (Escolar 2024, 349).

positions), architectural (stemming from interface design and choice architecture), or knowledge-based (as traders and developers typically possess far more insight into system functioning than end-users).[69] As Helberger and others observe, in digital society, these architectures are not merely passive environments but active producers of vulnerability. Dispositional and occurrent vulnerabilities are not incidental; rather, they are a direct product of the way digital systems are built and deployed.[70]

4.1 Architectural Vulnerability

The structural design of DAOs introduces distinct architectural vulnerabilities, many of which arise from their foundational reliance on smart contracts and pseudonymous participation.

DAOs make decisions either through on-chain or off-chain governance. On-chain governance means that proposals and votes are recorded directly on the blockchain, making the process transparent and unchangeable (for example, Compound Finance DAO and Uniswap DAO use this method to vote on upgrades or how to spend funds). In contrast, off-chain governance involves discussions that happen outside the blockchain, such as on forums or Discord servers, before any decisions are officially recorded on-chain.[71] No matter whether governance is on-chain or off-chain, DAOs often operate in an anonymous or pseudonymous manner, allowing participants to exercise token-based voting rights without revealing their real identities. While this anonymity supports privacy and decentralisation, it also opens the door to manipulation. Individuals with adverse reputations can re-enter the ecosystem under false identities,[72] and the lack of identifiable actors undermines accountability. The widespread pseudonymity creates significant information asymmetries between DAO founders or core developers and later participants or contributors, placing the latter at a disadvantage and complicating efforts to detect or prevent financial misconduct.[73]

Such asymmetries are not limited to identity. Founders (often developers) and early participants frequently set up, code and manage the DAO's governance rules, benefiting from early access and greater familiarity with its technical design.[74] They are the ones that, as visionaries, determine the purpose, drive the project forward, attract participants, select collaborators and establish strategic directions before

[69] Durovic and Kaprou (2024, 144).

[70] Helberger et al (2022, 19).

[71] Davidson (2025, 2). For more information on the distinction, see Davidson (2024).

[72] Naudts (2023, 14).

[73] WEF (2022, 8).

[74] While discussing the issue of who is responsible and liable for the actions of DAOs, the ECB report highlights the following about the developers: "Whether or not software developers in DAOs have an implicit fiduciary duty because their software coding affects the assets and interests of consumers is another subject of debate". Naudts (2023, 22).

raising capital.[75] Information asymmetries between founders and contributors[76] can lead to fraud and manipulation and make legal recourse challenging.[77] This dynamic leads to power imbalances that contradict the ideal of decentralisation. As some scholars have noted, despite their decentralised architecture, DAOs often replicate hierarchical structures (such as information asymmetry and power imbalance)—only in less visible forms.[78]

Another core architectural vulnerability stems from the nature of smart contracts themselves. Because DAOs are executed through immutable code, any divergence between on-chain execution and off-chain agreements can lead to disputes. Smart contracts are inherently rigid: once deployed, they are difficult to modify and cannot, unless expressly coded, adapt to evolving circumstances.[79] This lack of flexibility may result in the enforcement of contractual terms even when they no longer reflect the parties' intentions.[80] Even if a DAO's code is flawed, unlawful, or contrary to its intended purpose, it will still execute. In the absence of regulations mandating cybersecurity standards or monitoring protocols, these vulnerabilities can expose token holders to serious liability and leave them powerless to regain control of the DAO.[81] In addition, oracles—external data used to inform smart contracts—pose a further risk, as they lack the blockchain's reliability and are susceptible to manipulation or failure.[82]

The risk of code-based errors compounds these vulnerabilities. Smart contracts may contain bugs or logical flaws[83] that only become apparent after deployment. These errors can lead to a wrong execution of the terms or unintended outcomes, even if the code functions exactly as written.[84] Although not necessarily a failure of the technology per se, such outcomes can result in significant financial harm.[85] Some DAOs attempt to mitigate rigidity through off-chain governance mechanisms, which inserts human discretion into decision-making. However, this reintroduces many of the same challenges associated with centralised governance, such as reliance on dominant token holders and concerns over transparency and probity.[86]

---

[75] Villanueva Collao (2025, 7).

[76] "DAOs frequently use offshore business devices to manage specific projects in jurisdictions that offer limited protections to their members. In this sense, asymmetric information and new hierarchies are the desired outcomes among the founders and insiders of the organization, reducing the chances for members to access governance". Villanueva Collao (2025).

[77] WEF (2022). See also US Department of Treasury (2022, 2).

[78] See also Davidson (2025).

[79] Benetti and Piazza (2024, 6).

[80] Golub (2024, 294).

[81] Levin (2024, 465).

[82] Eliza (2017, 296).

[83] Poncibò and DiMatteo (2019, 121).

[84] Clifford Chance and EBRD (2018, 30), Erbguth (2019, 33).

[85] Davidson (2025, 12).

[86] Davidson (2025, 8).

Moreover, many DAO participants lack the technical expertise to read, audit, or understand the smart contracts governing their interactions. This creates a dependency on developers and auditors, deepening informational imbalances in both technological and legal literacy. The opacity of smart contract logic to the average user heightens the risk of exploitation and misinterpretation.[87]

In DAOs built on public blockchains, the identities of founders and participants may remain permanently obscured. This raises substantial barriers to legal redress. In most jurisdictions, consumer protection mechanisms rely on the ability to identify and hold a responsible party accountable.[88] Without a legally recognisable counterparty, participants may have no effective avenue for asserting their rights or recovering losses. This 'redress vulnerability' is further exacerbated by the high costs, procedural complexity, and jurisdictional uncertainty that often accompany attempts to resolve disputes involving decentralised systems.

In sum, the architectural foundations of DAOs introduce a range of vulnerabilities that challenge core legal and governance principles. The immutability of smart contracts, the opacity of code, the anonymity of participants, and the asymmetrical distribution of technical knowledge all contribute to an ecosystem in which power and responsibility are often misaligned.

4.2 Data-Driven Vulnerability

The pseudonymity and security features of blockchain technology are frequently mistaken for privacy. In reality, all transactions and governance activities recorded on a blockchain—including those within DAOs—are immutable and publicly accessible. While this transparency is often praised as a mechanism of trust and accountability, it simultaneously exposes participants to a range of data-driven vulnerabilities. Every action taken on-chain—casting of a vote, realisation of a token transfer, or proposal—is traceable and permanently recorded, allowing for the construction of detailed behavioural profiles over time.

This vulnerability is further compounded by using off-chain tools commonly integrated into DAO ecosystems. Platforms such as Snapshot, along with communication channels like Discord bots, collect and analyse behavioural data that can be linked to on-chain identities. The result is a hybrid surveillance environment, where seemingly anonymous users are subject to extensive behavioural tracking and profiling. In such settings, DAO participants may be exposed to targeted influence campaigns, sybil attacks, or the commodification of their behavioural data.[89]

Although DAOs may appear to be privacy-compliant due to the pseudonymity of blockchain addresses, this appearance is misleading. The accumulation and analysis

---

[87] Golub (2024, 294).

[88] Also see Parry and Şahin (2024, 15). It may be difficult for consumers to obtain redress in the event of a problem with the DAO due to its dispersed nature and lack of separate legal personality.

[89] WEF (2022, 12–13).

of on-chain and off-chain data effectively 'datafies' DAO participants. Their participation patterns—including voting frequency, proposal preferences, and interaction timings—can be used to infer personal traits, group affiliations, or strategic intentions. Over time, this opens the door to behavioural prediction and even conditioning, threatening user autonomy and the fairness of governance processes. In sum, while DAOs may lack centralised surveillance actors, their structural transparency and the use of external tools make participants highly vulnerable to data exploitation.

4.3 *Relational Vulnerability*

While DAOs reconfigure traditional organisational structures and aim to decentralise authority, they often result in hidden hierarchies that challenge their democratic aspirations. One of the central relational dynamics in DAOs is the issuance of tokens in place of traditional equity instruments. These tokens are frequently associated with governance rights and the expectation of economic returns. However, the legal relationship between token holders and the DAO is often undefined or entirely absent. This legal ambiguity increases the risk of misselling and unmet expectations, particularly among retail participants who may lack the knowledge or context to accurately assess the financial or governance implications of token ownership.[90]

As discussed in Sect. 3.3, the absence of formal corporate structures in many jurisdictions means that DAOs often exist without recognised legal personality. This creates uncertainty around questions of accountability and liability, especially when disputes arise. For uninformed or under-informed consumers, this structural opacity makes DAOs particularly risky, as there may be no identifiable entity—or even individual—to hold responsible in the event of harm or contractual failure.

The legal challenges presented by DAOs are compounded when viewed through the lens of private international law. As one scholar recently observed, digital vulnerabilities in decentralised systems often arise because fundamental private international law questions remain unanswered: Which law applies to a given transaction? Which court has jurisdiction? How are decisions recognised and enforced across borders? What cooperation frameworks exist to manage disputes involving decentralised actors?[91] The anonymity or pseudonymity of participants, the immaterial nature of digital assets, and the absence of clear territorial anchors all contribute to a fragmented and uncertain legal environment. Without a harmonised private international law framework, DLT-based transactions—including those involving DAOs—operate in a regulatory vacuum that leaves users exposed.[92]

These legal uncertainties intersect with governance issues to further deepen relational vulnerabilities. Participation in DAO governance is often low. As Bellavitis, Fisch, and Momtas (2022) report, two-thirds of token holders do not vote on

[90] Naudts (2023, 14).

[91] Escolar (2024, 328).

[92] Escolar (2024, 327).

proposals.[93] This low turnout creates a fertile environment for power consolidation, where a small group of large token holders—commonly referred to as "whales"—can exert disproportionate influence over outcomes.[94] This dynamic undermines the decentralisation ethos of DAOs and raises questions about fairness, legitimacy, and representation. A notable example occurred in July 2024, when the Compound Finance DAO approved a proposal to divert assets to another protocol, 'goldCOMP'. Although the transaction was ultimately reversed, it revealed critical weaknesses in the DAO's governance model and highlighted the potential for coordinated minority interests to steer decisions.[95]

Moreover, voter apathy is often exacerbated by the technical complexity of governance proposals and the coordination difficulties inherent in large, decentralised communities. In practice, many DAOs replicate well-known corporate governance problems, such as the dominance of majority shareholders or institutional investors. However, in the DAO context, these issues are further intensified by the pseudonymity and borderless nature of blockchain networks, where the identity, interests, and voting behaviour of major participants remain opaque and unaccountable.[96]

5 Addressing Digital Vulnerability in DAOs: Remedial Strategies

Mitigating digital vulnerability in the context of DAOs requires a multilayered approach that spans technological, legal, and ethical domains. This section outlines a structured framework of remedial strategies aimed at enhancing resilience, ensuring fairness, and strengthening trust within DAO ecosystems.

From a technical perspective, one of the key interventions involves embedding dispute resolution mechanisms directly into smart contract architecture. By designing contracts with features such as pause functions, soft-fork capabilities, and arbitration triggers, DAOs can mitigate the effects of malicious behaviour or coding errors without entirely undermining the principle of decentralisation. Complementing this, participatory governance design is essential. Involving users in the creation and ongoing evolution of governance frameworks—whether through deliberative mechanisms or structured community feedback loops—enhances procedural legitimacy and fosters greater inclusivity. Furthermore, implementing modular and adaptive governance structures, such as upgradeable smart contracts that include exit rights, veto thresholds, and layered voting mechanisms, allows DAOs to respond effectively to evolving community needs while preserving systemic stability.

On the legal and institutional front, the introduction of 'legal wrappers' can serve as a vital bridge between decentralised entities and traditional legal systems. These

[93] Bellavitis et al (2022, 187 f).

[94] See also US Department of Treasury (2022, 10–11), Ly and Shojaei (2025).

[95] Davidson (2025, 8).

[96] Davidson (2025, 12).

wrappers—facilitated through model laws or regulatory sandboxes—provide DAOs with an interface to operate within existing legal frameworks, thereby offering clarity in terms of rights, obligations, and enforcement.[97] A more robust and future-facing solution would be the formal recognition of legal personality for DAOs. Whether through adaptations of existing corporate structures or the creation of bespoke legal categories, such recognition would allow DAOs to enter into contracts, be held liable, and offer enforceable rights to third parties and participants alike. In parallel, the transnational nature of DAO activity necessitates the development of harmonised standards for dispute resolution. Establishing clear, interoperable mechanisms for both on-chain and off-chain adjudication would address current jurisdictional ambiguities and promote legal certainty across borders. In this regard, reform efforts in the domain of private international law must prioritise the digital economy and its specific vulnerabilities.

Ethical and data governance considerations also form a crucial pillar of this framework. While DAOs are often assumed to be privacy-enhancing due to blockchain's pseudonymity, the reality is more complex. Participants' activities—ranging from voting behaviour to transaction histories—are publicly accessible and can be exploited for profiling and manipulation. Accordingly, privacy-preserving technologies such as zero-knowledge proofs, cryptographic mixers, and decentralised identity protocols should be adopted to safeguard user identities while maintaining accountability. Beyond technological safeguards, DAOs should commit to ethical data governance by embedding principles such as data minimisation, purpose limitation, and auditable consent within their operational design. The establishment of community-driven data ethics charters can further institutionalise these commitments and serve as normative anchors in otherwise unregulated environments.

Finally, governance mechanisms must be designed to prevent capture and ensure fairness. The use of anti-concentration tools such as quadratic voting, identity-bound (or 'soulbound') tokens, and voting caps can help prevent dominance by large token holders and facilitate a more equitable distribution of influence. These measures are particularly important in light of the growing empirical evidence showing that voter participation in many DAOs is disproportionately low, enabling a small subset of actors to exert outsized control. Designing governance structures that proactively address these risks is essential for realising the democratic potential of DAOs and safeguarding against new forms of digital vulnerability.

6 Conclusion

In response to the growing complexities of the digital ecosystem, many scholars and regulators have argued for a reconceptualization of consumer vulnerability—one that reflects the universal and systemic nature in digitally mediated environments. In this evolving landscape, vulnerability is no longer confined to traditionally pre-defined

[97] Möslein and Ostrovski (2025, 255 f).

groups but is shaped by the structural, informational, and relational dynamics of digital platforms. All users, depending on the circumstances, can become vulnerable.

DAOs, as decentralised and code-governed entities, exemplify both the promise and the perils of Web3 innovation. They offer novel models of collective action, transparency, and disintermediation, yet also introduce a new spectrum of risk. These include architectural vulnerabilities rooted in the immutability and opacity of smart contracts; data-driven vulnerabilities arising from participant traceability and profiling; and relational vulnerabilities linked to legal ambiguity, governance, and unequal power dynamics. Together, these risks challenge foundational principles of accountability, equity, fairness and trust in digital environments.

Drawing on the qualitative findings of this research—as highlighted in the insights by the UK's Financial Conduct Authority (FCA) and the Information Commissioner's Office (ICO)[98]—it is evident that regulatory responses must evolve in tandem with technological innovation. First, the technology underpinning digital assets and decentralised finance offers features that consumers may value, but also presents novel risks that demand appropriate oversight. Second, transparency is essential. Consumers need clear information about the risks they face, how their data is processed, and what rights and remedies they retain. Without such transparency, confidence in digital asset markets—and in DAOs more specifically—may erode. Third, trust in how value and data are safeguarded remains critical. While digital assets are technologically distinct, the consumer expectations of security, fairness, and accountability remain consistent. Regulatory frameworks in financial services and data protection can play a central role in supporting DAO ecosystems to meet these expectations.

It is also essential that regulators develop a nuanced understanding of both the risks and benefits associated with DAOs and other decentralised structures. Such understanding will enable policymakers and stakeholders to design interventions that maximise privacy and consumer protection without undermining the utility, efficiency, and user-centric potential of decentralised technologies. A balanced approach—one that preserves the innovation enabled by DAOs while safeguarding user rights—is key to ensuring that these structures can serve the broader public interest.[99]

Until these concerns are addressed—through coherent legal recognition, global regulatory coordination, and the development of ethical and technological safeguards—the integration of DAOs into mainstream financial and governance systems will remain constrained. Without structural clarity and adequate consumer protections, DAOs risk remaining at the periphery of formal institutions.

Ultimately, the sustainable future of DAOs depends not only on their technical evolution but on the ability of regulators, developers, and communities to embed accountability, inclusiveness, and transparency at the core of decentralised governance.[100] The task ahead is to harness the transformative potential of DAOs while

---

[98] ICO and FCA (2024).

[99] ICO and FCA (2024, 12).

[100] See also Naudts (2023, 24).

ensuring they operate in ways that protect and empower all participants in the digital economy.[101]

References

Aragon (2023) DAO framework: how to code a DAO with Aragon Smart Contracts. Aragon Blog. Available at https://blog.aragon.org/dao-framework-how-to-code-a-dao-with-aragon-smart-contracts/

Bellavitis C, Fisch C, Momtaz PP (2022) The rise of decentralized autonomous organizations (DAOs): a first empirical glimpse. Venture Cap 25(2):187–203

Benetti Z, Piazza F (2024) Decentralised finance: a categorisation of smart contracts. ESMA Working Paper No 3. European Securities and Markets Authority, Paris. Available at https://www.esma.europa.eu/sites/default/files/2023-10/ESMA50-2085271018-3351_TRV_Article_Decentralised_Finance_A_Categorisation_of_Smart_Contracts.pdf

BEUC (2023) Towards European Digital fairness: framing response paper for the REFIT consultation. BEUC, Brussels. Available at https://www.beuc.eu/sites/default/files/publications/BEUC-X-2023-020_Consultation_paper_REFIT_consumer_law_digital_fairness.pdf

Bilski N (2019) Blockchain—technologie, smart contracts und selbstvollziehende Verträge. Available at https://papers.ssrn.com/3425805

Blocher W (2019) Fehlerhafte smart contracts. In: Braegelmann T, Kaulartz M (eds) Rechtshandbuch smart contracts. C.H. Beck, München, pp 113–133

Borgogno O (2022) Making decentralized autonomous organizations (DAOs) fit for legal life: mind the gap. Bank of Italy Occasional Paper No. 718. Available at https://ssrn.com/abstract=4462934

Boss S (2023) DAOs: Legal and empirical review. Amsterdam Law School Legal Studies Research Paper No. 2023–27. Available at https://papers.ssrn.com/4503234

Clock b Business Technology (2025) AI-Driven DAOs: The Future of Autonomous Organizations. Available at https://clockb.tech/ai-driven-daos-the-future-of-autonomous-organizations/.

Carron B, Botteron V (2019) How smart can a contract be? In: Kraus D, Obrist T, Hari O (eds) Blockchains, smart contracts, decentralised autonomous organisations and the law. Edward Elgar, Cheltenham, pp 101–143

CBI (2022) Decentralized Autonomous Organization (DAO) White Paper. Available at https://assets.ctfassets.net/c5bd0wqjc7v0/14KFHkWUtAi5NNmxblpSGd/2f4e411c01dddbea0938d17835b61a00/CBI-DAOWhitePaper_112822_v2.pdf

Cieplak J, Leefatt S (2017) Smart contracts: a smart way to automate performance. Geo Law Rev 417(1):417–427

Clifford Chance, EBRD (2018) Smart contracts: legal framework and proposed guidelines for lawmakers. Available at https://www.ebrd.com/

Cuccuru P (2017) Beyond bitcoin: an early overview on smart contracts. Int J Law Inf Technol 25(3):179–195

Davidson S (2025) The nature of the decentralised autonomous organisation. J Inst Econ (21:e5):1–14. https://doi.org/10.1017/S1744137424000341

Davidson S (2024) Decentralised autonomous organisations as commons. Available at https://ssrn.com/abstract=4795629

De Filippi P, Hassan S (2021), Decentralized autonomous organization. Internet Policy Rev 10:1–10. https://doi.org/10.14763/2021.2.1556

De Filippi P, Wright A. (2018) Blockchain and the law: the rule of code. Harvard University Press, Cambridge.

[101] OECD (2023, 28).

Dodsworth T et al (2023) Editorial: digital vulnerability. J Consum Policy 46(4):413–417
Dubnevych N (2021) DAO types: community DAO, service DAO & investment DAO and regulatory requirements for each. Legal Nodes. Available at https://legalnodes.com/article/dao-types
Durovic M, Kaprou E (2024) The new concept of digital vulnerability and the European Rules on unfair commercial practices. In: Crea C, De Franceschi A (eds) The new shapes of digital vulnerability in European private law. Nomos, Baden-Baden, pp 127–144
Mik E (2017) Smart contracts: terminology, technical limitations and real world complexity. Law, Innovation & Technology.
Erbguth J (2019) Transparenz von smart contracts. In: Fries M, Paal B (eds) Smart contracts. Mohr Siebeck, Tübingen, pp 25–32
Ernst and Young (2023) How to navigate tax and legal complexity associated with DAOs. In: EY Insights—Tax. Available at https://www.ey.com/en_gl/insights/tax/how-to-navigate-tax-and-legal-complexity-associated-with-daos
Escolar Goh G (2024) Addressing digital vulnerability through private international law. In: Crea C, De Franceschi A (eds) The new shapes of digital vulnerability in European private law. Nomos, Baden-Baden, pp 325–349
Golub J (2024) Digital vulnerability of consumers in the world of smart contracts—is European private international law "digitalised" enough? In: Crea C, De Franceschi A (eds) The new shapes of digital vulnerability in European private law. Nomos, Baden-Baden, pp 293–324
Grimmelmann J (2019) All smart contracts are ambiguous. Pa J Law Innov 2(1):1–22
Grochowski M (2024) Digital vulnerability in a post-consumer society. Subverting Paradigms? In: Crea C, De Franceschi A (eds) The new shapes of digital vulnerability in European private law. Nomos, Baden-Baden, pp 293–324
Guadamuz A (2019) All watched over by machines of loving grace: a critical look at smart contracts. Comput Law Secur Rev 35(6):1–16. Available at https://ssrn.com/abstract=3805473
Guillaume C, Riva S (2025) Blockchain dispute resolution for decentralized autonomous organizations: the rise of decentralized autonomous justice. In: Bonomi A, Lehmann M (eds) Blockchain and private international law. Brill, Leiden, pp 549–641
Helberger N, Sax M, Strycharz J, Micklitz H-W (2022) Choice architectures in the digital economy: towards a new understanding of digital vulnerability. J Consum Policy 45(2):175–200
Information Commissioner's Office (ICO) and Financial Conduct Authority (FCA) (2024) Consumer attitudes on the risks and benefits of engaging with digital assets. Available at https://www.drcf.org.uk/siteassets/drcf/pdf-files/consumers-and-digital-assets-ico-and-fca-joint-insights-paper?v=380464
Judge B, Nitzberg M, Russell S (2025) When code isn't law: rethinking regulation for artificial intelligence. Policy Soc 44(1):85–97
Karl J (2018) Die Vereinbarkeit von Smart Contracts mit dem deutschen Rechtssystem. Grin, Norderstedt
Kaulartz M, Heckmann J (2016) Smart contracts—Anwendungen der blockchain technologie. Comput Recht 32(9):620–624
Kolber AJ (2018) Not-so-smart blockchain contracts and artificial responsibility. Stanford Technol Law Rev 21(2):210–234
Lessig L (2000). Code is law: on liberty in cyberspace. Harvard Magazine (January/February). Available at https://www.harvardmagazine.com/2000/01/code-is-law-html
Levin R (2024) Bankrupting the matrix: DAOs and the code. Emory Bankr Dev J 40(3):455–510
Ly R, Shojaei A (2025) Decentralized autonomous organization in built environments: applications, potential and limitations. Inf Syst E-Bus Manag. https://doi.org/10.1007/s10257-025-00699-1
Mann M (2019) Komplexe smart contracts: die decentralized autonomous organization. In: Braegelmann T, Kaulartz M (eds) Rechtshandbuch smart contracts. C.H. Beck, München, pp 219–231
Mann M (2017) Die decentralized autonomous organization—ein neuer Gesellschaftstyp? Neue Z Gesellschaftsrecht 26:1014–1020

Möslein F, Ostrovski D (2025) Towards a European legal form for DAOs? In: Guillaume F, Riva S (eds) Decentralized autonomous organizations in the legal landscape. Edward Elgar, Cheltenham, pp 255–274

Mišćenić E (2024) Information, Transparency and Fairness for Consumers in the Digital Environment. In: Crea C, De Franceschi A (eds) The New Shapes of Digital Vulnerability in European Private Law. Nomos, Baden-Baden, p 89–125.

Naudts E (2023) The future of DAOs in finance. ECB Occasional Paper Series No 331. European Central Bank, Frankfurt am Main. Available at https://www.ecb.europa.eu/pub/pdf/scpops/ecb.op331~a03e416045.en.pdf.

Organisation for Economic Co-operation and Development (2023) Advancing accountability in AI: governing and managing risks throughout the lifecycle for trustworthy AI (OECD Digital Economy Papers No 349, OECD Publishing)

Parry R, Şahin H (2024) Cryptoassets, expectation gaps and consumer protection: the case of Turkey. Law Ethics Tech 2024(4):0011. https://doi.org/10.55092/let20240011.

Perera D, Barthe-Dejean J (2023) Arbitrating DAO disputes—A delectable can of worms? HFW Insights, 27 April 2023. Available at https://www.hfw.com/insights/arbitrating-dao-disputes-a-delectable-can-of-worms/

Poncibò C, DiMatteo LA (2019) Smart contracts: contractual and noncontractual remedies. In: DiMatteo LA, Cannarsa M, Poncibò C (eds) The Cambridge handbook of smart contracts, blockchain technology and digital platforms. Cambridge University Press, Cambridge, pp 118–140

Poretti P (2023) Touch screen justice and consumer vulnerability—a mixed blessing? EU Compar Law Issues Challenges Ser 7:144–162

Raskin M (2017) The law and legality of smart contracts. Geo Law Technol Rev 1:305–341

Rebrean M-L, Malgieri G (2025) Vulnerability in the AI Act: building an interpretation. In: FAccT '25: Proceedings of the 2025 ACM Conference on fairness, accountability, and transparency. Association for Computing Machinery, New York, pp 1985–1997

Riefa C (2022) Protecting vulnerable consumers in the digital single market. Eur Bus Law Rev 33(4):607–634

Riva S (2021) Decentralized autonomous organizations (DAOs) in the Swiss legal order. Yearb Priv Int Law 21:601–638

Rohr JG (2019) Smart contracts and traditional contract law, or: the law of the vending machine. Clev State Law Rev 67(1):71–92

Sax M, Helberger N (2024) Digital vulnerability and manipulation in the emerging digital framework. In: Helberger N et al (eds) Digital fairness for consumers. BEUC, Brussels, pp 10–24. Available at https://www.beuc.eu/reports/digital-fairness-consumers

Schillig M (2023) Decentralized autonomous organizations (DAOs) under English Law. Available at https://blogs.law.ox.ac.uk/oblb/blog-post/2023/03/decentralized-autonomous-organizations-daos-under-english-law

Scholz LH (2020) Algorithms and contract law. In: Barfield W (ed) The Cambridge handbook of the law of algorithms. Cambridge University Press, Cambridge, pp 141–152

Schuster E-P, Low KFK (2025) What do DAOs really contribute? In: Werbach K, Micheler E, Kremer B (eds) Foundations of decentralized organizations: blockchain and the future of corporate law. Oxford University Press (forthcoming)

Schuster E-P, Low KFK (2025) What do DAOs really contribute? LSE Legal Stud Working Paper No. 15/2025. Available at https://ssrn.com/abstract=5327229

Spindler G (2021) Blockchain Typen und ihre gesellschaftsrechtliche Einordnung. Recht Digital 1(7):309–317

Tjong Tjin Tai E (2019) Challenges of smart contracts. Implementing excuses. In: DiMatteo LA, Cannarsa M, Poncibò C (eds) The Cambridge handbook of smart contracts, blockchain technology and digital platforms. Cambridge University Press, Cambridge, pp 80–101

US Department of Treasury (2022) Crypto-Assets: Implications for Consumers, Investors, and Businesses. Published pursuant to Executive Order 14067. Available at https://home.treasury.gov/system/files/136/CryptoAsset_EO5.pdf
Verstraete M (2019) The stakes of smart contracts. Loy Univ Chicago Law J 50:743–795
Vigliotti MG, Jones H (2020) The executive guide to blockchain. Springer, Cham
Villanueva Collao V (2025) Decentralized(?), But far from disorganized: a comparative analysis of legal wrappers and the evolving structure of DAOs. Available at https://ssrn.com/abstract=5143035
von Hippel E, von Krogh Georg (2003) Open source software and the 'private-collective' innovation model: issues for organization science. Organization Science 14(2):209–223
Wang S et al (2019) Decentralized autonomous organizations: concept, model, and applications. IEEE Trans Comput Soc Syst 6(5):870–878
Weber RH (2019) Contractual duties and allocation of liability in automated digital contracts. In: Schulze R, Staudenmayer D (eds) Digital revolution: challenges for contract law in practice. Nomos, Baden-Baden, pp 163–187
Wilkens R, Falk R (2019) Smart Contracts Grundlagen, Anwendungsfelder und rechtliche Aspekte. Springer, Berlin
World Economic Forum (WEF) (2022) Decentralized autonomous organizations: beyond the hype. Crypto impact and sustainability accelerator & Wharton blockchain and digital asset project. Available at https://www3.weforum.org/docs/WEF_Decentralized_Autonomous_Organizations_Beyond_the_Hype_2022.pdf
Wright A (2021) The rise of decentralized autonomous organizations: opportunities and challenges. Stanford J Blockchain Law Policy 4(2):155–176

Conclusion

Remedies to Digital Vulnerability in European Private Law: Concluding Considerations of a Conference

Reiner Schulze

Abstract Based on the concluding remarks at the conference in Trieste, from which this volume emerged, this chapter deals with key concepts related to the conference topic and discusses the results of the conference with regard to five core areas of legislation and research on Digital Vulnerability: consumer protection, personal data protection, non-discrimination, intermediary services, and AI-related issues. It analyses a number of findings and their possible impact on the future development of EU protection instruments in these fields. In addition, it examines the overarching regulatory approaches that form the framework for the necessary adjustments to the protection instruments in line with technological and economic changes. This concerns in particular a stronger focus on structural and preventive protection mechanisms and the strengthening of cross-sectoral remedies for Digital Vulnerability, in addition to specific regulations for particularly vulnerable groups of people. In this context, it points out that provisions of the Consumer Acquis in particular can serve as a model for general provisions of European Private Law with regard to Digital Vulnerability. Finally, it emphasises the connection between the necessary further development of remedies and the transformation of the structures of European Private Law in the digital age.

Keywords Digital vulnerability · European private law · Consumer concept · AI contracting · Data protection

---

R. Schulze (✉)
Centre for European Private Law, University of Münster, Münster, Germany
e-mail: reiner.schulze@uni-muenster.de

C. Crea and M. Infantino (eds.), *Remedies to Digital Vulnerability in European Private Law*, https://doi.org/10.1007/978-3-032-19720-7_27

1 Introduction

The conference that this volume emerged from brought together experts from numerous countries to conclude the project 'Digital Vulnerability in European Private Law'.[1] This project (as its title suggests) focused on the relationship between two subjects, both of which are based on new and by no means completed developments: 'Digital Vulnerability' is the result of a profound technological, social and economic change that can be compared to the digital revolution of the twenty-first century and to the industrial revolution of the nineteenth century, and just as this once ushered in the 'industrial age', it has now initiated a 'digital age'. 'European Private Law' has emerged from the efforts towards European integration and thus from a fundamental change in the political, economic and legal profile of the European continent since the middle of the twentieth century and has recently, especially since the European Union's 'Digital Single Market Strategy',[2] increasingly turned to the consequences of digitalisation with new concepts and regulations.

In this thematic field of Digital Vulnerability in European Private Law, the conference documented in this volume, with its focus on 'remedies', has now introduced a specific focus that goes beyond the description of developments that have occurred and problems that have emerged. It has now turned to the task of considering legal approaches and possibilities for solutions to the problems and for future shaping of the law in the relevant areas.

With this thematic focus, this conference fulfilled its role as the conclusion of a trilogy of conferences in the context of the DiVE project. The first of these conferences was guided by the concern to define the contours of the research object of this project more precisely and made it possible to identify 'the new contours of Digital Vulnerability in European Private Law' more precisely.[3] On this basis, the second conference turned to the risks and opportunities of Artificial Intelligence as probably the greatest challenge in respect of Digital Vulnerability.[4] By focusing on the interaction of Human Vulnerability with Artificial Intelligence, it also deepened the theoretical foundations of the research in the project. After analysing the factual and legal starting positions and after the conceptual-theoretical clarifications at these two previous conferences, the third part of the trilogy now focuses on a legal-pragmatic perspective with the core question of what can and should be done in European Private Law to remedy Digital Vulnerability.

In the following, these three core concepts, which characterise the subject matter of the conference and this volume, will first be briefly considered: 'Digital Vulnerability', 'European Private Law' and 'remedies'. Based on the discussions at the

[1] 'Remedies to Digital Vulnerability in European Private Law', Conference in Trieste on 10 and 11 April 2025.

[2] European Commission (2015).

[3] 'Digital Vulnerability in European Private Law', Conference in Ferrara on 15 and 16 June 2023. The conference proceedings are published in Crea and De Franceschi (eds) (2024).

[4] 'Human Vulnerability in Interaction with AI', Conference in Rome on 16 and 17 May 2024. The conference proceedings are published in Amodio and Diurni (eds) (2025).

conference, six main tasks will then be addressed which arise with regard to remedies for Digital Vulnerability in European Private Law, even if this cannot fully reflect either the rich results of the conference nor the entire spectrum of challenges in these areas.

2 Core Concepts

2.1 *Digital Vulnerability—New Challenges for Legal Doctrine and Legislation*

Digital Vulnerability has been characterised when defining the starting positions of the DiVE project as a 'necessarily fluid concept'.[5] Such fluidity offers the disadvantage and at the same time the advantage of indeterminacy and openness for interpretations and concretisations that take into account the diversity and change of the objects to be included. With its orientation towards 'vulnerability', this open concept ties in with a term that links several branches of research in an interdisciplinary discourse and has also been in common use in law for some time.[6] It has gained crucial importance in case law and legal doctrine at the European and national levels, particularly with regard to the concept of consumer.[7]

The specification of this concept with regard to 'digital' vulnerability now turns to the new challenges that arise with regard to vulnerability from technological and thus economic and social change. Digital Vulnerability covers a wide range of different situations. It includes many different vulnerabilities that have only arisen as a result of digitalisation (for example, risks of 'computer addiction' of children and young people or, in terms of consumer protection, dependencies on the supply of digital content, for example, with regard to updating digital products).[8] However, the term also covers a variety of situations in which digitalisation affects vulnerabilities that already existed independently of it and reinforces or modifies them (for example, when advertising that specifically addresses minors and is aimed at their age-typical emotions and behaviours appears in digital social media alongside the corresponding print advertising).[9]

Moreover, the field of research described by the term 'Digital Vulnerability' for legal doctrine and the corresponding challenges for legislation and jurisprudence are

---

[5] Crea and De Franceschi (2024, 18).

[6] Crea and De Franceschi (2024, 17).

[7] Alexander (2025, mn 416).

[8] Note the recent corresponding development of consumer protection through the remedies pursuant to Art. 8, 11, 14 of the European Parliament and Council Directive (EU) 2019/770 on certain aspects concerning contracts for the supply of digital content and digital services (DCD).

[9] See Art. 28 of the European Parliament and Council Regulation (EU) 2022/2065 on a Single Market for Digital Services and amending Directive 2000/31/EC (Digital Services Act – DSA).

not limited either to one of the aspects described by traditional paradigms for the protection of vulnerable parties such as minors or discrimination[10] or to a single area of law such as consumer protection. Rather, it is one of the insights that the project has highlighted that Digital Vulnerability may affect almost everyone when taking into account the general risks to which individuals are exposed in the digital context, among other things, because of the common difficulties in understanding digital infrastructure.[11] To this extent, Digital Vulnerability is a general subject of private law, and the question of how to remedy it concerns not only specific areas but also the general provisions of private law. The spectrum in this regard ranges from general contract law with regard to Digital Vulnerability in the conclusion of contracts with AI[12] to, for example, the consideration of the liability of producers and operators for digital products in the context of tort law[13] or up to the general provisions on the protection of personal data, transparency of platforms, etc.

However, taking such general protection needs into account does not obviate the need to analyse situations of particular vulnerability and groups of persons requiring specific protection to provide for appropriate specific protection provisions and instruments (for example, with regard to the particularly high risk potential of certain types of artificial intelligence, the dominant market position of 'gatekeepers' or with regard to minors, dependent employees, patients, etc.). In other words, the generality of the need for protection must not obscure the requirements for special protection. An important task for future research on Digital Vulnerability will therefore be to determine the relationship between general protection instruments and those specific to particular sectors or groups of people.[14]

Against this background, 'Digital Vulnerability' should be seen as a cross-cutting issue that encompasses both general provisions of private law and various specific areas of protection and therefore affects almost all disciplines of private law. The studies on this topic include, to list just a few examples, consumer law (including its specialised areas such as the consumer insurance sector), product liability and tort law, restitution, unfair commercial practices, labour law, medical law, online dispute resolution and private international law.[15] For all these and other areas, phenomena that can be described with the term 'Digital Vulnerability' require analysis and the search for solutions by legal doctrine[16] to achieve appropriate remedies through case law or legislation in legal practice, where necessary.

---

[10] Crea and De Franceschi (2024, 17).

[11] See in this volume on this topic Infantino and Crea (2025).

[12] See below, Sect. 3.5.3.

[13] See below, Sect. 3.5.2.

[14] Insightful starting points on this can be found in this volume in Infantino and Crea (2025).

[15] For all these and other issues, see the contributions in the two volumes of the project listed above (fn 3 and 4), as well as in this volume.

[16] See in more detail Pasquale (2024, 21 ff), Pollicino (2024, 25 ff), Schulze (2024, 521, 525 ff).

2.2 *European Private Law—'Law in Progress'*

These challenges posed by digitalisation and the associated Digital Vulnerability are being met in Europe by a transformation of legal structures, characterised by the emergence and growth of common European law, especially supranational law of the European Union,[17] alongside the national law of the individual states. In recent years, this new European Union law has developed particularly in areas where changes brought about by digitalisation required legal responses—facilitated both by the openness of this 'young law in progress', whose structures are still emerging, to new subjects and concepts, and by the low penetration of national law in these new areas to date.[18]

However, the current inclusion of matters of private law in the turn of European law towards 'digital matters' can be built on earlier developments. As early as the 1960s, the first President of the European Commission, Walter Hallstein, stated in a seminal essay[19] that overcoming the obstacles to the free movement of persons, goods, services and capital requires that European Community legislation not be limited to matters of public law but also include private law; and it had introduced corresponding legislation for individual matters of private law.[20] Since the late twentieth century, the term 'European Private Law'—understood in various ways[21]—had developed into a common point of reference for various academic approaches and legal policy projects. This was prompted both by private law doctrine, which began to incorporate the legislation and case law of the European Communities into its studies of applicable private law, and by legal history, which drew on common traditions of European law, and by comparative law, which turned to the 'common principles' of national laws.[22] Not least guided by the desire to promote the coherence of the European Union's expanding legislation in the field of private law, the much-discussed 'Draft Common Frame of Reference'[23] was created.[24] These efforts to further develop the private law of the European Union have brought to the forefront of discussions the meaning of the term 'European Private Law' that refers to EU law. The term will also be used in this sense in the following.

---

[17] Overview of other forms of European law, such as the international law of the European Convention on Human Rights, e.g., in Schulze and Zoll (2021, ch 1 mn 18 ff).

[18] Schulze and Zoll (2021, ch 8 mn 8 ff).

[19] Hallstein (1964, 212).

[20] In particular in competition law and company law, and later also in consumer law; for an overview of this development, see Janssen, Lehmann, Schulze (2023, 11 ff), Twigg-Flesner (2010).

[21] See for an overview in Schulze and Zoll (2021, ch 1 mn 14 ff).

[22] For an overview of these developments, see Janssen, Lehmann, Schulze (2023, 13 ff), for the key concepts of 'common principles' and 'common core' (the latter being the basis for research by the 'Trento Common Core Project' since 1993), see Schulze and Zoll (2021, ch 1 mn 21).

[23] Von Bar, Clive, Schulte-Nölke (2019, 33).

[24] Largely based on previous drafts such as the 'Principles of European Contract Law' of the 'Lando Commission' (Lando and Beale (2000)), the 'Principles of Existing EU Contract Law' of the 'Acquis Group' (Research Group on the Existing EC Private Law (2007), Research Group on the Existing EC Private Law (2009)) and preparatory work by the 'Study Group on a European Civil Code'.

The European Commission's draft for a 'Common European Sales Law'[25] from 2011 marked the culmination and conclusion of this phase of efforts to achieve 'a more coherent European contract law'.[26] However, the withdrawal of this draft due to its rejection by a number of Member States was accompanied in the same European Commission document by the announcement of a 'new start'.[27] This 'new start'—which marked the beginning of the current phase of development of European Private Law—was, in a sense, a start into the digital age, as the European Commission presented a far-reaching programme for the further development of the internal market and related legislation in 2015 with its 'Digital Single Market Strategy'.[28] On this basis, European Private Law has expanded more than ever before in such a short period of time over the last five years through a series of EU legal acts and now covers numerous areas affected by digitalisation. These include, to highlight just a few examples, the distribution of digital content and services to consumers, including recourse in the transaction chain,[29] the sale of goods to consumers,[30] the cross-border portability of online content services,[31] geo-blocking,[32] the legal relationships of business users of internet platforms,[33] core areas of digital services law in the internal market[34] and competition law in digital markets,[35] and the broader area of data access and sharing.[36]

However, it is not only the scope of European legislation in the field of private law that has grown considerably in recent times, but also its intensity. While the regulations concerning consumer contracts for digital content and services and for the purchase of goods have been issued in the form of directives, the European Union has regulated most other matters relating to the Digital Single Market and the digital economy by means of regulations. Private law in these areas is therefore

[25] European Commission (2011).

[26] The title of the 2003 Action Plan by the European Commission was 'A more coherent European contract law': European Commission (2003).

[27] European Commission (2014).

[28] European Commission (2019).

[29] See above note 8.

[30] European Parliament and Council Directive (EU) 2019/771 on certain aspects concerning contracts for the sale of goods (SGD).

[31] European Parliament and Council Regulation (EU) 2017/1128 on cross-border portability of online content services in the internal market.

[32] European Parliament and Council Regulation (EU) 2018/302 on addressing unjustified geo-blocking and other forms of discrimination based on customers' nationality, place of residence or place of establishment within the internal market.

[33] European Parliament and Council Regulation (EU) 2019/1150 on promoting fairness and transparency for business users of online intermediation services.

[34] See above note 9.

[35] European Parliament and Council Regulation (EU) 2022/1925 on contestable and fair markets in the digital sector and amending Directives (EU) 2019/1937 and (EU) 2020/1828 (Digital Markets Act – DMA).

[36] European Parliament and Council Regulation (EU) 2023/2854 on harmonised rules on fair access to and use of data and amending Regulation (EU) 2017/2394 and Directive (EU) 2020/1828 (Data Act).

predominantly not merely harmonised national law but directly applicable uniform law of the European Union. In terms of scope and intensity, European Private Law has thus become of paramount importance for the legal responses to digitalisation and its consequences, including Digital Vulnerability. Accordingly, research into Digital Vulnerability should focus on the current status and future development of this European Private Law.

2.3 *Remedies—Addressing Legal Responses to the New Challenges*

Against this background, the issue of necessary and appropriate remedies in view of this vulnerability arises not only in relation to national law but also, and in particular, in relation to the development of law at the European level. At this level, the development and promotion of the internal market have been and continue to be of central importance for legislation, including in the field of private law. However, the focus on the functioning of the internal market has always been accompanied by legislative measures within the context of protection policies. This link between the development of the internal market and the consideration of various types of protection needs—from social policy (including with regard to employment relationships) to non-discrimination legislation to the protection of small and medium-sized enterprises and consumer protection—is in fact a characteristic feature of the understanding and legislative practice of European Private Law, in contrast to the concepts of private law that prevailed in some European countries at the end of the nineteenth century.[37]

In view of the current turn towards new issues and tasks in the context of digitalisation, it is consistent with this understanding of European Private Law to combine the focus on the Digital Single Market with consideration of the need for protection against the consequences of digitalisation. European Private Law can therefore provide the legal framework both for the development of the Digital Single Market and the promotion of the digital economy within its context and for protection against vulnerabilities created or exacerbated by digitalisation. In other words, European legislation in this field faces the dual task of creating favourable legal conditions for the development of the digital economy in terms of competitiveness and securing prosperity, while at the same time ensuring protection against the risks and vulnerabilities resulting from digitalisation. Taking sufficient account of the protective functions of European Private Law is therefore not only in line with the fundamental values of the Union, as laid down, inter alia, in the Charter of Fundamental Rights of the EU, but without it, stable development of the Digital Single Market and the digital economy is unlikely to be achieved, at least in the longer term.

This protective function of private law can take many forms at the European (as well as national) level. It can be expressed in preventive legislative measures

[37] Schulze (2024, 523).

(such as requirements for the design of digital products or the prohibition of certain uses of digital technologies) as well as in regulations that provide for responses to impairments that have occurred (such as rights of rescission and restitution or compensation for damages). In legal doctrine and legislation, a wide range of the instruments that can serve to fulfil such protective functions are described by the term 'remedies'. Originally more customary in common law and international sales law,[38] it is also used in several of the new legal acts relating to 'digital matters', although it is not generally defined in this legislation. It has gained considerable importance in recent European legislation, for example, in consumer protection, as in Art. 13 and 14 of the Digital Content Directive[39] and Art. 13 of the Sale of Goods Directive.[40]

In these provisions, the term 'remedies' refers to rights to which consumers are entitled in the specific circumstances described (e.g., in respect of a lack of conformity, the remedies of having the digital content or goods brought into conformity, receiving a price reduction or terminating the contract). However, in EU legislation, 'remedying' does not only refer to such possibilities for vulnerable parties to assert their rights individually. Rather, it can also cover the actions of institutions in favour of (collective) interests. Furthermore, the regulatory purposes of the provisions on 'remedies' cannot be clearly distinguished from the preventive protection functions in European Private Law. Rather, the reactive function of such provisions is regularly associated with a preventive effect, because the options for action provided for in them in the event of violations of protective provisions can also have a preventive effect on compliance with these provisions.[41]

Building on this broad understanding of the functions of remedies in EU legal acts—and, in part, going beyond it in view of the challenges posed by Digital Vulnerability—the research presented in this volume also does not use the term in an exclusively reactive sense. Rather, it takes into account that existing and possible future remedies for digital violations can and should also have a preventive effect. In this respect, it regards remedies both as instruments for 'healing' digital violations and as preventive measures designed to prevent Digital Vulnerabilities from being exploited and violations from occurring through the threat of legal consequences. In this respect, considerations in this volume on how to remedy Digital Vulnerability may even include the proposal for a fundamental shift toward protective 'ex ante designs'.[42]

The range of remedies that can be considered from this perspective with regard to Digital Vulnerability corresponds to the diversity of manifestations of Digital Vulnerability as discussed above.[43] On the one hand, this must include the potential of conventional protection instruments that have already been developed in consumer

---

[38] See, for example, the headings of Chapter 2: Sect. 3 and Chapter 3: Sect. 3 of the United Nations Convention on Contracts for the International Sale of Goods (CISG).

[39] See above note 8.

[40] See above note 30.

[41] See below Sect. 3.1.2.

[42] See in this volume Mišćenić and Namysłowska (2025); see also Sect. 3.1.2. below.

[43] See Sect. 2.1. above.

law and other areas before the new challenges posed by digitalisation, with a view to the new protection tasks resulting from digitalisation.[44] In this respect, the task is, for example, to further develop the instruments of information requirements and the right of withdrawal with regard to compensating for information asymmetries when using Artificial Intelligence, or to expand the arsenal of mandatory regulations on lack of conformity with regard to the distribution of digital products. On the other hand, it is necessary to explore which new approaches to protection can be developed precisely because of the technological change brought about by digitalisation. Accordingly, it is also important to address the technical and legal contours of specific protection instruments based on the use of digital technologies and, with regard to legislative measures, model contract clauses, dispositive norms, and mandatory provisions, for example, on the design of digital content and services and, in particular, on digital 'filters' to prevent certain types of impairments[45] and on integrated remedial functions in automated systems with regard to impairments to be avoided. In both respects, adapting conventional types of remedies and designing new types of remedies, digitisation is changing the instruments of private law.

3 Task Areas

3.1 Consumer Contracts and Consumer Concept

3.1.1 Recent Changes in Legislation

Based on the wide range of reflections and proposals put forward at the conference that gave rise to this volume on how to remedy Digital Vulnerability, five core areas can be identified—some of which are interlinked or overlap—in which these research findings can inspire not only legal doctrine and further research but also legal practice in case law and legislation (without such an outline claiming to be exhaustive).[46] Looking at the results of the present research therefore involves looking ahead to the tasks that will result from them, and the core areas to which these results can be assigned are also task areas for future research and legal practice.

Among these areas, the remedies available in consumer contracts relating to digital products or the use of the internet have drawn particular attention in view of their huge everyday significance and their particular role in the discussion of the concept of vulnerability in legal doctrine. In line with the particular importance of such consumer contracts, EU legislation began several years ago to adapt remedies to the

[44] As already outlined in the discussions at the first conference of the DiVE project; see Schulze (2024, 529 ff, 535 ff).

[45] Schulze (2024, 530).

[46] Additionally noteworthy are, for example, both the studies that concern related matters of enforcement (see below Sect. 4) and those that supplement issues in European Private Law with regard to public law (see in particular in this volume Rodin (2025) and Lisanti (2025)).

changes brought about by digitalisation, in particular through the 2019 Directive on the modernisation of consumer law[47] and the so-called 'twin directives', the Digital Content Directive[48] and the Sale of Goods Directive.[49] The implementation of the 'twin directives' has led to a far-reaching harmonisation of consumer contract law for the distribution of digital products and for the sale of goods in the EU member states.[50] In principle, all types of contracts with consumers for the provision of digital products and the sale of goods (with special provisions for goods with digital elements) are covered. Within this broad scope, the two directives have adapted the requirements for contractual conformity to technological change (for example, through criteria such as functionality and compatibility and, in particular, through update obligations)[51] and further developed the design of remedies, including the consequences of contract termination, by incorporating new legal instruments such as recovering digital content, preventing its use, and making digital content inaccessible into the Digital Content Directive.[52]

The EU has taken another important step toward adapting remedies to the changes brought about by digitalisation with the recent introduction of the 'withdrawal button', or, as it is now called, the 'withdrawal function'. This innovation, provided for in the amended version of the Consumer Rights Directive,[53] is intended to improve the exercise of one of the most important consumer rights in respect of off-premises contracts, including online contracts, in order to strengthen consumer protection. However, the study, which analyses these new provisions in detail,[54] shows that this strengthening of consumer protection has gaps, in particular due to the exclusion of some contractual constellations from the scope of application and the fact that risks with regard to the protection of personal data are not sufficiently taken into account (especially with regard to customer accounts for the use of the withdrawal function). The concrete proposals presented as a result of the critical analysis on the design of this important consumer protection instrument should prove to be practicable guidance for legal practice, such as focusing on the use of order confirmation emails with regard to access to the withdrawal function.[55]

---

[47] European Union Directive (EU) 2019/2161 of the European Parliament and of the Council of 27 November 2019 on the better enforcement and modernisation of Union consumer protection rules.

[48] See above note 8.

[49] See above note 30.

[50] Schulze and de Franceschi (2023).

[51] In connection with this, they have strengthened the role of objective requirements vis-à-vis contractual agreements (which in practice are often determined unilaterally by the trader); see in more detail Schulze and Staudenmayer (2025), as well as Art. 8 DCD mn 12 ff.

[52] For an overview of restitutionary remedies in European private law and an in-depth look at the relationship between digital vulnerability and restitutionary remedies, see in this volume Lutman (2025), in particular Sects. 2 and 5.

[53] European Parliament and Council Directive (EU) 2023/2673 amending Directive 2011/83/EU as regards financial services contracts concluded at a distance and repealing Directive 2002/65/EC.

[54] See in this volume Sein (2025).

[55] See in this volume Sein (2025), Sect. 4); see also the further proposals there.

3.1.2 Tasks for Further Research and Legislation

Changes to the General Framework

Even though European legislation has taken remarkable steps with these latest measures to adapt consumer contract remedies to the changes resulting from digitalisation, this does not in any way answer all questions regarding the remedies for consumer vulnerability in this area. This is apparent not only in relation to the potential need for improvement of the withdrawal function mentioned above. Rather, it remains to be considered whether more profound changes in the general framework of consumer protection are also necessary in order to adequately remedy Digital Vulnerabilities. In addition, the need to adapt remedies in consumer contract law to the changes brought about by digitalisation calls for consideration of a number of further issues. Only three of them that concern priority tasks for further research and legislation can be highlighted in the following: the harmonisation deficits in the toolbox of consumer contract law, particularly with regard to damages; the relationship between the concept of the 'average consumer' and the specific vulnerabilities of individual consumer groups; and finally, the key question of the suitability of the consumer concept with regard to Digital Vulnerability (and thus the contours of the personal scope of application of consumer protection remedies).

As far as the general framework of consumer protection is concerned, a number of studies assume that a fundamental shift is necessary in this regard. However, different objectives at different levels are being considered for such a shift. Two perspectives in particular can be distinguished in this regard. On the one hand, a significantly stronger foundation for consumer protection instruments in fundamental rights—beyond Art. 38 of the EU Charter of Fundamental Rights—is considered crucial[56] (including far-reaching direct applicability of those fundamental rights).[57] This view is in line with a tendency in the general debate on the relationship between fundamental rights and private law to assign a greater role to fundamental rights. The actual impact that such a paradigm shift in the recourse to fundamental rights may actually have on the legal structure of remedies in consumer protection beyond the theoretical foundation may differ between the various protection needs and areas and should best be considered concretely for the individual fields of investigation.

On the other hand, a shift toward 'structural protection' is proposed in view of the structural vulnerabilities caused by 'algorithmically shaped markets'.[58] The ex-ante instruments, which have been underdeveloped in consumer contract law from this perspective, are to become the core components of consumer protection for matters affected by digitalisation. This includes, in particular, information obligations and

[56] For more, see in this volume the programmatic explanations in Menyhárd (2025), in particular Sect. 4.2.

[57] See on this issue below Sect. 3.2.1.

[58] See in this volume Mišćenić and Namysłowska (2025).

transparency requirements on the one hand, and mandatory law containing 'per se prohibitions' on the other hand.[59]

However, the desired stronger focus on ex ante protection instruments also points to the task of conducting an in-depth analysis of the legal structures and their legal and economic impact in the interaction between ex ante and ex post protection mechanisms. Expanding the range of ex ante protection instruments is unlikely to be effective if it is not sufficiently coordinated with ex post intervention regulations.[60] With regard to the need for coordination or even integration of both protection perspectives, the studies on AI-driven Legal Tech tools[61] offer a convincing case study. Such conceptual considerations are likely to provide a forward-looking impetus that could accompany a probably rather gradual development of European legislation over a longer period of time.

In addition to addressing these issues of a shift towards a stronger focus on fundamental rights towards 'structural protection' through a stronger role for ex ante regimes, the need to adapt remedies in consumer contract law to the changes brought about by digitalisation calls for consideration of a number of further issues. Only three of them that concern priority tasks for further research and legislation can be highlighted here: the suitability of the consumer concept with regard to Digital Vulnerability (and thus the contours of the personal scope of application of consumer protection remedies); the relationship between the concept of the 'average consumer' and the specific vulnerabilities of individual consumer groups; and the harmonisation deficits in the toolbox of consumer contract law, particularly with regard to damages.

Harmonisation Deficits

Looking in detail at the arsenal of remedies available under EU private law, the need for considerable adaptation and supplementation is apparent. Against the backdrop of the Digital Vulnerabilities analysed at the project conferences, it goes well beyond the initial steps in recent legislation mentioned above. As several studies show in detail,[62] this already affects information obligations and transparency requirements in the pre-contractual stage and at the time of conclusion of the contract (including sanctions for violating them). However, adapting them to the digital environment is by no means necessarily equivalent to a mere extension. In view of the much-discussed problems of 'information overkill', more transparency can often be achieved with less information,[63] so that reducing information to content that is essential for consumers

[59] See in this volume Mišćenić and Namysłowska (2025, Sect. 3.3).

[60] On the critical analysis of the unintended effects of the AI Act on tort law, see in this volume Smorto (2025), as well as below Sect. 3.5.3.

[61] See in this volume Chieco (2025).

[62] See in this volume in particular Mišćenić and Namysłowska (2025), Legerén-Molina (2025), Menyhárd (2025).

[63] Mišćenić (2024, 125).

and can be realistically used in the circumstances remains a priority, also with regard to digital matters.

The further development of information requirements in the context of digitalisation also affects information that must be provided after the conclusion of the contract to protect the consumer during the performance of the contract. A significant example of this is information about updates that are necessary to ensure that a digital product can continue to be used. According to Art. 8(2) DCD, the trader must provide the consumer with such information regarding updates that are necessary to maintain the contractual conformity of digital content and digital services; Art. 7(3) SGD stipulates the same for goods with digital elements. However, the European legislator has so far only prescribed this 'two-track obligation structure', in which update obligations and information obligations are linked, for contracts with consumers. If future European legislation were to take into account corresponding protection needs beyond consumer law,[64] the information obligations relating to update obligations would also take on a more general significance.

Without even coming close to addressing all the other requirements for equipping the consumer protection toolbox with regard to Digital Vulnerabilities, at least one particularly notable example should be highlighted: The catalogue of remedies in the recently adopted EU directives does not contain any provisions on consumers' claims for damages in the event of non-performance or lack of conformity. This shortcoming in the harmonisation of consumer protection already exists in the Consumer Sales Directive. It has continued unabated in the adaptation of legislation to digitalisation, with even the rudimentary provision that Art. 14 of the Commission's proposal for the DCD had provided for in respect of damage to the consumer's digital environment being deleted during the legislative process.[65] However, in the case of digital products or goods with digital elements, just as with other goods (or even more so), the level of consumer protection can be negatively affected if the law on damages in a Member State is relatively restrictive (for example, if damages for defects and consequential damages are linked to fault and the burden of proof for fault is placed on the consumer). In order to respond to a lack of conformity on the part of the trader, the claim for damages is often much more useful to the consumer than his right to terminate the contract (especially if no equivalent digital products are available as an alternative). Preventively, too, damages are regularly the sharper sword to induce the other party to perform in accordance with the contract. Therefore, the more vulnerable the consumer is due to the trader's strong market position, the more important it would be for him to ensure a high level of consumer protection, especially with regard to damages. The development of remedies to protect consumers in the digital environment is therefore far from complete at the European level in this and other respects.

---

[64] See below Sect. 3.1.2.

[65] On this and the following, see Schulze (2019, 720 ff)

The 'Average Consumer' and the Specific Vulnerabilities

A key question for the design of protective instruments with regard to Digital Vulnerability in consumer law is also what standards they should be based on: should they focus on or even be limited to the model of the 'average consumer', or should the design of remedies also take into account the special vulnerabilities of individual consumer groups due to personal or external circumstances, and if so, to what extent and in what way? For consumer protection in the digital context, this thematic focus follows on from the discussions that have long been conducted independently of the consequences of digitisation, especially on the question of the extent to which the 'average consumer' can form the benchmark in consumer protection and whether and to what extent special protection needs of 'vulnerable consumers' should be taken into account.[66] As a result of digitalisation, this question has become even more important because existing vulnerabilities have intensified and new vulnerabilities have emerged based on risks inherent in the new technologies but also due to, for example, different levels of experience and skills of different groups of consumers in using these technologies. This has been demonstrated in detail by studies on the particular vulnerabilities of children,[67] older people, or persons who are particularly dependent for health reasons (including patients undergoing medical treatment),[68] but also, for example, employees in digitally permeated workplaces.[69] For these and other items, it is likely to be a priority, beyond the present analyses of the respective specific vulnerabilities, to determine in further investigations not only in more detail which specific form of remedy may be appropriate in each case, but also how these particular vulnerabilities are to be taken into account with regard to the application of remedies in judicial practice.

The Concept of the Consumer in the Face of Digital Vulnerability

Far beyond this aspect of the concept of consumer, however, the question ultimately arises as to whether the concept of the consumer as such still provides a suitable basis for remedying Digital Vulnerability in view of the profound technological and economic changes brought about by digitalisation. Against the background of the present studies on various fields of consumer protection, further discussion is therefore needed to consider the extent to which the traditional concept of the consumer in EU law adequately guarantees the protection needs of the parties covered by it when they use digital products or the internet and conclude corresponding contracts. Linked to this is the question of the extent to which the personal scope of consumer protection instruments should be extended to similar Digital Vulnerabilities and protection needs of parties other than those covered by this traditional concept of the consumer.

---

[66] See, for example, Lurger (2018, mn 13.)

[67] Pera and Rigazio (2024), Amram (2024).

[68] Amram (2024), Arcuri (2025).

[69] Wildhaber and Ebert (2024).

This question arises, for example, with regard to the update obligations, which in the 'twin directives' are limited to contracts with consumers in the traditional sense. Not all member states have followed this pattern.[70] Rather, there are good reasons to believe that corresponding protection needs may also exist in B2B contracts, so that the requirement for updating and the scope of application of the corresponding remedies should also be extended to contracts with users of digital products other than traditional consumers.[71] This extension of the personal scope of the updating obligations beyond the traditional concept of consumers should at least be appropriate where there is asymmetry between providers of digital products with a strong market position and small- or medium-sized enterprises as users of these products.[72] However, even such an extension to specific protection groups may fall short. Rather, it should be considered that updating is generally one of the typical obligations in contracts for digital products (regardless of the protection status of the respective customer) and should therefore be designed as a general provision for such contracts.

Such examples of protection needs that go beyond conventional consumer protection[73] give rise to general questions about the relationship between the concept of consumer and the protection of users of digital products and the internet. This question also arises from other perspectives. In particular, it seems doubtful whether the juxtaposition of consumer and trader is still appropriate for some digital matters, for example, in cooperative activities in which participants of digital content can be both 'consumers' and 'traders' in the traditional sense.[74] Future technological and economic change is likely to produce further such constellations that are difficult to grasp using conventional categories and require not only new approaches to describing the parties involved but also a corresponding further development of remedial approaches.

With regard to the consequences that such a further development of protection objectives and protection tools beyond the current scope of consumer protection may have for the role of consumer law in the legal system, different approaches are under consideration.[75] In particular, on the one hand, consideration is to be given to extending the concept of consumer protection in European law in such a way that certain user groups in need of protection that were not previously covered by it, such as small businesses, are included[76] (be it that the concept of 'consumer' is

[70] See, for example, for Austria, Zöchling-Jud (2023).

[71] See, for example, Beale (2016), Spindler and Sein (2019, 416), Schulze (2019, 702).

[72] This need for protection is recognised to a certain extent in recital 16 DCD by the reference that the Member States are free to extend the updating obligations to contracts with small and medium-sized enterprises; however, no legislative consequences have yet been drawn at the European level.

[73] See in this volume, for example, the references to the need for protection of both consumers in the traditional sense and other clients of lawyers, as well as lawyers themselves, with regard to AI-driven legal tech in Chieco (2025).

[74] See in this volume Aksoy (2025).

[75] See the observations based on the two previous DiVE conferences in Schulze (2024, 533 ff), Schulze (2025a).

[76] See critically on the narrow concept of consumer and on the question of its extension with regard to Digital Vulnerability, for example, Tereszkiewicz, Południak-Gierz, Walczak (2024).

extended accordingly, or be it that other user groups under their own designation—such as 'small businesses'—receive the same protection in respect of contracts for digital products or use of the Internet as consumers in the traditional sense). On the other hand, it is also worth considering the extent to which protection based on the concept of the consumer could take a back seat to general protection provisions under private law[77] in view of Digital Vulnerability. Ultimately, based on the model of a 'post-consumer society',[78] the question may arise as to whether the concept of the consumer is still appropriate at all for legal relationships in the 'digital world'.

However, it has been pointed out with good reason that even in the context of digitalisation, consumers may have specific protection needs and that therefore the further development of specific consumer protection provisions in addition to provisions with a broader personal scope for the protection of Internet users should be pursued.[79] Nevertheless, following this approach, some of the latest developments in European consumer law could not only be specific to this area but also set a pattern for general private law provisions on digital matters—for example, the update obligations just mentioned, which are generally relevant for contracts on digital products, or the provisions of the Digital Content Directive, which, as a result of termination, prohibit the further use of data and include the retrieval of content.[80]

3.2 Privacy, Especially Personal Data

3.2.1 Protection of Personal Data as a Fundamental Right

Another key area in which improving remedies for Digital Vulnerability has proven appropriate is privacy protection. The broad field of privacy protection—or, in the continental European conceptual tradition, the protection of personal rights—includes, among other things, many facets of self-determination, for example, the protection of private living space, confidential records and 'informational self-determination'.[81] In this context, the protection of personal data has played a central role in the studies of the DiVE project. These studies have revealed a wide range of situations in which Digital Vulnerability concerns personal data.[82]

---

[77] See in this volume Infantino and Crea (2025).

[78] Grochowski (2024).

[79] See, for example, Specht-Riemenschneider, El-Rifaai, Mehnert, Bodemann (2024), Schulze (2025b, 16).

[80] Twigg-Flesner (2025a, mn 36–78 and 2025b, mn 9–30).

[81] See, in regard to this term, already Bundesverfassungsgericht (Federal Constitutional Court) (1983) and later its further development with regard to digitalisation, Bundesverfassungsgericht (Federal Constitutional Court) (2008).

[82] See, among other things, the summaries based on the previous DiVE conferences: Schulze (2024) and Schulze (2025a).

This finding in the investigations corresponds to the fact that European law attaches great importance to the protection of personal data. The Charter of Fundamental Rights of the EU has given this protection a prominent place in its catalogue of Fundamental Rights (Art. 8 EU Charter of Fundamental Rights). On this basis, the General Data Protection Regulation (GDPR) constitutes a legal act of central importance in the EU's Acquis Communautaire for the protection of privacy with regard to its Digital Vulnerability.

Remedies Under the General Data Protection Regulation

Within the framework of the GDPR, which largely contains provisions of a public law nature, the right to compensation (Art. 82 GDPR) is one of the core provisions with a private law effect. As explained in more detail in this volume,[83] this right is available to any person who has suffered damage as a result of an infringement of the Regulation and is directed against any controller or processor involved in the processing of the data. The way in which the Court of Justice of the European Union has further developed this claim for damages, inter alia with regard to the concept of harm and the nature and extent of compensation, and the extent to which this reflects the specific contours of European law, is particularly clear in Japanese law due to the inclusion of a comparison with Japanese law in the relevant study (inter alia with regard to the different role of the apology in the context of remedies for a privacy violation in the two jurisdictions).[84]

The claim under Art. 82 GDPR is therefore likely to be one of the most important remedies in the European Private Law toolbox with regard to Digital Vulnerabilities. However, studies on the application of the GDPR nevertheless raise the question of whether the protective instruments in this legal act are sufficient from the perspective of the protection of fundamental rights, or whether additions or possibly even fundamental corrections to their design are necessary.[85] Based on the analysis of a case of data collection by a car manufacturer,[86] a study[87] describes the shortcomings of the current regulatory instruments from this fundamental rights perspective and attributes these largely to individualistic features such as the focus on the consent of the person concerned and the corresponding design of the remedies in the GDPR. It therefore argues—in a certain parallel to the proposals for a shift in consumer law towards 'structural protection'[88]—for a change of perspective in favour of 'privacy governance approaches that prioritise structural safeguards, default protections, and collective accountability over individual responsibility alone'.[89]

---

[83] See in this volume Milillo (2025).

[84] See in this volume Milillo (2025).

[85] See also the issues addressed below in Sect. 3.3. with regard to protection against discrimination.

[86] On the Australian Toyota case, see in this volume Pera and Rigazio (2025), Sect. 3.

[87] See in this volume Pera and Rigazio (2025).

[88] See above Sect. 3.1.2; see in this volume Mišćenić and Namysłowska (2025).

[89] See in this volume Pera and Rigazio (2025, Sect. 6).

Indeed, in particular, the strong focus in European data protection law on the consent of the person concerned may appear questionable in view of the numerous situations in which, for example, there is a lack of transparency regarding the consequences of consent or in which structural circumstances such as the position of the parties involved in the market do not in fact allow any alternative courses of action without disproportionate expense or other serious disadvantages for the person concerned. One of the most appealing, but also most challenging, tasks for future research will therefore probably be to concretise this focus on supplementary objective correctives for the 'consensus model' and on collective and structural protection mechanisms.

3.2.2 Compliance with Data Protection Under the Digital Market Act

The need to critically examine the weaknesses of the consensus model in protecting personal data is confirmed by research that has approached this issue from a completely different angle.[90] Based on the objectives and provisions of the Digital Market Act (DMA), the question also arises as to whether 'freely given consent' can be assumed when a dominant platform requires the consent of the person concerned to combine personal data from different services. Although Art. 5(2) DMA primarily aims to ensure competition and not necessarily to protect privacy by binding the combination of personal data to consent under the GDPR, this regulatory approach therefore increases the user's control over data.[91] However, with regard to this concern, it proves to be the 'Achilles heel in the personal data-related obligations'[92] under the DMA that the applicability of its Art. 5(2) is linked to the concept of consent under the GDPR. This problem is particularly evident in cases where, due to the platform's dominant market position, there are no equivalent alternatives for users (as recently seen in a European Commission's decision regarding Meta),[93] for example, if a platform with a dominant market position offers users no other option than 'consent or pay'. For such situations, it seems doubtful whether the actual conditions for a free decision by the user regarding control over their personal data really exist and, in this respect, whether the consent is based on a free decision, as is considered necessary in the conventional understanding. As a result of the analysis of the problematic consequences of the consensus approach in the context of the DMA, one possible approach to remedy at least some of these problems could be to understand and apply the provisions of this act in conjunction with other recent EU acts, in particular the Digital Services Act with its focus on a safe, predictable, and trusted online environment (Art. 1 DSA).[94] From this perspective, for example, the

[90] See in this volume Santoni (2025).

[91] See in this volume Santoni (2025) and de Franceschi (2025) Art 5 DMA mn 20.

[92] See in this volume Santoni (2025, Sect. 1).

[93] European Commission (2025); see also the opinion by the European Data Protection Board that the gatekeeper must provide a generally equivalent, free alternative EDPB (2024).

[94] See in this volume Santoni (2025, Sect. 6).

reference to the provisions of the latter act on dark patterns may offer an approach to correcting an overly broad understanding of the consensus approach with regard to practices nudging user consent in the application of the DMA.[95]

Although this research on the DMA differs from the aforementioned study on the GDPR in terms of its starting points and emphasis on remedies, the two may complement each other usefully in terms of further legal developments. This applies not only to the focus on two different subjects, which can provide impetus for each of them with regard to the problem of the consensus approach to personal Data Protection. Rather, each study primarily addresses a different actor in legal development: the proposals for the DMA are primarily aimed at changing the interpretation and application of existing law and can therefore mainly stimulate case law. In contrast, the considerations on the further development of the general structures of data protection law largely concern the development de lege lata and are therefore directed to the legislature. The protection of personal data is therefore addressed as a task for both the courts and—probably in the longer term—the legislature.

3.2.3 Sector-Specific Design of Remedies

The diversity of Digital Vulnerabilities that has emerged in the spectrum of investigations with regard to privacy also leads to an additional requirement in designing remedies: supplementing and modifying the general provisions for the protection of privacy with specific rules and instruments for the protection requirements in individual sectors. Just two examples from very different areas of life—which could stand for many more—are given here to illustrate this.

In the area of healthcare and medicine, Digital Vulnerabilities may arise that are often not recognised or not sufficiently recognised by the patients concerned prior to medical treatment but which later prove to have serious consequences. This may be the case, for example, when cardiac electronic devices are implanted, because such devices are embedded within complex digital ecosystems and expose patients to cybersecurity, data privacy, and medical autonomy risks.[96] With regard to remedies for such vulnerabilities, the study analysing this area recommends, above all, improving the information provided to patients, which should cover not only the direct health risks but also the risks arising from the digital technology used, including with regard to the protection of personal data and future technological changes. The study's findings indicate that, given the opacity of information in this regard and the asymmetry in physician–patient relations, the corresponding information requirements must go beyond the level currently specified by the GDPR. With these findings the study confirms for one of the forms of Digital Vulnerability in the medical field that the protection of self-determination and other aspects of privacy cannot be guaranteed by cross-sectoral regulations alone but requires specific investigation

[95] See in this volume Santoni (2025, Sect. 6).

[96] See in this volume Guiziou (2025).

and, if necessary, additional steps to safeguard specific design of remedies for the respective situations.

From a different perspective and in a completely different area, this is also confirmed for privacy in online land registers. Studies on this subject reveal risks—often overlooked by the public—that can arise from common access to land registers for privacy and, in particular, for the protection of personal data.[97] A comparison of a number of European countries provides several approaches to remedying the vulnerability associated with these risks through legal and technical measures. This not only offers an overview of possible courses of action that have been used (and could perhaps be used in other countries) to protect privacy in this specific sector at the national level in some countries. It also highlights the fact that, at the European law level, similar questions arise with regard to specific regulations for this sector against the background of the EU's concern to strengthen access to land information across the borders of the Member States. The design of protective measures that can remedy the vulnerability of privacy in such cross-border information on land registers thus becomes a task within the framework of European private law.

3.3 Non-Discrimination

As in the case of privacy, non-discrimination is protected by a fundamental right of the EU (Art. 21 EU Charter of Fundamental Rights). In accordance with the high status of this right in the EU legal system, numerous legal acts have been adopted that concern vulnerability to discrimination. They also extend to a considerable extent to matters of private law[98] and in this respect form one of the most relevant fundamental rights-based parts of European Private Law.

However, the impact of this legislation on protection against discrimination still shows considerable weaknesses, particularly with respect to the development of specific remedies for Digital Vulnerability in this field. The investigations have pointed to this from various perspectives, including with regard to the Digital Vulnerability of women in the 'femtech context'[99] and with regard to algorithmic discrimination.[100]

In the first respect, structural inequalities that can lead to the vulnerability of women in digital contexts are taken into consideration. As a result of a critical examination of the protective instruments in EU law, including the GDPR, from a

[97] See in this volume Kaczorowska (2025, Sect. 2).

[98] For example, Council of the European Union Directive 2000/43/EC of 29 June 2000 implementing the principle of equal treatment between persons irrespective of racial or ethnic origin; Council of the European Union Directive 2004/113/EC of 13 December 2004 implementing the principle of equal treatment between men and women in the access to and supply of goods and services.

[99] See in this volume Souto (2025).

[100] See in this volume Colombi Ciacchi, Berardi, Onaie, Singer (2025) and Masai, Carta, Arnaldi (2025).

gender-sensitive perspective, the study on this topic[101] has now identified several approaches for discussion with a view to further developing the design of remedies in this regard. In addition to suggestions for greater involvement of women in technological developments and regulatory processes, these include, in particular, proposals to amend Art. 9(1) of the GDPR (by introducing gender, sex and reproductive health as special categories requiring heightened protection) and to focus the activities of supervisory authorities more strongly on this area.[102]

With regard to algorithmic discrimination, the multitude and significance of the circumstances in which such discrimination is encountered indicate that this is one of the outstanding concerns in terms of Digital Vulnerability. The examples from legal practice include areas such as employment, banking and insurance, targeted advertising, pricing and retail.[103] In order to remedy such discrimination, one of the studies on this topic argues primarily for a resolute extension of the direct applicability of European fundamental rights, in particular Art. 21 (1) of the EU Charter of Fundamental Rights, in private law relationships beyond labour law.[104] Apart from the question of whether legal practice will follow this (not uncontroversial)[105] approach to the intended extent, however, it remains to be considered that it could serve both the legal certainty and efficiency of the protection instruments if appropriately designed private law provisions address the typical situations of algorithmic discrimination and define correspondingly tailored rights and legal remedies. In this respect, the design of protection against algorithmic discrimination remains a legislative task.

At least, for preventive action against such discrimination, European legislation has already recently provided an instrument that deserves special attention in the form of Fundamental Rights Impact Assessments (FRIA). Art. 27 of the AI Act provides for these assessments as a mandatory ex-ante procedure in order to be able to determine and evaluate the potential impact of artificial intelligence on fundamental rights. This evaluation is not solely geared towards protection against algorithmic discrimination but extends in general to the effects that the use of AI systems can have on fundamental rights (in accordance with the more detailed provisions in Art. 27). However, this broad context includes the prohibition of discrimination under Art. 21 of the EU Charter of Fundamental Rights and, in this respect, the assessment of possible algorithmic discrimination.

The combination of two studies now offers an in-depth presentation and analysis of the potential of such assessments to prevent algorithmic discrimination in contractual relationships. From a technological assessment perspective, the prerequisites and limits of the contribution that such assessments can make to assessing the social, economic and legal consequences of new technologies become apparent.[106] From a

---

[101] See in this volume Souto (2025).

[102] For these and other proposals, see in this volume the overview in Souto (2025, Sect. 5).

[103] See in detail in this volume Colombi Ciacchi, Berardi, Onaie, Singer (2025, Sect. 4).

[104] See in this volume Colombi Ciacchi, Berardi, Onaie, Singer (2025, Sect. 5).

[105] As it is taken into account in this volume by Colombi Ciacchi, Berardi, Onaie, Singer (2025, Sect. 5).

[106] See in this volume Masai, Carta, Arnaldi (2025).

legal perspective, an analysis of Art. 27 of the AI Act[107] addresses issues relating to the future application of this provision. It includes a comparison with an academic draft specifically focused on the impact of algorithms on discrimination, namely the 'Fundamental Rights and Algorithms Impact Assessment' (FRAIA) developed in the Netherlands.[108] It thus opens up a rich arsenal of suggestions that go beyond the provisions of Art. 27 of the AI Act and could possibly be taken into account in its future application or in legislative amendments.

3.4 *Intermediary Services Under the DSA*

Approaches in the Digital Services Act to remedy Digital Vulnerability with regard to the activities of intermediary services have already been discussed at the two previous conferences[109] and were also addressed at this conference in the above-mentioned contexts.[110] In addition, only the results of two further aspects of research in this field and related tasks should be highlighted here. Firstly, a study[111] explores the issue of liability of intermediary services in relation to consumer protection for situations such as misleading appearances regarding the role of the platform or consumer reviews and failure to comply with information obligations. Its analysis of the approaches adopted by the case law of the European Court of Justice with a view to strengthen consumer rights provides valuable impetus for further developments in case law in this field.

Secondly, the claim for damages provided for in Art. 54 DSA deserves special attention because, as in other areas,[112] the right to claim damages can be a particularly effective remedy, not only with an ex-post effect but also with a preventive effect in view of Digital Vulnerability. However, compared to Art. 82 GDPR, for example, a serious weakness of Art. 54 DSA is that its wording does not specify the substantive content of the right to compensation but merely refers to EU law and national law. To counteract this weakness, the present study develops an approach that derives from the analysis of the scope and content of technical due diligence obligations how these obligations influence the formulation of the right to compensation.[113] In this way, a nucleus of content for the claim for damages under Art. 54 DSA is outlined, as prescribed by European law. This approach therefore focuses on applying criteria inherent in the DSA regulations when considering damages, so that the protective aims of this legal act are not lost in the diversity of national tort laws. In this way, this study and the continuation of its approach through further research will also be

[107] See in this volume Colombi Ciacchi, Berardi, Onaie, Singer (2025).

[108] See in this volume Colombi Ciacchi, Berardi, Onaie, Singer (2025, Sect. 3).

[109] Schulze (2024; 2025a), Chapter 3.

[110] For example, above Sects. 2.1. and 3.2.2.

[111] See in this volume Legerén-Molina (2025).

[112] See above Sect. 3.1.2.

[113] See in this volume Kalogerakis (2025).

able to provide fruitful inspiration for case law given the need for at least a certain common core in the application of Art. 54 DSA.

3.5 Further AI-Related Task Areas

3.5.1 AI Characters

The particular challenges arising from the manifold and ever-growing uses of Artificial Intelligence with regard to Digital Vulnerability were the subject of the Rome conference, which dealt with the interaction between human vulnerability and Artificial Intelligence and whose findings are presented in a separate volume.[114] The Trieste conference has now expanded and deepened these findings, among other things—in addition to the topics already mentioned above in other contexts—for three items, each of which is at a different stage in terms of the preparation of appropriate remedies.

Firstly, research presented at the conference highlighted the risks that can arise from AI characters.[115] On this basis, the shortcomings of the legal framework of the EU—identified in a comparative analysis with the US, particularly with regard to specific safety standards—and the regulatory options addressed are now under discussion with a view to specifying possible legislative measures.

3.5.2 Liability for AI

Secondly, the issue of AI liability has come into focus both in terms of the recently revised Product Liability Directive[116] and in terms of the consequences of the new AI Act,[117] including its possible impact on operator liability. In the first respect, research on the example of liability for insurance robo-advisors points to uncertainties in the Product Liability Directive[118] (among other things, with regard to the boundaries between an adaptive algorithm and a 'defect' within the meaning of the Directive, and the only indirect consideration of pure economic loss). It remains to be seen to what extent case law will be able to overcome the problems identified by this research and to what extent legislative corrections will be necessary.

---

[114] See Amodio and Diurni (eds.) (2025).

[115] See in this volume Nunez Duffourc, Goel, Kennedy (2025).

[116] European Parliament and Council Directive (EU) 2024/2853 of 23 October 2024 on liability for defective products and repealing Council Directive 85/374/EEC.

[117] European Parliament and Council (2024) Regulation (EU) 2024/1689 of the European Parliament and of the Council of 13 June 2024 laying down harmonised rules on artificial intelligence and amending certain Union legislative acts (Artificial Intelligence Act).

[118] See in this volume Skalski and Tereszkiewicz (2025).

With regard to the AI Act, the assessment[119] of the consequences of this ex-ante instrument for ex-post liability for damages[120] leads to remarkable results in terms of current legal application and future legislation. Both with regard to considerations regarding the future design of AI liability at European level[121] and with regard to the application of European and national tort law provisions, the warning issued in this study will need to be taken into account, that the AI Act could have the unintended consequence of compliance with existing regulatory regimes preempting tort law provisions and thereby creating excessive protection for artificial intelligence with regard to liability matters.[122] These problems may suggest, in particular, that the EU's currently suspended legislative initiatives to create a harmonised framework for operator liability for artificial intelligence should be revisited in an improved form.

3.5.3 AI Contracting

Thirdly, the topic of AI contracting[123] has now been included, and, in this regard, the crucial problem of 'unexpected outcomes' has been addressed. This issue of 'unexpected outcomes' can arise when one or both parties use Artificial Intelligence to conclude contracts. It highlights a key aspect of the tension between private autonomy, which is intended to give people the power to shape their private affairs in a legally binding manner, on the one hand, and the autonomy of Artificial Intelligence, which is used to shape the legal relationships, on the other.[124] In this tension, the autonomous decisions made by Artificial Intelligence regarding the conclusion and content of contracts may deviate from the interests and expectations of the operator who wants to use artificial intelligence to exercise his private autonomy. Such 'unexpected outcomes' not only raise new questions about traditional theories of declaration of intent and legal transactions but also pose an urgent challenge for the practice of contracting.

Starting points for developing legal remedies with regard to such 'unexpected outcomes' can primarily be found in several recently presented drafts that propose model rules or principles for automated contracting.[125] The study in this volume[126] now provides an in-depth assessment that contributes, in particular, to clarifying the

---

[119] See in this volume Smorto (2025).

[120] On the task of coordinating ex ante instruments and ex post instruments, see also, for the specific area of AI-driven legal technology, in this volume Chieco (2025), as well as above Sect. 3.1.2.

[121] See in this regard Lohsse, Schulze, Staudenmayer (2023).

[122] See in this volume Smorto (2025, Sect. 7).

[123] For further information on this topic, see Lohsse, Schulze, Staudenmayer (2026).

[124] See Schulze (2025a, Sect. 5.2).

[125] UNCITRAL (2024) and ELI (2022, 2023).

[126] See in this volume Rodríguez de las Heras Ballell (2025).

question of the extent to which contractual remedies or liability rules are appropriate.[127] This not only lays a valuable foundation for leading the discussion of the drafts by legal scholars and practitioners to convincing results. Rather, at this stage of scholarly preparation, it does not seem too daring to assume that the time will also be ripe in the not-too-distant future for legislative decisions if the European Union or Member States wish to create regulations for this matter.

4 Outlook

Looking at the findings presented at the conference as a whole, a wealth of suggestions emerges from a variety of critical analyses. The spectrum of proposals ranges from remedies for Digital Vulnerabilities in specific areas (such as medical care)[128] to general regulations designed to remedy 'everyone's Digital Vulnerability' (or 'Universal Digital Vulnerability') caused by digital infrastructures[129] (for example, when concluding contracts or processing personal data).[130] It includes preventive measures,[131] reactive instruments, and the interaction of both.[132] Besides pointing to new technological approaches for remedies,[133] it presents numerous designs for adapting and further developing conventional remedies, such as information requirements before, during, and after the conclusion of a contract, rights of withdrawal, or claims for damages.

Such findings, of which only a few examples can be given here, can be found in large numbers in the conclusions above for the five areas that can be considered key to future research and legislation on Digital Vulnerability. However, even in the overviews of these key areas, it was not possible to mention all the remarkable research findings given the limited scope of this paper. This applies specifically to issues of enforcement. In this regard, two approaches should be highlighted here that are particularly noteworthy in the context of this final outlook. Firstly, a study has impressively demonstrated the role of agencies tasked with enforcement, including the problems of fragmentation in European legislation and the resulting distribution of tasks among the various agencies.[134] The references in its findings to the need to counteract the consequences of fragmentation in legislation through cooperation between the various agencies may prompt consideration of how greater coherence can

[127] See for the more detailed explanations in this volume Rodríguez de las Heras Ballell (2025).

[128] See in this volume Guiziou (2025).

[129] See in this volume Infantino and Crea (2025); see also above Sect. 2.1.

[130] See above Sect. 2.1.

[131] See, for example, in this volume Colombi Ciacchi, Berardi, Onaie, Singer (2025) and Masai, Carta, Arnaldi (2025), with regard to the assessments pursuant to Art. 27 AI Act.

[132] See above Sect. 3.1.2.

[133] See, for example, the references above under 2.3. to this issue, which requires more in-depth research.

[134] See in this volume de Conca (2025).

be achieved within the legislation itself. Another study addresses the shortcomings of the consensus model,[135] which have become apparent in areas such as the protection of personal data,[136] by proposing an EU-wide collective opt-out redress model. It thus pursues the idea of a structural shift away from the individualistic approach of current data protection law from an enforcement perspective. In this regard, as mentioned above,[137] the relationship between preventive and reactive measures in respect to the desired structural changes to remedies for Digital Vulnerability will also need to be further considered.

The wealth of research results obtained will prove useful in three ways for the development of remedies for Digital Vulnerability: for the interpretation and application of existing law, for the further development of legislation, and for future research. With regard to the interpretation and application of existing law, some studies offer a perspective with significant potential for the development of case law by paying particular attention to the role of fundamental rights, among other things, by advocating for the expansion of their direct application.[138] This applies in particular to the protection of personal data (Art. 8 of the EU Charter of Fundamental Rights) and non-discrimination (Art. 21 of the EU Charter of Fundamental Rights). Besides, the findings in the key task areas outlined above contain numerous suggestions for legal practice.[139] These range from suggestions on how data protection can be better taken into account when using the withdrawal function in consumer law[140] to, for example, the proposals for improvements of interpretation of Art. 54 DSA.[141] As these examples show, some of the research findings could prove useful, particularly for the upcoming application of recently enacted legislation.

As far as the findings de lege ferenda are concerned, the chain of proposed individual legislative measures covers all key areas in which Digital Vulnerability needs to be remedied—from the harmonisation of claims for damages in consumer law[142] to gender-sensitive remedies in data protection[143] and to 'unexpected outcomes' in the use of Artificial Intelligence[144] (to list just a few examples). Beyond this multitude of individual measures, a number of studies focus on profound changes in legislation. Besides the plea for legislation to also be more orientated towards

---

[135] See in this volume Aksoy (2025).

[136] See above Sect. 3.2.

[137] See above Sect. 3.1.

[138] See in this volume Menyhárd (2025), Pera and Rigazio (2025).

[139] See, for example, in this volume the suggestion of Santoni (2025) to interpret the DMA in the light of the DSA; see also above, Sect. 3.2.2.

[140] See the suggestions in this volume of Sein (2025) (which, however, are only partially directed at implementation de lege lata).

[141] Above Sect. 3.4.

[142] Above Sect. 3.1.2.

[143] Above Sect. 3.3.

[144] Above Sect. 3.5.3.

fundamental rights in the studies[145] and besides the proposal for an EU-wide collective redress,[146] two concerns stand out. Firstly, a shift towards preventive structural regulation is suggested in view of 'algorithmically shaped markets' (especially for consumer protection[147] and privacy protection).[148] Secondly, a stronger orientation towards cross-sectoral general provisions is proposed with regard to forms of Digital Vulnerability that can affect anyone.[149] For some of these general provisions, rules that are currently only applicable to specific sectors could serve as a model, in particular provisions from consumer law such as remedies for failure to update digital products or rules on the consequences of termination of contracts for digital products.[150] The further development of legislation in this direction is likely to make an important contribution to adapting not only specialised areas of private law but also provisions in its core areas to the changes brought about by digitalisation, thereby advancing the development of private law in line with the requirements of the digital age.

However, with regard to remedies for Digital Vulnerability involving such far-reaching changes to the legal framework, it is not only necessary to carefully take into account what is set out in detail in a study[151] with regard to lead times and the necessary intermediate steps in digital regulation. Rather, the legal basis would have to be examined just as carefully with regard to the EU's powers to enact such legislation, which cannot be specifically assigned to any of the protection policies usually referred to (such as consumer protection)—quite apart from the fact that the Member States must be willing to regulate core areas of private law at the European level in this respect. It may be encouraging, at least, that recognition of the advantages of common European responses to the cross-border challenges of digital transformation has led to a considerable expansion and intensification of European legislation on digital markets and the digital economy in recent years, including from data protection to product liability for software and provisions on remedies whose scope of application is not limited to specific groups of persons.[152] It therefore seems not excluded (although not certain) that this will continue and lead to further changes that will strengthen the cross-sectoral features of European private law.

As far as future research is concerned, building on the present findings, it will be possible to deepen the assessments regarding the prerequisites for Digital Vulnerability, the design of possible remedies and their social and legal effects, and to extend them to other subjects. In particular, at the stage now reached, the task is likely to be to examine in more detail the structural changes to the legal framework for remedies for Digital Vulnerability that have been mentioned and to refine the corresponding

[145] See in this volume Menyhárd (2025), as well as Pera and Rigazio (2025).

[146] See in this volume de Conca (2025).

[147] See in this volume Mišćenić and Namysłowska (2025).

[148] See in this volume Pera and Rigazio (2025).

[149] See in this volume Infantino and Crea (2025); see above Sect. 2.1.

[150] See above Sect. 3.1.2.

[151] See in this volume Pasquale and Jamali (2025).

[152] See above Sect. 2.2.

proposals so that they provide a concrete basis for the policy decisions that legislators have to make.

Linked to this, however, further tasks for research arise from the rapid increase in the number and scope of European legal acts on digital matters in recent years and the foreseeable ongoing expansion of European Private Law in this field. In particular, this development raises the task of ensuring the coherence of these provisions, which are spread across a large number of legal acts. In view of this continuing 'fragmentary' nature of European legislation, legal doctrine will have to contribute to ensuring the internal consistency and transparency of the regulatory framework as a whole in order to contribute in this way to legal certainty and equality in the application of the law and in the further development of the Acquis Communautaire.

With regard to remedies for Digital Vulnerability, cross-sectional studies can support this effort to achieve more coherence. Such studies can compare the design of specific remedies in different sectors and individual legal acts, thereby highlighting possible inconsistencies and providing suggestions for a harmonised approach. An example of such a cross-sectoral study is the study on restitution as a remedy for Digital Vulnerability.[153] Cross-sectoral comparative studies would also be appropriate for other remedies of significant importance for Digital Vulnerability. These include, for example, the various types of withdrawal from online contracting to Data Protection, or the information requirements under the various legal acts relating to digital contracting (including the issue of possible general criteria for their design).[154] The same applies—to mention just two further examples—to the nature and extent of damages, provided for in the various legal acts on digital matters, or to the remedies provided for in this newer legislation in respect of non-compliance with the provisions on fair and transparent general terms and conditions.

Such cross-sectoral studies can go beyond merely taking stock of the status quo of the Acquis Communautaire if they focus on harmonising and further developing the design of remedies across sectors where appropriate. For effective protection against Digital Vulnerability, it will be crucial in this further development to take into account the conclusions of the available research on overarching regulatory approaches, in particular with regard to the focus on structural protective measures and increased inclusion of remedies that are generally applicable, rather than only for specific groups of people. In this respect, adapting and expanding the remedies available in the Acquis Communautaire with regard to Digital Vulnerability to the ongoing changes resulting from digitalisation involves taking into account the profound structural changes facing European Private Law in the digital age. Addressing Digital Vulnerability therefore also means rethinking European Private Law.

---

[153] See in this volume Lutman (2025).

[154] See, for example, with regard to German and French consumer law, Micklitz and Specht-Riemenschneider (2025), as well as Aubert de Vincelles (2025).

References

Aksoy HC (2025) Empowering the vulnerable in the European Union: collective redress against digital exploitation. In this volume

Alexander M (2025) § 13 Verbraucher. In: Gsell H, Krüger R, Lorenz S, Reymann T (eds), Beck-online.Grosskommentar zum BGB. C.H. Beck, Munich

Amodio C, Diurni A (2025) Human vulnerability in interaction with AI in European private law. Springer, Cham

Amram D (2024) Standards to face children and patients digital vulnerabilities. In: Crea C, De Franceschi A (eds) The new shapes of digital vulnerability in European private law. Nomos, Baden-Baden, pp 439–468

Arcuri MA (2025) Human vulnerability in interaction with digital health. In: Amodio C, Diurni A (eds) Human vulnerability in interaction with AI in European private law. Springer, Cham

Aubert de Vincelles C (2025) Quelles limites aux instruments de protection du droit de la consommation? In: Mäsch G, Valierque J (eds) Quelles limites aux droits nationaux et européens de la consommation? 9e Journées Franco-allemandes, vol 40. Société de Législation Comparée, Paris, pp 45–64

Beale H (2016) The future of European contract law in the light of the European Commission's proposals for Directives on digital content and online sales. Revista De Internet, Derecho y Política 23:320

Bundesverfassungsgericht (Federal Constitutional Court) (1983) Judgment of 15 December 1983. Available at: https://www.bundesverfassungsgericht.de/SharedDocs/Entscheidungen/EN/1983/12/rs19831215_1bvr020983en.html

Bundesverfassungsgericht (Federal Constitutional Court) (2008) Judgment of 27 February 2008. Available at https://www.bundesverfassungsgericht.de/SharedDocs/Entscheidungen/EN/2008/02/rs20080227_1bvr037007en.html

Chieco G (2025) Digital vulnerability and AI-powered legal services. In this volume

Colombi Ciacchi A, Berardi G, Onaie A, Singer N (2025) Fundamental rights impact assessments under the AI act: a possible remedy to algorithmic discrimination in the private sector. In this volume

Crea C, De Franceschi A (eds) (2024) The new shapes of digital vulnerability in European private law. Nomos, Baden-Baden

Crea C, De Franceschi A (2024) 'Digital vulnerability in European private law'—towards a digital fairness. In: Crea C, De Franceschi A (eds) The new shapes of digital vulnerability in European private law. Nomos, Baden-Baden, pp 17–18

Infantino M, Crea C (2025) Digital vulnerability for all. In this volume.

De Conca S (2025) Strength in… fragmentation? A concise systemic look at the enforcement of the EU digital acquis, with some implications for vulnerability. In this volume

De Franceschi A (2025) Digital markets act. In: Schulze R, Staudenmayer D (eds) EU digital law. 2nd edn. Nomos, Baden-Baden, pp 991–1113

European Commission (2025) Commission finds Apple and Meta in breach of the Digital Markets Act. Press release, 23 April 2025. Available at: https://ec.europa.eu/commission/presscorner/api/files/document/print/en/ip_25_1085/IP_25_1085_EN.pdf

European Commission (2019) The European green deal. COM(2019) 640 final, Brussels, 11 December 2019

European Commission (2015) A digital single market strategy for Europe. COM(2015) 192 final, Brussels, 6 May 2015

European Commission (2014) Commission work program for 2015: A new start. COM(2014) 910 final, Brussels, 16 December 2014

European Commission (2011) Proposal for a regulation of the European Parliament and of the Council on a Common European Sales Law. COM(2011) 635 final, 2011/0284 (COD). Brussels, 11 October 2011

European Commission (2003) A more coherent European contract law—an action plan. COM(2003) 68 final, Brussels, 12 February 2003
European Data Protection Board (EDPB), Opinion no 4/2024 on the notion of main establishment of a controller in the Union under Art. 4.16(a) GDPR. Available at: https://www.edpb.europa.eu/our-work-tools/our-documents/opinion-board-art-64/opinion-042024-notion-main-establishment_en
European Law Institute (ELI) (2023) Interim Report, EU Consumer Law and Automated Decision-Making (ADM): Is EU Consumer Law Ready for ADM. Available at https://www.europeanlawinstitute.eu/fileadmin/user_upload/p_eli/Publications/ELI_Interim_Report_on_EU_Consumer_Law_and_Automated_Decision-Making.pdf
European Law Institute (ELI) (2022) Guiding Principles on Automated Decision-Making in the EU. Available at https://www.europeanlawinstitute.eu/fileadmin/user_upload/p_eli/Publications/ELI_Innovation_Paper_on_Guiding_Principles_for_ADM_in_the_EU.pdf
Grochowski M (2024) Digital vulnerability in a post-consumer society. Subverting paradigms?. In: Crea C, De Franceschi A (eds) The new shapes of digital vulnerability in European private law. Nomos, Baden-Baden, pp 201–226
Guiziou H (2025) Remedying vulnerability affecting patients' consent. The case of patients undergoing cardiac electronic device implantation. In this volume
Hallstein W (1964) Angleichung des Privat- und Prozessrechts in der EWG. RabelsZ 28:211–231
Janssen A, Lehmann M, Schulze R (2023) The future of European private law—an introduction. In: Janssen A, Lehmann M, Schulze R (eds) The future of European private law. Nomos, Baden-Baden, pp 11–40
Kaczorowska M (2025) Privacy and personal data protection in online land registers: a comparative and European perspective. In this volume
Kalogerakis MG (2025) Compensation for breach of technical requirements by the provider—a contribution to the establishment of liability under Article 54 DSA. In this volume
Lando O, Beale H (2000) The principles of European Contract Law. Part I & II. Wolters Kluwer, Alphen aan den Rijn
Legerén-Molina A (2025) Defective consent and platform liability under the digital services act: appearance, information duties and consumer reviews. In this volume
Lisanti M (2025) Algorithmic Governance of Territory and Market Dominion. The Role of Public Oversight. In this volume
Lohsse S, Schulze R, Staudenmayer D (eds) (2026) AI-Contracting. Münster Colloquia on EU Law and the Digital Economy IX. Nomos, Baden-Baden
Lohsse S, Schulze R, Staudenmayer D (eds) (2023) Liability for AI: Münster Colloquia on EU Law and the Digital Economy VII. Nomos, Baden-Baden
Lurger (2018) AEUV Art. 169. In: Streinz R, Michl W (eds) Beck'sche Kurzkommentare, Band 57, EUV/AEUV. C.H. Beck, Munich
Lutman K (2025) Restitution as a remedy to digital vulnerability in European Private Law. In this volume
Masai P, Carta L, Arnaldi S (2025) Governing AI through assessment: a critical analysis of FRIA from a technology assessment perspective. In this volume
Menyhárd A (2025) Digital vulnerability and private law remedies. In this volume
Milillo B (2025) Remedying data vulnerability in a global world: a comparison of the European Union and Japan's approach to compensation for data breaches. In this volume
Micklitz H-W, Specht-Riemenschneider L (2025) Potentiel d'amélioration du droit à l'information des consommateurs en Allemange. In: Mäsch G, Valierque J (eds) Quelles limites aux droits nationaux et européens de la consommation? 9e Journées Franco-allemandes, vol 40. Société de Législation Comparée, Paris, pp 29–44
Mišćenić E (2024) Information, transparency and fairness for consumers in the digital environment. In: Crea C, De Franceschi A (eds) The new shapes of digital vulnerability in European private law. Nomos, Baden-Baden, pp 89–126

Miščenić E, Namysłowska M (2025) From illusion to digital fairness: structural protection in EU consumer law. In this volume

Nunez Duffourc M, Goel R, Kennedy R (2025) Regulation of consumer safety risks from AI characters in the European Union and United States. In this volume

Pasquale F (2024) Enforcing and expanding legal protections for vulnerable subjects. In: Crea C, De Franceschi A (eds) The new shapes of digital vulnerability in European private law. Nomos, Baden-Baden, pp 21–24

Pasquale F, Jamali Z (2025) Rapidly remedying exploitation of digital vulnerability. Taking time seriously in digital regulation. In this volume

Pera A, Rigazio S (2024) Let the children play. smart toys and child vulnerability. In: Crea C, De Franceschi A (eds) The new shapes of digital vulnerability in European Private Law. Nomos, Baden-Baden, pp 413–438

Pera A, Rigazio S (2025) 'Baby, You Can Drive My Car' ...and I Will Know Everything About You! Privacy and data protection policy as remedy to our digital vulnerabilities. In this volume

Pollicino O (2024) Vulnerability in the digital age. In: Crea C, De Franceschi A (eds) The new shapes of digital vulnerability in European private law. Nomos, Baden-Baden, pp 25–28

Research Group on the Existing EC Private Law (2007) Principles of the existing EC contract law (acquis principles), contract I: Pre-contractual obligations, conclusion of contract, unfair terms. Sellier European Law Publishers, Munich

Research Group on the Existing EC Private Law (2009) Principles of the existing EC contract law (acquis principles), Contract II: general provisions, delivery of goods, package travel and payment services. Sellier European Law Publishers, Munich

Rodin S (2025) Proportionality analysis in 'digital' cases. In this volume

Rodríguez de las Heras Ballell T (2025) Digital vulnerability in automated contracting: the problem of unexpected outcomes. Contract-Law Remedies or Liability?. In this volume

Santoni G (2025) The role of individual autonomy in the pursuit of contestability in the digital market: consent and data portability in the digital markets act. In this volume

Schulze R (2025a) Human vulnerability in interaction with AI—conclusions. In: Amodio C, Diurni A (eds) Human vulnerability in interaction with AI in European private law. Springer, Cham

Schulze R (2025b) Propos Introductifs. In: Mäsch G, Valierque J (eds) Quelles limites aux droits nationaux et européens de la consommation? 9e Journées Franco-allemandes, vol 40. Société de Législation Comparée, Paris, pp 9–25

Schulze R (2024) Digital vulnerability in European private law—conclusions. In: Crea C, De Franceschi A (eds) The new shapes of digital vulnerability in European private law. Nomos, Baden-Baden, pp 521–536

Schulze R (2019) Die Digitale-Inhalte-Richtlinie—Innovation und Kontinuität im europäischen Vertragsrecht. ZEuP 4:695–722

Schulze R, de Franceschi A (2023) Harmonizing digital contract law. Nomos, Baden-Baden

Schulze R, Staudenmayer D (2025) EU digital law, 2nd edn. Nomos Baden-Baden

Schulze R, Zoll F (2021) European contract law, 3rd edn. Nomos, Baden-Baden

Sein K (2025) The new European withdrawal function: protecting consumers against 'Digital Traps'. In this volume

Skalski S, Tereszkiewicz P (2025) Robo-advisors as a product in the insurance sector. Considerations regarding enforceability. In this volume

Smorto G (2025) Regulating AI through standards and the risk of preempting liability. A transatlantic comparison. In this volume

Souto LM (2025) Women's digital vulnerability in the Femtech context: building up gender-sensitive remedies on data protection. In this volume

Specht-Riemenschneider L, El-Rifaai M, Mehnert V, Bodemann L (2024) IoT data sharing in B2C: how to better serve the consumer. In: Lohsse S, Schulze R, Staudenmayer D (eds) Private law and the data act. Münster Colloquia on EU Law and the Digital Economy VIII. Nomos, Baden-Baden, pp 59–96

Spindler G, Sein K (2019) Die endgültige Richtlinie über Verträge über digitale Inhalte und Dienstleistungen. MMR 7:415–420

Tereszkiewicz P, Południak-Gierz K, Walczak P (2024) The digital vulnerability of insurance consumers and personalised pricing of insurance products. In: Crea C, De Franceschi A (eds) The new shapes of digital vulnerability in European private law. Nomos, Baden-Baden, pp 383–412

Twigg-Flesner C (2010) The Cambridge companion to European Union private law. Cambridge University Press, Cambridge

Twigg-Flesner C (2025a) Digital content directive. Art. 16. In: Schulze R, Staudenmayer D (eds) EU digital law. 2nd edn. Nomos, Baden-Baden, pp 276–294

Twigg-Flesner C (2025b) Digital content directive. Art. 17. In: Schulze R, Staudenmayer D (eds) EU digital law. 2nd edn. Nomos, Baden-Baden, pp 294–303

UNCITRAL (2024) Model law on automated contracting. Available at https://uncitral.un.org/en/mlac

Von Bar C, Clive E, Schulte-Nölke H (eds) (2019) Principles, definitions and model rules of European private law: draft common frame of reference (DCFR). Outline Edition. Otto Schmidt, Köln

Wildhaber I, Ebert IL (2024) From digital vulnerability to data anxiety: the situation of employees in digitally permeated workplaces. In: Crea C, De Franceschi A (eds) The new shapes of digital vulnerability in European private law. Nomos, Baden-Baden, pp 469–498

Zöchling-Jud B (2023) The impact of EU directives 2019/770 and 2019/771. Austria. In: De Franceschi A, Schulze R (eds) Harmonizing digital contract law. Nomos, Baden-Baden, pp 33–67

MIX
Papier aus verantwortungsvollen Quellen
Paper from responsible sources
FSC® C105338

If you have any concerns about our products,
you can contact us on
ProductSafety@springernature.com

In case Publisher is established outside the EU,
the EU authorized representative is:
Springer Nature Customer Service Center GmbH
Europaplatz 3, 69115 Heidelberg, Germany

Printed by Libri Plureos GmbH
in Hamburg, Germany